Classics of
Organization Theory
Fourth Edition

Classics of
Organization Theory
Fourth Edition

Jay M. Shafritz
University of Pittsburgh

J. Steven Ott
University of Utah

Harcourt Brace College Publishers
Fort Worth   Philadelphia   San Diego
New York   Orlando   Austin   San Antonio
Toronto   Montreal   London   Sydney   Tokyo

Public Administration Editor: Jason Moore
Production: The Wheetley Company
Print Buyer: Karen Hunt
Cover Design: Andrew Ogus
Permissions Editor: Jeanne Bosschart
Copy Editor: The Wheetley Company
Composition: TCSystems, Inc.
Printer: Malloy Lithographing, Inc.

Library of Congress Cataloging-in-Publication Data

Classics of organization theory / [edited by] Jay M. Shafritz, J.
  Steven Ott. — 4th ed.
     p.   cm.
   Includes bibliographical references.
   ISBN 0-534-50417-5
   1. Organization. 2. Management.   I. Shafritz, Jay M.   II. Ott,
J. Steven.
HD31.C56   1996
658—dc20   95-21378
                                                        CIP

Printed in the United States of America

0-534-50417-5

789012345 066 111098765

Foreword

In this anthology of classical works in organization theory, Shafritz and Ott have captured the essence, if not all the details, of an extensive and intricate subject. This assertion requires asking ourselves, what is the "essence" of organization theory? Put another way, what was the fundamental problem that the classic writers were trying to resolve?

The answer to these questions is found in the fourth selection in this book, namely in Henry Towne's paper, "The Engineer as an Economist." One needs only to ponder Towne's title to find the motive behind most of the classicists' work. Ask yourself, what do engineers and economists have in common? Without too much effort I am sure you will conclude, "the quest for efficiency." Towne's linking of management with its root sciences of engineering and economics through the concept of efficiency ($E = O/I$) was a brilliant stroke that has to be one of the great monuments of managerial lucidity.

It is not as if the concept of efficiency had gone unnoticed before Towne wrote of it. Indeed, even in biblical times, Jethro, Moses' father-in-law, advised Moses to set up a chain of command and to delegate most of his decision making authority to lower levels, because trying to do it all himself was inefficient (Exodus: Chapter II 18:9). However, prior to Towne's work, there was little systematic knowledge of administration. As a matter of fact, the idea of "management" was barely realized and the notion of "executive" hardly understood.

But Towne wrote at a propitious time. He was driven by the Progressive Movement's reform endeavors and took the first steps to create a scientific body of thought that applied to the administration of public and private organizations. In this regard, the Scientific Management movement was a product of both Progressivism and Towne's attempt to get those people interested in management to contribute to the annual proceedings of the American Society of Mechanical Engineers. Frederick W. Taylor's epic paper "A Piece-Rate System," written in 1895, was a result of Towne's request.

Scientific Management was all about the efficiency of resource utilization based upon the collection of data and the rational analysis of that data. Organizational performance would be enhanced, so the scientific management pioneers believed, if management had at its disposal objective facts for making decisions, as opposed to the intuitive or rule of thumb methods used in the past. Thus science and rationality became the watchwords of efficiency.

But organization theory was more than "facts," as Bacon said, "like grapes, ripe and ready for plucking." Facts required a framework for understanding and this is where pertains the contributions, between the two World Wars, of the great builders of classical organizational theory. They are represented in this volume by

Max Weber, Chester I. Barnard, and Luther Gulick. These writers proposed two enduring themes in organization theory. The first theme is purely structural, that is, according to what methods and principles an organization arranges its functions to maximize *coordination*. This issue concerns the never-ending problem of achieving a balance between vertical and horizontal differentiation, in other words between hierarchy and the division of labor.

The second theme concerns *cooperation*, and it was a matter dear to Chester Barnard. He was the first practicing manager to recognize that the applied behavioral sciences could be useful to management as means to motivate workers and to encourage them to have a pleasing view of their work situation. Drawing in part upon the Hawthorne studies in human relations, Barnard's book, *The Functions of the Executive* became recognized as the paradigmatic statement of modern managerialism. He stressed that cooperation was based upon the mutual interest that workers and managers had in the success of an enterprise. But he went further to show that management had to be proactive in nurturing that sense of mutual interest by using the applied behavioral sciences to influence the attitudes and actions of subordinates.

Lest we risk losing the point, let me reemphasize that the great twin themes of coordination and cooperation in organization theory were in fact creatures of efficiency, that most fundamental of all organizational imperatives. These themes, blossoming in the interwar years, reached full bloom by midcentury, exemplified in the work of Herbert A. Simon, Richard M. Cyert, and James G. March. Drawing upon Barnard's inspiration, these writers viewed management as a process imbedded in a system of patterned relationships. During the 1960s, systems theory emerged and tried to do what Barnard had all along hoped to see done, to develop a general theory of interrelationships and interdependencies that explained the behavior of complex organizations.

Systems theory in management came to naught, however, largely because it did not move beyond the normative to include a descriptive, quantitative side that had any degree of generality. Through most of the 1970s, 1980s, and 1990s, organization theory fragmented with the theme of coordination pursued by the structuralists, the theme of cooperation explored by the behavioralists, and the idea of efficiency all but disappearing in the ensuing flood of specialist literature. The last chapters of this volume (Chapters V through IX) reflect this trend with subjects such as culture, gender, ecology, information technology, and on and on, tending to suggest that management is slipping into postmodern anarchy.

It takes a great deal of perspicacity to assemble a collection of readings that reflects the changes that organization theory went through during this century. The editors of this book deserve our admiration. One can hope that in their next edition the editors will find evidence in the literature that the field is rediscovering some of the fundamentals with which it began. This is not a plea for organizational revisionism, but for theoretical coherence.

William G. Scott
Professor of Management
University of Washington

Preface

Classics of Organization Theory is a collection of the most important works in organization theory, written by the most influential authors in the field. *Classics* doesn't just tell the reader what the "masters" said, it presents their works in their own words. These are theories that have withstood the test of time—the critically acclaimed masterworks in the field. Although it contains a sprinkling of important current works, its focus is the enduring classics. It tells the history of organization theory through the words of the great theorists.

Classics is designed to help people who are new to the field of organization theory "get into," understand, and appreciate its important themes, perspectives, and theories. Thus, we describe and explain what organization theory is, how it has developed, and how its development coincides with developments in other fields, as well as the contexts in which these great works were written.

Articles are organized chronologically within major perspectives or "schools" of organization theory. Each chapter focuses on one major perspective of organization theory. Readers thus can absorb themselves in one perspective at a time, before moving on to the next.

The chapters (and the major perspectives of organization theory) are:

- Classical Organization Theory
- Neoclassical Organization Theory
- Human Resource Theory, or the Organizational Behavior Perspective
- "Modern" Structural Organization Theory
- Systems Theory, Population Ecology, and Organizational Economics
- Power and Politics Organization Theory
- Organizational Culture and Sense-Making
- Organizational Culture Reform Movements
- Postmodernism and the Information Age.

Other features that help to make *Classics* "reader friendly" include:

- The *Introduction* explains why there are competing perspectives or frames for grouping theories of organization, and why we chose the particular framework that is used in *Classics*.
- The *Introduction* explains how theories of organization reflect what is going on in the world at the time (for example, World War II and the "flowerchild"/anti-establishment/self-development era of the 1960s); defines the criteria used for including and excluding works (for example, "Should the serious student of organization theory be expected to be able to identify this author

and his or her basic themes?"); and presents the organizing framework for the book.

- The *Introduction* contains a "Chronology" of important events and contributions to the field of organizational theory from 1491 B.C. into the 1990s. The "Chronology" allows one to see in one place the intellectual development of the myriad themes and perspectives of organization theory, and to comprehend the impact of time and context on the development of perspectives across the field.

- The opening pages of each chapter identify the central themes and issues of the perspective, contrasts the perspective with other perspectives, and briefly summarize the contributions each article has made to the field.

- Most of the articles have been shortened, to make them more readable—more so than in the third edition. The editing-down helps readers to focus on the central ideas that make the article a classic.

- Each chapter contains a bibliography of the most important books and articles from the perspective (whether or not the works are reproduced in *Classics*).

CHANGES FROM THE 3RD EDITION TO THE 4TH EDITION

The fourth edition retains "the essence" of the second and third editions. It has not been changed in level of writing, point of view, purpose, or emphasis. Its scope has been expanded to incorporate several exciting recent developments in the field. Some of the important additions include:

- organizational economics
- information technology (including "cyberspace" and "the information highway")
- postmodernism and chaos theory
- a feminist perspective
- diversity and multi-culturalism

Each edition of *Classics of Organization Theory* has required us to face up to a few difficult decisions about including or excluding particular schools of theory. For the third edition, our most difficult decision involved "human resource theory"—an enormous field that warrants books rather than a chapter. (See, for example, the second edition of *Classic Readings in Organizational Behavior*, by J. Steven Ott, a book of readings that is designed to accompany *Classics of Organization Theory*.)

For the fourth edition, our most difficult decision was whether to introduce several newer perspectives of organization theory—perspectives that have received wide attention in the media and the general public, as well as from practitioners and academicians. A number of friendly critics have repeatedly asked us to update the book's coverage—to bring the book "into the 1990s" by including more current theories and theorists. Other reviewers, though, have disagreed, urging us to resist the temptation to venture into ideas and writing that have not passed the test of time;

we should "keep *Classics* true to its title." Until now (with only a few exceptions), we have taken a firm position: *Classics* is a collection of enduring works by the great writers. We have softened our stand somewhat in this fourth edition. We attempt to walk a fine line that maintains the *classics* identity but still infuses a sprinkling of important newer works. Our more recent inclusions are mostly confined to the concluding three chapters. Thus, readers who want only "pure classics" of organization theory, probably should put this book down after reading Chapter VI. Those who also want exposure to well grounded works that represent the newer, evolving perspectives of organization, should venture into Chapters VII, VIII and IX.

Chapter-by-chapter, the following selections have been added and deleted:

CLASSICAL ORGANIZATION THEORY. (Chapter I in the 3rd and 4th editions.)

Deletion from the Third Edition

Charles Babbage, "On the Division of Labour" (1832)

NEOCLASSICAL ORGANIZATION THEORY. (Chapter II in the 3rd and 4th editions.)

Deletion from the Third Edition

James G. March & Herbert A. Simon, "Theories of Bureaucracy" (1958)

New Addition in the Fourth Edition

Chester I. Barnard, "The Economy of Incentives" (1938)

HUMAN RESOURCE THEORY, OR THE ORGANIZATIONAL BEHAVIOR PERSPECTIVE. (Chapter III in the 3rd and 4th editions.)

Deletions from the Third Edition

David C. McClelland, "That Urge to Achieve" (1966)

Chris Argyris, "Intervention Theory and Methods" (1970)

New Addition in the Fourth Edition

Taylor H. Cox, Jr., "Intergroup Conflict" (1993)

"MODERN" STRUCTURAL ORGANIZATION THEORY. (Chapter IV in the 3rd and 4th editions.)

Deletions from the Third Edition

Paul R. Lawrence & Jay W. Lorsch, "Organization-Environment Interface" (1969)

Stanley M. Davis & Paul R. Lawrence, "The Matrix Organization—Who Needs It?" (1977)

SYSTEMS THEORY, POPULATION ECOLOGY, AND ORGANIZATIONAL ECONOMICS. (Chapter V in the 3rd and 4th editions. "Organizational Economics" has been added in the fourth edition.)

Deletions from the Third Edition

Jay Galbraith, "Information Processing Model" (1973)

Eric Trist, "A Concept of Organizational Ecology" (1977)

New Additions in the Fourth Edition

William G. Scott, "Organization Theory: An Overview and an Appraisal (1961)

Michael C. Jensen & William H. Meckling, "Theory of the Firm: Managerial Behavior, Agency Costs and Ownership Structure" (1976)

Lex Donaldson, "The Ethereal Hand: Organizational Economics and Management Theory" (1990)

POWER AND POLITICS ORGANIZATION THEORY. (Chapter VII in the 3rd edition. Chapter VI in the 4th edition.)

Deletions from the Third Edition

David Mechanic, "Sources of Power of Lower Participants in Complex Organizations" (1962)

Anthony T. Cobb & Newton Margulies, "Organization Development: A Political Perspective" (1981)

New Addition in the Fourth Edition

John R. P. French, Jr., & Bertram Raven, "The Bases of Social Power" (1959)

ORGANIZATIONAL CULTURE AND SENSE-MAKING. (Chapter VIII in the 3rd edition. Chapter VII in the 4th edition. "Sense-making" has been added in the fourth edition.)

Deletions from the Third Edition

Burton R. Clark, "The Making of an Organizational Saga" (1970)

Meryl Reis Louis, "Organizations as Culture-Bearing Milieux" (1983)

Linda Smircich, "Organizations As Shared Meanings" (1983)

Thomas J. Sergiovanni, "Cultural and Competing Perspectives in Administrative Theory and Practice" (1984)

New Additions in the Fourth Edition

Meryl Reis Louis, "Surprise and Sensemaking: What Newcomers Experience in Entering Unfamiliar Organizational Settings" (1980)

Gareth Morgan, "Images of Organization" (1986)

Joan Acker, "Gendering Organizational Theory" (1992)

Harrison M. Trice & Janice M. Beyer, "Changing Organizational Cultures" (1993)

The chapter, "Multiple Constituencies/Market Organization Theory" has been eliminated in the fourth edition. Although multiple constituencies theories represent an important perspective, we decided that the two perspectives in chapters VIII and IX should take priority. Thus, the following articles have been deleted that were in the third edition.

Terry Connolly, Edward J. Conlon, & Stuart Jay Deutsch, "Organizational Effectiveness: A Multiple-Constituency Approach" (1980)

Michael Keeley, "Values in Organizational Theory and Management Education" (1983)

Ian Mitroff, "External Influences on Managers" (1983)

Oliver E. Williamson, "Understanding the Employment Relation" (1975)

The two new chapters "Organizational Culture Reform Movements" (Chapter VIII), and "Postmodernism and the Information Age" (Chapter IX) acknowledge the importance of two developments in the field that have attracted substantial attention from scholars, practitioners, and the popular press.

Selections in these two chapters include:

• ORGANIZATIONAL CULTURE REFORM MOVEMENTS

William G. Ouchi, "The Z Organization" (1981)

Thomas J. Peters & Robert H. Waterman, Jr., "In Search of Excellence: Simultaneous Loose-Tight Properties" (1982)

Peter M. Senge, "The Fifth Discipline: A Shift of Mind" (1990)

David Osborne & Ted Gaebler, "Reinventing Government: Introduction" (1992)

• POSTMODERNISM AND THE INFORMATION AGE

Shoshana Zuboff, "In the Age of the Smart Machine: The Limits of Hierarchy in an Informated Organization" (1988)

Karl E. Weick, Jr., "Technology as Equivoque: Sensemaking in New Technologies" (1990)

William Berqquist, "Postmodern Thought in a Nutshell: Where Art and Science Come Together" (1993)

L. Douglas Kiel, "Nonlinear Dynamical Analysis: Assessing Systems Concepts in a Government Agency" (1993)

Michael Hammer & James Champy, "Reengineering the Corporation: The Enabling Role of Information Technology" (1993)

ACKNOWLEDGMENTS

This fourth edition of *Classics of Organization Theory* has benefited immeasurably from the advice that we have received from our friendly critics of the third edition. Hopefully, it also has benefited from our maturing judgment and several years of additional pondering about organization theory. The rate of change and the degree of fragmentation in the field during the past 15 years, however, have been without precedent. Our confidence in our "maturing judgment" has been tested severely. Yet, this is a major part of the enjoyment that we derive from editing a book of classics in a dynamic and turbulent field.

Many people have contributed to this fourth edition, but three require special mention. First, Breena Coates, University of Pittsburgh, provided invaluable assistance in editing this edition. She helped to decide which articles should be retained, added, and deleted, as well as what to edit-out of articles.

Second, Chris C. Demchak, at the University of Arizona's College of Business and Public Administration, generously provided information and critiques that we used extensively in organizing and writing Chapter IX. We thank her deeply for her generous and sage advice—but we accept full responsibility for what we did with (or to) the information Chris provided. Finally, Peggy Gentles, University of Utah, managed the painstaking task of obtaining and coordinating the permissions in addition to helping with the editing task. Without the assistance that was provided by Breena Coates, Chris Demchak, and Peggy Gentles, the fourth edition would have been less professional and useful.

We also want to thank a number of people who provided support, ideas, and encouragement, including: Kevin Kearns, University of Pittsburgh; Al Hyde, American University; Ralph Hummel, University of Oklahoma; Jeffrey Pinto, University of Maine; Ted Hebert, Laurie DiPadova, and Peri Schwartz-Shea, University of Utah; Bill Russell, Monash University; and Peter Foot, Royal Naval College Greenwich.

David V. Day, The Pennsylvania State University; Dr. Gerard Fowler, St. Louis University; Dr. Ira Kaplan, Hofstra University; Dr. Esther Langston, University of Nevada-Las Vegas; Dr. Dorothy Marcic, Metropolitan State University; Dr. Thomas Marchigiano-Monroy, Rutgers-The State University of New Jersey; Dr. Scott Moore, Colorado State University; and Dr. Maria Papadakis, Syracuse University, all provided helpful suggestions and comments that helped shape the third edition. This fourth edition benefited from the comments of Joe Anderson, Northern

Arizona University; William G. Scott, University of Washington; and Mary Ellen Guy, University of Alabama, Birmingham.

We also collectively thank the authors and publishers of these classics for their permission to reproduce their work.

As with the prior editions, we sincerely solicit comments, ideas, and suggestions from the scholarly and practitioner communities. Given sufficient encouragement from readers and support from our publisher—and long enough lives—we will continue to revise *Classics of Organization Theory* as new theories and perspectives gain in importance.

Finally, we want to put readers on notice that changed standards of language are evident in some of the readings. Many terms and phrases that are sexist and racist by today's standards, were in common use twenty or thirty years ago. When it was possible to do so, offensive language was removed from articles by editing-out sentences or paragraphs. Some words and phrases, however, are essential to the text and could not be deleted.

Jay M. Shafritz
University of Pittsburgh

J. Steven Ott
University of Utah

Contents

Chapter III
Human Resource Theory, or the Organizational Behavior Perspective, 149

Chapter IV
"Modern" Structural Organization Theory, 203

Chapter V
Systems Theory, Population Ecology, and Organizational Economics, 254

Chapter VI
Power and Politics Organization Theory, 352

Chapter VII
Organizational Culture and Sense-making, 420

Introduction

This book is about organization theory. By *organization*, we mean a social unit with some particular purposes. By *theory*, we mean a proposition or set of propositions that seeks to explain or predict something. The something in this case is how groups and individuals behave in varying organizational structures and circumstances. This is obviously important information for any manager or leader to have. It is hardly an exaggeration to say that the world is ruled by the underlying premises of organization theory, and that it has been ever since humankind first organized itself for hunting, war, and even family life. Indeed, the newest thing about organization theory is the study of it.

Only in the twentieth century has intellectual substance and tradition been given to a field that was the instinctual domain of adventuresome entrepreneurs and cunning politicos. Organization theory lay largely dormant over the centuries until society found a practical use for it—to help manage the ever-burgeoning national (as opposed to local) industries and institutions that increasingly run the twentieth century. When the problems of managing an organization grew to be more than one head could cope with, the search for guidance on how to manage and arrange large-scale organizations became as noble a quest as the secular world of business could offer. If a commercial society ever had prophets, they were those pioneers of the scientific management movement who claimed that the path to ever-greater prosperity was to be found in the relentless search for the "one best way." They were offering society a theory—abstract guidance for those who knew where they wanted to go but didn't quite know how to get there. They already knew what Kurt Lewin would assert years later: "There is nothing so practical as a good theory" (Marrow, 1969).

Peter Drucker (1954) once observed that the thrust toward scientific management "may well be the most powerful as well as the most lasting contribution America has made to Western thought since the Federalist Papers." Of course, the scientific management movement was just the beginning of a continuous search for the most effective means by which people can be organized into social units in order to achieve the goals of their companies, their governments, or themselves. What was once said of the first atomic bomb is now said of the first U.S. voyage to the moon: It was as much an achievement of organization as it was of engineering and science.

Have our more recent theories of organization kept pace with our industrial and technical achievements? Maybe. But certainly yes when they are compared with the "primitive" notions of the scientific management movement. Yet many of the basics remain the same—remain as givens. The laws of physics and gravity do not change with intellectual fashions or technological advances; nor do the basic social and physical characteristics of people change. Just as those who would build space ships have to start by studying Newton, those who would design and manage organizations must start with Taylor and Fayol. The future will always build upon what is enduring from the past. That is the rationale for this book—to provide those who seek to understand and/or to advance organization theory with a convenient place to find the essentials, indeed the classics, of organization theory's past. However old some of these articles may be, they are not dated. A classic *is* a classic because it continues to be of value to each new generation of students and practitioners who study organizations.

The basic elements of organizations have remained relatively constant through history: Organizations (or their important constituencies) have purposes (which may be explicit or implicit), attract participants, acquire and allocate resources to accomplish goals, use some form of structure to divide and coordinate activities, and rely on certain members to lead or manage others. Although the elements of organizations have remained relatively constant, their purposes, structures, ways of doing things, and methods for coordinating activities have always varied widely. The variations largely (but not exclusively) reflect an organization's adaptation to its environment. Organizations are "open systems" that are influenced by and have an impact on the world around them. The world around organizations includes, for example, their sources of inputs (like raw materials, capital, and labor), markets, technology, politics, and the surrounding society's culture and subcultures. Inherently, organizations are part of the society and the culture in which they exist and function. Human behavior and thus organizational behavior is heavily influenced by culturally rooted beliefs, values, assumptions, and behavioral norms affecting all aspects of organizational life.

Theories about organizations do not develop in a vacuum. They reflect what is going on in the world—including the existing culture. Thus, contributions to organization theory vary over time and across cultures and subcultures. The advent of the factory system, World War II, the "flower child"/anti-establishment/self-development era of the 1960s, the computer/information society of the 1970s, and the pervasive uncertainties of the 1980s and 1990s all substantially influenced the evolution of organization theory. In order to truly understand organization theory as it exists today, one must appreciate the historical contexts through which it developed and the cultural milieus during and in which important contributions were made to its body of knowledge. In order to help readers place writings in their historical contexts, "A Chronology of Organization Theory," a review of the major events and publications in the field, follows this introduction.

CRITERIA FOR SELECTION

The editors are neither so vain nor so foolish as to assert that these are *the* classics of organization theory. The academic study of organization theory rests on a foundation of primary and secondary sciences: It draws significantly from such diverse disciplines as sociology, psychology, social psychology, cultural anthropology, political science, economics, business administration, and public administration. It draws with less force, but still importantly, from mathematics, statistics, systems theory, industrial engineering, philosophy and ethics, history, and the computer sciences. The field is so diverse that there can be no single definitive list of *the classics*. The editors readily admit that some important contributors and contributions to the field have not found their way into this collection. Omitting some was very painful. However, considerations of space and balance necessarily prevailed.

We used several criteria for making our selections. First, we asked ourselves, "Should the serious student of organization theory be expected to be able to identify these authors and their basic themes?" When the answer was yes, it was so because the contribution has long been, or is increasingly being recognized as, an important theme by a significant writer. Whereas we expect to be criticized for excluding other articles and writers, it will be more difficult to honestly criticize us for our inclusions; the writers and selections chosen are among the most widely quoted and reprinted theorists and theories in the field of organization theory. The exceptions are the articles chosen to represent the newer perspectives of organization theory—particularly organizational culture and sensemaking, and postmodernism. Most of the significant writing in these perspectives has been done since 1980, and some of the most impressive works are as recent as 1994. Obviously, new articles have not been quoted as extensively as those written ten, twenty, or thirty years earlier. Thus, we had to be more subjective when making our editorial decisions about inclusions and exclusions in these chapters. In our judgment, these selections will fare well against the test of time.

Although this is a book of classics, we continue to receive numerous requests to include some current and near-current management bestsellers. "How can *Classics of Organization Theory* fail to include 'modern management classics' such as *In Search of Excellence, Reinventing Government,* or *The Fifth Discipline?*" Other readers and reviewers, however, urge us to stay true to the book's purpose. "Stay with the time-tested classics. Don't try to be everything for everybody. Let other anthologies keep readers up-to-date with the current fads."

We have lived with this divided set of opinions through three editions. For this fourth edition, we decided to try something new. The last two chapters (Chapters VIII and IX) contain excerpts from four of the most important management movements since 1980:

- The quest for organizational excellence (Tom Peters and Robert Waterman, *In Search of Excellence,* 1982);
- Learning organizations (Peter Senge, *The Fifth Discipline,* 1992);
- *Reinventing Government* (David Osborne and Thomas Gaebler, 1992);
- Reengineering (Michael Hammer and James Champy, *Reengineering the Corporation,* 1993).

We hope to appease both points of view by including these modern management contributions. "Purists" can simply ignore Chapters VIII and IX. Pretend they are not included.

The second criterion is related to the first: Each article or portion of a book had to make a basic statement that has been echoed or attacked consistently over the years. In other words, the selection had to be important—significant in the sense that it must have been (or will be) an integral part of the foundation for the subsequent building of the field of organization theory.

The third criterion was that articles had to be readable. Those of you who have already had reason to peruse the literature of organization theory will appreciate the importance of this criterion. (We tried very hard to live by this, but we were not completely successful!)

The inclusion of articles from the more recent perspectives raises important questions about our choices of chapters for grouping theories and selections. For example, why did we establish separate chapters for power and politics and organizational culture, but not for natural selection? What is the basis for our distinction between the "modern" structuralists and the systemists? The answers to questions such as these reflect our own conceptual and historical construction of organization theory, tempered by the need to limit the size of this volume. It is crucially important, then, to understand where we, the authors/editors, "are coming from." Thus we have written rather lengthy historical and conceptual overviews for each chapter. Each presents a school or perspective of organization theory, and because there is no universally accepted set of schools or perspectives, a few words of explanation are needed here.

A FRAMEWORK: THE "PERSPECTIVES" OF ORGANIZATION THEORY

There is no such thing as *the* theory of organizations. Rather, there are many theories that attempt to explain and predict how organizations and the people in them will behave in varying organizational structures, cultures, and circumstances. Some theories of organization are compatible with and build upon others—in what they explain or predict, the aspects of organizations they consider to be important, their assumptions about organizations and the world at large from which they are created, and the methods for studying organizations that work well. They use the same language or jargon. These groupings of compatible theories and theorists usually are called alternately schools, perspectives, traditions, frameworks, models, paradigms or, occasionally, eras of organization theory. We use these terms interchangeably throughout this book.

Organization theorists from one school will quote and cite each other's works regularly. However, they usually ignore theorists and theories from other schools—or acknowledge them only negatively. In 1961, Harold Koontz described management theory as a "semantics jungle." In 1963, Arthur Kuriloff examined the various schools of organization theory and found that "each is at odds with others, each defends its own position, each claims that the others have major deficiencies." But that was 1963, and we have come a long way since then; or have we? Twenty years after Kuriloff's statement, Graham Astley and Andrew Van de Ven (1983) observed:

"The problem is that different schools of [organizational] thought tend to focus only on single sides of issues and use such different logics and vocabularies that they do not speak to each other directly." A year later, Lee Bolman and Terrence Deal (1984) remarked: "Within the social sciences, major schools of thought have evolved, each with its own view of organizations, its own well-defined concepts and assumptions, and its own ideas about how managers can best bring social collectives under control."

It is reasonable to conclude that not only is there no consensus on what constitutes knowledge in organization theory, but there is not likely to be any such consensus in the foreseeable future. Anyone who studies this subject is free to join the school of organization theory of his or her choice and is free to accept the philosophic boundaries of one group of serious thinkers over another. But before casting your lot with one school and excluding others, consider the options. Examine each school's strengths and weaknesses. See if its philosophy is in harmony with your already established beliefs, assumptions, and predispositions. You may find that no single perspective deserves your loyalty, that each contains important information and insights that are useful in differing circumstances. Remember these are schools with no tuition, no classes, and no grades. They exist only as intellectual constructs and as mutual support networks of organization theorists. They have one primary purpose: to organize and extend knowledge about organizations and how to study them.

Just as there is disagreement among the various frames about what makes organizations tick, there also are different views about the best way to group organization theories into schools. A few examples of different views on the schools of organization theory are summarized in Figure 1.

Each of the major frames of organization theory is associated with a period in time. For example, the classical school was at its prime in the 1920s and 1930s, and the neoclassical school in the 1940s and 1950s. Each school had its beginnings while another was dominant, gradually gained acceptance, and eventually replaced its predecessor as the dominant perspective. Some years later, another came along to challenge and eventually take its position. Once-dominant frames of organization theory may lose the center stage, but they do not die. Their thinking influences subsequent frames—even those that reject their basic assumptions and tenets. Important works from these earlier perspectives become the timeless classics.

This cycling of schools through struggling ascendancy, dominance, challenge by other schools, and reluctant decline is not unique to organization theory. Thomas Kuhn (1970) postulated that this dialectic process is common in all sciences—including physics, mathematics, and psychiatry. It is quite common for frames that are close to each other chronologically to have widely divergent basic assumptions about the object of their theories.

Despite their differences, most of the better-known approaches to grouping organization theories into schools (including those summarized in Figure 1) have commonalities. First, they group theories by their perspectives on organizations—in other words, by basic assumptions about humans and organizations and by

FIGURE 1 • A FEW EXAMPLES OF HOW SCHOLARS HAVE GROUPED
SCHOOLS OF ORGANIZATION THEORY

Author	Schools
Scott, W. G. (1961). Organization theory: An overview and an appraisal. *Academy of Management Journal.* Koontz, H. (1961). The management theory jungle. *Academy of Management Journal.*	The Classical Doctrine Neoclassical Theory Modern Theory Management Process School Empirical Approach (or Case Approach) Human Behavior School Social System School Decision Theory School Mathematics School

Hutchinson, J. G. (1967). *Organizations: Theory and classical concepts.* New York: Holt, Rinehart & Winston.	Scientific Management
	Environmental and Human Relations School
	Man as a Decision Maker
	Current Theories of Management
	   1. Operational School
	   2. Empirical School
	   3. Human Behavior School
	   4. Social Systems School
	   5. Decision Theory School
	   6. Mathematical School

Scott, W. G., & Mitchell, T. R. (1972). *Organization theory* (rev. ed.). Homewood, IL: Dorsey Press.	The Scientific Management Movement The Human Relations and Industrial Humanism Movements Classical Theory Neoclassical Critique The Systems Concept (Unlabeled, but including) Personality Dynamics and Motivation, Attitudes, and Group Dynamics Organization Processes (Communication Processes, Decision Processes, Balance and Conflict Processes, Status and Role Processes, Influence Processes, Leadership Processes, and Technological Processes) Organization Change
George, C. S. Jr., (1972). *The history of management thought.* Englewood Cliffs, NJ: Prentice-Hall.	Traditional School: Scientific Management Behavioral School Management Process School Quantitative School
Perrow, C. (1973, Summer). The short and glorious history of organizational theory. *Organizational Dynamics.*	Scientific Management Human Relations Bureaucracy ("A Comeback") Power, Conflict, and Decisions The Technological Qualification Goals, Environments, and Systems

(continued)

FIGURE 1 • A FEW EXAMPLES OF HOW SCHOLARS HAVE GROUPED
SCHOOLS OF ORGANIZATION THEORY (*Continued*)

Author	Schools
Pfeffer, J. (1981). *Power in organizations.* Marshfield, MA: Pitman.	Rational Choice Models Bureaucratic Models of Decision Making Decision Process Models Political Models
Bolman, L., & Deal, T. (1991). *Reframing organizations.* San Francisco: Jossey-Bass.	Structural Frame Human Resource Frame Political Frame Symbolic Frame

those aspects of organizations that they see as most important for understanding organizational behavior. Second, they usually group the theories by the period of time during which the most important contributions were written. However, there are other organization theorists who use different approaches for labeling them. For example, Harold Koontz in "The Management Theory Jungle Revisited" (1980) expanded his list from six to eleven approaches to the study of management and organizational theory. We find Koontz's categorization system, with its Interpersonal Behavior Approach, Cooperative Social System Approach, and Sociotechnical Systems Approach, to be far too detailed to be useful.

Graham Astley and Andrew Van de Ven (1983) use a very different logic to classify schools of organization "thought" into four basic views based on two analytical dimensions: the level of organizational analysis (micro or macro) and the emphasis placed on deterministic versus voluntaristic assumptions about human nature. Thus Astley and Van de Ven conclude that organization theories can be grouped into the cells of a two-by-two matrix (see Figure 2). Their voluntaristic-to-deterministic dimension (the horizontal continuum in Figure 2) classifies theories by their assumptions about individual organization members' autonomy and self-direction versus the assumption that behavior in organizations is determined by structural constraints. The macro-to-micro continuum (the vertical continuum in Figure 2) groups organization theories by their focus on communities of organizations or single organizations.

THE ORGANIZATION OF THIS BOOK

Although different approaches such as Astley and Van de Ven's (1983) and Koontz's (1980) are insightful and thought provoking, they are not well suited to a historical development of organization theory. And, it is our contention that the historical approach offers some clear advantages for the student. Organization theory tends to be somewhat cumulative—theorists and schools of theorists learn from and build upon each other's works. Sometimes the cumulative building of organization theory has been accomplished through the adoption of prior theorists' assumptions, logic,

FIGURE 2 · ASTLEY AND VAN DE VEN'S FOUR VIEWS
OF ORGANIZATION

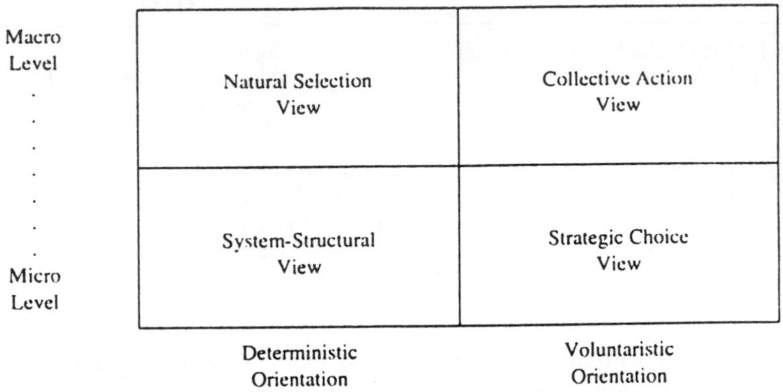

	Deterministic Orientation	Voluntaristic Orientation
Macro Level	Natural Selection View	Collective Action View
Micro Level	System-Structural View	Strategic Choice View

Examples of some representative organization theorists for each of the four views

System-Structural View: Gulick and Urwick (1937), Fayol (1949), Merton (1940), Blau and Scott (1962), Lawrence and Lorsch (1967), James D. Thompson (1967)
Strategic Choice View: Blau (1964), Feldman and March (1981), Strauss et al. (1963), Weick (1979), Bittner (1965)
Natural Selection View: Aldrich (1979), Hannan and Freeman (1977), Porter (1981), Pfeffer and Salancik (1978)
Collective Action View: Emery and Trist (1973), Hawley (1950, 1968), Schön (1971)

Adapted from Astley, W. G., & Van de Ven, A. H. (1983). Central perspectives and debates in organization theory. *Administrative Science Quarterly, 28.*

and empirical research methods and findings. In other instances, the building process has advanced by *rejecting* prior assumptions and theories (Kuhn, 1970). Thus, we have used a more traditional, historically oriented approach that allows the reader to follow the ebbs and flows within and between the perspectives. Within chapters, most selections are presented in chronological sequence so the reader can gain a sense of the evolution of thought in the field. Also, the reader can gain a quick overview of the historical development of organization theory by referring to the "Chronology of Organization Theory" that follows this Introduction. Our perspectives, or schools, and their corresponding chapters are:

Chapter I	Classical Organization Theory
Chapter II	Neoclassical Organization Theory
Chapter III	Human Resource Theory, or the Organizational Behavior Perspective
Chapter IV	"Modern" Structural Organization Theory
Chapter V	Systems Theory, Population Ecology, and Organizational Economics

Each perspective is described and discussed in the first pages of the respective chapters.

Although we have attempted to include only selections that fit into one school, many works span the boundaries, no matter how tightly the boundaries are defined and drawn. For example, Rosabeth Moss Kanter's writings (1977, 1983, and 1989) blend the power politics, human resource, and organizational culture perspectives. Cohen and March's (1974) concept of *organized anarchy* (reprinted here) bridges the power politics and the organizational culture perspectives. Argyris and Schön's (1978) notion of *theories for action* incorporates theory and research from the human resource and the organizational culture perspectives. Thus the reader should remember that the schools—and the chapters—reflect periods in time as well as perspectives of organizations.

REFERENCES

Al-Buraey, M. A. (1985). *Administrative development: An Islamic perspective*. London: Kegan Paul International.

Aldrich, H. (1979). *Organizations and environments*. Englewood Cliffs, NJ: Prentice-Hall.

Argyris, C., & Schön, D. A. (1978). *Organizational learning: A theory of action perspective*. Reading, MA: Addison-Wesley.

Astley, W. G., & Van De Ven, A. H. (1983, June). Central perspectives and debates in organization theory. *Administrative Science Quarterly, 28*, 245–270.

Bittner, E. (1965). The concept of organization. *Social Research, 32*(3), 239–255.

Blau, P. M. (1964). *Exchange and power in social life*. New York: Wiley.

Blau, P. M., & Scott, R. G. (1962). *Formal organizations*. San Francisco: Chandler.

Bolman, L. G., & Deal, T. E. (1984). *Modern approaches to understanding and managing organizations*. San Francisco: Jossey-Bass.

Bolman, L. G., & Deal, T. E. (1991). *Reframing organizations: Artistry, choice, and leadership*. San Francisco: Jossey-Bass.

Cohen, M. D., & March, J. G. (1974). *Leadership and ambiguity: The American college president*. New York: McGraw-Hill.

Deming, W. E. (1986). *Out of the crisis*. Cambridge, MA: M.I.T. Press.

Drucker, P. F. (1954). *The practice of management*. New York: Harper & Row.

Emery, F. E., and Trist, E. L. (1973). *Towards a social ecology: Contextual appreciations of the future in the present*. New York: Plenum.

Fayol, H. (1949). *General and industrial management*. London: Pitman. (Original work published 1916)

Feldman, M. S., & March, J. G. (1981). Information in organizations as signal and symbol. *Administrative Science Quarterly, 26,* 171–186.

George, C. S., Jr. (1972). *The history of management thought.* Englewood Cliffs, NJ: Prentice-Hall.

Gulick, L., & Urwick, L. (Eds.) (1937). *Papers on the science of administration.* New York: Institute of Public Administration.

Hammer, M., & Champy, J. (1993). *Reengineering the corporation: A manifesto for business revolution.* New York: HarperCollins.

Hannan, M., & Freeman, J. (1977). The population ecology of organizations. *American Journal of Sociology, 82,* 929–964.

Hawley, A. (1950). *Human ecology: A theory of community structure.* New York: Ronald Press.

Hawley, A. (1968). Human ecology. In D. L. Sills (Ed.). *The international encyclopedia of the social sciences* (Vol. 4, pp. 328–337). New York: Crowell-Collier & Macmillan.

Hutchinson, J. G. (1967). *Organizations: Theory and classical concepts.* New York: Holt, Rinehart & Winston.

Ibn Khaldun. (1969). *The muqaddimah: An introduction to history* (trans. by F. Rosenthal, ed. and abridged by N. J. Dawood). Princeton, NJ: Bollingen Series/Princeton University Press.

Kanter, R. M. (1977). *Men and women of the corporation.* New York: Basic Books.

Kanter, R. M. (1983). *The change masters.* New York: Simon & Schuster.

Kanter, R. M. (1989). *When giants learn to dance.* New York: Simon & Schuster.

Koontz, H. (1961). The management theory jungle. *Academy of Management Journal, 4,* 174–188.

Koontz, H. (1980). The management theory jungle revisited. *Academy of Management Review, 5,* 175–187.

Kuhn, T. S. (1970). *The structure of scientific revolutions* (2nd ed., enlarged.) Chicago: University of Chicago Press.

Lawrence, P. R., & Lorsch, J. W. (1967). *Organization and environment.* Cambridge, MA: Harvard University Press.

Marrow, A. J. (1969). *The practical theorist: The life and works of Kurt Lewin.* New York: Basic Books.

Merton, R. K. (1940). Bureaucratic structure and personality. *Social Forces, 18,* 560–568.

Nadler, D. A., Gerstein, M. S., & Shaw, R. B. (Eds.) (1992). *Organizational architecture: Designs for changing organizations.* San Francisco: Jossey-Bass.

Osborne, D., & Gaebler, T. (1992). *Reinventing government.* Reading, MA: Addison-Wesley.

Ott, J. S. (1996). *Classic readings in organizational behavior* (2nd. ed.). Belmont, CA: Wadsworth.

Perrow, C. (1973, Summer). The short and glorious history of organizational theory. *Organizational Dynamics.*

Peters, T. J., & Waterman, R. H., Jr. (1982). *In search of excellence: Lessons from America's best-run companies.* New York: Harper & Row.

Pfeffer, J. (1981). *Power in organizations.* Marshfield, MA: Pitman.

Pfeffer, J., & Salancik, G. R. (1978). *The external control of organizations: A resource dependence perspective.* New York: Harper & Row.

Porter, M. E. (1981). The contributions of industrial organization to strategic management. *Academy of Management Review, 6,* 609–620.

Schön, D. A. (1971). *Beyond the stable state*. New York: Basic Books.

Scott, W. G. (1961, April). Organization theory: An overview and an appraisal. *Academy of Management Journal*, 7–26.

Scott, W. G., & Mitchell, T. R. (1972). *Organization theory* (rev. ed.). Chicago: Dorsey Press.

Senge, P. M. (1990). *The fifth discipline: The art & practice of the learning organization*. New York: Doubleday Currency.

Strauss, A., Schatzman, L., Erlich, D., Bucher, R., & Sabshin, M. (1963). The hospital and its negotiated order. In E. Friedson (Ed.), *The hospital in modern society* (pp. 147–169). New York: Free Press.

Thompson, J. D. (1967). *Organizations in action*. New York: McGraw-Hill.

Weick, K. E. (1979). *The social psychology of organizing* (2nd ed.). Reading, MA: Addison-Wesley.

Wren, D. A. (1972). *The evolution of management thought*. New York: Ronald Press.

A CHRONOLOGY OF ORGANIZATION THEORY

1491 B.C.

- During the exodus from Egypt, Jethro, the father-in-law of Moses, urges Moses to delegate authority over the tribes of Israel along hierarchical lines.

500 B.C.

- Sun Tzu's *The Art of War* recognizes the need for hierarchical organization, interorganization communications, and staff planning.

400 B.C.

- Socrates argues for the universality of management as an art unto itself.

360 B.C.

- Aristotle in *The Politics* asserts that the specific nature of executive powers and functions cannot be the same for all states (organizations), but must reflect their specific cultural environment.

370 B.C.

- Xenophon records the first known description of the advantages of the division of labor when he describes an ancient Greek shoe factory.

770

- Abu Yusuf, an important pioneering Muslim scholar, explores the administration of essential Islamic government functions, including public financial policy, taxation, and criminal justice, in *Kitab al-Kharaj (The Book of Land Taxes)*. (Year is approximate.)

1058

- *Al-Ahkam As-Sultaniyyah (The Governmental Rules)*, by al-Mawardi, examines Islamic constitutional law, theoretical and practical aspects of Muslim political thought and behavior, and the behavior of politicians and administrators in Islamic states.

1093

- Al Ghazali emphasizes the role of Islamic creed and teachings for the improvement of administrative and bureaucratic organization in Muslim states, particularly the qualifications and duties of rulers, ministers, and secretaries, in *Ihya 'Ulum ad-Din (The Revival of the Religious Sciences)* and *Nasihat al-Muluk (Counsel for Kings)*. (Year is approximate.)

1300

- In *As-Siyasah ash-Shariyyah (The Principles of Religious Government)*, ibn Taymiyyah, "the father of Islamic administration," uses the scientific method to outline the principles of administration within the framework of Islam, including: the right man for the right job, patronage, and the spoils system. (Year is approximate.)

1377

- *The Muqaddimah: An Introduction to History*, by Muslim scholar ibn Khaldun, argues that methods for organizational improvement can be developed through the study of the science of culture. Ibn Khaldun specifically introduces conceptions of formal and informal organization, organizations as natural organisms with limits beyond which they cannot grow, and *esprit de corps*.

1513

- Machiavelli, in *The Discourses*, urges the principle of unity of command: "It is better to confide any expedition to a single man of ordinary ability, rather than to two, even though they are men of the highest merit, and both having equal ability."

1532

- Machiavelli's book of advice to all would-be leaders, *The Prince*, is published five years after its author's death; it will become the progenitor of all "how to succeed" books that advocate practical rather than moral actions.

1776

- Adam Smith's *The Wealth of Nations* discusses the optimal organization of a pin factory; this becomes the most famous and influential statement of the economic rationale of the factory system and the division of labor.

1813

- Robert Owen, in his "Address to the Superintendents of Manufactories," puts forth the revolutionary idea that managers should pay as much attention to their "vital machines" (employees) as to their "inanimate machines."

1832

- Charles Babbage's *On the Economy of Machinery and Manufactures* anticipates many of the notions of the scientific management movement, including "basic principles of management" such as the division of labor.

1855
- Daniel C. McCallum, in his annual report as superintendent of the New York and Erie Railroad Company, states his six basic principles of administration; the first was to use internally generated data for managerial purposes.

1885
- Captain Henry Metcalfe, the manager of an army arsenal, published *The Cost of Manufactures and the Administration of Workshops, Public and Private*, which asserts that there is a "science of administration" that is based upon principles discoverable by diligent observation.

1886
- Henry R. Towne's paper "The Engineer as an Economist," read to the American Society of Mechanical Engineers, encourages the scientific management movement.

1902
- Vilfredo Pareto becomes the "father" of the concept of "social systems"; his societal notions would later be applied by Elton Mayo and the human relationists in an organizational context.

1903
- Frederick W. Taylor publishes *Shop Management*.

1904
- Frank B. and Lillian M. Gilbreth marry; they then proceed to produce many of the pioneering works on time and motion study, scientific management, applied psychology, and twelve children.

1910
- Louis D. Brandeis, an associate of Frederick W. Taylor (and later Supreme Court Justice), coins and popularizes the term *scientific management* in his Eastern Rate Case testimony before the Interstate Commerce Commission by arguing that railroad rate increases should be denied because the railroads could save "a million dollars a day" by applying scientific management methods.

1911
- Frederick W. Taylor publishes *The Principles of Scientific Management*.

1912
- Harrington Emerson publishes *The Twelve Principles of Efficiency*, which puts forth an interdependent but coordinated management system.

1913
- Hugo Munsterberg's *Psychology and Industrial Efficiency* calls for the application of psychology to industry.

1914

- Robert Michels, in his analysis of the workings of political parties and labor unions, *Political Parties*, formulates his iron law of oligarchy: "Who says organization, says oligarchy."

1916

- In France, Henri Fayol publishes his *General and Industrial Management*, the first complete theory of management.

1922

- Max Weber's structural definition of bureaucracy is published posthumously; it uses an "ideal-type" approach to extrapolate from the real world the central core of features that characterizes the most fully developed form of bureaucratic organization.

1924

- Hawthorne studies begin at the Hawthorne Works of the Western Electric Company in Chicago; they last until 1932 and lead to new thinking about the relationships among work environment, human motivation, and productivity.

1926

- Mary Parker Follett, in calling for "power with" as opposed to "power over," anticipates the movement toward more participatory management styles.

1931

- Mooney and Reiley, in *Onward Industry* (republished in 1939 as *The Principles of Organization*), show how the newly discovered "principles of organization" have really been known since ancient times.

1933

- Elton Mayo's *The Human Problems of an Industrial Civilization* is the first major report on the Hawthorne studies, the first significant call for a human relations movement.

1937

- Luther Gulick's "Notes on the Theory of Organization" draws attention to the functional elements of the work of an executive with his mnemonic device POSDCORB.

1938

- Chester I. Barnard's *The Functions of the Executive*, his sociological analysis of organizations, encourages and foreshadows the postwar revolution in thinking about organizational behavior.

1939

- Roethlisberger and Dickson publish *Management and the Worker*, the definitive account of the Hawthorne studies.

1940

- Robert K. Merton's article "Bureaucratic Structure and Personality" proclaims that Max Weber's "ideal-type" bureaucracy has inhibiting dysfunctions leading to inefficiency and worse.

1941

- James Burnham, in *The Managerial Revolution*, asserts that as the control of large organizations passes from the hands of the owners into the hands of professional administrators, the society's new governing class will be the possessors not of wealth but of technical expertise.

1943

- Abraham Maslow's "needs hierarchy" first appears in his *Psychological Review* article, "A Theory of Human Motivation."

1946

- Herbert A. Simon's "The Proverbs of Administration" attacks the principles approach to management for being inconsistent and often inapplicable.

1947

- National Training Laboratories for Group Development (now called the NTL Institute for Applied Behavioral Science) is established to do research on group dynamics and later, sensitivity training.

- Herbert A. Simon's *Administrative Behavior* urges that a true scientific method be used in the study of administrative phenomena, that the perspective of logical positivism should be used in dealing with questions of policy making, and that decision making is the true heart of administration.

1948

- Dwight Waldo publishes *The Administrative State*, which attacks the "gospel of efficiency" that dominated administrative thinking prior to World War II.

- In their *Human Relations* article "Overcoming Resistance to Change," Lester Coch and John R. P. French, Jr., note that employees resist change less when the need for it is effectively communicated to them and when the workers are involved in planning the changes.

- Norbert Wiener coins the term *cybernetics* in his book with the same title, which becomes a critical foundation concept for the systems school of organizational theory.

1949

- Philip Selznick, in *TVA and the Grass Roots*, discovers "co-optation" when he examines how the Tennessee Valley Authority subsumed new external elements into its policy-making process in order to prevent those elements from becoming a threat to the organization.

- In his *Public Administration Review* article "Power and Administration," Norton E. Long finds that power is the lifeblood of administration, and that

managers had to more than just apply the scientific method to problems—
they had to attain, maintain, and increase their power or risk failing in
their mission.

- Rufus E. Miles, Jr., of the Bureau of the Budget first states Miles' Law:
"Where you stand depends on where you sit."

- Air Force Captain Edsel Murphy first states Murphy's Law: "If anything can
go wrong, it will."

1950

- George C. Homans publishes *The Human Group*, the first major application
of "systems" to organizational analysis.

1951

- Kurt Lewin proposes a general model of change consisting of three phases,
"unfreezing, change, refreezing," in his *Field Theory in Social Science*; this
model becomes the conceptual frame for organization development.

- Ludwig von Bertalanffy's article "General Systems Theory: A New Approach
to the Unity of Science" is published in *Human Biology*; his concepts will
become *the* intellectual basis for the systems approach to organizational
thinking.

1954

- Peter Drucker's book, *The Practice of Management*, popularizes the concept
of management by objectives.

- Alvin Gouldner's *Patterns of Industrial Bureaucracy* describes three possible
responses to a formal bureaucratic structure: "mock," where the formal rules
are ignored by both management and labor; "punishment-centered," where
management seeks to enforce rules that workers resist; and "representative,"
where rules are both enforced and obeyed.

1956

- William H. Whyte, Jr., first profiles *The Organization Man*, an individual
within an organization who accepts its values and finds harmony in conforming to its policies.

- In the premier issue of *Administrative Science Quarterly*, Talcott Parsons'
article "Suggestions for a Sociological Approach to the Theory of Organizations" defines an organization as a social system that focuses on the attainment of specific goals and contributes, in turn, to the accomplishment of
goals of the larger organization or society itself.

- Kenneth Boulding's *Management Science* article, "General Systems Theory—
The Skeleton of Science," integrates Wiener's concept of cybernetics with
von Bertalanffy's general systems theory; this will become the most quoted
introduction to the systems concept of organization.

1957

- C. Northcote Parkinson discovers his law that "work expands so as to fill the time available for its completion."

- Chris Argyris asserts in his first major book, *Personality and Organization,* that there is an inherent conflict between the personality of a mature adult and the needs of modern organizations.

- Douglas M. McGregor's article "The Human Side of Enterprise" distills the contending traditional (authoritarian) and humanistic managerial philosophies into Theory X and Theory Y; applies the concept of "self-fulfilling prophesies" to organizational behavior.

- Philip Selznick in *Leadership in Administration* anticipates many of the 1980s notions of "transformational leadership" when he asserts that the function of an institutional leader is to help shape the environment in which the institution operates and to define new institutional directions through recruitment, training, and bargaining.

- Alvin W Gouldner, in "Cosmopolitans and Locals," identifies two latent social roles that tend to manifest themselves in organizations: "cosmopolitans," who have small loyalty to the employing organization, high commitment to specialized skills, and an outer-reference group orientation; and "locals," who have high loyalty to the employing organization, a low commitment to specialized skills, and an inner-reference group orientation.

1958

- March and Simon, in *Organizations,* seek to inventory and classify all that is worth knowing about the behavioral revolution in organization theory.

- Leon Festinger, the father of cognitive dissonance theory, writes "The Motivating Effect of Cognitive Dissonance," which becomes the theoretical foundation for the "inequity theories of motivation."

- Robert Tannenbaum and Warren H. Schmidt's *Harvard Business Review* article "How to Choose a Leadership Pattern" describes "democratic management" and devises a leadership continuum ranging from authoritarian to democratic.

1959

- Charles A. Lindblom's "The Science of 'Muddling Through'" rejects the rational model of decision making in favor of incrementalism.

- Herzberg, Mausner, and Snyderman's *The Motivation to Work* puts forth the motivation-hygiene theory of worker motivation.

- Cyert and March postulate that power and politics impact on the formation of organizational goals; their "A Behavioral Theory of Organizational Objectives" is an early precursor of the power and politics school.

- John R. P. French and Bertram Raven identify five bases of power (expert, referent, reward, legitimate, and coercive) in their article "The Bases of

Social Power." They argue that managers should not rely on coercive and expert power bases, as they are least effective.

1960
- Richard Neustadt's *Presidential Power* asserts that the president's (or any executive's)essential power is that of persuasion.
- Herbert Kaufman's *The Forest Ranger* shows how organizational and professional socialization can develop the will and capacity to conform in employees.

1961
- Victor A. Thompson's *Modern Organization* finds that there is "an imbalance between ability and authority" causing bureaucratic dysfunctions all over the place.
- Harold Koontz's "The Management Theory Jungle" describes thinking about management as a "semantics jungle."
- Burns and Stalker's *The Management of Innovation* articulates the need for different types of management systems (organic or mechanistic) under differing circumstances.
- Rensis Likert's *New Patterns of Management* offers an empirically based defense of participatory management and organization development techniques.
- William G. Scott's *Academy of Management Journal* article, "Organization Theory: An Overview and an Appraisal," articulates the relationship between systems theory and organization theory and the distinction between micro and macro perspectives in the development of theory.
- Amatai Etzioni, in *A Comparative Analysis of Complex Organizations*, argues that organizational effectiveness is affected by the match between an organization's goal structure and its compliance structure.

1962
- Robert Presthus' *The Organizational Society* presents his threefold classification of patterns of organizational accommodation: "upward-mobiles," who identify and accept the values of the organization; "indifferents," who reject such values and find personal satisfaction off the job; and "ambivalents," who want the rewards of organizational life but can't cope with the demands.
- Blau and Scott, in their *Formal Organizations: A Comparative Approach*, assert that all organizations include both a formal and informal element, and that it is impossible to know and understand the true structure of a formal organization without a similar understanding of its parallel informal organization.
- David Mechanic's *Administrative Science Quarterly* article "Sources of Power of Lower Participants in Complex Organizations" anticipates the power and politics perspective of organization theory.

1963

- Strauss, Schatzman, Bucher, Erlich, and Sabshin describe the maintenance of order in a hospital as a dynamic process operating within a framework of negotiated "contracts" among people and groups with different expectations and interests, in "The Hospital and Its Negotiated Order."
- Cyert and March, in *A Behavioral Theory of the Firm*, demonstrate that corporations tend to "satisfice" rather than engage in economically rational profit-maximizing behavior.

1964

- Blake and Mouton's *The Managerial Grid* uses a graphic gridiron to explain management styles and their potential impacts on an organization development program.
- Michel Crozier in *The Bureaucratic Phenomenon* defines a bureaucracy as "an organization which cannot correct its behavior by learning from its errors."
- Bertram M. Gross publishes his two-volume *The Managing of Organizations*, a historical analysis of thinking about organizations from ancient times to the present.

1965

- Don K. Price publishes *The Scientific Estate*, in which he posits that decisional authority flows inexorably from the executive suite to the technical office.
- Robert L. Kahn's *Organizational Stress* is the first major study of the mental health consequences of organizational role conflict and ambiguity.
- James G. March edits the huge *Handbook of Organizations*, which sought to summarize all existing knowledge on organization theory and behavior.

1966

- Katz and Kahn, in *The Social Psychology of Organizations*, seek to unify the findings of behavioral science on organizational behavior through open systems theory.
- *Think Magazine* publishes David C. McClelland's article "That Urge to Achieve," in which he identifies two groups of people: the majority of whom are not concerned about achieving, and the minority who are challenged by the opportunity to achieve. This notion becomes a premise for future motivation studies.
- Warren Bennis, in *Changing Organizations*, sounds the death knell for bureaucratic institutions because they are inadequate for a future that will demand rapid organizational change, participatory management, and the growth of a more professionalized work force.

1967

- James D. Thompson's *Organizations in Action* seeks to close the gap between open and closed systems theory by suggesting that organizations deal with the uncertainty of their environments by creating specific elements designed to cope with the outside world while other elements are able to focus on the rational nature of technical operations.

- Anthony Downs' *Inside Bureaucracy* seeks to develop laws and propositions that would aid in predicting the behavior of bureaus and bureaucrats.

- John Kenneth Galbraith's *The New Industrial State* asserts that the control of modern corporations has passed to the technostructure and that this technostructure is more concerned with stability than profits.

- Antony Jay, in *Management and Machiavelli*, applies Machiavelli's political principles (from *The Prince*) to modern organizational management.

1968

- Harold Wilensky's *Organizational Intelligence* presents the pioneering study of the flow and perception of information in organizations.

- In *Group Dynamics*, Dorwin Cartwright and Alvin Zander propose that the systematic study of group dynamics would advance knowledge of the nature of groups; how they are organized; and relationships among individuals, other groups, and larger institutions.

- John P. Campbell and M.D. Dunnette's "Effectiveness of T-Group Experiences in Managerial Training and Development," appearing in *Psychological Bulletin*, provides a critical review of T-Group literature. They conclude that "an individual's positive feelings about his T-Group experiences" cannot be scientifically measured, nor should they be based entirely on "existential grounds."

- Walker and Lorsch grapple with the perennial structural issue of whether to design organizations by product or function in their *Harvard Business Review* article, "Organizational Choice: Product vs. Function."

- Frederick Herzberg's *Harvard Business Review* article "One More Time, How Do You Motivate Employees?" catapults *motivators* or *satisfiers* and *hygiene factors* into the forefront of organizational motivation theory.

1969

- Laurence J. Peter promulgates his principle that "in a hierarchy every employee tends to rise to his level of incompetence."

- Lawrence and Lorsch, in *Organization and Environment*, call for a contingency theory that can deal with the appropriateness of different theories under differing circumstances; they state that organizations must solve the problem of simultaneous differentiation and integration.

- Paul Hersey and Kenneth R. Blanchard's "Life Cycle Theory of Leadership," appearing in *Training and Development Journal*, asserts that the appropriate leadership style for a given situation depends upon the employee's education and experience levels, achievement motivation, and willingness to accept responsibility by the subordinates.

1970

- Burton Clark's *The Distinctive College* identifies ways that three colleges created and maintained their distinctiveness through the management of symbols.
- In "Expectancy Theory," John P. Campbell, Marvin D. Dunnette, Edward E. Lawler III, and Karl E. Weick, Jr., articulate the *expectancy theories of motivation*. People are motivated by calculating how much they want something, how much of it they think they will get, how likely it is their actions will cause them to get it, and how much others in similar circumstances have received.
- Chris Argyris writes *Intervention Theory and Methods*, which becomes one of the most widely cited and enduring works on organizational consulting for change that is written from the organizational behavior/organization development perspective.

1971

- Graham T. Allison's *Essence of Decision* demonstrates the inadequacies of the view that the decisions of a government are made by a "single calculating decisionmaker" who has control over the organizations and officials within his government.
- Irving Janis' "Groupthink," first published in *Psychology Today*, proposes that group cohesion can lead to the deterioration of effective group decision-making efforts.

1972

- Wildcat strike at General Motors Lordstown, Ohio, automobile assembly plant calls national attention to the dysfunctions of dehumanized and monotonous work.
- Harlan Cleveland, in *The Future Executive*, asserts that decision making in the future will call for "continuous improvisation on a general sense of direction."
- Charles Perrow's *Complex Organizations* is a major defense of bureaucratic forms of organization and an attack on those writers who think that bureaucracy can be easily, fairly, or inexpensively replaced.
- Kast and Rosenzweig, in their *Academy of Management Journal* article "General Systems Theory: Applications for Organization and Management," assess the level of successful application of general systems theory in organizations and advocate a contingency theory as a less abstract and more applicable theoretical approach.

1973

- Jay Galbraith, in *Designing Complex Organizations*, articulates the systems/contingency view that the amount of information an organization needs is a function of the levels of its uncertainty, interdependence of units and functions, and adaptation mechanisms.

1974

- In a report for the Carnegie Commission on Higher Education, Michael Cohen and James March introduce the phrase *organized anarchies* to communicate why colleges and universities are distinctive organizational forms with uniquely difficult leadership needs and problems. The report was published as the book, *Leadership and Ambiguity: The American College President*.
- Robert J. House and Terrance R. Mitchell's *Journal of Contemporary Business* article "Path-Goal Theory of Leadership" offers path-goal theory as a useful tool for explaining the effectiveness of certain leadership styles in given situations.
- Victor H. Vroom's *Organizational Dynamics* article "A New Look at Managerial Decision-Making" develops a useful model whereby leaders can perform a diagnosis of a situation to determine which leadership style is most appropriate.
- Steven Kerr's *Academy of Management Journal* article "On the Folly of Rewarding A, While Hoping for B" substantiates that many organizational reward systems are "fouled up"—they pay off for behaviors other than those they are seeking.

1975

- Oliver E. Williamson analyzes organizational decisions to produce products and services internally or to purchase them externally using economic market models, and assesses the implications of such decisions on, for example, organizational authority, in *Markets and Hierarchies: Analysis and Antitrust Implications*.
- *Behavior in Organizations*, by Lyman Porter, Edward Lawler III, and Richard Hackman, examines how individual–organizational relationships emerge and grow, including how groups can exert influence on individuals in organizations and how such social influences relate to work effectiveness.

1976

- Michael Maccoby psychoanalytically interviews 250 corporate managers and discovers "The Gamesman," a manager whose main interest lies in "competitive activity where he can prove himself a winner."
- Jensen and Meekling describe an organization as simply an extension of and a means for satisfying the interests of the multiple individuals and groups that affect and are affected by it, in "Agency Costs and the Theory of the Firm."
- In "A Concept of Organizational Ecology," Eric Trist proposes a concept of organizational population ecology based on the field that is created by a number of organizations whose interrelations comprise a system. The system is the field as a whole, not its component organizations.

1977

- Hannan and Freeman's article "The Population Ecology of Organizations" proposes a new unit of analysis for understanding organizations: the "population of organizations."

- Salancik and Pfeffer's article "Who Gets Power—and How They Hold on to It" explains how power and politics help organizations adapt to their environment by reallocating critical resources to subunits that are performing tasks most vital to organizational survival.

- In *Matrix*, Davis and Lawrence caution against using a matrix form of organization unless there exist specific organizational conditions that are conducive to its success.

- Rosabeth Moss Kanter, in *Men and Women of the Corporation*, describes the unique problems women encounter with power and politics in organizations.

1978

- Thomas J. Peters' *Organizational Dynamics* article "Symbols, Patterns, and Settings: An Optimistic Case for Getting Things Done" is the first major analysis of symbolic management in organizations to gain significant attention in the "mainstream" literature of organization theory.

1979

- Rosabeth Moss Kanter's *Harvard Business Review* article "Power Failure in Management Circuits" identifies organizational positions that tend to have power problems—then argues that powerlessness is often more of a problem than power for organizations.

- *Structuring Organizations* is published, the first book in Henry Mintzberg's integrative series on "The Theory of Management Policy."

1980

- Connolly, Conlon, and Deutsch argue that evaluations of organizational effectiveness should employ multiple criteria that reflect the diverse interests of the various constituencies that are involved with organizations, in "Organizational Effectiveness: A Multiple-Constituency Approach."

- Meryl Reis Louis's *Administrative Science Quarterly* article, "Surprise and Sense Making: What Newcomers Experience in Entering Unfamiliar Organizational Settings," proposes that sense-making by newcomers usually must rely on inadequate sources of information which can lead them astray.

1981

- In "Organization Development: A Political Perspective," Anthony Cobb and Newton Margulies argue that organization development (OD) has developed more political sensitivity and sophistication than most critics realize, but that political activity by OD practitioners is fraught with serious utilitarian and values problems.

- Jeffrey Pfeffer's *Power in Organizations* integrates the tenets and applications of the power and politics school of organization theory.

- Thomas Ouchi's *Theory Z* and Pascale and Athos' *The Art of Japanese Management* popularize the Japanese management "movement."

1982

- Organizational culture becomes "hot" in the general business literature with such books as Peters and Waterman's *In Search of Excellence*, Deal and Kennedy's *Corporate Culture*, and *Business Week*'s cover story on "Corporate Culture."

1983

- Henry Mintzberg's *Power in and Around Organizations* molds the power and politics school of organizational theory into an integrative theory of management policy.

- In *The Change Masters*, Rosabeth Moss Kanter defines *change masters* as architects of organizational change; they are the right people in the right places at the right time.

- Meryl R. Louis' article "Organizations as Cultural-Bearing Milieux" becomes the first readable, integrative statement of the organizational cultural school's assumptions and positions.

- "Values in Organizational Theory and Management Education," by Michael Keeley, proposes that organizations exist by virtue of agreement on joint activities to achieve separate purposes of important constituencies, not to achieve organizational goals or purposes.

- Ian Mitroff's *Stakeholders of the Organizational Mind* explains how the perceptions of internal and external organizational stakeholders influence organizational behavior—particularly, decision making about complex problems of organizational policy and design.

- Pondy, Frost, Morgan, and Dandridge edit the first definitive volume on symbolic management, *Organizational Symbolism*.

- Linda Smircich's article "Organizations as Shared Meanings" examines how systems of commonly shared meanings develop and are sustained in organizations through symbolic communications processes, and also how these shared meanings provide members of an organizational culture with a sense of commonality and a distinctive character.

1984

- Sergiovanni and Corbally edit the first notable collection of papers on the organizational culture perspective, *Leadership and Organizational Culture*. Sergiovanni's opening chapter "Cultural and Competing Perspectives in Administrative Theory and Practice" clearly articulates the fundamental underlying assumptions of the organizational culture and symbolic management perspective.

- Siehl and Martin report the findings of the first major quantitative and qualitative empirical study of organizational culture in their "The Role of Symbolic Management: How Can Managers Effectively Transmit Organizational Culture?"

1985

- Edgar Schein writes the most comprehensive and integrative statement of the organizational culture school in his *Organizational Culture and Leadership*.

- In *The Irrational Organization*, Nils Brunsson postulates that rationality may lead to good decisions, but it decreases the probability of organizational action and change.

- *Administrative Development*, by Muhammad A. Al-Buraey, combines Western methodology and technique with Islamic substance, values, and ethics, to demonstrate how the Islamic perspective (as a system and a way of life) is an important moving force in the process and realization of administrative development world-wide.

1986

- *Corporate Culture: Diagnosis and Change*, by Desmond Graves, presents the first serious methodological treatise on "diagnosing" organizational culture.

- Michael Harmon and Richard Mayer write a comprehensive text that applies organization theory in the public sector, *Organization Theory for Public Administration*.

- Gareth Morgan's *Images of Organization* develops the art of reading and understanding organizations starting from the premise that our theories of organization are based on distinctive but partial mental images or metaphors.

1988

- Michael Keeley combines and extends his previous essays on multiple constituencies, organizational purposes, systems of justice, values, and organizational worth into the first comprehensive statement of *A Social-Contract Theory of Organizations*.

- Quinn and Cameron compile *Paradox and Transformation*, an important collection of essays on the necessity for managing with paradoxes in complex organizations, rather than necessarily trying to eliminate them.

- The *American Journal of Sociology* publishes a heated debate between the leading proponents and detractors of population ecology of organization theory.

- *In the Age of the Smart Machine*, by Shoshana Zuboff, examines the effects of information technology change on authority and hierarchy—on people and organizations.

1989

- Rosabeth Moss Kanter's book *When Giants Learn to Dance* examines how organizations can gain the advantages of smallness (flexibility) and size (staying power) at the same time.

- *Developing Corporate Character*, by Alan Wilkins, explains how it is difficult but possible to change elements of an organizational culture without destroying the positive aspects of the culture that already exist.

1990

- Sally Helgesen creates *diary studies* that explore how women leaders make decisions and gather and disperse information in organizations. Helgesen suggests that "women may be the new Japanese" of management, in *The Female Advantage*.

- "In Praise of Hierarchy," by Elliott Jaques, argues that critics of hierarchy are misguided. Instead of needing new organizational forms, we need to learn how to manage hierarchies better.

- In *Organizations, Uncertainties and Risk*, James F. Short, Jr., and Lee Clarke describe how organizational behavior is impacted by decision making under risk and uncertainty, and how, in turn, risk and uncertainty in the general society affect the decision making of organizations.

- Paul S. Goodman and Lee S. Sproull describe how organizational behavior is affected by new technologies. They argue that the impacts of technology are so profound that organizations must find new ways of conducting enterprise in order to survive the new techno/business climate; in *Technology and Organizations*.

- Allan R. Cohen and David L. Bradford's book, *Influence Without Authority* discusses an alternative method of work achievement based on the law of reciprocity that leads to organizational self-empowerment and the mutual advantage of participants.

- *Symbols and Artifacts: Views of the Corporate Landscape*, by Pasquale Gagliardi, focuses on corporate artifacts: buildings, objects, images, and forms that go into the making of corporate cultures. Gagliardi presents social constructivist, phenomenological, and interpretive views of reality.

- Peter Senge's highly influential book, *The Fifth Discipline*, describes organizations with "learning disabilities" and how "learning organizations" defy the odds to overcome them.

- David Ulrich and Dale Lake develop a theory of inside competition that emphasizes organizational capability. Their book, *Organizational Capability: Competing from the Inside Out*, explains what "capability" is and how to develop competitiveness based on management action.

- Lex Donaldson's *Academy of Management Review* article, "The Ethereal Hand: Organizational Economics and Management Theory," demonstrates the potentialities and pitfalls of organizational economics.

- Karl Weick's chapter, "Technology as Equivoque: Sensemaking in New Technologies," examines cognitive processes that people use in their struggle to adapt to work in environments where important events are unpredictable and chaotic; in Goodman and Sproull's book, *Technology and Organizations*.

1991

- Robert G. Lord and Karen J. Maher frame leadership in terms of how organizational "commandants" process information—rational, limited-capacity, expert, and cybernetic—and relate this to how other participants in the leader's environment process information about him or her; in, *Information Processing: Linking Perceptions and Performance*.

- Kathleen D. Ryan and Daniel K. Oestreich's book, *Driving Fear Out of the Workplace: How to Overcome the Invisible Barriers to Quality, Productivity, and Innovation*, explains the relationship between fear and workplace productivity. Management should take responsibility for fear in the workplace, starting with themselves, and then enlist the efforts of all organizational participants.

- Manfred Kets de Vries demonstrates how individuals' rational and irrational behavior patterns influence organizations; in *Organizations on the Couch*.

1992

- Thierry C. Pauchant and Ian I. Mitroff explore crisis-prone organizations and the psychological and emotional factors that enable managers to ignore the possibility of pending crises, in *Transforming The Crisis-Prone Organization*.

- Jeffrey Pfeffer's book, *Managing With Power*, describes how to consolidate power and use it for constructive organizational goals. The book teaches managers how to use power for advantage, to stop fearing it, and to realize that if they do not use power, someone else will.

- Barbara Czarniawska-Joerges explains sensemaking in organizational life—even when organizational behavior does not make sense. Her ideas as proposed in *Exploring Complex Organizations: A Cultural Perspective* constitute a cross-cultural and cross-contextual analysis of sense-making in large organizations.

- *Organizational Architecture*, by David Nadler, Marc Gerstein, and Robert Shaw, uses architecture as a metaphor to identify evolving forms and features of effective organizations of the future, including: autonomous work teams, high-performance work systems, spinouts, networks, self-designed organizations, and fuzzy boundaries.

- In *Creating Corporate Culture: From Discord to Harmony*, Charles Hampden-Turner studies organizations facing challenges from evolving cultures, using the perspective of "core dilemmas." Dilemmas are two "lemmas" or propositions located on an axis with the organization located in between.

- "Gendering Organization Theory" by Joan Acker, asserts that ordinary activities in organizations are not gender-neutral. They perpetuate the "gendered substructure within the organization itself and within the wider society"—as well as in organization theory; in A. J. Mills and P. Pancred, *Gendering Organizational Analysis*.

- David Osborne & Ted Gaebler's best-selling book, *Reinventing government: How the entrepreneurial spirit is transforming the public sector*, claims that public agencies are designed to protect against politicians and bureaucrats gaining too much power or misusing public money. Instead, we need "entrepreneurial government."

- Ralph D. Stacey's book, *Managing the Unknowable: Strategic Boundaries Between Order and Chaos*, challenges the view that organizational success stems from stability, harmony, predictability and stable equilibrium. Managers should embrace "unbounded instability," because disorder, chance, and irregularity can be beneficial.

- Richard Beckhard and Wendy Pritchard's *Changing the Essence* discusses leadership behaviors that are necessary for initiating and managing fundamental organizational change.

1993

- William Bergquist's book, *The Postmodern Organization*, looks comparatively at premodern, modern, and postmodern notions of five dimensions of organizational life: size and complexity, mission and boundaries, leadership, communication, and capital and worker values.

- *Cultural Diversity in Organizations*, by Taylor Cox, Jr., examines the potential benefits and the difficulties that may accrue to an organization from cultural diversity.

- Ian I. Mitroff and Harold A. Linstone examine four ways of knowing, or inquiry systems designed to assist decision making, in *The Unbounded Mind: Breaking the Chains of Traditional Business Thinking*.

- *Reengineering the Corporation*, by Michael Hammer and James Champy, describes how to radically redesign a company's processes, organization, and culture to achieve a quantum leap in performance.

- In *The Corporate Closet*, James D. Woods and Jay H. Lucas explore what it is like to be gay in the corporate world and how to manage sexual identity in the workplace. They encourage openness in corporate practices, such as listing sexual preference, as well as with gender and ethnicity in training, recruiting, and retention programs.

- In a *Public Administration Review* article, "Nonlinear Dynamical Analysis: Assessing Systems Concepts in a Government Agency," L. Douglas Kiel suggests that nonlinear dynamics, or chaos theory, can be applied to public agencies because human organizations are nonlinear systems.

- Harrison M. Trice and Janice M. Beyer write the most comprehensive treatise on organizational culture, *The Cultures of Work Organizations*.

1994

- *Managing Chaos and Complexity in Government*, by L. Douglas Kiel, applies chaos theory to self-organization in public management. Kiel shows how the deep structures and processes of agency dynamics can foster learning and coping with risk and uncertainty.

CHAPTER I

Classical Organization Theory

No single date can be pinpointed as the beginning of serious thinking about how organizations work and how they should be structured and managed. One can trace writings about management and organizations as far back as the known origins of commerce. A lot can be learned from the early organizations of the Muslims, Hebrews, Greeks, and Romans. If we were to take the time, we could make the case that much of what we know about organization theory has its origins in ancient and medieval times. After all, it was Aristotle who first wrote of the importance of culture to management systems, ibn Taymiyyah who used the scientific method to outline the principles of administration within the framework of Islam, and Machiavelli who gave the world the definitive analysis of the use of power.

In order to give the reader a sense of organization theory's deep roots in earlier eras, we offer two examples of ancient wisdom on organization management. The first of our ancient examples is from the Book of Exodus, Chapter 18 (see Box 1), in which Jethro, Moses' father-in-law, chastises Moses for failing to establish an organization through which he could delegate his responsibility for the administration of justice. In Verse 25, Moses accepts Jethro's advice; he "chose able men out of all Israel, and made them heads over the people, rulers of thousands, rulers of hundreds, rulers of fifties, and rulers of tens." Moses continued to judge the "hard cases," but his rulers judged "every small matter" themselves. This concept of "management by exception" would later be developed for modern audiences by Frederick Winslow Taylor.

In the second ancient example (see the first selection in this chapter), Socrates anticipates the arguments for "generic management" and "principles of management" as he explains to Nicomachides that a leader who "knows what he needs, and is able to provide it, [can] be a good president, whether he have the direction of a chorus, a family, a city, or an army" (Xenophon, 1869). Socrates lists and discusses the duties of all good presidents—of public and private institutions—and emphasizes the similarities. This is the first known statement that organizations as entities are basically alike; that a manager who could cope well with one would be equally adept at coping with others—even though their purposes and functions might be widely disparate.

Box 1

Exodus Chapter 18

13 And it came to pass on the morrow, that Moses sat to judge the people: and the people stood by Moses from the morning unto the evening.

14 And when Moses' father-in-law saw all that he did to the people, he said, "What *is* this thing that thou doest to the people? why sittest thou thyself alone, and all the people stand by thee from morning unto even?"

15 And Moses said unto his father-in-law, "Because the people come unto me to inquire of God:

16 When they have a matter, they come unto me; and I judge between one and another, and I do make *them* know the statutes of God, and his laws."

17 And Moses' father-in-law said unto him, "The thing that thou doest is not good.

18 Thou wilt surely wear away, both thou, and this people that *is* with thee: for this thing *is* too heavy for thee: thou art not able to perform it thyself alone.

19 Hearken now unto my voice, I will give thee counsel, and God shall be with thee: Be thou for the people to God-ward, that thou mayest bring the causes unto God:

20 And thou shalt teach them ordinances and laws, and shalt shew them the way wherein they must walk, and the work that they must do.

21 Moreover thou shalt provide out of all the people able men, such as fear God, men of truth, hating covetousness; and place *such* over them, *to be* rulers of thousands, *and* rulers of hundreds, rulers of fifties, and rulers of tens:

22 And let them judge the people at all seasons: and it shall be, *that* every great matter they shall bring unto thee, but every small matter they shall judge: so shall it be easier for thyself, and they shall bear *the burden* with thee.

23 If thou shall do this thing, and God command thee *so*, then thou shalt be able to endure, and all this people shall also go to their place in peace."

24 So Moses hearkened to the voice of his father-in-law, and did all that he had said.

25 And Moses chose able men out of all Israel, and made them heads over the people, rulers of thousands, rulers of hundreds, rulers of fifties, and rulers of tens.

26 And they judged the people at all seasons: the hard cases they brought unto Moses, but every small matter they judged themselves.

27 And Moses let his father-in-law depart; and he went his way into his own land.

Although it is always great fun to delve into the wisdom of the ancients, most analysts of the origins of organization theory view the beginnings of the factory system in Great Britain in the eighteenth century as the birthpoint of complex economic organizations and, consequently, of the field of organization theory.

Classical organization theory, as its name implies, was the first theory of its kind, is considered traditional, and continues to be the base upon which other schools of organization theory have built. Thus, an understanding of classical organization theory is essential not only because of its historical interest but also, more importantly, because subsequent analyses and theories presume a knowledge of it.

The classical school dominated organization theory into the 1930s and remains highly influential today (Merkle, 1980). Over the years, classical organization theory expanded and matured. Its basic tenets and assumptions, however, which were rooted in the industrial revolution of the 1700s and the professions of mechanical engineering, industrial engineering, and economics, have never changed. They were only expanded upon, refined, and made more sophisticated. These fundamental tenets are that:

1. Organizations exist to accomplish production-related and economic goals.
2. There is one best way to organize for production, and that way can be found through systematic, scientific inquiry.
3. Production is maximized through specialization and division of labor.
4. People and organizations act in accordance with rational economic principles.

The evolution of any theory must be viewed in context. The beliefs of early management theorists about how organizations worked or should work were a direct reflection of the societal values of their times. And the times were harsh. It was well into the twentieth century before the industrial workers of the United States and Europe began to enjoy even limited "rights" as organization citizens. Workers were viewed not as individuals but as the interchangeable parts in an industrial machine whose parts were made of flesh only when it was impractical to make them of steel.

The advent of power-driven machinery and hence the modern factory system spawned our current concepts of economic organizations and organization for production. Power-driven equipment was expensive. Production workers could not purchase and use their own equipment as they had their own tools. Remember the phrase for being fired—"get the sack." It comes from the earliest days of the industrial revolution when a dismissed worker literally was given a sack in which to gather up his tools. Increasingly, workers without their own tools and often without any special skills had to gather for work where the equipment was— in factories. Expensive equipment had to produce enough output to justify their acquisition and maintenance costs.

The advent of the factory system presented managers of organizations with an unprecedented array of new problems. Managers had to arrange for heavy infusions of capital, plan and organize for reliable large-scale production, coordinate and control activities of large numbers of people and functions, contain costs (this was hardly a concern under "cottage industry" production), and maintain a trained and motivated work force.

Under the factory system, organizational success resulted from well-organized production systems that kept machines busy and costs under control. Industrial and mechanical engineers—and their machines—were the keys to production. Organizational structures and production systems were needed to take best advantage of the machines. Organizations, it was thought, should work like machines, using people, capital, and machines as their parts. Just as industrial engineers sought to design "the best" machines to keep factories productive, industrial and mechanical engineering-type thinking dominated theories about "the best way" to organize for production. Thus, the first theories of organizations were concerned primarily with the anatomy—or structure—of formal organizations. This was the milieu, or the environment, the mode of thinking, that shaped and influenced the tenets of classical organization theory.

Centralization of equipment and labor in factories, division of specialized labor, management of specialization, and economic paybacks on factory equipment all were concerns of the Scottish economist Adam Smith's work *An Inquiry into the Nature and Causes of the Wealth of Nations* (1776). The historian Arnold Toynbee (1956) identified Adam Smith (1723-1790) and James Watt (1736-1819) as the two people who were most responsible for pushing the world into industrialization. Watt, of course, invented the steam engine.

Smith, who is considered the "father" of the academic discipline of economics, provided the intellectual foundation for laissez-faire capitalism. *The Wealth of Nations* (1776) devotes its first chapter, "Of the Division of Labour," to a discussion of the optimum organization of a pin factory. Why? Because specialization of labor was one of the pillars of Smith's "invisible hand" market mechanism in which the greatest rewards would go to those who were the most efficient in the competitive marketplace. Traditional pin makers could produce only a few dozen pins a day. When organized in a factory with each worker performing a limited operation, they could produce tens of thousands a day. Smith's "Of the Division of Labour" is reprinted here because, coming as it did at the dawn of the Industrial Revolution, it is the most famous and influential statement on the economic rationale of the factory system. Smith revolutionized thinking about economics and organizations. Thus we have operationally defined 1776, the year in which *Wealth of Nations* was published, as the beginning point of organization theory as an applied science and academic discipline. Besides, 1776 was a good year for other events as well.

In 1856 Daniel C. McCallum (1815-1878), the visionary general superintendent of the New York and Erie Railroad, elucidated general principles of organization that "may be regarded as settled and necessary." His principles included division of responsibilities, power commensurate with responsibilities, and a reporting system that allowed managers to know promptly if responsibilities were "faithfully executed" and to identify errors and "delinquent" subordinates. McCallum, who is also credited with creating the first modern organization chart, had an enormous influence on the managerial development of the American railroad industry.

In systematizing America's first big business before the Civil War, McCallum provided the model principles and procedures of management for the big businesses that would follow after the war. He became so much *the* authority on running railroads that, as a major general during the Civil War, he was chosen to run the Union's military rail system. Although McCallum was highly influential as a practitioner, he was no scholar, and the only coherent statement of his general principles comes from an annual report he wrote for the New York and Erie Railroad. Excerpts from his "Superintendent's Report" of March 25, 1856, are reprinted here.

During the 1800s, two practicing managers in the United States independently discovered that generally applicable principles of administration could be determined through systematic, scientific investigation—about thirty years before Taylor's *The Principles of Scientific Management* or Fayol's *General and Industrial Management*. The first, Captain Henry Metcalfe (1847-1917) of the United States Army's Frankford Arsenal in Philadelphia, urged managers to record production events and experiences systematically so that they could use the information to improve production processes. He published his propositions in *The Cost of Manufactures and the Administration of Workshops, Public and Private* (1885), which also pioneered in applying "pre-scientific management" methods to the problems of managerial control and asserted that there is a "science of administration" based upon principles discoverable by diligent observation. Although Metcalfe's work is important historically, it is so similar to that of Taylor's and others that it is not included here as a selection.

The second prescientific management advocate of the 1880s was Henry R. Towne (1844-1924), co-founder and president of the Yale & Towne Manufacturing Company. In 1886, Towne proposed that shop management was of equal importance to engineering management and that the American Society of Mechanical Engineers (ASME) should take a leadership role in establishing a multicompany, engineering/ management "database" on shop practices or "the management of works." The information could then be shared among established and new enterprises. Several years later, his proposal was adopted by ASME. His paper presented to the society, entitled "The Engineer as an Economist," was published in *Transactions of the American Society of Mechanical Engineers* (1886) and is reprinted here. Historians have often considered Towne's paper the first "call" for scientific management.

Interestingly, Towne had several significant associations with Frederick Winslow Taylor. The two of them were fellow draftsmen at the Midvale Steel works during the 1880s. Towne gave Taylor one of his first true opportunities to succeed at applying scientific management principles at Yale & Towne in 1904. Towne also nominated Taylor for the presidency of ASME in 1906, and thus provided him with an international forum for advocating scientific management. (Upon election, Taylor promptly reorganized the ASME according to scientific management principles.)

While the ideas of Adam Smith, Frederick Winslow Taylor, and others are still dominant influences on the design and management of organizations, it was Henri Fayol (1841-1925), a French executive engineer, who developed the first comprehensive theory of management. While Taylor was tinkering with the technology employed by the individual worker, Fayol was theorizing about all of the elements necessary to organize and manage a major corporation. Fayol's major work, *Administration Industrielle et Generale* (published in France in 1916), was almost ignored in the United States until Constance Storr's English translation, *General and Industrial Management*, appeared in 1949. Since that time, Fayol's theoretical contributions have been widely recognized and his work is considered fully as significant as that of Taylor.

Fayol believed that his concept of management was universally applicable to every type of organization. Whereas he had six principles: technical (production of goods), commercial (buying, selling, and exchange activities), financial (raising and using capital), security (protection of property and people), accounting, and managerial (coordination, control, organization, planning, and command of people); Fayol's primary interest and emphasis was on his final principle—managerial. His managerial principle addressed such variables as division of work, authority and responsibility, discipline, unity of command, unity of direction, subordination of individual interest to general interest, remuneration of personnel, centralization, scalar chains, order, equity, stability of personnel tenure, initiative, and esprit de corps. Reprinted here is Fayol's "General Principles of Management," a chapter from his *General and Industrial Management*.

About one hundred years after Adam Smith declared the factory to be the most appropriate means of mass production, Frederick Winslow Taylor and a group of his followers were "spreading the gospel" that factory workers could be much more productive if their work was designed scientifically. Taylor, the acknowledged father of the scientific management movement, pioneered the development of time-and-motion studies, originally under the name "Taylorism" or the "Taylor system." "Taylorism" or its successor scientific management was not a single invention but rather a series of methods and organizational arrangements designed by Taylor and his associates to increase the efficiency and speed of machine-shop production. Premised upon the notion that there was "one best way" of accomplishing any given task, Taylor's scientific management sought to increase output by discovering the fastest, most efficient, and least fatiguing production methods.

The job of the scientific manager, once the "one best way" was found, was to impose this procedure upon his or her organization. Classical organization theory derives from a corollary of this proposition. If there was one best way to accomplish any given production task, then correspondingly, there must also be one best way to accomplish any task of social organization—including organizing firms. Such principles of social organization were assumed to exist and to be waiting to be discovered by diligent scientific observation and analysis.

Scientific management, as espoused by Taylor, also contained a powerful, puritanical, social message. Taylor (1911) offered scientific management as the way for firms to increase profits, get rid of unions, "increase the thrift and virtue of the working classes," and raise productivity so that the broader society could enter a new era of harmony based on higher consumption of mass-produced goods by members of the laboring classes.

Scientific management emerged as a national movement during a series of events in 1910. The railroad companies in the eastern states filed for increased freight rates with the Interstate Commerce Commission. The railroads had been receiving poor press, being blamed for many things including a cost-price squeeze that was bankrupting farmers. Thus the rate hearings received extensive media coverage. Louis D. Brandeis, a self-styled populist lawyer who would later be a Supreme Court justice, took the case against the railroads without pay. Brandeis called in Harrington Emerson, a consultant who had "systematized" the Santa Fe Railroad, to testify that the railroads did not need increased rates: They could "save a million dollars a day" by using what Brandeis initially called "scientific management" methods (Urwick, 1956). At first, Taylor was reluctant to use the phrase because it sounded too academic. But the ICC hearings meant that the national scientific management boom was underway, and Taylor was its leader.

Taylor had a profound—almost revolutionary—effect on the fields of business and public administration. Taylor gained credence for the notion that organizational operations could be planned and controlled systematically by experts using scientific principles. Many of Taylor's concepts and precepts are still in use today. The legacy of scientific management is substantial. Taylor's best known work is his 1911 book *The Principles of Scientific Management*, but he also wrote numerous accounts on the subject. Reprinted here is an article, also entitled "The Principles of Scientific Management," which was the summary of an address given by him on March 3, 1915, two weeks prior to his death.

Several of Taylor's associates subsequently gained wide recognition including, for example, Frank (1868-1924) and Lillian (1878-1972) Gilbreth of *Cheaper by the Dozen* (1948) and "therblig" (Spriegel & Myers, 1953) fame; Henry Laurence Gantt (1861-1919), who invented the Gantt chart for planning work output (Alford, 1932); and Carl G. Barth (1860-1939) who, among his other accomplishments, in 1908 convinced the dean of the new Harvard Business School to adopt "Taylorism" as the "foundation concept" of modern management (Urwick, 1956).

In contrast with the fervent advocates of scientific management, Max Weber (1864-1920) was a brilliant analytical sociologist who happened to study bureaucratic organizations. Bureaucracy has emerged as a dominant feature of the contemporary world. Virtually everywhere one looks in both developed and developing nations, economic, social, and political life are influenced extensively by bureaucratic organizations. Typically *bureaucracy* is used to refer to a specific set of structural arrangements. It is also used to refer to specific patterns of behavior—patterns that are not restricted to formal bureaucracies. It is widely assumed that the structural characteristics of organizations properly defined as "bureaucratic" influence the behavior of individuals—whether clients or bureaucrats—who interact with them. Contemporary thinking along these lines began with the work of Max Weber. His analysis of bureaucracy, first published in 1922, remains the single most influential statement and the point of departure for all further analyses on the subject (including those of the "modern structuralists" in Chapter IV).

Drawing upon studies of ancient bureaucracies in Egypt, Rome, China, and the Byzantine Empire, as well as on the more modern ones emerging in Europe during the nineteenth and early part of the twentieth centuries, Weber used an "ideal-type" approach to extrapolate from the real world the central core of features characteristic of the most fully developed bureaucratic form of organization. Weber's "Bureaucracy," which is included here, is neither a description of reality nor a statement of normative preference. In fact, Weber feared the potential implications of bureaucracies. Rather, his "ideal-type" bureaucracy is merely an identification of the major variables or features that characterize this type of social institution.

Luther Gulick's "Notes on the Theory of Organization," which clearly was influenced by the work of Henry Fayol, is one of the major statements of the "principles" approach to managing the functions of organizations. It appeared in *Papers on the Science of Administration,* a collection that he and Lyndall Urwick edited in 1937. It was here that Gulick introduced his famous mnemonic, POSDCORB, which stood for the seven major functions of executive management—planning, organizing, staffing, directing, coordinating, reporting, and budgeting. Gulick's principles of administration also included unity of command and span of control. Overall, the *Papers* was a statement of the "state of the art" of organization theory. The study of organizations through analysis of management functions continues within the field of organization theory.

Daniel A. Wren (1972) once observed that "the development of a body of knowledge about how to manage has . . . evolved within a framework of the economic, social, and political facets of various cultures. Management thought is both a process in and a product of its cultural environment." The selections we have chosen to represent the classical school of organization theory vividly demonstrate Wren's thesis. Looking through 1992 lenses, it is tempting to denigrate the contributions of the classicalists—to view them as narrow and simplistic. In the context of their times, however, they were brilliant pioneers. Their thinking provided invaluable foundations for the field of organization theory, and their influence upon organization theory and theorists continues today.

REFERENCES

Al-Buraey, M. A. (1985). *Administrative development: An Islamic perspective.* London: Kegan Paul International.

Alford, L. P. (1932). *Henry Laurence Gantt: Leader in industry.* New York: Harper & Row.

Babbage, C. (1832). *On the economy of machinery and manufactures.* Philadelphia, PA: Carey & Lea.

Fayol, H. (1949). *General and industrial management* (C. Storrs, Trans.) London: Pitman. (Original work published 1916)

George, C. S., Jr. (1972). *The history of management thought.* (2nd ed.). Englewood Cliffs, NJ: Prentice-Hall.

Gilbreth, F. B., Jr., & Carey, E. G. (1948). *Cheaper by the dozen.* New York: Grosset & Dunlap.

Gulick, L. (1937). Notes on the theory of organization. In L. Gulick & L. Urwick (Eds.), *Papers on the science of administration* (pp. 3-13). New York: Institute of Public Administration.

McCallum, D.C. (1856). Superintendent's report, March 25, 1856. In *Annual report of the New York and Erie Railroad Company for 1855.* In A. D. Chandler, Jr. (Ed.), *The railroads* (pp. 101-108). New York: Harcourt Brace Jovanovich.

Merkle, J. A. (1980). *Management and ideology: The legacy of the international scientific management movement.* Berkeley, CA: University of California Press.

Metcalfe, H. (1885). *The cost of manufactures and the administration of workshops, public and private.* New York: Wiley.

Smith, A. (1776). Of the division of labour. In A. Smith, *The wealth of nations* (chap. 1).

Spriegel, W. R., & Myers, C. E. (Eds.). (1953). *The writings of the Gilbreths.* Homewood, IL: Irwin.

Taylor, F. W. (1911). *The principles of scientific management.* New York: Norton.

Taylor, F. W. (1916, December). The principles of scientific management. *Bulletin of the Taylor Society.* An abstract of an address given by the late Dr. Taylor before the Cleveland Advertising Club, March 3, 1915.

Towne, H. R. (1886, May). The engineer as an economist. *Transactions of the American Society of Mechanical Engineers, 7,* 428-432. Paper presented at a meeting of the Society, Chicago, IL.

Toynbee, A. (1956). *The industrial revolution.* Boston: Beacon Press. (Original publication 1884).

Urwick, L. (1956). *The golden book of management.* London: Newman, Neame.

Weber, M. (1922). Bureaucracy. In H. Gerth & C. W. Mills (Eds.), *Max Weber: Essays in sociology.* Oxford, UK: Oxford University Press.

Wren, D. A. (1972). *The evolution of management thought.* New York: Ronald Press.

Xenophon. (1869). *The memorabilia of Socrates,* (Rev. J. S. Watson, Trans.) New York: Harper & Row.

1
Socrates Discovers Generic Management

Seeing Nicomachides, one day, coming from the assembly for the election of magistrates, he asked him, "Who have been chosen generals, Nicomachides?"

"Are not the Athenians the same as ever, Socrates?" he replied; "for they have not chosen me, who am worn out with serving on the list, both as captain and centurion, and with having received so many wounds from the enemy (he then drew aside his robe, and showed the scars of the wounds), but have elected Antisthenes, who has never served in the heavy-armed infantry, nor done anything remarkable in the cavalry, and who indeed knows nothing, but how to get money."

"It is not good, however, to know this," said Socrates, "since he will then be able to get necessaries for the troops?"

"But merchants," replied Nicomachides, "are able to collect money; and yet would not on that account, be capable of leading an army."

"Antisthenes, however," continued Socrates, "is given to emulation, a quality necessary in a general. Do you not know that whenever he has been chorus-manager he has gained the superiority in all his choruses?"

"But, but Jupiter," rejoined Nicomachides, "there is nothing similar in managing a chorus and an army. "

"Yet Antisthenes," said Socrates, "though neither skilled in music nor in teaching a chorus, was able to find out the best masters in these departments."

"In the army, accordingly," exclaimed Nicomachides, "he will find others to range his troops for him, and others to fight for him!"

"Well, then," rejoined Socrates, "if he finds out and selects the best men in military affairs, as he has done in the conduct of his choruses, he will probably attain superiority in this respect also; and it is likely that he will be more willing to spend money for a victory in war on behalf of the whole state, than for a victory with a chorus in behalf of his single tribe."

"Do you say, then, Socrates," said he, "that it is in the power of the same man to manage a chorus well, and to manage an army well?"

"I say," said Socrates, "that over whatever a man may preside, he will, if he knows what he needs, and is able to provide it, to be a good president, whether he have the direction of a chorus, a family, a city, or an army."

"By Jupiter, Socrates," cried Nicomachides, "I should never have expected to hear from you that good managers of a family would also be good generals."

"Come, then," proceeded Socrates, "let us consider what are the duties of each of them, that we may understand whether they are the same, or are in any respect different."

"By all means."

"Is it not, then, the duty of both," asked Socrates, "to render those under their command obedient and submissive to them?"

"Unquestionably."

"Is it not also the duty of both to intrust various employments to such as are fitted to execute them?"

Source: Xenophon, The Anabasis or Expedition of Cyrus and the Memorabilia of Socrates, trans. J. S. Watson (New York: Harper & Row, 1869), 430-433.

"That is also unquestionable."

"To punish the bad, and to honor the good, too, belongs, I think, to each of them."

"Undoubtedly."

"And is it not honorable in both to render those under them well-disposed toward them?"

"That also is certain."

"And do you think it for the interest of both to gain for themselves allies and auxiliaries or not?"

"It assuredly is for their interest."

"Is it not proper for both' also to be careful of their resources?"

"Assuredly."

"And is it not proper for both, therefore, to be attentive and industrious in their respective duties?"

"All these particulars," said Nicomachides, "are common alike to both; but it is not common to both to fight."

"Yet both have doubtless enemies," rejoined Socrates.

"That is probably the case," said the other.

"Is it not for the interest of both to gain the superiority over those enemies?"

"Certainly; but to say something on that point, what, I ask, will skill in managing a household avail, if it be necessary to fight?"

"It will doubtless in that case, be of the greatest avail," said Socrates; "for a good manager of a house, knowing that nothing is so advantageous or profitable as to get the better of your enemies when you contend with them, nothing so unprofitable and prejudicial as to be defeated, will zealously seek and provide every thing that may conduce to victory, will carefully watch and guard against whatever tends to defeat, will vigorously engage if he sees that his force is likely to conquer, and, what is not the least important point, will cautiously avoid engaging if he finds himself insufficiently prepared. Do not, therefore, Nicomachides," he added, "despise men skillful in managing a household; for the conduct of private affairs differs from that of public concerns only in magnitude; in other respects they are similar; but what is most to be observed, is, that neither of them are managed without men, and that private matters are not managed by one species of men, and public matters by another; for those who conduct public business make use of men not at all differing in nature from those whom the managers of private affairs employ; and those who know how to employ them conduct either public or private affairs judiciously, while those who do not know will err in the management of both."

2
Of the Division of Labour
Adam Smith

The greatest improvement in the productive powers of labour, and the greater part of the skill, dexterity, and judgment with which it is any where directed, or applied, seem to have been the effects of the division of labour.

The effects of the division of labour, in the general business of society, will be more easily understood, by considering in what manner it operates in some particular manufactures. It is commonly supposed to be carried furthest in some very trifling ones; not perhaps that it really is carried further in them than in others of more importance: but in those trifling manufactures which are destined to supply the small wants of but a small number of people, the whole number of workmen must necessarily be small; and those employed in every different branch of the work can often be collected into the same workhouse, and placed at once under the view of the spectator. In those great manufactures, on the contrary, which are destined to supply the great wants of the great body of the people, every different branch of the work employs so great a number of workmen, that it is impossible to collect them all into the same workhouse. We can seldom see more, at one time, than those employed in one single branch. Though in such manufactures, therefore, the work may really be divided into a much greater number of parts, than in those of a more trifling nature, the division is not near so obvious, and has accordingly been much less observed.

To take an example, therefore, from a very trifling manufacture; but one in which the division of labour has been very often taken notice of, the trade of the pin-maker; a workman not educated to this business (which the division of labour has rendered a distinct trade), nor acquainted with the use of the machinery employed in it (to the invention of which the same division of labour has probably given occasion), could scarce, perhaps, with his utmost industry, make one pin in a day, and certainly could not make twenty. But in the way in which this business is now carried on, not only the whole work is a peculiar trade, but it is divided into a number of branches, of which the greater part are likewise peculiar trades. One man draws out the wire, another straights it, a third cuts it, a fourth points it, a fifth grinds it at the top for receiving the head; to make the head requires two or three distinct operations; to put it on, is a peculiar business, to whiten the pins is another; it is even a trade by itself to put them into the paper; and the important business of making a pin is, in this manner, divided into about eighteen distinct operations, which, in some manufactories, are all performed by distinct hands, though in others the same man will sometimes perform two or three of them. I have seen a small manufactory of this kind where ten men only were employed, and where some of them consequently performed two or three distinct operations. But

Source: Adam Smith, *The Wealth of Nations* (1776), Chapter 1. Footnotes omitted.

though they were very poor, and therefore but indifferently accommodated with the necessary machine, they could, when they exerted themselves, make among them about twelve pounds of pins in a day. There are in a pound upwards of four thousand pins of a middling size. Those ten persons, therefore, could make among them upwards of forty-eight thousand pins in a day. Each person, therefore, making a tenth part of forty-eight thousand pins, might be considered as making four thousand eight hundred pins in a day. But if they had all wrought separately and independently, and without any of them having been educated to this peculiar business, they certainly could not each of them have made twenty, perhaps not one pin in a day; that is, certainly, not the two hundred and fortieth, perhaps not the four thousand eight hundredth part of what they are at present capable of performing, in consequence of a proper division and combination of their different operations.

In every other art and manufacture, the effects of the division of labour are similar to what they are in this very trifling one; though, in many of them, the labour can neither be so much subdivided, nor reduced to so great a simplicity of operation. The division of labour, however, so far as it can be introduced, occasions, in every art, a proportionable increase of the productive powers of labour. The separation of different trades and employments from one another, seems to have taken place, in consequence of this advantage. This separation too is generally carried furthest in those countries which enjoy the highest degree of industry and improvement; what is the work of one man in a rude state of society, being generally that of several in an improved one. In every improved society, the farmer is generally nothing but a farmer; the manufacturer,

nothing but a manufacturer. The labour too which is necessary to produce any one complete manufacture, is almost always divided among a great number of hands. How many different trades are employed in each branch of the linen and woollen manufactures, from the growers of the flax and the wool, to the bleachers and smoothers of the linen, or to the dyers and dressers of the cloth! The nature of agriculture, indeed, does not admit of so many subdivisions of labour, nor of so complete a separation of one business from another, as manufactures. It is impossible to separate so entirely, the business of the grazier from that of the corn-farmer, as the trade of the carpenter is commonly separated from that of the smith. The spinner is almost always a distinct person from the weaver; but the ploughman, the harrower, the sower of the seed, and the reaper of the corn, are often the same. The occasions for those different sorts of labour returning with the different seasons of the year, it is impossible that one man should be constantly employed in any one of them. This impossibility of making so complete and entire a separation of all the different branches of labour employed in agriculture, is perhaps the reason why the improvement of the productive powers of labour in this art, does not always keep pace with their improvement in manufactures. The most opulent nations, indeed, generally excel all their neighbours in agriculture as well as in manufactures; but they are commonly more distinguished by their superiority in the latter than in the former. Their lands are in general better cultivated, and having more labour and expence bestowed upon them, produce more in proportion to the extent and natural fertility of the ground. But this superiority of produce is seldom much more than in proportion to the superiority of labour and expence. In agriculture, the labour of the rich country is not always much more productive than that of the poor; or, at least, it is never so much more productive, as it commonly is in manufactures. The corn of the rich country, therefore, will not always, in the same degree of goodness, come cheaper to market than that of the poor. The corn of Poland, in the same degree of goodness is as cheap as that of France, notwithstanding the superior opulence and improvement of the latter country. The corn of France is, in the corn provinces, fully as good, and most years nearly about the same price with the corn of England, though, in opulence and improvement, France is perhaps inferior to England. The corn lands of England, however, are better cultivated than those of France, and the corn lands of France are said to be much better cultivated than those of Poland. But though the poor country, notwithstanding the inferiority of its cultivation, can, in some measure, rival the rich in the cheapness and goodness of its corn, it can pretend to no such competition in its manufactures; at least if those manufactures suit the soil, climate, and situation of the rich country. The silks of France are better and cheaper than those of England, because the silk manufacture, at least under the present high duties upon the importation of raw silk, does not so well suit the climate of England as that of France. But the hardware and the coarse woollens of England are beyond all comparison superior to those of France, and much cheaper too in the same degree of goodness. In Poland there are said to be scarce any manufactures of any kind, a few of those coarser household manufactures excepted, without which no country can well subsist.

This great increase of the quantity of work, which, in consequence of the division of labour, the same number of people are capable of performing, is owing to three different circumstances; first, to the increase of dexterity in every particular workman; secondly, to the saving of the time which is commonly lost in passing from one species of work to another; and lastly, to the invention of a great number of machines which facilitate and abridge labour, and enable one man to do the work of many.

First, the improvement of the dexterity of the workman necessarily increases the quantity of the work he can perform; and the division of labour, by reducing every man's business to some one simple operation, and by making this operation the sole employment of his life, necessarily increases very much the dexterity of the workman. A common smith, who, though accustomed to handle the hammer, has never been used to make nails, if upon some particular occasion he is obliged to attempt it, will scarce, I am assured, be able to make above two or three hundred nails in a day, and those too very bad ones. A smith who has been accustomed to make nails, but whose sole or principal business has not been that of a nailer, can seldom with his utmost diligence make more than eight hundred or a thousand nails in a day. I have seen several boys under twenty years of age who had never exercised any other trade but that of making nails, and who, when they exerted themselves, could make, each of them, upwards of two thousand three hundred nails in a day. The making of a nail, however, is by no means one of the simplest operations. The same person blows the bellows, stirs or mends the fire as there is occasion, heats the iron, and forges every part of the nail: In forging the head too he is obliged to change his tools. The different operations into which the making of a pin, or of a metal button, is subdivided, are all of them much more simple, and the dexterity of the person, of whose life it has been the sole business to perform them, is usually much greater. The rapidity with which some of the operations of those manufactures are performed, exceeds what the human hand could, by those who had never seen them, be supposed capable of acquiring.

Secondly, the advantage which is gained by saving the time commonly lost in passing from one sort of work to another, is much greater than we should at first view be apt to imagine it. It is impossible to pass very quickly from one kind of work to another, that is carried on in a different place, and with quite different tools. A country weaver, who cultivates a small farm, must lose a good deal of time in passing from his loom to his field, and from the field to his loom. When the two trades can be carried on in the same workhouse, the loss of time is no doubt much less. It is even in this case, however, very considerable. A man commonly saunters a little in turning his hand from one sort of employment to another. When he first begins the new work he is seldom very keen and hearty; his mind, as they say, does not go to it, and from some time he rather trifles than applies to good purpose. The habit of sauntering and of indolent careless application, which is naturally, or rather necessarily acquired by every country workman who is obliged to change his work and his tools every half hour, and to apply his hand in twenty different ways almost every day of his life; renders him almost always slothful and lazy, and incapable of any vigorous application even on the most pressing occasions. Independent, therefore, of his deficiency in point of dexterity, this cause alone must always reduce considerably the quantity of work which he is capable of performing.

Thirdly, and lastly, every body must be sensible how much labour is facilitated and abridged by the application of proper machinery. It is unnecessary to give any example. I shall only observe,

therefore, that the invention of all those machines by which labour is so much facilitated and abridged, seems to have been originally owing to the division of labour. Men are much more likely to discover easier and readier methods of attaining any object, when the whole attention of their minds is directed towards that single object, than when it is dissipated among a great variety of things. But in consequence of the division of labour, the whole of every man's attention comes naturally to be directed towards some one very simple object. It is naturally to be expected, therefore, that some one or other of those who are employed in each particular branch of labour should soon find out easier and readier methods of performing their own particular work, wherever the nature of it admits of such improvement. A great part of the machines made use of in those manufactures in which labour is most subdivided, were originally the inventions of common workmen, who, being each of them employed in some very simple operation, naturally turned their thoughts towards finding out easier and readier methods of performing it. Whoever has been much accustomed to visit such manufactures, must frequently have been shewn very pretty machines, which were the inventions of such workmen, in order to facilitate and quicken their own particular part of the work. In the first fire-engines, a boy was constantly employed to open and shut alternately the communication between the boiler and the cylinder, according as the piston either ascended or descended. One of those boys, who loved to play with his companions, observed that, by tying a string from the handle of the valve which opened this communication to another part of the machine, the valve would open and shut without his assistance, and leave him at liberty to divert himself with his playfellows. One of the greatest improvements that has been made upon this machine, since it was first invented, was in this manner the discovery of a boy who wanted to save his own labour.

All the improvements in machinery, however, have by no means been the inventions of those who had occasion to use the machines. Many improvements have been made by the ingenuity of the makers of the machines, when to make them become the business of a peculiar trade; and some by that of those who are called philosophers or men of speculation, whose trade it is not to do any thing, but to observe every thing; and who, upon that account, are often capable of combining together the powers of the most distant and dissimilar objects. In the progress of society, philosophy or speculation becomes, like every other employment, the principal or sole trade and occupation of a particular class of citizens. Like every other employment too, it is subdivided into a great number of different branches, each of which affords occupation to a peculiar tribe or class of philosophers; and this subdivision of employment in philosophy, as well as in every other business, improves dexterity, and saves time. Each individual becomes more expert in his own peculiar branch, more work is done upon the whole, and the quantity of science is considerably increased by it.

It is the great multiplication of the productions of all the different arts, in consequence of the division of labour, which occasions, in a well-governed society, that universal opulence which extends itself to the lowest ranks of the people. Every workman has a great quantity of his own work to dispose of beyond what he himself has occasion for; and every other workman being exactly in the same situation, he is enabled to exchange a great quantity of his own goods for a great quantity, or, what comes to

the same thing, for the price of a great quantity of theirs. He supplies them abundantly with what they have occasion for, and they accommodate him as amply with what he has occasion for, and a general plenty diffuses itself through all the different ranks of the society.

Observe the accommodation of the most common artificer or day-labourer in a civilized and thriving country, and you will perceive that the number of people of whose industry a part, though but a small part, has been employed in procuring him his accommodation, exceeds all computation. The woollen coat, for example, which covers the day-labourer, as coarse and rough as it may appear, is the produce of the joint labour of a great multitude of workmen. The shepherd, the sorter of the wool, the woolcomber or carder, the dyer, the scribbler, the spinner, the weaver, the fuller, the dresser, with many others, must all join their different arts in order to complete even this homely production. How many merchants and carriers, besides, must have been employed in transporting the materials from some of those workmen to others who often live in a very distant part of the country! How much commerce and navigation in particular, how many ship-builders, sailors, sail-makers, rope-makers, must have been employed in order to bring together the different drugs made use of by the dyer, which often come from the remotest corners of the world! What a variety of labour too is necessary in order to produce the tools of the meanest of those workmen! To say nothing of such complicated machines as the ship of the sailor, the mill of the fuller, or even the loom of the weaver, let us consider only what a variety of labour is requisite in order to form that very simple machine, the shears with which the shepherd clips the wool. The miner, the builder of the furnace for smelting the ore, the feller of the timber, the burner of the charcoal to be made use of in the smelting-house, the brick-maker, the brick-layer, the work-men who attend the furnace, the millwright, the forger, the smith, must all of them join their different arts in order to produce them. Were we to examine, in the same manner, all the different parts of his dress and household furniture, the coarse linen shirt which he wears next his skin, the shoes which cover his feet, the bed which he lies on, and all the different parts which compose it, the kitchen grate at which he prepares his victuals, the coals which he makes use of for that purpose, dug from the bowels of the earth, and brought to him perhaps by a long sea and a long land carriage, all the other utensils of his kitchen, all the furniture of his table, the knives and forks, the earthen or pewter plates upon which he serves up and divides his victuals, the different hands employed in preparing his bread and his beer, the glass window which lets in the heat and the light, and keeps out the wind and the rain, with all the knowledge and art requisite for preparing that beautiful and happy invention, without which these northern parts of the world could scarce have afforded a very comfortable habitation, together with the tools of all the different workmen employed in producing those different conveniences; if we examine, I say, all these things, and consider what a variety of labour is employed about each of them, we shall be sensible that without the assistance and cooperation of many thousands, the very meanest person in a civilized country could not be provided, even according to, what we very falsely imagine, the easy and simple manner in which he is commonly accommodated. Compared, indeed, with the more extravagant luxury of the great, his accommodation must no doubt appear extremely simple and easy; and yet it may be true, perhaps, that the accommodation of an European prince does not always so much exceed that of an industrious and frugal peasant, as the accommodation of the latter exceeds that of many an African king. . . .

3
Superintendent's Report

OFFICE GENERAL SUP'T N.Y. &
ERIE R. R.
NEW YORK, MARCH 25, 1856

HOMER RAMSDELL, ESQ.
PRESIDENT OF THE NEW YORK AND
ERIE RAILROAD COMPANY:

SIR:

The magnitude of the business of this road, its numerous and important connections, and the large number of employés engaged in operating it, have led many, whose opinions are entitled to respect, to the conclusion, that a proper regard to details, which enter so largely into the elements of success in the management of all railroads, cannot possibly be attained by any plan that contemplates its organization as a whole; and in proof of this position, the experience of shorter roads is referred to, the business operations of which have been conducted much more economically.

Theoretically, other things being equal, a long road should be operated for a less cost per mile than a short one. This position is so clearly evident and so generally admitted, that its truth may be assumed without offering any arguments in support of it; and, notwithstanding the reverse, so far as *practical* results are considered, has generally been the case, we must look to other causes than the mere difference in length of roads for a solution of the difficulty.

A Superintendent of a road fifty miles in length can give its business his personal attention, and may be almost constantly upon the line engaged in the direction of its details; each employé is familiarly known to him, and all questions in relation to its business are at once presented and acted upon; and any system, however imperfect, may under such circumstances prove comparatively successful.

In the government of a road five hundred miles in length a very different state of things exists. Any system which might be applicable to the business and extent of a short road, would be found entirely inadequate to the wants of a long one; and I am fully convinced, that in the want of a system perfect in its details, properly adapted and vigilantly enforced, lies the true secret of their failure; and that this disparity of cost per mile in operating long and short roads, is not produced by *a difference in length*, but is in proportion to the perfection of the system adopted.

Entertaining these views, I had the honor, more than a year since, to submit for your consideration and approval a plan for the more effective organization of this department. The system then proposed has to some extent been introduced, and experience, so far, affords the strongest assurances that when fully carried out, the most satisfactory results will be obtained.

In my opinion a system of operations, to be efficient and successful, should be such as to give to the principal and responsible head of the running department a complete daily history of details in all their minutiae. Without such su-

Source: Daniel C. McCallum, "Superintendent's Report," March 25, 1856, in *Annual Report of the New York and Erie Railroad Company for 1855* (New York, 1856).

pervision, the procurement of a satisfactory annual statement must be regarded as extremely problematical. The fact that dividends are earned without such control does not disprove the position, as in many cases the extraordinarily remunerative nature of an enterprise may ensure satisfactory returns under the most loose and inefficient management.

It may be proper here to remark that in consequence of that want of adaptation before alluded to, we cannot avail ourselves to any great extent of the plan of organization of shorter lines in framing one for this, nor have we any precedent or experience upon which we can fully rely in doing so. Under these circumstances, it will scarcely be expected that we can at once adopt any plan of operations which will not require amendment and a reasonable time to prove its worth.

A few general principles, however, may be regarded as settled and necessary in its formation, amongst which are:

1. A proper division of responsibilities.
2. Sufficient power conferred to enable the same to be fully carried out, that such responsibilities may be real in their character.
3. The means of knowing whether such responsibilities are faithfully executed.
4. Great promptness in the report of all derelictions of duty, that evils may be at once corrected.
5. Such information, to be obtained through a system of daily reports and checks that will not embarrass principal officers, nor lessen their influence with their subordinates.
6. The adoption of a system, as a whole, which will not only enable the General Superintendent to detect errors immediately, but will also point out the delinquent.

4
The Engineer as Economist
Henry R. Towne

The monogram of our national initials, which is the symbol of our monetary unit, the dollar, is almost as frequently conjoined to the figures of an engineer's calculations as are the symbols indicating feet, minutes, pounds, or gallons. The final issue of his work, in probably a majority of cases, resolves itself into a question of dollars and cents, of relative or absolute values. This statement, while true in regard to the work of all engineers, applies particularly to that of the mechanical engineer, for the reason that his functions, more frequently than in the case of others, include the executive duties of organizing and superintending the operations of industrial establishments, and of directing the labor of the artisans whose organized efforts yield the fruition of his work.

To insure the best results, the organization of productive labor must be directed and controlled by persons having not only good executive ability, and possessing the practical familiarity of a mechanic or engineer with the goods produced and the processes employed, but having also, and equally, a practical knowledge of how to observe, record, analyze and compare essential facts in relation to wages, supplies, expense accounts, and all else that enters into or affects the economy of production and the cost of the product. There are many good mechanical engineers;—there are

also many good "business men";—but the two are rarely combined in one person. But this combination of qualities, together with at least some skill as an accountant, either in one person or more, is essential to the successful management of industrial works, and has its highest effectiveness if united in one person, who is thus qualified to supervise, either personally or through assistants, the operations of all departments of a business, and to subordinate each to the harmonious development of the whole.

Engineering has long been conceded a place as one of the modern arts, and has become a well-defined science, with a large and growing literature of its own, and of late years has subdivided itself into numerous and distinct divisions, one of which is that of mechanical engineering. It will probably not be disputed that the matter of shop management is of equal importance with that of engineering, as affecting the successful conduct of most, if not all, of our great industrial establishments, and that the *management of works* has become a matter of such great and far-reaching importance as perhaps to justify its classification also as one of the modern arts. The one is a well-defined science, with a distinct literature, with numerous journals and with many associations for the interchange of experience; the other is unorganized, is almost without literature, has

Source: *Transactions of The American Society of Mechanical Engineers*, Vol. 7 (Paper presented at May 1886 meeting of the Society, Chicago), 428-432.

no organ or medium for the interchange of experience, and is without association or organization of any kind. A vast amount of accumulated experience in the art of workshop management already exists, but there is no record of it available to the world in general, and each old enterprise is managed more or less in its own way, receiving little benefit from the parallel experience of other similar enterprises, and imparting as little of its own to them; while each new enterprise, starting *de novo* and with much labor, and usually at much cost for experience, gradually develops a more or less perfect system of its own, according to the ability of its managers, receiving little benefit or aid from all that may have been done previously by others in precisely the same field of work.

Surely this condition of things is wrong and should be remedied. But the remedy must not be looked for from those who are "business men" or clerks and accountants only; it should come from those whose training and experience has given them an understanding of both sides (viz.: the mechanical and the clerical) of the important questions involved. It should originate, therefore, from those who are also engineers, and, for the reasons above indicated, particularly from mechanical engineers. Granting this, why should it not originate from, and be promoted by The American Society of Mechanical Engineers?

To consider this proposition more definitely, let us state the work which requires to be done. The questions to be considered, and which need recording and publication as conducing to discussion and the dissemination of useful knowledge in this specialty, group themselves under two principal heads, namely: Shop Management, and Shop Accounting. A third head may be named

which is subordinate to, and partly included in each of these, namely: Shop Forms and Blanks. Under the head of Shop Management fall the questions of organization, responsibility, reports, systems of contract and piece work, and all that relates to the executive management of works, mills and factories. Under the head of Shop Accounting fall the questions of time and wages systems, determination of costs, whether by piece or day-work, the distribution of the various expense accounts, the ascertainment of profits, methods of bookkeeping, and all that enters into the system of accounts which relates to the manufacturing departments of a business, and to the determination and record of its results.

There already exists an enormous fund of information relating to such matters, based upon actual and most extensive experience. What is now needed is a medium for the interchange of this experience among those whom it interests and concerns. Probably no better way for this exists than that obtaining in other instances, namely, by the publication of papers and reports, and by meetings for the discussion of papers and interchange of opinions.

The subject thus outlined, however distinct and apart from the primary functions of this society, is, nevertheless, germane to the interests of most, if not all, of its members. Conceding this, why should not the function of the society be so enlarged as to embrace this new field of usefulness? This work, if undertaken, may be kept separate and distinct from the present work of the society by organizing a new "section" (which might be designated the "Economic Section"), the scope of which would embrace all papers and discussions relating to the topics herein referred to. The meetings of this section could be held either separately from, or immediately following the regular meetings of the society, and its papers could appear as a supplement to the regular transactions. In this way all interference would be avoided with the primary and chief business of the society, and the attendance at the meetings of the new section would naturally resolve itself into such portion of the membership as is interested in the objects for which it would be organized.

As a single illustration of the class of subjects to be covered by the discussions and papers of the proposed new section, and of the benefit to be derived therefrom, there may be cited the case of a manufacturing establishment in which there are now in use, in connection with the manufacturing accounts and exclusive of the ordinary commercial accounts, some twenty various forms of special record and account books, and more than one hundred printed forms and blanks. The primary object to which all of these contribute is the systematic recording of the operations of the different departments of the works, and the computation therefrom of such statistical information as is essential to the efficient management of the business, and especially to increased economy of production. All of these special books and forms have been the outgrowth of experience extending over many years, and represent a large amount of thoughtful planning and intelligent effort at constant development and improvement. The methods thus arrived at would undoubtedly be of great value to others engaged in similar operations, and particularly to persons engaged in organizing and starting new enterprises. It is probable that much, if not all, of the information and experience referred to would be willingly made public through such a channel as is herein suggested,

particularly if such action on the part of one firm or corporation would be responded to in like manner by others, so that each member could reasonably expect to receive some equivalent for his contributions by the benefit which he would derive from the experience of others.

In the case of the establishment above referred to, a special system of contract and piece-work has been in operation for some fifteen years, the results from which, in reducing the labor cost on certain products without encroaching upon the earnings of the men engaged, have been quite striking. A few of these results selected at random, are indicated by the accompanying diagram (Figure 1), the diagonal lines on which represent the fluctuations in the labor cost of certain special products during the time covered by the table, the vertical scale representing values.

Undoubtedly a portion of the reductions thus indicated resulted from improved appliances, larger product, and increased experience, but after making due allowance for all of these, there remains a large portion of the reduction which, to the writer's knowledge, is fairly attributable to the operation of the peculiar piece-work system adopted. The details and operations of this system would probably be placed before the society, in due time, through the channel of the proposed new section, should the latter take definite form. Other, and probably much more valuable, information and experience relating to systems of contract and piece-work would doubtless be contributed by other members, and in the aggregate a great amount of information of a most valuable character would thus be made available to the whole membership of the society.

In conclusion, it is suggested that if the plan herein proposed commends

FIGURE 1

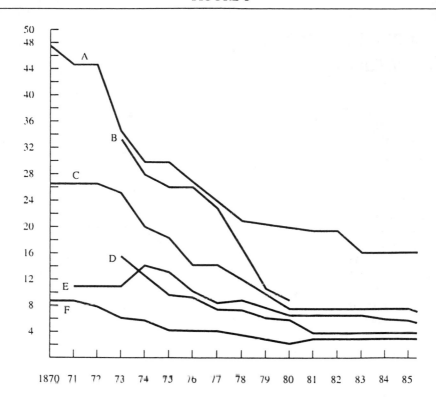

itself favorably to the members present at the meeting at which it is presented, the subject had best be referred to a special committee, by whom it can be carefully considered, and by whom, if it seems expedient to proceed further, the whole matter can be matured and formulated in an orderly manner, and thus be so presented at a future meeting as to enable the society then intelligently to act upon the question, and to decide whether or not to adopt the recommendations made by such committee.

5
General Principles of Management
Henri Fayol

The managerial function finds its only outlet through the members of the organization (body corporate). Whilst the other functions bring into play material and machines the managerial function operates only on the personnel. The soundness and good working order of the body corporate depend on a certain number of conditions termed indiscriminately principles, laws, rules. For preference I shall adopt the term principles whilst dissociating it from any suggestion of rigidity, for there is nothing rigid or absolute in management affairs, it is all a question of proportion. Seldom do we have to apply the same principle twice in identical conditions; allowance must be made for different changing circumstances, for men just as different and changing and for many other variable elements.

Therefore principles are flexible and capable of adaptation to every need; it is a matter of knowing how to make use of them, which is a difficult art requiring intelligence, experience, decision and proportion. Compounded of tact and experience, proportion is one of the foremost attributes of the manager. There is no limit to the number of principles of management, every rule or managerial procedure which strengthens the body corporate or facilitates its functioning has a place among the principles so long, at least, as experience confirms its worthiness. A change in the state of affairs can be responsible for change of rules which had been engendered by that state.

I am going to review some of the principles of management which I have most frequently had to apply; viz.—

1. Division of work.
2. Authority and responsibility.
3. Discipline.
4. Unity of command.
5. Unity of direction.
6. Subordination of individual interest to the general interest.
7. Remuneration of personnel.
8. Centralization.
9. Scalar chain (line of authority).
10. Order.
11. Equity.
12. Stability of tenure of personnel.
13. Initiative.
14. Esprit de corps.

1. DIVISION OF WORK

Specialization belongs to the natural order; it is observable in the animal world, where the more highly developed the creature the more highly differentiated its organs; it is observable in human societies where the more important the body corporate[1] the closer is the relationship between structure and function. As society grows, so new organs develop destined to replace the single one performing all functions in the primitive state.

The object of division of work is to produce more and better work with the same effort. The worker always on the same part, the manager concerned always with the same matters, acquire an

Source: Henri Fayol, *General and Industrial Management*, trans. Constance Storrs (London: Pitman Publishing, Ltd., 1949), 19-42. (Original work published 1916.) Reprinted by permission.

ability, sureness, and accuracy which increase their output. Each change of work brings in its train an adaptation which reduces output. Division of work permits reduction in the number of objects to which attention and effort must be directed and has been recognized as the best means of making use of individuals and of groups of people. It is not merely applicable to technical work, but without exception to all work involving a more or less considerable number of people and demanding abilities of various types, and it results in specialization of functions and separation of powers. Although its advantages are universally recognized and although possibility of progress is inconceivable without the specialized work of learned men and artists, yet division of work has its limits which experience and a sense of proportion teach us may not be exceeded.

2. AUTHORITY AND RESPONSIBILITY

Authority is the right to give orders and the power to exact obedience. Distinction must be made between a manager's official authority deriving from office and personal authority, compounded of intelligence, experience, moral worth, ability to lead, past services, etc. In the make up of a good head personal authority is the indispensable complement of official authority. Authority is not to be conceived of apart from responsibility, that is apart from sanction—reward or penalty—which goes with the exercise of power. Responsibility is a corollary of authority, it is its natural consequence and essential counterpart, and wheresoever authority is exercised responsibility arises.

The need for sanction, which has its origin in a sense of justice, is strengthened and increased by this consideration, that in the general interest useful actions have to be encouraged and their opposite discouraged. Application of sanction to acts of authority forms part of the conditions essential for good management, but it is generally difficult to effect, especially in large concerns. First, the degree of responsibility must be established and then the weight of the sanction. Now, it is relatively easy to establish a workman's responsibility for his acts and a scale of corresponding sanctions; in the case of a foreman it is somewhat difficult, and proportionately as one goes up the scalar chain of businesses, as work grows more complex, as the number of workers involved increases, as the final result is more remote, it is increasingly difficult to isolate the share of the initial act of authority in the ultimate result and to establish the degree of responsibility of the manager. The measurement of this responsibility and its equivalent in material terms elude all calculation.

Sanction, then, is a question of kind, custom, convention, and judging it one must take into account the action itself, the attendant circumstances and potential repercussions. Judgment demands high moral character, impartiality and firmness. If all these conditions are not fulfilled there is a danger that the sense of responsibility may disappear from the concern.

Responsibility valiantly undertaken and borne merits some consideration; it is a kind of courage everywhere much appreciated. Tangible proof of this exists in the salary level of some industrial leaders, which is much higher than that of civil servants of comparable rank but carrying no responsibility. Nevertheless, generally speaking, responsibility is feared as much as authority is sought after, and fear of responsibility paralyses much initiative and destroys many good qualities. A good leader should possess and infuse into those around him courage to accept responsibility.

The best safeguard against abuse of authority and against weakness on the part of a higher manager is personal integrity and particularly high moral character of such a manager, and this integrity, it is well known, is conferred neither by election nor ownership.

3. DISCIPLINE

Discipline is in essence obedience, application, energy, behaviour, and outward marks of respect observed in accordance with the standing agreements between the firm and its employees, whether these agreements have been freely debated or accepted without prior discussion, whether they be written or implicit, whether they derive from the wish of the parties to them or from rules and customs, it is these agreements which determine the formalities of discipline.

Discipline, being the outcome of different varying agreements, naturally appears under the most diverse forms; obligations of obedience, application, energy, behavior, vary, in effect, from one firm to another, from one group of employees to another, from one time to another. Nevertheless, general opinion is deeply convinced that discipline is absolutely essential for the smooth running of business and that without discipline no enterprise could prosper.

This sentiment is very forcibly expressed in military hand-books, where it runs that "Discipline constitutes the chief strength of armies." I would approve unreservedly of this aphorism were it followed by this other, "Discipline is what leaders make it." The first one inspires respect for discipline, which is a good thing, but it tends to eclipse from view the responsibility of leaders, which is undesirable, for the state of discipline of any group of people depends essentially on the worthiness of its leaders.

When a defect in discipline is apparent or when relations between superiors and subordinates leave much to be desired, responsibility for this must not be cast heedlessly, and without going further afield, on the poor state of the team, because the ill mostly results from the ineptitude of the leaders. That, at all events, is what I have noted in various parts of France, for I have always found French workmen obedient and loyal provided they are ably led.

In the matter of influence upon discipline, agreements must set side by side with command. It is important that they be clear and, as far as possible, afford satisfaction to both sides. This is not easy. Proof of that exists in the great strikes of miners, railwaymen, and civil servants which, in these latter years, have jeopardized national life at home and elsewhere and which arose out of agreements in dispute or inadequate legislation.

For half a century a considerable change has been effected in the mode of agreements between a concern and its employees. The agreements of former days fixed by the employer alone are being replaced, in ever increasing measure, by understandings arrived at by discussion between an owner or group of owners and workers' associations. Thus each individual owner's responsibility has been reduced and is further diminished by increasingly frequent state intervention in labour problems. Nevertheless, the setting up of agreements binding a firm and its employees from which disciplinary formalities emanate, should remain one of the chief preoccupations of industrial heads.

The well-being of the concern does not permit, in cases of offence against discipline, of the neglect of certain sanctions capable of preventing or minimizing their recurrence. Experience and tact on the part of a manager are put to the proof in the choice and degree of sanctions to be used, such as remonstrances, warning, fines, suspensions, demotion, dismissal. Individual people and attendant circumstances must be taken into account. In fine, discipline is respect for agreements which are directed at achieving obedience, application, energy, and the outward marks of respect. It is incumbent upon managers at high levels as much as upon humble employees, and the best means of establishing and maintaining it are—

1. Good superiors at all levels.
2. Agreements as clear and fair as possible.
3. Sanctions (penalties) judiciously applied.

4. UNITY OF COMMAND

For any action whatsoever, an employee should receive orders from one superior only. Such is the rule of unity of command, arising from general and ever-present necessity and wielding an influence on the conduct of affairs, which to my way of thinking, is at least equal to any other principle whatsoever. Should it be violated, authority is undermined, discipline is in jeopardy, order disturbed and stability threatened. This rule seems fundamental to me and so I have given it the rank of principle. As soon as two superiors wield their authority over the same person or department, uneasiness makes itself felt and should the cause persist, the disorder increases, the malady takes on the appearance of an animal organism troubled by a foreign body, and the following consequences are to be observed: either the dual command ends in disappearance or elimination of one of the superiors and organic well-being is restored, or else the organism continues to wither away. In no case is there adaptation of the social organism to dual command.

Now dual command is extremely common and wreaks havoc in all concerns, large or small, in home and in state. The evil is all the more to be feared in that it worms its way into the social organism on the most plausible pretexts. For instance—

(a) In the hope of being better understood or gaining time or to put a stop forthwith to an undesirable practice, a superior S^2 may give orders directly to an employee E without going via the superior S^1. If this mistake is repeated there is dual command with its consequences, *viz.*, hesitation on the part of the subordinate, irritation and dissatisfaction on the part of the superior set aside, and disorder in the work. It will be seen later that it is possible to bypass the scalar chain when necessary, whilst avoiding the drawbacks of dual command.

(b) The desire to get away from the immediate necessity of dividing up authority as between two colleagues, two friends, two members of one family, results at times in dual command reigning at the top of a concern right from the outset. Exercising the same powers and having the same authority over the same men, the two colleagues end up inevitably with dual command and its consequences. Despite harsh lessons, instances of this sort are still numerous. New colleagues count on their mutual regard, common interest, and good sense to save them from every conflict, every serious disagreement and, save for rare exceptions, the illusion is short-lived. First an awkwardness makes itself felt, then a certain irritation and, in time, if dual command exists, even hatred. Men cannot bear dual command. A judicious assignment of duties would have reduced the danger without entirely banishing it, for between two superiors on the same footing there must always be some question ill-defined. But it is riding for a fall to set up a business organization with two superiors on equal footing without assigning duties and demarcating authority.

(c) Imperfect demarcation of departments also leads to dual command: two superiors issuing orders in a sphere which each thinks his own, constitutes dual command.

(d) Constant linking up as between different departments, natural intermeshing of functions, duties often badly defined, create an everpresent danger of dual command. If a knowledgeable superior does not put it in order, footholds are established which later upset and compromise the conduct of affairs.

In all human associations, in industry, commerce, army, home, state, dual command is a perpetual source of conflicts, very grave sometimes, which have special claim on the attention of superiors of all ranks.

5. UNITY OF DIRECTION

This principle is expressed as: one head and one plan for a group of activities having the same objective. It is the condition essential to unity of action, coordination of strength and focusing of effort. A body with two heads is in the social as in the animal sphere a monster, and has difficulty in surviving. Unity of direction (one head one plan) must not be confused with unity of command (one employee to have orders from one superior only). Unity of direction is provided for by sound organization of the body corporate, unity of command turns on the functioning of the personnel. Unity of command cannot exist without unity of direction, but does not flow from it.

6. SUBORDINATION OF INDIVIDUAL INTEREST TO GENERAL INTEREST

This principle calls to mind the fact that in a business the interest of one em-

ployee or group of employees should not prevail over that of the concern, that the interest of the home should come before that of its members and that the interest of the state should have pride of place over that of one citizen or group of citizens.

It seems that such an admonition should not need calling to mind. But ignorance, ambition, selfishness, laziness, weakness, and all human passions tend to cause the general interest to be lost sight of in favour of individual interest and a perpetual struggle has to be waged against them. Two interests of a different order, but claiming equal respect, confront each other and means must be found to reconcile them. That represents one of the great difficulties of management. Means of effecting it are—

1. Firmness and good example on the part of superiors.
2. Agreements as fair as is possible.
3. Constant supervision.

7. REMUNERATION OF PERSONNEL

Remuneration of personnel is the price of services rendered. It should be fair and, as far as is possible, afford satisfaction both to personnel and firm (employee and employer). The rate of remuneration depends, firstly, on circumstances independent of the employer's will and employee's worth, viz. cost of living, abundance or shortage of personnel, general business conditions, the economic position of the business, and after that it depends on the value of the employee and mode of payment adopted. Appreciation of the factors dependent on the employer's will and on the value of employees, demands a fairly good knowledge of business, judgement, and impartiality. Later on in connection with selecting personnel we shall deal with assessing the value of employees; here only the mode of payment is under consideration as a factor operation on remuneration. The method of payment can exercise considerable influence on business progress, so the choice of this method is an important problem. It is also a thorny problem which in practice has been solved in widely different ways, of which so far none has proved satisfactory. What is generally looked for in the method of payment is that—

1. It shall assure fair remuneration.
2. It shall encourage keenness by rewarding well-directed effort.
3. It shall not lead to overpayment going beyond reasonable limits.

I am going to examine briefly the modes of payment in use for workers, junior managers, and higher managers.

Workers

The various modes of payment in use for workers are—

1. Time rates.
2. Job rates.
3. Piece rates.

These three modes of payment may be combined and give rise to important variations by the introduction of bonuses, profit-sharing schemes, payment in kind, and nonfinancial incentives.

1. Time rates. Under this system the workman sells the employer, in return for a predetermined sum, a day's work under definite conditions. This system has the disadvantage of conducing to negligence and of demanding constant supervision. It is inevitable where the work done is not susceptible to measurement and in effect it is very common.

2. Job rates. Here payment made turns upon the execution of a definite job set in advance and may be independent of the length of the job. When payment is due only on condition that the job be completed during the normal work spell, this method merges into time rate. Payment by daily job does not require as close a supervision as payment

by the day, but it has the drawback of levelling the output of good workers down to that of mediocre ones. The good ones are not satisfied, because they feel that they could earn more; the mediocre ones find the task set too heavy.

3. Piece rates. Here payment is related to work done and there is no limit. This system is often used in workshops where a large number of similar articles have to be made, and is found where the product can be measured by weight, length, or cubic capacity, and in general is used wherever possible. It is criticized on the grounds of emphasizing quantity at the expense of quality and of provoking disagreements when rates have to be revised in the light of manufacturing improvements. Piece-work becomes contract work when applied to an important unit of work. To reduce the contractor's risk, sometimes there is added to the contract price a payment for each day's work done.

Generally, piece rates give rise to increased earnings which act for some time as a stimulus, then finally a system prevails in which this mode of payment gradually approximates to time rates for a pre-arranged sum.

The above three modes of payment are found in all large concerns; sometimes time rates prevail, sometimes one of the other two. In a workshop the same workman may be seen working now on piece rates, not on time rates. Each one of these methods had its advantages and drawbacks, and their effectiveness depends on circumstances and the ability of superiors. Neither method nor rate of payment absolves management from competence and tact, and keenness of workers and peaceful atmosphere of the workshop depend largely upon it.

Bonuses

To arouse the worker's interest in the smooth running of the business, sometimes an increment in the nature of a bonus is added to the time-, job- or piece-rate: for good time keeping, hard work, freedom from machine breakdown output, cleanliness, etc. The relative importance, nature and qualifying conditions of these bonuses are very varied. There are to be found the small daily supplement, the monthly sum, the annual award, shares or portions of shares distributed to the most meritorious, and also even profit-sharing schemes such as, for example certain monetary allocations distributed annually among workers in some large firms. Several French collieries started some years back the granting of a bonus proportional to profits distributed or to extra profits. No contract is required from the workers save that the earning of the bonus is subject to certain conditions, for instance, that there shall be no strike during the year, or that absenteeism shall not have exceeded a given number of days. This type of bonus introduced an element of profit-sharing into miners' wages without any prior discussion as between workers and employer. The workman did not refuse a gift, largely gratuitous, on the part of the employer, that is, the contract was a unilateral one. Thanks to a successful trading period the yearly wages have been appreciably increased by the operation of the bonus. But what is to happen in lean times? This interesting procedure is as yet too new to be judged, but obviously it is no general solution of the problem. . . .

Profit-Sharing

1. Workers. The idea of making workers share in profits is a very attractive one and it would seem that it is from there that harmony as between Capital and Labour should come. But the practical formula for such sharing has not yet been found. Workers' profit-sharing has hitherto come up against insurmountable difficulties of application in the case of large concerns. Firstly, let us note that it cannot exist in enterprises having no monetary objective (State services, religion, philanthropic, scientific societies) and also that it is not possible in the case of businesses running at a loss. Thus profit-sharing is excluded from a great number of concerns. There remain the prosperous business concerns and of these latter the desire to reconcile and harmonize workers' and employers' interests is nowhere so great as in French mining and metallurgical industries. Now, in these industries I know of no clear application of workers' profit-sharing, whence it may be concluded forthwith that the matter is difficult, if not impossible. It is very difficult indeed. Whether a business is making a profit or not the worker must have an immediate wage assured him, and a system which would make workers' payment depend entirely on eventual future profit is unworkable. But perhaps a part of wages might come from business profits. Let us see. Viewing all contingent factors, the workers' greater or lesser share of activity or ability in the final outcome of a large concern is impossible to assess and is, moreover, quite insignificant. The portion accruing to him of distributed dividend would at the most be a few centimes on a wage of five francs for instance, that is to say the smallest extra effort, the stroke of a pick or of a file operating directly on his wage, would prove of greater advantage to him. Hence the worker has no interest in being rewarded by a share in profits proportionate to the effect he has upon profits. It is worthy of note that, in most large concerns, wages increases, operative now for some twenty years, represent a total sum greater than the amount of capital shared out. In effect, unmodified real profit-sharing by workers of large concerns has not yet entered the sphere of practical business politics.

2. *Junior Managers.* Profit-sharing for foremen, superintendents, engineers, is scarcely more advanced than for workers. Nevertheless the influence of these employees on the results of a business is quite considerable, and if they are not consistently interested in profits the only reason is that the basis for participation is difficult to establish. Doubtless managers have no need of monetary incentive to carry out their duties, but they are not indifferent to material satisfactions and it must be acknowledged that the hope of extra profit is capable of arousing their enthusiasm. So employees at middle levels should, where possible, be induced to have an interest in profits. It is relatively easy in businesses which are starting out or on trial, where exceptional effort can yield outstanding results. Sharing may then be applied to overall business profits or merely to the running of the particular department of the employee in question. When the business is of long standing and well run the zeal of a junior manager is scarcely apparent in the general outcome, and it is very hard to establish a useful basis on which he may participate. In fact, profit-sharing among junior managers in France is very rare in large concerns. Production or workshop output bonuses—not to be confused with profit-sharing—are much more common.

3. *Higher Managers.* It is necessary to go right up to top management to find a class of employee with frequent interest in the profits of large-scale French concerns. The head of the business, in view of his knowledge, ideas, and actions, exerts considerable influence on general results, so it is quite natural to try and provide him with an interest in them. Sometimes it is possible to establish a close connection between his personal activity and its effects. Nevertheless, generally speaking, there exist other influences quite independent of the personal capability of the manager which can influence results to a greater extent than can his personal activity. If the manager's salary were exclusively dependent upon profits, it might at times be reduced to nothing. There are besides, businesses being built up, wound up, or merely passing through temporary crisis, wherein management depends no less on talent than in the case of prosperous ones, and wherein profit-sharing cannot be a basis for remuneration for the manager. In fine, senior civil servants cannot be paid on a profit-sharing basis. Profit-sharing, then, for either higher managers or workers is not a general rule of remuneration. To sum up, then: profit-sharing is a mode of payment capable of giving excellent results in certain cases, but is not a general rule. It does not seem to me possible, at least for the present, to count on this mode of payment for appeasing conflict between Capital and Labour. Fortunately, there are other means which hitherto have been sufficient to maintain relative social quiet. Such methods have not lost their power and it is up to managers to study them, apply them, and make them work well.

Payment in Kind, Welfare Work, Non-Financial Incentives

Whether wages are made up of money only or whether they include various additions such as heating, light, housing, food, is of little consequence provided that the employee be satisfied.

From another point of view, there is no doubt that a business will be better served in proportion as its employees are more energetic, better educated, more conscientious and more permanent. The employer should have regard, if merely in the interests of the business, for the health, strength, education, morale, and stability of his personnel. These elements of smooth running are not acquired in the workshop alone, they are formed and developed as well, and particularly, outside it, in the home and school, in civil and religious life. Therefore, the employer comes to be concerned with his employees outside the works and here the question of proportion comes up again. Opinion is greatly divided on this point. Certain unfortunate experiments have resulted in some employers stopping short their interest, at the works gate and at the regulation of wages. The majority consider that the employer's activity may be used to good purpose outside the factory confines provided that there be discretion and prudence, that it be sought after rather than imposed, be in keeping with the general level of education and taste of those concerned and that it have absolute respect for their liberty. It must be benevolent collaboration, not tyrannical stewardship, and therein lies an indispensable condition of success. . . .

8. CENTRALIZATION

Like division of work, centralization belongs to the natural order; this turns on the fact that in every organism, animal or social, sensations converge towards the brain or directive part, and from the brain or directive part orders are sent out which set all parts of the organism in movement. Centralization is not a system of management good or bad of itself, capable of being adopted or discarded at the whim of managers or of circumstances; it is always present to a greater or less extent. The question of centralization or decentralization, is a simple question of proportion, it is a matter of finding the optimum degree for the particular concern. In small firms, where the manager's orders go directly to subordinates there is absolute centralization; in large concerns, where a long scalar chain is interposed between manager

and lower grades, orders and counter-information too, have to go through a series of intermediaries. Each employee, intentionally or unintentionally, puts something of himself into the transmission and execution of orders and of information received too. He does not operate merely as a cog in a machine. What appropriate share of initiative may be left to intermediaries depends on the personal character of the manager, on his moral worth, on the reliability of his subordinates, and also on the condition of the business. The degree of centralization must vary according to different cases. The objective to pursue is the optimum utilization of all faculties of the personnel.

If the moral worth of the manager, his strength, intelligence, experience, and swiftness of thought allow him to have a wide span of activities he will be able to carry centralization quite far and reduce his seconds in command to mere executive agents. If, conversely, he prefers to have greater recourse to the experience, opinions, and counsel of his colleagues whilst reserving to himself the privilege of giving general directives, he can effect considerable decentralization.

Seeing that both absolute and relative value of manager and employees are constantly changing, it is understandable that the degree of centralization or decentralization may itself vary constantly. It is a problem to be solved according to circumstances, to the best satisfaction of the interests involved. It arises, not only in the case of higher authority, but for superiors at all levels and not one but can extend or confine, to some extent, his subordinates' initiative.

The finding of the measure which shall give the best overall yield: that is the problem of centralization or decentralization. Everything which goes to increase the importance of the subordinate's rôle is decentralization, everything which goes to reduce it is centralization.

9. SCALAR CHAIN

The scalar chain is the chain of superiors ranging from the ultimate authority to the lowest ranks. The line of authority is the route followed—via every link in the chain—by all communications which start from or go to the ultimate authority. This path is dictated both by the need for some transmission and by the principle of unity of command, but it is not always the swiftest. It is even at times disastrously lengthy in large concerns, notably in governmental ones. Now, there are many activities whose success turns on speedy execution, hence respect for the line of authority must be reconciled with the need for swift action.

Let us imagine that section F has to be put into contact with section P in a business whose scalar chain is represented by the double ladder G-A-Q thus—

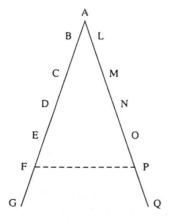

By following the line of authority the ladder must be climbed from F to A and then descended from A to P, stopping at each rung, then ascended again from P to A, and descended once more from A to F, in order to get back to the starting point. Evidently it is much simpler and quicker to go directly from F to P by making use of FP as a "gang plank" and that is what is most often done. The scalar principle will be safeguarded if managers E and O have authorized their respective subordinates F and P to treat directly, and the position will be fully regularized if F and P inform their respective superiors forthwith of what they have agreed upon. So long as F and P remain in agreement, and so long as their actions are approved by their immediate superiors, direct contact may be maintained, but from the instant that agreement ceases or there is no approval from the superiors direct contact comes to an end, and the scalar chain is straightway resumed. Such is the actual procedure to be observed in the great majority of businesses. It provides for the usual exercise of some measure of initiative at all levels of authority. In the small concern, the general interest, viz. that of the concern proper, is easy to grasp, and the employer is present to recall this interest to those tempted to lose sight of it. In government enterprise the general interest is such a complex, vast, remote thing, that it is not easy to get a clear idea of it, and for the majority of civil servants the employer is somewhat mythical and unless the sentiment of general interest be constantly revived by higher authority, it becomes blurred and weakened and each section tends to regard itself as its own aim and end and forgets that it is only a cog in a big machine, all of whose parts must work in concert. It becomes isolated, cloistered, aware only of the line of authority.

The use of the "gang plank" is simple, swift, sure. It allows the two employees F and P to deal at one sitting, and in a few hours, with some question or other which via the scalar chain would pass through twenty transmissions, inconvenience many people, involve masses of paper, lose weeks or months to get to a conclusion less satisfactory generally than the one which could have been obtained via direct contact as between F and P.

Is it possible that such practices, as ridiculous as they are devastating, could be in current use? Unfortunately there can be little doubt of it in government department affairs. It is usually acknowledged that the chief cause is fear of responsibility. I am rather of the opinion that it is insufficient executive capacity on the part of those in charge. If supreme authority A insisted that his assistants B and L made use of the "gang plank" themselves and made its use incumbent upon their subordinates C and M, the habit and courage of taking responsibility would be established and at the same time the custom of using the shortest path.

It is an error to depart needlessly from the line of authority, but it is an even greater one to keep to it when detriment to the business ensues. The latter may attain extreme gravity in certain conditions. When an employee is obliged to choose between the two practices, and it is impossible for him to take advice from his superior, he should be courageous enough and feel free enough to adopt the line dictated by the general interest. But for him to be in this frame of mind there must have been previous precedent, and his superiors must have set him the example—for example must always come from above.

10. ORDER

The formula is known in the case of material things "A place for everything and everything in its place." The formula is the same for human order. "A place for everyone and everyone in his place."

Material Order

In accordance with the preceding definition, so that material order shall prevail, there must be a place appointed for each thing and each thing must be in its appointed place. Is that enough? Is it not also necessary that the place shall have been well chosen? The object of order must be avoidance of loss of material, and for this object to be completely realized not only must things be in their place suitably arranged but also the place must have been chosen so as to facilitate all activities as much as possible. If this last condition be unfulfilled, there is merely the appearance of order. Appearance of order may cover over real disorder. I have seen a works yard used as a store for steel ingots in which the material was well stacked, evenly arranged and clean and which gave a pleasing impression of orderliness. On close inspection it could be noted that the same heap included five or six types of steel intended for different manufacture all mixed up together. Whence useless handling, lost time, risk of mistakes because each thing was not in its place. It happens, on the other hand, that the appearance of disorder may actually be true order. Such is the case with papers scattered about at a master's whim which a well-meaning but incompetent servant re-arranges and sticks in neat piles. The master can no longer find his way about them. Perfect order presupposes a judiciously chosen place and the appearance of order is merely a false or imperfect image of real order. Cleanliness is a corollary of orderliness, there is no appointed place for dirt. A diagram representing the entire premises divided up into as many sections as there are employees responsible facilitates considerably the establishing and control of order.

Social Order

For social order to prevail in a concern there must, in accordance with the definition, be an appointed place for every employee and every employee be in his appointed place. Perfect order requires, further, that the place be suitable for the employee and the employee for the place—in English idiom, "The right man in the right place."

Thus understood, social order presupposes the successful execution of the two most difficult managerial activities: good organization and good selection. Once the posts essential to the smooth running of the business have been decided upon and those to fill such posts have been selected, each employee occupies that post wherein he can render most service. Such is perfect social order "A place for each one and each one in his place." That appears simple, and naturally we are so anxious for it to be so that when we hear for the twentieth time a government departmental head assert this principle, we conjure up straightway a concept of perfect administration. This is a mirage.

Social order demands precise knowledge of the human requirements and resources of the concern and a constant balance between these requirements and resources. Now this balance is most difficult to establish and maintain and all the more difficult the bigger the business, and when it has been upset and individual interests resulted in neglect or sacrifice of the general interest, when ambition, nepotism, favouritism, or merely ignorance, has multiplied positions without good reason or filled them with incompetent employees, much talent and strength of will and more persistence than current instability of ministerial appointments presupposes, are required in order to sweep away abuses and restore order. . . .

11. EQUITY

Why equity and not justice? Justice is putting into execution established conventions, but conventions cannot fore-

see everything, they need to be interpreted or their inadequacy supplemented. For the personnel to be encouraged to carry out its duties with all the devotion and loyalty of which it is capable it must be treated with kindliness, and equity results from the combination of kindliness and justice. Equity excludes neither forcefulness nor sternness and the application of it requires much good sense, experience, and good nature.

Desire for equity and equality of treatment are aspirations to be taken into account in dealing with employees. In order to satisfy these requirements as much as possible without neglecting any principle or losing sight of the general interest, the head of the business must frequently summon up his highest faculties. He should strive to instil a sense of equity throughout all levels of the scalar chain.

12. STABILITY OF TENURE OF PERSONNEL

Time is required for an employee to get used to new work and succeed in doing it well, always assuming that he possesses the requisite abilities. If when he has got used to it, or before then, he is removed, he will not have had time to render worthwhile service. If this be repeated indefinitely the work will never be properly done. The undesirable consequences of such insecurity of tenure are especially to be feared in large concerns, where the settling in of managers is generally a lengthy matter. Much time is needed indeed to get to know men and things in a large concern in order to be in a position to decide on a plan of action, to gain confidence in oneself, and inspire it in others. Hence it has often been recorded that a mediocre manager who stays is infinitely preferable to outstanding managers who merely come and go.

Generally the managerial personnel of prosperous concerns is stable, that of unsuccessful ones is unstable. Instability of tenure is at one and the same time cause and effect of bad running. The apprenticeship of a higher manager is generally a costly matter. Nevertheless, changes of personnel are inevitable; age, illness, retirement, death, disturb the human make-up of the firm, certain employees are no longer capable of carrying out their duties, whilst others become fit to assume greater responsibilities. In common with all the other principles, therefore, stability of tenure and personnel is also a question of proportion.

13. INITIATIVE

Thinking out a plan and ensuring its success is one of the keenest satisfactions for an intelligent man to experience. It is also one of the most powerful stimulants of human endeavour. This power of thinking out and executing is what is called initiative, and freedom to propose and to execute belongs too, each in its way, to initiative. At all levels of the organizational ladder zeal and energy on the part of employees are augmented by initiative. The initiative of all, added to that of the manager, and supplementing it if need be, represents a great source of strength for businesses. This is particularly apparent at difficult times; hence it is essential to encourage and develop this capacity to the full.

Much tact and some integrity are required to inspire and maintain everyone's initiative, within the limits imposed, by respect for authority and for discipline. The manager must be able to sacrifice some personal vanity in order to grant this sort of satisfaction to subordinates. Other things being equal, moreover, a manager able to permit the exercise of initiative on the part of subordinates is infinitely superior to one who cannot do so.

14. ESPRIT DE CORPS

"Union is strength." Business heads would do well to ponder on this proverb. Harmony, union among the personnel of a concern, is great strength in that concern. Effort, then, should be made to establish it. Among the countless methods in use I will single out specially one principle to be observed and two pitfalls to be avoided. The principle to be observed is unity of command; the dangers to be avoided are (a) a misguided interpretation of the motto "divide and rule," (b) the abuse of written communications.

(a) *Personnel must not be split up.* Dividing enemy forces to weaken them is clever, but dividing one's own team is a grave sin against the business. Whether this error results from inadequate managerial capacity or imperfect grasp of things, or from egoism which sacrifices general interest to personal interest, it is always reprehensible because harmful to the business. There is no merit in sowing dissension among subordinates; any beginner can do it. On the contrary, real talent is needed to coordinate effort, encourage keenness, use each man's abilities, and reward each one's merit without arousing possible jealousies and disturbing harmonious relations.

(b) *Abuse of written communications.* In dealing with a business matter or giving an order which requires explanation to complete it, usually it is simpler and quicker to do so verbally than in writing. Besides, it is well known that differences and misunderstandings which a conversation could clear up, grow more bitter in writing. Thence it follows that, wherever possible, contacts should be verbal; there is a gain in speed, clarity and harmony. Nevertheless, it happens in some firms that employees of neighbouring departments with numerous points of contact, or even employees within a department, who could quite easily meet, only communicate with each other in writing. Hence arise increased work and complications and delays harmful to the business. At the same time, there is to be observed a certain animosity prevailing between different departments or different employees within a department. The system of written communications usually brings this result. There is a way of putting an end to this deplorable system and that is to forbid all communications in writing which could easily and advantageously be replaced by verbal ones. There again, we come up against a question of proportion. . . .

There I bring to an end this review of principles, not because the list is exhausted—this list has no precise limits—but because to me it seems at the moment especially useful to endow management theory with a dozen or so well-established principles, on which it is appropriate to concentrate general discussion. The foregoing principles are those to which I have most often had recourse. I have simply expressed my personal opinion in connection with them. Are they to have a place in the management code which is to be built up? General discussion will show.

This code is indispensable. Be it a case of commerce, industry, politics, religion, war, or philanthropy, in every concern there is a management function to be performed, and for its performance there must be principles, that is to say ac-

knowledged truths regarded as proven on which to rely. And it is the code which represents the sum total of these truths at any given moment.

Surprise might be expressed at the outset that the eternal moral principles, the laws of the Decalogue and Commandments of the Church are not sufficient guide for the manager, and that a special code is needed. The explanation is this: the higher laws of religious or moral order envisage the individual only, or else interests which are not of this world, whereas management principles aim at the success of associations of individuals and at the satisfying of economic interests. Given that the aim is different, it is not surprising that the means are not the same. There is no identity, so there is no contradiction. Without principles one is in darkness and chaos; interest, experience, and proportion are still very handicapped, even with the best principles. The principle is the lighthouse fixing the bearings, but it can only serve those who already know the way into port.

NOTE

1. "*Body corporate.*" Fayol's term "corps social,"· meaning all those engaged in a given corporate activity in any sphere, is best rendered by this somewhat unusual term because (*a*) it retains his implied biological metaphor; (*b*) it represents the structure as distinct from the process of organization. The term will be retained in all contexts where these two requirements have to be met. (Translator's note.)

6

The Principles of Scientific Management

Frederick Winslow Taylor

By far the most important fact which faces the industries of our country, the industries, in fact, of the civilized world, is that not only the average worker, but nineteen out of twenty workmen throughout the civilized world firmly believe that it is for their best interests to go slow instead of to go fast. They firmly believe that it is for their interest to give as little work in return for the money that they get as is practical. The reasons for this belief are twofold, and I do not believe that the workingmen are to blame for holding these fallacious views.

If you will take any set of workmen in your own town and suggest to those men that it would be a good thing for them in their trade if they were to double their output in the coming year, each man turn out twice as much work and become twice as efficient, they would say, "I don't know anything about other people's trades; what you are saying about increasing efficiency being a good thing may be good for other trades, but I know that the only result if you come to our trade would be that half of us would be out of a job before the year was out." That to the average workingman is an axiom; it is not a matter subject to debate at all. And even among the average business men of this country that opinion is almost universal. They firmly believe that that would be the result of a great increase in efficiency, and yet directly the opposite is true.

THE EFFECT OF LABOR-SAVING DEVICES

Whenever any labor-saving device of any kind has been introduced into any trade—go back into the history of any trade and see it—even though that labor-saving device may turn out ten, twenty, thirty times that output that was originally turned out by men in that trade, the result has universally been to make work for more men in that trade, not work for less men.

Let me give you one illustration. Let us take one of the staple businesses, the cotton industry. About 1840 the power loom succeeded the old hand loom in the cotton industry. It was invented many years before, somewhere about 1780 or 1790, but it came in very slowly. About 1840 the weavers of Manchester, England, saw that the power loom was coming, and they knew it would turn out three times the yardage of cloth in a day that the hand loom turned out. And what did they do, these five thousand weavers of Manchester, England, who saw starvation staring them in the face? They broke into the establishments into which those machines were being introduced, they smashed them, they did everything possible to stop the introduction of the power loom. And the same result followed that follows every attempt to interfere with the introduction of any labor-saving device, if it is really a

Source: Bulletin of the Taylor Society (December 1916). An abstract of an address given by the late Dr. Taylor before the Cleveland Advertising Club, March 3, 1915, two weeks prior to his death. It was repeated the following day at Youngstown, Ohio, and this presentation was Dr. Taylor's last public appearance.

labor-saving device. Instead of stopping the introduction of the power loom, their opposition apparently accelerated it, just as opposition to scientific management all over the country, bitter labor opposition today, is accelerating the introduction of it instead of retarding it. History repeats itself in that respect. The power loom came right straight along.

And let us see the result in Manchester. Just what follows in every industry when any labor-saving device is introduced. Less than a century has gone by since 1840. The population of England in that time has now more than doubled. Each man in the cotton industry in Manchester, England, now turns out, at a restricted estimate ten yards of cloth for every yard of cloth that was turned out in 1840. In 1840 there were 5,000 weavers in Manchester. Now there are 265,000. Has that thrown men out of work? Has the introduction of labor-saving machinery, which has multiplied the output per man by tenfold, thrown men out of work?

What is the real meaning of this? All that you have to do is to bring wealth into this world and the world uses it. That is the real meaning. The meaning is that where in 1840 cotton goods were a luxury to be worn only by rich people when they were hardly ever seen on the street, now every man, woman, and child all over the world wears cotton goods as a daily necessity.

Nineteen-twentieths of the real wealth of this world is used by the poor people, and not the rich, so that the workingman who sets out as a steady principle to restrict output is merely robbing his own kind. That group of manufacturers which adopts as a permanent principle restriction of output, in order to hold up prices, is robbing the world. The one great thing that marks the improvement of this world is measured by the enormous increase in output of the individuals in this world. There is fully twenty times the output per man now that there was three hundred years ago. That marks the increase in the real wealth of the world; that marks the increase of the happiness of the world, that gives us the opportunity for shorter hours, for better education, for amusement, for art, for music, for everything that is worthwhile in this world—goes right straight back to this increase in the output of the individual. The workingmen of today live better than the king did three hundred years ago. From what does the progress the world has made come? Simply from the increase in the output of the individual all over the world.

THE DEVELOPMENT OF SOLDIERING

The second reason why the workmen of this country and of Europe deliberately restrict output is a very simple one. They, for this reason, are even less to blame than they are for the other. If, for example, you are manufacturing a pen, let us assume for simplicity that a pen can be made by a single man. Let us say that the workman is turning out ten pens per day, and that he is receiving $2.50 a day for his wages. He has a progressive foreman who is up to date, and that foreman goes to the workman and suggests, "Here, John, you are getting $2.50 a day, and you are turning out ten pens. I would suggest that I pay you 25 cents for making that pen." The man takes the job, and through the help of his foreman, through his own ingenuity, through his increased work, through his interest in his business, through the help of his friends, at the end of the year he finds himself turning out twenty pens instead of ten. He is happy, he is making $5, instead of $2.50 a day. His foreman is happy because, with the same room, with the same men he had before, he has doubled the output of his department, and the manufacturer himself is sometimes happy, but not often. Then someone on the board of directors asks to see the payroll, and he finds that we are paying $5 a day where other similar mechanics are only getting $2.50, and in no uncertain terms he announces that we must stop ruining the labor market. We cannot pay $5 a day when the standard rate of wages is $2.50; how can we hope to compete with surrounding towns? What is the result? Mr. Foreman is sent for, and he is told that he has got to stop ruining the labor market of Cleveland. And the foreman goes back to his workman in sadness, in depression, and tells his workman, "I am sorry, John, but I have got to cut the price down for that pen; I cannot let you earn $5 a day; the board of directors has got on to it, and it is ruining the labor market; you ought to be willing to have the price reduced. You cannot earn more than $3 or $2.75 a day, and I will have to cut your wages so that you will only get $3 a day." John, of necessity accepts the cut, but he sees to it that he never makes enough pens to get another cut.

CHARACTERISTICS OF THE UNION WORKMAN

There seem to be two divergent opinions about the workmen of this country. One is that a lot of the trade unions' workmen, particularly in this country, have become brutal, have become dominating, careless of any interests but their own, and are a pretty poor lot. And the other opinion which those same trade unionists hold of themselves is that they are pretty close to little gods. Whichever view you may hold of the workingmen of this country, and my personal view of them is that they are a pretty fine lot of fellows, they are just about the same as you and I. But whether you hold the bad opinion or the good opinion, it makes no

difference. Whatever the workingmen of this country are or whatever they are not, they are not fools. And all that is necessary is for a workingman to have but one object lesson, like that I have told you, and he soldiers for the rest of his life.

There are a few exceptional employers who treat their workmen differently, but I am talking about the rule of the country. Soldiering is the absolute rule with all workmen who know their business. I am not saying it is for their interest to soldier. You cannot blame them for it. You cannot expect them to be large enough minded men to look at the proper view of the matter. Nor is the man who cuts the wages necessarily to blame. It is simply a misfortune in industry.

THE DEVELOPMENT OF SCIENTIFIC MANAGEMENT

There has been, until comparatively recently, no scheme promulgated by which the evils of rate cutting could be properly avoided, so soldiering has been the rule.

Now the first step that was taken toward the development of those methods, of those principles, which rightly or wrongly have come to be known under the name of scientific management—the first step that was taken in an earnest endeavor to remedy the evils of soldiering; an earnest endeavor to make it unnecessary for workmen to be hypocritical in this way, to deceive themselves, to deceive their employers, to live day in and day out a life of deceit, forced upon them conditions—the very first step that was taken toward the development was to overcome that evil. I want to emphasize that, because I wish to emphasize the one great fact relating to scientific management, the greatest factor: namely, that scientific management is no new set of theories that has been tried on by any one at every step. Scientific management at every step has been an evolution, not a theory. In all cases the practice has preceded the theory, not succeeded it. In every case one measure after another has been tried out, until the proper remedy has been found. That series of proper eliminations, that evolution, is what is called scientific management. Every element of it has had to fight its way against the elements that preceded it, and prove itself better or it would not be there tomorrow.

All the men that I know of who are in any way connected with scientific management are ready to abandon any scheme, and theory in favor of anything else that could be found that is better. There is nothing in scientific management that is fixed. There is no one man, or group of men, who have invented scientific management.

What I want to emphasize is that all of the elements of scientific management are an evolution, not an invention. Scientific management is in use in an immense range and variety of industries. Almost every type of industry in this country has scientific management working successfully. I think I can safely say that on the average in those establishments in which scientific management has been introduced, the average workman is turning out double the output he was before. I think that is a conservative statement.

THE WORKMEN THE CHIEF BENEFICIARIES

Three or four years ago I could have said there were about fifty thousand men working under scientific management, but now I know there are many more. Company after company is coming under it, many of which I know nothing about. Almost universally they are working successfully. This increasing of the output per individual in the trade, results, of course, in cheapening the product; it results, therefore, in larger profit usually to the owners of the business; it results also, in many cases, in a lowering of the selling price, although that has not come to the extent it will later. In the end the public gets the good. Without any question, the large good which so far has come from scientific management has come to the worker. To the workmen has come, practically right off as soon as scientific management is introduced, an increase in wages amounting from 33 to 100 percent, and yet that is not the greatest good that comes to the workmen from scientific management. The great good comes from the fact that, under scientific management, they look upon their employers as the best friends they have in the world; the suspicious watchfulness which characterizes the old type management, the semi-antagonism, or the complete antagonism between workmen and employers is entirely superseded, and in its place comes genuine friendship between both sides. That is the greatest good that has come under scientific management. As a proof of this in the many businesses in which scientific management has been introduced, I know of not one single strike of workmen working under it after it had been introduced, and only two or three while it was in process of introduction. In this connection I must speak of the fakers, those who have said they can introduce scientific management into a business in six months or a year. That is pure nonsense. There have been many strikes stirred up by that type of man. Not one strike has ever come, and I do not believe ever will come, under scientific management.

WHAT SCIENTIFIC MANAGEMENT IS

What is scientific management? It is no efficiency device, nor is it any group of efficiency devices. Scientific management is no new scheme for paying men, it is no bonus system, no piecework system, no premium system of payment; it is no new method of figuring costs. It is no one of the various elements by which it is commonly known, by which people refer to it. It is not time study nor man study. It is not the printing of a ton or two of blanks and unloading them on a company and saying, "There is your system, go ahead and use it." Scientific management does not exist and cannot exist until there has been a complete mental revolution on the part of the workmen working under it, as to their duties toward themselves and toward their employers, and a complete mental revolution in the outlook for the employers, toward their duties, toward themselves, and toward their workmen. And until this great mental change takes place, scientific management does not exist. Do you think you can make a great mental revolution in a large group of workmen in a year, or do you think you can make it in a large group of foremen and superintendents in a year? If you do, you are very much mistaken. All of us hold mighty close to our ideas and principles in life, and we change very slowly toward the new, and very properly too.

Let me give you an idea of what I mean by this change in mental outlook. If you are manufacturing a hammer or a mallet, into the cost of that mallet goes a certain amount of raw materials, a certain amount of wood and metal. If you will take the cost of the raw materials and then add to it that cost which is frequently called by various names— overhead expenses, general expense, indirect expense; that is, the proper share of taxes, insurance, light, heat, salaries of officers and advertising—and you have a sum of money. Subtract that sum from the selling price, and what is left over is called the surplus. It is over this surplus that all of the labor disputes in the past

have occurred. The workman naturally wants all he can get. His wages come out of that surplus. The manufacturer wants all he can get in the shape of profits, and it is from the division of this surplus that all the labor disputes have come in the past—the equitable division.

The new outlook that comes under scientific management is this: The workmen, after many object lessons, come to see and the management come to see that this surplus can be made so great, providing both sides will stop their pulling apart, will stop their fighting and will push as hard as they can to get as cheap an output as possible, that there is no occasion to quarrel. Each side can get more than ever before. The acknowledgement of this fact represents a complete mental revolution. . . .

WHAT SCIENTIFIC MANAGEMENT WILL DO

I am going to try to prove to you that the old style of management has not a ghost of a chance in competition with the principles of scientific management. Why? In the first place, under scientific management, the initiative of the workmen, their hard work, their goodwill, their best endeavors are obtained with absolute regularity. There are cases all the time where men will soldier, but they become the exception, as a rule, and they give their true initiative under scientific management. That is the least of the two sources of gain. The greatest source of gain under scientific management comes from the new and almost unheard-of duties and burdens which are voluntarily assumed, not by the workmen, but by the men on the management side. These are the things which make scientific management a success. These new duties, these new burdens undertaken by the management have rightly or wrongly been divided into four groups, and have been called the principles of scientific management.

The first of the great principles of scientific management, the first of the new burdens which are voluntarily undertaken by those on the management side is the deliberate gathering together of the great mass of traditional knowledge which, in the past, has been in the heads of the workmen, recording it, tabulating it, reducing it in most cases to rules, laws, and in many cases to mathematical formulae, which, with these new laws, are applied to the cooperation of the management to the work of the workmen. This results in an immense increase in the output, we may say, of the two. The gathering in of this great mass of traditional knowledge, which is done by the means of motion study, time study, can be truly called the science.

Let me make a prediction. I have before me the first book, so far as I know, that has been published on motion study and on time study. That is, the motion study and time study of the cement and concrete trades. It contains everything relating to concrete work. It is of about seven hundred pages and embodies the motions of men, the time and the best way of doing that sort of work. It is the first case in which a trade has been reduced to the same condition that engineering data of all kinds have been reduced, and it is this sort of data that is bound to sweep the world.

I have before me something which has been gathering for about fourteen years, the time or motion study of the machine shop. It will take probably four or five years more before the first book will be ready to publish on that subject. There is a collection of sixty or seventy thousand elements affecting machine-shop work. After a few years, say three, four or five years more, someone will be ready to publish the first book giving the laws of the movements of men in the machine shop—all the laws, not only a few of

them. Let me predict, just as sure as the sun shines, that is going to come in every trade. Why? Because it pays, for no other reason. That results in doubling the output in any shop. Any device which results in an increased output is bound to come in spite of all opposition, whether we want it or not. It comes automatically.

THE SELECTION OF THE WORKMAN

The next of the four principles of scientific management is the scientific selection of the workman, and then his progressive development. It becomes the duty under scientific management of not one, but of a group of men on the management side, to deliberately study the workmen who are under them; study them in the most careful, thorough and painstaking way; and not just leave it to the poor, overworked foreman to go out and say, "Come on, what do you want? If you are cheap enough I will give you a trial."

That is the old way. The new way is to take a great deal of trouble in selecting the workmen. The selection proceeds year after year. And it becomes the duty of those engaged in scientific management to know something about the workmen under them. It becomes their duty to set out deliberately to train the workmen in their employ to be able to do a better and still better class of work than ever before, and to then pay them higher wages than ever before. This deliberate selection of the workmen is the second of the great duties that devolve on the management under scientific management.

BRINGING TOGETHER THE SCIENCE AND THE MAN

The third principle is the bringing together of this science of which I have spoken and the trained workmen. I say bringing because they don't come together unless someone brings them. Select and train your workmen all you may, but unless there is someone who will make the men and the science come together, they will stay apart. The "make" involves a great many elements. They are not all disagreeable elements. The most important and largest way of "making" is to do something nice for the man whom you wish to make come together with the science. Offer him a plum, something that is worthwhile. There are many plums offered to those who come under scientific management—better treatment, more kindly treatment, more consideration for their wishes, and an opportunity for them to express their wants freely. That is one side of the "make." An equally important side is, whenever a man will not do what he ought, to either make him do it or stop it. If he will not do it, let him get out. I am not talking of any mollycoddle. Let me disabuse your minds of any opinion that scientific management is a mollycoddle scheme. . . .

THE PRINCIPLE OF THE DIVISION OF WORK

The fourth principle is the plainest of all. It involves a complete re-division of the work of the establishment. Under the old scheme of management, almost all of the work was done by the workmen. Under the new, the work of the establishment is divided into two large parts. All of that work which formerly was done by the workmen alone is divided into two large sections, and one of those sections is handed over to the management. They do a whole division of the work formerly done by the workmen. It is this real cooperation, this genuine division of the work between the two sides, more than any other element

which accounts for the fact that there never will be strikes under scientific management. When the workman realizes that there is hardly a thing he does that does not have to be preceded by some act of preparation on the part of management, and when that workman realizes when the management falls down and does not do its part, that he is not only entitled to a kick, but that he can register that kick in the most forcible possible way, he cannot quarrel with the men over him. It is teamwork. There are more complaints made every day on the part of the workmen that the men on the management side fail to do their duties than are made by the management that the men fail. Every one of the complaints of the men have to be heeded, just as much as the complaints from the management that the workmen do not do their share. That is characteristic of scientific management. It represents a democracy, co-operation, a genuine division of work which never existed before in this world.

THE PROOF OF THE THEORY

I am through now with the theory. I will try to convince you of the value of these four principles by giving you some practical illustrations. I hope that you will look for these four elements in the illustrations. I shall begin by trying to show the power of these four elements when applied to the greatest kind of work I know of that is done by man. The reason I have heretofore chosen pig-iron for an illustration is that it is the lowest form of work that is known.

A pig of iron weighs about ninety-two pounds on an average. A man stoops down and, with no other implement than his hands, picks up a pig of iron, walks a few yards with it, and drops it on a pile. A large part of the community has the impression that scientific management is chiefly handling pig-iron. The reason I first chose pig-iron for an illustration is that, if you can prove to any one the strength, the effect, of those four principles when applied to such rudimentary work as handling pig-iron, the presumption is that it can be applied to something better. The only way to prove it is to start at the bottom and show those four principles all along the line. I am sorry I cannot, because of the lack of time, give you the illustration of handling pig-iron. Many of you doubt whether there is much of any science in it. I am going to try to prove later with a high class mechanic that the workman who is fit to work at any type of work is almost universally incapable of understanding the principles without the help of some one else. I will use shoveling because it is a shorter illustration, and I will try to show what I mean by the science of shoveling, and the power which comes to the man who knows the science of shoveling. It is a high art compared with pig-iron handling.

THE SCIENCE OF SHOVELING

When I went to the Bethlehem Steel Works, the first thing I saw was a gang of men unloading rice coal. They were a splendid set of fellows, and they shoveled fast. There was no loafing at all. They shoveled as hard as you could ask any man to work. I looked with the greatest of interest for a long time, and finally they moved off rapidly down into the yard to another part of the yard and went right at handling iron ore. One of the main facts connected with that shoveling was that the work those men were doing was that, in handling the rice coal, they had on their shovels a load of 3¾ pounds, and when the same men went to handling ore with the same shovel, they had over 38 pounds on their shovels. Is it asking too much of anyone to inquire whether 3¾ pounds is the right load for a shovel, or whether 38 pounds is the right load for a shovel? Surely if one is right the other must be wrong. I think that is a self-evident fact, and yet I am willing to bet that that is what workmen are doing right now in Cleveland.

That is the old way. Suppose we notice that fact. Most of us do not notice it because it is left to the foreman. At the Midvale works, we had to find out these facts. What is the old way of finding them out? The old way was to sit down and write one's friends and ask them the questions. They got answers from contractors about what they thought it ought to be, and then they averaged them up, or took the most reliable man, and said, "That is all right; now we have a shovel load of so much." The more common way is to say, "I want a good shovel foreman." They will send for the foreman of the shovelers and put the job up to him to find what is the proper load to put on a shovel. He will tell you right off the bat. I want to show you the difference under scientific management.

Under scientific management you ask no one. Every little trifle,—here is nothing too small,—becomes the subject of experiment. The experiments develop into a law; they save money; they increase the output of the individual and make the thing worthwhile. How is this done? What we did in shoveling experiments was to deliberately select two first class shovelers, the best we knew how to get. We brought them into the office and said, "Jim and Mike, you two fellows are both good shovelers. I have a proposition to make to you. I am going to pay you double wages if you fellows will go out and do what I want you to do. There will be a young chap go along with you with a pencil and a piece of paper, and he will tell you to do a lot of fool things, and you will do them, and he will write down a lot of fool things, and you will think it is a joke, but it is nothing of the kind. Let me tell you one thing: if you fellows think that you can fool that chap you are very much mistaken, you cannot fool him at all. Don't get it through your heads you can fool him. If you take this double wages, you will be straight and do what you are told." They both promised and did exactly what they were told. What we told them was this: "We want you to start in and do whatever shoveling you are told to do and work at just the pace, all day long, that when it comes night you are going to be good and tired, but not tired out. I do not want you exhausted or anything like that, but properly tired. You know what a good day's work is. In other words, I do not want any loafing business or any overwork business. If you find yourself overworked and getting too tired, slow down." Those men did that and did it in the most splendid kind of way day in and day out. We proved their cooperation because they were in different parts of the yard, and they both got near enough the same results. Our results were duplicated.

I have found that there are a lot of schemes among my working friends, but no more among them than among us. They are good, straight fellows if you only treat them right, and put the matter up squarely to them. We started in at a pile of material, with a very large shovel. We kept innumerable accurate records of all kinds, some of them useless. Thirty or forty different items were carefully observed about the work of those two men. We counted the number of shovelfuls thrown in a day. We found with a weight of between thirty-eight and thirty-nine pounds on the shovel, the man made a pile of material of a certain height. We then cut off the shovel, and he shoveled

again and with a thirty-four pound load his pile went up and he shoveled more in a day. We again cut off the shovel to thirty pounds, and the pile went up again. With twenty-six pounds on the shovel, the pile again went up, and at twenty-one and one-half pounds the men could do their best. At twenty pounds the pile went down, at eighteen it went down, at fourteen it went down, so that they were at the peak of twenty-one and one-half pounds. There is a scientific fact. A first class shoveler ought to take twenty-one and one-half pounds on his shovel in order to work to the best possible advantage. You are not giving that man a chance unless you give him a shovel which will hold twenty-one pounds.

The men in the yard were run by the old fashioned foreman. He simply walked about with them. We at once took their shovels away from them. We built a large labor tool room which held ten to fifteen different kinds of shoveling implements so that for each kind of material that was handled in that yard, all the way from rice coals, ashes, coke, all the way up to ore, we would have a shovel that would just hold twenty-one pounds, or average twenty-one. One time it would hold eighteen, the next twenty-four, but it will average twenty-one.

When you have six hundred men laboring in the yard, as we had there, it becomes a matter of quite considerable difficulty to get, each day, for each one of those six hundred men, engaged in a line one and one-half to two miles long and a half mile wide, just the right shovel for shoveling material. That requires organization to lay out and plan for those men in advance. We had to lay out the work each day. We had to have large maps on which the movements of the men were plotted out a day in advance. When each workman came in the morning, he took out two pieces of paper. One of the blanks gave them a statement of the implements which they had to use, and the part of the yard in which they had to work. That required organization planning in advance.

One of the first principles we adopted was that no man in that labor gang could work on the new way unless he earned sixty percent higher wages than under the old plan. It is only just to the workman that he shall know right off whether he is doing his work right or not. He must not be told a week or month after, that he fell down. He must know it the next morning. So the next slip that came out of the pigeon hole was either a white or yellow slip. We used the two colors because some of the men could not read. The yellow slip meant that he had not earned his sixty per cent higher wages. He knew that he could not stay in that gang and keep on getting yellow slips.

TEACHING THE MEN

I want to show you again the totally different outlook there is under scientific management by illustrating what happened when that man got his yellow slips. Under the old scheme, the foreman could say to him, "You are no good, get out of this; no time for you, you cannot earn sixty percent higher wages; get out of this! Go!" It was not done politely, but the foreman had no time to palaver. Under the new scheme what happened? A teacher of shoveling went down to see that man. A teacher of shoveling is a man who is handy with a shovel, who has made his mark in life with a shovel, and yet who is a kindly fellow and knows how to show the other fellow what he ought to do. When that teacher went there he said, "See here, Jim, you have a lot of those yellow slips, what is the

matter with you? What is up? Have you been drunk? Are you tired? Are you sick? Anything wrong with you? Because if you are tired or sick we will give you a show somewhere else." "Well, no, I am all right." "Then if you are not sick, or there is nothing wrong with you, you have forgotten how to shovel. I showed you how to shovel. You have forgotten something, now go ahead and shovel and I will show you what is the matter with you." Shoveling is a pretty big science, it is not a little thing.

If you are going to use the shovel right you should always shovel off an iron bottom; if not an iron bottom, a wooden bottom; and if not a wooden bottom a hard dirt bottom. Time and again the conditions are such that you have to go right into the pile. When that is the case, with nine out of ten materials it takes more trouble and more time and more effort to get the shovel into the pile than to do all the rest of the shoveling. That is where the effort comes. Those of you again who have taught the art of shoveling will have taught your workmen to do this. There is only one way to do it right. Put your forearm down onto the upper part of your leg, and when you push into the pile, throw your weight against it. That relieves your arm of work. You then have an automatic push, we will say, about eighty pounds, the weight of your body thrown on to it. Time and again we would find men whom we had taught to shovel right were going at it in the same old way, and of course, they could not do a day's work. The teacher would simply stand over that fellow and say, "There is what is the matter with you, Jim, you have forgotten to shovel into the pile."

You are not interested in shoveling, you are not interested in whether one way or the other is right, but I do hope to interest you in the difference of the mental attitude of the men who are teaching under the new system. Under the new system, if a man falls down, the presumption is that it is our fault at first, that we probably have not taught the man right, have not given him a fair show, have not spent time enough in showing him how to do his work.

Let me tell you another thing that is characteristic of scientific management. In my day, we were smart enough to know when the boss was coming, and when he came up we were apparently really working. Under scientific management, there is none of that pretense. I cannot say that in the old days we were delighted to see the boss coming around. We always expected some kind of roast if he came too close. Under the new, the teacher is welcomed; he is not an enemy, but a friend. He comes there to try to help the man get bigger wages, to show him how to do something. It is the great mental change, the change in the outlook that comes, rather than the details of it.

DOES SCIENTIFIC MANAGEMENT PAY?

It took the time of a number of men for about three years to study the art of shoveling in that yard at the Bethlehem Steel Works alone. They were carefully trained college men, and they were busy all the time. That costs money, the tool room costs money, the clerks we had to keep there all night figuring up how much the men did the day before cost money, the office in which the men laid out and planned the work cost money. The very fair and proper question, the only question to ask is "Does it pay?" because if scientific management does not pay in dollars and cents, it is the rankest kind of nonsense. There is nothing philanthropic about it. It has got to

pay, because business which cannot be done on a profitable basis, ought not to be done on a philanthropic basis, for it will not last. At the end of three and one-half years we had a very good chance to know whether or not it paid.

Fortunately in the Bethlehem Steel Works they had records of how much it cost to handle the materials under the old system, where the single foreman led a group of men around the works. It costs them between seven and eight cents a ton to handle materials, on an average throughout the year. After paying for all this extra work I have told you about, it cost between three and four cents a ton to handle materials, and there was a profit of between seventy-five and eighty thousand dollars a year in that yard by handling those materials in the new way. What the men got out of it was this: Under the old system there were between four and six hundred men handling the material in that yard, and when we got through there were about one hundred and forty. Each one was earning a great deal more money. We made careful investigation and found they were almost all saving money, living better, happier; they are the most contented set of laborers to be seen anywhere. It is only by this kind of justification, justification of a profit for both sides, an advantage to both sides, that scientific management can exist.

I would like to give you one more illustration. I want to try to prove to you that even the highest class mechanic cannot possibly understand the philosophy of his work, cannot possibly understand the laws under which he has to operate. There is a man who has had a high school education, an ingenious fellow who courts variety in life, to whom it is pleasant to change from one kind of work to another. He is not a cheap man, he is rather a high grade man among the machinists of this country. The case of which I am going to tell you is one in which my friend Barth went to introduce scientific management in the works of an owner, who, at between 65 and 70 years of age, had built up his business from nothing to almost five thousand men. They had a squabble, and after they got through, Mr. Barth made the proposition, "I will take any machine that you use in your shop, and I will show you that I can double the output of that machine." A very fair machine was selected. It was a lathe on which the workman had been working about twelve years. The product of that shop is a patented machine with a good many parts, 350 men working making those parts year in and year out. Each man had ten or a dozen parts a year.

The first thing that was done was in the presence of the foreman, the superintendent and the owner of the establishment. Mr. Barth laid down the way in which all of the parts were to be machined on that machine by the workman. Then Mr. Barth, with one of his small slide rules, proceeded to analyze the machine. With the aid of this analysis, which embodies the laws of cutting metals, Mr. Barth was able to take his turn at the machine; his gain was from two and one-half times to three times the amount of work turned out by the other man. This is what can be done by science as against the old rule of thumb knowledge. That is not exaggeration; the gain is as great as that in many cases.

Let me tell you something. The machines of this country, almost universally in the machine shops of our country, are speeded two or three hundred percent wrong. I made that assertion before the tool builders in Atlantic City. I said,

"Gentlemen, in your own shops, many of your machines are two and three hundred percent wrong in speeds. Why? Because you have guessed at it." I am trying to show you what are the losses under the old opinions, the difference between knowledge on the one hand and guesswork on the other.

In 1882, at the end of a long fight with the machinists of the Midvale Steel Works, I went there as a laborer, and finally became a machinist after serving my apprenticeship outside. I finally got into the shop, and worked up to the place of a clerk who had something wrong with him. I then did a little bit more work than the others were doing, not too much. They came to me and said, "See here, Fred, you are not going to be a piecework hog." I said, "You fellows mean that you think I am not going to try to get any more work off these machines? I certainly am. Now I am on the other side, and I am going to be straight with you, and I will tell you so in advance." They said, "All right then, we will give you fair notice you will be outside the fence inside of six weeks." Let me tell you gentlemen, if any of you have been through a fight like that, trying to get workmen to do what they do not want to do, you will know the meanness of it, and you will never want to go into another one. I never would have gone into it if I had known what was ahead of me. After the meanest kind of a bitter fight, at the end of three years, we fairly won out and got a big increase in output. I had no illusion at the end of that time as to my great ability or anything else. I knew that those workmen knew about ten times as much as I did about doing the work. I set out deliberately to get on our side some of that knowledge that those workmen had.

Mr. William Sellers was the president, and he was a man away beyond his generation in progress. I went to him and said, "I want to spend quite a good deal of money trying to educate ourselves on the management side of our works. I do not know much of anything, and I am just about in the same condition as all the rest of the foremen around here." Very reluctantly, I may say, he allowed us to start to spend money. That started the study of the art of cutting metals. At the end of six months, from the standpoint of how to cut the metal off faster, the study did not amount to anything, but we unearthed a gold mine of information. Mr. Sellers laughed at me, but when I was able to show him the possibilities that lay ahead of us, the number of things we could find out, he said, "Go ahead." So until 1889, that experiment went straight ahead day in and day out. That was done because it paid in dollars and cents.

After I left the Midvale Steel Works, we had no means of figuring those experiments except the information which we had already gotten. Ten different machines were built to develop the art of cutting metals, so that almost continuously from 1882 for twenty-six years, all sorts of experiments went on to determine the twelve great elements that go to make up the art of cutting metals. I am trying to show you just what is going to take place in every industry throughout this world. You must know those facts if you are going to manufacture cheaply, and the only way to know them is to pay for them . . .

THE EFFECT ON
THE WORKMAN

Almost every one says, "Why, yes, that may be a good thing for the manufacturer, but how about the workmen? You are taking all the initiative away from that workman, you are making a machine out of him; what are you doing for him? He becomes merely a part of the machine." That is the almost universal impression. Again let me try to sweep aside the fallacy of that view by an illustration. The modern surgeon without a doubt is the finest mechanic in the world. He combines the greatest manual dexterity with the greatest knowledge of implements and the greatest knowledge of materials on which he is working. He is a true scientist, and he is a very highly skilled mechanic.

How does the surgeon teach his trade to the young men who come to the medical school? Does he say to them, "Now, young men, we belong to an older generation than you do, but the new generation is going to far outstrip anything that has been done in our generation; therefore, what we want of you is your initiative. We must have your brains, your thought, with your initiative. Of course, you know we old fellows have certain prejudices. For example, if we were going to amputate a leg, when we come down to the bone we are accustomed to take a saw, and we use it in that way and saw the bone off. But, gentlemen, do not let that fact one minute interfere with your originality, with your initiative, if you prefer an axe or a hatchet." Does the surgeon say this? He does not. He says, "You young men are going to outstrip us, but we will show you how. You shall not use a single implement in a single way until you know just which one to use, and we will tell you which one to use, and until you know how to use it, we will tell you how to use that implement, and after you have learned to use that implement our way, if you then see any defects in the implements, any defects in the method, then invent; but, invent so that you can invent upwards. Do not go inventing things which we discarded years ago."

That is just what we say to our young men in the shops. Scientific management makes no pretense that there is any finality in it. We merely say that the collective work of thirty or forty men in this trade through eight or ten years has gathered together a large amount of data. Every man in the establishment must start that way, must start our way, then if he can show us any better way, I do not care what it is, we will make an experiment to see if it is better. It will be named after him, and he will get a prize for having improved on one of our standards. There is the way we make progress under scientific management. There is your justification for all this. It does not dwarf initiative, it makes true initiative. Most of our progress comes through our workmen, but comes in a legitimate way.

7

Bureaucracy

Max Weber

1. CHARACTERISTICS OF BUREAUCRACY

Modern officialdom functions in the following specific manner:

I. There is the principle of fixed and official jurisdictional areas, which are generally ordered by rules, that is, by laws or administrative regulations.

1. The regular activities required for the purposes of the bureaucratically governed structure are distributed in a fixed way as official duties.

2. The authority to give the commands required for the discharge of these duties is distributed in a stable way and is strictly delimited by rules concerning the coercive means, physical, sacerdotal, or otherwise, which may be placed at the disposal of officials.

3. Methodical provision is made for the regular and continuous fulfillment of these duties and for the execution of the corresponding rights; only persons who have the generally regulated qualifications to serve are employed.

In public and lawful government these three elements constitute "bureaucratic authority." In private economic domination, they constitute bureaucratic "management." Bureaucracy, thus understood, is fully developed in political and ecclesiastical communities only in the modern state, and, in the private economy, only in the most advanced institutions of capitalism. Permanent and public office authority, with fixed jurisdiction, is not the historical rule but rather the exception. This is so even in large political structures such as those of the ancient Orient, the Germanic and Mongolian empires of conquest, or of many feudal structures of state. In all these cases, the ruler executes the most important measures through personal trustees, table-companions, or court-servants. Their commissions and authority are not precisely delimited and are temporarily called into being for each case.

II. The principles of office hierarchy and of levels of graded authority mean a firmly ordered system of super- and subordination in which there is a supervision of the lower offices by the higher ones. Such a system offers the governed the possibility of appealing the decision of a lower office to its higher authority, in a definitely regulated manner. With the full development of the bureaucratic type, the office hierarchy is monocratically organized. The principle of hierarchical office authority is found in all bureaucratic structures: in state and ecclesiastical structures as well as in large party organizations and private enterprises. It does not matter for the character of bureaucracy whether its authority is called "private" or "public."

When the principle of jurisdictional "competency" is fully carried through, hierarchical subordination—at least in

Source: From *From Max Weber: Essays in Sociology* edited and translated by H. H. Gerth and C. Wright Mills eds.. Copyright © 1946 by Oxford University Press, Inc.; renewed 1973 by Hans H. Gerth. Reprinted by permission of the publisher. Footnotes omitted.

public office—does not mean that the "higher" authority is simply authorized to take over the business of the "lower." Indeed, the opposite is the rule. Once established and having fulfilled its task, an office tends to continue in existence and be held by another incumbent.

III. *The management of the modern office is based upon written documents ("the files"), which are preserved in their original or draught form.* There is, therefore, a staff or subaltern officials and scribes of all sorts. The body of officials actively engaged in a "public" office, along with the respective apparatus of material implements and the files, make up a "bureau." In private enterprise, "the bureau" is often called "the office."

In principle, the modern organization of the civil service separates the bureau from the private domicile of the offical, and, in general, bureaucracy segregates official activity as something distinct from the sphere of private life. Public monies and equipment are divorced from the private property of the official. This condition is everywhere the product of a long development. Nowadays, it is found in public as well as in private enterprises; in the latter, the principle extends even to the leading entrepreneur. In principle, the executive office is separated from the household, business from private correspondence, and business assets from private fortunes. The more consistently the modern type of business management has been carried through the more are these separations the case. The beginnings of this process are to be found as early as the Middle Ages.

It is the peculiarity of the modern entrepreneur that he conducts himself as the "first official" of his enterprise, in the very same way in which the ruler of a specifically modern bureaucratic state spoke of himself as "the first servant" of the state. The idea that the bureau activities of the state are intrinsically different in character from the management of private economic offices is a continental European notion and, by way of contrast, is totally foreign to the American way.

IV. *Office management, at least all specialized office management—and such management is distinctly modern—usually presupposes thorough and expert training.* This increasingly holds for the modern executive and employee of private enterprises, in the same manner as it holds for the state official.

V. *When the office is fully developed, official activity demands the full working capacity of the official, irrespective of the fact that his obligatory time in the bureau may be firmly delimited.* In the normal case, this is only the product of a long development, in the public as well as in the private office. Formerly, in all cases, the normal state of affairs was reversed: official business was discharged as a secondary activity.

VI. *The management of the office follows general rules, which are more or less stable, more or less exhaustive, and which can be learned.* Knowledge of these rules represents a special technical learning which the officials possess. It involves jurisprudence, or administrative or business management.

The reduction of modern office management to rules is deeply embedded in its very nature. The theory of modern public administration, for instance, assumes that the authority to order certain matters by decree—which has been legally granted to public authorities—does not entitle the bureau to regulate the matter by commands given for each case, but only to regulate the matter abstractly. This stands in extreme contrast to the regulation of all relationships through individual privileges and bestowals of favor, which is absolutely dominant in patrimonialism, at least in so far as such relationships are not fixed by sacred tradition.

2. THE POSITION OF THE OFFICIAL

All this results in the following for the internal and external position of the official:

I. *Office holding is a "vocation."* This is shown, first, in the requirement of a firmly prescribed course of training, which demands the entire capacity for work for a long period of time, and in the generally prescribed and special examinations which are prerequisites of employment. Furthermore, the position of the official is in the nature of a duty. This determines the internal structure of his relations, in the following manner: Legally and actually, office holding is not considered a source to be exploited for rents or emoluments, as was normally the case during the Middle Ages and frequently up to the threshold of recent times. Nor is office holding considered a usual exchange of services for equivalents, as is the case with free labor contracts. Entrance into an office, including one in the private economy, is considered an acceptance of a specific obligation of faithful management in return for a secure existence. It is decisive for the specific nature of modern loyalty to an office that, in the pure type, it does not establish a relationship to a *person*, like the vassal's or disciple's faith in feudal or in patrimonial relations of authority. Modern loyalty is devoted to impersonal and functional purposes. Behind the functional purposes, of course, "ideas of culture-values" usually stand. These are *ersatz* for the earthly or supramundane personal master: ideas such as "state," "church," "community," "party," or "enterprise" are thought of

as being realized in a community; they provide an ideological halo for the master.

The political official—at least in the fully developed modern state—is not considered the personal servant of a ruler. Today, the bishop, the priest, and the preacher are in fact no longer, as in early Christian times, holders of purely personal charisma. The supra-mundane and sacred values which they offer are given to everybody who seems to be worthy of them and who asks for them. In former times, such leaders acted upon the personal command of their master; in principle, they were responsible only to him. Nowadays, in spite of the partial survival of the old theory, such religious leaders are officials in the service of a functional purpose, which in the present-day "church" has become routinized and, in turn, ideologically hallowed.

II. *The personal position of the official is patterned in the following way:*

1. Whether he is in a private office or a public bureau, the modern official always strives and usually enjoys a distinct *social esteem* as compared with the governed. His social position is guaranteed by the prescriptive rules of rank order and, for the political official, by special definitions of the criminal code against "insults of officials" and "contempt" of state and church authorities.

The actual social position of the official is normally highest where, as in old civilized countries, the following conditions prevail: a strong demand for administration by trained experts; a strong and stable social differentiation, where the official predominantly derives from socially and economically privileged strata because of the social distribution of power; or where the costliness of the required training and status conventions are binding upon him. The possession of educational certificates—to be discussed elsewhere—are usually linked with qualification for office. Naturally, such certificates or patents enhance the "status element" in the social position of the official. For the rest this status factor in individual cases is explicitly and impassively acknowledged; for example, in the prescription that the acceptance or rejection of an aspirant to an official career depends upon the consent ("election") of the members of the official body. This is the case in the German army with the officer corps. Similar phenomena, which promote this guild-like closure of officialdom, are typically found in patrimonial and, particularly, in prebendal officialdoms of the past. The desire to resurrect such phenomena in changed forms is by no means infrequent among modern bureaucrats. For instance, they have played a role among the demands of the quite proletarian and expert officials (the *tretyj* element) during the Russian revolution.

Usually the social esteem of the officials as such is especially low where the demand for expert administration and the dominance of status conventions are weak. This is especially the case in the United States; it is often the case in new settlements by virtue of their wide fields for profitmaking and the great instability of their social stratification.

2. The pure type of bureaucratic official is *appointed* by a superior authority. An official elected by the governed is not a purely bureaucratic figure. Of course, the formal existence of an election does not by itself mean that no appointment hides behind the election—in the state, especially, appointment by party chiefs. Whether or not this is the case does not depend upon legal statutes but upon the way in which the party mechanism functions. Once firmly organized, the parties can turn a formally free

election into the mere acclamation of a candidate designated by the party chief. As a rule, however, a formally free election is turned into a fight, conducted according to definite rules, for votes in favor of one of two designated candidates.

In all circumstances, the designation of officials by means of an election among the governed modifies the strictness of hierarchical subordination. In principle, an official who is so elected has an autonomous position opposite the superordinate official. The elected official does not derive his position "from above" but "from below," or at least not from a superior authority of the official hierarchy but from powerful party men ("bosses"), who also determine his further career. The career of the elected official is not, or at least not primarily, dependent upon his chief in the administration. The official who is not elected but appointed by a chief normally functions more exactly, from a technical point of view, because, all other circumstances being equal, it is more likely that purely functional points of consideration and qualities will determine his selection and career. As laymen, the governed can become acquainted with the extent to which a candidate is expertly qualified for office only in terms of experience, and hence only after his service. Moreover, in every sort of selection of officials by election, parties quite naturally give decisive weight not to expert considerations but to the services a follower renders to the party boss. This holds for all kinds of procurement of officials by elections, for the designation of formally free, elected officials by party bosses when they determine the slate of candidates, or the free appointment by a chief who has himself been elected. The contrast, however, is relative: substantially similar conditions hold where legitimate monarchs and their subordinates appoint officials, except that the influence of the followings are then less controllable.

Where the demand for administration by trained experts is considerable, and the party followings have to recognize an intellectually developed, educated, and freely moving "public opinion," the use of unqualified officials falls back upon the party in power at the next election. Naturally, this is more likely to happen when the officials are appointed by the chief. The demand for a trained administration now exists in the United States, but in the large cities, where immigrant votes are "corralled," there is, of course, no educated public opinion. Therefore, popular elections of the adminisrative chief and also of his subordinate officials usually endanger the expert qualification of the official as well as the precise functioning of the bureaucratic mechanism. It also weakens the dependence of the officials upon the hierarchy. This holds at least for the large administrative bodies that are difficult to supervise. The superior qualification and integrity of federal judges, appointed by the President, as over against elected judges in the United States is well known, although both types of officials have been selected primarily in terms of party considerations. The great changes in American metropolitan administrations demanded by reformers have proceeded essentially from elected mayors working with an apparatus of officials who were appointed by them. These reforms have thus come about in a "Caesarist" fashion. Viewed technically, as an organized form of authority, the efficiency of "Caesarism," which often grows out of democracy, rests in general upon the position of the "Caesar" as a free trustee of the masses (of the army or of the citizenry), who is unfettered by tradition. The "Caesar" is thus the unrestrained master of a body of highly qualified military officers and officials whom he selects freely and personally without regard to tradition or to any other considerations. This "rule of the personal genius," however, stands in contradiction to the formally "democratic" principle of a universally elected officialdom.

3. Normally, the position of the official is held for life, at least in public bureaucracies; and this is increasingly the case for all similar structures. As a factual rule, *tenure for life* is presupposed, even where the giving of notice or periodic reappointment occurs. In contrast to the worker in a private enterprise, the official normally holds tenure. Legal or actual life-tenure, however, is not recognized as the official's right to the possession of office, as was the case with many structures of authority in the past. Where legal guarantees against arbitrary dismissal or transfer are developed, they merely serve to guarantee a strictly objective discharge of specific office duties free from all personal considerations. In Germany, this is the case for all juridical and, increasingly, for all administrative officials.

Within the bureaucracy, therefore, the measure of "independence," legally guaranteed by tenure, is not always a source of increased status for the official whose position is thus secured. Indeed, often the reverse holds, especially in old cultures and communities that are highly differentiated. In such communities, the stricter the subordination under the arbitrary rule of the master, the more it guarantees the maintenance of the conventional seigneurial style of living for the official. Because of the very absence of these legal guarantees of tenure, the conventional esteem for the official may rise in the same way as, during the Middle Ages, the esteem of the nobility of office rose at the expense of esteem for the freemen, and as the king's judge surpassed that of the people' s judge. In

Germany, the military officer or the administrative official can be removed from office at any time, or at least far more readily than the "independent judge," who never pays with loss of his office for even the grossest offense against the "code of honor" or against social conventions of the salon. For this very reason, if other things are equal, in the eyes of the master stratum the judge is considered less qualified for social intercourse than are officers and administrative officials, whose greater dependence on the master is a greater guarantee of their conformity with status conventions. Of course, the average official strives for a civil-service law, which would materially secure his old age and provide increased guarantees against his arbitrary removal from office. This striving, however, has its limits. A very strong development of the "right to the office" naturally makes it more difficult to staff them with regard to technical efficiency, for such a development decreases the career opportunities of ambitious candidates for office. This makes for the fact that officials, on the whole, do not feel their dependency upon those at the top. This lack of a feeling of dependency, however, rests primarily upon the inclination to depend upon one's equals rather than upon the socially inferior and governed strata. The present conservative movement among the Badenia clergy, occasioned by the anxiety of a presumably threatening separation of church and state, has been expressly determined by the desire not to be turned "from a master into a servant of the parish."

4. The official receives the regular *pecuniary* compensation of a normally fixed *salary* and the old age security provided by a pension. The salary is not measured like a wage in terms of work done, but according to "status," that is, according to the kind of function (the "rank") and, in addition, possibly, according to the length of service. The relatively great security of the official's income, as well as the rewards of social esteem, make the office a sought-after position, especially in countries which no longer provide opportunities for colonial profits. In such countries, this situation permits relatively low salaries for officials.

5. The official is set for a "*career*" within the hierarchical order of the public service. He moves from the lower, less important, and lower paid to the higher positions. The average official naturally desires a mechanical fixing of the conditions of promotion: if not of the offices, at least of the salary levels. He wants these conditions fixed in terms of "seniority," or possibly according to grades achieved in a developed system of expert examinations. Here and there, such examinations actually form a character *indelebilis* of the official and have lifelong effects on his career. To this is joined the desire to qualify the right to office and the increasing tendency toward status group closure and economic security. All of this makes for a tendency to consider the offices as "prebends" of those who are qualified by educational certificates. The necessity of taking general personal and intellectual qualifications into consideration, irrespective of the often subaltern character of the education certificate, has led to a condition in which the highest political offices, especially the positions of "ministers," are principally filled without reference to such certificates.

8

Notes on the Theory of Organization

Luther Gulick

Every large-scale or complicated enterprise requires many men to carry it forward. Wherever many men are thus working together the best results are secured when there is a division of work among these men. The theory of organization, therefore, has to do with the structure of co-ordination imposed upon the work-division units of an enterprise. Hence it is not possible to determine how an activity is to be organized without, at the same time, considering how the work in question is to be divided. Work division is the foundation of organization; indeed, the reason for organization.

1. THE DIVISION OF WORK

It is appropriate at the outset of this discussion to consider the reasons for and the effect of the division of work. It is sufficient for our purpose to note the following factors.

Why Divide Work?

Because men differ in nature, capacity and skill, and gain greatly in dexterity by specialization; Because the same man cannot be at two places at the same time; Because the range of knowledge and skill is so great that a man cannot within his life-span know more than a small fraction of it. In other words, it is a question of human nature, time, and space.

In a shoe factory it would be possible to have 1,000 men each assigned to making complete pairs of shoes. Each man

would cut his leather, stamp in the eyelets, sew up the tops, sew on the bottoms, nail on the heels, put in the laces, and pack each pair in a box. It might take two days to do the job. One thousand men would make 500 pairs of shoes a day. It would also be possible to divide the work among these same men, using the identical hand methods, in an entirely different way. One group of men would be assigned to cut the leather, another to putting in the eyelets, another to stitching up the tops, another to sewing on the soles, another to nailing on the heels, another to inserting the laces and packing the pairs of shoes. We know from common sense and experience that there are two great gains in this latter process: first, it makes possible the better utilization of the varying skills and aptitudes of the different workmen, and encourages the development of specialization; and second, it eliminates the time that is lost when a workman turns from a knife, to a punch, to a needle and awl, to a hammer, and moves from table to bench, to anvil, to stool. Without any pressure on the workers, they could probably turn out twice as many shoes in a single day. There would be additional economies, because inserting laces and packing could be assigned to unskilled and low-paid workers. Moreover, in the cutting of the leather there would be less spoilage because the less skillful pattern cutters would be eliminated and assigned to other work. It would also be possible

Source: Luther Gulick and Lyndall Urwick, eds., *Papers on the Science of Administration* (New York: Institute of Public Administration, 1937), 3-13. Reprinted with permission.

to cut a dozen shoe tops at the same time from the same pattern with little additional effort. All of these advances would follow, without the introduction of new labor saving machinery.

The introduction of machinery accentuates the division of work. Even such a simple thing as a saw, a typewriter, or a transit requires increased specialization, and serves to divide workers into those who can and those who cannot use the particular instrument effectively. Division of work on the basis of the tools and machines used in work rests no doubt in part on aptitude, but primarily upon the development and maintenance of skill through continued manipulation.

Specialized skills are developed not alone in connection with machines and tools. They evolve naturally from the materials handled, like wood, or cattle, or paint, or cement. They arise similarly in activities which center in a complicated series of interrelated concepts, principles, and techniques. These are most clearly recognized in the professions, particularly those based on the application of scientific knowledge, as in engineering, medicine, and chemistry. They are none the less equally present in law, ministry, teaching, accountancy, navigation, aviation, and other fields.

The nature of these subdivisions is essentially pragmatic, in spite of the fact that there is an element of logic underlying them. They are therefore subject to a gradual evolution with the advance of science, the invention of new machines, the progress of technology and the change of the social system. In the last analysis, however, they appear to be based upon differences in individual human beings. But it is not to be concluded that the apparent stability of "human nature," whatever that may be, limits the probable development of specialization. The situation is quite the reverse. As each field of knowledge and work is advanced, constituting a continually larger

and more complicated nexus of related principles, practices and skills, any individual will be less and less able to encompass it and maintain intimate knowledge and facility over the entire area, and there will thus arise a more minute specialization because knowledge and skill advance while man stands still. Division of work and integrated organization are the bootstraps by which mankind lifts itself in the process of civilization.

The Limits of Division

There are three clear limitations beyond which the division of work cannot to advantage go. The first is practical and arises from the volume of work involved in man-hours. Nothing is gained by subdividing work if that further subdivision results in setting up a task which requires less than the full time of one man. This is too obvious to need demonstration. The only exception arises where space interferes, and in, such cases the part-time expert must fill in his spare time at other tasks, so that as a matter of fact a new combination is introduced.

The second limitation arises from technology and custom at a given time and place. In some areas nothing would be gained by separating undertaking from the custody and cleaning of churches, because by custom the sexton is the undertaker; in building construction it is extraordinarily difficult to redivide certain aspects of electrical and plumbing work and to combine them in a more effective way, because of the jurisdictional conflicts of craft unions; and it is clearly impracticable to establish a division of cost accounting in a field in which no technique of costing has yet been developed.

This second limitation is obviously elastic. It may be changed by invention and by education. If this were not the fact, we should face a static division of labor. It should be noted, however, that a marked change has two dangers. It greatly restricts the labor market from which workers may be drawn and greatly lessens the opportunities open to those who are trained for the particular specialization.

The third limitation is that the subdivision of work must not pass beyond physical division into organic division. It might seem far more efficient to have the front half of the cow in the pasture grazing and the rear half in the barn being milked all of the time, but this organic division would fail. Similarly there is no gain from splitting a single movement or gesture like licking an envelope, or tearing apart a series of intimately and intricately related activities.

It may be said that there is in this an element of reasoning in a circle; that the test here applied as to whether an activity is organic or not is whether it is divisible or not—which is what we set out to define. This charge is true. It must be a pragmatic test. Does the division work out? Is something vital destroyed and lost? Does it bleed?

The Whole and the Parts

It is axiomatic that the whole is equal to the sum of its parts. But in dividing up any "whole," one must be certain that every part, including unseen elements and relationships, is accounted for. The marble sand to which the Venus de Milo may be reduced by a vandal does not equal the statue, though every last grain be preserved; nor is a thrush just so much feathers, bones, flesh and blood; nor a typewriter merely so much steel, glass, paint, and rubber. Similarly a piece of work to be done cannot be subdivided into the obvious component parts without great danger that the central design, the operating relationships, the imprisoned idea, will be lost. . . .

When one man builds a house alone he plans as he works; he decides what to do first and what next, that is, he "co-ordinates the work." When many men work together to build a house this part of the work, the co-ordinating, must not be lost sight of.

In the "division of the work" among the various skilled specialists, a specialist in planning and coordination must be sought as well. Otherwise, a great deal of time may be lost, workers may get in each other's way, material may not be on hand when needed, things may be done in the wrong order, and there may even be a difference of opinion as to where the various doors and windows are to go. It is self-evident that the more the work is subdivided, the greater is the danger of confusion, and the greater is the need of overall supervision and coordination. Co-ordination is not something that develops by accident. It must be won by intelligent, vigorous, persistent, and organized effort.

2. THE CO-ORDINATION OF WORK

If subdivision of work is inescapable, co-ordination becomes mandatory. There is, however, no one way to co-ordination. Experience shows that it may be achieved in two primary ways. These are:

1. By organization, that is, by interrelating the subdivisions of work by allotting them to men who are placed in a structure of authority, so that the work may be co-ordinated by orders of superiors to subordinates, reaching from the top to the bottom of the entire enterprise.
2. By the dominance of an idea, that is, the development of intelligent singleness of purpose in the minds and wills of those who are working together as a group, so that each worker will of his own accord fit his task into the whole with skill and enthusiasm.

These two principles of co-ordination are not mutually exclusive, in fact, no enterprise is really effective without the extensive utilization of both.

Size and time are the great limiting factors in the development of coordination. In a small project, the problem is not difficult; the structure of authority is simple, and the central purpose is real to every worker. In a large complicated enterprise, the organization becomes involved, the lines of authority tangled, and there is danger that the workers will forget that there is any central purpose, and so devote their best energies only to their own individual advancement and advantage.

The interrelated elements of time and habit are extraordinarily important in coordination. Man is a creature of habit. When an enterprise is built up gradually from small beginnings the staff can be "broken in" step by step. And when difficulties develop, they can be ironed out, and the new method followed from that point on as a matter of habit, with the knowledge that that particular difficulty will not develop again. Routines may even be mastered by drill as they are in the army. When, however, a large new interprise must be set up or altered overnight, then the real difficulties of coordination make their appearance. The factor of habit, which is thus an important foundation of co-ordination when time is available, becomes a serious handicap when time is not available, that is, when rules change. The question of co-ordination therefore must be approached with different emphasis in small and in large enterprises; in simple and in complex situations; in stable and in new or changing organizations.

Co-ordination through Organization

Organization as a way of co-ordination requires the establishment of a system of authority whereby the central purpose or objective of an enterprise is translated into reality through the combined efforts of many specialists, each working in his own field at a particular time and place.

It is clear from long experience in human affairs that such a structure of authority requires not only many men at work in many places at selected times, but also a single directing executive authority.[1] The problem of organization thus becomes the problem of building up between the executive at the center and the subdivisions of work on the periphery of an effective network of communication and control.

The following outline may serve further to define the problem:

I. First Step: Define the job to be done, such as the furnishing of pure water to all of the people and industries within a given area at the lowest possible cost;

II. Second Step: Provide a director to see that the objective is realized;

III. Third Step: Determine the nature and number of individualized and specialized work units into which the job will have to be divided. As has been seen above, this subdivision depends partly upon the size of the job (no ultimate subdivision can generally be so small as to require less than the full time of one worker) and upon the status of technological and social development at a given time;

IV. Fourth Step: Establish and perfect the structure of authority between the director and the ultimate work subdivisions.

It is this fourth step which is the central concern of the theory of organization. It is the function of this organization (IV) to enable the director (II) to co-ordinate and energize all of the subdivisions of work (III) so that the major objective (I) may be achieved efficiently.

The Span of Control

In this undertaking we are confronted at the start by the inexorable limits of human nature. Just as the hand of man can span only a limited number of notes on the piano, so the mind and will of man can span but a limited number of immediate managerial contacts. The problem has been discussed brilliantly by Graicunas in his paper included in this collection. The limit of control is partly a matter of the limits of knowledge, but even more is it a matter of the limits of time and of energy. As a result the executive of any enterprise can personally direct only a few persons. He must depend upon these to direct others, and upon them in turn to direct still others, until the last man in the organization is reached. . . .

But when we seek to determine how many immediate subordinates the director of an enterprise can effectively supervise, we enter a realm of experience which has not been brought under sufficient scientific study to furnish a final answer. Sir Ian Hamilton says, "The nearer we approach the supreme head of the whole organization, the more we ought to work towards groups of three; the closer we get to the foot of the whole organization (the Infantry of the Line), the more we work towards groups of six."[2]

The British Machinery of Government Committee of 1918 arrived at the conclusions that "The Cabinet should be small in number—preferably ten or, at most, twelve."[3]

Henri Fayol said "[In France] a minister has twenty assistants, where the Administrative Theory says that a manager at the head of a big undertaking should not have more than five or six."[4]

Graham Wallas expressed the opinion that the cabinet should not be increased "beyond the number of ten or twelve at which organized oral discussion is most efficient."[5]

Léon Blum recommended for France a prime minister with a technical cabinet modelled after the British War Cabinet, which was composed of five members.[6]

It is not difficult to understand why there is this divergence of statement among authorities who are agreed on the fundamentals. It arises in part from the differences in the capacities and work habits of individual executives observed, and in part from the noncomparable character of the work covered. It would seem that insufficient attention has been devoted to three factors, first, the element of diversification of function; second, the element of time; and third, the element of space. A chief of public works can deal effectively with more direct subordinates than can the general of the army, because all of his immediate subordinates in the department of public works will be in the general field of engineering, while in the army there will be many different elements, such as communications, chemistry, aviation, ordinance, motorized service, engineering, supply, transportation, etc., each with its own technology. The element of time is also of great significance as has been indicated above. In a stable organization the chief executive can deal with more immediate subordinates than in a new or changing organization. Similarly, space influences the span of control. An organization located in one building can be supervised through more immediate subordinates than can the same organization if scattered in several cities. When scattered there is not only need for more supervision, and therefore more supervisory personnel, but also for a fewer number of contacts with the chief executive because of the increased difficulty faced by the chief executive in learning sufficient details about a far-flung organization to do an intelligent job. The failure to attach sufficient importance to these variables has served to limit the scientific validity of the statements which have been made that one man can supervise but three, or five, or eight, or twelve immediate subordinates.

These considerations do not, however, dispose of the problem. They indicate rather the need for further research. But without further research we may conclude that the chief executive of an organization can deal with only a few immediate subordinates; that this number is determined not only by the nature of the work, but also by the nature of the executive; and that the number of immediate subordinates in a large, diversified and dispersed organization must be even less than in a homogeneous and unified organization to achieve the same measure of coordination.

One Master

From the earliest times it has been recognized that nothing but confusion arises under multiple command. "A man cannot serve two masters" was adduced as a theological argument because it was already accepted as a principle of human relation in everyday life. In administration this is known as the principle of "unity of command."[7] The principle may be stated as follows: A workman subject to orders from several superiors will be confused, inefficient, and irresponsible; a workman subject to orders from but one superior may be methodical, efficient, and responsible. Unity of command thus refers to those who are commanded, not to those who issue the commands.[8]

The significance of this principle in the process of co-ordination and organization must not be lost sight of. In building a structure of co-ordination, it is often tempting to set up more than one boss for a man who is doing work which has more than one relationship. Even as

great a philosopher of management as Taylor fell into this error in setting up separate foremen to deal with machinery, with materials, with speed, etc., each with the power of giving orders directly to the individual workman.[9] The rigid adherence to the principle of unity of command may have its absurdities; these are, however, unimportant in comparison with the certainty of confusion, inefficiency and irresponsibility which arise from the violation of the principle.

Technical Efficiency

There are many aspects of the problem of securing technical efficiency. Most of these do not concern us here directly. They have been treated extensively by such authorities as Taylor, Dennison, and Kimball, and their implications for general organization by Fayol, Urwick, Mooney, and Reiley. There is, however, one efficiency concept which concerns us deeply in approaching the theory of organization. It is the principle of homogeneity.

It has been observed by authorities in many fields that the efficiency of a group working together is directly related to the homogeneity of the work they are performing, of the processes they are utilizing, and of the purposes which actuate them. From top to bottom, the group must be unified. It must work together.

It follows from this (1) that any organizational structure which brings together in a single unit work divisions which are non-homogeneous in work, in technology, or in purpose will encounter the danger of friction and inefficiency; and (2) that a unit based on a given specializaton cannot be given technical direction by a layman.

In the realm of government it is not difficult to find many illustrations of the unsatisfactory results of non-homogeneous administrative combinations. It is generally agreed that agricultural development and education cannot be administered by the same men who enforce pest and disease control, because the success of the former rests upon friendly co-operation and trust of the farmers, while the latter engenders resentment and suspicion. Similarly, activities like drug control established in protection of the consumer do not find appropriate homes in departments dominated by the interests of the producer. In the larger cities and in states it has been found that hospitals cannot be so well administered by the health department directly as they can be when set up independently in a separate department, or at least in a bureau with an extensive autonomy, and it is generally agreed that public welfare administration and police administration require separation, as do public health administration and welfare administration, though both of these combinations may be found in successful operation under special conditions. No one would think of combining water supply and public education, or tax administration and public recreation. In every one of these cases, it will be seen that there is some element either of work to be done, or of the technology used, or of the end sought which is non-homogeneous.

Another phase of the combination of incompatible functions in the same office may be found in the common American practice of appointing unqualified laymen and politicians to technical positions or to give technical direction to highly specialized services. As Dr. Frank J. Goodnow pointed out a generation ago, we are faced here by two heterogeneous functions, "politics" and "administration," the combination of which cannot be undertaken within the structure of the administration without producing inefficiency.

Caveamus Expertum

At this point a word of caution is necessary. The application of the principle of homogeneity has its pitfalls. Every highly trained technician, particularly in the learned professions, has a profound sense of omniscience and a great desire for complete independence in the service of society. When employed by government he knows exactly what the people need better than they do themselves, and he knows how to render this service. He tends to be utterly oblivious of all other needs, because, after all, is not his particular technology the road to salvation? Any restraint applied to him is "limitation of freedom," and any criticism "springs from ignorance and jealousy." Every budget increase he secures is "in the public interest," while every increase secured elsewhere is "a sheer waste." His efforts and maneuvers to expand are "public education" and "civic organization," while similar efforts by others are "propaganda" and "politics."

Another trait of the expert is his tendency to assume knowledge and authority in fields in which he has no competence. In this particular, educators, lawyers, priests, admirals, doctors, scientists, engineers, accountants, merchants and bankers are all the same—having achieved technical competence or "success" in one field, they come to think this competence is a general quality detachable from the field and inherent in themselves. They step without embarrassment into other areas. They do not remember that the robes of authority of one kingdom confer no sovereignty in another; but that there they are merely a masquerade.

The expert knows his "stuff." Society needs him, and must have him more and more as man' s technical knowledge becomes more and more extensive. But history shows us that the common man is a better judge of his own needs in the long run than any cult of experts. Kings and ruling classes, priests and prophets, soldiers and lawyers, when permitted to rule rather than serve mankind, have in the end done more to check the advance of human welfare than they have to advance it. The true place of the expert is, as A. E. said so well, "on tap, not on top." The essential validity of democracy rests upon this philosophy, for democracy is a way of government in which the common man is the final judge of what is good for him.

Efficiency is one of the things that is good for him because it makes life richer and safer. That efficiency is to be secured more and more through the use of technical specialists. These specialists have no right to ask for, and must not be given freedom from supervisory control, but in establishing that control, a government which ignores the conditions of efficiency cannot expect to achieve efficiency.

3. ORGANIZATIONAL PATTERNS

Organization Up or Down?

One of the great sources of confusion in the discussion of the theory of organization is that some authorities work and think primarily from the top down, while others work and think from the bottom up. This is perfectly natural because some authorities are interested primarily in the executive and in the problems of central management, while others are interested primarily in individual services and activities. Those who work from the top down regard the organization as a system of subdividing the enterprise under the chief executive, while those who work from the bottom up, look upon organization as a system of combining the individual units of work into aggregates which are in turn subordinated to the chief executive. It may be argued that either approach leads to a consideration of the entire problem, so that it is of no great significance which way the organization is viewed. Certainly it makes this very important practical difference: those who work from the top down must guard themselves from the danger of sacrificing the effectiveness of the individual services in their zeal to achieve a model structure at the top, while those who start from the bottom, must guard themselves from the danger of thwarting co-ordination in their eagerness to develop effective individual services.

In any practical situation the problem of organization must be approached from both top and bottom. This is particularly true in the reorganization of a going concern. May it not be that this practical necessity is likewise the sound process theoretically? In that case one would develop the plan of an organization or reorganization both from the top downward and from the bottom upward, and would reconcile the two at the center. In planning the first subdivisions under the chief executive, the principle of the limitation of the span of control must apply; in building up the first aggregates of specialized functions, the principle of homogeneity must apply. If any enterprise has such an array of functions that the first subdivisions from the top down do not readily meet the first aggregations from the bottom up, then additional divisions and additional aggregates must be introduced, but at each further step there must be a less and less rigorous adherence to the two conflicting principles until their juncture is effected. . . .

Organizing the Executive

The effect of the suggestion presented above is to organize and institutionalize the executive function as such so that it may be more adequate in a complicated situation. This is in reality not a new idea. We do not, for example, expect the chief executive to write his own letters.

We give him a private secretary, who is part of his office and assists him to do this part of his job. This secretary is not a part of any department, he is a subdivision of the executive himself. In just this way, though on a different plane, other phases of the job of the chief executive may be organized.

Before doing this, however, it is necessary to have a clear picture of the job itself. This brings us directly to the question, "What is the work of the chief executive? What does he do?"

The answer is POSDCORB.

POSDCORB is, of course, a made-up word designed to call attention to the various functional elements of the work of a chief executive because "administration" and "management" have lost all specific content.[10] POSDCORB is made up of the initials and stands for the following activities:

Planning, that is working out in broad outline the things that need to be done and the methods for doing them to accomplish the purpose set for the enterprise;

Organizing, that is the establishment of the formal structure of authority through which work subdivisions are arranged, defined and co-ordinated for the defined objective;

Staffing, that is the whole personnel function of bringing in and training the staff and maintaining favorable conditions of work;

Directing, that is the continuous task of making decisions and embodying them in specific and general orders and instructions and serving as the leader of the enterprise;

Co-ordinating, that is the all important duty of interrelating the various parts of the work;

Reporting, that is keeping those to whom the executive is responsible informed as to what is going on, which thus includes keeping himself and his subordinates informed through records, research, and inspection;

Budgeting, with all that goes with budgeting in the form of fiscal planning, accounting, and control.

This statement of the work of a chief executive is adapted from the functional analysis elaborated by Henri Fayol in his "Industrial and General Administration." It is believed that those who know administration intimately will find in this analysis a valid and helpful pattern, into which can be fitted each of the major activities and duties of any chief executive.

If these seven elements may be accepted as the major duties of the chief executive, it follows that they *may* be separately organized as subdivisions of the executive. The need for such subdivision depends entirely on the size and complexity of the enterprise. In the largest enterprises, particularly where the chief executive is as a matter of fact unable to do the work that is thrown upon him, it may be presumed that one or more parts of POSDCORB should be suborganized.

NOTES

1. I.e., when *organization is the basis of coordination*. Wherever the central executive authority is composed of several who exercise their functions jointly by majority vote, as on a board, this is from the standpoint of organization still a "single authority"; where the central executive is in reality composed of several men acting freely and independently, then organization cannot be said to be the basis of co-ordination; it is rather the dominance of an idea and falls under the second principle stated above.

2. Sir Ian Hamilton, "The Soul and Body of an Army." Arnold, London, 1921, p. 230.

3. Great Britain. Ministry of Reconstruction. Report of the Machinery of Government Committee. H. M. Stationery Office, London, 1918, p. 5.

4. Henri Fayol, "The Administrative Theory in the State." Address before the Second International Congress of Administrative Sci-

ence at Brussels, September 13, 1923. Paper IV in this collection.

5. Graham Wallas, "The Great Society." Macmillan, London and New York, 1919, p. 264.

6. Léon Blum, "La Réforme Gouvernementale." Grasset, Paris, 1918. Reprinted in 1936, p. 59.

7. Henri Fayol, "Industrial and General Administration." English translation by J. A. Coubrough. International Management Association, Geneva, 1930.

8. Fayol terms the latter "unity of direction."

9. Frederick Winslow Taylor, "Shop Management;" Harper and Brothers, New York and London, 1911, p. 99.

10. See Minutes of the Princeton Conference on Training for the Public Service, 1935, p. 35. See also criticism of this analysis in Lewis Meriam, "Public Service and Special Training," University of Chicago Press, 1936, pp. 1, 2, 10 and 15, where this functional analysis is misinterpreted as a statement of qualifications for appointment.

CHAPTER II

Neoclassical Organization Theory

There is no precise definition of *neoclassical* in the context of organization theory. The general connotation is that of a theoretical perspective that revises and/ or is critical of classical organization theory—particularly for minimizing issues related to the humanness of organizational members, coordination needs among administrative units, internal-external organizational relations, and organizational decision processes. The major writers of the classical school did their most significant work before World War II. The Neoclassical writers gained their reputations as organization theorists by attacking the classical writers from the end of the war through the 1950s. Because classical theories were, to a large measure, derived intellectually rather than empirically, their artificial assumptions left them vulnerable to attack. Theorists of the classical period thought that organizations should be based on universally applicable, scientific principles.

In spite of their frequent and vigorous attacks upon the classicalists, the neoclassicalists did not develop a body of theory that could adequately replace the classical school. The neoclassical school modified, added to, and somewhat extended classical theory. It attempted to blend assumptions of classical theory with concepts that subsequently were used by later organization theorists from all subsequent schools. The neoclassical school attempted to save classical theory by introducing modifications based upon research findings in the behavioral sciences. It did not have a bona fide theory of its own. To a great extent, it was an "anti-school."

Despite its limitations, the neoclassical school was very important in the historical development of organization theory. But, like a rebellious teenager, neoclassical theory could not permanently stand on its own. It was a transitional, somewhat reactionary school. Why then was the neoclassical school so important? First, because it initiated the theoretical movement away from the oversimplistic mechanistic views of the classical school. The neoclassicalists challenged some of the basic tenets of the classical school *head on*. And, remember, the classical school was the only school at that time. Organization theory and classical organization theory were virtually synonomous.

Secondly, in the process of challenging the classical school, the neoclassicalists raised issues and initiated theories that became central to the foundations of most of the schools that have followed. The neoclassical school was a critically important forerunner. Most serious post-1960 articles from *any* school of organization theory cite neoclassical theorists. All of the neoclassical selections that we have chosen to include in this chapter are important precursors of the human relations, "modern" structural, systems, multiple constituency, power and politics, and organizational culture perspectives of organization theory.

Chester Barnard's purposes in writing *The Functions of the Executive* (1938) were ambitious. He sought to create a comprehensive theory of behavior in formal organizations that was centered on the need for people in organizations to cooperate—to enlist others to help accomplish tasks that individuals could not accomplish alone. In Barnard's view, cooperation holds an organization together. Thus, the responsibility of an executive is (1) to create and maintain a sense of purpose and a *moral code* for the organization—a set of ethical visions that established "*right* or *wrong* in a moral sense, of deep feeling, of innate conviction, not arguable; emotional, not intellectual in character" (1938, p. 266); (2) to establish systems of formal and informal communication; and (3) to ensure the willingness of people to cooperate.

In "The Economy of Incentives," the chapter reprinted here from *The Functions of the Executive,* Barnard argues that individuals must be induced to cooperate, or the result will be dissolution of the organization, changes of organizational purpose, or failure of cooperation. The executive needs to employ different strategies for inducing cooperation: to find and use objective positive incentives and ways to reduce negative incentives, but also to "change the state of mind, or attitudes, or motives so that the available objective incentives can become effective." The latter approach, Barnard refers to as "persuasion," and "in every type of organization, for whatever purpose, several incentives are necessary, and some degree of persuasion likewise, in order to secure and maintain the contributions to organization that are required."

Herbert A. Simon was the first neoclassicalist to seriously challenge the tenets of classical organization theory. In his widely quoted 1946 *Public Administration Review* article "The Proverbs of Administration" (the first selection in this chapter), Simon is devastating in his criticism of the classical approach to "general principles of management," such as those proposed by Fayol, Gulick, and others, as being inconsistent, conflicting, and inapplicable to many of the administrative situations facing managers. He suggests that such "principles" as "span of control" and "unity of command" can, with equal logic, be applied in diametrically opposed ways to the same set of circumstances. Simon concludes that the so-called principles of administration are instead proverbs of administration. The basic themes of the article later were incorporated in his landmark book *Administrative Behavior* (1947).

One of the major themes of the neoclassical organization theorists was that organizations did not and could not exist as self-contained islands isolated from their environments. As might be expected, the first significant efforts to "open up" organizations (theoretically speaking) came from analysts whose professional identities required them to take a broad view of things—sociologists.

One such sociologist, Philip Selznick, in his 1948 *American Sociological Review* article, "Foundations of the Theory of Organization" (which is reprinted here), asserts that while it is possible to describe and design organizations in a purely rational manner, such efforts can never hope to cope with the nonrational aspects of organizational behavior. In contrast with the classical theorists, Selznick maintains that organizations consist of individuals whose goals and aspirations might not necessarily coincide with the formal goals of the organization, rather than consist of simply a number of positions for management to control. Selznick is perhaps best known for his concept of "cooptation," which describes the process of an organization bringing and subsuming new elements into its policy-making process in order to prevent such elements from becoming a threat to the organization or its mission. The fullest account of Selznick's "co-optation" is found in *TVA and the Grass Roots*, his 1949 case study of how the Tennessee Valley Authority first gained local support for its programs. Selznick's approach to studying organizations and his intellectual distinction between the concepts of "organization" and "institution" have been lauded as models of organizational theory's insightfulness and usefulness by such writers on organizational culture as Ott (1989), Pedersen and Sorensen (1989), Siehl and Martin (1984), Walker (1986), and Wilkins (1983; 1989).

We have focused on Philip Selznick here, but many other sociologists made important contributions to the neoclassical school and to the general development of the field of organization theory. For example:

- Melville Dalton (1950; 1959) focused on structural frictions between line and staff units and between the central office of an organization and geographically dispersed facilities. His work drew attention to some of the universal ingredients of conflict within organizations and to problems of educating and socializing managers.

- Talcott Parsons introduced an approach to the analysis of formal organizations using the general theory of social systems. In his 1956 article "Suggestions for a Sociological Approach to the Theory of Organizations," Parsons defined an organization as a social system that focuses on the attainment of specific goals and contributes, in turn, to the accomplishment of goals of a more comprehensive system, such as the larger organization or even society itself.

- William F. Whyte (1948) studied human relations in the restaurant business in order to understand and describe stresses that result from interrelations and status differences in the workplace.

As we mentioned earlier, Herbert Simon and his associates at the Carnegie Institute of Technology (now, Carnegie-Mellon University) also were major developers of theories of organizational decision making. Simon was a firm believer that decision making should be the focus of a new "administrative science." For example, Simon (1947) asserted that organizational theory is, in fact, the theory of the bounded rationality of human beings who "satisfice" because they do not have the intellectual capacity to maximize. Simon (1960) also drew a distinction between "programmed" and "unprogrammed" organizational decisions and highlighted the importance of the distinction for management information systems. His work on administrative science and decision making went in two major directions: first, he was a pioneer in developing the "science" of improved organizational decision making through quantitive methods, such as operations research and computer technology. Secondly, and perhaps even more important, was his leadership in studying the processes by which administrative organizations make decisions. Herbert Simon's extensive contributions continue to influence the field of organization theory in the 1990s.

Two of Simon's colleagues at Carnegie Tech during the early 1960s, R. M. Cyert and James G. March, analyze the impact of power and politics on the establishment of organizational goals in "A Behavioral Theory of Organizational Objectives" (reprinted here). This was a perspective that did not receive serious attention from organizational theorists until the mid-1970s. Cyert and March discuss the formation and activation of coalitions, as well as negotiations to impose coalitions' demands on the organization. The article subsequently was merged into their widely cited 1963 book *A Behavioral Theory of the Firm*, which postulated that corporations tended to "satisfice" rather than engage in economically rational profit-maximizing behavior.

The neoclassical school played a very important role in the evolution of organization theory. Its writers provided the intellectual and empirical impetus to break the classicalists' simplistic, mechanically oriented, monopolistic dominance of the field. Neoclassicalists also paved the way—opened the door—for the soon-to-follow explosions of thinking from the human relations, "modern" structural, systems, power and politics, and organizational culture perspectives of organizations.

REFERENCES

Barnard, C. I. (1938, 1968). *The functions of the executive.* Cambridge, MA: Harvard University Press.

Cyert, R. M., & March, J. G. (1959). Behavioral theory of organizational objectives. In M. Haire (Ed.), *Modern organization theory* (pp. 76–90). New York: Wiley.

Cyert, R. M., & March, J. G. (1963). *A behavioral theory of the firm.* Englewood Cliffs, NJ: Prentice-Hall.

Dalton, M. (1950, June). Conflicts between staff and line managerial officers. *American Sociological Review*, 342–351.

Dalton, M. (1959). *Men who manage.* New York: Wiley.

Durkheim, E. (1947). *The division of labor in society.* George Simpson (Trans). New York: Free Press. (Original work published 1893)

Etzioni, A. (1961). *A comparative analysis of complex organizations.* New York: Free Press.

Gordon, C. W., & Babchuk, N. (1959). A typology of voluntary associations. *American Sociological Review, 24,* 22–29.

Ott, J. S. (1989). *The organizational culture perspective.* Pacific Grove, CA: Brooks/Cole.

Parsons, T. (1956, June). Suggestions for a sociological approach to the theory of organizations. *Administrative Science Quarterly, 1*, 63–85.

Pedersen, J. S., & Sorensen, J. S. (1989). *Organisational cultures in theory and practice.* Aldershot, UK: Gower Publishing Company.

Selznick, P. (1948). Foundations of the theory of organization. *American Sociological Review, 13*, 25–35.

Siehl, C., & Martin, J. (1984). The role of symbolic management: How can managers effectively transmit organizational culture? In J. G. Hunt, D. M. Hosking, C. A. Schriesheim, & R. Stewart (Eds.), *Leaders and managers* (pp. 227–269). New York: Pergamon Press.

Simon, H. A. (1946, Winter). The proverbs of administration. *Public Administration Review, 6*, 53–67.

Simon, H. A. (1947). *Administrative behavior.* New York: Macmillan.

Simon, H. A. (1957). *Administrative behavior* (2nd ed.). New York: Macmillan.

Simon, H. A. (1960). *The new science of management decisions.* New York: Harper & Row.

Walker, W. E. (1986). *Changing organizational culture: Strategy, structure, and professionalism in the U. S. General Accounting Office.* Knoxville, TN: The University of Tennessee Press.

Whyte, W. F. (1948). *Human relations in the restaurant business.* New York: McGraw-Hill.

Wilkins, A. A. (1983). Organizational stories as symbols which control the organization. In L. R. Pondy, P. J. Frost, G. Morgan, & T. C. Dandridge (Eds.), *Organizational symbolism* (pp. 93–107). Greenwich, CT: JAI Press.

Wilkins, A. A. (1989). *Developing corporate character.* San Francisco: Jossey-Bass.

9
The Economy of Incentives
Chester I. Barnard

[An] essential element of organizations is the willingness of persons to contribute their individual efforts to the coöperative system. The power of coöperation, which is often spectacularly great when contrasted with that even of large numbers of individuals unorganized, is nevertheless dependent upon the willingness of individuals to coöperate and to contribute their efforts to the coöperative system. The contributions of personal efforts which constitute the energies of organizations are yielded by individuals because of incentives. The egotistical motives of self-preservation and of self-satisfaction are dominating forces; on the whole, organizations can exist only when consistent with the satisfaction of these motives, unless, alternatively, they can change these motives. The individual is always the basic strategic factor in organization. Regardless of his history or his obligations he must be induced to coöperate, or there can be no coöperation.

It needs no further introduction to suggest that the subject of incentives is fundamental in formal organizations and in conscious efforts to organize. Inadequate incentives mean dissolution, or changes of organization purpose, or failure of cooperation. Hence, in all sorts of organizations the affording of adequate incentives becomes the most definitely emphasized task in their existence. It is probably in this aspect of executive work that failure is most pronounced, though the causes may be due either to inadequate understanding or to the breakdown of the effectiveness of organization.

I

The net satisfactions which induce a man to contribute his efforts to an organization result from the positive advantages as against the disadvantages which are entailed.[1] It follows that a net advantage may be increased or a negative advantage made positive either by increasing the number or the strength of the positive inducements or by reducing the number or the strength of the disadvantages. It often occurs that the positive advantages are few and meager, but the burdens involved are also negligible, so that there is a strong net advantage. Many "social" organizations are able to exist under such a state of affairs. Conversely, when the burdens involved are numerous or heavy, the offsetting positive advantages must be either numerous or powerful.

Hence, from the viewpoint of the organization requiring or seeking contribu-

[1] The method of statement convenient for this exposition should not be allowed to mislead. Only occasionally as to most persons and perhaps as to all persons is the determination of satisfactions and dissatisfactions a matter of logical thought.

Source: Reprinted by permission from *Functions of the Executive* by Chester I. Barnard, Cambridge, Mass.: Harvard University Press, Copyright © 1938, 1968 by the President and Fellows of Harvard College, © renewed 1966 by Grace F. Noera Barnard.

tions from individuals, the problem of effective incentives may be either one of finding positive incentives or of reducing or eliminating negative incentives or burdens. For example, employment may be made attractive either by reducing the work required—say, by shortening hours or supplying tools or power, that is, by making conditions of employment less onerous—or by increasing positive inducement, such as wages.

In practice, although there are many cases where it is clear which side of the "equation" is being adjusted, on the whole specific practices and conditions affect both sides simultaneously or it is impossible to determine which they affect. Most specific factors in so-called working conditions may be viewed either as making employment positively attractive or as making work less onerous. We shall, therefore, make no attempt to treat specific inducements as increasing advantages or as decreasing disadvantages; but this underlying aspect is to be kept in mind.

More important than this is the distinction between the objective and the subjective aspects of incentives. Certain common positive incentives, such as material goods and in some senses money, clearly have an objective existence; and this is true also of negative incentives like working hours, conditions of work. Given a man of a certain state of mind, of certain attitudes, or governed by certain motives, he can be induced to contribute to an organization by a given combination of these objective incentives, positive or negative. It often is the case, however, that the organization is unable to offer objective incentives that will serve as an inducement to that state of mind, or to those attitudes, or to one governed by those motives. The only alternative then available is to change the state of mind, or attitudes, or motives,

so that the available objective incentives can become effective.

An organization can secure the efforts necessary to its existence, then, either by the objective inducements it provides or by changing states of mind. It seems to me improbable that any organization can exist as a practical matter which does not employ both methods in combination. In some organizations the emphasis is on the offering of objective incentives—this is true of most industrial organizations. In others the preponderance is on the state of mind—this is true of most patriotic and religious organizations.

We shall call the processes of offering objective incentives "the method of incentives"; and the processes of changing subjective attitudes "the method of persuasion." Using these new terms, let us repeat what we have said: In commercial organizations the professed emphasis is apparently almost wholly on the side of the method of incentives. In religious and political organizations the professed emphasis is apparently almost wholly on the side of persuasion. But in fact, especially if account be taken of the different kinds of contributions required from different individuals, both methods are used in all types of organizations. Moreover, the centrifugal forces of individualism and the competition between organizations for individual contributions result in both methods being ineffective, with few exceptions, for more than short periods or a few years.

I. THE METHOD OF INCENTIVES

We shall first discuss the method of incentives. It will facilitate our consideration of the subject if at the outset we distinguish two classes of incentives: first those that are specific and can be specifically offered to an individual; and second, those that are general, not personal, that cannot be specifically offered. We shall call the first class specific inducements, the second general incentives.

The specific inducements that may be offered are of several classes, for example: (*a*) material inducements; (*b*) personal non-material opportunities; (*c*) desirable physical conditions; (*d*) ideal benefactions. General incentives afforded are, for example: (*e*) associational attractiveness; (*f*) adaptation of conditions to habitual methods and attitudes; (*g*) the opportunity of enlarged participation; (*h*) the condition of communion. Each of these classes of incentives is known under various names, and the list does not purport to be complete, since our purpose now is illustrative. But to accomplish this purpose it is necessary briefly to discuss the incentives named.

(*a*) Material inducements are money, things, or physical conditions that are offered to the individual as inducements to accepting employment, compensation for service, reward for contribution. Under a money economy and the highly specialized production of material goods, the range and profusion of material inducements are very great. The complexity of schedules of money compensation, the difficulty of securing the monetary means of compensation, and the power of exchange which money gives in organized markets, have served to exaggerate the importance of money in particular and material inducements in general as incentives to personal contributions to organized effort. It goes without elaboration that where a large part of the time of an individual is devoted to one organization, the physiological necessities—food, shelter, clothing—require that material inducements should be present in most cases; but these requirements are so limited that they are satisfied with small quantities. The unaided power of material incentives, when the

minimum necessities are satisfied, in my opinion is exceedingly limited as to most men, depending almost entirely for its development upon persuasion. Notwithstanding the great emphasis upon material incentives in modern times and especially in current affairs, there is no doubt in my mind that, unaided by other motives, they constitute weak incentives beyond the level of the bare physiological necessities.

To many this view will not be readily acceptable. The emphasis upon material rewards has been a natural result of the success of technological developments—relative to other incentives it is the material things which have been progressively easier to produce, and therefore to offer. Hence there has been a forced cultivation of the love of material things among those above the level of subsistence. Since existing incentives seem always inadequate to the degree of coöperation and of social integration theoretically possible and ideally desirable, the success of the sciences and the arts of material production would have been partly ineffective, and in turn would have been partly impossible, without inculcating the desire of the material. The most significant result of this situation has been the expansion of population, most of which has been necessarily at the bare subsistence level, at which level material inducements are, on the whole, powerful incentives. This has perpetuated the illusion that beyond this subsistence level material incentives are also the most effective.[2]

[2] It has been suggested to me that the illusion is also a result of the neglect of motives and the excessive imputation of logical processes in men by the earlier economists, and in purely theoretical economics. This was associated with the deterministic and especially the utilitarian doctrines of the greater part of the nineteenth century, and with the materialistic philosophies of Marx and others.

A concurrent result has been the creation of sentiments in individuals that they *ought* to want material things. The inculcation of "proper" ambitions in youth have greatly stressed material possessions as an evidence of good citizenship, social adequacy, etc. Hence, when underlying and governing motives have not been satisfied, there has been strong influence to rationalize the default as one of material compensation, and not to be conscious of the controlling motives or at least not to admit them.

Yet it seems to me to be a matter of common experience that material rewards are ineffective beyond the subsistence level excepting to a very limited proportion of men; that most men neither work harder for more material things, nor can be induced thereby to devote more than a fraction of their possible contribution to organized effort. It is likewise a matter of both present experience and past history that many of the most effective and powerful organizations are built up on incentives in which the materialistic elements, above bare subsistence, are either relatively lacking or absolutely absent. Military organizations have been relatively lacking in material incentives. The greater part of the work of political organizations is without material incentive. Religious organizations are characterized on the whole by material sacrifice. It seems to me to be definitely a general fact that even in purely commercial organizations material incentives are so weak as to be almost negligible except when reinforced by other incentives, and then only because of wholesale general persuasion in the form of salesmanship and advertising.

It will be noted that the reference has been to material incentives rather than to money. What has been said requires some, but not great, qualification with reference to money as an incentive— solely for the reason that money in our

economy may be used as the indirect means of satisfying non-materialistic motives—philanthropic, artistic, intellectual, and religious motives for example—and because money income becomes an index of social status, personal development, etc.

(*b*) Inducements of a personal, non-materialistic character are of great importance to secure coöperative effort above the minimum material rewards essential to subsistence. The opportunities for distinction, prestige, personal power,[3] and the attainment of dominating position are much more important than material rewards in the development of all sorts of organizations, including commercial organizations. In various ways this fact applies to many types of human beings, including those of limited ability and children. Even in strictly commercial organizations, where it is least supposed to be true, money without distinction, prestige, position, is so utterly ineffective that it is rare that greater income can be made to serve even temporarily as an inducement if accompanied by suppression of prestige. At least for short periods inferior material rewards are often accepted if assurance of distinction is present; and usually the presumption is that material rewards ought to follow or arise from or even are made necessary by the attainment of distinction and prestige. There is unlimited experience to show that among many men, and especially among women, the real value of differences of money rewards lies in the recognition or distinction assumed to be conferred thereby, or to be procured therewith—one of the reasons why differentials either in money income or in material possessions are a source of jealousy and disruption if not

---

[3] Largely an illusion, but a very dear one to some.

accompanied by other factors of distinction.

(c) Desirable physical conditions of work are often important conscious, and more often important unconscious, inducements to coöperation.

(d) Ideal benefactions as inducements to coöperation are among the most powerful and the most neglected. By ideal benefaction I mean the capacity of organizations to satisfy personal ideals usually relating to non-material, future, or altruistic relations. They include pride of workmanship, sense of adequacy, altruistic service for family or others, loyalty to organization in patriotism, etc., aesthetic and religious feeling. They also include the opportunities for the satisfaction of the motives of hate and revenge, often the controlling factor in adherence to and intensity of effort in some organizations.

All of these inducements—material rewards, personal nonmaterial opportunities, desirable physical conditions, and ideal benefactions—may be and frequently are definitely offered as inducements to contribute to organizations. But there are other conditions which cannot usually be definitely offered, and which are known or recognized by their absence in particular cases. Of these I consider associational attractiveness as exceedingly, and often critically, important.

(e) By associational attractiveness I mean social compatibility. It is in many cases obvious that racial hostility, class antagonism, and national enmities absolutely prevent cooperation, in others decrease its effectiveness, and in still others make it impossible to secure coöperation except by great strengthening of other incentives. But it seems clear that the question of personal compatibility or incompatibility is much more far-reaching in limiting coöperative effort than is recognized, because an intimate knowledge of particular organizations is usually necessary to understand its precise character. When such an intimate knowledge exists, personal compatibility or incompatibility is so thoroughly sensed, and the related problems are so difficult to deal with, that only in special or critical cases is conscious attention given to them. But they can be neglected only at peril of disruption. Men often will not work at all, and will rarely work well, under other incentives if the social situation *from their point of view* is unsatisfactory. Thus often men of inferior education cannot work well with those of superior education, and vice versa. Differences not merely of race, nation, religion, but of customs, morals, social status, education, ambition, are frequently controlling. Hence, a powerful incentive to the effort of almost all men is favorable associational conditions from their viewpoint. . . .

(f) Another incentive of the general type is that of customary working conditions and conformity to habitual practices and attitudes. This is made obvious by the universal practice, in all kinds of organizations, of rejecting recruits trained in different methods or possessing "foreign" attitudes. It is taken for granted that men will not or cannot do well by strange methods or under strange conditions. What is not so obvious is that men will frequently not attempt to coöperate if they recognize that such methods or conditions are to be accepted.

(g) Another indirect incentive that we may regard as of general and often of controlling importance is the opportunity for the feeling of enlarged participation in the course of events. It affects all classes of men under some conditions. It is sometimes, though not necessarily, related to love of personal distinction and prestige. Its realization is the feeling of importance of result of effort because of the importance of the coöperative effort as a whole. Thus, *other things being equal,* many men prefer association with large organizations, organizations which they regard as useful, or organizations they regard as effective, as against those they consider small, useless, ineffective.

(*h*) The most intangible and subtle of incentives is that which I have called the condition of communion. It is related to social compatibility, but is essentially different. It is the feeling of personal comfort in social relations that is sometimes called solidarity, social integration, the gregarious instinct, or social security (in the original, not in its present debased economic, sense). It is the opportunity for comradeship, for mutual support in personal attitudes. The need for communion is a basis of informal organization that is essential to the operation of every formal organization. It is likewise the basis for informal organization within but hostile to formal organization.[4]

It is unnecessary for our purpose to exhaust the list of inducements and incentives to coöperative contributions of individuals to organization. Enough has

[4] Referring to this paragraph, one of my valued correspondents, an army officer of long experience in active service, writes to the effect that I do not relatively emphasize this incentive sufficiently. Speaking of comradeship he says: "I was impressed, somewhat to my innocent surprise, during 1918, by the influence of this factor. I came out of the war with the definite impression that it was perhaps the strongest constructive moral factor, stronger than patriotism, and in many cases stronger than religion." He quotes Professor Joergensenson of Denmark, in his treatise appearing (with other contributions) in the Interparliamentary Union's book *What Would Be the Character of a New War?* as saying: "In the opinion of many experts these feelings [of brotherhood and comradeship among the troops] constituted the most important source of inner strength from a psychological point of view, and helped the soldiers to bear the sufferings and perils of the battlefield."

been said to suggest that the subject of incentives is important and complex when viewed in its objective aspects. One fact of interest now is that different men are moved by different incentives or combinations of incentives, and by different incentives or combinations at different times. Men are unstable in their desires, a fact partly reflecting the instability of their environments. A second fact is that organizations are probably never able to offer all the incentives that move men to coöperative effort, and are usually unable to offer adequate incentives. To the reasons for this fact we shall advert later; but a result of it to which we shall turn our attention now is the necessity of persuasion.

II. THE METHOD OF PERSUASION

If an organization is unable to afford incentives adequate to the personal contributions it requires it will perish unless it can by persuasion so change the desires of enough men that the incentives it can offer will be adequate. Persuasion in the broad sense in which I am here using the word includes: (*a*) the creation of coercive conditions; (*b*) the rationalization of opportunity; (*c*) the inculcation of motives.

(*a*) Coercion is employed both to exclude and to secure the contribution of individuals to an organization. Exclusion is often intended to be exclusion permanently and nothing more. It is an aspect of competition or hostility between organizations or between organizations and individuals. . . . I suppose it is generally accepted that no superior permanent or very complex system of coöperation can be supported to a great extent merely by coercion.

(*b*) The rationalization of opportunity is a method of persuasion of much greater importance in most modern activities. Even under political and economic regimes in which coercion of individuals is at least temporarily and in some degree the basic process of persuasion, as in Russia, Germany, and Italy, it is observed that the processes of rationalization of other incentives, that is, propaganda, are carried on more extensively than anywhere else.

The rationalization of incentives occurs in two degrees; the general rationalization that is an expression of social organization as a whole and has chiefly occurred in connection with religious and political organizations, and the specific rationalization that consists in attempting to convince individuals or groups that they "ought," "it is to their interest," to perform services or conform to requirements of specific organizations.

The general rationalization of incentives on a noteworthy scale has occurred many times. The rationalization of religious motives as a basis of the Crusades is one of the most striking. The rationalization of communist doctrine in Russia is another. The rationalization of hate as a means of increasing organization (national) "solidarity" is well known. One of the most interesting of these general rationalizations is that of materialistic progress, to which we have already referred. It is an important basis of the characteristic forms of modern western organization. In its most general form it consists in the cult of science as a means to material ends, the glorification of inventions and inventive talent, including patent legislation; and the exaltation of the exploitation of land, forests, mineral resources, and of the means of transportation. In its more obvious current forms it consists in extensive and intensive salesmanship, advertising, and propaganda concerning the satisfactions to be had from the use of material products. . . .

Specific rationalization of incentives is the process of personal appeal to "join" an organization, to accept a job or position, to undertake a service, to contribute to a cause. It is the process of proselyting or recruiting that is commonly observed in connection with industrial, military, political, and religious organizations. It consists in emphasizing opportunities for satisfaction that are offered, usually in contrast with those available otherwise; and in attempting to elicit interest in those incentives which are most easily or most outstandingly afforded.

The background of the individual to whom incentives are rationalized consists of his physiological requirements, his geographical and social location, and the general rationalization and especially the social influences to which he has previously been subjected by his society, his government, and his church. . . .

This brief[5] discussion of the incentives has been a necessary introduction to the considerations that are important to our study of the subject of organization and the executive functions. The processes concerned are each of them difficult in themselves, and are subject to highly developed techniques and skills.

---

[5] Among other matters it has not been necessary to develop here are those of fraud, trickery, and "economic compulsion," as related either to force of social pressures. At periods or in specific situations all have been important, and in the aggregate at any time no doubt are substantial. In principle, however, it is usually evident that, like direct coercion, they all involve disadvantages or sacrifices that offset their advantages; and it is doubtful if they often are the dominant factors in coöperation. On the contrary they arise from and are chiefly evidence of non-coöperation. They are disruptive, not integrating, methods.

Their importance as a whole arises from the inherent difficulty that organizations experience either in supplying incentives or in exercising persuasion. The most appropriate phrase to apply to this inherent difficulty is "economy of incentives"; but it should be understood that "economy" is used in a broad sense and refers not merely to material or monetary economy.

II

In the economy of incentives we are concerned with the net effects of the income and outgo of things resulting from the production of objective incentives and the exercise of persuasion. An organization which makes material things the principal incentive will be unable long to offer this kind of incentive if it is unable to secure at least as much material or money as it pays out. This is the ordinary economic aspect which is well understood. But the same principle applies to other incentives. The possibilities of offering non-material opportunities, desirable conditions, ideal benefactions, desirable associations, stability of practice, enlarged participation, or communion advantages are limited and usually insufficient, so that the utmost economy is ordinarily essential not only in the material sense but in the broader sense as well. The limitations are due not alone to the relationship of the organization to the external physical environment, but also to its relationship to the social environment, and to its internal efficiency.

A complete exposition of the economy of incentives would among other things involve some duplication of the theories of general economics, rewritten from the point of view of organization. This is not the place to attempt such an exposition; but as the economy of

incentives as a whole in terms of organization is not usually stressed in economic theory[6] and is certainly not well understood, I shall attempt to indicate the outlines of the theory. It will be convenient to do this with reference to organizations of three radically different purposes: (a) an industrial organization; (b) a political organization; and (c) a religious organization.

(a) In an industrial organization the purpose[7] is the production of material goods, or services. For the sake of simplicity we may assume that it requires no capital. It secures material production by applying the energies of men to the physical environment. These energies will result in a gross production; but if the inducements offered to secure these energies are themselves material, and are sufficient, then it will pay out of its production something on this account. If the amount paid out is no more than the production the organization can survive; but if the amount paid out is more than the production, it must cease, since it cannot then continue to offer inducements.

Whether this occurs depends upon the combined effect of four factors; the

---

[6] I think it doubtful that many of the aspects of the economy of incentives have any place in theoretical economics.

[7] The purpose is *not* profit, notwithstanding that business men, economists, ecclesiastics, politicians, labor unions, persistently misstate the purpose. Profit may be essential to having a supply of inducements to satisfy the motives of that class of contributors usually called owners or investors whose contributions in turn were essential to the supply of inducements to other classes of contributors. The possibilities of profit and their realization in some degree are necessary in some economies as conditions under which a continuing supply of incentives is possible; but the objective purpose of no organization is profit, but services. Among industrialists this has been most emphasized by Mr. Ford and some utility organizations.

difficulties of the environment, the effectiveness of organization effort, the internal efficiency of organization, and the amount of inducements paid. Obviously many cooperative efforts fail because the environment is too resistant, others because the organization is ineffective, others because internal losses are large, others because the price paid for services is too large. Within the range of ordinary experience, these are mutually dependent variables, or mutually interacting factors. Under very favorable environmental conditions, relative ineffectiveness and relative internal inefficiency with high outgo for inducements are possible. Under unfavorable conditions, effectiveness, efficiency, and low inducements are necessary.

In most cases the limitations of conditions, of effectiveness, and of efficiency permit only limited material inducements; and both effectiveness and efficiency require an output of individual energies that cannot be elicited from most men by material inducements in any event. Hence, in practice other inducements also must be offered. But in such an organization such inducements in some degree, and usually to a considerable degree, require again material inducements. Thus, satisfactory physical conditions of work mean material inducements to factors not directly productive; satisfactory social conditions mean the rejection of some of those best able to contribute the material production and acceptance of some less able. Almost every type of incentive that can be, or is, necessary will itself in some degree call for material outgo, so that the question is one of choice of methods and degree of emphasis upon different incentives to find the most efficient combination of incentives determined from the material viewpoint. Hence, the various incentives are in competition with each other even from the material point of view.

But the economy of incentives in an industrial organization only begins with the analysis of incentives from the standpoint of material; that is, dollars and cents, costs. The non-material incentives often conflict with each other or are incompatible. Thus opportunity for personal prestige as an incentive for one person necessarily involves a relative depression of others; so that if this incentive is emphasized as to one person, it must be in conjunction with other persons to whom personal prestige is relatively an unimportant inducement.

The difficulties of finding the workable balance of incentives is so great that recourse must be had to persuasion. But persuasion in connection with an industrial effort itself involves material outgo. Thus if coercion is the available method of persuasion, the maintenance of force for this purpose is involved; and if the contribution that can be secured by coercion is limited, as it usually is, except for short periods, the cost of coercion exceeds its effect. The limited efficiencies of slavery systems is an example.

If the method of persuasion is rationalization, either in the form of general propaganda[8] or that of specific argument to individuals (including processes of "selection"), again the overhead cost is usually not negligible. When the general social conditioning is favorable, of course, it is a windfall like favorable physical environment.

(b) A political organization is not ordinarily productive in the materialistic sense. The motives which lie at its roots are ideal benefactions and community

[8] General propaganda of industrial concerns usually relates to that class of contributors to organizations known as consumers.

satisfactions. Such organizations appear not to survive long unless they can afford these incentives; yet it is obvious that every extensive political organization requires the use of "inferior" incentives. Of these, opportunity for personal prestige and material rewards are most prominent. Hence the necessity, under all forms of political organization, for obtaining great supplies of material inducements for use either in the form of direct payments or of "paying jobs." Accordingly, a striking characteristic of political organizations has been the necessity for securing material contributions from "members" either to capture the opportunities to secure additional material (through taxation) or for direct payment (as in campaigns). But here again the balancing of incentives is necessary. For the limitations of material resources, the impossibility of giving more than is received, the discrimination between recipients as respects either material benefits or prestige granted, all tend either to destroy the vital idealism upon which political organization is based or to minimize the *general* material advantages which are perhaps an alternative basis of political organization in many cases.

It is hardly necessary to add that persuasion in its many forms is an important aspect of political recruiting—and that much of the material expenditure goes for this purpose; but this thereby decreases the material available as an incentive to intensive efforts of the "faithful."

(c) In religious organizations the predominant incentives[9] appear to be ideal benefactions and the communion of "kindred spirits," although inferior incentives no doubt often are effective.

[9] That is, without taking into account supernatural benefactions.

The fundamental contributions required of members are intensity of faith and loyalty to organization. A most important effort of religious organizations has been persuasion, known as missionary or proselyting effort. But both the maintenance of organization and missionary effort (and coercion when this is used) require material means, so that superficially, and often primarily, members are required by various methods to make material contributions to permit great material expenditures. . . .

It will be evident, perhaps, without more elaborate illustration, that in every type of organization, for whatever purpose, several incentives are necessary, and some degree of persuasion likewise, in order to secure and maintain the contributions to organization that are required. It will also be clear that, excepting in rare instances, the difficulties of securing the means of offering incentives, of avoiding conflict of incentives, and of making effective persuasive efforts; are inherently great; and that the determination of the precise combination of incentives and of persuasion that will be both effective and feasible is a matter of great delicacy. Indeed, it is so delicate and complex that rarely, if ever, is the scheme of incentives determinable in advance of application. It can only evolve; and the questions relating to it become chiefly those of strategic factors from time to time in the course of the life of the organization. It is also true, of course, that the scheme of incentives is probably the most unstable of the elements of the coöperative system, since invariably external conditions affect the possibilities of material incentives; and human motives are likewise highly variable. Thus incentives represent the final residual of all the conflicting forces involved in organization, a very slight change in underlying forces often making a great change in the power of incentives; and yet it is only by the incentives that the effective balancing of these forces is to be secured, if it can be secured at all. . . . Since all incentives are costly to organization, and the costs tend to prevent its survival, and since the balancing of organization outgo and income is initially to be regarded as impossible without the utmost economy, the distribution of incentives must be proportioned to the value and effectiveness of the various contributions sought.

This is only too much accepted as respects material incentives, that is, material things or money payment. No enduring or complex formal organization of any kind seems to have existed without differential material payments, though material compensation may be indirect to a considerable extent. This seems true up to the present even though contrary to the expressed attitude of the organization or not in harmony with its major purpose, as often in the case of churches and socialistic states.

The same doctrine applies in principle and practice even more to non-material incentives. The hierarchy of positions, with gradation of honors and privileges, which is the universal accompaniment of all complex organization, is essential to the adjustment of non-material incentives to induce the services of the most able individuals or the most valuable potential contributors to organization, and it is likewise necessary to the maintenance of pride of organization, community sense, etc., which are important general incentives to all classes of contributors.

10

The Proverbs of Administration

Herbert A. Simon

A fact about proverbs that greatly enhances their quotability is that they almost always occur in mutually contradictory pairs. "Look before you leap!"—but "He who hesitates is lost."

This is both a great convenience and a serious defect—depending on the use to which one wishes to put the proverbs in question. If it is a matter of rationalizing behavior that has already taken place or justifying action that has already been decided upon, proverbs are ideal. Since one is never at a loss to find one that will prove his point or the precisely contradictory point, for that matter—they are a great help in persuasion, political debate, and all forms of rhetoric.

But when one seeks to use proverbs as the basis of a scientific theory, the situation is less happy. It is not that the propositions expressed by the proverbs are insufficient; it is rather that they prove too much. A scientific theory should tell what is true but also what is false. If Newton had announced to the world that particles of matter exert either an attraction or a repulsion on each other, he would not have added much to scientific knowledge. His contribution consisted in showing that an attraction was exercised and in announcing the precise law governing its operation.

Most of the propositions that make up the body of administrative theory today share, unfortunately, this defect of proverbs. For almost every principle one can find an equally plausible and acceptable contradictory principle. Although the two principles of the pair will lead to exactly opposite organizational recommendations, there is nothing in the theory to indicate which is the proper one to apply.[1]

It is the purpose of this paper to substantiate this sweeping criticism of administrative theory, and to present some suggestions—perhaps less concrete than they should be—as to how the existing dilemma can be solved.

SOME ACCEPTED ADMINISTRATIVE PRINCIPLES

Among the more common "principles" that occur in the literature of administration are these:

1. Administrative efficiency is increased by a specialization of the task among the group.
2. Administrative efficiency is increased by arranging the members of the group in a determinate hierarchy of authority.
3. Administrative efficiency is increased by limiting the span of control at any point in the hierarchy to a small number.
4. Administrative efficiency is increased by grouping the workers, for purposes of control, according to (a) purpose, (b) process, (c) clientele, or (d) place. (This is really an elaboration of the first principle but deserves separate discussion.)

Source: Reprinted with permission from *Public Administration Review* © (Winter 1946): 6, 53-67. © 1946 by the American Society for Public Administration (ASPA), 1120 G Street NW, Suite 700, Washington, DC 20005. All rights reserved.

Since these principles appear relatively simple and clear, it would seem that their application to concrete problems of administrative organization would be unambiguous and that their validity would be easily submitted to empirical test. Such, however, seems not to be the case. To show why it is not, each of the four principles just listed will be considered in turn.

Specialization. Administrative efficiency is supposed to increase with an increase in specialization. But is this intended to mean that *any* increase in specialization will increase efficiency? If so, which of the following alternatives is the correct application of the principle in a particular case?

1. A plan of nursing should be put into effect by which nurses will be assigned to districts and do all nursing within that district, including school examinations, visits to homes of school children, and tuberculosis nursing.

2. A functional plan of nursing should be put into effect by which different nurses will be assigned to school examinations, visits to homes of school children, and tuberculosis nursing. The present method of generalized nursing by districts impedes the development of specialized skills in the three very diverse programs.

Both of these administrative arrangements satisfy the requirement of specialization—the first provides specialization by place; the second, specialization by function. The principle of specialization is of no help at all in choosing between the two alternatives.

It appears that the simplicity of the principle of specialization is a deceptive simplicity—a simplicity which conceals fundamental ambiguities. For "specialization" is not a condition of efficient administration; it is an inevitable characteristic of all group effort, however efficient or inefficient that effort may be. Specialization merely means that different persons are doing different things— and since it is physically impossible for two persons to be doing the same thing in the same place at the same time, two persons are always doing different things.

The real problem of administration, then, is not to "specialize," but to specialize in that particular manner and along those particular lines which will lead to administrative efficiency. But, in thus rephrasing this "principle" of administration, there has been brought clearly into the open its fundamental ambiguity: "Administrative efficiency is increased by a specialization of the task among the group in the direction which will lead to greater efficiency."

Further discussion of the choice between competing bases of specialization will be undertaken after two other principles of administration have been examined.

Unity of Command. Administrative efficiency is supposed to be enhanced by arranging the members of the organization in a determinate hierarchy of authority in order to preserve "unity of command."

Analysis of this "principle" requires a clear understanding of what is meant by the term "authority." A subordinate may be said to accept authority whenever he permits his behavior to be guided by a decision reached by another, irrespective of his own judgment as to the merits of that decision.

In one sense the principle of unity of command, like the principle of specialization, cannot be violated; for it is physically impossible for a man to obey two contradictory commands —that is what is meant by "contradictory commands." Presumably, if unity of command is a principle of administration, it must assert something more than this physical impossibility. Perhaps it asserts this: that it is undesirable to place a member of an organization in a position where he receives orders from more than one superior. This is evidently the meaning that Gulick attaches to the principle when he says,

> The significance of this principle in the process of co-ordination and organization must not be lost sight of. In building a structure of co-ordination, it is often tempting to set up more than one boss for a man who is doing work which has more than one relationship. Even as great a philosopher of management as Taylor fell into this error in setting up separate foremen to deal with machinery, with materials, with speed, etc., each with the power of giving orders directly to the individual workman. The rigid adherence to the principle of unity of command may have its absurdities; these are, however, unimportant in comparison with the certainty of confusion, inefficiency and irresponsibility which arise from the violation of the principle.[2]

Certainly the principle of unity of command, thus interpreted, cannot be criticized for any lack of clarity or any ambiguity. The definition of authority given above should provide a clear test whether, in any concrete situation, the principle is observed. The real fault that must be found with this principle is that it is incompatible with the principle of specialization. One of the most important uses to which authority is put in organization is to bring about specialization in the work of making decisions, so that each decision is made at a point in the organization where it can be made most expertly. As a result, the use of authority permits a greater degree of expertness to be achieved in decision making than would be possible if each operative employee had himself to make all the decisions upon which his activity is predicated. The individual fireman does not decide whether to use a two-inch hose or a fire extinguisher; that is decided for him by his officers, and the

decision is communicated to him in the form of a command.

However, if unity of command, in Gulick's sense, is observed, the decisions of a person at any point in the administrative hierarchy are subject to influence through only one channel of authority; and if his decisions are of a kind that require expertise in more than one field of knowledge, then advisory and informational services must be relied upon to supply those premises which lie in a field not recognized by the mode of specialization in the organization. For example, if an accountant in a school department is subordinate to an educator, and if unity of command is observed, then the finance department cannot issue direct orders to him regarding the technical, accounting aspects of his work. Similarly, the director of motor vehicles in the public works department will be unable to issue direct orders on care of motor equipment to the fire-truck driver.[3]

Gulick, in the statement quoted above, clearly indicates the difficulties to be faced if unity of command is not observed. A certain amount of irresponsibility and confusion are almost certain to ensue. But perhaps this is not too great a price to pay for the increased expertise that can be applied to decisions. What is needed to decide the issue is a principle of administration that would enable one to weigh the relative advantages of the two courses of action. But neither the principle of unity of command nor the principle of specialization is helpful in adjudicating the controversy. They merely contradict each other without indicating any procedure for resolving the contradiction. . . .

The principle of unity of command is perhaps more defensible if narrowed down to the following: In case two authoritative commands conflict, there should be a single determinate person whom the subordinate is expected to obey; and the sanctions of authority should be applied against the subordinate only to enforce his obedience to that one person.

If the principle of unity of command is more defensible when stated in this limited form, it also solves fewer problems. In the first place, it no longer requires, except for settling conflicts of authority, a single hierarchy of authority. Consequently, it leaves unsettled the very important question of how authority should be zoned in a particular organization (i.e., the modes of specialization) and through what channels it should be exercised. Finally, even this narrower concept of unity of command conflicts with the principle of specialization, for whenever disagreement does occur and the organization members revert to the formal lines of authority, then only those types of specialization which are represented in the hierarchy of authority can impress themselves on decisions. If the training officer of a city exercises only functional supervisions over the police training officer, then in case of disagreement with the police chief, specialized knowledge of training problems will be subordinated or ignored. That this actually occurs is shown by the frustration so commonly expressed by functional supervisors at their lack of authority to apply sanctions.

Span of Control. Administrative efficiency is supposed to be enhanced by limiting the number of subordinates who report directly to any one administrator to a small number—say six. This notion that the "span of control" should be narrow is confidently asserted as a third incontrovertible principle of administration. The usual common-sense arguments for restricting the span of control are familiar and need not be repeated here. What is not so generally recognized is that a contradictory proverb of administration can be stated which, though it

is not so familiar as the principle of span of control, can be supported by arguments of equal plausibility. The proverb in question is the following: Administrative efficiency is enhanced by keeping at a minimum the number of organizational levels through which a matter must pass before it is acted upon.

This latter proverb is one of the fundamental criteria that guide administrative analysis in procedures simplification work. Yet in many situations the results to which this principle leads are in direct contradiction to the requirements of the principle of span of control, the principle of unity of command, and the principle of specialization. The present discussion is concerned with the first of these conflicts. To illustrate the difficulty, two alternative proposals for the organization of a small health department will be presented—one based on the restriction of span of control, the other on the limitation of number of organization levels:

1. The present organization of the department places an administrative overload on the health officer by reason of the fact that all eleven employees of the department report directly to him and the further fact that some of the staff lack adequate technical training. Consequently, venereal disease clinic treatments and other details require an undue amount of the health officer's personal attention.

It has previously been recommended that the proposed medical officer be placed in charge of the venereal disease and chest clinics and all child hygiene work. It is further recommended that one of the inspectors be designated chief inspector and placed in charge of all the department's inspectional activities and that one of the nurses be designated as head nurse. This will relieve the health commissioner of considerable detail and will leave him greater freedom to plan and supervise the health program as a whole, to conduct health education, and to coordinate the work of the department with that of other community agencies. If the department were thus organized, the effectiveness of all employees could be substantially increased.

2. The present organization of the department leads to inefficiency and excessive red tape by reason of the fact that an unnecessary supervisory level intervenes between the health officer and the operative employees, and that those four of the twelve employees who are best trained technically are engaged largely in "overhead" administrative duties. Consequently, unnecessary delays occur in securing the approval of the health officer on matters requiring his attention, and too many matters require review and re-review.

The medical officer should be left in charge of the venereal disease and chest clinics and child hygiene work. It is recommended, however, that the position of chief inspector and head nurse be abolished and that the employees now filling these positions perform regular inspectional and nursing duties. The details of work scheduling now handled by these two employees can be taken care of more economically by the secretary to the health officer, and, since broader matters of policy have, in any event, always required the personal attention of the health officer, the abolition of these two positions will eliminate a wholly unnecessary step in review, will allow an expansion of inspectional and nursing services, and will permit at least a beginning to be made in the recommended program of health education. The number of persons reporting directly to the health officer will be increased to nine, but since there are few matters requiring the coordination of these employees, other than the work schedules and policy questions referred to above,

this change will not materially increase his work load.

The dilemma is this: in a large organization with complex interrelations between members, a restricted span of control inevitably produces excessive red tape, for each contact between organization members must be carried upward until a common superior is found. If the organization is at all large, this will involve carrying all such matters upward through several levels of officials for decision and then downward again in the form of orders and instructions—a cumbersome and time-consuming process.

The alternative is to increase the number of persons who are under the command of each officer, so that the pyramid will come more rapidly to a peak, with fewer intervening levels. But this, too, leads to difficulty, for if an officer is required to supervise too many employees, his control over them is weakened.

If it is granted, then, that both the increase and the decrease in span of control has some undesirable consequences, what is the optimum point? Proponents of a restricted span of control have suggested three, five, even eleven, as suitable numbers, but nowhere have they explained the reasoning which led them to the particular number they selected. The principle as stated casts no light on this very crucial question. One is reminded of current arguments about the proper size of the national debt.

Organization by Purpose, Process, Clientele, Place. Administrative efficiency is supposed to be increased by grouping workers according to (a) purpose, (b) process, (c) clientele, or (d) place. But from the discussion of specialization it is clear that this principle is internally inconsistent; for purpose, process, clientele, and place are competing bases of organization, and at any given point of division the advantages of three must be sacrificed to secure the advantages of the fourth. If the major departments of a city, for example, are organized on the basis of major purpose, then it follows that all the physicians, all the lawyers, all the engineers, all the statisticians will not be located in a single department exclusively composed of members of their profession but will be distributed among the various city departments needing their services. The advantages of organization by process will thereby be partly lost.

Some of these advantages can be regained by organizing on the basis of process *within* the major departments. Thus there may be an engineering bureau within the public works department, or the board of education may have a school health service as a major division of its work. Similarly, within small units there may be division by area or by clientele: e.g., a fire department will have separate companies located throughout the city, while a welfare department may have intake and case work agencies in various locations. Again, however, these major types of specialization cannot be simultaneously achieved, for at any point in the organization it must be decided whether specialization at the next level will be accomplished by distinction of major purpose, major process, clientele, or area.

The conflict may be illustrated by showing how the principle of specialization according to purpose would lead to a different result from specialization according to clientele in the organization of a health department.

1. Public health administration consists of the following activities for the prevention of disease and the maintenance of healthful conditions: (1) vital statistics; (2) child hygiene—prenatal, maternity, postnatal, infant, preschool, and school health programs; (3) communicable disease control; (4) inspection of milk, foods, and drugs; (5) sanitary inspection; (6) laboratory service; (7) health education.

One of the handicaps under which the health department labors is the fact that the department has no control over school health, that being an activity of the county board of education, and there is little or no coordination between that highly important part of the community health program and the balance of the program which is conducted by the city-county health unit. It is recommended that the city and county open negotiations with the board of education for the transfer of all school health work and the appropriation therefor to the joint health unit. . . .

2. To the modern school department is entrusted the care of children during almost the entire period that they are absent from the parental home. It has three principal responsibilities toward them: (1) to provide for their education in useful skills and knowledge and in character; (2) to provide them with wholesome play activities outside school hours; (3) to care for their health and to assure the attainment of minimum standards of nutrition.

One of the handicaps under which the school board labors is the fact that, except for school lunches, the board has no control over child health and nutrition, and there is little or no coordination between that highly important part of the child development program and the balance of the program which is conducted by the board of education. It is recommended that the city and county open negotiations for the transfer of all health work for children of school age to the board of education.

Here again is posed the dilemma of choosing between alternative, equally plausible, administrative principles. But this is not the only difficulty in the present case, for a closer study of the situation shows there are fundamental ambiguities in the meanings of the key terms—"purpose," "process," "clientele," and "place."

"Purpose" may be roughly defined as the objective or end for which an activity is carried on; "process" as a means for accomplishing a purpose. Processes, then, are carried on in order to achieve purposes. But purposes themselves may generally be arranged in some sort of hierarchy. A typist moves her fingers in order to type; types in order to reproduce a letter, reproduces a letter in order that an inquiry may be answered. Writing a letter is then the purpose for which the typing is performed; while writing a letter is also the process whereby the purpose of replying to an inquiry is achieved. It follows that the same activity may be described as purpose or as process.

This ambiguity is easily illustrated for the case of an administrative organization. A health department conceived as a unit whose task it is to care for the health of the community is a purpose organization; the same department conceived as a unit which makes use of the medical arts to carry on its work is a process organization. In the same way, an education department may be viewed as a purpose (to educate) organization, or a clientele (children) organization; the forest service as a purpose (forest conservation), process (forest management), clientele (lumbermen and cattlemen utilizing public forests), or area (publicly owned forest lands) organization. When concrete illustrations of this sort are selected, the lines of demarcation between these categories become very hazy and unclear indeed.

"Organization by major purpose," says Gulick, ". . . serves to bring together in

a single large department all of those who are at work endeavoring to render a particular service."[4] But what is a particular service? Is fire protection a single purpose, or is it merely a part of the purpose of public safety?—or is it a combination of purposes including fire prevention and fire fighting? It must be concluded that there is no such thing as a purpose, or a unifunctional (single-purpose) organization. What is to be considered a single function depends entirely on language and techniques.[5] If the English language has a comprehensive term which covers both of two subpurposes it is natural to think of the two together as a single purpose. If such a term is lacking, the two subpurposes become purposes in their own right. On the other hand, a single activity may contribute to several objectives, but since they are technically (procedurally) inseparable, the activity is considered a single function or purpose.

The fact, mentioned previously, that purposes form a hierarchy, each subpurpose contributing to some more final and comprehensive end, helps to make clear the relation between purpose and process. "Organization by major process," says Gulick, ". . . tends to bring together in a single department all of those who are at work making use of a given special skill or technology, or are members of a given profession."[6] Consider a simple skill of this kind—typing. Typing is a skill which brings about a means-end coordination of muscular movements, but a very low level in the means-end hierarchy. The content of the typewritten letter is indifferent to the skill that produces it. The skill consists merely in the ability to hit the letter "*t*" quickly whenever the letter "*t*" is required by the content and to hit the letter "*a*" whenever the letter "*a*" is required by the content.

There is, then, no essential difference between a "purpose" and a "process," but only a distinction of degree. A "process" is an activity whose immediate purpose is at a low level in the hierarchy of means and ends, while a "purpose" is a collection of activities whose orienting value or aim is at a high level in the means-end hierarchy.

Next consider "clientele" and "place" as bases of organization. These categories are really not separate from purpose, but a part of it. A complete statement of the purpose of a fire department would have to include the area served by it: "to reduce fires losses on property in the city of X." Objectives of an administrative organization are phrased in terms of a service to be provided and an area for which it is provided. Usually, the term "purpose" is meant to refer only to the first element, but the second is just as legitimately an aspect of purpose. Area of service, of course, may be a specified clientele quite as well as a geographical area. In the case of an agency which works on "shifts," time will be a third dimension of purpose—to provide a given service in a given area (or to a given clientele) during a given time period.

With this clarification of terminology, the next task is to reconsider the problem of specializing the work of an organization. It is no longer legitimate to speak of a "purpose" organization, a "process" organization, a "clientele" organization, or an "area" organization. The same unit might fall into any one of these four categories, depending on the nature of the larger organizational unit of which it was a part. A unit providing public health and medical services for school-age children in Multnomah County might be considered (1) an "area" organization if it were part of a unit providing the same service for the state of Oregon; (2) a "clientele" organization if it were

part of a unit providing similar services for children of all ages; (3) a "purpose" or a "process" organization (it would be impossible to say which) if it were part of an education department.

It is incorrect to say that Bureau A is a process bureau; the correct statement is that Bureau A is a process bureau *within* Department X.[7] This latter statement would mean that Bureau A incorporates all the processes of a certain kind in Department X, without reference to any special subpurposes, subareas, or subclientele of Department X. Now it is conceivable that a particular unit might incorporate all processes of a certain kind but that these processes might relate to only certain particular subpurposes of the department purpose. In this case, which corresponds to the health unit in an education department mentioned above, the unit would be specialized by both purpose and process. The health unit would be the only one in the education department using the medical art (process) and concerned with health (subpurpose).

Even when the problem is solved of proper usage for the terms "purpose," "process," "clientele," and "area," the principles of administration give no guide as to which of these four competing bases of specialization is applicable in any particular situation. The British Machinery of Government Committee had no doubts about the matter. It considered purpose and clientele as the two possible bases of organization and put its faith entirely in the former. Others have had equal assurance in choosing between purpose and process. The reasoning which leads to these unequivocal conclusions leaves something to be desired. The Machinery of Government Committee gives this sole argument for its choice:

Now the inevitable outcome of this method of organization [by clientele] is a tendency to Lilliputian administration. It is impossible that the specialized service which each Department has to render to the community can be of as high a standard when its work is at the same time limited to a particular class of persons and extended to every variety of provision for them, as when the Department concentrates itself on the provision of the particular service only by whomsoever required, and looks beyond the interest of comparatively small classes.[8]

The faults in this analysis are obvious. First, there is no attempt to determine how a service is to be recognized. Second, there is a bald assumption, absolutely without proof, that a child health unit, for example, in a department of child welfare could not offer services of "as high a standard" as the same unit if it were located in a department of health. Just how the shifting of the unit from one department to another would improve or damage the quality of its work is not explained. Third, no basis is set forth for adjudicating the competing claims of purpose and process—the two are merged in the ambiguous term "service." It is not necessary here to decide whether the committee was right or wrong in its recommendation; the important point is that the recommendation represented a choice, without any apparent logical or empirical grounds, between contradictory principles of administration. . . .

These contradictions and competitions have received increasing attention from students of administration during the past few years. For example, Gulick, Wallace, and Benson have stated certain advantages and disadvantages of the several modes of specialization, and have considered the conditions under which one or the other mode might best be adopted.[9] All this analysis has been at a theoretical level—in the sense that data have not been employed to demonstrate the superior effectiveness claimed for the different modes. But though theoretical, the analysis has lacked a theory. Since no comprehensive framework has been constructed within which the discussion could take place, the analysis has tended either to the logical one-sidedness which characterizes the examples quoted above or to inconclusiveness.

The Impasse of Administrative Theory. The four "principles of administration" that were set forth at the beginning of this paper have now been subjected to critical analysis. None of the four survived in very good shape, for in each case there was found, instead of an unequivocal principle, a set of two or more mutually incompatible principles apparently equally applicable to the administrative situation.

Moreover, the reader will see that the very same objections can be urged against the customary discussions of "centralization" versus "decentralization," which usually conclude, in effect, that "on the one hand, centralization of decision-making functions are desirable; on the other hand, there are definite advantages in decentralization."

Can anything be salvaged which will be useful in the construction of an administrative theory? As a matter of fact, almost everything can be salvaged. The difficulty has arisen from treating as "principles of administration" what are really only criteria for describing and diagnosing administrative situations. Closet space is certainly an important item in the design of a successful house; yet a house designed entirely with a view to securing a maximum of closet space— all other considerations being forgotten —would be considered, to say the least, somewhat unbalanced. Similarly, unity of command, specialization by purpose, and decentralization are all items to be considered in the design of an efficient administrative organization. No single one of these items is of sufficient importance to suffice as a guiding principle for the administrative analyst. In the design of administrative organizations, as in their operation, overall efficiency must be the guiding criterion. Mutually imcompatible advantages must be balanced against each other, just as an architect weighs the advantages of additional closet space against the advantages of a larger living room.

This position, if it is a valid one, constitutes an indictment of much current writing about administrative matters. As the examples cited in this chapter amply demonstrate, much administrative analysis proceeds by selecting a single criterion and applying it to an administrative situation to reach a recommendation; while the fact that equally valid, but contradictory, criteria exist which could be applied with equal reason, but with a different result, is conveniently ignored. A valid approach to the study of administration requires that *all* the relevant diagnostic criteria be identified; that each administrative situation be analyzed in terms of the entire set of criteria; and that research be instituted to determine how weights can be assigned to the several criteria when they are, as they usually will be, mutually incompatible.

AN APPROACH TO ADMINISTRATIVE THEORY

This program needs to be considered step by step. First, what is included in the description of administrative situations for purposes of such an analysis? Second, how can weights be assigned to the various criteria to give them their proper place in the total picture?

The Description of Administrative Situations. Before a science can develop principles, it must possess concepts. Before a law of gravitation could be formu-

lated, it was necessary to have the notions of "acceleration" and "weight." The first task of administrative theory is to develop a set of concepts that will permit the description in terms relevant to the theory of administrative situations. These concepts, to be scientifically useful, must be operational; that is, their meanings must correspond to empirically observable facts or situations. The definition of *authority* given earlier in this paper is an example of an operational definition.

What is a scientifically relevant description of an organization? It is a description that, so far as possible, designates for each person in the organization what decisions that person makes and the influences to which he is subject in making each of these decisions. Current descriptions of administrative organizations fall far short of this standard. For the most part, they confine themselves to the allocation of *functions* and the formal structure of *authority*. They give little attention to the other types of organizational influence or to the system of communications. . . .[10]

Consider the term "centralization." How is it determined whether the operations of a particular organization are "centralized" or "decentralized"? Does the fact that field offices exist prove anything about decentralization? Might not the same decentralization take place in the bureaus of a centrally located office? A realistic analysis of centralization must include a study of the allocation of decisions in the organization and the methods of influence that are employed by the higher levels to affect the decisions at the lower levels. Such an analysis would reveal a much more complex picture of the decision-making process than any enumeration of the geographical locations of organizational units at the different levels.

Administrative description suffers currently from superficiality, oversimplification, lack of realism. It had confined itself too closely to the mechanism of authority and has failed to bring within its orbit the other, equally important, modes of influence on organizational behavior. It has refused to undertake the tiresome task of studying the actual allocation of decision-making functions. It has been satisfied to speak of "authority," "centralization," "span of control," "function," without seeking operational definitions of these terms. Until administrative description reaches a higher level of sophistication, there is little reason to hope that rapid progress will be made toward the identification and verification of valid administrative principles.

Does this mean that a purely formal description of an administrative organization is impossible—that a relevant description must include an account of the content of the organization's decisions? This is a question that is almost impossible to answer in the present state of knowledge of administrative theory. One thing seems certain: content plays a greater role in the application of administrative principles than is allowed for in the formal administrative theory of the present time. This is a fact that is beginning to be recognized in the literature of administration. If one examines the chain of publications extending from Mooney and Reilley, through Gulick and the President's Committee controversy, to Schuyler Wallace and Benson, he sees a steady shift of emphasis from the "principles of administration" themselves to a study of the *conditions* under which competing principles are respectively applicable. Recent publications seldom say that "organization should be by purpose," but rather that "under such and such conditions purpose organization is desirable." It is to these condi-

tions which underlie the application of the proverbs of administration that administrative theory and analysis must turn in their search for really valid principles to replace the proverbs.

The Diagnosis of Administrative Situations. Before any positive suggestions can be made, it is necessary to digress a bit and to consider more closely the exact nature of the propositions of administrative theory. The theory of administration is concerned with how an organization should be constructed and operated in order to accomplish its work efficiently. A fundamental principle of administration, which follows almost immediately from the rational character of "good" administration, is that among several alternatives involving the same expenditure that one should always be selected which leads to the greatest accomplishment of administrative objectives; and among several alternatives that lead to the same accomplishment that one should be selected which involves the least expenditure. Since this "principle of efficiency" is characteristic of any activity that attempts rationally to maximize the attainment of certain ends with the use of scarce means, it is as characteristic of economic theory as it is of administrative theory. The "administrative man" takes his place alongside the classical "economic man."[11]

Actually, the "principle" of efficiency should be considered a definition rather than a principle: it is a definition of what is meant by "good" or "correct" administrative behavior. It does not tell *how* accomplishments are to be maximized, but merely states that this maximization is the aim of administrative activity, and that administrative theory must disclose under what conditions the maximization takes place.

Now what are the factors that determine the level of efficiency which is achieved by an administrative organization? It is not possible to make an exhaustive list of these but the principal categories can be enumerated. Perhaps the simplest method of approach is to consider the single member of the administrative organization and ask what the limits are to the quantity and quality of his output. These limits include (a) limits on his ability to perform and (b) limits on his ability to make correct decisions. To the extent that these limits are removed, the administrative organization approaches its goal of high efficiency. Two persons, given the same skills, the same objectives and values, the same knowledge and information, can rationally decide only upon the same course of action. Hence, administrative theory must be interested in the factory that will determine with what skills, values, and knowledge the organization member undertakes his work. These are the "limits" to rationality with which the principles of administration must deal.

On one side, the individual is limited by those skills, habits, and reflexes which are no longer in the realm of the conscious. His performance, for example, may be limited by his manual dexterity or his reaction time or his strength. His decision-making processes may be limited by the speed of his mental processes, his skill in elementary arithmetic, and so forth. In this area, the principles of administration must be concerned with the physiology of the human body and with the laws of skill-training and of habit. This is the field that has been most successfully cultivated by the followers of Taylor and in which has been developed time-and-motion study and the therblig.

On a second side, the individual is limited by his values and those conceptions of purpose which influence him in making decisions. If his loyalty to the organization is high, his decisions may evidence sincere acceptance of the ob-

jectives set for the organization; if that loyalty is lacking, personal motives may interfere with his administrative efficiency. If his loyalties are attached to the bureau by which he is employed, he may sometimes make decisions that are inimical to the larger unit of which the bureau is a part. In this area the principles of administration must be concerned with the determinants of loyalty and morale, with leadership and initiative, and with the influences that determine where the individual's organizational loyalties will be attached.

On a third side, the individual is limited by the extent of his knowledge of things relevant to his job. This applies both to the basic knowledge required in decision-making—a bridge designer must know the fundamentals of mechanics—and to the information that is required to make his decisions appropriate to the given situation. In this area, administrative theory is concerned with such fundamental questions as these: What are the limits on the mass of knowledge that human minds can accumulate and apply? How rapidly can knowledge be assimilated? How is specialization in the administrative organization to be related to the specializations of knowledge that are prevalent in the community's occupational structure? How is the system of communication to channel knowledge and information to the appropriate decision-points? What types of knowledge can, and what types cannot, be easily transmitted? How is the need for intercommunication of information affected by the modes of specialization in the organization? This is perhaps the *terra incognita* of administrative theory, and undoubtedly its careful exploration will cast great light on the proper application of the proverbs of administration.

Perhaps this triangle of limits does not completely bound the area of rationality, and other sides need to be added to the figure. In any case, this enumeration will serve to indicate the kinds of considerations that must go into the construction of valid and noncontradictory principles of administration.

An important fact to be kept in mind is that the limits of rationality are variable limits. Most important of all, consciousness of the limits may in itself alter them. Suppose it were discovered in a particular organization, for example, that organizational loyalties attached to small units had frequently led to a harmful degree of intraorganizational competition. Then, a program which trained members of the organization to be conscious of their loyalties, and to subordinate loyalties to the smaller group to those of the large, might lead to a very considerable alteration of the limits in that organization.[12]

A related point is that the term "rational behavior" as employed here, refers to rationality when that behavior is evaluated in terms of the objectives of the larger organization; for, as just pointed out, the difference in direction of the individual's aims from those of the larger organization is just one of those elements of nonrationality with which the theory must deal.

A final observation is that, since administrative theory is concerned with the nonrational limits of the rational, it follows that the larger the area in which rationality has been achieved the less important is the exact form of the administrative organization. For example, the function of plan preparation, or design, if it results in a written plan that can be communicated interpersonally without difficulty, can be located almost anywhere in the organization without affecting results. All that is needed is a procedure whereby the plan can be given authoritative status, and this can be provided in a number of ways. A discussion,

then, of the proper location for a planning or designing unit is apt to be highly inconclusive and is apt to hinge on the personalities in the organization and their relative enthusiasm, or lack of it, toward the planning function rather than upon any abstract principles of good administration.[13]

On the other hand, when factors of communication or faiths or loyalty are crucial to the making of a decision, the location of the decision in the organization is of great importance. The method of allocating decisions in the army, for instance, automatically provides (at least in the period prior to the actual battle) that each decision will be made where the knowledge is available for coordinating it with other decisions.

Assigning Weights to the Criteria. A first step, then, in the overhauling of the proverbs of administration is to develop a vocabulary, along the lines just suggested, for the description of administrative organization. A second step, which has also been outlined, is to study the limits of rationality in order to develop a complete and comprehensive enumeration of the criteria that must be weighed in evaluating an administrative organization. The current proverbs represent only a fragmentary and unsystematized portion of these criteria.

When these two tasks have been carried out, it remains to assign weights to the criteria. Since the criteria, or "proverbs," are often mutually competitive or contradictory, it is not sufficient merely to identify them. Merely to know, for example, that a specified change in organization will reduce the span of control is not enough to justify the change. This gain must be balanced against the possible resulting loss of contact between the higher and lower ranks of the hierarchy.

Hence, administrative theory must also be concerned with the question of the weights that are to be applied to these criteria—to the problems of their relative importance in any concrete situation. This question is not one that can be solved in a vacuum. Arm-chair philosophizing about administration—of which the present paper is an example— has gone about as far as it can profitably go in this particular direction. What is needed now is empirical research and experimentation to determine the relative desirability of alternative administrative arrangements.

The methodological framework for this research is already at hand in the principle of efficiency. If an administrative organization whose activities are susceptible to objective evaluation be subjected to study, then the actual change in accomplishment that results from modifying administrative arrangements in these organizations can be observed and analyzed.

There are two indispensable conditions to successful research along these lines. First, it is necessary that the objectives of the administrative organization under study be defined in concrete terms so that results, expressed in terms of these objectives, can be accurately measured. Second, it is necessary that sufficient experimental control be exercised to make possible the isolation of the particular effect under study from other disturbing factors that might be operating on the organization at the same time.

These two conditions have seldom been even partially fulfilled in so-called "administrative experiments." The mere fact that a legislature passes a law creating an administrative agency, that the agency operates for five years, that the agency is finally abolished, and that a historical study is then made of the agency's operations is not sufficient to make of that agency's history an "administrative experiment." Modern American legislation is full of such "experiments" which furnish orators in neigh-

boring states with abundant ammunition when similar issues arise in their bailiwicks, but which provide the scientific investigator with little or nothing in the way of objective evidence, one way or the other. . . .

Perhaps the program outlined here will appear an ambitious or even a quixotic one. There should certainly be no illusions, in undertaking it, as to the length and deviousness of the path. It is hard to see, however, what alternative remains open. Certainly neither the practitioner of administration nor the theoretician can be satisfied with the poor analytic tools that the proverbs provide him. Nor is there any reason to believe that a less drastic reconversion than that outlined here will rebuild those tools to usefulness.

It may be objected that administration cannot aspire to be a "science"; that by the nature of its subject it cannot be more than an "art." Whether true or false, this objection is irrelevant to the present discussion. The question of how "exact" the principles of administration can be made is one that only experience can answer. But as to whether they should be logical or illogical there can be no debate. Even an "art" cannot be founded on proverbs.

NOTES

1. Lest it be thought that this deficiency is peculiar to the science—or "art"—of administration, it should be pointed out that the same trouble is shared by most Freudian psychological theories, as well as by some sociological theories.

2. Luther Gulick, "Notes on the Theory of Organization," in Luther Gulick and L. Urwick (eds.), *Papers on the Science of Administration* (Institute of Public Administration, Columbia University, 1937), p. 9.

3. This point is discussed in Herbert A. Simon, "Decision-Making and Administrative Organization," 4 *Public Administration Review* 20-21 (Winter, 1944).

4. Gulick and Urwick (eds.), *op. cit.*, p. 21.

5. If this is correct, then any attempt to prove that certain activities belong in a single department because they relate to a single purpose is doomed to fail. See, for example, John M. Gaus and Leon Wolcott, *Public Administration and the U.S. Department of Agriculture* (Public Administration Service, 1940).

6. *Op. cit.*, p. 23.

7. This distinction is implicit in most of Gulick's analysis of specialization. However, since he cites as examples single departments within a city, and since he usually speaks of "grouping activities" rather than "dividing work," the relative character of these categories is not always apparent in this discussion (*op. cit.*, pp. 15-30).

8. *Report of the Machinery of Government Committee* (H. M. Stationery Office, 1918).

9. Gulick, "Notes on the Theory of Organization," pp. 21-30; Schuyler Wallace, *Federal Departmentalization* (Columbia University Press, 1941); George C. S. Benson, "International Administrative Organization," 1 *Public Administration Review* 473-486 (Autumn, 1941).

10. The monograph by Macmahon, Millett, and Ogden, op. cit., perhaps approaches nearer than any other published administrative study to the sophistication required in administrative description. See, for example, the discussion on pp. 233-236 of headquarters-field relationships.

11. For an elaboration of the principle of efficiency and its place in administrative theory see Clarence E. Ridley and Herbert A. Simon, *Measuring Municipal Activities* (International City Managers' Association, 2nd ed., 1943), particularly Chapter 1 and the preface to the second edition.

12. For an example of the use of such training, see Herbert A. Simon and William Divine, "Controlling Human Factors in an Administrative Experiment," 1 *Public Administration Review* 487-492 (Autumn, 1941).

13. See, for instance, Robert A. Walker, *The Planning Function in Urban Government* (University of Chicago Press, 1941), pp. 166-175. Walker makes out a strong case for attaching the planning agency to the chief executive. But he rests his entire case on the rather slender reed that "as long as the planning agency is outside the governmental structure . . . planning will tend to encounter resistance from public officials as an invasion of their responsibility and jurisdiction." This "resistance" is precisely the type of nonrational loyalty which has been referred to previously, and which is certainly a variable.

11
Foundations of the Theory of Organization
Philip Selznick

Trades unions, governments, business corporations, political parties, and the like are formal structures in the sense that they represent rationally ordered instruments for the achievement of stated goals. "Organization," we are told, "is the arrangement of personnel for facilitating the accomplishment of some agreed purpose through the allocation of functions and responsibilities."[1] Or, defined more generally, formal organization is "a system of consciously coordinated activities or forces of two or more persons."[2] Viewed in this light, formal organization is the structural expression of rational action. The mobilization of technical and managerial skills requires a pattern of coordination, a systematic ordering of positions and duties which defines a chain of command and makes possible the administrative integration of specialized functions. In this context *delegation* is the primordial organization act, a precarious venture which requires the continuous elaboration of formal mechanisms of coordination and control. The security of all participants, and of the system as a whole, generates a persistent pressure for the institutionalization of relationships, which are thus removed from the uncertainties of individual fealty or sentiment. Moreover, it is necessary for the relations within the structure to be determined in such a way that individuals will be interchangeable and the organization will thus be free of dependence upon personal qualities.[3] In this way, the formal structure becomes subject to calculable manipulation, an instrument of rational action.

But as we inspect these formal structures we begin to see that they never succeed in conquering the nonrational dimensions of organizational behavior. The latter remain at once indispensable to the continued existence of the system of coordination and at the same time the source of friction, dilemma, doubt, and ruin. This fundamental paradox arises from the fact that rational action systems are inescapably imbedded in an institutional matrix, in two significant senses: (1) the action system—or the formal structure of delegation and control which is its organizational expression—is itself only an aspect of a concrete social structure made up of individuals who may interact as *wholes*, not simply in terms of their formal roles within the system; (2) the formal system, and the social structure within which it finds concrete existence, are alike subject to the pressure of an institutional environment to which some overall adjustment must be made. The formal administrative design can never adequately or fully reflect the concrete organization to which it refers, for the obvious reason that no abstract plan or pattern can— or may, if it is to be useful—exhaustively describe an empirical totality. At the same time, that which is not included

Source: From *American Sociological Review* 13 (1948): 25-35. Copyright © 1948 American Sociological Association. Reprinted by permission.

in the abstract design (as reflected, for example, in a staff-and-line organization chart) is vitally relevant to the maintenance and development of the formal system itself.

Organization may be viewed from two standpoints which are analytically distinct but which are empirically united in a context of reciprocal consequences. On the one hand, any concrete organizational system is an economy; at the same time, it is an adaptive social structure. Considered as an economy, organization is a system of relationships which define the availability of scarce resources *and* which may be manipulated in terms of efficiency and effectiveness. It is the economic aspect of organization which commands the attention of management technicians and, for the most part, students of public as well as private administration.[4] Such problems as the span of executive control, the role of staff or auxiliary agencies, the relation of headquarters to field offices, and the relative merits of single or multiple executive boards are typical concerns of the science of administration. The coordinative scalar, and functional principles, as elements of the theory of organization, are products of the attempt to explicate the most general features of organization as a "technical problem" or, in our terms, as an economy.

Organization as an economy is, however, necessarily conditioned by the organic states of the concrete structure, outside of the systematics of delegation and control. This becomes especially evident as the attention of leadership is directed toward such problems as the legitimacy of authority and the dynamics of persuasion. It is recognized implicitly in action and explicitly in the work of a number of students that the possibility of manipulating the system of coordination depends on the extent to which that system is operating within an envi-

ronment of effective inducement to individual participants and of conditions in which the stability of authority is assured. This is in a sense the fundamental thesis of Barnard's remarkable study, *The Functions of the Executive*. It is also the underlying hypothesis which makes it possible for Urwick to suggest that "proper" or formal channels in fact function to "confirm and record" decisions arrived at by more personal means.[5] We meet it again in the concept of administration as a process of education, in which the winning of consent and support is conceived to be a basic function of leadership.[6] In short, it is recognized that control and consent cannot be divorced even within formally authoritarian structures.

The indivisibility of control and consent makes it necessary to view formal organizations as *cooperative* systems, widening the frame of reference of those concerned with the manipulation of organizational resources. At the point of action, of executive decision, the economic aspect of organization provides inadequate tools for control over the concrete structure. This idea may be readily grasped if attention is directed to the role of the individual within the organizational economy. From the standpoint of organization as a formal system, persons are viewed functionally, in respect to their *roles*, as participants in assigned segments of the cooperative system. But in fact individuals have a propensity to resist depersonalization, to spill over the boundaries of their segmentary roles, to participate as *wholes*. The formal systems (at an extreme, the disposition of "rifles" at a military perimeter) cannot take account of the deviations thus introduced, and consequently break down as instruments of control when relied upon alone. The whole individual raises new problems for the organization, partly because of the needs of his own personality, partly because he brings with him a set of established habits as well, perhaps, as commitments to special groups outside of the organization.

Unfortunately for the adequacy of formal systems of coordination, the needs of individuals do not permit a singleminded attention to the stated goals of the system within which they have been assigned. The hazard inherent in the act of delegation derives essentially from this fact. Delegation is an organizational act, having to do with formal assignments to functions and powers. Theoretically, these assignments are made to roles or official positions, not to individuals as such. In fact, however, delegation necessarily involves concrete individuals who have interests and goals which do not always coincide with the goals of the formal system. As a consequence, individual personalities may offer resistance to the demands made upon them by the official conditions of delegation. These resistances are not accounted for within the categories of coordination and delegation, so that when they occur they must be considered as unpredictable and accidental. Observations of this type of situation within formal structures are sufficiently commonplace. A familiar example is that of delegation to a subordinate who is also required to train his own replacement. The subordinate may resist this demand in order to maintain unique access to the "mysteries" of the job, and thus insure his indispensability to the organization.

In large organizations, deviations from the formal system tend to become institutionalized, so that "unwritten laws" and informal associations are established. Institutionalization removes such deviations from the realm of personality differences, transforming them into a persistent structural aspect of formal organizations.[7] These institutionalized

rules and modes of informal cooperation are normally attempts by participants in the formal organization to control the group relations which form the environment of organizational decisions. The informal patterns (such as cliques) arise spontaneously, are based on personal relationships, and are usually directed to the control of some specific situation. They may be generated anywhere within a hierarchy, often with deleterious consequences for the formal goals of the organization, but they may also function to widen the available resources of executive control and thus contribute to rather than hinder the achievement of the stated objectives of the organization. The deviations tend to force a shift away from the purely formal system as the effective determinant of behavior to (1) a condition in which informal patterns buttress the formal, as through the manipulation of sentiment within the organization in favor of established authority; or (2) a condition wherein the informal controls effect a consistent modification of formal goals, as in the case of some bureaucratic patterns.[8] This trend will eventually result in the formalization of erstwhile informal activities, with the cycle of deviation and transformation beginning again on a new level.

The relevance of informal structures to organizational analysis underlines the significance of conceiving of formal organizations as cooperative systems. When the totality of interacting groups and individuals becomes the object of inquiry, the latter is not restricted by formal, legal, or procedural dimensions. The *state of the system* emerges as a significant point of analysis, as when an internal situation charged with conflict qualifies and informs actions ostensibly determined by formal relations and objectives. A proper understanding of the organizational process must make it possible to interpret changes in the formal system—new appointments or rules or reorganizations—in their relation to the informal and unavowed ties of friendship, class loyalty, power cliques, or external commitment. This is what it means "to know the score." . . .

To recognize the sociological relevance of formal structures is not, however, to have constructed a theory of organization. It is important to set the framework of analysis, and much is accomplished along this line when, for example, the nature of authority in formal organizations is reinterpreted to emphasize the factors of cohesion and persuasion as against legal or coercive sources.[9] This redefinition is logically the same as that which introduced the conception of the self as social. The latter helps make possible, but does not of itself fulfill, the requirements for a dynamic theory of personality. In the same way, the definition of authority as conditioned by sociological factors of sentiment and cohesion—or more generally the definition of formal organizations as cooperative systems—only sets the stage, as an initial requirement, for the formulation of a theory of organization.

STRUCTURAL-FUNCTIONAL ANALYSIS

Cooperative systems are constituted of individuals interacting as wholes in relation to a formal system of coordination. The concrete structure is therefore a resultant of the reciprocal influences of the formal and informal aspects of organization. Furthermore, this structure is itself a totality, an adaptive "organism" reacting to influences upon it from an external environment. These considerations help to define the objects of inquiry; but to progress to a system of predicates *about* these objects it is necessary to set forth an analytical method which seems to

be fruitful and significant. The method must have a relevance to empirical materials, which is to say, it must be more specific in its reference than discussions of the logic or methodology of social science.

The organon which may be suggested as peculiarly helpful in the analysis of adaptive structures has been referred to as "structural-functional analysis."[10] This method may be characterized in a sentence: *Structural-functional analysis relates contemporary and variable behavior to a presumptively stable system of needs and mechanisms*. This means that a given empirical system is deemed to have basic needs, essentially related to self-maintenance; the system develops repetitive means of self-defense; and day-to-day activity is interpreted in terms of the function served by that activity for the maintenance and defense of the system. Put thus generally, the approach is applicable on any level in which the determinate "states" of empirically isolable systems undergo self-impelled and repetitive transformations when impinged upon by external conditions. This self-impulsion suggests the relevance of the term "dynamic," which is often used in referring to physiological, psychological, or social systems to which this type of analysis has been applied.[11]

It is a postulate of the structural-functional approach that the basic need of all empirical systems is the maintenance of the integrity and continuity of the system itself. Of course, such a postulate is primarily useful in directing attention to a set of "derived imperatives" or needs which are sufficiently concrete to characterize the system at hand.[12] It is perhaps rash to attempt a catalogue of these imperatives for formal organizations, but some suggestive formulation is needed in the interests of setting forth the type of analysis under discussion. In formal organizations, the "maintenance of the system" as a generic need may be specified in terms of the following imperatives:

1. *The security of the organization as a whole in relation to social forces in its environment.* This imperative requires continuous attention to the possibilities of encroachment and to the forestalling of threatened aggressions or deleterious (though perhaps unintended) consequences from the actions of others.

2. *The stability of the lines of authority and communication.* One of the persistent reference-points of administrative decision is the weighing of consequences for the continued capacity of leadership to control and to have access to the personnel or ranks.

3. *The stability of informal relations within the organization.* Ties of sentiment and self-interest are evolved as unacknowledged but effective mechanisms of adjustment of individuals and subgroups to the conditions of life within the organization. These ties represent a cementing of relationships which sustains the formal authority in day-to-day operations and widens opportunities for effective communication.[13] Consequently, attempts to "upset" the informal structure, either frontally or as an indirect consequence of formal reorganization, will normally be met with considerable resistance.

4. *The continuity of policy and of the sources of its determination.* For each level within the organization, and for the organization as a whole, it is necessary that there be a sense that action taken in the light of a given policy will not be placed in continuous jeopardy. Arbitrary or unpredictable changes in policy undermine the significance of (and therefore the attention to) day-to-day action by injecting a note of capriciousness. At the same time, the organization will seek stable roots (or firm statutory authority or

popular mandate) so that a sense of the permanency and legitimacy of its acts will be achieved.

5. *A homogeneity of outlook with respect to the meaning and role of the organization.* The minimization of disaffection requires a unity derived from a common understanding of what the character of the organization is meant to be. When this homogeneity breaks down, as in situations of internal conflict over basic issues, the continued existence of the organization is endangered. On the other hand, one of the signs of "healthy" organization is the ability to effectively orient new members and readily slough off those who cannot be adapted to the established outlook.

This catalogue of needs cannot be thought of as final, but it approximates the stable system generally characteristic of formal organizations. These imperatives are derived, in the sense that they represent the conditions for survival or self-maintenance of cooperative systems of organized action. An inspection of these needs suggests that organizational survival is intimately connected with the struggle for relative prestige, both for the organization and for elements and individuals within it. It may therefore be useful to refer to a *prestige-survival motif* in organizational behavior as a shorthand way of relating behavior needs, especially when the exact nature of the needs remains in doubt. However, it must be emphasized that prestige-survival in organizations does not derive simply from like motives in individuals. Loyalty and self-sacrifice may be individual expressions of organizational or group egotism and self-consciousness.

The concept of organizational need directs analysis to the *internal relevance* of organizational behavior. This is especially pertinent with respect to discretionary action undertaken by agents manifestly in pursuit of formal goals. The question then becomes one of relating the specific act of discretion to some presumptively stable organizational need. In other words, it is not simply action plainly oriented internally (such as inservice training) but also action presumably oriented externally which must be inspected for its relevance to internal conditions. This is of prime importance for the understanding of bureaucratic behavior, for it is of the essence of the latter that action formally undertaken for substantive goals be weighed and transformed in terms of its consequences for the position of the officialdom. . . .

The setting of structural-functional analysis as applied to organizations requires some qualification, however. Let us entertain the suggestion that the interesting problem in social science is not so much why men act the way they do as why men in certain circumstances *must* act the way they do. This emphasis upon constraint, if accepted, releases us from an ubiquitous attention to behavior in general, and especially from any undue fixation upon statistics. On the other hand, it has what would seem to be salutary consequence of focusing inquiry upon certain necessary relationships of the type "if . . . then," for example: If the cultural level of the rank and file members of a formally democratic organization is below that necessary for participation in the formulation of policy, then there will be pressure upon the leaders to use the tools of demagogy.

Is such a statement universal in its applicability? Surely not in the sense that one can predict without remainder the nature of all or even most political groups in a democracy. Concrete behavior is a resultant, a complex vector, shaped by the operation of a number of such general constraints. But there is a test of general applicability: it is that of noting whether the relation made ex-

plicit must be *taken into account* in action. This criterion represents an empirical test of the significance of social generalizations. If a theory is significant it will state a relation which will either (1) be taken into account as an element of achieving control; or (2) be ignored only at the risk of losing control and will evidence itself in a ramification of objective or unintended consequences.[14] It is a corollary of this principle of significance that investigation must search out the underlying factors in organizational action, which requires a kind of intensive analysis of the same order as psychoanalytic probing.

A frame of reference which invites attention to the constraints upon behavior will tend to highlight tensions and dilemmas, the characteristic paradoxes generated in the course of action. The dilemma may be said to be the handmaiden of structural-functional analysis, for it introduces the concept of *commitment* or *involvement* as fundamental to organizational analysis. A dilemma in human behavior is represented by an inescapable commitment which cannot be reconciled with the needs of the organism or the social system. There are many spurious dilemmas which have to do with verbal contradictions, but inherent dilemmas to which we refer are of a more profound sort, for they reflect the basic nature of the empirical system in question. An economic order committed to profit as its sustaining incentive may, in Marxist terms, sow the seed of its own destruction. Again, the anguish of man, torn between finitude and pride, is not a matter of arbitrary and replaceable assumptions but is a reflection of the psychological needs of the human organism, and is concretized in his commitment to the institutions which command his life; he is in the world and of it, inescapably involved in its goals and demands; at the same time, the needs of the spirit are compelling, proposing modes of salvation which have continuously disquieting consequences for worldly involvements. In still another context, the need of the human organism for affection and response necessitates a commitment to elements of the culture which can provide them; but the rule of the super-ego is uncertain since it cannot be completely reconciled with the need for libidinal satisfaction. . . .

Organizational analysis, too, must find its selective principle; otherwise the indiscriminate attempts to relate activity functionally to needs will produce little in the way of significant theory. Such a principle might read as follows: *Our frame of reference is to select out those needs which cannot be fulfilled within approved avenues of expression and thus must have recourse to such adaptive mechanisms as ideology and to the manipulation of formal processes and structures in terms of informal goals.* This formulation has many difficulties, and is not presented as conclusive, but it suggests the kind of principle which is likely to separate the quick and the dead, the meaningful and the trite, in the study of cooperative systems in organized action.[15]

The frame of reference outlined here for the theory of organization may now be identified as involving the following major ideas: (1) the concept of organizations as cooperative systems, adaptive social structures, made up of interacting individuals, subgroups, and informal plus formal relationships; (2) structural-functional analysis, which relates variable aspects of organization (such as goals) to stable needs and self-defensive mechanisms; (3) the concept of recalcitrance as a quality of the tools of social action, involving a break in the continuum of adjustment and defining an environment of constraint, commitment, and tension. This frame of reference is suggested as providing a specifiable *area*

of relations within which predicates in the theory of organization will be sought, and at the same time setting forth principles of selection and relevance in our approach to the data of organization.

It will be noted that we have set forth this frame of reference within the overall context of social action. The significance of events may be defined by their place and operational role in a means-end scheme. If functional analysis searches out the elements important for the maintenance of a given structure, and that structure is one of the materials to be manipulated in action, then that which is functional in respect to the structure is also functional in respect to the action system. This provides a ground for the significance of functionally derived theories. At the same time, relevance to control in action is the empirical test of their applicability or truth.

CO-OPTATION AS A MECHANISM OF ADJUSTMENT

The frame of reference stated above is in fact an amalgam of definition, resolution, and substantive theory. There is an element of *definition* on conceiving of formal organizations as cooperative systems, though of course the interaction of informal and formal patterns is a question of fact; in a sense, we are *resolving* to employ structural-functional analysis on the assumption that it will be fruitful to do so, though here, too, the specification of needs or derived imperatives is a matter for empirical inquiry; and our predication of recalcitrance as a quality of the tools of action is itself a *substantive theory,* perhaps fundamental to a general understanding of the nature of social action.

A theory of organization requires more than a general frame of reference, though the latter is indispensable to inform the approach of inquiry to any given set of materials. What is necessary is the construction of generalizations concerning transformations within and among cooperative systems. These generalizations represent, from the standpoint of particular cases, possible predicates which are relevant to the materials as we know them in general, but which are not necessarily controlling in all circumstances. A theory of transformations in organization would specify those states of the system which resulted typically in predictable, or at least understandable, changes in such aspects of organization as goals, leadership, doctrine, efficiency, effectiveness, and size. These empirical generalizations would be systematized as they were related to the stable needs of the cooperative system.

Changes in the characteristics of organizations may occur as a result of many different conditions, not always or necessarily related to the processes of organization as such. But the theory of organization must be selective, so that explanations of transformations will be sought within its own assumptions or frame of reference. Consider the question of size. Organizations may expand for many reasons—the availability of markets, legislative delegations, the swing of opinion—which may be accidental from the point of view of the organizational process. To explore changes in size (as of, say, a trades union) as related to changes in nonorganizational conditions may be necessitated by the historical events to be described, but it will not of itself advance the frontiers of the theory of organization. However, if "the innate propensity of all organizations to expand" is asserted as a function of "the inherent instability of incentives"[16] then transformations have been stated within the terms of the theory of organization itself. It is likely that in many cases the generalization in question may represent only a

minor aspect of the empirical changes, but these organizational relations must be made explicit if the theory is to receive development.

In a frame of reference which specifies needs and anticipates the formulation of a set of self-defensive responses or mechanisms, the latter appear to constitute one kind of empirical generalization or "possible predicate" within the general theory. The needs of organizations (whatever investigation may determine them to be) are posited as attributes of all organizations, but the responses to disequilibrium will be varied. The mechanisms used by the system in fulfillment of its needs will be repetitive and thus may be described as a specifiable set of assertions within the theory of organization, but any given organization may or may not have recourse to the characteristic modes of response. Certainly no given organization will employ all of the possible mechanisms which are theoretically available. When Barnard speaks of an "innate propensity of organization to expand," he is in fact formulating one of the general mechanisms, namely, expansion, which is a characteristic mode of response available to an organization under pressure from within. These responses necessarily involve a transformation (in this case, size) of some structural aspect of the organization.

Other examples of the self-defensive mechanisms available to organizations may derive primarily from the response of these organizations to the institutional environments in which they live. The tendency to construct ideologies, reflecting the need to come to terms with major social forces, is one such mechanism. Less well understood as a mechanism of organizational adjustment is what we may term *co-optation*. Some statement of the meaning of this concept may aid in clarifying the foregoing analysis.

Co-optation is the process of absorbing new elements into the leadership or policy-determining structure of an organization as a means of averting threats to its stability or existence. This is a defensive mechanism, formulated as one of a number of possible predicates available for the interpretation of organizational behavior. Co-optation tells us something about the process by which an institutional environment impinges itself upon an organization and effects changes in its leadership and policy. Formal authority may resort to co-optation under the following general conditions:

1. When there exists a hiatus between consent and control, so that the legitimacy of the formal authority is called into question. The "indivisibility" of consent and control refers, of course, to an optimum situation. Where control lacks an adequate measure of consent, it may revert to coercive measures or attempt somehow to win the consent of the governed. One means of winning consent is to co-opt elements into the leadership or organization, usually elements which in some way reflect the sentiment, or possess the confidence of the relevant public or mass. As a result, it is expected that the new elements will lend respectability or legitimacy to the organs of control and thus reestablish the stability of formal authority. This process is widely used, and in many different contexts. It is met in colonial countries, where the organs of alien control reaffirm their legitimacy by co-opting native leaders into the colonial administration. We find it in the phenomenon of "crisis-patriotism" wherein formally disfranchised groups are temporarily given representation in the councils of government in order to win their solidarity in a time of national stress. Co-optation is presently being considered by the United States Army in its study of proposals to give enlisted personnel representation in the court-martial machinery—a clearly adaptive response to stresses made explicit during the war, the lack of confidence in the administration of army justice. The "unity" parties of totalitarian states are another form of co-optation; company unions or some employee representation plans in industry are still another. In each of these cases, the response of formal authority (private or public, in a large organization or a small one) is an attempt to correct a state of imbalance by *formal* measures. It will be noted, moreover, that what is shared is the *responsibility* for power rather than power itself. These conditions define what we shall refer to as *formal co-optation*.

2. Co-optation may be a response to the pressure of specific centers of power. This is not necessarily a matter of legitimacy or of a general and diffuse lack of confidence. These may be well established; and yet organized forces which are able to threaten the formal authority may effectively shape its structure and policy. The organization in respect to its institutional environment—or the leadership in respect to its ranks—must take these forces into account. As a consequence, the outside elements may be brought into the leadership or policy-determining structure, may be given a place as a recognition of and concession to the resources they can independently command. The representation of interests through administrative constituencies is a typical example of this process. Or, within an organization, individuals upon whom the group is dependent for funds or other resources may insist upon and receive a share in the determination of policy. This form of cooperation is typically expressed in informal terms, for the problem is not one of responding to a state of imbalance with respect to the "people as a whole" but rather one of

meeting the pressure of specific individuals or interest-groups which are in a position to enforce demands. The latter are interested in the substance of power and not its forms. Moreover, an open acknowledgement of capitulation to specific interests may itself undermine the sense of legitimacy of the formal authority within the community. Consequently, there is a positive pressure to refrain from explicit recognition of the relationship established. This form of the co-optative mechanism, having to do with the sharing of power as a response to specific pressures, may be termed *informal co-optation*.

Co-optation reflects a state of tension between formal authority and social power. The former is embodied in a particular structure and leadership, but the latter has to do with subjective and objective factors which control the loyalties and potential manipulability of the community. Where the formal authority is an expression of social power, its stability is assured. On the other hand, when it becomes divorced from the sources of social power its continued existence is threatened. This threat may arise from the sheer alienation of sentiment or from the fact that other leaderships have control over the sources of social power. Where a formal authority has been accustomed to the assumption that its constituents respond to it as individuals, there may be a rude awakening when organization of those constituents on a non-governmental basis creates nuclei of power which are able effectively to demand a sharing of power.[17]

The significance of co-optation for organizational analysis is not simply that there is a change in or a broadening of leadership, and that this is an adaptive response, but also that *this change is consequential for the character and role of the organization*. Co-optation involves com-

mitment, so that the groups to which adaptation has been made constrain the field of choice available to the organization or leadership in question. The character of the co-opted elements will necessarily shape (inhibit or broaden) the modes of action available to the leadership which has won adaptation and security at the price of commitment. The concept of co-optation thus implicitly sets forth the major points of the frame of reference outlined above: it is an adaptive response of a cooperative system to a stable need, generating transformations which reflect constraints enforced by the recalcitrant tools of action.

NOTES

1. John M. Gaus, "A Theory of Organization in Public Administration," in *The Frontiers of Public Administration* (Chicago: University of Chicago Press, 1936), p. 66.

2. Chester I. Barnard, *The Functions of the Executive* (Cambridge: Harvard University Press, 1938), p. 73.

3. Cf. Talcott Parsons' generalization (after Max Weber) of the "law of the increasing rationality of action systems," in *The Structure of Social Action* (New York: McGraw-Hill, 1937), p. 752.

4. See Luther Gulick and Lydall Urwick (eds.), *Papers on the Science of Administration* (New York: Institute of Public Administration, Columbia University, 1937); Lydall Urwick, *The Elements of Administration* (New York, Harper, 1943); James D. Mooney and Alan C. Reiley, *The Principles of Organization* (New York: Harper, 1939); H. S. Dennison, *Organization Engineering* (New York: McGraw-Hill, 1931).

5. Urwick, *The Elements of Administration, op. cit.*, p. 47.

6. See Gaus, *op. cit.* Studies of the problem of morale are instances of the same orientation, having received considerable impetus in recent years from the work of the Harvard Business School group.

7. The creation of informal structures within various types of organizations has received explicit recognition in recent years. See F. J. Roethlisberger and W. J. Dickson, *Manage-*

ment and the Worker (Cambridge: Harvard University Press, 1941), p. 524; also Barnard, *op. cit.*, c. ix; and Wilbert E. Moore, *Industrial Relations and the Social Order* (New York: Macmillan, 1946), chap. xv.

8. For an analysis of the latter in these terms, see Philip Selznick, "An Approach to a Theory of Bureaucracy," *American Sociological Review* 8 (February, 1943).

9. Robert Michels, "Authority," *Encyclopedia of the Social Sciences* (New York: Macmillan, 1931), pp. 319ff.; also Barnard, *op cit.*, c. xii.

10. For a presentation of this approach having a more general reference than the study of formal organizations, see Talcott Parsons, "The Present Position and Prospects of Systematic Theory in Sociology," in Georges Gurvitch and Wilbert E. Moore (ed.), *Twentieth Century Sociology* (New York: The Philosophical Library, 1945).

11. "Structure" refers to both the relationships within the system (formal plus informal patterns in organization) and the set of needs and modes of satisfaction which characterize the given type of empirical system. As the utilization of this type of analysis proceeds, the concept of "need" will require further clarification. In particular, the imputation of a "stable set of needs" to organizational systems must not function as a new instinct theory. At the same time, we cannot avoid using these inductions as to generic needs, for they help us to stake out our area of inquiry. The author is indebted to Robert K. Merton who has, in correspondence, raised some important objections to the use of the term "need" in this context.

12. For "derived imperative" see Bronislaw Malinowski, *The Dynamics of Culture Change* (New Haven: Yale University Press, 1945), pp. 44ff. For the use of "need" in place of "motive" see the same author's *A Scientific Theory of Culture* (Chapel Hill: University of North Carolina Press, 1944), pp. 89-90.

13. They may also *destroy* those relationships, as noted above, but the need remains, generat-

ing one of the persistent dilemmas of leadership.

14. See R. M. MacIver's discussion of the "dynamic assessment" which "brings the external world selectively into the subjective realm, conferring on it subjective significance for the ends of action." *Social Causation* (Boston: Ginn, 1942), chaps. 11, 12. The analysis of this assessment within the context of organized action yields the implicit knowledge which guides the choice among alternatives. See also Robert K. Merton, "The Unanticipated Consequences of Purposive Social Action," *American Sociological Review* 1 (December, 1936).

15. This is not meant to deprecate the study of organizations as *economies* or formal systems. The latter represent an independent level, abstracted from organizational structures as cooperative or adaptive systems ("organisms").

16. Barnard, *op. cit.*, pp. 158-159.

17. It is perhaps useful to restrict the concept of co-optation to formal organizations, but in fact it probably reflects a process characteristic of all group leaderships. This has received some recognition in the analysis of class structure, wherein the ruling class is interpreted as protecting its own stability by absorbing new elements. Thus Michels made the point that "an aristocracy cannot maintain an enduring stability by sealing itself off hermetically." See Robert Michels, *Umschichtungen in den herrschenden Klassen nach dem Kriege* (Stuttgart: Kohlhammer, 1934), p. 39; also Gaetano Mosca, *The Ruling Class* (New York: McGraw-Hill, 1939), p. 413ff. The alliance or amalgamation of classes in the face of a common threat may be reflected in formal and informal co-optative responses among formal organizations sensitive to class pressures. In a forthcoming volume, *TVA and the Grass Roots*, the author has made extensive use of the concept of co-optation in analyzing some aspects of the organizational behavior of a government agency.

12
A Behavioral Theory of Organizational Objectives
Richard M. Cyert & James G. March

Organizations make decisions. They make decisions in the same sense in which individuals make decisions: The organization as a whole behaves as though there existed a central coordination and control system capable of directing the behavior of the members of the organization sufficiently to allow the meaningful imputation of purpose to the total system. Because the central nervous system of most organizations appears to be somewhat different from that of the individual system, we are understandably cautious about viewing organization decision-making in quite the same terms as those applied to individual choice. Nevertheless, organizational choice is a legitimate and important focus of research attention.

As in theories of individual choice, theories of organizational decision-making fall into two broad classes. Normative theorists—particularly economic theorists of the firm—have been dedicated to the improvement of the rationality of organizational choice. Recent developments in the application of mathematics to the solution of economic decision-problems are fully and effectively in such a tradition (Cooper, Hitch, Baumol, Shubik, Schelling, Valavanis, and Ellsberg, 1958). The empirical theory of organizational decision-making has a much more checkered tradition and is considerably less well-developed (March and Simon, 1958).

The present efforts to develop a behavioral theory of organizational decision-making represent attempts to overcome the disparity between the importance of decision-making in organizations and our understanding of how, in fact, such decisions are made. The research as a whole, as well as that part of it discussed below, is based on three initial commitments. The first of these is to develop an explicitly empirical theory rather than a normative one. Our interest is in understanding how complex organizations make decisions, not how they ought to do so. Without denying the importance of normative theory, we are convinced that the major current needs are for empirical knowledge.

The second commitment is to focus on the classic problems long explored in economic theory—pricing, resource allocation, and capital investment. This commitment is intended to overcome some difficulties with existing organization theory. By introducing organizational propositions into models of rather complex systems, we are driven to increase the precision of the propositions considerably. At present, anyone taking existing organization theory as a base for predicting behavior within organizations finds that he can make a number of rather important predictions of the general form: If x varies, y will vary. Only rarely will he find either the parameters of the functions or more elaborate predictions for situations in which the *ceteris paribus* assumptions are not met.

The third commitment is to approximate in the theory the process by which decisions are made by organizations. This commitment to a process-oriented theory is not new. It has typified many organization theorists in the past (Marshall, 1919; Weber, 1947). The sentiment that one should substitute observation for assumption whenever possible seems, a priori, reasonable. Traditionally, the major dilemma in organization theory has been between putting into the theory all the features of organizations we think are relevant and thereby making the theory unmanageable, or pruning the model down to a simple system, thereby making it unrealistic. So long as we had to deal primarily with classical mathematics, there was, in fact, little we could do. With the advent of the computer and use of simulation, we have a methodology that will permit us to expand considerably the emphasis on actual process without losing the predictive precision essential to testing (Cyert and March, 1959).

In models currently being developed there are four major subsystems. Since they operate more or less independently, it is possible to conceive them as the four basic subtheories required for a behavioral theory of organizational decision-making; first, the theory of organizational objectives; second, the theory of organizational expectations; third, the theory of organizational choice; fourth, the theory of organizational implementation. In this paper we discuss the first of these only, the theory of organizational objectives.

THE ORGANIZATION AS A COALITION

Let us conceive the organization as a coalition. It is a coalition of individuals, some of them organized into subcoalitions. In the business organization, one immediately thinks of such coalition members as managers, workers, stockholders, suppliers, customers, lawyers, tax collectors, etc. In the governmental organization, one thinks of such members as administrators, workers, appointive officials, elective officials, legislators, judges, clientele, etc. In the voluntary charitable organization, one thinks of paid functionaries, volunteers, donors, donees, etc.

This view of an organization as a coalition suggests, of course, several different recent treatments of organization theory in which a similar basic position is adopted. In particular, inducements-contributions theory (Barnard, 1938; Simon, 1947), theory of games (von Neumann and Morgenstern, 1947), and theory of teams (Marschak, in this volume). Each of these theories is substantially equivalent on this score. Each specifies:

1. That organizations include individual participants with (at least potentially) widely varying preference orderings.
2. That through bargaining and side payments the participants in the organization enter into a coalition agreement for purposes of the game. This agreement specifies a joint preference-ordering (or organizational objective) for the coalition.
3. That thereafter the coalition can be treated as a single strategist, entrepreneur, or what have you.

Such a formulation permits us to move immediately to modern decision theory, which has been an important part of recent developments in normative organization theory. In our view, however, a joint preference ordering is not a particularly good description of actual organization goals. Studies of organizational objectives suggest that to the extent to which there is agreement on objectives, it is agreement on highly ambiguous goals (Truman, 1951; Kaplan, Dirlam, and Lanzillotti, 1958). Such agreement is undoubtedly important to choice within the organization, but it is a far cry from a clear preference ordering. The studies suggest further that behind this agreement on rather vague objectives there is considerable disagreement and uncertainty about subgoals; that organizations appear to be pursuing one goal at one time and another (partially inconsistent) goal at another; and that different parts of the organization appear to be pursuing different goals at the same time (Kaplan, Dirlam, and Lanzillotti, 1958; Selznick, 1949). Finally, the studies suggest that most organization objectives take the form of an aspiration level rather than an imperative to "maximize" or "minimize," and that the aspiration level changes in reponse to experience (Blau, 1955; Alt, 1949).

In the theory to be outlined here, we consider three major ways in which the objectives of a coalition are determined. The first of these is the bargaining process by which the composition and general terms of the coalition are fixed. The second is the internal organizational process of control by which objectives are stabilized and elaborated. The third is the process of adjustment to experience, by which coalition agreements are altered in response to environmental changes. Each of these processes is considered, in turn, in the next three sections of the paper.

FORMATION OF COALITION OBJECTIVES THROUGH BARGAINING

A basic problem in developing a theory of coalition formation is the problem of handling side payments. No matter how we try we simply cannot imagine that the side payments by which organizational coalitions are formed even remotely satisfy the requirements of unrestricted transferability of utility. Side payments are made in many forms: money, personal treatment, authority, organization policy, etc. A winning coalition does not

have a fixed booty which it then divides among its members. Quite to the contrary, the total value of side payments available for division among coalition members is a function of the composition of the coalition; and the total utility of the actual side payments depends on the distribution made within the coalition. There is no conservation of utility.

For example, if we can imagine a situation in which any dyad is a viable coalition (e.g., a partnership to exploit the proposition that two can live more cheaply in coalition than separately), we would predict a greater total utility for those dyads in which needs were complementary than for those in which they were competitive. Generally speaking, therefore, the partitioning of the adult population into male-female dyads is probably more efficient from the point of view of total utility accruing to the coalition than is a partition into sexually homogeneous pairs.

Such a situation makes game theory as it currently exists virtually irrelevant for a treatment of organizational side payments (Luce and Raiffa, 1957). But the problem is in part even deeper than that. The second requirement of such theories as game theory, theory of teams, and inducements-contributions theory, is that after the side payments are made, a joint preference ordering is defined. All conflict is settled by the side-payment bargaining. The employment-contract form of these theories, for example, assumes that the entrepreneur has an objective. He then purchases whatever services he needs to achieve the objective. In return for such payments, employees contract to perform whatever is required of them—at least within the range of permissible requirements. For a price, the employee adopts the "organization" goal.

One strange feature of such a conception is that it describes a coalition asymmetrically. To what extent is it arbitrary that we call wage payments "costs" and dividend payments "profits"—rather than the other way around? Why is it that in our quasi-genetic moments we are inclined to say that in the beginning there was a manager and he recruited workers and capital? For the development of our own theory we make two major arguments. First, the emphasis on the asymmetry has seriously confused our understanding of organizational goals. The confusion arises because ultimately it makes only slightly more sense to say that the goals of a business organization is to maximize profit than it does to say that its goal is to maximize the salary of Sam Smith, Assistant to the Janitor.

Second, despite this there are important reasons for viewing some coalition members as quite different from others. For example, it is clear that employees and management make somewhat different demands on the organization. In their bargaining, side payments appear traditionally to have performed the classical function of specifying a joint preference ordering. In addition, some coalition members (e.g., many stockholders) devote substantially less time to the particular coalition under consideration than do others. It is this characteristic that has usually been used to draw organizational boundaries between "external" and "internal" members of the coalition. Thus, there are important classes of coalition members who are passive most of the time. A condition of such passivity must be that the payment demands they make are of such a character that most of the time they can be met rather easily.

Although we thereby reduce substantially the size and complexity of the coalition relevant for most goal-setting, we are still left with something more complicated than an individual entrepreneur. It is primarily through bargaining

within this active group that what we call organizational objectives arise. Side payments, far from being incidental distribution of a fixed, transferable booty, represent the central process of goal specification. That is, a significant number of these payments are in the form of policy commitments.

The distinction between demands for monetary side payments and demands for policy commitments seems to underlie management-oriented treatments of organizations. It is clear that in many organizations this distinction has important ideological and therefore affective connotations. Indeed, the breakdown of the distinction in our generation has been quite consistently violent. Political party-machines in this country have changed drastically the ratio of direct monetary side payments (e.g., patronage, charity) to policy commitments (e.g., economic legislation). Labor unions are conspicuously entering into what has been viewed traditionally as the management prerogatives of policy-making, and demanding payments in that area. Military forces have long since given up the substance—if not entirely the pretense—of being simply hired agents of the regime. The phenomenon is especially obvious in public (Dahl and Lindblom, 1953; Simon, Smithburg, and Thompson, 1950) and voluntary (Sills, 1957; Messinger, 1955) organizations; but all organizations use policy side payments. The marginal cost to other coalition members is typically quite small.

This trend toward policy side payments is particularly observable in contemporary organizations, but the important point is that we have never come close to maintenance of a sharp distinction in the kinds of payments made and demanded. Policy commitments have (one is tempted to say always) been an important part of the method by which coalitions are formed. In fact, an organization that does not use such devices can exist in only a rather special environment.

To illustrate coalition formation under conditions where the problem is not scarce resources for side payments, but varying complementarities of policy demands, imagine a nine-man committee appointed to commission a painting for the village hall. The nine members make individually the following demands:

Committeeman A: The painting must be an abstract monotone.
Committeeman B: The painting must be an impressionistic oil.
Committeeman C: The painting must be small and oval in shape.
Committeeman D: The painting must be small and in oil.
Committeeman E: The painting must be square in shape and multicolored.
Committeeman F: The painting must be an impressionistic square.
Committeeman G: The painting must be a monotone and in oil.
Committeeman H: The painting must be multicolored and impressionistic.
Committeeman I: The painting must be small and oval.

In this case, each potential coalition member makes two simple demands. Assuming that five members are all that are required to make the decision, there are three feasible coalitions. A, C, D, G, and I can form a coalition and commission a small, oval, monotone, oil abstract. B, C, D, H, and I can form a coalition and commission a small, oval, multicolored, impressionistic oil. B, D, E, F, and H can form a coalition and commission a small, square, multicolored, impressionistic oil.

Committeeman D, it will be noted, is in the admirable position of being included in every possible coalition. The reason is clear; his demands are completely consistent with the demands of everyone else.

Obviously at some level of generality the distinction between money and policy payments disappears because any side payment can be viewed as a policy constraint. When we agree to pay someone $35,000 a year, we are constrained to that set of policy decisions that will allow such a payment. Any allocation of scarce resources (such as money) limits the alternatives for the organization. But the scarcity of resources is not the only kind of problem. Some policy demands are strictly inconsistent with other demands. Others are completely complementary. If I demand of the organization that John Jones be shot and you demand that he be sainted, it will be difficult for us both to stay in the organization. This is not because either bullets or haloes are in short supply or because we don't have enough money for both.

To be sure, the problems of policy consistency are in *principle* amenable to explicit optimizing behavior. But they add to the computational difficulties facing the coalition members and make it even more obvious why the bargaining leading to side payment and policy agreements is only slightly related to the bargaining anticipated in a theory of omniscient rationality. The tests of short-run feasibility that they represent lead to the familiar complications of conflict, disagreement, and rebargaining.

In the process of bargaining over side payments many of the organizational objectives are defined. Because of the form the bargaining takes, the objectives tend to have several important attributes. First, they are imperfectly rationalized. Depending on the skill of the leaders involved, the sequence of demands leading to the new bargaining, the aggressiveness of various parts of the organization, and the scarcity of resources, the new demands will be tested for consistency with existing policy. But this testing is normally far from complete. Second, some objectives are stated in the form of aspiration-level constraints. Objectives arise in this form when demands which are consistent with the coalition are stated in this form. For example, the demand, "We must allocate ten percent of our total budget to research." Third, some objectives are stated in a nonoperational form. In our formulation such objectives arise when potential coalition members have demands which are nonoperational or demands which can be made nonoperational. The prevalence of objectives in this form can be explained by the fact that nonoperational objectives are consistent with virtually any set of objectives.

STABILIZATION
AND ELABORATION
OF OBJECTIVES

The bargaining process goes on more or less continuously, turning out a long series of commitments. But a description of goal formation simply in such terms is not adequate. Organizational objectives are, first of all, much more stable than would be suggested by such a model, and secondly, such a model does not handle very well the elaboration and clarification of goals through day-to-day bargaining.

Central to an understanding of these phenomena is again an appreciation for the limitations of human capacities and time to devote to any particular aspect of the organizational system. Let us return to our conception of a coalition having monetary and policy side payments. These side-payment agreements are incomplete. They do not anticipate effectively all possible future situations, and they do not identify all considerations that might be viewed as important by the coalition members at some future time. Nevertheless, the coalition members are motivated to operate under the agreements and to develop some mutual control-systems for enforcing them.

One such mutual control-system in many organizations is the budget. A budget is a highly explicit elaboration of previous commitments. Although it is usually viewed as an asymmetric control-device (i.e., a means for superiors to control subordinates), it is clear that it represents a form of mutual control. Just as there are usually severe costs to the department in exceeding the budget, so also are there severe costs to other members of the coalition if the budget is not paid in full. As a result, budgets in every organization tend to be self-confirming.

A second major, mutual control-system is the allocation of functions. Division of labor and specialization are commonly treated in management textbooks simply as techniques of rational organization. If, however, we consider the allocation of functions in much the way we would normally view the allocation of resources during budgeting, a somewhat different picture emerges. When we define the limits of discretion, we constrain the individual or subgroup from acting outside those limits. But at the same time, we constrain any other members of the coalition from prohibiting action within those limits. Like the allocation of resources in a budget, the allocation of discretion in an organization chart is largely self-confirming.

The secondary bargaining involved in such mutual control-systems serves to elaborate and revise the coalition agreements made on entry (Thompson and McEwen, 1958). In the early life of an organization, or after some exceptionally drastic organizational upheaval, this elaboration occurs in a context where very little is taken as given. Relatively deliberate action must be taken on everything from pricing policy to paperclip policy. Reports from individuals who have lived through such early stages emphasize the lack of structure that typifies settings for day-to-day decisions (Simon, 1953).

In most organizations most of the time, however, the elaboration of objectives occurs within much tighter constraints. Much of the situation is taken as given. This is true primarily because organizations have memories in the form of precedents, and individuals in the coalition are strongly motivated to accept the precedents as binding. Whether precedents are formalized in the shape of an official standard-operating-procedure or are less formally stored, they remove from conscious consideration many agreements, decisions, and commitments that might well be subject to renegotiation in an organization without a memory (Cyert and March, 1960). Past bargains become precedents for present situations. A budget becomes a precedent for future budgets. An allocation of functions becomes a precedent for future allocations. Through all the well-known mechanisms, the coalition agreements of today are institutionalized into semipermanent arrangements. A number of administrative aphorisms come to mind: an unfilled position disappears; see an empty office and fill it up; there is nothing temporary under the sun. As a result of organizational precedents, objectives exhibit much greater stability than would typify a pure bargaining situation.

The "accidents" of organizational genealogy tend to be perpetuated.

CHANGES IN OBJECTIVES THROUGH EXPERIENCE

Although considerably stabilized by memory and institutionalization-phenomena, the demands made on the coalition by individual members do change with experience. Both the nature of the demands and their quantitative level vary over time.

Since many of the requirements specified by individual participants are in the form of attainable goals rather than general maximizing constraints, objectives are subject to the usual phenomena associated with aspiration levels. As an approximation to the aspiration-level model, we can take the following set of propositions:

1. In the steady state, aspiration level exceeds achievement by a small amount.
2. Where achievement increases at an increasing rate, aspiration level will exhibit short-run lags behind achievement.
3. Where achievement decreases, aspiration level will be substantially above achievement.

These propositions derive from simpler assumptions requiring that current aspiration be an optimistic extrapolation of past achievement and past aspiration. Although such assumptions are sometimes inappropriate, the model seems to be consistent with a wide range of human goal-setting behavior (Lewin, Dembo, Festinger, and Sears, 1944). Two kinds of achievement are, of course, important. The first is the achievement of the participant himself. The second is the achievement of others in his reference group (Festinger, 1954).

Because of these phenomena, our theory of organizational objectives must allow for drift in the demands of members of the organization. No one doubts that aspirations with respect to monetary compensation vary substantially as a function of payments received. So also do aspirations regarding advertising budget, quality of product, volume of sales, product mix, and capital investment. Obviously, until we know a great deal more than we do about the parameters of the relation between achievement and aspiration we can make only relatively weak predictions. But some of these predictions are quite useful, particularly in conjunction with search theory (Cyert, Dill, and March, 1958).

For example, two situations are particularly intriguing. What happens when the rate of improvement in the environment is great enough so that it outruns the upward adjustment of aspiration? Second, what happens when the environment becomes less favorable? The general answer to both of these questions involves the concept of organizational slack (Cyert and March, 1956). When the environment outruns aspiration-level adjustment, the organization secures, or at least has the potentiality of securing, resources in excess of its demands. Some of these resources are simply not obtained—although they are available. Others are used to meet the revised demands of those members of the coalition whose demands adjust most rapidly—usually those most deeply involved in the organization. The excess resources would not be subject to very general bargaining because they do not involve allocation in the face of scarcity. Coincidentally perhaps, the absorption of excess resources also serves to delay aspiration-level adjustment by passive members of the coalition.

When the environment becomes less favorable, organizational slack represents a cushion. Resource scarcity brings on renewed bargaining and tends to cut heavily into the excess payments introduced during plusher times. It does not necessarily mean that precisely those demands that grew abnormally during better days are pruned abnormally during poorer ones; but in general we would expect this to be approximately the case.

Some attempts have been made to use these very simple propositions to generate some meaningful empirical predictions. Thus, we predict that, discounting for the economies of scale, relatively successful firms will have higher unit-costs than relatively unsuccessful ones. We predict that advertising expenditures will be a function of sales in the previous time period at least as much as the reverse will be true.

The nature of the demands also changes with experience in another way. We do not conceive that individual members of the coalition will have a simple listing of demands, with only the quantitative values changing over time. Instead we imagine each member as having a rather disorganized file case full of demands. At any point in time, the member attends to only a rather small subset of his demands, the number and variety depending again on the extent of his involvement in the organization and on the demands of his other commitments on his attention.

Since not all demands are attended to at the same time, one important part of the theory of organizational objectives is to predict when particular units in the organization will attend to particular goals. Consider the safety goal in a large corporation. For the safety engineers, this is a very important goal most of the time. Other parts of the organization rarely even consider it. If, however, the organization has some drastic experience (e.g., a multiple fatality), attention to a safety goal is much more widespread and safety action quite probable.

Whatever the experience, it shifts the attention-focus. In some (as in the safety example), adverse experience suggests a problem area to be attacked. In others, solutions to problems stimulate attention to a particular goal. An organization with an active personnel-research department will devote substantial attention to personnel goals not because it is necessarily a particularly pressing problem but because the subunit keeps generating solutions that remind other members of the organization of a particular set of objectives they profess.

The notion of attention-focus suggests one reason why organizations are successful in surviving with a large set of unrationalized goals. They rarely see the conflicting objectives simultaneously. For example, let us reconsider the case of the pair of demands that John Jones be either (a) shot or (b) sainted. Quite naturally, these were described as inconsistent demands. Jones cannot be simultaneously shot and sainted. But the emphasis should be on *simultaneously*. It is quite feasible for him to be first shot and then sainted, or vice versa. It is logically feasible because a halo can be attached as firmly to a dead man as to a live one and a saint is as susceptible to bullets as a sinner. It is organizationally feasible because the probability is low that both of these demands will be attended to simultaneously.

The sequential attention to goals is a simple mechanism. A consequence of the mechanism is that organizations ignore many conditions that outside observers see as direct contradictions. They are contradictions only if we imagine a well-established, joint preference ordering or omniscient bargaining. Neither condition exists in an organization. If we assume that attention to goals is limited, we can explain the absence of any strong pressure to resolve apparent internal inconsistencies. This is not to argue that

all conflicts involving objectives can be resolved in this way, but it is one important mechanism that deserves much more intensive study.

CONSTRUCTING A PREDICTIVE THEORY

Before the general considerations outlined above can be transformed into a useful predictive theory, a considerable amount of precision must be added. The introduction of precision depends, in turn, on the future success of research into the process of coalition formation. Nevertheless, some steps can be taken now to develop the theory. In particular, we can specify a general framework for a theory and indicate its needs for further development.

We assume a set of coalition members, actual or potential. Whether these members are individuals or groups of individuals is unimportant. Some of the possible subsets drawn from this set are viable coalitions. That is, we will identify a class of combinations of members such that any of these combinations meet the minimal standards imposed by the external environment on the organization. Patently, therefore, the composition of the viable set of coalitions will depend on environmental conditions.

For each of the potential coalition members we require a set of demands. Each such individual set is partitioned into an active part currently attended to and an inactive part currently ignored. Each demand can be characterized by two factors; first, its marginal resource requirements, given the demands of all possible other combinations of demands from potential coalition members; second, its marginal consistency with all possible combinations of demands from potential coalition members.

For each potential coalition member we also require a set of problems, partitioned similarly into an active and an inactive part.

This provides us with the framework of the theory. In addition, we need five basic mechanisms. First, we need a mechanism that changes the quantitative value of the demands over time. In our formulation, this becomes a version of the basic aspiration-level and mutual control theory outlined earlier.

Second, we need an attention-focus mechanism that transfers demands among the three possible states; active set, inactive set, not-considered set. We have said that some organizational participants will attend to more demands than other participants and that for all participants some demands will be considered at one time and others at other times. But we know rather little about the actual mechanisms that control this attention factor.

Third, we need a similar attention-focus mechanism for problems. As we have noted, there is a major interaction between what problems are attended to and what demands are attended to, but research is also badly needed in this area.

Fourth, we need a demand-evaluation procedure that is consistent with the limited capacities of human beings. Such a procedure must specify how demands are checked for consistency and for their resource demands. Presumably, such a mechanism will depend heavily on a rule that much of the problem is taken as given and only incremental changes are considered.

Fifth, we need a mechanism for choosing among the potentially viable coalitions. In our judgment, this mechanism will probably look much like the recent suggestions of game theorists that only small changes are evaluated at a time (Luce and Raiffa, 1957).

Given these five mechanisms and some way of expressing environmental resources, we can describe a process for the determination of objectives in an organization that will exhibit the important attributes of organizational goal-determination. At the moment, we can approximate some of the required functions. For example, it has been possible to introduce into a complete model a substantial part of the first mechanism, and some elements of the second, third, and fourth (Cyert, Feigenbaum, and March, 1959). Before the theory can develop further, however, and particularly before it can focus intensively on the formation of objectives through bargaining and coalition formation (rather than on the revision of such objectives and the selective attention to them), we require greater empirical clarification of the phenomena involved.

REFERENCES

Alt, R. M. (1949). The internal organization of the firm and price formation: An illustrative case. *Quarterly J. of Econ.*, 63, 92–110.

Barnard, C. I. (1938). *The functions of the executive*. Cambridge: Harvard University Press.

Blau, P. M. (1955). *The dynamics of bureaucracy.* Chicago: University of Chicago Press.

Cooper, W. W., Hitch, C., Baumol, W. J., Shubik, M., Schelling, T. C., Valavanis, S., & Ellsberg, D. (1958). Economics and operations research: A symposium. *The Rev. of Econ. and Stat.*, 40, 195–229.

Cyert, R. M., & March, J. G. (1956). Organizational factors in the theory of oligopoly. *Quarterly J. of Econ.*, 70, 44–64.

Cyert, R. M., Dill, W. R., & March, J. G. (1958). The role of expectations in business decision making. *Adm. Sci. Quarterly*, 3, 307–340.

Cyert, R. M., & March, J. G. (1959). Research on a behavioral theory of the firm. *Management Rev.*

Cyert, R. M., Feigenbaum, E. A., & March, J. G. (1959). Models in a behavioral theory of the firm. *Behavioral Sci.*, 4, 81–95.

Cyert, R. M., & March, J. G. (1960). Business operating procedure. In B. von H. Gilmer (ed.), *Industrial psychology.* New York: McGraw-Hill.

Dahl, R. A., & Lindblom, C. E. (1953). *Politics, economics, and welfare.* New York: Harper.

Festinger, L. (1954). A theory of social comparison processes. *Human Relations, 7,* 117–140.

Kaplan, A. D. H., Dirlam, J. B., & Lanzillotti, R. F. (1958). *Pricing in big business.* Washington: Brookings Institution.

Lewin, L., Dembo, T., Festinger, L., & Sears, P. (1944). Level of aspiration. In J. M. Hunt (ed.), *Personality and the behavior disorders.* (Vol I). New York: Ronald Press.

Luce, R. D., & Raiffa, H. (1957). *Games and decisions.* New York: Wiley.

March, J. G., & Simon, H. A. (1958). *Organizations.* New York: Wiley.

Marshall, A. (1919). *Industry and trade.* London: Macmillan.

Messinger, S. L. (1955). Organizational transformation: A case study of a declining social movement. *Amer. sociol. Rev., 20,* 3–10.

Selznick, P. (1949). *TVA and the grass roots.* Berkeley: University of California Press.

Sills, D. L. (1957). *The volunteers.* Glencoe, IL: Free Press.

Simon, H. A. (1947). Administrative behavior. New York: Macmillan.

Simon, H. A., Smithburg, D. W., & Thompson, V. A. (1950). *Public administration.* New York: Knopf.

Simon, H. A. (1953). Birth of an organization: The economic cooperation administration. *Public Adm. Rev., 13,* 227–236.

Thompson, J. D., & McEwen, W. J. (1958). Organizational goals and environment: Goal setting as an interaction process. *Amer. sociol. rev., 23,* 23–31.

Truman, D. B. (1951). *The governmental process.* New York: Knopf.

Von Neumann, J., & Morgenstern, O. (1947). *Theory of games and economic behavior.* (2nd ed.) Princeton, NJ: Princeton University Press.

Weber, M. (1947). *The theory of social and economic organization* (A. M. Henderson & T. Parsons, Trans.). New York: Oxford University Press.

CHAPTER III

Human Resource Theory, or The Organizational Behavior Perspective

Students and practitioners of management have always been interested in and concerned with the behavior of people in organizations. But fundamental assumptions about the behavior of people at work did not change dramatically from the beginnings of humankind's attempts to organize until only a few decades ago. Using the traditional "the boss knows best" mind-set (set of assumptions), Hugo Münsterberg (1863–1916), the German-born psychologist whose later work at Harvard would earn him the title of "father" of industrial or applied psychology, pioneered the application of psychological findings from laboratory experiments to practical matters. He sought to match the abilities of new hires with a company's work demands, to positively influence employee attitudes toward their work and their company, and to understand the impact of psychological conditions on employee productivity (H. Münsterberg, 1913; M. Münsterberg, 1922). Münsterberg's approach characterized how the behavioral sciences tended to be applied in organizations well into the 1950s. During and following World War II, the armed services were particularly active in conducting and sponsoring research into how the military could best *find and shape people to fit its needs*.

In contrast to the Hugo Münsterberg-type perspective on organizational behavior, the 1960s, 1970s, and 1980s "modern breed" of applied behavioral scientists have focused their attention on seeking to answer questions such as how organizations could and should allow and encourage their people to grow and develop. From this perspective, it is *assumed* that organizational creativity, flexibility, and prosperity flow naturally from employee growth and development. The essence of the relationship between organization and people is redefined from dependence to codependence. People are considered to be as or more important than the organization itself. The organizational behavior methods and techniques of the 1960s, 1970s, and 1980s could not have been used in Münsterberg's days *because we didn't believe (assume) that codependence was the "right" relationship between an organization and its employees*.

Although practitioners and researchers have been interested in the behavior of people inside organizations for a very long time, it has only been since about

1957—when our basic assumptions about the relationship between organizations and people truly began to change—that the organizational behavior perspective, or human resource theory, came into being. Those who see organizations through the "lenses" of the organizational behavior perspective focus on people, groups, and the relationships among them and the organizational environment. Because the organizational behavior perspective places a very high value on humans as individuals, things typically are done very openly and honestly, providing employees with maximum amounts of accurate information so they can make informed decisions with free will about their future (Argyris, 1970).

Human resource theory draws on a body of research and theory built around the following assumptions:

1. Organizations exist to serve human needs (rather than the reverse).
2. Organizations and people need each other. (Organizations need ideas, energy, and talent; people need careers, salaries, and work opportunities.)
3. When the fit between the individual and the organization is poor, one or both will suffer: individuals will be exploited, or will seek to exploit the organizations, or both.
4. A good fit between individual and organization benefits both: human beings find meaningful and satisfying work, and organizations get the human talent and energy that they need (Bolman & Deal, 1991, p. 121).

No other perspective of organizations has ever had such a wealth of research findings and methods at its disposal.

The one most significant set of events that preceded and presaged a conscious theory (and field) of organizational behavior was the multiyear work done by the Elton Mayo team at the Hawthorne plant of the Western Electric Company beginning in 1927 (Mayo, 1933; Roethlisberger & Dixon, 1939). It is important to note that the Mayo team began its work trying to fit into the mold of classical organization theory thinking. The team phrased its questions in the language and concepts industry was accustomed to using in order to see and explain problems such as: productivity in relationship to such factors as the amount of light, the rate of flow of materials, and alternative wage payment plans. The Mayo team succeeded in making significant breakthroughs in understanding only after it redefined the Hawthore problems as social psychological problems—problems conceptualized in such terms as interpersonal relations in groups, group norms, control over one's own environment, and personal recognition. It was only after the Mayo team achieved this breakthrough that it became the "grandfather"—the direct precursor—of the field of organizational behavior and human resource theory. The Hawthorne studies laid the foundation for a set of assumptions that would be fully articulated and would displace the assumptions of classical organization theory twenty years later. The Hawthorne experiments were the emotional and intellectual wellspring of the organizational behavior perspective and modern theories of motivation. The Hawthorne experiments showed that complex, interactional variables make the difference in motivating people—things like attention paid to workers as individuals, workers' control over their own work, differences between individuals' needs, management's willingness to listen, group norms, and direct feedback.

According to human resource theory, the organization is not the independent variable to be manipulated in order to change behavior (as a dependent variable)— even though organizations pay employees to help them achieve organizational goals. Instead, the organization must be seen as the context in which behavior occurs. It is both an independent and dependent variable. The organization influences human behavior just as behavior shapes the organization. The interactions shape conceptualizations of jobs, human communication and interaction in work groups, the impact of participation in decisions about one's own work, roles (in general), and the roles of leaders.

It should be evident that human resource organization theory is an enormous field of study supported by a large body of literature both because it addresses numerous subfields and because it has so much research available for use. In this chapter, we can only introduce a few of its most important ideas and best-known authors. For a more thorough presentation, we suggest the second edition of J. Steven Ott's (1996) anthology *Classic Readings in Organizational Behavior* (2d. ed.). Ott groups the literature of human resource theory by its most pervasive themes:

- Motivation
- Group and intergroup behavior
- Leadership
- Work teams and empowerment
- Effects of the work environment on individuals
- Power and influence
- Organizational change processes [including the subfield of organization development (OD)]

In this chapter, we have limited the selections to a few classic readings on leadership, motivation, group dynamics, and organizational change. The first article reprinted here is a truly pioneering treatise on the situational or contingency approach to leadership, "The Giving of Orders," by Mary Parker Follett. Follett discusses how orders should be given in any organization: They should be depersonalized "to unite all concerned in a study of the situation, to discover the law of the situation and obey that." Follett thus argues for a participatory leadership style, whereby employees and employers cooperate to assess the situation and decide what should be done at that moment—in that situation. Once the "law" of the situation is discovered, "the employee can issue it to the employer as well as employer to employee." This manner of giving orders facilitates better attitudes within an organization because nobody is necessarily under another person; rather, all take their cues from the situation.

All discussions of motivation start with Abraham Maslow. His hierarchy of needs stands alongside the Hawthorne experiments and Douglas McGregor's Theory

X and Theory Y as *the* departure points for studying motivation in organizations. An overview of Maslow's basic theory of needs is presented here from his 1943 *Psychological Review* article "A Theory of Human Motivation." Maslow's theoretical premises can be summarized in a few phrases:

- All humans have needs that underlie their motivational structure
- As lower levels of needs are satisfied, they no longer "drive" behavior
- Satisfied needs are not motivators
- As lower level needs of workers become satisfied, higher order needs take over as the motivating forces

Maslow's theory has been attacked frequently. Few empirical studies have supported it, and it oversimplifies the complex structure of human needs and motivations. Several modified needs hierarchies have been proposed over the years that reportedly are better able to withstand empirical testing (for example, Alderfer, 1969). But, despite the criticisms and the continuing advances across the spectrum of applied behavioral sciences, Abraham Maslow's theory continues to occupy a most honored and prominent place in organizational behavior and management textbooks.

Between 1957 and 1960, the organizational behavior perspective literally exploded onto the organization scene. On April 9, 1957, Douglas M. McGregor delivered the Fifth Anniversary Convocation address to the School of Industrial Management at the Massachusetts Institute of Technology. He titled his address "The Human Side of Enterprise." McGregor expanded his talk into some of the most influential articles and books on organizational behavior and organization theory. In "The Human Side of Enterprise," McGregor articulated how managerial assumptions about employees become self-fulfilling prophesies. He labeled his two sets of contrasting assumptions Theory X and Theory Y, but they are more than just theories. McGregor had articulated the basic assumptions of the organizational behavior perspective.

"The Human Side of Enterprise" is a cogent articulation of the basic assumptions of the organizational behavior perspective. Theory X and Theory Y are contrasting basic managerial assumptions about employees that, in McGregor's words, become self-fulfilling prophesies. Managerial assumptions cause employee behavior. Theory X and Theory Y are ways of seeing and thinking about people that, in turn, affect their behavior. Thus, "The Human Side of Enterprise" (1957b), which is reprinted in this chapter, is a landmark theory of motivation.

Theory X assumptions represent a restatement of the tenets of the scientific management movement. For example, Theory X holds that human beings inherently dislike work and will avoid it if possible. Most people must be coerced, controlled, directed, or threatened with punishment to get them to work toward the achievement of organizational objectives; and humans prefer to be directed, to avoid responsibility, and will seek security above all else. These assumptions serve as polar opposites to McGregor's Theory Y.

Theory Y assumptions postulate, for example, that people do not inherently dislike work; work can be a source of satisfaction. People will exercise self-direction and self-control if they are committed to organization objectives. People are willing to seek and to accept responsibility; avoidance of responsibility is not natural, it is a consequence of experiences. The intellectual potential of most humans is only partially utilized at work.

Irving Janis' 1971 article "Groupthink," is a study of pressures for conformance—the reasons that social conformity is encountered so frequently in groups. Janis examines high-level decision makers and decision making during times of major fiascoes: the 1962 Bay of Pigs, the Johnson administration's decision to escalate the Vietnam War, and the 1941 failure to prepare for the attack on Pearl Harbor. Groupthink is "the mode of thinking that persons engage in when *concurrence seeking* becomes so dominant in a cohesive in-group that it tends to override realistic appraisal of alternative courses of action . . . the desperate drive for consensus at any cost that suppresses dissent among the mighty in the corridors of power." Janis identifies eight symptoms of groupthink that are relatively easy to observe:

- An illusion of invulnerability
- Collective construction of rationalizations that permit group members to ignore warnings or other forms of negative feedback
- Unquestioning belief in the morality of the in-group
- Strong, negative, stereotyped views about the leaders of enemy groups
- Rapid application of pressure against group members who express even momentary doubts about virtually any illusions the group shares
- Careful, conscious, personal avoidance of deviation from what appears to be a group consensus
- Shared illusions of unanimity of opinion
- Establishment of *mindguards*—people who "protect the leader and fellow members from adverse information that might break the complacency they shared about the effectiveness and morality of past decisions."

Janis concludes with an assessment of the negative influence of groupthink on executive decision making (including overestimation of the group's capability and self-imposed isolation from new or opposing information and points of view), as well as preventive and remedial steps for dealing with groupthink.

The final reading in this chapter, "Intergroup Conflict" (1993), by Taylor Cox, Jr., a chapter from his groundbreaking book, *Cultural Diversity in Organizations: Theory, Research & Practice.* "Intergroup Conflict" suggests that a great deal of interpersonal conflict in organizations may be analyzed from an intergroup perspective, because "group identities are an integral part of the individual personality. Therefore, much of what is commonly referred to as 'personality clash' may actually be a manifestation of group identity-related conflict" (p. 138). Five sources of intergroup conflict are particularly important in the context of cultural diversity in organizations: competing goals, competition for resources, cultural differences, power discrepancies, and assimilation versus preservation of microcultural identity. Cox concludes with a listing of approaches for managing intergroup conflict in organizations and an assessment of the sources of diversity-related conflict that each of the approaches is most effective in addressing.

The organizational behavior perspective is the most optimistic of all perspectives or theories of organization. Building from Douglas McGregor's Theory X and Theory Y assumptions, organizational behavior has assumed that under the right circumstances, people and organizations will grow and prosper together. The ultimate worth of people is an overarching value of the human relations movement— a worthy end in and of itself—not simply a means or process for achieving a higher-order organizational end. Individuals and organizations are not necessarily antagonists. Managers can learn to unleash previously stifled energies and creativities. The beliefs, values, and tenets of organizational behavior are noble, uplifting, and exciting. They hold a promise for humankind, especially those who will spend their lifetime working in organizations.

As one would expect of a very optimistic and humanistic set of assumptions and values, they (and the strategies of organizational behavior) became strongly normative (prescriptive). For many organizational behavior practitioners of the 1960s, 1970s, and 1980s the perspective's assumptions and methods became a cause. Hopefully, through the choice of articles and the introductions to each chapter, this volume communicates these optimistic tenets and values, and articulates the logical and emotional reasons why the organizational behavior perspective developed into a virtual movement. This is the true essence of *organizational behavior*.

REFERENCES

Alderfer, J. S. (1969). An empirical test of a new theory of human needs. *Organizational Behavior and Human Performance, 4,* 142–175.

Argyris, C. (1962). *Interpersonal competence and organizational effectiveness.* Homewood, IL: The Dorsey Pres and Richard D. Irwin.

Argyris, C. (1970). *Intervention theory and method.* Reading, MA: Addison-Wesley.

Argyris, C. (1990). *Overcoming organizational defenses: Facilitating organizational learning.* Boston: Allyn & Bacon.

Bell, N E., & Staw, B. M. (1989). People as sculptors versus sculpture: The roles of personality and personal control in organizations. In M. B. Arthur, D. T. Hall, & B. S. Lawrence (Eds.), *Handbook of career theory* (pp. 232–251). Cambridge, UK: Cambridge University Press.

Bennis, W. G. (1976). *The unconscious conspiracy: Why leaders can't lead.* New York: AMACOM.

Bolman, L. G., & Deal, T. E. (1991). *Reframing organizations.* San Francisco: Jossey-Bass.

Cohen, A. R., Fink, S. L., Gadon, H., & Willits, R. D. (1988). *Effective behavior in organizations (4th ed.).* Homewood, IL: Irwin.

Cox, T. H., Jr. (1993). *Cultural diversity in organizations: Theory, research & practice.* San Francisco: Berrett-Koehler.

Follett, M. P. (1926). The giving of orders. In H. C. Metcalf (Ed.), *Scientific foundations of business administration.* Baltimore, MD: Williams & Wilkins.

Haire, M. (1954). Industrial social psychology. In G. Lindzey (Ed.), *Handbook of social psychology, Volume II: Special fields and applications* (pp. 1104–1123). Reading, MA: Addison-Wesley.

Hersey, P., & Blanchard, K. H. (1982). *Management of organizational behavior: Utilizing human resources* (4th ed.). Englewood Cliffs, NJ: Prentice-Hall.

Janis, I. L. (November 1971). Groupthink. *Psychology Today,* 44–76.

Lewin, K. (1947). Frontiers in group dynamics: Concept, method and reality in social science: Social equilibrium and social change. *Human Relations, 1,* 5–41.

Lewin, K. (1948). *Resolving social conflicts.* New York: Harper.

Maslow, A. H. (1943). A theory of human motivation. *Psychological Review, 50.*

Mayo, G. E. (1933). *The human problems of an industrial civilization.* Boston, MA: Harvard Business School, Division of Research.

McGregor, D. M. (1957a, April). The human side of enterprise. Address to the Fifth Anniversary Convocation of the School of Industrial Management, Massachusetts Institute of Technology. In *Adventure in thought and action.* Cambridge, MA: M.I.T. School of Industrial Management, 1957. Reprinted in W. G. Bennis, E. H. Schein, & C. McGregor (Eds.), (1966). *Leadership and motivation: Essays of Douglas McGregor* (pp. 3–20). Cambridge, MA: The M.I.T. Press.

McGregor, D. M. (November 1957b). The human side of enterprise. *Management Review,* 22–28, 88–92.

McGregor, D. M. (1960). *The human side of enterprise.* New York: McGraw-Hill.

Münsterberg, H. (1913). *Psychology and industrial efficiency.* Boston: Houghton Mifflin Company.

Münsterberg, M. (1922). *Hugo Münsterberg, His life and work.* New York: Appleton.

Ott, J. S. (Ed.). (1996). *Classic readings in organizational behavior.* (2d. ed.). Belmont, CA: Wadsworth.

Porter, L. W., Lawler, E. E. III, & Hackman, J. R. (1975). Social influences on work effectiveness. In L. W. Porter, E. E. Lawler III, & J. R. Hackman, *Behavior in organizations* (pp. 403–422). New York: McGraw-Hill.

Roethlisberger, F. J., & Dixon, W. J. (1939). *Management and the worker.* Cambridge, MA: Harvard University Press.

Wren, D. A. (1972). *The evolution of management thought.* New York: Ronald Press.

13
The Giving of Orders
Mary Parker Follett

To some men the matter of giving orders seems a very simple affair; they expect to issue their own orders and have them obeyed without question. Yet, on the other hand, the shrewd common sense of many a business executive has shown him that the issuing of orders is surrounded by many difficulties; that to demand an unquestioning obedience to orders not approved, not perhaps even understood, is bad business policy. Moreover, psychology, as well as our own observation, shows us not only that you cannot get people to do things most satisfactorily by ordering them or exhorting them; but also that even reasoning with them, even convincing them intellectually, may not be enough. Even the "consent of the governed" will not do all the work it is supposed to do, an important consideration for those who are advocating employee representation. For all our past life, our early training, our later experience, all our emotions, beliefs, prejudices, every desire that we have, have formed certain habits of mind that the psychologists call habit-patterns, action-patterns, motor-sets.

Therefore it will do little good merely to get intellectual agreement; unless you change the habit-patterns of people, you have not really changed your people. . . .

If we analyse this matter a little further we shall see that we have to do three things. I am now going to use psychological language: (1) build up certain atti-tudes; (2) provide for the release of these attitudes; (3) augment the released response as it is being carried out. What does this mean in the language of business? A psychologist has given us the example of the salesman. The salesman first creates in you the attitude that you want his article; then, at just the "psychological" moment, he produces his contract blank which you may sign and thus release that attitude; then if, as you're preparing to sign, some one comes in and tells you how pleased he has been with his purchase of this article, that augments the response which is being released.

If we apply this to the subject of orders and obedience, we see that people can obey an order only if previous habit patterns are appealed to or new ones created. . . .

This is an important consideration for us, for from one point of view business success depends largely on this—namely, whether our business is so organized and administered that it tends to form certain habits, certain mental attitudes. It has been hard for many old-fashioned employers to understand that *orders will not take the place of training.* I want to italicize that. Many a time an employer has been angry because, as he expressed it, a workman "wouldn't" do so and so, when the truth of the matter was that the workman couldn't, actually couldn't, do as ordered because he could not go contrary to life-long habits. This

Source: Henry C. Metcalf, ed., *Scientific Foundations of Business Administration* (Baltimore: Williams & Wilkins Co., 1926). Copyright © 1926 The Williams & Wilkins Co. Footnotes omitted.

whole subject might be taken up under the heading of education, for there we could give many instances of the attempt to make arbitrary authority take the place of training. In history, the aftermath of all revolutions shows us the results of the lack of training.

. . . A boy may respond differently to the same suggestion when made by his teacher and when made by his schoolmate. Moreover, he may respond differently to the same suggestion made by the teacher in the schoolroom and made by the teacher when they are taking a walk together. Applying this to the giving of orders, we see that the place in which orders are given, the circumstances under which they are given, may make all the difference in the world as to the response which we get. Hand them down a long way from President or Works Manager and the effect is weakened. One might say that the strength of favourable response to an order is in inverse ratio to the distance the order travels. Production efficiency is always in danger of being affected whenever the long-distance order is substituted for the face-to-face suggestion. There is, however, another reason for that which I shall consider in a moment.

. . . I should say that the giving of orders and the receiving of orders ought to be a matter of integration through circular behaviour, and that we should seek methods to bring this about.

Psychology has another important contribution to make on this subject of issuing orders or giving directions: before the integration can be made between order-giver and order-receiver, there is often an integration to be made within one or both of the individuals concerned. There are often two dissociated paths in the individual; if you are clever enough to recognize these, you can sometimes forestall a Freudian conflict, make the integration appear before there is an acute stage. . . .

Business administration has often to consider how to deal with the dissociated paths in individuals or groups, but the methods of doing this successfully have been developed much further in some departments than in others. We have as yet hardly recognized this as part of the technique of dealing with employees, yet the clever salesman knows that it is the chief part of his job. The prospective buyer wants the article and does not want it. The able salesman does not suppress the arguments in the mind of the purchaser against buying, for then the purchaser might be sorry afterwards for his purchase, and that would not be good salesmanship. Unless he can unite, integrate, in the purchaser's mind, the reasons for buying and the reasons for not buying, his future sales will be imperilled, he will not be the highest grade salesman.

Please note that this goes beyond what the psychologist whom I quoted at the beginning of this section told us. He said, "The salesman must create in you the attitude that you want his article." Yes, but only if he creates this attitude by integration, not by suppression.

Apply all this to orders. An order often leaves the individual to whom it is given with two dissociated paths; an order should seek to unite, to integrate, dissociated paths. Court decisions often settle arbitrarily which of two ways is to be followed without showing a possible integration of the two, that is, the individual is often left with an internal conflict on his hands. This is what both courts and business administration should try to prevent, the internal conflicts of individuals or groups.

. . . Probably more industrial trouble has been caused by the manner in which orders are given than in any other way. In the *Report on Strikes and Lockout*, a British Government publication, the cause of a number of strikes is given as "alleged harassing conduct of the foreman," "alleged tyrannical conduct of an under-foreman," "alleged overbearing conduct of officials." The explicit statement, however, of the tyranny of superior officers as the direct cause of strikes is I should say, unusual, yet resentment smoulders and breaks out in other issues. And the demand for better treatment is often explicit enough. We find it made by the metal and wood-working trades in an aircraft factory, who declared that any treatment of men without regard to their feelings of self-respect would be answered by a stoppage of work. We find it put in certain agreements with employers the "the men must be treated with proper respect, and threats and abusive language must not be used."

What happens to man, *in* a man, when an order is given in a disagreeable manner by foreman, head of department, his immediate superior in store, bank or factory? The man addressed feels that his self-respect is attacked, that one of his most inner sanctuaries is invaded. He loses his temper or becomes sullen or is on the defensive; he begins thinking of his "rights"—a fatal attitude for any of us. In the language we have been using, the wrong behaviour pattern is aroused, the wrong motor-set; that is, he is now "set" to act in a way which is not going to benefit the enterprise in which he is engaged.

There is a more subtle psychological point here, too; the more you are "bossed" the more your activity of thought will take place within the bossing-pattern, and your part in that pattern seems usually to be opposition to the bossing.

This complaint of the abusive language and the tyrannical treatment of the one just above the worker is an old story to us all, but there is an opposite extreme which is far too little considered. The immediate superior officer is often so close to the worker that he does not exercise the proper duties of his position. Far from taking on himself an aggressive authority, he has often evaded one of the chief problems of his job: how to do what is implied in the fact that he has been put in a position over others. . . .

Now what is our problem here? How can we avoid the two extremes: too great bossism in giving orders, and practically no orders given? I am going to ask how *you* are avoiding these extremes. My solution is to depersonalize the giving of orders, to unite all concerned in a study of the situation, to discover the law of the situation and obey that. Until we do this I do not think we shall have the most successful business administration. This is what does take place, what has to take place, when there is a question between two men in positions of equal authority. The head of the sales departments does not give orders to the head of the production department, or vice versa. Each studies the market and the final decision is made as the market demands. This is, ideally, what should take place between foremen and the rank and file, between any head and his subordinates. One *person* should not give orders to another *person*, but both should agree to take their orders from the situation. If orders are simply part of the situation, the question of someone giving and someone receiving does not come up. Both accept the orders given by the situation. Employers accept the orders given by the situation; employees accept the orders given by the situation. This gives, does it not, a slightly different aspect to the whole of business administration through the entire plant?

We have here, I think, one of the largest contributions of scientific management: it tends to depersonalize orders. From one point of view, one might call the essence of scientific management the attempt to find the law of the situation. With scientific management the managers are as much under orders as the workers, for both obey the law of the situation. Our job is not how to get people to obey orders, but how to devise methods by which we can best *discover* the order integral to a particular situation. When that is found, the employee can issue it to the employer, as well as employer to employee. This often happens easily and naturally. My cook or my stenographer point out the law of the situation, and I, if I recognize it as such, accept it, even although it may reverse some "order" I have given.

If those in supervisory positions should depersonalize orders, then there would be no overbearing authority on the one hand, nor on the other that dangerous *laissez-aller* which comes from the fear of exercising authority. Of course we should exercise authority, but always the authority of the situation. I do not say that we have found the way to a frictionless existence, far from it, but we now understand the place which we mean to give to friction. We intend to set it to work for us as the engineer does when he puts the belt over the pulley. There will be just as much, probably more, room for disagreement in the method I am advocating. The situation will often be seen differently, often be interpreted differently. But we shall know what to do with it, we shall have found a method of dealing with it.

I call it depersonalizing because there is not time to go any further into the matter. I think it really is a matter of *repersonalizing*. We, persons, have relations with each other, but we should find them in and through the whole situation. We cannot have any sound relations with each other as long as we take them out of that setting which gives them their meaning and value. This divorcing of persons and the situation does a great deal of harm. I have just said that

scientific management depersonalizes; the deeper philosophy of scientific management shows us personal relations within the whole setting of that thing of which they are a part. . . .

I said above that we should substitute for the long-distance order the face-to-face suggestion. I think we can now see a more cogent reason for this than the one then given. It is not the face-to-face suggestion that we want so much as the joint study of the problem, and such joint study can be made best by the employee and his immediate superior or employee and special expert on that question.

I began this talk by emphasizing the advisability of preparing in advance the attitude necessary for the carrying out of orders, and in the previous paper we considered preparing the attitude for integration; but we have now, in our consideration of the joint study of situations, in our emphasis on obeying the law of the situation, perhaps got a little beyond that, or rather we have now to consider in what sense we wish to take the psychologist's doctrine of prepared-in-advance attitudes. . . .

We should not try to create the attitude we *want*, although that is the usual phrase, but the attitude required for co-operative study and decision. This holds good even for the salesman. We said above that when the salesman is told that he should create in the prospective buyer the attitude that he wants the article, he ought also to be told that he should do this by integration rather than by suppression. We have now a hint of *how* he is to attain this integration.

I have spoken of the importance of changing some of the language of business personnel relations. We considered whether the words "grievances," complaints," or Ford's "trouble specialists" did not arouse the wrong behaviour-patterns. I think "order" certainly does.

If that word is not to mean any longer external authority, arbitrary authority, but the law of the situation, then we need a new word for it. It is often the order that people resent as much as the thing ordered. People do not like to be ordered even to take a holiday. I have often seen instances of this. The wish to govern one's own life is, of course, one of the most fundamental feelings in every human being. To call this "the instinct of self-assertion," "the instinct of initiative," does not express it wholly. I think it is told in the life of some famous American that when he was a boy and his mother said, "Go get a pail of water," he always replied, "I won't," before taking up the pail and fetching the water. This is significant; he resented the command, the command of a person; but he went and got the water, not, I believe, because he had to, but because he recognized the demand of the situation. *That*, he knew he had to obey; *that*, he was willing to obey. And this kind of obedience is not opposed to the wish to govern one's self, but each is involved in the other; both are part of the same fundamental urge at the root of one's being. We have here something far more profound than "the egoistic impulse" or "the instinct of self-assertion." We have the very essence of the human being.

This subject of orders has led us into the heart of the whole question of authority and consent. When we conceive of authority and consent as parts of an inclusive situation, does that not throw a flood of light on this question? The point of view here presented gets rid of several dilemmas which have seemed to puzzle people in dealing with consent. The feeling of being "under" someone, of "subordination," of "servility," of being "at the will of another," comes out again and again in the shop stewards movement and in the testimony before the Coal Commission. One man said before the Coal Commission, "It is all right to work with anyone; what is disagreeable is to feel too distinctly that you are working *under* anyone." *With* is a pretty good preposition, not because it connotes democracy, but because it connotes functional unity, a much more profound conception than that of democracy as usually held. The study of the situation involves the *with* preposition. Then Sadie is not left alone by the head of the cloak department, nor does she have to obey her. The head of the department says, "Let's see how such cases had better be handled, then we'll abide by that." Sadie is not under the head of the department, but both are *under* the situation.

Twice I have had a servant applying for a place ask me if she would be treated as a menial. When the first woman asked me that, I had no idea what she meant, I thought perhaps she did not want to do the roughest work, but later I came to the conclusion that to be treated as a menial meant to be obliged to be under someone, to follow orders without using one's own judgment. If we believe that what heightens self-respect increases efficiency, we shall be on our guard here.

Very closely connected with this is the matter of pride in one's work. If an order goes against what the craftsman or the clerk thinks is the way of doing his work which will bring the best results, he is justified in not wishing to obey that order. Could not that difficulty be met by a joint study of the situation? It is said that it is characteristic of the British workman to feel, "I know my job and won't be told how." The peculiarities of the British workman might be met by a joint study of the situation, it being understood that he probably has more to contribute to that study than anyone else. . . .

There is another dilemma which has to be met by everyone who is in what is called a position of authority: how can you expect people merely to obey orders and at the same time to take that degree of responsibility which they should take? Indeed, in my experience, the people who enjoy following orders blindly, without any thought on their own part, are those who like thus to get rid of responsibility. But the taking of responsibility, each according to his capacity, each according to his function in the whole . . . , this taking of responsibility is usually the most vital matter in the life of every human being, just as the allotting of responsibility is the most important part of business administration.

A young trade unionist said to me, "how much dignity can I have as a mere employee?" He can have all the dignity in the world if he is allowed to make his fullest contribution to the plant *and to assume definitely the responsibility therefor.*

I think one of the gravest problems before us is how to make the reconciliation between receiving orders and taking responsibility. And I think the reconciliation can be made through our conception of the law of the situation. . . .

We have considered the subject of symbols. It is often very apparent that an order is a symbol. The referee in the game stands watch in hand and says, "Go." It is an order, but order only as symbol. I may say to an employee, "Do so and so," but I should say it only because we have both agreed, openly or tacitly, that that which I am ordering done is the best thing to be done. The order is then a symbol. And if it is a philosophical and psychological truth that we owe obedience only to a functional unity to which we are contributing, we should remember that a more accurate way of stating that would be to say that our obligation is to a unifying, to a process.

This brings us now to one of our most serious problems in this matter of orders.

It is important, but we can touch on it only briefly; it is what we spoke of . . . as the evolving situation. I am trying to show here that the order must be integral to the situation and must be recognized as such. But we saw that the situation was always developing. If the situation is never stationary, then the order should never be stationary, so to speak; how to prevent it from being so is our problem. The situation is changing while orders are being carried out. How is the order to keep up with the situation? External orders never can, only those drawn fresh from the situation.

Moreover, if taking a *responsible* attitude toward experience involves recognizing the evolving situation, a *conscious* attitude toward experience means that we note the change which the developing situation makes in ourselves; the situation does not change without changing us.

. . . When I asked a very intelligent girl what she thought would be the result of profit sharing and employee representation in the factory where she worked, she replied joyfully, "We shan't need foremen any more." While her entire ignoring of the fact that the foreman has other duties than keeping workers on their jobs was amusing, one wants to go beyond one's amusement and find out what this objection to being watched really means. . . .

I have seen similar instances cited. Many workmen feel that being watched is unbearable. What can we do about it? How can we get proper supervision without this watching which a worker resents? Supervision is necessary; supervision is resented—how are we going to make the integration there? Some say, "Let the workers elect the supervisors." I do not believe in that.

There are three other points closely connected with the subject of this paper which I should like merely to point out.

First, when and how do you point out mistakes, misconduct? One principle can surely guide us here: don't blame for the sake of blaming, make what you have to say accomplish something; say it in that form, at that time, under those circumstances, which will make it a real education to your subordinate. Secondly, since it is recognized that the one who gives the orders is not as a rule a very popular person, the management sometimes tries to offset this by allowing the person who has this onus upon him to give any pleasant news to the workers, to have the credit of any innovation which the workers very much desire. One manager told me that he always tried to do this. I suppose that this is good behaviouristic psychology, and yet I am not sure that it is a method I wholly like. It is quite different, however, in the case of a mistaken order having been given; then I think the one who made the mistake should certainly be the one to rectify it, not as a matter of strategy, but because it is better for him too. It is better for all of us not only to acknowledge our mistakes, but to do something about them. If a foreman discharges someone and it is decided to reinstate the man, it is obviously not only good tactics but a square deal to the foreman to allow him to do the reinstating.

There is, of course, a great deal more to this matter of giving orders than we have been able to touch on; far from exhausting the subject, I feel that I have only given hints. I have been told that the artillery men suffered more mentally in the war than others, and the reason assigned for this was that their work was directed from a distance. The combination of numbers by which they focused their fire was telephoned to them. The result was also at a distance. Their activity was not closely enough connected with the actual situation at either end.

14
A Theory of Human Motivation
Abraham H. Maslow

I. INTRODUCTION

In a previous paper [13] various propositions were presented which would have to be included in any theory of human motivation that could lay claim to being definitive. These conclusions may be briefly summarized as follows:

1. The integrated wholeness of the organism must be one of the foundation stones of motivation theory.
2. The hunger drive (or any other physiological drive) was rejected as a centering point or model for a definitive theory of motivation. Any drive that is somatically based and localizable was shown to be atypical rather than typical in human motivation.
3. Such a theory should stress and center itself upon ultimate or basic goals rather than partial or superficial ones, upon ends rather than means to these ends. Such a stress would imply a more central place for unconscious than for conscious motivations.
4. There are usually available various cultural paths to the same goal. Therefore conscious, specific, local-cultural desires are not as fundamental in motivation theory as the more basic, unconscious goals.
5. Any motivated behavior, either preparatory or consummatory, must be understood to be a channel through which many basic needs may be simultaneously expressed or satisfied. Typically an act has *more* than one motivation.
6. Practically all organismic states are to be understood as motivated and as motivating.
7. Human needs arrange themselves in hierarchies of prepotency. That is to say, the appearance of one need usually rests on the prior satisfaction of another, more pre-potent need. Man is a perpetually wanting animal. Also no need or drive can be treated as if it were isolated or discrete; every drive is related to the state of satisfaction or dissatisfaction of other drives.
8. *Lists* of drives will get us nowhere for various theoretical and practical reasons. Furthermore any classification of motivations must deal with the problem of levels of specificity or generalization of the motives to be classified.
9. Classifications of motivations must be based upon goals rather than upon instigating drives or motivated behavior.
10. Motivation theory should be human-centered rather than animal-centered.
11. The situation or the field in which the organism reacts must be taken into account but the field alone can rarely serve as an exclusive explanation for behavior. Furthermore the field itself must be interpreted in terms of the organism. Field theory cannot be a substitute for motivation theory.
12. Not only the integration of the organism must be taken into account, but also the possibility of isolated, specific, partial or segmental reactions.

It has since become necessary to add to these another affirmation.

13. Motivation theory is not synonymous with behavior theory. The motivations are only one class of determi-

Source: From *Psychological Review* 50 (1943): 370–396.

nants of behavior. While behavior is almost always motivated, it is also almost always biologically, culturally and situationally determined as well.

The present paper is an attempt to formulate a positive theory of motivation which will satisfy these theoretical demands and at the same time conform to the known facts, clinical and observational as well as experimental. It derives most directly, however, from clinical experience. This theory is, I think, in the functionalist tradition of James and Dewey, and is fused with the holism of Wertheimer [19], Goldstein [6], and Gestalt Psychology, and with the dynamicism of Freud [4] and Adler [1]. This fusion or synthesis may arbitrarily be called a 'general-dynamic' theory.

It is far easier to perceive and to criticize the aspects in motivation theory than to remedy them. Mostly this is because of the very serious lack of sound data in this area. I conceive this lack of sound facts to be due primarily to the absence of a valid theory of motivation. The present theory then must be considered to be a suggested program or framework for future research and must stand or fall, not so much on facts available or evidence presented, as upon researches yet to be done, researches suggested perhaps, by the questions raised in this paper.

II. THE BASIC NEEDS

The 'Physiological' Needs. The needs that are usually taken as the starting point for motivation theory are the so-called physiological drives. Two recent lines of research make it necessary to revise our customary notions about these needs, first, the development of the concept of homeostasis, and second, the finding that appetites (preferential choices among foods) are a fairly effi-cient indication of actual needs or lacks in the body.

Homeostasis refers to the body's automatic efforts to maintain a constant, normal state of the blood stream. Cannon [2] has described this process for (1) the water content of the blood, (2) salt content, (3) sugar content, (4) protein content, (5) fat content, (6) calcium content, (7) oxygen content, (8) constant hydrogen-ion level (acid-base balance) and (9) constant temperature of the blood. Obviously this list can be extended to include other minerals, the hormones, vitamins, etc.

Young in a recent article [21] has summarized the work on appetite in its relation to body needs. If the body lacks some chemical, the individual will tend to develop a specific appetite or partial hunger for that food element. . . .

It should be pointed out again that any of the physiological needs and the consummatory behavior involved with them serve as channels for all sorts of other needs as well. That is to say, the person who thinks he is hungry may actually be seeking more for comfort, or dependence, than for vitamins or proteins. Conversely, it is possible to satisfy the hunger need in part by other activities such as drinking water or smoking cigarettes. In other words, relatively isolable as these physiological needs are, they are not completely so.

Undoubtedly these physiological needs are the most prepotent of all needs. What this means specifically is, that in the human being who is missing everything in life in an extreme fashion, it is most likely that the major motivation would be the physiological needs rather than any others. A person who is lacking food, safety, love, and esteem would most probably hunger for food more strongly than for anything else.

If all the needs are unsatisfied, and the organism is then dominated by the physiological needs, all other needs may become simply nonexistent or be pushed into the background. . . . For the man who is extremely and dangerously hungry, no other interests exist but food. He dreams food, he remembers food, he thinks about food, he emotes only about food, he perceives only food and he wants only food. The more subtle determinants that ordinarily fuse with the physiological drives in organizing even feeding, drinking or sexual behavior, may not be so completely overwhelmed as to allow us to speak at this time (but *only* at this time) of pure hunger drive and behavior, with the one unqualified aim of relief.

Another peculiar characteristic of the human organism when it is dominated by a certain need is that the whole philosophy of the future tends also to change. For our chronically and extremely hungry man, Utopia can be defined very simply as a place where there is plenty of food. He tends to think that, if only he is guaranteed food for the rest of his life, he will be perfectly happy and will never want anything more. Life itself tends to be defined in terms of eating. Anything else will be defined as unimportant. Freedom, love, community feeling, respect, philosophy, may all be waved aside as fripperies which are useless since they fail to fill the stomach. Such a man may fairly be said to live by bread alone.

It cannot possibly be denied that such things are true but their *generality* can be denied. Emergency conditions are, almost by definition, rare in the normally functioning peaceful society. . . .

At once other (and 'higher') needs emerge and these, rather than physiological hungers, dominate the organism. And when these in turn are satisfied, again new (and still 'higher') needs emerge and so on. This is what we mean by saying that the basic human needs are organized into a hierarchy of relative prepotency.

One main implication of this phrasing is that gratification becomes as important a concept as deprivation in motivation theory, for it releases the organism from the domination of a relatively more physiological need, permitting thereby the emergence of other more social goals. The physiological needs, along with their partial goals, when chronically gratified cease to exist as active determinants or organizers of behavior. They now exist only in a potential fashion in the sense that they may emerge again to dominate the organism if they are thwarted. But a want that is satisfied is no longer a want. The organism is dominated and its behavior organized only by unsatisfied needs. If hunger is satisfied, it becomes unimportant in the current dynamics of the individual. . . .

The Safety Needs. If the physiological needs are relatively well gratified, there then emerges a new set of needs, which we may categorize roughly as the safety needs. All that has been said of the physiological needs is equally true, although in lesser degree, of these desires. The organism may equally well be wholly dominated by them. They may serve as the almost exclusive organizers of behavior, recruiting all the capacities of the organism in their service, and we may then fairly describe the whole organism as a safety-seeking mechanism. Again we may say of the receptors, the effectors, of the intellect and the other capacities that they are primarily safety-seeking tools. Again, as in the hungry man, we find that the dominating goal is a strong determinant not only of his current world-outlook and philosophy but also of his philosophy of the future. Practically everything looks less important than safety, (even sometimes the physiological needs which being satisfied, are now underestimated). A man, in this state, if it is extreme enough and chronic enough, may be characterized as living almost for safety alone.

Although in this paper we are interested primarily in the needs of the adult, we can approach an understanding of his safety needs perhaps more efficiently by observation of infants and children, in whom these needs are much more simple and obvious. One reason for the clearer appearance of the threat or danger reaction in infants, is that they do not inhibit this reaction at all, whereas adults in our society have been taught to inhibit it at all costs. Thus even when adults do feel their safety threatened we may not be able to see this on the surface. Infants will react in a total fashion and as if they were endangered, if they are disturbed or dropped suddenly, startled by loud noises, flashing light, or other unusual sensory stimulation, by rough handling, by general loss of support in the mother's arms, or by inadequate support.[1]

In infants we can also see a much more direct reaction to bodily illnesses of various kinds. Sometimes these illnesses seem to be immediately and *per se* threatening and seem to make the child feel unsafe. For instance, vomiting, colic or other sharp pains seem to make the child look at the whole world in a different way. At such a moment of pain, it may be postulated that, for the child, the appearance of the whole world suddenly changes from sunniness to darkness, so to speak, and becomes a place in which anything at all might happen, in which previously stable things have suddenly become unstable. Thus a child who because of some bad food is taken ill may, for a day or two, develop fear, nightmares, and a need for protection and reassurance never seen in him before his illness.

Another indication of the child's need for safety is his preference for some kind of undisrupted routine or rhythm. He seems to want a predictable, orderly world. For instance, injustice, unfairness, or inconsistency in the parents seems to make a child feel anxious and unsafe. This attitude may be not so much because of the injustice *per se* or any particular pains involved, but rather because this treatment threatens to make the world look unreliable, or unsafe, or unpredictable. Young children seem to thrive better under a system which has at least a skeletal outline of rigidity, in which there is a schedule of a kind, some sort of routine, something that can be counted upon, not only for the present but also far into the future. Perhaps one could express this more accurately by saying that the child needs an organized world rather than an unorganized or unstructured one. . . .

From these and similar observations, we may generalize and say that the average child in our society generally prefers a safe, orderly, predictable, organized world, which he can count on, and in which unexpected, unmanageable or other dangerous things do not happen, and in which, in any case, he has all-powerful parents who protect and shield him from harm.

That these reactions may so easily be observed in children is in a way a proof of the fact that children in our society, feel too unsafe (or, in a word, are badly brought up). Children who are reared in an unthreatening, loving family do *not* ordinarily react as we have described above [17]. In such children the danger reactions are apt to come mostly to objects or situations that adults too would consider dangerous.[2]

The healthy, normal, fortunate adult in our culture is largely satisfied in his safety needs. The peaceful, smoothly running, 'good' society ordinarily makes its members feel safe enough from wild animals, extremes of temperature, criminals, assault and murder, tyranny, etc.

Therefore, in a very real sense, he no longer has any safety needs as active motivators. Just as a sated man no longer feels hungry, a safe man no longer feels endangered. If we wish to see these needs directly and clearly we must turn to neurotic or near-neurotic individuals, and to the economic and social underdogs. In between these extremes, we can perceive the expressions of safety needs only in such phenomena as, for instance, the common preference for a job with tenure and protection, the desire for a savings account, and for insurance of various kinds (medical, dental, unemployment, disability, old age).

Other broader aspects of the attempt to seek safety and stability in the world are seen in the very common preference for familiar rather than unfamiliar things, or for the known rather than the unknown. The tendency to have some religion or world-philosophy that organizes the universe and the men in it into some sort of satisfactorily coherent, meaningful whole is also in part motivated by safety-seeking. Here too we may list science and philosophy in general as partially motivated by the safety needs (we shall see later that there are also other motivations to scientific, philosophical or religious endeavor).

Otherwise the need for safety is seen as an active and dominant mobilizer of the organism's resources only in emergencies, *e.g.*, war, disease, natural catastrophes, crime waves, societal disorganization, neurosis, brain injury, chronically bad situation. . . .

The neurosis in which the search for safety takes its clearest form is in the compulsive-obsessive neurosis. Compulsive-obsessives try frantically to order and stabilize the world so that no unmanageable, unexpected or unfamiliar dangers will ever appear [14]. They hedge themselves about with all sorts of ceremonials, rules and formulas so that every possible contingency may be provided for and so that no new contingencies may appear. They are much like the brain injured cases, described by Goldstein [6], who manage to maintain their equilibrium by avoiding everything unfamiliar and strange and by ordering their restricted world in such a neat, disciplined, orderly fashion that everything in the world can be counted upon. . . .

The Love Needs. If both the physiological and the safety needs are fairly well gratified, then there will emerge the love and affection and belongingness needs, and the whole cycle already described will repeat itself with this new center. Now the person will feel keenly, as never before, the absence of friends, or a sweetheart, or a wife, or children. He will hunger for affectionate relations with people in general, namely, for a place in his group, and he will strive with great intensity to achieve this goal. He will want to attain such a place more than anything else in the world and may even forget that once, when he was hungry, he sneered at love. . . .

One thing that must be stressed at this point is that love is not synonymous with sex. Sex may be studied as a purely physiological need. Ordinarily sexual behavior is multi-determined, that is to say, determined not only by sexual but also by other needs chief among which are the love and affection needs. Also not to be overlooked is the fact that the love needs involve both giving *and* receiving love.[3]

The Esteem Needs. All people in our society (with a few pathological exceptions) have a need or desire for a stable, firmly based, (usually) high evaluation of themselves, for self-respect, or self-esteem, and for the esteem of others. By firmly based self-esteem, we mean that which is soundly based upon real capacity, achievement and respect from others. These needs may be classified into two subsidiary sets. These are, first, the desire for strength, for achievement, for adequacy, for confidence in the face of the world, and for independence and freedom.[4] Secondly, we have what we may call the desire for reputation or prestige (defining it as respect or esteem from other people), recognition, attention, importance or appreciation.[5] These needs have been relatively stressed by Alfred Adler and his followers, and have been relatively neglected by Freud and the psychoanalysts. More and more today however there is appearing widespread appreciation of their central importance.

Satisfaction of the self-esteem need leads to feelings of self-confidence, worth, strength, capability and adequacy of being useful and necessary in the world. But thwarting of these needs produces feelings of inferiority, of weakness and of helplessness. These feelings in turn give rise to either basic discouragement or else compensatory or neurotic trends. An appreciation of the necessity of basic self-confidence and an understanding of how helpless people are without it, can be easily gained from a study of severe traumatic neurosis [8].[6]

The Need for Self-Actualization. Even if all these needs are satisfied, we may still often (if not always) expect that a new discontent and restlessness will soon develop, unless the individual is doing what he is fitted for. A musician must make music, an artist must paint, a poet must write, if he is to be ultimately happy. What a man can be, he must be. This need we may call self-actualization.

This term, first coined by Kurt Goldstein, is being used in this paper in a much more specific and limited fashion. It refers to the desire for self-fulfillment, namely, to the tendency for him to become actualized in what he is potentially. This tendency might be phrased as the desire to become more and more what one is, to become everything that one is capable of becoming.

The specific form that these needs will take will of course vary greatly from person to person. In one individual it may take the form of the desire to be an ideal mother, in another it may be expressed athletically, and in still another it may be expressed in painting pictures or in inventions. It is not necessarily a creative urge although in people who have any capacities for creation it will take this form.

The clear emergence of these needs rests upon prior satisfaction of the physiological, safety, love and esteem needs. We shall call people who are satisfied in these needs, basically satisfied people, and it is from these that we may expect the fullest (and healthiest) creativeness.[7] Since, in our society, basically satisfied people are the exception, we do not know much about self-actualization, either experimentally or clinically. It remains a challenging problem for research.

The Preconditions for the Basic Need Satisfactions. There are certain conditions which are immediate prerequisites for the basic need satisfactions. Danger to these is reacted to almost as if it were a direct danger to the basic needs themselves. Such conditions as freedom to speak, freedom to do what one wishes so long as no harm is done to others, freedom to express one's self, freedom to investigate and seek for information, freedom to defend one's self, justice, fairness, honesty, orderliness in the group are examples of such preconditions for basic need satisfactions. Thwarting in these freedoms will be reacted to with a threat or emergency response. These conditions are not ends in themselves but they are *almost* so since they are so closely related to the basic needs, which are apparently the only ends in themselves. These conditions are defended because without them the basic satisfactions are quite impossible, or at least, very severely endangered.

If we remember that the cognitive capacities (perceptual, intellectual, learning) are a set of adjustive tools, which have, among other functions, that of satisfaction of our basic needs, then it is clear that any danger to them, any deprivation or blocking of their free use, must also be indirectly threatening to the basic needs themselves. Such a statement is a partial solution of the general problems of curiosity, the search for knowledge, truth and wisdom, and the ever-persistent urge to solve the cosmic mysteries.

We must therefore introduce another hypothesis and speak of degrees of closeness to the basic needs, for we have already pointed out that *any* conscious desires (partial goals) are more or less important as they are more or less close to the basic needs. The same statement may be made for various behavior acts. An act is psychologically important if it contributes directly to satisfaction of basic needs. The less directly it so contributes, or the weaker this contribution is, the less important this act must be conceived to be from the point of view of dynamic psychology. A similar statement may be made for the various defense or coping mechanisms. Some are very directly related to the protection or attainment of the basic needs, other are only weakly and distantly related. Indeed if we wished, we could speak of more basic and less basic defense mechanisms, and then affirm that danger to the more basic defenses is more threatening than danger to less basic defenses (always remembering that this is so only because of their relationship to the basic needs). . . .

III. FURTHER CHARACTERISTICS OF THE BASIC NEEDS

The Degree of Fixity of the Hierarchy of Basic Needs. We have spoken so far as if this hierarchy were a fixed order but actually it is not nearly as rigid as we may have implied. It is true that most of the people with whom we have worked have seemed to have these basic needs in about the order that has been indicated. However, there have been a number of exceptions.

(1) There are some people in whom, for instance, self-esteem seems to be more important than love. This most common reversal in the hierarchy is usually due to the development of the notion that the person who is most likely to be loved is a strong or powerful person, one who inspires respect or fear, and who is self confident or aggressive. Therefore such people who lack love and seek it, may try hard to put on a front of aggressive, confident behavior. But essentially they seek high self-esteem and its behavior expressions more as a means-to-an-end than for its own sake; they seek self-assertion for the sake of love rather than for self-esteem itself.

(2) There are other, apparently innately creative people in whom the drive to creativeness seems to be more important than any other counter-determinant. Their creativeness might appear not as self-actualization released by basic satisfaction, but in spite of lack of basic satisfaction.

(3) In certain people the level of aspiration may be permanently deadened or lowered. That is to say, the less prepotent goals may simply be lost, and may disappear forever, so that the person who has experienced life at a very low level, i.e., chronic unemployment, may continue to be satisfied for the rest of his life if only he can get enough food.

(4) The so-called 'psychopathic personality' is another example of permanent loss of the love needs. These are people who, according to the best data available [9], have been starved for love in the earliest months of their lives and have simply lost forever the desire and

the ability to give and to receive affection (as animals lose sucking or peck-
ing reflexes that are not exercised soon
enough after birth).

(5) Another cause of reversal of the
hierarchy is that when a need has been
satisfied for a long time, this need may
be underevaluated. . . .

(6) Another partial explanation of
apparent reversals is seen in the fact that
we have been talking about the hierarchy of prepotency in terms of consciously
felt wants or desires rather than behavior. Looking at behavior itself may give
us the wrong impression. What we have
claimed is that the person will *want* the
more basic of two needs when deprived
in both. There is no necessary implication here that he will act upon his desires. Let us say again that there are many
determinants of behavior other than the
needs and desires.

(7) Perhaps more important than all
these exceptions are the ones that involve ideals, high social standards, high
values and the like. With such values
people become martyrs; they will give
up everything for the sake of a particular
ideal, or value. These people may be understood, at least in part, by reference to
one basic concept (or hypothesis) which
may be called 'increased frustration-
tolerance through early gratification.'
People who have been satisfied in their
basic needs throughout their lives, particularly in their earlier years, seem to
develop exceptional power to withstand
present or future thwarting of these
needs simply because they have strong,
healthy character structure as a result of
basic satisfaction. They are the 'strong'
people who can easily weather disagreement or opposition, who can swim
against the stream of public opinion and
who can stand up for the truth at great
personal cost. It is just the ones who
have loved and been well loved, and who
have had many deep friendships who can

hold out against hatred, rejection or per-
secution.

I say all this in spite of the fact that
there is a certain amount of sheer habitu-
ation which is also involved in any full
discussion of frustration tolerance. For
instance, it is likely that those persons
who have been accustomed to relative
starvation for a long time, are partially
enabled thereby to withstand food deprivation. What sort of balance must be
made between these two tendencies, of
habitation on the one hand, and of past
satisfaction breeding present frustration
tolerance on the other hand, remains
to be worked out by further research.
Meanwhile we may assume that they are
both operative, side by side, since they
do not contradict each other. In respect
to this phenomenon of increased frustration tolerance, it seems probable that
the most important gratifications come
in the first two years of life. That is to
say, people who have been made secure
and strong in the earliest years, tend to
remain secure and strong thereafter in
the face of whatever threatens.

Degrees of Relative Satisfaction. So far,
our theoretical discussion may have
given the impression that these five sets
of needs are somehow in a step-wise, all-
or-none relationships to each other. We
have spoken in such terms as the following: "If one need is satisfied, then another emerges." This statement might
give the false impression that a need
must be satisfied 100 per cent before the
next need emerges. In actual fact, most
members of our society who are normal,
are partially satisfied in all their basic
needs and partially unsatisfied in all their
basic needs at the same time. A more
realistic description of the hierarchy
would be in terms of decreasing percentages of satisfaction as we go upon the
hierarchy of prepotency. For instance, if
I may assign arbitrary figures for the sake
of illustration, it is as if the average citi-

zen is satisfied perhaps 85 per cent in his physiological needs, 70 per cent in his safety needs, 50 per cent in his love needs, 40 per cent in his self-esteem needs, and 10 per cent in his self-actualization needs.

As for the concept of emergence of a new need after satisfaction of the prepotent need, this emergence is not a sudden, saltatory phenomenon but rather a gradual emergence by slow degrees from nothingness. For instance, if prepotent need A is satisfied only 10 per cent then need B may not be visible at all. However, as this need A becomes satisfied 25 per cent, need B may emerge 5 per cent, as need A becomes satisfied 75 per cent need B may emerge 90 per cent, and so on.

Unconscious Character of Needs. These needs are neither necessarily conscious nor unconscious. On the whole, however, in the average person, they are more often unconscious rather than conscious. . . .

Cultural Specificity and Generality of Needs. This classification of basic needs makes some attempt to take account of the relative unity behind the superficial differences in specific desires from one culture to another. Certainly in any particular culture an individual's conscious motivational content will usually be extremely different from the conscious motivational content of an individual in another society. However, it is the common experience of anthropologists that people, even in different societies, are much more alike than we would think from our first contact with them, and that as we know them better we seem to find more and more of this commonness. . . .

Multiple Motivations of Behavior. These needs must be understood *not* to be *exclusive* or single determiners of certain kinds of behavior. An example may be found in any behavior that seems to be physiologically motivated, such as

eating, or sexual play or the like. The clinical psychologists have long since found that any behavior may be a channel through which flow various determinants. Or to say it in another way, most behavior is multi-motivated. Within the sphere of motivational determinants any behavior tends to be determined by several or *all* of the basic needs simultaneously rather than by only one of them. The latter would be more an exception than the former. Eating may be partially for the sake of filling the stomach, and partially for the sake of comfort and amelioration of other needs. One may make love not only for pure sexual release, but also to convince one's self of one's masculinity, or to make a conquest, to feel powerful, or to win more basic affection. As an illustration, I may point out that it would be possible (theoretically if not practically) to analyze a single act of an individual and see in it the expression of his physiological needs, his safety needs, his love needs, his esteem needs and self-actualization. This contrasts sharply with the more naive brand of trait psychology in which one trait or one motive accounts for a certain kind of act, *i.e.*, an aggressive act is traced solely to a trait of aggressiveness.

Multiple Determinants of Behavior. Not all behavior is determined by the basic needs. We might even say that not all behavior is motivated. There are many determinants of behavior other than motives.[8] For instance, one other important class of determinants is the so-called 'field' determinants. Theoretically, at least, behavior may be determined completely by the field, or even by specific isolated external stimuli, as in association of ideas, or certain conditioned reflexes. If in response to the stimulus word 'table,' I immediately perceive a memory image of a table, this response certainly has nothing to do with my basic needs.

Secondly, we may call attention again to the concept of 'degree of closeness to the basic needs' or 'degree of motivation.' Some behavior is highly motivated, other behavior is only weakly motivated. Some is not motivated at all (but all behavior is determined).

Another important point[9] is that there is a basic difference between expressive behavior and coping behavior (functional striving, purposive goal seeking). An expressive behavior does not try to do anything; it is simply a reflection of the personality. A stupid man behaves stupidly, not because he wants to, or tries to, or is motivated to, but simply because he *is* what he is. The same is true when I speak in a bass voice rather than tenor or soprano. The random movements of a healthy child, the smile on the face of a happy man even when he is alone, the springiness of the healthy man's walk, and the erectness of his carriage are other examples of expressive, non-functional behavior. Also the *style* in which a man carries out almost all his behavior, motivated as well as unmotivated, is often expressive.

We may then ask, is *all* behavior expressive or reflective of the character structure? The answer is 'No.' Rote, habitual, automatized, or conventional behavior may or may not be expressive. The same is true for most 'stimulus-bound' behaviors.

It is finally necessary to stress that expressiveness of behavior, and goal-directedness of behavior are not mutually exclusive categories. Average behavior is usually both.

Goals as Centering Principle in Motivation Theory. It will be observed that the basic principle in our classification has been neither the instigation nor the motivated behavior but rather the functions, effects, purposes, or goals of the behavior. It has been proven sufficiently by various people that this is the most suitable point for centering any motivation theory.[10]

Animal- and Human-Centering. This theory starts with the human being rather than any lower and presumably 'simpler' animal. Too many of the findings that have been made in animals have been proven to be true for animals but not for the human being. There is no reason whatsoever why we should start with animals in order to study human motivation. . . .

Motivation and the Theory of Psychopathogenesis. The conscious motivational content of everyday life has, according to the foregoing, been conceived to be relatively important or unimportant accordingly as it is more or less closely related to the basic goals. A desire for an ice cream cone might actually be an indirect expression of a desire for love. If it is, then this desire for the ice cream cone becomes extremely important motivation. If however the ice cream is simply something to cool the mouth with, or a casual appetitive reaction, then the desire is relatively unimportant. Everyday conscious desires are to be regarded as symptoms, as *surface indicators of more basic needs*. If we were to take these superficial desires at their face value we would find ourselves in a state of complete confusion which could never be resolved, since we would be dealing seriously with symptoms rather than with what lay behind the symptoms.

Thwarting of unimportant desires produces no psychopathological results; thwarting of a basically important need does produce such results. Any theory of psychopathogenesis must then be based on a sound theory of motivation. A conflict or a frustration is not necessarily pathogenic. It becomes so only when it threatens or thwarts the basic needs, or partial needs that are closely related to the basic needs [10].

The Role of Gratified Needs. It has been pointed out above several times that our needs usually emerge only when more prepotent needs have been gratified. Thus gratification has an important role in motivation theory. Apart from this, however, needs cease to play an active determining or organizing role as soon as they are gratified.

What this means is that, *e.g.*, a basically satisfied person no longer has the needs for esteem, love, safety, etc. . . .

It is such considerations as these that suggest the bold postulation that a man who is thwarted in any of his basic needs may fairly be envisaged simply as a sick man. This is a fair parallel to our designation as 'sick' of the man who lacks vitamins or minerals. Who is to say that a lack of love is less important than a lack of vitamins? Since we know the pathogenic effects of love starvation, who is to say that we are invoking value-questions in an unscientific or illegitimate way, any more than the physician does who diagnoses and treats pellagra or scurvy? If I were permitted this usage, I should then say simply that a healthy man is primarily motivated by his needs to develop and actualize his fullest potentialities and capacities. If a man has any other basic needs in any active, chronic sense, then he is simply an unhealthy man. He is as surely sick as if he had suddenly developed a strong salt-hunger or calcium hunger.[11]

If this statement seems unusual or paradoxical the reader may be assured that this is only one among many such paradoxes that will appear as we revise our ways of looking at man's deeper motivations. When we ask what man wants of life, we deal with his very essence.

IV. SUMMARY

(1) There are at least five sets of goals, which we may call basic needs. These are briefly physiological, safety, love, esteem, and self-actualization. In addition, we are motivated by the desire to achieve or maintain the various conditions upon which these basic satisfactions rest and by certain more intellectual desires.

(2) These basic goals are related to each other, being arranged in a hierarchy of prepotency. This means that the most prepotent goal will monopolize consciousness and will tend of itself to organize the recruitment of the various capacities of the organism. The less prepotent needs are minimized, even forgotten or denied. But when a need is fairly well satisfied, the next prepotent ('higher') need emerges, in turn to dominate the conscious life and to serve as the center of organization of behavior, since gratified needs are not active motivators.

Thus man is a perpetually wanting animal. Ordinarily the satisfaction of these wants is not altogether mutually exclusive, but only tends to be. The average member of our society is most often partially satisfied and partially unsatisfied in all of his wants. The hierarchy principle is usually empirically observed in terms of increasing percentages of nonsatisfaction as we go up the hierarchy. Reversals of the average order of the hierarchy are sometimes observed. Also it has been observed that an individual may permanently lose the higher wants in the hierarchy under special conditions. There are not only ordinarily multiple motivations for usual behavior, but in addition many determinants other than motives.

(3) Any thwarting or possibility of thwarting of these basic human goals, or danger to the defenses which protect them, or to the conditions upon which they rest, is considered to be a psychological threat. With a few exceptions, all psychopathology may be partially traced to such threats. A basically thwarted

man may actually be defined as a 'sick' man, if we wish.

(4) It is such basic threats which bring about the general emergency reactions. . . .

NOTES

1. As the child grows up, sheer knowledge and familiarity as well as better motor development make these 'dangers' less and less dangerous and more and more manageable. Throughout life it may be said that one of the main conative functions of education is this neutralizing of apparent dangers through knowledge, e.g., I am not afraid of thunder because I know something about it.

2. A 'test battery' for safety might be confronting the child with a small exploding firecracker, or with a bewhiskered face, having the mother leave the room, putting him upon a high ladder, a hypodermic injection, having a mouse crawl up to him, etc. Of course I cannot seriously recommend the deliberate use of such 'tests' for they might very well harm the child being tested. But these and similar situations come up by the score in the child's ordinary day-to-day living and may be observed. There is no reason why these stimuli should not be used with, for example, young chimpanzees.

3. For further details see [12].

4. Whether or not this particular desire is universal we do not know. The crucial question, especially important today, is "Will men who are enslaved and dominated, inevitably feel dissatisfied and rebellious?" We may assume on the basis of commonly known clinical data that a man who has known true freedom (not paid for by giving up safety and security but rather built on the basis of adequate safety and security) will not willingly or easily allow his freedom to be taken away from him. But we do not know that this is true for the person born into slavery. The events of the next decade should give us our answer. See discussion of this problem in [5].

5. Perhaps the desire for prestige and respect from others is subsidiary to the desire for self-esteem or confidence in oneself. Observation of children seems to indicate that this is so, but clinical data give no clear support for such a conclusion.

6. For more extensive discussion of normal self-esteem, as well as for reports of various researchers, see [11].

7. Clearly creative behavior, like painting, is like any other behavior in having multiple determinants. It may be seen in 'innately creative' people whether they are satisfied or not, happy or unhappy, hungry or sated. Also it is clear that creative activity may be compensatory, ameliorative or purely economic. It is my impression (as yet unconfirmed) that it is possible to distinguish that artistic and intellectual products of basically satisfied people from those of basically unsatisfied people by inspection alone. In any case, here to we must distinguish, in a dynamic fashion, the overt behavior itself from its various motivations or purposes.

8. I am aware that many psychologists and psychoanalysts use the term 'motivated' and 'determined' synonymously, e.g., Freud. But I consider this an obfuscating usage. Sharp distinctions are necessary for clarity of thought, and precision in experimentation.

9. To be discussed fully in a subsequent publication.

10. The interested reader is referred to the very excellent discussion of this point in Murray's *Explorations in Personality* [15].

11. If we were to use the word 'sick' in this way, we should then also have to face squarely the relations of man to his society. One clear implication of our definition would be that (1) since a man is to be called sick who is basically thwarted, and (2) since such basic thwarting is made possible ultimately only by forces outside the individual, then (3) sickness in the individual must come ultimately from a sickness in the society. The 'good' or healthy society would then be defined as one that permitted man's highest purposes to emerge by satisfying all his prepotent basic needs.

REFERENCES

1. Adler, A. *Social interest*. London: Faber & Faber, 1938.

2. Cannon, W. B. *Wisdom of the body*. New York: Norton, 1932.

3. Freud, A. *The ego and the mechanisms of defense*. London: Hogarth, 1937.

4. Freud, S. *New introductory lectures on psychoanalysis*. New York: Norton, 1933.

5. Fromm, E. *Escape from freedom.* New York: Farrar and Rinehart, 1941.

6. Goldstein, K. *The organism.* New York: American Book Co., 1939.

7. Horney, K. *The neurotic personality of our time.* New York: Norton, 1937.

8. Kardiner, A. *The traumatic neuroses of war.* New York: Hoeber, 1941.

9. Levy, D. M. Primary effect of hunger. *Amer. J. Psychiat.,* 1937, 94, 643–652.

10. Maslow, A. H. Conflict, frustration, and the theory of threat. *J. abnorm. (soc.) Psychol.,* 1943, 38, 81–86.

11. ———. Dominance, personality and social behavior in women. *J. soc. Psychol.,* 1939, 10, 3–39.

12. ———. The dynamics of psychological security-insecurity. *Character & Pers.,* 1942, 10, 331–344.

13. ———. A preface to motivation theory. *Psychosomatic Med.,* 1943, 5, 85–92.

14. ———, & Mittlemann, B. *Principles of abnormal psychology.* New York: Harper & Bros., 1941.

15. Murray, H. A., *et al. Explorations in personality.* New York: Oxford University Press, 1938.

16. Plant, J. *Personality and the cultural pattern.* New York: Commonwealth Fund, 1937.

17. Shirley, M. Children's adjustments to a strange situation. *J. abnorm. (soc.) Psychol.,* 1942, 37, 201–217.

18. Tolman, E. C. *Purposive behavior in animals and men.* New York: Century, 1932.

19. Wertheimer, M. Unpublished lectures at the New School for Social Research.

20. Young, P. T. *Motivation of behavior.* New York: Wiley, 1936.

21. ———. The experimental analysis of appetite. *Psychol. Bull.,* 1941, 38, 129–164.

15
The Human Side of Enterprise
Douglas Murray McGregor

It has become trite to say that industry has the fundamental know-how to utilize physical science and technology for the material benefit of mankind, and that we must now learn how to utilize the social sciences to make our human organizations truly effective.

To a degree, the social sciences today are in a position like that of the physical sciences with respect to atomic energy in the thirties. We know that past conceptions of the nature of man are inadequate and, in many ways, incorrect. We are becoming quite certain that, under proper conditions, unimagined resources of creative human energy could become available within the organizational setting. . . .

MANAGEMENT'S TASK: THE CONVENTIONAL VIEW

The conventional conception of management's task in harnessing human energy to organizational requirements can be stated broadly in terms of three propositions. In order to avoid the complications introduced by a label, let us call this set of propositions "Theory X":

1. Management is responsible for organizing the elements of productive enterprise—money, materials, equipment, people—in the interest of economic ends.

2. With respect to people, this is a process of directing their efforts, motivating them, controlling their actions, modifying their behavior to fit the needs of the organization.

3. Without this active intervention by management, people would be passive—even resistant—to organizational needs. They must therefore be persuaded, rewarded, punished, controlled—their activities must be directed. This is management's task. We often sum it up by saying that management consists of getting things done through other people.

Behind this conventional theory there are several additional beliefs—less explicit, but widespread:

4. The average man is by nature indolent—he works as little as possible.

5. He lacks ambition, dislikes responsibility, prefers to be led.

6. He is inherently self-centered, indifferent to organizational needs.

7. He is by nature resistant to change.

8. He is gullible, not very bright, the ready dupe of the charlatan and the demagogue.

The human side of economic enterprise today is fashioned from propositions and beliefs such as these. Conventional organization structures and managerial policies, practices, and programs reflect these assumptions.

In accomplishing its task—with these assumptions as guides—management has conceived of a range of possibilities.

Source: Reprinted by permission of the publisher, from "The Human Side of Enterprise" by Douglas Murray McGregor, *Management Review*, November, 1957. Copyright © 1957 by the American Management Association, New York. All rights reserved.

Note: This article is based on an address by Dr. McGregor before the Fifth Anniversary Convocation of the M.I.T. School of Industrial Management.

At one extreme, management can be "hard" or "strong." The methods for directing behavior involve coercion and threat (usually disguised), close supervision, tight controls over behavior. At the other extreme, management can be "soft" or "weak." The methods for directing behavior involve being permissive, satisfying people's demands, achieving harmony. Then they will be tractable, accept direction.

This range has been fairly completely explored during the past half century, and management has learned some things from the exploration. There are difficulties in the "hard" approach. Force breeds counter-forces: restriction of output, antagonism, militant unionism, subtle but effective sabotage of management objectives. This "hard" approach is especially difficult during times of full employment.

There are also difficulties in the "soft" approach. It leads frequently to the abdication of management—to harmony, perhaps, but to indifferent performance. People take advantage of the soft approach. They continually expect more but they give less and less.

Currently, the popular theme is "firm but fair." This is an attempt to gain the advantages of both the hard and the soft approaches. It is reminiscent of Teddy Roosevelt's "speak softly and carry a big stick."

IS THE CONVENTIONAL VIEW CORRECT?

. . . The social scientist does not deny that human behavior in industrial organization today is approximately what management perceives it to be. He has, in fact, observed it and studied it fairly extensively. But he is pretty sure that this behavior is *not* a consequence of man's inherent nature. It is a consequence rather of the nature of industrial organizations, of management philoso-phy, policy, and practice. The conventional approach of Theory X is based on mistaken notions of what is cause and what is effect.

Perhaps the best way to indicate why the conventional approach of management is inadequate is to consider the subject of motivation.

PHYSIOLOGICAL NEEDS

Man is a wanting animal—as soon as one of his needs is satisfied, another appears in its place. This process is unending. It continues from birth to death. . . .

A *satisfied need is not a motivator of behavior!* This is a fact of profound significance that is regularly ignored in the conventional approach to the management of people. Consider your own need for air: Except as you are deprived of it, it has no appreciable motivating effect upon your behavior.

SAFETY NEEDS

When the physiological needs are reasonably satisfied, needs at the next higher level begin to dominate man's behavior—to motivate him. These are called *safety needs*. They are needs for protection against danger, threat, deprivation. Some people mistakenly refer to these as needs for security. However, unless man is in a dependent relationship where he fears arbitrary deprivation, he does not demand security. The need is for the "fairest possible break." When he is confident of this, he is more than willing to take risks. But when he feels threatened or dependent, his greatest need is for guarantees, for protection, for security.

The fact needs little emphasis that, since every industrial employee is in a dependent relationship, safety needs may assume considerable importance. Arbitrary management actions, behavior which arouses uncertainty with respect to continued employment or which reflects favoritism or discrimination, unpredictable administration of policy—these can be powerful motivators of the safety needs in the employment relationship *at every level,* from worker to vice president.

SOCIAL NEEDS

When man's physiological needs are satisfied and he is no longer fearful about his physical welfare, his *social needs* become important motivators of his behavior—needs for belonging, for association, for acceptance by his fellows, for giving and receiving friendship and love.

Management knows today of the existence of these needs, but it often assumes quite wrongly that they represent a threat to the organization. Many studies have demonstrated that the tightly knit, cohesive work group may, under proper conditions, be far more effective than an equal number of separate individuals in achieving organization goals.

Yet management, fearing group hostility to its own objectives, often goes to considerable lengths to control and direct human efforts in ways that are inimical to the natural "groupiness" of human beings. When man's social needs—and perhaps his safety needs, too—are thus thwarted, he behaves in ways which tend to defeat organizational objectives. He becomes resistant, antagonistic, uncooperative. But this behavior is a consequence, not a cause.

EGO NEEDS

Above the social needs—in the sense that they do not become motivators until lower needs are reasonably satisfied—are the needs of greatest significance to management and to man himself. They

are the *egoistic needs,* and they are of two kinds:

1. Those needs that relate to one's self-esteem—needs for self-confidence, for independence, for achievement, for competence, for knowledge.
2. Those needs that relate to one's reputation—needs for status, for recognition, for appreciation, for the deserved respect of one's fellows.

Unlike the lower needs, these are rarely satisfied: man seeks indefinitely for more satisfaction of these needs once they have become important to him. But they do not appear in any significant way until physiological, safety, and social needs are all reasonably satisfied.

The typical industrial organization offers few opportunities for the satisfaction of these egoistic needs to people at lower levels in the hierarchy. The conventional methods of organizing work, particularly in mass-production industries, give little heed to these aspects of human motivation. If the practices of scientific management were deliberately calculated to thwart these needs, they could hardly accomplish this purpose better than they do.

SELF-FULFILLMENT NEEDS

Finally—a capstone, as it were, on the hierarchy of man's needs—there are what we may call the *needs for self-fulfillment.* These are the needs for realizing one's own potentialities, for continued self-development, for being creative in the broadest sense of that term.

It is clear that the conditions of modern life give only limited opportunity for these relatively weak needs to obtain expression. The deprivation most people experience with respect to other lower-level needs diverts their energies into the struggle to satisfy *those* needs, and the needs for self-fulfillment remain dormant.

MANAGEMENT AND MOTIVATION

We recognize readily enough that a man suffering from a severe-dietary deficiency is sick. The deprivation of physiological needs has behavioral consequences. The same is true—although less well recognized—of deprivations of higher-level needs. The man whose needs for safety, association, independence, or status are thwarted is sick just as surely as the man who has rickets. And his sickness will have behavioral consequences. We will be mistaken if we attribute his resultant passivity, his hostility, his refusal to accept responsibility to his inherent "human nature." These forms of behavior are *symptoms* of illness—of deprivation of his social and egoistic needs.

The man whose lower-level needs are satisfied is not motivated to satisfy those needs any longer. For practical purposes they exist no longer. Management often asks, "Why aren't people more productive? We pay good wages, provide good working conditions, have excellent fringe benefits and steady employment. Yet people do not seem to be willing to put forth more than minimum effort."

The fact that management has provided for these physiological and safety needs has shifted the motivational emphasis to the social and perhaps to the egoistic needs. Unless there are opportunities *at work* to satisfy these higher-level needs, people will be deprived; and their behavior will reflect this deprivation. Under such conditions, if management continues to focus its attention on physiological needs, its efforts are bound to be ineffective.

People *will* make insistent demands for more money under these conditions. It becomes more important than ever to buy the material goods and services which can provide limited satisfaction of the thwarted needs. Although money

has only limited value in satisfying many higher-level needs, it can become the focus of interest if it is the *only* means available.

THE CARROT-AND-STICK APPROACH

The carrot-and-stick theory of motivation (like Newtonian physical theory) works reasonably well under certain circumstances. The *means* for satisfying man's physiological and (within limits) his safety needs can be provided or withheld by management. Employment itself is such a means, and so are wages, working conditions, and benefits. By these means the individual can be controlled so long as he is struggling for subsistence.

But the carrot-and-stick theory does not work at all once man has reached an adequate subsistence level and is motivated primarily by higher needs. Management cannot provide a man with self-respect, or with the respect of his fellows, or with the satisfaction of needs for self-fulfillment. It can create such conditions that he is encouraged and enabled to seek such satisfactions for *himself*, or it can thwart him by failing to create those conditions.

But this creation of conditions is not "control." It is not a good device for directing behavior. And so management finds itself in an odd position. The high standard of living created by our modern technological know-how provides quite adequately for the satisfaction of physiological and safety needs. The only significant exception is where management practices have not created confidence in a "fair break"—and thus where safety needs are thwarted. But by making possible the satisfaction of low-level needs, management has deprived itself of the ability to use as motivators the devices on which conventional theory has taught it to rely—rewards, promises, incentives, or threats and other coercive devices.

The philosophy of management by direction and control—*regardless of whether it is hard or soft*—is inadequate to motivate because the human needs on which this approach relies are today unimportant motivators of behavior. Direction and control are essentially useless in motivating people whose important needs are social and egoistic. Both the hard and the soft approach fail today because they are simply irrelevant to the situation.

People, deprived of opportunities to satisfy at work the needs which are now important to them, behave exactly as we might predict—with indolence, passivity, resistance to change, lack of responsibility, willingness to follow the demagogue, unreasonable demands for economic benefits. It would seem that we are caught in a web of our own weaving.

A NEW THEORY OF MANAGEMENT

For these and many other reasons, we require a different theory of the task of managing people based on more adequate assumptions about human nature and human motivation. I am going to be so bold as to suggest the broad dimensions of such a theory. Call it "Theory Y," if you will.

1. Management is responsible for organizing the elements of productive enterprise—money, materials, equipment, people—in the interest of economic ends.
2. People are *not* by nature passive or resistant to organizational needs. They have become so as a result of experience in organizations.
3. The motivation, the potential for development, the capacity for assuming responsibility, the readiness to direct behavior toward organizational goals

are all present in people. Management does not put them there. It is a responsibility of management to make it possible for people to recognize and develop these human characteristics for themselves.

4. The essential task of management is to arrange organizational conditions and methods of operation so that people can achieve their own goals *best* by directing *their own* efforts toward organizational objectives.

This is a process primarily of creating opportunities, releasing potential, removing obstacles, encouraging growth, providing guidance. It is what Peter Drucker has called "management by objectives" in contrast to "management by control." It does *not* involve the abdication of management, the absence of leadership, the lowering of standards, or the other characteristics usually associated with the "soft" approach under Theory X.

SOME DIFFICULTIES

It is no more possible to create an organization today which will be a full, effective application of this theory than it was to build an atomic power plant in 1945. There are many formidable obstacles to overcome.

The conditions imposed by conventional organization theory and by the approach of scientific management for the past half century have tied men to limited jobs which do not utilize their capabilities, have discouraged the acceptance of responsibility, have encouraged passivity, have eliminated meaning from work. Man's habits, attitudes, expectations—his whole conception of membership in an industrial organization—have been conditioned by his experience under these circumstances.

People today are accustomed to being directed, manipulated, controlled in industrial organizations and to finding satisfaction for their social, egoistic, and self-fulfillment needs away from the job. This is true of much of management as well as of workers. Genuine "industrial citizenship"—to borrow again a term from Drucker—is a remote and unrealistic idea, the meaning of which has not even been considered by most members of industrial organizations.

Another way of saying this is that Theory X places exclusive reliance upon external control of human behavior, while Theory Y relies heavily on self-control and self-direction. It is worth noting that this difference is the difference between treating people as children and treating them as mature adults. After generations of the former, we cannot expect to shift to the latter overnight.

STEPS IN THE RIGHT DIRECTION

Before we are overwhelmed by the obstacles, let us remember that the application of theory is always slow. Progress is usually achieved in small steps. Some innovative ideas which are entirely consistent with Theory Y are today being applied with some success.

Decentralization and Delegation

These are ways of freeing people from the too-close control of conventional organization, giving them a degree of freedom to direct their own activities, to assume responsibility, and, importantly, to satisfy their egoistic needs. In this connection, the flat organization of Sears, Roebuck and Company provides an interesting example. It forces "management by objectives," since it enlarges the number of people reporting to a manager until he cannot direct and control them in the conventional manner.

Job Enlargement

This concept, pioneered by I.B.M. and Detroit Edison, is quite consistent with Theory Y. It encourages the acceptance of responsibility at the bottom of the organization; it provides opportunities for satisfying social and egoistic needs. In fact, the reorganization of work at the factory level offers one of the more challenging opportunities for innovation consistent with Theory Y.

Participation and Consultative Management

Under proper conditions, participation and consultative management provide encouragement to people to direct their creative energies toward organizational objectives, give them some voice in decisions that affect them, provide significant opportunities for the satisfaction of social and egoistic needs. . . .

Performance Appraisal

Even a cursory examination of conventional programs of performance appraisal within the ranks of management will reveal how completely consistent they are with Theory X. In fact, most such programs tend to treat the individual as though he were a product under inspection on the assembly line.

A few companies—among them General Mills, Ansul Chemical, and General Electric—have been experimenting with approaches which involve the individual in setting "targets" or objectives *for himself* and in a *self*-evaluation of performance semiannually or annually. Of course, the superior plays an important leadership role in this process—one, in fact, which demands substantially more competence than the conventional approach. The role is, however, considerably more congenial to many managers than the role of "judge" or "inspector" which is usually forced upon them. Above all, the individual is encouraged to take a greater responsibility for planning and appraising his own contribution to organizational objectives; and the accompanying effects on egoistic and self-fulfillment needs are substantial.

APPLYING THE IDEAS

The not infrequent failure of such ideas as these to work as well as expected is often attributable to the fact that a management has "bought the idea" but applied it within the framework of Theory X and its assumptions.

Delegation is not an effective way of exercising management by control. Participation becomes a farce when it is applied as a sales gimmick or a device for kidding people into thinking they are important. Only the management that has confidence in human capacities and is itself directed toward organizational objectives rather than toward the preservation of personal power can grasp the implications of this emerging theory. Such management will find and apply successfully other innovative ideas as we move slowly toward the full implementation of a theory like Y.

THE HUMAN SIDE OF ENTERPRISE

. . . The ingenuity and the perseverance of industrial management in the pursuit of economic ends have changed many scientific and technological dreams into commonplace realities. It is now becoming clear that the application of these same talents to the human side of enterprise will not only enhance substantially these materialistic achievements, but will bring us one step closer to "the good society."

16

Groupthink: The Desperate Drive for Consensus at Any Cost

Irving L. Janis

"How could we have been so stupid?" President John F. Kennedy asked after he and a close group of advisers had blundered into the Bay of Pigs invasion. For the last two years I have been studying that question, as it applies not only to the Bay of Pigs decision-makers but also to those who led the United States into such other major fiascoes as the failure to be prepared for the attack on Pearl Harbor, the Korean War stalemate and the escalation of the Vietnam War.

Stupidity certainly is not the explanation. The men who participated in making the Bay of Pigs decision, for instance, comprised one of the greatest arrays of intellectual talent in the history of American Government—Dean Rusk, Robert McNamara, Douglas Dillon, Robert Kennedy, McGeorge Bundy, Arthur Schlesinger Jr., Allen Dulles and others.

It also seemed to me that explanations were incomplete if they concentrated only on disturbances in the behavior of each individual within a decision-making body: temporary emotional states of elation, fear, or anger that reduce a man's mental efficiency, for example, or chronic blind spots arising from a man's social prejudices or idiosyncratic biases.

I preferred to broaden the picture by looking at the fiascoes from the standpoint of group dynamics as it has been explored over the past three decades, first by the great social psychologist Kurt Lewin and later in many experimental situations by myself and other behavioral scientists. My conclusion after poring over hundreds of relevant documents—historical reports about formal group meetings and informal conversations among the members—is that the groups that committed the fiascoes were victims of what I call "groupthink."

"Groupy." In each case study, I was surprised to discover the extent to which each group displayed the typical phenomena of social conformity that are regularly encountered in studies of group dynamics among ordinary citizens. For example, some of the phenomena appear to be completely in line with findings from social-psychological experiments showing that powerful social pressures are brought to bear by the members of a cohesive group whenever a dissident begins to voice his objections to a group consensus. Other phenomena are reminiscent of the shared illusions observed in encounter groups and friendship cliques when the members simultaneously reach a peak of "groupy" feelings.

Above all, there are numerous indications pointing to the development of group norms that bolster morale at the expense of critical thinking. One of the most common norms appears to be that of remaining loyal to the group by stick-

Source: From "Groupthink" by Irving L. Janis. Reprinted with permission from *Psychology Today Magazine.* Copyright © 1971 (Sussex Publishers, Inc.).

ing with the policies to which the group has already committed itself, even when those policies are obviously working out badly and have unintended consequences that disturb the conscience of each member. This is one of the key characteristics of groupthink.

1984. I use the term groupthink as a quick and easy way to refer to the mode of thinking that persons engage in when *concurrence-seeking* becomes so dominant in a cohesive ingroup that it tends to override realistic appraisal of alternative courses of action. Groupthink is a term of the same order as the words in the newspeak vocabulary George Orwell used in his dismaying world of 1984. In that context, groupthink takes on an invidious connotation. Exactly such a connotation is intended, since the term refers to a deterioration in mental efficiency, reality testing and moral judgments as a result of group pressures.

The symptoms of groupthink arise when the members of decision-making groups become motivated to avoid being too harsh in their judgments of their leaders' or their colleagues' ideas. They adopt a soft line of criticism, even in their own thinking. At their meetings, all the members are amiable and seek complete concurrence on every important issue, with no bickering or conflict to spoil the cozy, "we-feeling" atmosphere.

Kill. Paradoxically, soft-headed groups are often hard-hearted when it comes to dealing with outgroups or enemies. They find it relatively easy to resort to dehumanizing solutions—they will readily authorize bombing attacks that kill large numbers of civilians in the name of the noble cause of persuading an unfriendly government to negotiate at the peace table. They are unlikely to pursue the more difficult and controversial issues that arise when alternatives to a harsh military solution come up for discussion. Nor are they inclined to raise ethical issues that carry the implication that *this fine group of ours, with its humanitarianism and its high-minded principles, might be capable of adopting a course of action that is inhumane and immoral.*

Norms. There is evidence from a number of social-psychological studies that as the members of a group feel more accepted by the others, which is a central feature of increased group cohesiveness, they display less overt conformity to group norms. Thus we would expect that the more cohesive a group becomes, the less the members will feel constrained to censor what they say out of fear of being socially punished for antagonizing the leader or any of their fellow members.

In contrast, the groupthink type of conformity tends to increase as group cohesiveness increases. Groupthink involves nondeliberate suppression of critical thoughts as a result of internalization of the group's norms, which is quite different from deliberate suppression on the basis of external threats of social punishment. The more cohesive the group, the greater the inner compulsion on the part of each member to avoid creating disunity, which inclines him to believe in the soundness of whatever proposals are promoted by the leader or by a majority of the group's members.

In a cohesive group, the danger is not so much that each individual will fail to reveal his objections to what the others propose but that he will think the proposal is a good one, without attempting to carry out a careful, critical scrutiny of the pros and cons of the alternatives. When groupthink becomes dominant, there also is considerable suppression of deviant thoughts, but it takes the form of each person's deciding that his misgivings are not relevant and should be set aside, that the benefit of the doubt regarding any lingering uncertainties should be given to the group consensus.

Stress. I do not mean to imply that all cohesive groups necessarily suffer from groupthink. All ingroups may have a mild tendency toward groupthink, displaying one or another of the symptoms from time to time, but it need not be so dominant as to influence the quality of the group's final decision. Neither do I mean to imply that there is anything necessarily inefficient or harmful about group decisions in general. On the contrary, a group whose members have properly defined roles, with traditions concerning the procedures to follow in pursuing a critical inquiry, probably is capable of making better decisions than any individual group member working alone.

The problem is that the advantages of having decisions made by groups are often lost because of powerful psychological pressures that arise when the members work closely together, share the same set of values and, above all, face a crisis situation that puts everyone under intense stress.

The main principle of groupthink, which I offer in the spirit of Parkinson's Law, is this: *The more amiability and esprit de corps there is among the members of a policy-making ingroup, the greater the danger that independent critical thinking will be replaced by groupthink, which is likely to result in irrational and dehumanizing actions directed against outgroups.*

Symptoms. In my studies of high-level governmental decision-makers, both civilian and military, I have found eight main symptoms of groupthink.

1. *Invulnerability.* Most or all of the members of the ingroup share an illusion of invulnerability that provides for them some degree of reassurance about obvious dangers and leads them to become over-optimistic and willing to take extraordinary risks. It also causes them to fail to respond to clear warnings of danger.

The Kennedy ingroup, which uncritically accepted the Central Intelligence Agency's disastrous Bay of Pigs plan, operated on the false assumption that they could keep secret the fact that the United States was responsible for the invasion of Cuba. Even after news of the plan began to leak out, their belief remained unshaken. They failed even to consider the danger that awaited them: a worldwide revulsion against the U.S.

A similar attitude appeared among the members of President Lyndon B. Johnson's ingroup, the "Tuesday Cabinet," which kept escalating the Vietnam War despite repeated setbacks and failures. "There was a belief," Bill Moyers commented after he resigned, "that if we indicated a willingness to use our power, they [the North Vietnamese] would get the message and back away from an all-out confrontation. . . . There was a confidence—it was never bragged about, it was just there—that when the chips were really down, the other people would fold."

A most poignant example of an illusion of invulnerability involves the ingroup around Admiral H. E. Kimmel, which failed to prepare for the possibility of a Japanese attack on Pearl Harbor despite repeated warnings. Informed by his intelligence chief that radio contact with Japanese aircraft carriers had been lost, Kimmel joked about it: "What, you don't know where the carriers are? Do you mean to say that they could be rounding Diamond Head (at Honolulu) and you wouldn't know it?" The carriers were in fact moving full-steam toward Kimmel's command post at the time. Laughing together about a danger signal, which labels it as a purely laughing matter, is a characteristic manifestation of groupthink.

2. *Rationale*. As we see, victims of group-think ignore warnings; they also collectively construct rationalizations in order to discount warnings and other forms of negative feedback that, taken seriously, might lead the group members to reconsider their assumptions each time they recommit themselves to past decisions. Why did the Johnson ingroup avoid reconsidering its escalation policy when time and again the expectations on which they based their decisions turned out to be wrong? James C. Thomson, Jr., a Harvard historian who spent five years as an observing participant in both the State Department and the White House, tells us that the policymakers avoided critical discussion of their prior decisions and continually invented new rationalizations so that they could sincerely recommit themselves to defeating the North Vietnamese.

In the fall of 1964, before the bombing of North Vietnam began, some of the policymakers predicted that six weeks of air strikes would induce the North Vietnamese to seek peace talks. When someone asked, "What if they don't?" the answer was that another four weeks certainly would do the trick. . . .

3. *Morality*. Victims of groupthink believe unquestioningly in the inherent morality of their ingroup; this belief inclines the members to ignore the ethical or moral consequences of their decisions.

Evidence that this symptom is at work usually is of a negative kind—the things that are left unsaid in group meetings. At least two influential persons had doubts about the morality of the Bay of Pigs adventure. One of them, Arthur Schlesinger, Jr., presented his strong objections in a memorandum to President Kennedy and Secretary of State Rusk but suppressed them when he attended meetings of the Kennedy team. The other, Senator J. William Fulbright, was not a member of the group, but the Presi-

dent invited him to express his misgivings in a speech to the policymakers. However, when Fulbright finished speaking the President moved on to other agenda items without asking for reactions of the group.

David Kraslow and Stuart H. Loory, in *The Secret Search for Peace in Vietnam*, report that during 1966 President Johnson's ingroup was concerned primarily with selecting bomb targets in North Vietnam. They based their selections on four factors—the military advantage, the risk to American aircraft and pilots, the danger of forcing other countries into the fighting, and the danger of heavy civilian casualties. At their regular Tuesday luncheons, they weighed these factors the way school teachers grade examination papers, averaging them out. Though evidence on this point is scant, I suspect that the group's ritualistic adherence to a standardized procedure induced the members to feel morally justified in their destructive way of dealing with the Vietnamese people—after all, the danger of heavy civilian casualties from U.S. air strikes was taken into account on their checklists.

4. *Stereotypes*. Victims of groupthink hold stereotyped views of the leaders of enemy groups: they are so evil that genuine attempts at negotiating differences with them are unwarranted, or they are too weak or too stupid to deal effectively with whatever attempts the ingroup makes to defeat their purposes, no matter how risky the attempts are.

Kennedy's groupthinkers believed that Premier Fidel Castro's air force was so ineffectual that obsolete B-26's could knock it out completely in a surprise attack before the invasion began. They also believed that Castro's army was so weak that a small Cuban-exile brigade could establish a well-protected beachhead at the Bay of Pigs. In addition, they believed that Castro was not smart enough to put down any possible internal uprisings in support of the exiles. They were wrong on all three assumptions. Though much of the blame was attributable to faulty intelligence, the point is that none of Kennedy's advisers even questioned the CIA planners about these assumptions.

The Johnson advisers' sloganistic thinking about "the Communist apparatus" that was "working all around the world" (as Dean Rusk put it) led them to overlook the powerful nationalistic strivings of the North Vietnamese government and its efforts to ward off Chinese domination. The crudest of all stereotypes used by Johnson's inner circle to justify their policies was the domino theory ("If we don't stop the Reds in South Vietnam, tomorrow they will be in Hawaii and next week they will be in San Francisco," Johnson once said). The group so firmly accepted this stereotype that it became almost impossible for any adviser to introduce a more sophisticated viewpoint.

In the documents on Pearl Harbor, it is clear to see that the Navy commanders stationed in Hawaii had a naive image of Japan as a midget that would not dare to strike a blow against a powerful giant.

5. *Pressure.* Victims of groupthink apply direct pressure to any individual who momentarily expresses doubts about any of the group's shared illusions or who questions the validity of the arguments supporting a policy alternative favored by the majority. This gambit reinforces the concurrence-seeking norm that loyal members are expected to maintain.

President Kennedy probably was more active than anyone else in raising skeptical questions during the Bay of Pigs meetings, and yet he seems to have encouraged the group's docile, uncritical acceptance of defective arguments in favor of the CIA's plan. At every meeting,

he allowed the CIA representatives to dominate the discussion. He permitted them to give their immediate refutations in response to each tentative doubt that one of the others expressed, instead of asking whether anyone shared the doubt or wanted to pursue the implications of the new worrisome issue that had just been raised. And at the most crucial meeting, when he was calling on each member to give his vote for or against the plan, he did not call on Arthur Schlesinger, the one man there who was known by the President to have serious misgivings.

Historian Thomson informs us that whenever a member of Johnson's ingroup began to express doubts, the group used subtle social pressures to "domesticate" him. To start with, the dissenter was made to feel at home provided that he lived up to two restrictions: 1) that he did not voice his doubts to outsiders, which would play into the hands of the opposition; and 2) that he kept his criticisms within the bounds of acceptable deviation, which meant not challenging any of the fundamental assumptions that went into the group's prior commitments. One such "domesticated dissenter" was Bill Moyers. When Moyers arrived at a meeting, Thomson tells us, the President greeted him with, "Well, here comes Mr. Stop-the-Bombing."

6. *Self-Censorship.* Victims of groupthink avoid deviating from what appears to be group consensus; they keep silent about their misgivings and even minimize to themselves the importance of their doubts.

As we have seen, Schlesinger was not at all hesitant about presenting his strong objections to the Bay of Pigs plan in a memorandum to the President and the Secretary of State. But he became keenly aware of his tendency to suppress objections at the White House meetings.

"In the months after the Bay of Pigs, I bitterly reproached myself for having kept so silent during those crucial discussions in the cabinet room," Schlesinger writes in *A Thousand Days*, "I can only explain my failure to do more than raise a few timid questions by reporting that one's impulse to blow the whistle on this nonsense was simply undone by the circumstances of the discussion."

7. *Unanimity*. Victims of groupthink share an illusion of unanimity within the group concerning almost all judgments expressed by members who speak in favor of the majority view. This symptom results partly from the preceding one, whose effects are augmented by the false assumption that any individual who remains silent during any part of the discussion is in full accord with what the others are saying.

When a group of persons who respect each other's opinions arrives at a unanimous view, each member is likely to feel that the belief must be true. This reliance on consensual validation within the group tends to replace individual critical thinking and reality testing, unless there are clear-cut disagreements among the members. In contemplating a course of action such as the invasion of Cuba, it is painful for the members to confront disagreements within their group, particularly if it becomes apparent that there are widely divergent views about whether the preferred course of action is too risky to undertake at all. Such disagreements are likely to arouse anxieties about making a serious error. Once the sense of unanimity is shattered, the members no longer can feel complacently confident about the decision they are inclined to make. Each man must then face the annoying realization that there are troublesome uncertainties and he must diligently seek out the best information he can get in order to decide for himself exactly how serious

the risks might be. This is one of the unpleasant consequences of being in a group of hardheaded, critical thinkers.

To avoid such an unpleasant state, the members often become inclined, without quite realizing it, to prevent latent disagreements from surfacing when they are about to initiate a risky course of action. The group leader and the members support each other in playing up the areas of convergence in their thinking, at the expense of fully exploring divergencies that might reveal unsettled issues. . . .

8. *Mindguards*. Victims of groupthink sometimes appoint themselves as mindguards to protect the leader and fellow members from adverse information that might break the complacency they shared about the effectiveness and morality of past decisions. At a large birthday party for his wife, Attorney General Robert F. Kennedy, who had been constantly informed about the Cuban invasion plan, took Schlesinger aside and asked him why he was opposed. Kennedy listened coldly and said, "You may be right or you may be wrong, but the President has made his mind up. Don't push it any further. Now is the time for everyone to help him all they can."

Rusk also functioned as a highly effective mindguard by failing to transmit to the group the strong objections of three "outsiders" who had learned of the invasion plan—Undersecretary of State Chester Bowles, USIA Director Edward R. Murrow, and Rusk's intelligence chief, Roger Hilsman. Had Rusk done so, their warnings might have reinforced Schlesinger's memorandum and jolted some of Kennedy's ingroup, if not the President himself, into reconsidering the decision.

Products. When a group of executives frequently displays most or all of these interrelated symptoms, a detailed study of their deliberations is likely to reveal a number of immediate consequences. These consequences are, in effect, products of poor decision-making practices because they lead to inadequate solutions to the problems under discussion.

First, the group limits its discussions to a few alternative courses of action (often only two) without an initial survey of all the alternatives that might be worthy of consideration.

Second, the group fails to reexamine the course of action initially preferred by the majority after they learn of risks and drawbacks they had not considered originally.

Third, the members spend little or no time discussing whether there are nonobvious gains they may have overlooked or ways of reducing the seemingly prohibitive costs that made rejected alternatives appear undesirable to them.

Fourth, members make little or no attempt to obtain information from experts within their own organizations who might be able to supply more precise estimates of potential losses and gains.

Fifth, members show positive interest in facts and opinions that support their preferred policy, and they tend to ignore facts and opinions that do not.

Sixth, members spend little time deliberating about how the chosen policy might be hindered by bureaucratic inertia, sabotaged by political opponents, or temporarily derailed by common accidents. Consequently, they fail to work out contingency plans to cope with foreseeable setbacks that could endanger the overall success of their chosen course.

Support. The search for an explanation of why groupthink occurs has led me through a quagmire of complicated theoretical issues in the murky area of human motivation. My belief, based on recent social psychological research, is that we can best understand the various symptoms of groupthink as a mutual effort among the group members to maintain self-esteem and emotional equanimity by providing social support to each other, especially at times when they share responsibility for making vital decisions.

Even when no important decision is pending, the typical administrator will begin to doubt the wisdom and morality of his past decisions each time he receives information about setbacks, particularly if the information is accompanied by negative feedback from prominent men who originally had been his supporters. It should not be surprising, therefore, to find that individual members strive to develop unanimity and esprit de corps that will help bolster each other's morale, to create an optimistic outlook about the success of pending decisions, and to reaffirm the positive value of past policies to which all of them are committed.

Pride. Shared illusions of invulnerability, for example, can reduce anxiety about taking risks. Rationalizations help members believe that the risks are really not so bad after all. The assumption of inherent morality helps the members to avoid feelings of shame or guilt. Negative stereotypes function as stress-reducing devices to enhance a sense of moral righteousness as well as pride in a lofty mission.

The mutual enhancement of self-esteem and morale may have functional value in enabling the members to maintain their capacity to take action, but it has maladaptive consequences insofar as concurrence-seeking tendencies interfere with critical, rational capacities and lead to serious errors of judgment.

While I have limited my study to decision-making bodies in government, groupthink symptoms appear in business, industry and any other field where small, cohesive groups make the decisions. It is vital, then, for all sorts of people—and especially group leaders—

to know what steps they can take to prevent groupthink.

Remedies. To counterpoint my case studies the major fiascoes, I have also investigated two highly successful group enterprises, the formulation of the Marshall Plan in the Truman Administration and the handling of the Cuban missile crisis by President Kennedy and his advisers. I have found it instructive to examine the steps Kennedy took to change his group's decision-making processes. These changes ensured that the mistakes made by his Bay of Pigs ingroup were not repeated by the missile-crisis ingroup, even though the membership of both groups was essentially the same.

The following recommendations for preventing groupthink incorporate many of the good practices I discovered to be characteristic of the Marshall Plan and missile crisis groups:

1. The leader of a policy-forming group should assign the role of critical evaluator to each member, encouraging the group to give high priority to open airing of objections and doubts. This practice needs to be reinforced by the leader's acceptance of criticism of his own judgments in order to discourage members from soft-pedaling their disagreements and from allowing their striving for concurrence to inhibit critical thinking.

2. When the key members of a hierarchy assign a policy-planning mission to any group within their organization, they should adopt an impartial stance instead of stating preferences and expectations at the beginning. This will encourage open inquiry and impartial probing of a wide range of policy alternatives.

3. The organization routinely should set up several outside policy-planning and evaluation groups to work on the same policy question, each deliberating

under a different leader. This can prevent the insulation of an ingroup.

4. At intervals before the group reaches a final consensus, the leader should require each member to discuss the group's deliberations with associates in his own unit of the organization—assuming that those associates can be trusted to adhere to the same security regulations that govern the policy-makers—and then to report back their reactions to the group.

5. The group should invite one or more outside experts to each meeting on a staggered basis and encourage the experts to challenge the views of the core members.

6. At every general meeting of the group, whenever the agenda calls for an evaluation of policy alternatives, at least one member should play devil's advocate, functioning as a good lawyer in challenging the testimony of those who advocate the majority position.

7. Whenever the policy issue involves relations with a rival nation or organization, the group should devote a sizable block of time, perhaps an entire session, to a survey of all warning signals from the rivals and should write alternative scenarios on the rivals' intentions.

8. When the group is surveying policy alternatives for feasibility and effectiveness, it should from time to time divide into two or more subgroups to meet separately, under different chairmen, and then come back together to hammer out differences.

9. After reaching a preliminary consensus about what seems to be the best policy, the group should hold a "second-chance" meeting at which every member expresses as vividly as he can all his residual doubts, and rethinks the entire issue before making a definitive choice.

How. These recommendations have their disadvantages. To encourage the open airing of objections, for instance, might lead to prolonged and costly debates when a rapidly growing crisis requires immediate solution. It also could cause rejection, depression and anger. A leader's failure to set a norm might create cleavage between leader and members that could develop into a disruptive power struggle if the leader looks on the emerging consensus as anathema. Setting up outside evaluation groups might increase the risk of security leakage. Still, inventive executives who know their way around the organizational maze probably can figure out how to apply one or another of the prescriptions successfully, without harmful side effects.

They also could benefit from the advice of outside experts in the administrative and behavioral sciences. Though these experts have much to offer, they have had few chances to work on policymaking machinery within large organizations. As matters now stand, executives innovate only when they need new procedures to avoid repeating serious errors that have deflated their self-images.

In this era of atomic warheads, urban disorganization and ecocatastrophes, it seems to me that policymakers should collaborate with behavioral scientists and give top priority to preventing groupthink and its attendant fiascoes.

17
Intergroup Conflict
Taylor H. Cox, Jr.

INTERGROUP CONFLICT DEFINED

Although writers have offered numerous different definitions of conflict, they seem to agree that conflict is an overt expression of tensions between the goals or concerns of one party and those of another. Thus the core of conflict is opposing interests of the involved parties (Rummell, 1976). In this chapter we are concerned with conflict between groups. Since all groups are composed of individuals and conflict behavior is frequently enacted by individuals, intergroup conflict may be conceived as a special case of interpersonal conflict. Intergroup conflict in the context of cultural diversity has two distinguishing features: (1) group boundaries and group differences are involved, and (2) the conflict is directly or indirectly related to culture group identities.

Concerning the second point, there are at least two reasons why a great deal of observed interpersonal conflict may be analyzed from an intergroup perspective. First group identities are an integral part of the individual personality. Therefore, much of what is commonly referred to as "personality clash" may actually be a manifestation of group identity-related conflict. Second, there are clear cases in which the basis of conflict is endemic to the groups as well as, or instead of, the individuals involved. For example, considerable conflict has arisen in parts of Florida and California over the extent to which education will be conducted exclusively in English. The main parties to the conflict are Hispanic Americans (the majority of whom are bilingual but have Spanish as their first language) and non-Hispanic Americans, who by and large are monolingual English speakers. In this instance, the source of the conflict itself has roots in the different culture identities of the parties.

Also in the context of cultural diversity in organizations, it may be useful to note that intergroup conflict occurs between the majority group and the various minority groups represented as well as among the minority groups themselves. In the following section, sources of intergroup conflict in the context of cultural diversity in organizations will be addressed.

SOURCES OF INTERGROUP CONFLICT

As indicated in the definition above, the core element of conflict is opposing interests. A study of literature on intergroup dynamics in organizations reveals myriad issues, attitudes, and behaviors around which opposing interest may develop (Alderfer, Alderfer, Tucker, & Tucker, 1980; Landis & Boucher, 1987; Arnold & Feldman, 1986; Daft & Steers, 1986). In the context of cultural diversity in organizations, however, five stand out to me as particularly important. They are:

1. Competing goals
2. Competition for resources
3. Cultural differences
4. Power discrepancies
5. Assimilation versus preservation of microcultural identity

Competing Goals

As previously indicated, common goals is one of the defining characteristics of culture groups. Indeed, this characteristic applies to groups of any kind. In multicultural social systems, the various groups represented may develop competing goals which then become the basis of intergroup conflict. This insight into intergroup conflict has been addressed extensively by Campbell (1965) and by Sherif (1966) in their discussions of "realistic group conflict theory.". . .

. . . The point to be made here is that organizational functions are often characterized by very different systems of norms, goal priorities, work styles, and so on. In other words, they may be viewed as having different occupational cultures. The difference in cultures between them, partly manifested in different goals, sets the stage for intergroup conflict.

Competition for Resources

A second source of intergroup conflict is disagreement about the allocation of resources. In some cases, such as conflict between American Indians and White Americans, the bases of these conflicts are embedded in the history of intergroup relations. In other cases, such as tensions between men and women over access to executive jobs, the conflict is more directly embedded in organizational issues. Several examples will be offered.

Intergroup conflict over resources is illustrated by a recent consulting project I was involved in at a plant site of a large international telecommunications company. Several years ago, the plant hired a significant number of Laotian immigrants. Subsequently there was a major downsizing in which several hundred employees were relocated or lost their jobs. Many of the local Laotian workers survived these cuts. In interviews with African American, Hispanic Americans, and White American workers at the plant, all of whom are native-born, a great deal of resentment was expressed toward the plant's management and toward the Laotians themselves over the loss of jobs to "outsiders." The Laotians that I talked to were also aware of this resentment and held a certain amount of hostility of their own toward what they regarded as unfair treatment by the native-born Americans. The conflict had persisted over a period of several years and was a hindrance to the effective functioning of self-managed work-teams that the plant was trying to implement.

The resource in contention in the above example (jobs) is frequently a source of intergroup conflict related to diversity. This can be seen, for example, in the recent events in European cities where immigrants, most of them non-white, are increasingly being harassed by natives who view them as unwelcome outsiders who are threatening their access to employment (see, for example, "Germans," 1991). It has also been identified as a major source of conflict between black and white Americans as well as between blacks and other racioethnic minorities. . . .

Cultural Differences

Intergroup conflict between diverse groups may also occur because of misunderstandings and misperceptions that are related to the different worldviews of culture groups. For example, Alderfer and Smith (1982) and Daft and Steers (1986) are among those citing cognitive differences between groups as a primary source of potential conflict. Alderfer and Smith describe the nature of these differences in the following way: "[Groups] condition their members' perceptions of objective and subjective phenomena and transmit a set of propositions . . . to explain the nature of experiences encountered by members and to influence relations with other groups" (p. 40).

Alderfer and Smith provide one of the most startling examples of different cognitive orientations between groups from their data on perceptions of race relations in a large organization. In a study of 2,000 managers in a large corporation, they found that perceptions between whites and blacks were dramatically different. For example, they found that while 62 percent of black men and 53 percent of black women agreed that qualified whites were promoted in the company more rapidly than equally qualified blacks, the percent agreement among whites was only 4 and 7 percent respectively for men and women. They also asked the same subjects if they agreed that qualified blacks are promoted more rapidly than equally qualified whites. Here the percentages tended to be reversed, with agreement by only 12 to 13 percent of blacks versus 75 to 82 percent of whites. Since the statements are mutually exclusive, these data give a striking portrayal of how members of different groups in the same organization can see events very differently. Another revealing finding from this study concerns perceptions of the nature of two support groups in the organization. The Black Managers Association was composed of black managers of all organization levels and restricted its membership to blacks. The Foreman's Club was composed of first-level supervisors, nearly all of whom were white; however, membership was open to anyone at the specified organization level. Nearly half of the white women (45 percent) and more than half of the white men (64 percent) viewed the Black Manager's Association

as "essentially a racist organization." This compared to only 25 and 16 percent respectively for black women and men. Alternatively, a majority of blacks (both men and women) viewed the Foreman's Club as essentially racist, while less than 20 percent of whites held this view. One could argue that the differences in eligibility criteria between the two support groups left the Black Managers Association more vulnerable to charges of racism, but the point here is to note how differently whites and blacks viewed the two organizations.

These types of organizational support groups have become increasingly common in recent years (Cox, 1991) and therefore these data are relevant to one of the most ubiquitous consequences of cultural diversity in organizations. I contend that it is not the existence of such organizational support groups per se that creates conflict but rather the differences in how they are perceived. Reconciling such differences in perceptions therefore is a critical challenge for organization development work related to cultural diversity. . . .

Power Discrepancies

Majority groups as defined [here] hold advantages over minority groups in the power structure of organizations. As numerous writers have noted, this discrepancy of power is a primary source of potential conflict (Landis & Boucher, 1987; Alderfer &: Smith, 1982; Randolph & Blackburn, 1989). The logic of this is straightforward. Stated simply, the "power approach" argues that intergroup hostility and antagonism are natural results of competition between groups for control of the economic, political, and social structures of social systems (Giles & Evans, 1986). On a general level, a core manifestation of the power perspective is tension between minority groups and the majority group over whether to change or preserve the status quo. . . .

The power approach to explaining intergroup conflict is illustrated in tensions between majority and minority group members over the use of affirmative action in promotion decisions. Most minority group members are favorable toward affirmative action as one method to promote a redistribution of power in organizations, while many majority group members oppose it as an unwarranted and misguided policy of reverse discrimination. . . . Suffice to say, however, majority group backlash against affirmative action and similar practices are among the most serious forms of intergroup conflict in organizations. . . .

Minority Group Density. Minority group density refers to the percentage representation of a minority group in the total population of a social system. A considerable amount of research in the political science and social science fields has addressed the effects of minority group density on majority-minority relations in diverse groups (Blalock, 1967; Giles & Evans, 1986). Much of the research has focused on how minority group density affects the behavior of majority group members toward minorities. Specifically of interest has been the "minority-group-size-inequality hypothesis" (MGSI) which holds that majority group members tend to lower levels of support for, and increase levels of discrimination against, minorities when their percentage representation increases beyond a certain, relatively low, threshold (Blalock, 1967; Blau, 1977). The essence of the argument is that majority members are less favorable toward minorities when their numbers are relatively large because they perceive them as a threat to their established power.

Blalock's empirical data on the MGSI hypothesis were largely taken from records of voting behavior among whites, and on educational and economic inequality between blacks and whites in the southern United States. He concluded that the level of educational and economic disadvantage for blacks, and the level of support for politically conservative candidates among whites, was systematically related to the percentage representation of blacks in the local area. Consistent with the MGSI hypothesis, Blalock concluded that the aforementioned conditions were more favorable toward blacks in those areas where they had small representations (Blalock, 1967). . . .

A second example is Ott's study (1989) of 297 women in two Dutch police departments. Ott found that male attitudes toward the presence of women shifted from neutral to negative when their numbers reached a critical mass (15-20 percent).

In another relevant study, Hoffman (1985) examined communications patterns in ninety-six groups with varying percentages of black and white government-agency supervisors. He predicted that communication would improve in higher-density groups because there would be less isolation and stereotyping of blacks in groups where they represented a larger percentage of the group. He found, however, that only formal communications such as in staff meetings increased in the higher-density groups. Communication on the interpersonal level actually declined as the percent non-white increased. . . .

Collectively the theory and research of MGSI provide considerable support for the idea that the distribution of power is key to majority-minority group conflict. Promotion decisions are a primary mechanism by which organizations define participation in the formal influence structure, and therefore changes here simultaneously pose a threat to the existing power structure and an opportu-

nity for those who are relatively powerless.

Conformity Versus Identity Affirmation

The final source of interconflict to be
discussed here is the tension between
majority and minority group members
over the preservation of minority group
identity. One perspective on this source
of conflict that I have found very useful
is provided by Ashforth and Mael (1989)
in their discussion of high-status versus
low-status groups in organization: "The
identity of a low-status group is implicitly threatened by a high-status
group. . . . A high-status group, however, is less likely to feel threatened and
thus less in need of positive affirmation.
Accordingly, while a low-status group
may go to great lengths to differentiate
itself from a high-status group, the latter
may be relatively unconcerned about
such comparisons and form no strong
impression about the low-status group.
This indifference of the high-status
group is, perhaps, the greatest threat to
the identity of the low-status group because the latter's identity remains socially unvalidated" (p. 33).

Status is not defined by the authors
but, based on the examples they give,
appears to be closely related to the relative power and prestige of groups. Thus
the majority group in an organization
has higher status than minority groups
by definition. Having made this clarification, we can identify several important
insights in the above quotation. First,
it points out that minority groups will
usually be much more aware of, and more
concerned with, the preservation of
group identity than majority group members will. Not feeling a need for "positive
affirmation" themselves, they often will
not understand or appreciate that members of minority groups do feel this need.
The constant efforts of minority groups

to affirm themselves may annoy majority
group members, who view these efforts
as needless differentiations that serve
no useful purpose. A prime example of
this in organizations is the reaction of
majority group members to support
groups formed by minority group
members. . . . Many majority group
members view these organizations with
disdain. The difference in perspective regarding the need for, and desirability of,
such groups often becomes the focus of
intergroup tensions.

The prevalence of minority support
groups throughout history attests to the
fact that minority group members in majority organizations often feel a need to
form such groups and their purposes are
often expressly understood to include
protection against a perceived threat to
survival of the group (i.e., the groups are
to some degree a reaction to being in
a lower-status situation). Thus, in the
groups of which I have been a member
or had occasion to observe, the role of
the group in identity affirmation has
been explicitly acknowledged. On the
other hand, my experience has been that
majority group members often fail to realize that their opposition to minority
support groups is, in part, a result of their
insensitivity to the identity threat that
minorities feel. The last statement of the
Ashforth and Mael quotation gets at
this. They refer to the indifference of
the high-status group toward efforts of
minority groups to differentiate and affirm themselves. As suggested previously, I have observed numerous cases
where the attitude has gone beyond indifference to a hostility toward efforts of
the minority group to differentiate itself.
The refusal by members of a majority
group to acknowledge the need for support groups leaves differences unvalidated, which minorities are quite sensitive to but majorities, by and large, are
not. Thus Ashforth and Mael have hit

upon an important, albeit subtle, insight into sources of intergroup conflict in organizations related to identity preservation. . . .

A final example of intergroup conflict related to identity preservation is the frequent disagreement over the use of non-majority-group languages in organizations. In my own work, this was illustrated most recently in interviews at the plant site of a large telecommunications company, referred to earlier, that employs a significant number of Laotians. Considerable tensions between Laotian and non-Laotian members of the organization existed. As previously reported some of this was due to conflict over jobs. However, a second dimension was the preference among many of the non-Laotian members for the use of English only in communications in the workplace. Some Laotians felt that this represented an unwarranted denial of their opportunity for cultural expression as well as simply a loss of communication facility when conversing with others who knew their native language. The basis of concern among some about the use of the Laotian language revolved around a discomfort with not being able to understand proximate communication, even when it was directed to someone else, and a concern that it tended to interfere with developing English language skills. . . .

APPROACHES TO MANAGING INTERGROUP CONFLICT

Thus far in this chapter I have reviewed five primary sources of intergroup conflict related to cultural diversity in organizations. There is no question that the potential for increased conflict is a possible downside of increased diversity in workgroups. However, since diversity in many situations is a fact of life and not

a choice, and since the potential benefits of diversity appear to be greater than the potential costs (Cox & Blake, 1991), the challenge for organizations is to manage the conflict. In this final section, I will briefly discuss suggestions for minimizing diversity-related intergroup conflict.

Management writers have identified common approaches to the resolution of intergroup conflict in organizations (Arnold & Feldman, 1986; Randolph & Blackburn, 1989). Table 1 shows a list of the most commonly mentioned strategies, along with my assessment of the sources of diversity-related conflict that they are most effective in addressing.

Competing Goals

As Table 1 indicates, most of the strategies offer some potential for addressing conflict resulting from competing goals. I will discuss two examples. Competing goals between marketing and manufacturing might be addressed by restructuring the organization into cross-functional workteams whose organizational rewards depend upon collaboration and joint outcomes. One of the most promising resolution techniques is to get both departments to focus attention on superordinate organizational goals such as profits and market share rather than on those of their individual departments. As a final example, bargaining and mediation have historically been used to resolve competing interests of management and labor groups, although not always successfully, especially in recent years.

An application of superordinate goals and of smoothing that seems especially pertinent to gender, racioethnic, and nationality diversity in organizations is to capitalize on the shared group identity of the common employer. To do this successfully, minority as well as majority members of organizations have to identify with the employer and have some

TABLE 1 • MANAGING CONFLICT IN DIVERSE WORKGROUPS.

Resolution Strategies	Source of Conflict				
	Competitive Goals	Resources	Cultural Differences	Power Discrepancies	Identity Affirmation
Collaboration/negotiation/bargaining	X			X	X
Alter situation/context (e.g., organization redesign)	X	X		X	X
Procedures/rules/policies		X		X	X
Alter personnel			X		X
Alter/redefine the issues of contention	X		X		
Hierarchial appeal	X			X	
Smoothing (emphasize similarities, play down conflict)	X				
Superordinate goals	X	X			
Structured interactions	X	X	X	X	X
Integrative problem solving (mediation + compromise)	X				X

degree of confidence that the goals of the organization and those of the microculture group are compatible if not mutually supportive.

Competition for Resources

As noted earlier, one of the most common manifestations of resource competition in the context of cultural diversity is competition over jobs. Obviously a great deal of conflict potential is eliminated when jobs are more plentiful. Thus to the extent that overall job opportunities can be expanded, the climate of intergroup relations will be improved immeasurably. Unfortunately, the expansion of resources is often not possible, especially in the short term.

In many organizations, hiring policies—such as Xerox's Balanced Workforce Plan—attempt to formally acknowledge group identities such as gender, racioethnicity, and nationality in regulating the competition for jobs. The goal is to ensure equal competition, although . . . the reaction to such plans among majority group members often heightens intergroup conflict related to job competition. Xerox has been somewhat successful at minimizing and resolving conflict related to their plan partly by paying a lot of attention to how the plan has been communicated.

The utility of superordinate goals for resolving resource-based conflict can be illustrated by considering the case of two departments vying for a larger share of a limited training budget. If both can be encouraged to plan on the basis of the training priorities of the overall organization, it may help to resolve the conflict.

Finally, as with all of the sources of conflict, structured interaction to discuss the points of contention, gain a better appreciation of the other party's perspective, and promote mutual understanding is a potentially valuable tool for re-

solving conflict based on resource competition.

Cultural Differences

Here I recommend three strategies for conflict resolution related to cultural differences, beginning with altering personnel. One way to achieve this goal is by educating existing personnel to obtain a better knowledge of cultural differences. Another way is to hire and promote persons with tolerant and flexible personalities who will productively support cultural-diversity change initiatives in the organization. Stated simply, people who are more tolerant and accepting of difference will produce less conflict when confronted with cultural differences than people who are not. The problem of intergroup conflict is partly due to emotional or affective reactions of individuals.

Redefining issues can also aid in cultural conflict resolution. An example of this is promoting the mindset that cultural differences present opportunities rather than problems to be solved. For example, Blau (1977) argues that increased intergroup experience stimulates intellectual endeavors. One way that this kind of redefinition is illustrated in the language of organizational relations is in the preference for the "valuing" of diversity rather than "tolerating" diversity.

Structured interaction is also usable in resolving conflict related to cultural differences. An example is the use of interdepartmental task forces. Although such groups normally have a specific work task to accomplish, time may be spent initially on activities designed to help representatives of the various departments get to know the culture of the other departments better. Familiarity with the language and norms of the other groups is likely to facilitate the work on the task. Even informal meetings may be of great value. For example, during a recent consulting project with a research and development firm, several engineers and scientists spoke about how some of them had used cross-disciplinary meetings as a means of gaining understanding about the differences between their functions and how they viewed their role in the overall mission of the firm. These persons reported that the meetings had proved valuable in reducing misconceptions between the groups and that joint projects and cross-functional communications had increased as a result.

Power Discrepancies

The earlier discussion of this factor made it clear that power differences between majority and minority members of organizations are perhaps the most deadly of the conflict sources. Power discrepancies are sometimes resolved by negotiations, such as those currently under way between the government of South Africa and the African National Congress over representation of Black and White South Africans in the new government under a democratic model. Power differences may also be resolved by policies, such as designated representation of minority groups in government bodies. For example, a minimum of four seats are reserved for Maoris in the New Zealand legislature.

Another policy with obvious power redistribution objectives is affirmative action in promotion decisions. Although controversial, there is no denying the impact of affirmative action in changing and diversifying the authority structure of an organization. The substantial results of Xerox's Balanced Workforce Plan and U.S. West's Pluralism Performance Effort are two cases in point.

An example of an organization redesign to assist in resolving intergroup power conflicts is the creation of diverse groups of advisers to give direct input

to senior management. U.S. West and Equitable Life Insurance are examples of companies that have created these. To the extent that such groups address issues beyond diversity, they hold the potential to make modest shifts in the power structure of organizations, even though they do not change the fundamental authority hierarchy per se.

It may also be useful to redefine issues as a means of conflict reduction. For example, what is the primary motive for using affirmative action in promotion decisions? Is it to right the wrongs of past discrimination, to address the discrimination of the present, to meet social responsibility objectives, or to meet economic responsibilities of the organization? . . . I submit that how these questions are answered, and the extent to which their answers are understood and embraced by members of organizations, has much to do with the success in resolving power-based conflict in organizations.

Finally, planned interactions between groups to discuss the existence of power discrepancies, their effects, and what to do about them are advised for majority-minority situations of all kinds.

Conflict over Conformity Versus Affirmative Identity

In this last category, a number of strategies are indicated in Table 1 as potentially effective. First, since some combination of assimilation to majority group norms and preservation of microculture norms is expected, the techniques of negotiation and compromise seem at least theoretically relevant. One example is the extent to which organizations adapt the work environment to accommodate a particular disability of an employee or potential employee. In many instances the level of accommodation will not eliminate all barriers to full participation. However, some compromise may be reached that reduces the potential for conflict between persons with disabilities seeking accommodation and fully able members who may feel that the cost of accommodations places an undue burden on the financial and social resources of the firm.

In some instances, mediation may be of help in resolving intergroup differences related to conformity. One example is when consultants on workforce diversity are asked to assist in improving relations between identity-based employee support groups and the senior management of organizations. This work includes increasing awareness among senior management of the importance of identity affirmation by members of minority groups, as well as increasing sensitivity among support-group members of senior management concerns over the existence and purposes of these groups.

An example of a structural/environmental change that organizations can make to alter conflict potential related to conformity is the selection of a mode of acculturation. . . . [S]uffice to say here that an organization's choice of whether to approach acculturation using a pluralism or a traditional assimilation model has many implications for the identity-based conflict under discussion here.

Another type of identity-related conflict that was discussed above is disagreement over the use of alternative languages. Organizations may wish to address this type of conflict by establishing a policy statement about the use of alternative languages in the workplace that is sensitive to the concerns of both groups. Companies such as Esprit De Corp., Economy Color Card, and Pace Foods are examples of firms that have taken what I consider to be a sound approach by supporting the learning of alternative languages by English-only speakers and the formal use of non-

English languages under some conditions such as in published policy manuals (Cox, 1991).

Concerning altering personnel, the same points made earlier in this section about cultural differences apply here. Intolerant, narrow-minded people will tend to expand the scope of behaviors for which pressure is applied to conform to the norms of the majority group. It is true that restricting the hiring of persons in minority groups to those who do not have a strong concern with the preservation of microcultural identity may eliminate some potential intergroup conflict by creating a more culturally homogeneous organization. This approach is not recommended, however, because it is out of step with worldwide labor-force demographic trends and because it brings other, unaffordable costs, such as the loss of divergent cultural perspectives to enhance problem solving. . . .

REFERENCES

Alderfer, C. P., Alderfer, C. J., Tucker, L., & Tucker, R. (1980). Diagnosing race relations in management. *Journal of Applied Behavioral Science, 16,* 135–166.

Alderfer, C. P., & Smith, K. K. (1982). Studying intergroup relations embedded in organizations. *Administrative Science Quarterly 27,* 5–65.

Arnold, H., & Feldman, D. (1986). *Organizational behavior.* New York: McGraw-Hill.

Ashforth, B., & Mael, F. (1989). Social identity theory and the organization. *Academy of Management Review, 14*(1), 20–39.

Blalock, H., Jr. (1967). *Toward a theory of minority-group relations.* New York: Wiley.

Blau, P.M. (1977). A macrosociological theory of social structure. *American Journal of Sociology, 83,* 26–54.

Campbell, D. T. (1965). Ethnocentric and other altruistic motives. In D. Levine (Ed.), *Nebraska symposium on motivation* (pp. 283–311). Lincoln: University of Nebraska Press.

Cox, T. H. (1991). The multicultural organization. *The Executive, 5*(2), 34–47.

Cox, T. H., & Blake, S. (1991). Managing cultural diversity: Implications for organizational competitiveness. *The Executive, 5*(3), 45–56.

Daft, R., & Steers, R. (1986). *Organizations: A micro/macro approach.* Glenview, IL: Scott-Foresman.

Germans try to stem right wing attacks against foreigners. (1991, December 4). *Wall Street Journal.*

Giles, M. W., & Evans, A. (1986). The power approach to intergroup hostility. *Journal of Conflict Resolution, 30*(3), 469–486.

Hoffman, E. (1985). The effect of race ratio composition on the frequency of organizational communication. *Social Psychology Quarterly, 48*(1), 17–26.

Landis, D., & Boucher, J. (1987). Themes and models of conflict. In J. Boucher, D. Landis, & K. A. Clark (Eds.), *Ethnic conflict: International perspectives* (pp. 18–32). Newbury Park, CA: Sage.

Ott, E. M. (1989). Effects of the male-female ratio. *Psychology of Women Quarterly, 13,* 41–57.

Randolph, W. A., & Blackburn, R. S. (1989). *Managing organizational behavior.* Homewood, IL: Richard D. Irwin.

Rummell, R. J. (1976). *Understanding conflict and war.* New York: Wiley.

Sherif, M. (1966). *Group conflict and cooperation.* London: Routledge & Kegan Paul.

CHAPTER IV

"Modern" Structural Organization Theory

Usually when someone refers to the structure of an organization, that person is talking about the relatively stable relationships among the positions, groups of positions (units), and work processes that make up the organization. Structural organization theory is concerned with vertical differentiations—hierarchical levels of organizational authority and coordination, and horizontal differentiations between organizational units—for example, between product or service lines, geographical areas, or skills. The organization chart is the ever-present "tool" of a structural organization theorist.

Why do we use the label "modern" to modify structural organization theory? Most organizational theorists from the classical school were structuralists. They focused their attention on the structure—or design—of organizations and their production processes. Some examples that are reprinted in Chapter I include those by Adam Smith, Henri Fayol, Daniel McCallum, Frederick Winslow Taylor, and Max Weber. Thus we use the word "modern" (always in quotation marks) merely to differentiate between the structural organization theorists of the 1960s and 1970s and the pre-World War II classical school structuralists.

The "modern" structuralists are concerned with many of the same issues that the classical structuralists were, but their theories have been influenced by and have benefited greatly from advancements in organization theory since World War II. Modern structuralists' roots are in the thinking of Fayol, Taylor, Gulick, and Weber, and their underlying tenets are quite similar: Organizational efficiency is the essence of organizational rationality; the goal of rationality is to increase the production of wealth in terms of real goods and services. However, "modern" structural theories also have been influenced substantially by the neoclassical, human relations-oriented, and systems theorists of organization.

Bolman and Deal (1991) identify the basic assumptions of the structural perspective:

1. Organizations are rational institutions whose primary purpose is to accomplish established objectives; rational organizational behavior is achieved best through systems of defined rules and formal authority. Organizational control and coordination are key for maintaining organizational rationality.

2. There is a "best" structure for any organization—or at least a most appropriate structure— in light of its given objectives, the environmental conditions surrounding it (for example, its markets, the competition, and the extent of government regulation), the nature of its products and/or services (the "best" structure for a management consulting firm probably is substantially different from that for a certified public accounting firm), and the technology of the production processes (a coal mining company has a different "best structure" than the "high tech" manufacturer of computer microcomponents).

3. Specialization and the division of labor increase the quality and quantity of production—particularly in highly skilled operations and professions.

4. Most problems in an organization result from structural flaws and can be solved by changing the structure.

What sorts of practical issues are best addressed by "modern" structural organization theory? Is it useful? The most immediate issue in the design of any organization is the question of structure. What should it look like? How should it work? How will it deal with the most common structural questions of specialization, departmentalization, span of control, and the coordination and control of specialized units?

Tom Burns and G. M. Stalker of the Tavistock Institute in London—which is widely acknowledged as the birthplace of the "socio-technical approach" to organizations—developed their widely cited theory of "mechanistic and organic systems" of organization while examining rapid technological change in the British and Scottish electronics industry in the post–World War II years. Their account of "Mechanistic and Organic Systems" from their 1961 book, *The Management of Innovation,* is reprinted here.

Burns and Stalker found that stable conditions may suggest the use of a mechanistic form of organization where a traditional pattern of hierarchy, reliance on formal rules and regulations, vertical communications, and structured decision making is possible. However, more dynamic conditions—situations in which the environment changes rapidly—require the use of an organic form of organization where there is less rigidity, more participation, and more reliance on workers to define and redefine their positions and relationships. For example, technological creativity, an essential ingredient in an organic system, requires an organizational climate and management systems that are supportive of innovation. The impacts of these two organizational forms on individuals are substantially different. Supervisors and managers find that the mechanistic form provides them with a greater sense of security in dealing with their environment than the organic form, which introduces much greater uncertainty. Bums and Stalker conclude that either form of organization may be appropriate in particular situations.

In "The Concept of Formal Organization," a chapter from their 1962 book *Formal Organizations: A Comparative Approach,* Peter M. Blau and W. Richard Scott assert that all organizations include both a formal and informal element. The informal organization by its nature is rooted in the formal structure and supports its formal organization by establishing norms for the operation of the organization—

which cannot always be spelled out by rules and policies. For these reasons, Blau and Scott maintain that it is impossible to know and understand the true structure of a formal organization without a similar understanding of its parallel informal organization. Clearly, Blau and Scott were influenced by the "classical philosopher" Chester Barnard's 1938 book *The Functions of the Executive*, in which he held that:

> informal organization, although comprising the processes of society which are unconscious as contrasted with those of formal organizations which are conscious, has two important classes of effects: (*a*) it establishes certain attitudes, understandings, customs, habits, institutions, and (*b*) it creates the condition under which formal organization may arise.

Arthur H. Walker and Jay W. Lorsch, in their 1968 *Harvard Business Review* article "Organizational Choice: Product vs. Function," grapple with one of the perennial questions facing those who would design organizations: Should an organization be structured according to product or function? "Should all specialists in a given function be grouped under a common boss, regardless of differences in products they are involved in, or should the various functional specialists working on a single product be grouped together under the same superior?" Walker and Lorsch tackle this problem by examining two firms in the same industry—one organized by product and the other by function. They conclude that either structural arrangement can be appropriate, depending upon the organization's environment and the nature of the organization itself.

In 1776, Adam Smith advocated the division of labor to increase the effectiveness of the factory system of production. In 1922, Max Weber described two strong and opposing forces that have an impact on all organizations: the need for division of labor and specialization, and the need for centralizing authority. Division of labor is an inevitable consequence of specialization by skills, products, or processes. Most "modern" structuralists now use the word *differentiation*—which means essentially the same thing as specialization but also reflects increased appreciation of the myriad and rapidly changing external environmental forces with which organizations interact (for example, different markets, sociopolitical cultures, regulatory environments, technologies, competition, and the economy). Thus, complex differentiation is essential for organizational effectiveness as well as efficiency. However, differentiation *means* diverse forces that "pull organizations apart." Differentiation increases the need for organizational coordination and control that, in the language of "modern" structuralists, is labeled "integration."

Henry Mintzberg emerged as one of the most widely respected management and organizational theorists of the 1970s and 1980s. Since the 1960s, Mintzberg has been compiling a theory of management policy—a field of management and organization theory that has lacked attention. An adaptation of his early conceptual model of management policy is in Figure 1. The model demonstrates why Mintzberg is so influential: He is synthesizing many schools of organization and management theory—and doing so with coherence. His 1979 book *The Structuring of Organizations* addresses the first component of the model. (His 1983 book *Power in and Around*

FIGURE 1 • MINTZBERG'S BASIC MODEL OF MANAGEMENT POLICY

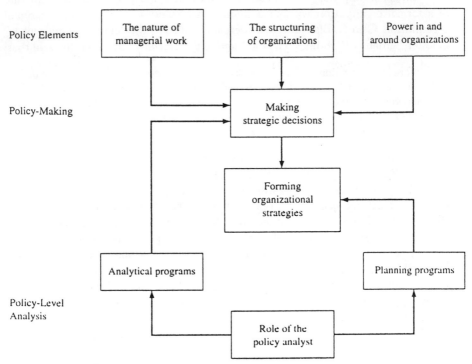

Source: Adapted from Mintzberg, H. (1979). *The Structuring of Organizations* (p. iv). Englewood Cliffs, NJ: Prentice-Hall.

Organizations addresses the second component of the model. A chapter from it is reprinted in our Chapter VI.) In his chapter "Five Basic Parts of the Organization," which is reprinted here, Mintzberg uses James D. Thompson's (1967) concepts of "pooled, sequential, and reciprocal organizational coupling" to create a model of organizations with five interdependent parts: the strategic apex, the middle line, the operating core, the technostructure, and the support staff. His model is a creative and useful departure from traditional views of formal organization structure.

From the mid-1960s until well into the late 1980s, the historical attacks against the bureaucratic form of organization were renewed and expanded. For example, in *Changing Organizations* (1966), Warren Bennis predicted that bureaucratic organizations as we know them will disappear within this century because they are unable to adapt to rapidly changing environments. Alvin Toffler's chapter in *Future Shock* (1970), "Organization: The Coming Ad-hocracy," reflects Bennis' thinking, and Bennis and Philip Slater's *The Temporary Society* (1968) extended Bennis' (1966) theme to predict a rise in democracy within organizations as well as in general society. Frederick Thayer (1981) identifies hierarchy as *the* root cause of alienation in organizations. Yet, all theories of organizational democracy are based on the assumption that hierarcy is desirable, necessary, and inevitable. Peter Drucker (1988) predicted flatter, more information-based, task- and mission-focused organizations. Edgar Schein (1989) foresees that information technology will eliminate the need for most functions currently performed by supervisors and thus eliminate the need for hierarchical arrangements. However, as much as we may need new non-hierarchical models, "we may have difficulty inventing them because of the automatic tendency to think hierarchically" (p. 63).

Is the bureaucratic form of organization on an inevitable road to extinction? Is it being replaced by systems of temporary democratic networks or structures without hierarchical layers of authority, responsibility, and accountability? If so, the trend isn't apparent yet. In fact, bureaucracy appears to be holding its own quite well in practice—even if not in the mainstream literature of organization theory. A small body of literature has even developed within the discipline of public administration that justifies the bureaucratic form of organization because of its efficiency and its promotion of equity and representativeness (Kaufman, 1977; Krislov & Rosenbloom, 1981; Goodsell, 1983).

Elliott Jaques, whose studies of organizations and structure have spanned more than forty years—from the Tavistock Institute's socio-technical systems "Glacier Project" (1950) to the present, has asserted himself as a foremost defender of the hierarchical-bureaucratic form of organization in the early 1990s. Jaques contends that those who argue against hierarchy are "simply wrong, and all their proposals are based on an inadequate understanding of not only hierarchy but also human nature." Hierarchical layers enable organizations to cope with discontinuities in mental and physical complexities, thereby separating tasks into manageable series of steps: "What we need is not some new kind of organization. What we need is managerial hierarchy that understands its own nature and purpose." According to Jaques, hierarchy is *the* best alternative for large organizations: "We need to stop casting about fruitlessly for organizational Holy Grails and settle down to the hard work of putting our managerial hierarchies in order."

REFERENCES

Barnard, C. I. (1938). *The functions of the executive.* Cambridge, MA: Harvard University Press.

Bennis, W. G. (1966). *Changing organizations.* New York: McGraw-Hill.

Bennis, W. G., & Slater, P. E. (1968). *The temporary society.* New York: Harper & Row.

Blau, P. M., & Scott, W. R. (1962). *Formal organizations: A comparative approach.* San Francisco: Jossey-Bass.

Bolman, L. G., & Deal, T. E. (1991). *Reframing organizations: Artistry, choice, and leadership.* San Francisco: Jossey-Bass.

Burns, T., & Stalker, G. M. (1961). *The management of innovation.* London: Tavistock Publications.

Crozier, M. (1964). *The bureaucratic phenomenon*. Chicago: University of Chicago Press.

Davis, S. M., & Lawrence, P. R. (1977). *Matrix*. Reading, MA: Addison-Wesley.

Drucker, P. F. (1988, January-February). The coming of the new organization. *Harvard Business Review*, 45–53.

Etzioni, A. (1961). *A comparative analysis of complex organizations*. Englewood Cliffs, NJ: Prentice-Hall.

Goodsell, C. T. (1983). *The case for bureaucracy: A public administration polemic*. Chatham, NJ: Chatham House.

Jaques, E. (1950). Collaborative group methods in a wage negotiation situation (The Glacier Project—I). *Human Relations, 3*(3).

Jaques, E. (1990, January-February). In praise of hierarchy. *Harvard Business Review*, 127–133.

Kaufman, H. (1977). *Red tape*. Washington, DC: Brookings Institution.

Krislov, S., & Rosenbloom, D. H. (1981). *Representative bureaucracy and the American political system*. New York: Praeger.

Lawrence, P. R., & Lorsch, J. W. (1969). *Developing organizations*. Reading, MA: Addison-Wesley.

Mintzberg, H. (1979). *The structuring of organizations*. Englewood Cliffs, NJ: Prentice-Hall.

Mintzberg. H. (1983). *Power in and around organizations*. Englewood Cliffs, NJ: Prentice-Hall.

Schein, E. H. (1989, Winter). Reassessing the "divine rights" of managers. *Sloan Management Review, 30*(2), 63–68.

Thayer, F. C. (1981). *An end to hierarchy and competition: Administration in the post-affluent world* (2d ed.). New York: New Viewpoints.

Thompson, J. D. (1967). *Organizations in action*. New York: McGraw-Hill.

Thompson, V. A. (1961). *Modern organization*. New York: Knopf.

Toffler, A. (1970). *Future Shock*. New York: Random House.

Walker, A. H., & Lorsch, J. W. (1968, November-December). Organizational choice: Product vs. function. *Harvard Business Review, 46*, 129–138.

18
Mechanistic and Organic Systems
Tom Burns and G. M. Stalker

We are now at the point at which we may set down the outline of the two management systems which represent for us . . . the two polar extremities of the forms which such systems can take when they are adapted to a specific rate of technical and commercial change. The cases we have tried to establish from the literature, as from our research experience . . . , is that the different forms assumed by a working organization do exist objectively and are not merely interpretations offered by observers of different schools. ·

Both types represent a "rational" form of organization, in that they may both, in our experience, be explicitly and deliberately created and maintained to exploit the human resources of a concern in the most efficient manner feasible in the circumstances of the concern. Not surprisingly, however, each exhibits characteristics which have been hitherto associated with different kinds of interpretation. For it is our contention that empirical findings have usually been classified according to sociological ideology rather than according to the functional specificity of the working organization to its task and the conditions confronting it.

We have tried to argue that these are two formally contrasted forms of management system. These we shall call the mechanistic and organic forms.

A mechanistic management system is appropriate to stable conditions. It is characterized by:

(*a*) the specialized differentiation of functional tasks into which the problems and tasks facing the concern as a whole are broken down;

(*b*) the abstract nature of each individual task, which is pursued with techniques and purposes more or less distinct from those of the concern as a whole; *i.e.*, the functionaries tend to pursue the technical improvement of means, rather than the accomplishment of the ends of the concern;

(*c*) the reconciliation, for each level in the hierarchy, of these distinct performances by the immediate superiors, who are also, in turn, responsible for seeing that each is relevant in his own special part of the main task.

(*d*) the precise definition of rights and obligations and technical methods attached to each functional role;

(*e*) the translation of rights and obligations and methods into the responsibilities of a functional position;

(*f*) hierarchic structure of control, authority, and communication;

(*g*) a reinforcement of the hierarchic structure by the location of knowledge of actualities exclusively at the top of the hierarchy, where the final reconciliation of distinct tasks and assessment of relevance is made.[1]

Source: From Tom Burns and G. M. Stalker, *The Management of Innovation* (London: Tavistock Publications, 1961), 119–125. Reprinted by permission. References omitted; footnotes retained.

(*h*) a tendency for interaction between members of the concern to be vertical, *i.e.*, between superior and subordinate;

(*i*) a tendency for operations and working behavior to be governed by the instructions and decisions issued by superiors;

(*j*) insistence on loyalty to the concern and obedience to superiors as a condition of membership;

(*k*) a greater importance and prestige attaching to internal (local) than to general (cosmopolitan) knowledge, experience, and skill.

The *organic* form is appropriate to changing conditions, which give rise constantly to fresh problems and unforeseen requirements for action which cannot be broken down or distributed automatically arising from the functional roles defined within a hierarchic structure. It is characterized by:

(*a*) the contributive nature of special knowledge and experience to the common task of the concern;

(*b*) the "realistic" nature of the individual task, which is seen as set by the total situation of the concern;

(*c*) the adjustment and continual redefinition of individual tasks through interaction with others;

(*d*) the shedding of "responsibility" as a limited field of rights, obligations and methods (Problems may not be posted upwards, downwards or sideways as being someone else's responsibility);

(*e*) the spread of commitment to the concern beyond any technical definition;

(*f*) a network structure of control, authority, and communication. The sanctions which apply to the individual's conduct in his working role derive more from presumed community of interest with the rest of the working organization

in the survival and growth of the firm, and less from a contractual relationship between himself and a nonpersonal corporation, represented for him by an immediate superior;

(*g*) omniscience no longer imputed to the head of the concern; knowledge about the technical or commercial nature of the here and now task may be located anywhere in the network; this location becoming the ad hoc centre of control authority and communication;

(*h*) a lateral rather than a vertical direction of communication through the organization, communication between people of different rank, also, resembling consultation rather than command;

(*i*) a content of communication which consists of information and advice rather than instructions and decisions;

(*j*) commitment to the concern's task and to the "technological ethos" of material progress and expansion is more highly valued than loyalty and obedience;

(*k*) importance and prestige attach to affiliations and expertise valid in the industrial and technical and commercial milieux external to the firm.

One important corollary to be attached to this account is that while organic systems are not hierarchic in the same sense as are mechanistic, they remain stratified. Positions are differentiated according to seniority—*i.e.*, greater expertise. The lead in joint decisions is frequently taken by seniors, but it is an essential presumption of the organic system that the lead, *i.e.*, "authority," is taken by whoever shows himself most informed and capable, *i.e.*, the "best authority." The location of authority is settled by consensus.

A second observation is that the area of commitment to the concern—the extent to which the individual yields himself as a resource to be used by the working organization—is far more extensive in organic than in mechanistic systems. Commitment, in fact, is expected to approach that of the professional scientist to his work, and frequently does. One further consequence of this is that it becomes far less feasible to distinguish "informal" from "formal" organization.

Thirdly, the emptying out of significance from the hierarchic command system, by which co-operation is ensured and which serves to monitor the working organization under a mechanistic system, is countered by the development of shared beliefs about the values and goals of the concern. The growth and accretion of institutionalized values, beliefs, and conduct, in the form of commitments, ideology, and manners, around an image of the concern in its industrial and commercial setting make good the loss of formal structure.

Finally, the two forms of systems represent a polarity, not a dichotomy; there are, as we have tried to show, intermediate stages between the extremities empirically known to us. Also, the relation of one form to the other is elastic, so that a concern oscillating between relative stability and relative change may also oscillate between the two forms. A concern may (and frequently does) operate with a management system which includes both types.

The organic form, by departing from the familiar clarity and fixity of the hierarchic structure, is often experienced by the individual manager as an uneasy, embarrassed, or chronically anxious quest for knowledge about what he should be doing, or what is expected of him, and similar apprehensiveness about what others are doing. Indeed, as we shall see later, this kind of response is necessary if the organic form of organization is to work effectively. Understandably, such anxiety finds expression in resentment when the apparent confusion

besetting him is not explained. In these situations, all managers some of the time, and many managers all of the time, yearn for more definition and structure.

On the other hand, some managers recognize a rationale of nondefinition, a reasoned basis for the practice of those successful firms in which designation of status, function, and line of responsibility and authority has been vague or even avoided.

The desire for more definition is often in effect a wish to have the limits of one's task more neatly defined—to know what and when one doesn't have to bother about as much as to know what one does have to. It follows that the more definition is given, the more omniscient the management must be, so that no functions are left whole or partly undischarged, no person is overburdened with undelegated responsibility, or left without the authority to do his job properly. To do this, to have all the separate functions attached to individual roles fitting together and comprehensively, to have communication between persons constantly maintained on a level adequate to the needs of each functional role, requires rules or traditions of behavior proved over a long time and an equally fixed, stable task. The omniscience which may then be credited to the head of the concern is expressed throughout its body through the lines of command, extending in a clear, explicitly titled hierarchy of officers and subordinates.

The whole mechanistic form is instinct with this twofold principle of definition and dependence which acts as the frame within which action is conceived and carried out. It works, unconsciously, almost in the smallest minutiae of daily activity. "How late is late?" The answer to this question is not to be found in the rule book, but in the superior. Late is when the boss thinks it is late.

Is he the kind of man who thinks 8:00 is the time, and 8:01 is late? Does he think that 8:15 is all right occasionally if it is not a regular thing? Does he think that everyone should be allowed a 5-minute grace after 8:00 but after that they are late?

Settling questions about how a person's job is to be done in this way is nevertheless simple, direct, and economical of effort. We shall, in a later chapter, examine more fully the nature of the protection and freedom (in other respects than his job) which this affords the individual.

One other feature of mechanistic organization needs emphasis. It is a necessary condition of its operation that the individual "works on his own," functionally isolated; he "knows his job," he is "responsible for seeing it's done." He works at a job which is in a sense artificially abstracted from the realities of the situation the concern is dealing with, the accountant "dealing with the costs side," the works manager "pushing production," and so on. As this works out in practice, the rest of the organization becomes part of the problem situation the individual has to deal with in order to perform successfully; *i.e.*, difficulties and problems arising from work or information which has been handed over the "responsibility barrier" between two jobs or departments are regarded as "really" the responsibility of the person from whom they were received. As a design engineer put it,

> When you get designers handing over designs completely to production, it's "their responsibility" now. And you get tennis games played with the responsibility for anything that goes wrong. What happens is that you're constantly getting unsuspected faults arising from characteristics which you didn't think important in the design. If you get to hear of these through a sales person, or a production person, or

somebody to whom the design was handed over to in the dim past, then, instead of being a design problem, it's an annoyance caused by that particular person, who can't do his own job—because you'd thought you were finished with that one, and you're on to something else now.

When the assumptions of the form of organization make for preoccupation with specialized tasks, the chances of career success, or of greater influence, depend rather on the relative importance which may be attached to each special function by the superior whose task it is to reconcile and control a number of them. And, indeed, to press the claims of one's job or department for a bigger share of the firm's resources is in many cases regarded as a mark of initiative, of effectiveness, and even of "loyalty to the firm's interests." The state of affairs thus engendered squares with the role of the superior, the man who can see the wood instead of just the trees, and gives it the reinforcement of the aloof detachment belonging to a court of appeal. The ordinary relationship prevailing between individual managers "in charge of" different functions is one of rivalry, a rivalry which may be rendered innocuous to the persons involved by personal friendship or the norms of sociability, but which turns discussion about the situations which constitute the real problems of the concern—how to make the products more cheaply, how to sell more, how to allocate resources, whether to curtail activity in one sector, whether to risk expansion in another and so on—into an arena of conflicting interests.

The distinctive feature of the second, organic system is the pervasiveness of the working organization as an institution. In concrete terms, this makes itself felt in a preparedness to combine with others in serving the general aims of the concern. Proportionately to the rate and extent of change, the less can the omniscience appropriate to command organizations be ascribed to the head of the organization; for executives, and even operatives, in a changing firm it is always theirs to reason why. Furthermore, the less definition can be given to status roles, and modes of communication, the more do the activities of each member of the organization become determined by the real tasks of the firm as he sees them than by instruction and routine. The individual's job ceases to be self-contained; the only way in which "his" job can be done is by his participating continually with others in the solution of problems which are real to the firm, and put in a language of requirements and activities meaningful to them all. Such methods of working put much heavier demands on the individual. . . .

We have endeavored to stress the appropriateness of each system to its own specific set of conditions. Equally, we desire to avoid the suggestion that either system is superior under all circumstances to the other. In particular, nothing in our experience justifies the assumption that mechanistic systems should be superseded by organic in conditions of stability.[2] The beginning of administrative wisdom is the awareness that there is no one optimum type of management system.

NOTES

1. This functional attribute to the head of a concern often takes on a clearly expressive aspect. It is common enough for concerns to instruct all people with whom they deal to address correspondence to the firm (*i.e.*, to its formal head) and for all outgoing letters and orders to be signed by the head of the concern. Similarly, the printed letter heading used by Government departments carries instructions for the replies to be addressed to the Secretary, etc. These instructions are not always taken seriously, either by members of the organization or their correspondents, but in one company this practice was insisted upon and was taken to somewhat unusual lengths; *all* correspondence was delivered to the managing director, who would thereafter distribute excerpts to members of the staff, synthesizing their replies into the letter of reply which he eventually sent. Telephone communication was also controlled by limiting the number of extensions, and by monitoring incoming and outgoing calls.

2. A recent instance of this assumption is contained in H. A. Shepard's paper addressed to the Symposium on the Direction of Research Establishments, 1956. "There is much evidence to suggest that the optimal use of human resources in industrial organizations requires a different set of conditions, assumptions, and skills from those traditionally present in industry. Over the past twenty-five years, some new orientations have emerged from organizational experiments, observations, and inventions. The new orientations depart radically from doctrines associated with 'Scientific Management' and traditional bureaucratic patterns.

The central emphases in this development are as follows:

1. Wide participation in decision-making, rather than centralized decision-making.
2. The face-to-face group, rather than the individual, as the basic unit of organization.
3. Mutual confidence, rather than authority, the integrative force in organization.
4. The supervisor as the agent for maintaining intragroup and intergroup communication, rather than as the agent of higher authority.
5. Growth of members of the organization to greater responsibility, rather than external control of the member's performance or their tasks."

19
The Concept of Formal Organization
Peter M. Blau and W. Richard Scott

SOCIAL ORGANIZATION AND FORMAL ORGANIZATIONS

Although a wide variety of organizations exists, when we speak of an organization it is generally quite clear what we mean and what we do not mean by this term. We may refer to the American Medical Association as an organization, or to a college fraternity; to the Bureau of Internal Revenue, or to a union; to General Motors, or to a church; to the Daughters of the American Revolution, or to an army. But we would not call a family an organization, nor would we so designate a friendship clique, or a community, or an economic market, or the political institutions of a society. What is the specific and differentiating criterion implicit in our intuitive distinction of organizations from other kinds of social groupings or institutions? It has something to do with how human conduct becomes socially organized, but it is not, as one might first suspect, whether or not social controls order and organize the conduct of individuals, since such social controls operate in both types of circumstances.

Before specifying what is meant by formal organization, let us clarify the general concept of social organization. "Social organization" refers to the ways in which human conduct becomes socially organized, that is, to the observed regularities in the behavior of people that are due to the social conditions in which they find themselves rather than to their physiological or psychological characteristics as individuals. The many social conditions that influence the conduct of people can be divided into two main types, which constitute the two basic aspects of social organizations: (1) the structure of social relations in a group or larger collectivity of people, and (2) the shared beliefs and orientations that unite the members of the collectivity and guide their conduct.

The conception of structure or system implies that the component units stand in some relation to one another and, as the popular expression "The whole is greater than the sum of its parts" suggests, that the relations between units add new elements to the situation.[1] This aphorism, like so many others, is a half-truth. The sum of fifteen apples, for example, is no more than fifteen times one apple. But a block of ice is more than the sum of the atoms of hydrogen and oxygen that compose it. In the case of the apples, there exist no linkages or relations between the units comprising the whole. In the case of the ice, however, specific connections have been formed between H and O atoms and among H_2O molecules that distinguish ice from hydrogen and oxygen, on the one hand, and from water, on the other. Similarly, a busload of passengers does not constitute a group, since no social relations unify individuals into a common structure.[2] But a busload of club

Source: From Peter M. Blau and W. Richard Scott, *Formal Organizations: A Comparative Approach*, (Chandler Publishing, 1962), 2–8. Copyright © 1962 by Peter M. Blau and W. Richard Scott. Reprinted by permission of the authors.

members on a Sunday outing is a group, because a network of social relations links the members into a social structure, a structure which is an emergent characteristic of the collectivity that cannot be reduced to the attributes of its individual members. In short, a network of social relations transforms an aggregate of individuals into a group (or an aggregate of groups into a larger social structure), and the group is more than the sum of the individuals composing it since the structure of social relations is an emergent element that influences the conduct of individuals.

To indicate the nature of social relations, we can briefly dissect this concept. Social relations involve, first, patterns of social interaction: the frequency and duration of the contacts between people, the tendency to initiate these contacts, the direction of influence between persons, the degree of cooperation, and so forth. Second, social relations entail people's sentiments to one another, such feelings of attraction, respect, and hostility. The differential distribution of social relations in a group, finally, defines its status structure. Each member's status in the group depends on his relations with the others—their sentiments toward and interaction with him. As a result, integrated members become differentiated from isolates, those who are widely respected from those who are not highly regarded, and leaders from followers. In addition to these relations between individuals within groups, relations also develop between groups, relations that are a source of still another aspect of social status, since the standing of the group in the larger social system becomes part of the status of any of its members. An obvious example is the significance that membership in an ethnic minority, say, Puerto Rican, has for an individual's social status.

The networks of social relations between individuals and groups, and the status structure defined by them, constitute the core of the social organization to a collectivity, but not the whole of it. The other main dimension of social organization is a system of shared beliefs and orientations, which serve as standards for human conduct. In the course of social interaction common notions arise as to how people should act and interact and what objectives are worthy of attainment. First, common values crystallize, values that govern the goals for which men strive—their ideals and their ideas of what is desirable—such as our belief in democracy or the importance financial success assumes in our thinking. Second, social norms develop—that is, common expectations concerning how people ought to behave—and social sanctions are used to discourage violations of these norms. These socially sanctioned rules of conduct vary in significance from moral principles or mores, as Sumner calls them, to mere customs or folkways. If values define the ends of human conduct, norms distinguish behavior that is a legitimate means for achieving these ends from behavior that is illegitimate. Finally, aside from the norms to which everybody is expected to conform, differential role expectations also emerge, expectations that become associated with various social positions. Only women in our society are expected to wear skirts, for example. Or, the respected leader of a group is expected to make suggestions, and the other members will turn to him in times of difficulties, whereas group members who have not earned the respect of others are expected to refrain from making suggestions and generally to participate little in group discussions.

These two dimensions of social organization—the networks of social relations and the shared orientations—are often referred to as the social structure and the culture, respectively.[3] Every society has a complex social structure and a complex culture, and every community within a society can be characterized by these two dimensions of social organization, and so can every group within a community (except that the specific term "culture" is reserved for the largest social systems). The prevailing cultural standards and the structure of social relations serve to organize human conduct in the collectivity. As people conform more or less closely to the expectations of their fellows, and as the degree of their conformity in turn influences their relations with others and their social status, and as their status in further turn affects their inclinations to adhere to social norms and their chances to achieve valued objectives, their patterns of behavior become socially organized.

In contrast to the social organization that emerges whenever men are living together, there are organizations that have been deliberately established for a certain purpose.[4] If the accomplishment of an objective requires collective effort, men set up an organization designed to coordinate the activities of many persons and to furnish incentives for others to join them for this purpose. For example, business concerns are established in order to produce goods that can be sold for a profit, and workers organize unions in order to increase their bargaining power with employers. In these cases, the goals to be achieved, the rules the members of the organization are expected to follow, and the status structure that defines the relations between them (the organizational chart) have not spontaneously emerged in the course of social interaction but have been had consciously designed a priori to anticipate and guide interaction and activities. Since the distinctive characteristic of these organizations is that they have been formally established for the explicit purpose of achieving certain goals, the term "formal organization" is used to

designate them. And this formal establishment for explicit purpose is the criterion that distinguishes our subject matter from the study of social organization in general.

FORMAL ORGANIZATION AND INFORMAL ORGANIZATION

The fact that an organization has been formally established, however, does not mean that all activities and interactions of its members conform strictly to the official blueprint. Regardless of the time and effort devoted by management to designing a rational organization chart and elaborate procedure manuals, this official plan can never completely determine the conduct and social relations of the organization's members. Stephen Vincent Benét illustrates this limitation when he contrasts the military blueprint with military action:

If you take a flat map
And move wooden blocks upon it strategically,
The thing looks well, the blocks behave as they should.
The science of war is moving live men like blocks.
And getting the blocks into place at a fixed moment.
But it takes time to mold your men into blocks
And flat maps turn into country where creeks and gullies
Hamper you wooden squares. They stick in the brush,
They are tired and rest, they straggle after ripe blackberries.
And you cannot lift them up in your hand and move them.[5]

In every formal organization there arise informal organizations. The constituent groups of the organization, like all groups, develop their own practices, values, norms, and social relations as their members live and work together. The roots of these informal systems are embedded in the formal organization itself and nurtured by the very formality of its arrangements. Official rules must be general to have sufficient scope to cover the multitude of situations that may arise. But the application of these general rules to particular cases often poses problems of judgment, and informal practices tend to emerge that provide solutions for these problems. Decisions not anticipated by official regulations must frequently be made, particularly in times of change, and here again unofficial practices are likely to furnish guides for decisions long before the formal rules have been adapted to the changing circumstances. Moreover, unofficial norms are apt to develop that regulate performance and productivity. Finally, complex networks of social relations and informal status structures emerge, within groups and between them, which are influenced by many factors besides the organizational chart, for example by the background characteristics of various persons, their abilities, their willingness to help others, and their conformity to group norms. But to say that these informal structures are not completely determined by the formal institutions is not to say that they are entirely independent of it. For informal organizations develop in response to the opportunities created and the problems posed by their environment, and the formal organization constitutes the immediate environment of the groups within it.

When we speak of formal organizations in this book, we do not mean to imply that attention is confined to formally instituted patterns; quite the contrary. It is impossible to understand the nature of a formal organization without investigating the networks of informal relations and the unofficial norms as well as the formal hierarchy of authority and the official body of rules, since the formally instituted and the informally emerging patterns are inextricably intertwined. The distinction between the formal and the informal aspects of organizational life is only an analytical one and should not be reified; there is only one actual organization. Note also that one does not speak of the informal organization of a family or of a community. The term "informal organization" does not refer to all types of emergent patterns of social life but only to those that evolve within the framework of a formally established organization. Excluded from our purview are social institutions that have evolved without explicit design; included are the informally emerging as well as the formally instituted patterns within formally established organizations.

The decision of the members of a group to formalize their endeavors and relations by setting up a specific organization, say, a social and athletic club, is not fortuitous. If a group is small enough for all members to be in direct social contact, and if it has no objectives that require coordination of activities, there is little need for explicit procedures or a formal division of labor. But the larger the group and the more complex the task it seeks to accomplish, the greater are the pressures to become explicitly organized.[6] Once a group of boys who merely used to hang around a drugstore decide to participate in the local baseball league, they must organize a team. And the complex coordination of millions of soldiers with thousands of specialized duties in a modern army requires extensive formalized procedures and a clear-cut authority structure.

Since formal organizations are often very large and complex, some authors refer to them as "large-scale" or as "complex" organizations. But we have eschewed these terms as misleading in two respects. First, organizations vary in size and complexity, and using these variables as defining criteria would result in such odd expressions as "a small large-scale organization" or "a very complex complex organization." Second, although formal organizations often become very large and complex, their size and complexity do not rival those of the social organization of a modern society, which includes such organizations and their relations with one another in addition to other nonorganizational patterns. (Perhaps the complexity of formal organizations is so much emphasized because it is man-made whereas the complexity of societal organization has slowly emerged, just as the complexity of modern computers is more impressive than that of the human brain. Complexity by design may be more conspicuous than complexity by growth or evolution.)

The term "bureaucratic organization" which also is often used, calls attention to the fact that organizations generally possess some sort of administrative machinery. In an organization that has been formally established, a specialized administrative staff usually exists that is responsible for maintaining the organization as a going concern and for coordinating the activities of its members. Large and complex organizations require an especially elaborate administrative apparatus. In a large factory, for example, there is not only an industrial work force directly engaged in production but also an administration composed of executive, supervisory, clerical, and other staff personnel. The case of a government agency is more complicated, because such an agency is part of the administrative arm of the nation. The entire personnel of, say, a law-enforcement agency is engaged in administration, but administration of different kinds; whereas operating officials administer the law and thereby help maintain social order in the society, their superiors and the auxiliary staff administer agency procedures and help maintain the organization itself.

One aspect of bureaucratization that has received much attention is the elaboration of detailed rules and regulations that the members of the organization are expected to faithfully follow. Rigid enforcement of the minutiae of extensive official procedures often impedes effective operations. Colloquially, the term "bureaucracy" connotes such rule-encumbered inefficiency. In sociology, however, the term is used neutrally to refer to the administrative aspects of organizations. If bureaucratization is defined as the amount of effort devoted to maintaining the organization rather than to directly achieving its objectives, all formal organizations have at least a minimum of bureaucracy—even if this bureaucracy involves no more than a secretary-treasurer who collects dues. But wide variations have been found in the degree of bureaucratization in organizations, as indicated by the amount of effort devoted to administrative problems, the proportion of administrative personnel, the hierarchical character of the organization, or the strict enforcement of administrative procedures and rigid compliance with them.

NOTES

1. For a discussion of some of the issues raised by this assertion, see Ernest Nagel, "On the statement 'The Whole Is More Than the Sum of Its Parts'," Paul F. Lazarsfeld and Morris Rosenberg (eds.), *The Language of Social Research* (Glencoe, IL: Free Press, 1955), pp. 519–527.

2. A purist may, concededly, point out that all individuals share the role of passenger and

so are subject to certain generalized norms, courtesy for example.

3. See the recent discussion of these concepts by Kroeber and Parsons, who conclude by defining culture as "transmitted and created content and patterns of values, ideas, and other symbolic meaningful systems" and social structure or system as "the specifically relational system of interaction among individuals and collectivities." A. L. Kroeber and Talcott Parsons, "The Concepts of Culture and of Social System," *American Sociological Review*, 23 (1958), p. 583.

4. Sumner makes this distinction between, in his terms, *crescive* and *enacted* social institutions. William Graham Sumner, *Folkways* (Boston: Ginn, 1907), p. 54.

5. From *John Brown's Body*. Holt, Rinehart & Winston, Inc. Copyright, 1927, 1928, by Stephen Vincent Benét. Copyright renewed, 1955, 1956, by Rosemary Carr Benét.

6. For a discussion of size and its varied effects on the characteristics of social organization, see Theodore Caplow, "Organizational Size," *Administrative Science Quarterly*, 1 (1957), pp. 484–505.

20
Organizational Choice: Product versus Function
Arthur H. Walker & Jay W. Lorsch

Of all the issues facing a manager as he thinks about the form of his organization, one of the thorniest is the question of whether to group activities primarily by product or by function. Should all specialists in a given function be grouped under a common boss, regardless of differences in products they are involved in, or should the various functional specialists working on a single product be grouped together under the same superior?

In talks with managers we have repeatedly heard them anguishing over this choice. For example, recently a divisional vice president of a major U.S. corporation was contemplating a major organizational change. After long study, he made this revealing observation to his subordinate managers:

> We still don't know which choice will be the best one. Should the research, engineering, marketing, and production people be grouped separately in departments for each function? Or would it be better to have them grouped together in product departments, each department dealing with a particular product group?
>
> We were organized by product up until a few years ago. Then we consolidated our organization into specialized functional departments, each dealing with all of our products. Now I'm wondering if we wouldn't be better off to divide our operations again into product units. Either way I can see advantages and disadvantages, trade-offs. What criteria should I use? How can we predict what the outcomes will be if we change?

Companies that have made a choice often feel confident that they have resolved this dilemma. Consider the case of a large advertising agency that consolidated its copy, art, and television personnel into a "total creative department." Previously they had reported to group heads in their areas of specialization. In a memo to employees the company explained the move:

> Formation of the "total creative" department completely tears down the walls between art, copy, and television people. Behind this move is the realization that for best results all creative people, regardless of their particular specialty, must work together under the most intimate relationship as total advertising people, trying to solve creative problems together from start to finish.
>
> The new department will be broken into five groups reporting to the senior vice president and creative director, each under the direction of an associate creative director. Each group will be responsible for art, television, and copy in their accounts.

But our experience is that such reorganizations often are only temporary. The issues involved are so complex that many managements oscillate between these two choices or try to effect some compromise between them.

In this article we shall explore—from the viewpoint of the behavioral scientist—some of the criteria that have been used in the past to make these choices, and present ideas from recent studies that suggest more relevant criteria for making the decision. We hope to provide a way of thinking about these problems that will lead to the most sensible decisions for the accomplishment of organizational goals.

The dilemma of products versus function is by no means new; managers have been facing the same basic question for decades. As large corporations like Du Pont and General Motors grew, they found it necessary to divide their activities among product divisions.[1] Following World War II, as companies expanded their sales of existing products and added new products and businesses, many of them implemented a transition from functional organizations handling a number of different products to independently managed product divisions. These changes raised problems concerning divisionalization, decentralization, corporate staff activities, and the like.

As the product divisions grew and prospered, many companies extended the idea of product organization further down in their organizations under such labels as "the unit management concept." Today most of the attention is still being directed to these changes and innovations *within* product or market areas below the divisional level.

We are focusing therefore on these organizational issues at the middle and lower echelons of management, particularly on the crucial questions being faced by managers today within product divisions. The reader should note, however, that a discussion of these issues is immensely complicated by the fact that a choice at one level of the corporate structure affects the choices and criteria for choice at other levels. Nonetheless, the ideas we suggest in this article are directly relevant to organizational choice at any level.

ELEMENTS TO CONSIDER

To understand more fully the factors that make these issues so difficult, it is useful to review the criteria often relied on in making this decision. Typically, managers have used technical and economic criteria. They ask themselves, for instance, "Which choice will minimize payroll costs?" Or, "Which will best utilize equipment and specialists?" This approach not only makes real sense in the traditional logic of management, but it has strong support from the classical school of organization theorists. Luther Gulick, for example, used it in arguing for organization by function:

> It guarantees the maximum utilization of up-to-date technical skill and . . . makes it possible in each case to make use of the most effective divisions of work and specialization. . . . [It] makes possible also the economies of the maximum use of labor-saving machinery and mass production. . . . [It] encourages coordination in all of the technical and skilled work of the enterprise. . . . [It] furnishes an excellent approach to the development of central coordination and control.[2]

In pointing to the advantages of the product basis of organization, two other classical theorists used the same approach:

> Product or product line is an important basis for departmentalizing, because it permits the maximum use of personal skills and specialized knowledge, facilitates the employment of specialized capital and makes easier a certain type of coordination.[3]

In sum, these writers on organization suggested that the manager should make the choice based on three criteria:

1. Which approach permits maximum use of special technical knowledge?
2. Which provides the most efficient utilization of machinery and equipment?
3. Which provides the best hope of obtaining the required control and coordination?

There is nothing fundamentally wrong with these criteria as far as they go, and, of course, managers have been using them. But they fail to recognize the complex set of trade-offs involved in these decisions. As a consequence, managers make changes that produce unanticipated results and may even reduce the effectiveness of their organization. For example:

A major manufacturer of corrugated containers a few years ago shifted from a product basis to a functional basis. The rationale for the decision was that it would lead to improved control of production costs and efficiencies in production and marketing. While the organization did accomplish these aims, it found itself less able to obtain coordination among its local sales and production units. The functional specialists now reported to the top officers in charge of production and sales, and there was no mechanism for one person to coordinate their work below the level of division management. As a result, the company encountered numerous problems and unresolved conflicts among functions and later returned to the product form.

This example pinpoints the major trade-off that the traditional criteria omit. Developing highly specialized functional units makes it difficult to achieve coordination or integration among these units. On the other hand, having product units as the basis for organization promotes collaboration between specialists, but the functional specialists feel less identification with functional goals.

BEHAVIORISTS' FINDINGS

We now turn to some new behavioral science approaches to designing organization structure. . . . Studies[4] have highlighted three other important factors about specialization and coordination:

• As we have suggested, the classical theorists saw specialization in terms of grouping similar activities, skills, or even equip-

ment. They did not look at its psychological and social consequences. . . . Behavioral scientists (including the authors) have found that there is an important relationship between a unit's or individual's assigned activities and the unit members' patterns of thought and behavior. Functional specialists tend to develop patterns of behavior and thought that are in tune with the demands of their jobs and their prior training, and as a result these specialists (e.g., industrial engineers and production supervisors) have different ideas and orientation about what is important in getting the job done. This is called *differentiation*, which simply means the differences in behavior and thought patterns that develop among different specialists in relation to their respective tasks. Differentiation is necessary for functional specialists to perform their jobs effectively.

• Differentiation is closely related to achievement of coordination, or what behavioral scientists call *integration*. This means collaboration between specialized units or individuals. Recent studies have demonstrated that is an inverse relationship between differentiation and integration: the more two functional specialists (or their units) differ in their patterns of behavior and thought, the more difficult it is to bring about integration between them. Nevertheless, this research has indicated, achievement of both differentiation and integration is essential if organizations are to perform effectively.

• While achievement of both differentiation and integration is possible, it can occur only when well-developed means of communication among specialists exist in the organization and when the specialists are effective in resolving the inevitable cross-functional conflicts.

These recent studies, then, point to certain related questions that managers must consider when they choose between a product or functional basis of organization.

1. How will the choice affect differentiation among specialists? Will it allow the necessary differences in view-

point to develop so that specialized tasks can be performed effectively?

2. How does the decision affect the prospects of accomplishing integration? Will it lead, for instance, to greater differentiation, which will increase the problems of achieving integration?

3. How will the decision affect the ability of organization members to communicate with each other, resolve conflicts, and reach the necessary joint decisions?

There appears to be a connection between the appropriate extent of differentiation and integration and the organization's effectiveness in accomplishing its economic goals. What the appropriate pattern is depends on the nature of external factors—markets, technology, and so on—facing the organization, as well as the goals themselves. The question of how the organizational pattern will affect individual members is equally complex. Management must consider how much stress will be associated with a certain pattern and whether such stress should be a serious concern.

To explore in more detail the significance of modern approaches to organizational structuring, we shall describe one recent study conducted in two manufacturing plants—one organized by *product*, the other on a *functional* basis.[5]

PLANT F AND PLANT P

The two plants where this study was conducted were selected because they were closely matched in several ways. They were making the same product; their markets, technology, and even raw materials were identical. The parent companies were also similar: both were large, national corporations that developed, manufactured, and marketed many consumer products. In each case divisional and corporate headquarters were located more than 100 miles from the facilities

studied. The plants were separated from other structures at the same site, where other company products were made.

Both plants had very similar management styles. They stressed their desire to foster employees' initiative and autonomy and placed great reliance on selection of well-qualified department heads. They also identified explicitly the same two objectives. The first was to formulate, package, and ship the products in minimum time at specified levels of quality and at minimum costs—that is, within existing capabilities. The second was to improve the capabilities of the plant.

In each plant there were identical functional specialists involved with the manufacturing units and packing unit, as well as quality control, planning and scheduling, warehousing, industrial engineering, and plant engineering. In Plant F (with the *functional* basis of organization), only the manufacturing departments and the planning and scheduling function reported to the plant manager responsible for the product (see Figure 1). All other functional specialists reported to the staff of the divisional manufacturing manager, who was also responsible for plants manufacturing other products. At Plant P (with the *product* basis of organization), all functional specialists with the exception of plant engineering reported to the plant manager (see Figure 2).

State of Differentiation

In studying differentiation, it is useful to focus on the functional specialists' differences in outlook in terms of: orientation toward goals, orientation toward time, and perception of the formality of organization.

Goal Orientation. The bases of organization in the two plants had a marked effect on the specialists' differentiated goal orientations. In Plant F they focused

FIGURE 1 · ORGANIZATIONAL CHART AT PLANT F

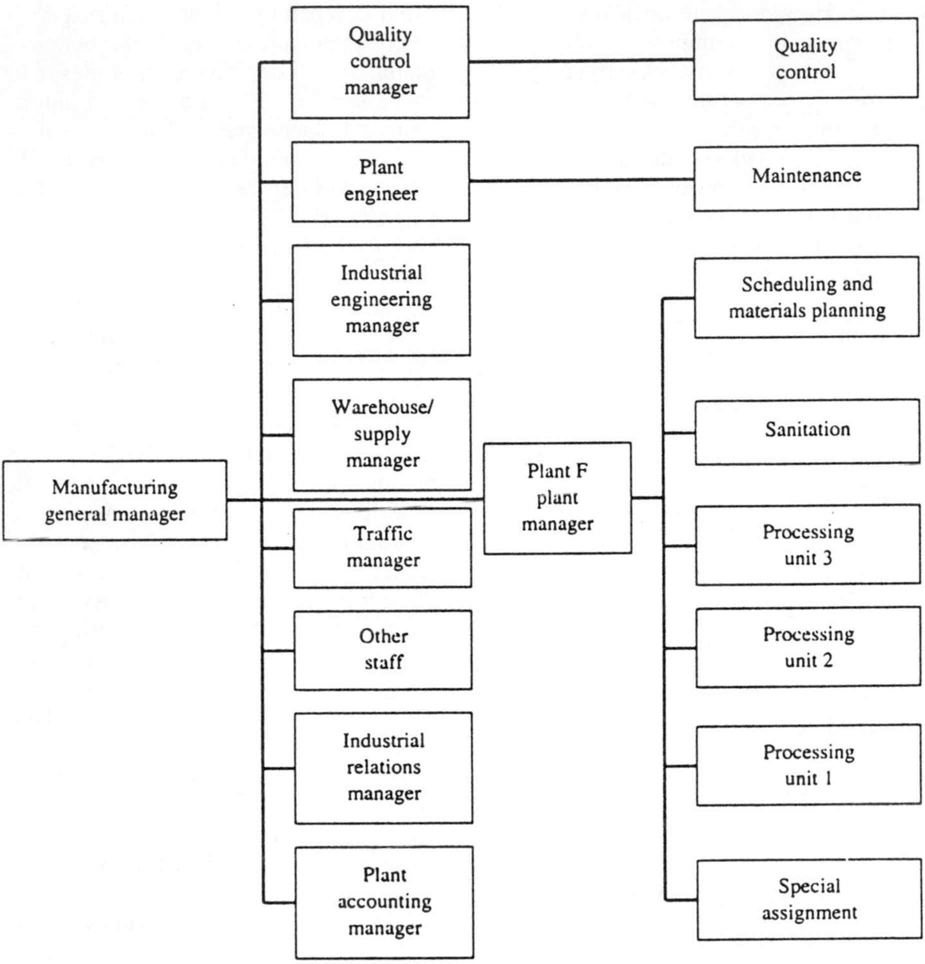

sharply on their specialized goals and objectives. For example, quality control specialists were concerned almost exclusively with meeting quality standards, industrial engineers with methods improvements and cost reduction, and scheduling specialists with how to meet requirements. An industrial engineer in Plant F indicated this intensive interest in his own activity:

> We have 150 projects worth close to a million dollars in annual savings. I guess

I've completed some that save as much as $90,000 a year. Right now I'm working on cutting departmental costs. You need a hard shell in this work. No one likes to have his costs cut, but that is my job.

That these intense concerns with specialized objectives were expected is illustrated by the apologetic tone of a comment on production goals by an engineering supervisor at Plant F:

> At times we become too much involved in production. It causes a change in heart.

FIGURE 2 · ORGANIZATIONAL CHART AT PLANT P

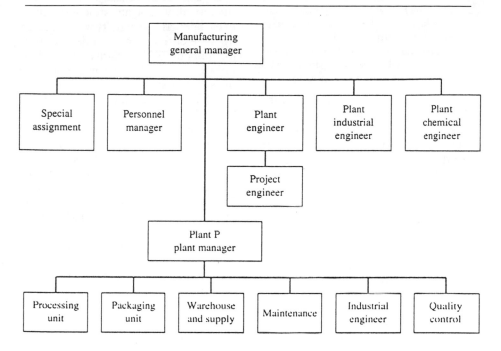

We are interested in production, but not at the expense of our own standards of performance. If we get too much involved, then we may become compromised.

A final illustration is when production employees stood watching while members of the maintenance department worked to start a new production line, and a production supervisor remarked:

I hope that they get that line going soon. Right now, however, my hands are tied. Maintenance has the job. I can only wait. My people have to wait, too.

This intense concern with one set of goals is analogous to a rifle shot; in a manner of speaking, each specialist took aim at one set of goals and fired at it. Moreover, the specialists identified closely with their counterparts in other plants and at divisional headquarters. As one engineer put it:

We carry the ball for them (the central office). We carry a project through and get it working right.

At Plant P the functional specialists' goals were more diffuse—like buckshot. Each specialist was concerned not only with his own goals, but also with the operation of the entire plant. For example, in contrast to the Plant F production supervisor's attitude about maintenance, a Plant P maintenance manager said, under similar circumstances:

We're all interested in the same thing. If I can help, I'm willing. If I have a mechanical problem, there is no member of the operating department who wouldn't go out of his way to solve it.

Additional evidence of this more diffuse orientation toward goals is provided by comments such as these which came from Plant P engineers and managers:

We are here for a reason—to run this place the best way we know how. There is no reluctance to be open and frank despite various backgrounds and ages.

The changeovers tell the story. Everyone shows willingness to dig in. The whole plant turns out to do cleaning up.

Because the functional specialists at Plant F focused on their individual goals, they had relatively wide differences in goals and objectives. Plant P's structure, on the other hand, seemed to make functional specialists more aware of common product goals and reduced differences in goal orientation. Yet, as we shall see, this lesser differentiation did not hamper their performance.

Time Orientation. The two organizational bases had the opposite effect, however, on the time orientation of functional managers. At Plant F, the specialists shared a concern with short-term issues (mostly daily problems). The time orientation of specialists at Plant P was more differentiated. For example, its production managers concentrated on routine matters, while planning and industrial engineering focused on issues that needed solution within a week, and quality control specialists worried about even longer-term problems.

The reason is not difficult to find. Since Plant P's organization led its managers to identify with product goals, those who could contribute to the solution of longer-term problems became involved in these activities. In Plant F, where each unit focused on its own goals, there was more of a tendency to worry about getting daily progress. On the average, employees of Plant P reported devoting 30 percent of their time to daily problems, while at Plant F this figure was 49 percent. We shall have more to say shortly about how these factors influenced the results achieved in the two plants.

Organizational Formality. In the study, the formality of organizational structure in each functional activity was measured by three criteria: clarity of definition of job responsibilities, clarity of dividing lines between jobs, and importance of rules and procedures.

It was found that at Plant F there were fewer differences among functional activities in the formality of organization structure than at Plant P. Plant F employees reported that a uniform degree of structure existed across functional specialities; job responsibilities were well defined, and the distinctions between jobs were clear. Similarly, rules and procedures were extensively relied on. At Plant P, on the other hand, substantial differences in the formality of organization existed. Plant engineers and industrial engineers, for example, were rather vague about their responsibilities and about the dividing line between their jobs and other jobs. Similarly, they reported relatively low reliance on rules and procedures. Production managers, on the other hand, noted that their jobs were well defined and that rules and procedures were more important to them.

The effects of these two bases of organization on differentiation along these three dimensions are summarized in Figure 3. Overall, differentiation was greater between functional specialists at Plant P than at Plant F.

Integration Achieved

While the study found that both plants experienced some problems in accomplishing integration, these difficulties were more noticeable at Plant F. Collaboration between maintenance and production personnel and between production and scheduling was a problem there. In Plant P the only relationship where integration was unsatisfactory was that between production and quality control specialists. Thus Plant P seemed to be

FIGURE 3 · DIFFERENTIATION IN PLANTS F AND P

Dimensions of Differentiation	Plant F	Plant P
Goal orientation	More differentiated and focused	Less differentiated and more diffuse
Time orientation	Less differentiated and shorter term	More differentiated and lnger term
Formality of structure	Less differentiated, with more formality	More differentiated, with less formality

getting slightly better integration in spite of the greater differentiation among specialists in that organization. Since differentiation and integration are basically antagonistic, the only way managers at Plant P could get both was by being effective at communication and conflict resolution. They were better at this than were managers at Plant F.

Communication Patterns. In Plant P, communication among employees was more frequent, less formal, and more often of a face-to-face nature than was the case with Plant F personnel. One Plant P employee volunteered:

> Communications are no problem around here. You can say it. You can get an answer.

Members of Plant F did not reflect such positive feelings. They were heard to say:

> Why didn't they tell me this was going to happen? Now they've shut down the line.
> When we get the information, it is usually too late to do any real planning. We just do our best.

The formal boundaries outlining positions that were more prevalent at Plant F appeared to act as a damper on communication. The encounters observed were often a succession of two-man conversations, even though more than two may have been involved in a problem. The telephone and written memoranda were

more often employed than at Plant P, where spontaneous meetings involving several persons were frequent, usually in the cafeteria.

Dealing with Conflict. In both plants, *confrontation* of conflict was reported to be more typical than either the use of power to force one's own position or an attempt to *smooth* conflict by "agreeing to disagree." There was strong evidence, nevertheless, that in Plant P managers were coming to grips with conflicts more directly than in Plant F. Managers at Plant F reported that more conflicts were being smoothed over. They worried that issues were often not getting settled. As they put it:

> We have too many nice guys here.
> If you can't resolve an issue, you go to the plant manager. But we don't like to bother him often with small matters. We should be able to settle them ourselves. The trouble is we don't. So it dies.

Thus, by ignoring conflict in the hope it would go away, or by passing it to a higher level, managers at Plant F often tried to smooth over their differences. While use of the management hierarchy is one acceptable way to resolve conflict, so many disagreements at Plant F were pushed upstairs that the hierarchy became overloaded and could not handle all the problems facing it. So it responded by dealing with only the more immediate and pressing ones.

At Plant P the managers uniformly reported that they resolved conflicts themselves. There was no evidence that conflicts were being avoided or smoothed over. As one manager said:

> We don't let problems wait very long. There's no sense to it. And besides, we get together frequently and have plenty of chances to discuss differences over a cup of coffee.

As this remark suggests, the quicker resolution of conflict was closely related to the open and informal communication pattern prevailing at Plant P. In spite of greater differentiation in time and orientation and structure, then, Plant P managers were able to achieve more satisfactory integration because they could communicate and resolve conflict effectively.

Performance and Attitudes

Before drawing some conclusions from the study of these two plants, it is important to make two more relevant comparisons between them—their effectiveness in terms of the goals set for them and the attitudes of employees.

Plant Performance. As we noted before, the managements of the two plants were aiming at the same two objectives: maximizing current output within existing capabilities and improving the capabilities of the plant. Of the two facilities, Plant F met the first objective more effectively; it was achieving a higher production rate with greater efficiency and at less cost than was Plant P. In terms of the second objective, however, Plant P was clearly superior to Plant F; the former's productivity had increased by 23 percent from 1963 to 1966 compared with the latter's increment of only 3 percent. One key manager at Plant F commented:

> There has been a three- or four-year effort to improve our capability. Our expecta-

tions have simply not been achieved. The improvement in performance is just not there. We are still where we were three years ago. But our targets for improvements are realistic.

By contrast, a key manager at Plant P observed:

> Our crews have held steady, yet our volume is up. Our quality is consistently better too.

Another said:

> We are continuing to look for and find ways to improve and consolidate jobs.

Employee Attitudes. Here, too, the two organizations offer a contrast, but the contrast presents a paradoxical situation. Key personnel at Plant P appeared to be more deeply involved in their work than did managers at Plant F, and they admitted more often to feeling stress and pressure than did their opposite numbers at Plant F. But Plant F managers expressed more satisfaction with their work than did those at Plant P; they liked the company and their jobs more than did managers at Plant P.

Why Plant P managers felt more involved and had a higher level of stress, but were less satisfied than Plant F managers, can be best explained by linking these findings with the others we have reported.

Study Summary

The characteristics of these two organizations are summarized in Figure 4. The nature of the organization at Plant F seemed to suit its stable but high rate of efficiency. Its specialists concentrated on their own goals and performed well, on the whole. The jobs were well defined and managers worked within procedures and rules. The managers were concerned primarily with short-term matters. They were not particularly effective in communicating with each other and in resolving conflict. But this was not

FIGURE 4 • OBSERVED CHARACTERISTICS OF THE
TWO ORGANIZATIONS

Characteristics	Plant F	Plant P
Differentiation	Less differentiation except in goal orientation	Greater differentiation in structure and time orientation
Integration	Somewhat less effective	More effective
Conflict management	Confrontation, but also "smoothing over" and avoidance; rather restricted communicaiton pattern	Confrontation of conflict; open, face-to-face communication
Effectiveness	Efficient, stable production; but less successful in improving plant capabilities	Successful in improving plant capabilities, but less effective in stable production
Employee attitudes	Prevalent feeling of satisfaction, but less feeling of stress and involvement	Prevalent feeling of stress and involvement, but less satisfaction

very important to achieve steady, good performance, since the coordination necessary to meet this objective could be achieved through plans and procedures and through the manufacturing technology itself.

As long as top management did not exert much pressure to improve performance dramatically, the plant's managerial hierarchy was able to resolve the few conflicts arising from daily operations. And as long as the organization avoided extensive problem solving, a great deal of personal contact was not very important. It is not surprising therefore that the managers were satisfied and felt relatively little pressure. They attended strictly to their own duties, remained uninvolved, and got the job done. For them, this combination was satisfying. And higher management was pleased with the facility's production efficiency.

The atmosphere at Plant P, in contrast, was well suited to the goal of improving plant capabilities, which it did very well. There was less differentiation between goals, since the functional specialists to a degree shared the product

goals. Obviously, one danger in this form of organization is the potential attraction of specialist managers to total goals to the extent that they lose sight of their particular goals and become less effective in their jobs. But this was not a serious problem at Plant P.

Moreover, there was considerable differentiation in time orientation and structure; some specialists worked at the routine and programmed tasks in operating the plant, while others concentrated on longer-term problems to improve manufacturing capability. The latter group was less constrained by formal procedures and job definitions, and this atmosphere was conducive to problem solving. The longer time orientation of some specialists, however, appeared to divert their attention from maintaining schedules and productivity. This was a contributing factor to Plant P's less effective current performance.

In spite of the higher degree of differentiation in these dimensions, Plant P managers were able to achieve the integration necessary to solve problems that hindered plant capability. Their shared goals and a common boss encouraged them to deal directly with each other and confront their conflicts. Given this pattern, it is not surprising that they felt very involved in their jobs. Also they were under stress because of their great involvement in their jobs. This stress could lead to dissatisfaction with their situation. Satisfaction for its own sake, however, may not be very important; there was no evidence of higher turnover of managers at Plant P.

Obviously, in comparing the performance of these two plants operating with similar technologies and in the same market, we might predict that, because of its greater ability to improve plant capabilities, Plant P eventually will reach a performance level at least as high as Plant F's. While this might occur in time, it should not obscure one important point: the functional organization seems to lead to better results in a situation where stable performance of a routine task is desired, while the product organization leads to better results in situations where the task is less predictable and requires innovative problem solving.

CLUES FOR MANAGERS

How can the manager concerned with the function versus product decision use these ideas to guide him in making the appropriate choice? The essential step is identifying the demands of the task confronting the organization.

Is it a routine, repetitive task? Is it one where integration can be achieved by plan and conflict managed through the hierarchy? This was the way the task was implicitly defined at Plant F. If this is the nature of the task, or, to put it another way, if management is satisfied with this definition of the task, then the functional organization is quite appropriate. While it allows less differentiation in time orientation and structure,

it does encourage differentiation in goal orientation. This combination is important for specialists to work effectively in their jobs.

Perhaps even more important, the functional structure also seems to permit a degree of integration sufficient to get the organization's work done. Much of this can be accomplished through paper systems and through the hardware of the production line itself. Conflict that comes up can more safely be dealt with through the management hierarchy, since the difficulties of resolving conflict are less acute. This is so because the tasks provide less opportunity for conflict and because the specialists have less differentiated viewpoints to overcome. This form of organization is less psychologically demanding for the individuals involved.

On the other hand, if the task is of a problem-solving nature, or if management defines it this way, the product organization seems to be more appropriate. This is especially true where there is a need for tight integration among specialists. As illustrated at Plant P, the product organization form allows the greater differentiation in time orientation and structure that specialists need to attack problems. While encouraging identification with superordinate goals, this organizational form does allow enough differentiation in goals for specialists to make their contributions.

Even more important, to identify with product ends and have a common boss encourages employees to deal constructively with conflict, communicate directly and openly with each other, and confront their differences, so they can collaborate effectively. Greater stress and less satisfaction for the individual may be unavoidable, but it is a small price to pay for the involvement that accompanies it.

The manager's problem in choosing between product and functional forms is complicated by the fact that in each organization there are routine tasks and tasks requiring problem solving, jobs requiring little interdependence among specialists and jobs requiring a great deal. Faced with these mixtures, many companies have adopted various compromises between product and functional bases. They include (in ascending order of structural complexity):

1. *The use of cross-functional teams to facilitate integration.* These teams provide some opportunity for communication and conflict resolution and also a degree of the common identification with product goals that characterizes the product organization. At the same time, they retain the differentiation provided by the functional organization.

2. *The appointment of full-time integrators or coordinators around a product.* These product managers or project managers encourage the functional specialists to become committed to product goals and help resolve conflicts between them. The specialists still retain their primary identification with their functions.[6]

3. *The "matrix" or grid organization, which combines the product and functional forms by overlaying them.* Some managers wear functional hats and are involved in the day-to-day, more routine activities. Naturally, they identify with functional goals. Others, wearing product or project hats, identify with total product goals and are more involved in the problem-solving activity required to cope with long-range issues and to achieve cross-functional coordination.

These compromises are becoming popular because they enable companies to deal with multiple tasks simultaneously. But we do not propose them as a panacea, because they make sense only for those situations where the differentiation and integration required by the sum of all the tasks make a middle approach necessary. Further, the complexity of interpersonal plus organizational relationships in these forms and the ambiguity associated with them make them difficult to administer effectively and psychologically demanding on the persons involved.

In our view, the only solution to the product versus function dilemma lies in analysis of the multiple tasks that must be performed, the differences between specialists, the integration that must be achieved, and the mechanisms and behavior required to resolve conflict and arrive at these states of differentiation and integration. This analysis provides the best hope of making a correct product or function choice or of arriving at some appropriate compromise solution.

NOTES

1. For a historical study of the organizational structure of U.S. corporations, see Alfred D. Chandler, Jr., *Strategy and Structure* (Cambridge: The M.I.T. Press, 1962).

2. Luther Gulick, "Notes on the Theory of Organization," in *Papers on the Science of Administration,* edited by Luther Gulick and Lyndall F. Urwick (New York Institute of Public Administration, 1917), pp. 23–24.

3. Harold D. Koontz, and C. J. O'Donnell, *Principles of Management* (New York, McGraw-Hill, 2nd ed. 1959), p. 111.

4. See Paul R. Lawrence and Jay W. Lorsch, *Organization and Environment* (Boston, Division of Research, Harvard Business School, 1967); and Eric J. Miller and A. K. Rice, *Systems of Organization* (London, Tavistock Publications, 1967).

5. Arthur H. Walker, *Behavioral Consequences of Contrasting Patterns of Organization* (Boston, Harvard Business School, unpublished doctoral dissertation, 1967).

6. See Paul R. Lawrence and Jay W. Lorsch, "New Management Job: The Integrator," HBR November-December 1967, p. 142.

21

The Five Basic Parts of the Organization

Henry Mintzberg

[Previously] organizations were described in terms of their use of the coordinating mechanisms. We noted that, in theory, the simplest organization can rely on mutual adjustment to coordinate its basic work of producing a product or service. Its *operators*—those who do this basic work—are largely self-sufficient.

As the organization grows, however, and adopts a more complex division of labor among its operators, the need is increasingly felt for direct supervision. Another brain—that of a *manager*—is needed to help coordinate the work of the operators. So, whereas the division of labor up to this point has been between the operators themselves, the introduction of a manager introduces a first *administrative* division of labor in the structure—between those who do the work and those who supervise it. And as the organization further elaborates itself, more managers are added—not only managers of operators but also managers of managers. An administrative *hierarchy* of authority is built.

As the process of elaboration continues, the organization turns increasingly to standardization as a means of coordinating the work of its operators. The responsibility for much of this standardization falls on a third group, composed of *analysts*. Some, such as work study analysts and industrial engineers, concern themselves with the standardization of work processes; others, such as

quality control engineers, accountants, planners, and production schedulers, focus on the standardization of outputs; while a few, such as personnel trainers, are charged with the standardization of skills (although most of this standardization takes place outside the organization, before the operators are hired). The introduction of these analysts brings a second kind of adminstrative division of labor to the organization, between those who do and who supervise the work, and those who standardize it. Whereas in the first case managers assume responsibility from the operators for some of the coordination of their work by substituting direct supervision for mutual adjustment, the analysts assumed responsibility from the managers (and the operators) by substituting standardization for direct supervision (and mutual adjustment). Earlier, some of the control over the work was removed from the operator; now it begins to be removed from the manager as well, as the systems designed by the analysts take increasing responsibility for coordination. The analyst "institutionalizes" the manager's job.

We end up with an organization that consists of a core of operators, who do the basic work of producing the products and services, and an *administrative* component of managers and analysts, who take some of the responsibility for coordinating their work. This leads us to the conceptual description of the organiza-

Source: Henry Mintzberg, *The Structure of Organizations,* © 1979, pp. 18–34. Reprinted by permission of Prentice-Hall, Englewood Cliffs, New Jersey.

tion shown in Figure 1. This figure will be used repeatedly throughout the book, sometimes overlaid to show flows, sometimes distorted to illustrate special structures. It emerges, in effect, as the "logo," or symbol, of the book.

At the base of the logo is the *operating core*, wherein the operators carry out the basic work of the organization—the input, processing, output, and direct support tasks associated with producing the products or services. Above them sits the administrative component, which is shown in three parts. First, are the managers, divided into two groups. Those at the very top of the hierarchy, together with their own personal staff, form the *strategic apex*. And those below, who join the strategic apex to the operating core through the chain of command (such as it exists), make up the *middle line*. To their left stands the *technostructure*, wherein the analysts carry out their work of standardizing the work of others, in addition to applying their analytical techniques to help the organization adapt to its environment. Finally, we add a fifth group, the *support staff*, shown to the right of the middle line. This staff support the functioning of the operating core indirectly, that is, outside the basic flow of operating work. The support staff goes largely unrecognized in the literature of organizational structuring, yet a quick glance at the chart of virtually any large organization indicates that it is a major segment, one that should not be confused with the other four. Examples of support groups in a typical manufacturing firm are research and development, cafeteria, legal council, payroll, public relations, and mailroom.

Figure 1 shows a small strategic apex connected by a flaring middle line to a large, flat operating core. These three parts of the organization are shown in one uninterrupted sequence to indicate that they are typically connected through a single line of formal authority. The technostructure and the support

FIGURE 1 • THE FIVE BASIC PARTS OF ORGANIZATIONS

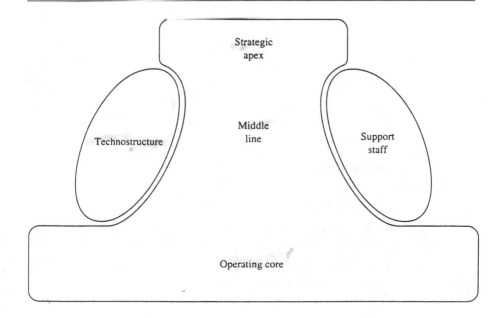

Strategic apex

Technostructure

Middle line

Support staff

Operating core

staff are shown off to either side to indicate that they are separate from this main line of authority, and influence the operating core only indirectly.

It might be useful at this point to relate this scheme to some terms commonly used in organizations. The term "middle management," although seldom carefully defined, generally seems to include all members of the organization not at the strategic apex or in the operating core. In our scheme, therefore, "middle management" would comprise three distinct groups—the middle-line managers, the analysts, and the support staff. To avoid confusion, however, the term *middle level* will be used here to describe these three groups together, the term "management" being reserved for the managers of the strategic apex and the middle line.

The word "staff" should also be put into this context. In the early literature, the term was used in contrast to "line": in theory, line positions had formal authority to make decisions, while staff positions did not; they merely advised those who did. (This has sometimes been referred to as "functional" authority, in contrast to the line's formal or "hierarchical" authority.) Allen (1955), for example, delineates the staff's major activities as (1) providing advice, counsel, suggestions, and guidance on planning objectives, policies, and procedures to govern the operations of the line departments on how best to put decisions into practice; and (2) performing specific service activities for the line, for example, installing budgeting systems and recruiting line personnel, "which may include making decisions that the line has asked it to make" (p. 348). As we shall see later, this distinction between line and staff holds up in some kinds of structures and breaks down in others. Nevertheless, the distinction between line and staff is of some use to us, and we shall retain the terms here though in somewhat modified form. *Staff* will be used to refer to the technostructure *and* the support staff, those groups shown on either side in Figure 1. *Line* will refer to the central part of Figure 1, those managers in the flow of formal authority from the strategic to the operating core. Note that this definition does not mention the power to decide or advise. As we shall see, the support staff does not primarily advise; it has distinct functions to perform and decisions to make, although these relate only indirectly to the functions of the operating core. The chef in the plant cafeteria may be engaged in a production process, but it has nothing to do with the basic manufacturing process. Similarly, the technostructure's power to advise sometimes amounts to the power to decide, but that is outside the flow of formal authority that oversees the operating core.[1]

Some conceptual ideas of James D. Thompson. Before proceeding with a more detailed description of each of the five basic parts of the organization, it will be helpful to introduce at this point some of the important conceptual ideas of James D. Thompson (1967). To Thompson, "Uncertainty appears as the fundamental problem for complex organizations, and coping with uncertainty, as the essence of the administrative process" (p. 159). Thompson describes the organization in terms of a "technical core," equivalent to our operating core, and a group of "boundary spanning units." In his terms, the organization reduces uncertainty by sealing off this core from the environment so that the operating activities can be protected. The boundary spanning units face the environment directly and deal with its uncertainties. For example, the research department interprets the confusing scientific environment for the organization, while the public relations department placates a hostile social environment. . . .

Thompson also introduces a conceptual scheme to explain the *interdependencies* among organizational members. He distinguishes three ways in which the work can be coupled, shown in Figure 2. First is *pooled coupling,* where members share common resources but are otherwise independent. Figure 2(a) could represent teachers in a school who share common facilities and budgets but work alone with their pupils. In *sequential coupling,* members work in series, as in a relay race where the baton passes from runner to runner. Figure 2(b) could represent a mass production factory, where raw materials enter at one end, are sequentially fabricated and machined, then fed into an assembly line at various points, and finally emerge at the other end as finished products. In *reciprocal coupling,* the members feed their work back and forth among themselves; in effect each receives inputs from and provides outputs to the others. "This is illustrated by the airline which contains both operations and maintenance units. The production of the maintenance unit is an input for operations, in the form of a serviceable aircraft; and the product (or by-product) of operations is an input for maintenance, in the form of an aircraft needing maintenance" (Thompson, 1967, p. 55). Figure 2(c) could be taken to represent this example, or one in a hospital in which the nurse "preps" the patient, the surgeon operates, and the nurse then takes care of the postoperative care.

Clearly, pooled coupling involves the least amount of interdependence among members. Anyone can be plucked out; and, as long as there is no great change in the resources available, the others can continue to work uninterrupted. Pulling out a member of a sequentially coupled organization, however, is like breaking a link in a chain—the whole activity must cease to function. Reciprocal coupling is, of course, more interdependent still, since a change in one task affects not only those farther along but also those behind.

Now let us take a look at each of the five parts of the organization.

THE OPERATING CORE

The operating core of the organization encompasses those members—the operators—who perform the basic work related directly to the production of products and services. The operators perform four prime functions: (1) They *secure the inputs* for production. For example, in a manufacturing firm, the purchasing department buys the raw materials and the receiving department takes it in the door. (2) They *transform the inputs into outputs.* Some organizations transform raw materials, for example, by chopping down trees and converting them to pulp and then paper. Others transform individual parts into complete units, for example, by assembling typewriters, while still others transform information or people, by writing consulting reports, educating students, cutting hair, or curing illness. (3) They *distribute the outputs,* for example, by selling and physically distributing what comes out of the transformation process. (4) They *provide direct support* to the input, transformation, and output functions, for example, by performing maintenance on the operating machines and inventorying the raw materials.

Since it is the operating core that the other parts of the organization seek to protect, standardization is generally carried furthest here. How far, of course, depends on the work being done: assemblers in automobile factories and professors in universities are both operators,

FIGURE 2 • POOLED, SEQUENTIAL, AND RECIPROCAL COUPLING OF WORK

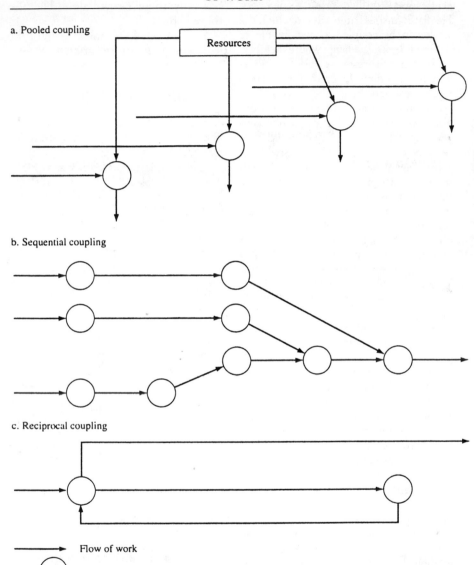

a. Pooled coupling

b. Sequential coupling

c. Reciprocal coupling

Flow of work

Task

although the work of the former is far more standardized than that of the latter.

The operating core is the heart of every organization, the part that produces the essential outputs that keep it alive. But except for the very smallest one, organizations need to build *administrative* components. The administrative component comprises the strategic apex, middle line, and technostructure.

THE STRATEGIC APEX

At the other end of the organization lies the strategic apex. Here are found those people charged with overall responsibility for the organization—the chief executive officer (whether called president, superintendent, Pope, or whatever), and any other top-level managers whose concerns are global. Included here as well are those who provide direct support to the top managers-their secretaries, assistants, and so on.[2] In some organizations, the strategic apex includes the executive committee (because it mandate is global even if its members represent specific interests); in others, it includes what is known as the chief executive office—two or three individuals who share the job of chief executive.

The strategic apex is charged with ensuring that the organization serve its mission in an effective way, and also that it serve the needs of those people who control or otherwise have power over the organization (such as owners, government agencies, unions of the employees, pressure groups). This entails three sets of duties. One already discussed is that of direct supervision. To the extent that the organization relies on this mechanism of coordination, it is the managers of the strategic apex and middle line who effect it. Among the managerial roles (Mintzberg, 1973) associated with direct supervision are resource allocator, including the design of the structure itself, the assignment of people and resources to tasks, the issuing of work orders, and the authorization of major decisions made by the employees; disturbance handler, involving the resolution of conflicts, exceptions, and disturbances sent up the hierarchy for resolution; monitor, involving the review of employees' activities; disseminator, involving the transmission of information to employees; and leader, involving the staffing of the organization and the motivating and rewarding of them. In its essence, direct supervision at the strategic apex means ensuring that the whole organization function smoothly as a single integrated unit.

But there is more to managing an organization than direct supervision. That is why even organizations with a minimal need for direct supervision, for example the very smallest that can rely on mutual adjustment, or professional ones that rely on formal training, still need managers. The second set of duties of the strategic apex involves the management of the organization's boundary conditions—its relationships with its environment. The managers of the strategic apex must spend a good deal of their time acting in the roles of spokesman, in informing influential people in the environment about the organization's activities; liaison, to develop high-level contact for the organization, and monitor, to tap these for information and to serve as the contact point for those who wish to influence the organization's goals; negotiator, when major agreements must be reached with outside parties; and sometimes even figurehead, in carrying out ceremonial duties, such as greeting important customers. (Someone once defined the manager, only half in jest, as that person who sees the visitors so that everyone else can get their work done.)

The third set of duties relates to the development of the organization's strategy. Strategy may be viewed as a mediating force between the organization and its environment. Strategy formulation therefore involves the interpretation of the environment and the development of consistent patterns in streams of organizational decisions ("strategies") to deal with it. Thus, in managing the boundary conditions of the organization, the managers of the strategic apex develop an understanding of its environment; and in carrying out the duties of direct supervision, they seek to tailor a strategy to its strengths and its needs, trying to maintain a pace of change that is responsive to the environment without being disruptive to the organization. Specifically, in the entrepreneur role, the top managers search for effective ways to carry out the organization's "mission" (i.e., its production of basic products and services), and sometimes even seek to change that mission. . . .

In general, the strategic apex takes the widest, and as a result the most abstract, perspective of the organization. Work at this level is generally characterized by a minimum of repetition and standardization, considerable discretion, and relatively long decision-making cycles. Mutual adjustment is the favored mechanism for coordination among the managers of the strategic apex itself.

THE MIDDLE LINE

The strategic apex is joined to the operating core by the chain of middle-line managers with formal authority. This chain runs from the senior managers just below the strategic apex to the *first-line supervisors* (e.g., the shop foremen), who have direct authority over the operators, and embodies the coordinating mechanism that we have called direct supervision. Figure 3 shows one famous chain of authority, that of the U.S. Army, from

four-star general at the strategic apex to sergeant as first-line supervisor. This particular chain of authority is *scalar*, that is, it runs in a single line from top to bottom. But as we shall see later, not all need be: some divide and rejoin; a "subordinate" can have more than one "superior."

What do all these levels of managers do? If the strategic apex provides overall direction and the operating core produces the products or services, why does the organization need this whole chain of middle-line managers? One answer seems evident. To the extent that the organization is large and reliant on direct supervision for coordination, it requires middle-line managers. In theory, one manager—the chief executive at the strategic apex—can supervise all the operators. In practice, however, direct supervision requires close personal contact between manager and operator, with the result that there is some limit to the number of operators any one manager can supervise—his so-called span of control. Small organizations can get along with one manager (at the strategic apex); bigger ones require more (in the middle-line). As Moses was told in the desert:

> Thous shalt provide out of all the people able men, such as fear God, men of truth, hating covetousness; and place such over them, to be rulers of thousands, and rulers of hundreds, ruler of fifties, and rulers of tens: and let them judge the people at all seasons: and it shall be, that every great matter they shall bring unto thee, but every small matter they shall judge: so shall it be easier for thyself, and they shall bear the burden with thee. If thou shalt do this thing, and God command thee so, then thou shalt be able to endure, and all this people shall also go to their place in peace (Exodus 18:21–24).

Thus, an organizational *hierarchy* is built as a first-line supervisor is put in charge of a number of operators to form

FIGURE 3 · THE SCALAR CHAIN OF COMMAND IN THE U.S. ARMY

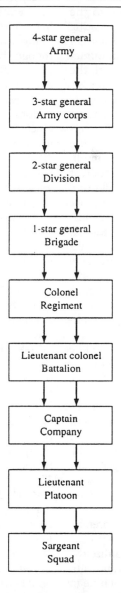

a basic organizational unit, another manager is put in charge of a number of these units to form a higher level unit, and so on until all the remaining units can come under a single manager at the strategic apex—designated the "chief executive officer"—to form the whole organization.

In this hierarchy, the middle-line manager performs a number of tasks in the flow of direct supervision above and below him. He collects "feedback" information on the performance of his own unit and passes some of this up to the managers above him, often aggregating it in the process. The sales manager of the machinery firm may receive information on every sale, but he reports to the district sales manager only a monthly total. He also intervenes in the flow of decisions. Flowing up are disturbances in the unit, proposals for change, decisions requiring authorization. Some the middle-line manager handles himself, while others he passes on up for action at a higher level in the hierarchy. Flowing down are resources that he must allocate in his unit, rules and plans that he must elaborate and projects that he must implement there. For example, the strategic apex in the Postal Service may decide to implement a project to sell "domestograms." Each regional manager and, in turn, each district manager must elaborate the plan as it applies to his geographical area.

But like the top manager, the middle manager is required to do more than simply engage in direct supervision. He, too, has boundary conditions to manage, horizontal ones related to the environment of his own unit. That environment may include other units within the larger organization as well as groups outside the organization. The sales manager must coordinate by mutual adjustment with the managers of production and of research, and he must visit some of the organization's customers. The foreman must spend a good deal of time with the industrial engineers who standardize the work processes of the operators and with the supplier installing a new machine in his shop, while the plant manager may spend his time with the production scheduler and the architect designing a new factory. In effect, each middle-line manager maintains liaison contacts with the other managers, analysts, support staffers, and outsiders whose work is in-

terdependent with that of his own unit. Furthermore, the middle-line manager, like the top manager, is concerned with formulating the strategy for his unit, although this strategy is, of course, significantly affected by the strategy of the overall organization.

In general, the middle-line manager performs all the managerial roles of the chief executive, but in the context of managing his own unit (Mintzberg, 1973). He must serve as a figurehead for his unit and lead its members; develop a network of liaison contacts; monitor the environment and his unit's activities and transmit some of the information he receives into his own unit, up the hierarchy, and outside the chain of command; allocate resources within his unit; negotiate with outsiders; initiate strategic change; and handle exceptions and conflicts.

Managerial jobs do, however, shift in orientation as they descend in the chain of authority. There is clear evidence that the job becomes more detailed and elaborated, less abstract and aggregated, more focused on the work flow itself. Thus, the "real-time" roles of the manager—in particular, negotiation and the handling of disturbances—become especially important at lower levels in the hierarchy (Mintzberg, 1973, pp. 110-113). Martin (1956) studied the decisions made by four levels of production managers in the chain of authority and concluded that at each successively lower level, the decisions were more frequent, of shorter duration, and less elastic, ambiguous, and abstract; solutions tended to be more pat or predetermined; the significance of events and interrelationships was more clear; in general, lower-level decision making was more structured.

Figure 4 shows the line manager in the middle of a field of forces. Sometimes these forces become so great—especially

FIGURE 4 · THE LINE MANAGER IN THE MIDDLE

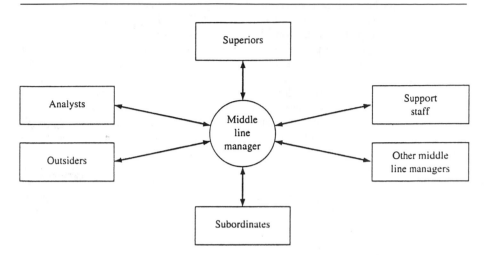

those of the analysts to institutionalize his job by the imposition of rules on the unit—that the individual in the job can hardly be called a "manager" at all, in the sense of really being "in charge" of an organizational unit. This is common at the level of first-line supervisor—for example, the foreman in some mass production manufacturing firms and branch managers in some large banking systems.

THE TECHNOSTRUCTURE

In the technostructure we find the analysts (and their supporting clerical staff) who serve the organization by affecting the work of others. These analysts are removed from the operating work flow—they may design it, plan it, change it, or train the people who do it, but they do not do it themselves. Thus, the technostructure is effective only when it can use its analytical techniques to make the work of others more effective.[3]

Who makes up the technostructure? There are the analysts concerned with adaptation, with changing the organization to meet environmental change, and

those concerned with control, with stabilizing and standardizing patterns of activity in the organization (Katz and Kahn, 1966). In this book we are concerned largely with the control analysts, those who focus their attention directly on the design and functioning of structure. The control analysts of the technostructure serve to effect standardization in the organization. This is not to say that operators cannot standardize their own work, just as everyone establishes his or her own procedure for getting dressed in the morning, or that managers cannot do it for them. But in general, the more standardization an organization uses, the more it relies on its technostructure. Such standardization reduces the need for direct supervision, in effect enabling clerks to do what managers once did.

We can distinguish three types of control analysts who correspond to the three forms of standardization: work study analysts (such as industrial engineers), who standardize work processes; planning and control analysts (such as long-range planners, budget analysts, and accountants), who standardize outputs; and personnel analysts (including trainers and recruiters), who standardize skills.

In a fully developed organization, the technostructure may perform at all levels of the hierarchy. At the lowest levels of the manufacturing firm, analysts standardize the operating work flow by scheduling production, carrying out time-and-method studies of the operator's work, an instituting systems of quality control. At middle levels, they seek to standardize the intellectual work of the organization (e.g., by training middle managers) and carry out operations research studies of informational tasks. On behalf of the strategic apex, they design strategic planning systems and develop financial systems to control the goals of major units.

While the analysts exist to standardize the work of others, their own work would appear to be coordinated with others largely through mutual adjustment. (Standardization of skills does play a part in this coordination, however, because analysts are typically highly trained specialists.) Thus, analysts spend a good deal of their time in informal communication. Guetzkow (1965, p. 537), for example, notes that staff people typically have wider communication contacts than line people, and my review of the literature on managerial work (Mintzberg, 1973, pp. 116-118) showed some evidence that staff managers pay more attention to the information processing roles—monitor, disseminator, spokesman—than do line managers.

SUPPORT STAFF

A glance at the chart of almost any large contemporary organization reveals a great number of units, all specialized, that exist to provide support to the organization outside the operating work flow. Those comprise the *support staff*. For ex-

ample, in a university, we find the alma mater fund, building and grounds department, museum, university press, bookstore, printing service, payroll department, janitorial service, endowment office, mailroom, real estate office, security department, switchboard, athletics department, student placement office, student residence, faculty club, guidance service, and chaplainery. None is a part of the operating core, that is, none engages in teaching or research, or even supports it directly (as does, say, the computing center or the library), yet each exists to provide indirect support to these basic missions. In the manufacturing firm, these units run the gamut from legal counsel to plant cafeteria. . . .

The support units can be found at various levels of the hierarchy, depending on the receivers of their service. In most manufacturing firms, public relations and legal counsel are located near the top, since they tend to serve the strategic apex directly. At middle levels are found the units that support the decisions made there, such as industrial relations, pricing, and research and development. And at the lower levels are found the units with more standardized work, that akin to the work of the operating core—cafeteria, mailroom, reception, payroll. Figure 5 shows all these support groups overlaid on our logo, together with typical groups from the other four parts of the organization, again using the manufacturing firm as our example.

Because of the wide variations in the types of support units, we cannot draw a single definitive conclusion about the favored coordinating mechanism for all of them. Each unit relies on whatever mechanism is most appropriate for itself—standardization of skills in the office of legal counsel, mutual adjustment in the research laboratory, standardization of work processes in the cafeteria.

FIGURE 5 · SOME MEMBERS AND UNITS OF THE PARTS OF THE MANUFACTURING FIRM

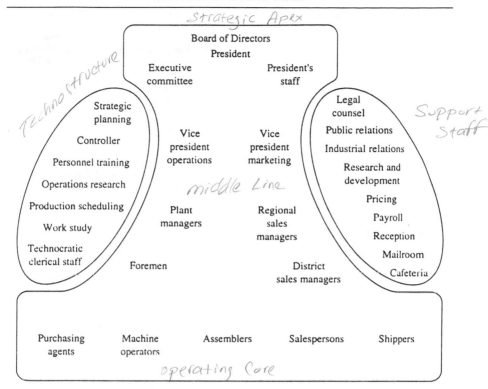

However, because many of the support units are highly specialized and rely on professional staff, standardization of skills may be the single most important coordinating mechanism. . . .

The most dramatic growth in organizations in recent decades has been in these staff groups, both the technostructure and the support staff. For example, Litterer (1973, pp. 584-585), in a study of thirty companies, noted the creation of 292 new staff units between 1920 and 1960, nearly ten units per company. More than half these units were in fact created between 1950 and 1960.

Organizations have always had operators and top managers, people to do the basic work and people to hold the whole

system together. As they grew, typically they first elaborated their middle-line component, on the assumption in the early literature that coordination had to be effected by direct supervision. But as standardization became an accepted coordinating mechanism, the technostructure began to emerge. The work of Frederick Taylor gave rise to the "scientific management" movement of the 1920s, which saw the hiring of many work study analysts. Just after World War II, the establishing of operations research and the advent of the computer pushed the influence of the technostructure well into the middle levels of the organization, and with the more recent popularity of techniques such as strategic planning and sophisticated financial controls, the technostructure has entrenched itself firmly at the highest levels of the organization as well. And the growth of the support staff has perhaps been even more dramatic, as all kinds of specializations developed during this century—scientific research in a wide number of fields, industrial relations, public relations and many more. Organizations have sought increasingly to bring these as well as the more traditional support functions such as maintenance and cafeteria within their boundaries. Thus, the ellipses to the left and right in the logo have become great bulges in many organizations. Joan Woodward (1965, p. 60) found in her research that firms in the modem process industries (such as oil refining) averaged one staff member for less than three operators, and in some cases the staff people actually outnumbered the operators by wide margins.[4]

NOTES

1. There are other, completely different, uses of the term "staff" that we are avoiding here. The military "chiefs of staff" are really managers of the strategic apex; the hospital "staff" physicians are really operators. Also, the introduction of the line/staff distinction here is not meant to sweep all of its problems under the rug, only to distinguish those involved directly from those involved peripherally with the operating work of organizations. By our definition, the production and sales functions in the typical manufacturing firm are clearly line activities, marketing research and public relations clearly staff. To debate whether engineering is line or staff—does it serve the operating core indirectly or is it an integral part of it?—depends on the importance one imputes to engineering in a particular firm. There is a gray area between line and staff: where it is narrow, for many organizations, we retain the distinction; where it is wide, we shall explicitly discard it.

2. Our subsequent discussion will focus only on the managers of the strategic apex, the work

of the latter group being considered an integral part of their own.

3. This raises an interesting point: that the techno-structure has a built-in commitment to change, to perpetual improvement. The modern organization's obsession with change probably derives in part at least from large and ambitious technostructures seeking to ensure their own survival. The perfectly stable organization has no need for a technostructure.

4. Woodward's tables and text here are very confusing, owing in part at least to some line errors in the page makeup. The data cited above are based on Figure 18, page 60, which seems to have the title that belongs to Figure 17 and which seems to relate back to Figure 7 on page 28, not to Figure 8 as Woodward claims.

REFERENCES

Allen, L. A. (1955, September). The line-staff relationship. *Management Record*, 346–349, 374–376.

Guetzkow, H. (1965). Communications in organizations. In J. G. March (Ed.), *Handbook of organizations* (Chap. 12). Chicago: Rand McNally.

Katz, D., & Kahn, R. L. (1966). *The social psychology of organizations*. New York: Wiley.

Kaufman, H., & Seidman, D. (1970). The morphology of organization. *Administrative Science Quarterly*, 439–445.

Litterer, J. A. (1973). *The analysis of organizations* (2nd ed.). New York: Wiley. Used with permission.

Martin, N. H. (1956). Differential decisions in the management of an industrial plant. *The Journal of Business*, 249–260.

Mintzberg, H. (1973). The nature of managerial work. New York: Harper & Row.

———. (1978). Patterns in strategy formation. *Management Science*, 934–948.

Thompson, J. D. (1967). *Organizations in action*. New York: McGraw-Hill.

Woodward, J. (1965). *Industrial organization: Theory and practice*. New York: Oxford University Press. Used with permission.

22
In Praise of Hierarchy
Elliott Jaques

At first glance, hierarchy may seem difficult to praise. Bureaucracy is a dirty word even among bureaucrats, and in business there is a widespread view that managerial hierarchy kills initiative, crushes creativity, and has therefore seen its day. Yet 35 years of research have convinced me that managerial hierarchy is the most efficient, the hardiest, and in fact the most natural structure ever devised for large organizations. Properly structured, hierarchy can release energy and creativity, rationalize productivity, and actually improve morale. Moreover, I think most managers know this intuitively and have only lacked a workable structure and a decent intellectual justification for what they have always known could work and work well.

As presently practiced, hierarchy undeniably has its drawbacks. One of business's great contemporary problems is how to release and sustain among the people who work in corporate hierarchies the thrust, initiative, and adaptability of the entrepreneur. This problem is so great that it has become fashionable to call for a new kind of organization to put in place of managerial hierarchy, an organization that will better meet the requirements of what is variously called the Information Age, the Services Age, or the Post-Industrial Age.

As vague as the description of the age is the definiton of the kind of new organization required to suit it. Theorists tell us it ought to look more like a symphony orchestra or a hospital or perhaps the British raj. It ought to function by means of primus groups or semiautonomous work teams or matrix overlap groups. It should be organic or entrepreneurial or tight-loose. It should hinge on skunk works or on management by walking around or perhaps on our old friend, management by objective.

All these approaches are efforts to overcome the perceived faults of hierarchy and find better ways to improve morale and harness human creativity. But the theorists' belief that our changing world requires an alternative to hierarchical organization is simply wrong, and all their proposals are based on an inadequate understanding of not only hierarchy but also human nature.

Hierarchy is not to blame for our problems. Encouraged by gimmicks and fads masquerading as insights, we have burdened our managerial systems with a makeshift scaffolding of inept structures and attitudes. What we need is not simply a new, flatter organization but an understanding of how managerial hierarchy functions—how it relates to the complexity of work and how we can use it to achieve a more effective deployment of talent and energy.

The reason we have a hierarchical organization of work is not only that tasks occur in lower and higher degrees of complexity—which is obvious—but also that there are sharp discontinuities in complexity that separate tasks into a series of steps or categories—which is not so obvious. The same discontinuities occur with respect to mental work and to the breadth and duration of accountability. The hierarchical kind of organization we call bureaucracy did not emerge accidentally. It is the only form of organization that can enable a company to employ large numbers of people and yet preserve unambiguous accountability for the work they do. And that is why, despite its problems, it has so doggedly persisted.

Hierarchy has not had its day. Hierarchy never did have its day. As an organizational system, managerial hierarchy has never been adequately described and has just as certainly never been adequately used. The problem is not to find an alternative to a system that once worked well but no longer does; the problem is to make it work efficiently for the first time in its 3,000-year history.

WHAT WENT WRONG . . .

There is no denying that hierarchical structure has been the source of a great deal of trouble and inefficiency. Its misuse has hampered effective management and stifled leadership, while its track record as a support for entrepreneurial energy has not been exemplary. We might almost say that successful businesses have had to succeed despite hierarchical organization rather than because of it.

One common complaint is excessive layering—too many rungs on the ladder. Information passes through too many people, decisions through too many levels, and managers and subordinates are too close together in experience and ability, which smothers effective leadership, cramps accountability, and promotes buck passing. Relationships grow stressful when managers and subordinates bump elbows, so to speak, within the same frame of reference.

Another frequent complaint is that few managers seem to add real value to the work of their subordinates. The fact that the breakup value of many large corporations is greater than their share value shows pretty clearly how much value corporate managers can *subtract* from their subsidiary businesses, but in fact few of us know exactly what managerial added value would look like as it was occurring.

Many people also complain that our present hierarchies bring out the nastier aspects of human behavior, like greed, insensitivity, careerism, and self-importance. These are the qualities that have sent many behavioral scientists in search of cooperative, group-oriented, nonhierarchical organizational forms. But are they the inevitable companions of hierarchy, or perhaps a product of the misuse of hierarchy that would disappear if hierarchy were properly understood and structured?

. . . AND WHAT CONTINUES TO GO WRONG

The fact that so many of hierarchy's problems show up in the form of individual misbehavior has led to one of the most widespread illusions in business, namely, that a company's managerial leadership can be significantly improved solely by doing psychotherapeutic work on the personalities and attitudes of its managers. Such methods can help individuals gain greater personal insight, but I doubt that individual insight, personality matching, or even exercises in group dynamics can produce much in the way of organizational change or an overall improvement in leadership effectiveness. The problem is that our managerial hierarchies are so badly designed as to defeat the best effort even of psychologically insightful individuals.

Solutions that concentrate on groups, on the other hand, fail to take into account the real nature of employment systems. People are not employed in groups. They are employed individually, and their employment contracts—real or implied—are individual. Group members may insist in moments of great esprit de corps that the group as such is the author of some particular accomplishment, but once the work is completed, the members of the group look for individual recognition and individual progression in their careers. And it is not groups but individuals whom the company will hold accountable. The only true group is the board of directors, with its corporate liability.

None of the group-oriented panaceas face this issue of accountability. All the theorists refer to group authority, group decisions, and group concensus, none of them to group accountability. Indeed, they avoid the issue of accountability altogether, for to hold a group accountable, the employment contract would have to be with the group, not with the individuals, and companies simply do not employ groups as such.

To understand hierarchy, you must first understand employment. To be employed is to have an ongoing contract that holds you accountable for doing work of a given type for a specified number of hours per week in exchange for payment. Your specific tasks within that given work are assigned to you by a person called your manager (or boss or supervisor), who *ought to be held accountable* for the work you do.

If we are to make our hierarchies function properly, it is essential to place the emphasis on *accountability for getting work done*. This is what hierarchical systems ought to be about. Authority is a secondary issue and flows from accountability in the sense that there should be just that amount of authority needed to discharge the accountability. So if a group is to be given authority, its members must be held accountable as a group, and unless this is done, it is very hard to take so-called group decisions seriously. If the CEO or the manager of the group is held accountable for outcomes, then in the final analysis, he or she will have to agree with group decisions or have the authority to block them, which means that the group never really had decision-making power to begin with. Alternatively, if groups are allowed to make decisions without their manager's seal of approval, then accountability as such will suffer, for if a group does badly, the group is never fired. (And it would be shocking if it were.)

In the long run, therefore, group authority *without* group accountability is dysfunctional, and group authority *with* group accountability is unacceptable. So images of organizations that are more like symphony orchestras or hospitals or the British raj are surely nothing more than metaphors to express a desired feeling of togetherness—the togetherness produced by a conductor's baton, the shared concern of doctors and nurses for their patients, or the apparent unity of the British civil service in India.

In employment systems, after all, people are not mustered to play together as their manager beats time. As for hospitals, they are the essence of everything bad about burearcratic organization. They function in spite of the system, only because of the enormous professional devotion of their staffs. The Indian civil service was in many ways like a hospital, its people bound together by the struggle to survive in a hostile environment. Managers do need authority, but authority based appropriately on the accountabilities they must discharge.

WHY HIERARCHY?

The bodies that govern companies, unions, clubs, and nations all employ people to do work, and they all organize these employees in managerial hierarchies, systems that allow organizations to hold people accountable for getting assigned work done. Unfortunately, we often lose sight of this goal and set up the organizational layers in our managerial hierarchies to accomodate pay brackets and facilitate career development instead. If work happens to get done as well, we consider that a useful bonus.

But if our managerial hierarchical organizations tend to choke so readily on debilitating bureaucratic practices, how do we explain the persistence and continued spread of this form of organization for more than 3,000 years? And why has the determined search for alternatives proved so fruitless?

The answer is that managerial hierarchy is and will remain the *only* way to structure unified working systems with hundreds, thousands, or tens of thousands of employees, for the very good reason that managerial hierarchy is the expression of two fundamental characteristics of real work. First, the tasks we carry out are not only more or less complex but they also become more complex as they separate out into discrete categories or types of complexity. Second, the same is true of the mental work that people do on the job, for as this work grows more complex, it too separates out into distinct categories or types of mental activity. In turn, these two characteristics permit hierarchy to meet four of any organization's fundamental needs: to add real value to work as it moves through the organization, to identify and nail down accountability at each stage of

the value-adding process, to place people with the necessary competence at each organizational layer, and to build a general consensus and acceptance of the managerial structure that achieves these ends.

HIERARCHICAL LAYERS

The complexity of the problems encountered in a particular task, project, or strategy is a function on the variables involved—their number, their clarity or ambiguity, the rate at which they change, and, overall, the extent to which they are distinct or tangled. Obviously, as you move higher in a managerial hierarchy the most difficult problems you have to contend with become increasingly complex. The biggest problems faced by the CEO of a large corporation are vastly more complex than those encountered on the shop floor. The CEO must cope not only with a huge array of often amorphous and constantly changing data but also with variables so tightly interwoven that they must be disentangled before they will yield useful information. Such variables might include the cost of capital, the interplay of corporate cash flow, the structure of the international competitive market, the uncertainties of Europe after 1992, the future of Pacific Rim development, social developments with respect to labor, political developments in Eastern Europe, the Middle East, and the Third World, and technological research and change.

That the CEO's and the lathe operator's problems are different in quality as well as quantity will come as no surprise to anyone. The question is—and always has been—where does the change in quality occur? On a continuum of complexity from the bottom of the structure to the top, where are the discontinuities that will allow us to identify layers of hierarchy that are distinct and separable, as different as ice is from water and water from steam? I spent years looking for the answer, and what I found was somewhat unexpected.

My first step was to recognize the obvious, that the layers have to do with manager-subordinate relationships. The manager's position is in one layer and the subordinate's is in the next layer below. What then sets the necessary distance between? This question cannot be answered without knowing just what it is that a manager does.

The managerial role has three critical features. First, and *most* critical, every manager must be held accountable not only for the work of subordinates but also for adding value to their work. Second, every manager must be held accountable for sustaining a team of subordinates capable of doing this work. Third, every manager must be held accountable for setting direction and getting subordinates to follow willingly, indeed enthusiastically. In brief, every manager is accountable for work and leadership.

In order to make accountability possible, managers must have enough authority to ensure that their subordinates can do the work assigned to them. This authority must include at least these four elements: (1) the right to veto any applicant who, in the manager's opinion, falls below the minimum standards of ability; (2) the power to make work assignments; (3) the power to carry out performance appraisals and, within the limits of company policy, to make decisions—not recommendations—about raises and merit rewards; and (4) the authority to initiate removal—at least from the manager's own team—of anyone who seems incapable of doing the work.

But defining the basic nature of the managerial role reveals only part of what a managerial layer means. It cannot tell us how wide a managerial layer should be, what the difference in responsibility should be between a manager and a subordinate, or, most important, where the break should come between one managerial layer and another. Fortunately, the next step in the research process supplied the missing piece of the puzzle.

RESPONSIBILITY AND TIME

This second step was the unexpected and startling discovery that the level of responsibility in any organizational role—whether a manager's or an individual contributor's—can be objectively measured in terms of the target completion time of the *longest* task, project, or program assigned to that role. The more distant the target completion date of the longest task or program, the heavier the weight of responsibility is felt to be. I call this measure the responsibility time span of the role. For example, a supervisor whose principal job is to plan tomorrow's production assignments and next week's work schedule but who also has ongoing responsibility for uninterrupted production supplies for the month ahead has a responsibility time span of one month. A foreman who spends most of his time riding herd on this week's production quotas but who must also develop a program to deal with the labor requirements of next year's retooling has a responsibility time span of a year or a little more. The advertising vice president who stays late every night working on next week's layouts but who also has to begin making contingency plans for the expected launch of two new local advertising media campaigns three years hence has a responsibility time span of three years.

To my great surprise, I found that in all types of managerial organizations in many different countries over 35 years, people in roles at the same time span experience the same weight of responsibility and declare the same level of pay to be fair, regardless of their occupation or actual pay. The time-span range runs from a day at the bottom of a large corporation to more than 20 years at the top, while the felt-fair pay ranges from $15,000 to $1 million and more.

Armed with my definition of a manager and my time-span measuring instrument, I then bumped into the second surprising finding—repeatedly confirmed—about layering in managerial hierarchies: the boundaries between successive managerial layers occur at certain specific time-span increments, just as ice changes to water and water to steam at certain specific temperatures. And the fact that everyone in the hierarchy, regardless of status, seems to see these boundaries in the same places suggests that the boundaries reflect some universal truth about human nature.

The illustration below, "Managerial Hierarchy in Fiction and in Fact," shows the hierarchical structure of part of a department at one company I studied, along with the approximate responsibility time span for each position. The longest task for manager A was more than five years, while for B, C, and D, the longest task fell between two and five years. Note also that according to the organization chart, A is the designated manager of B, B of C, and C of D.

In reality, the situation was quite different. Despite the managerial roles specified by the company, B, C, and D all described A as their "real" boss. C complained that B was "far too close" and "breathing down my neck." D had the same complaint about C. B and C also admitted to finding it very difficult to manage their immediate subordinates, C and D respectively, who seemed to do better if treated as colleagues and left alone.

In short, there appeared to be a cutoff at five years, such that those with responsibility time spans of less than five years felt they needed a manager with a responsibility time span of more than five years. Manager D, with a time span of two to three years, did not feel that C, with a time span of three to four, was distant enough hierarchically to take order from. D felt the same way about B. Only A filled the bill for *any* of the other three.

As the responsibility time span increased in the example from two years to three to four and approached five, no one seemed to perceive a qualitative difference in the nature of the responsibility that a manager discharged. Then, suddenly, when a manager had responsibility for tasks and projects that exceeded five years in scope, everyone seemed to perceive a difference not only in the scope of responsibility but also in its quality and in the kind of work and worker required to discharge it.

I found several such discontinuities that appeared consistently in more than 100 studies. Real managerial and hierarchical boundaries occur at time spans of three months, one year, two years, five years, ten years, and twenty years.

These natural discontinuities in our perception of the responsibility time span create hierarchical strata that people in different companies, countries, and circumstances all seem to regard as genuine and acceptable. The existence of such boundaries has important impli-

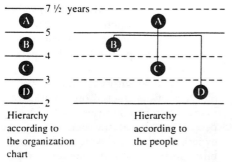

Hierarchy according to the organization chart

Hierarchy according to the people

cations in nearly every sphere of organizational management. One of these is performance appraisal. Another is the capacity of managers to add value to the work of their subordinates.

The only person with the perspective and authority to judge and communicate personal effectiveness is an employee's accountable manager, who, in most cases, is also the only person from whom an employee will accept evaluation and coaching. This accountable manager must be the supervisor one real layer higher in the hierarchy, not merely the next higher employee on the pay scale.

As I suggested earlier, part of the secret to making hierarchy work is to distinguish carefully between hierarchical layers and pay grades. The trouble is that companies need two to three times as many pay grades as they do working layers, and once they've established the pay grades, which are easy to describe and set up, they fail to take the next step and set up a different managerial hierarchy based on responsibility rather than salary. The result is too many layers.

My experience with organizations of all kinds in many different countries has convinced me that effective value-adding managerial leadership of subordinates can come only from an individual one category higher in cognitive capacity, working one category higher in problem complexity. By contrast, wherever managers and subordinates are in the same layer—separated only by pay grade—subordinates see the boss as too close, breathing down their necks, and they identify their "real" boss as the next manager at a genuinely higher level of cognitive and task complexity. This kind of overlayering is what produces the typical symptoms of bureaucracy in its worst form—too much passing problems up and down the system, bypassing, poor task setting, frustrated subordinates, anxious managers, wholly inadequate performance appraisals, "personality problems" everywhere, and so forth.

LAYERING AT COMPANY X

Companies need more than seven pay grades—as a rule, many more. But seven hierarchical layers is enough or more than enough for all but the largest corporations.

Let me illustrate this pattern of hierarchical layering with the case of two divisions of Company X, a corporation with 32,000 employees and annual sales of $7 billion. As shown in "Two Divisions of Corporation X," on page 252, the CEO sets strategic goals that look ahead as far as 25 years and manages executive vice presidents with responsibility for 12- to 15-year development programs. One vice president is accountable for several strategic business units, each with a president who works with critical tasks of up to 7 years duration.

One of these units (Y Products) employs 2,800 people, has annual sales of $250 million, and is engaged in the manufacture and sale of engineering products, with traditional semiskilled shop-floor production at Layer I. The other unit (Z Press) publishes books and employs only 88 people. Its funding and negotiations with authors are in the hands of a general editor at Layer IV, assisted by a small group of editors at Layer III, each working on projects that may take up to 18 months to complete.

So the president of Y Products manages more people, governs a greater share of corporate resources, and earns a lot more money for the parent company than does the president of Z Press. Yet the two presidents occupy the same hierarchical layer, have similar authority, and take home comparable salaries. This is neither coincidental nor unfair. It is natural, correct, and efficient.

TWO DIVISIONS OF CORPORATION X

	Layer	Time Span	Felt-Fair Pay*
CEO	VII	20 years	$1,040
EVP EVP EVP EVP	VI	10 years	520
President President President	V	5 years	260
General Manager General Editor General Manager General Manager	IV	2 years	130
Unit Managers Editors	III	1 year	68
First-Line Managers	II	3 months	38
Technicians and Operators Typists	I	1 day	20

* (In thousands of dollars)

It is the level of responsibility, *measured in terms of time span*, that tells you how many layers you need in an enterprise—not the number of subordinates or the magnitude of sales or profits. These factors may have a marginal influence on salary; they have no bearing at all on hierarchical layers.

CHANGES IN THE QUALITY OF WORK

The widespread and striking consistency of this underlying pattern of true managerial layers leads naturally to the question of why it occurs. Why do people perceive a sudden leap in status from,

say, four-and-a-half years to five and from nine to ten?

The answer goes back to the earlier discussion of complexity. As we go higher in a managerial hierarchy, the most difficult problems that arise grow increasingly complex, and, as the complexity of a task increases, so does the complexity of the mental work required to handle it. What I found when I looked at this problem over the course of ten years was that this complexity, like responsibility time span, also occurs in leaps or jumps. In other words, the most difficult tasks found within any given layer are all characterized by the same type or category of complexity, just as water remains in the same liquid state from 0° to 100° Celsius, even though it ranges from very cold to very hot. (A few degress cooler or hoter and water changes in state, to ice or steam.)

It is this suddenly increased level of necessary mental capacity, experience, knowledge, and mental stamina that allows managers to add value to the work of their subordinates. What they add is a new perspective, one that is broader, more experienced, and, most important, one that extends further in time. If, at Z Press, the editors at Layer III find and develop manuscripts into books with market potential, it is their general editor at Layer IV who fits those books into the press's overall list, who thinks ahead to their position on next year's list and later allocates resources to their production and marketing, and who makes projections about the publishing and book-buying trends of the next two to five years.

It is also this sudden change in the quality, not just the quantity, of managerial work that subordinates accept as a natural and appropriate break in the continuum of hierarchy. It is why they accept the boss's authority and not just the boss's power.

So the whole picture comes together. Managerial hierarchy or layering is the only effective organizational form for deploying people and tasks at complementary levels, where people can do the tasks assigned to them, where the people in any given layer can add value to the work of those in the layer below them, and, finally, where this stratification of management strikes everyone as necessary and welcome.

What we need is not some new kind of organization. What we need is managerial hierarchy that understands its own nature and purpose. Hierarchy is the best structure for getting work done in big organizations. Trying to raise efficiency and morale without first setting this structure to rights is like trying to lay bricks without mortar. No amount of exhortation, attitudinal engineering, incentive planning, or even leadership will have any permanent effect unless we understand what hierarchy is and why and how it works. We need to stop casting about fruitlessly for organizational Holy Grails and settle down to the hard work of putting our managerial hierarchies in order.

CHAPTER V

Systems Theory, Population Ecology, and Organizational Economics

S ince World War II, the social sciences have used systems analysis to examine their assertions about human behavior. The field of management, which to the extent that it deals with human resources can be said to be a social science, has been no exception. In fact, the systems perspective began to dominate organization theory in 1966–1967, when two of the most influential modern works in organization theory appeared: Robert Katz and Daniel Kahn's *The Social Psychology of Organizations* (1966), which articulated the concept of organizations as *open systems*; and James D. Thompson's coherent statement of the rational systems/contingency perspective of organizations, in *Organizations in Action* (1967).

Perhaps the field of organization theory was simply ripe for advancement in the late 1960s. The human relations orientation had lost much of its vigor, and the cultural milieu was moving away from the introspective, self-developmental, optimism of the "flower-child generation" and the "T-groups" of the early 1960s. Society was becoming enamored with computers, statistics, heuristic models, information systems, and measurement. Whatever the reasons may have been, Katz and Kahn and James D. Thompson provided the intellectual basis for the systems perspective to emerge as *the* mainstream of organization theory.

Systems theories of organization have two major conceptual themes or components: (1) applications to organizations of Ludwig von Bertalanffy's (1951) general systems theory, and (2) the use of quantitative tools and techniques to understand complex relationships among organizational and environmental variables and, thereby, to optimize decisions. Each theme is considered in the paragraphs that follow.

A *system* is any organized collection of parts united by prescribed interactions and designed for the accomplishment of specific goals or general purposes (Boulding, 1956). Thus, it is easy to see why general systems theory provides an important perspective for understanding modern organizations. Systems theory views an organization as a complex set of dynamically intertwined and interconnected elements, including its inputs, processes, outputs, feedback loops, and the environment in which it operates and with which it continuously interacts. A change in any element of the system causes changes in other elements. The interconnections tend to be complex, dynamic, and often unknown; thus when management makes decisions involving one organizational element, unanticipated impacts usually occur throughout the organizational system. Systems theorists study these interconnections, frequently using organizational decision processes and information and control systems as their focal points of analysis.

Whereas classical organization theory tends to be one-dimensional and somewhat simplistic, systems theories tend to be multidimensional and complex in their assumptions about organizational cause-and-effect relationships. The classicalists viewed organizations as static structures; systems theorists see organizations as always-changing processes of interactions among organizational and environmental elements. Organizations are not static, but rather are in constantly shifting states of dynamic equilibrium. They are adaptive systems that are integral parts of their environments. Organizations must adjust to changes in their environment if they are to survive; in turn, virtually all of their decisions and actions affect their environment.

Norbert Wiener's classic model of an organization as an adaptive system, from his 1948 book *Cybernetics*, epitomizes these basic theoretical perspectives of the systems perspective (see Figure 1). *Cybernetics*, a Greek word meaning *steersman*, was used by Wiener to mean the multidisciplinary study of the structures and functions of control and information processing systems in animals and machines. The basic concept behind cybernetics is self-regulation—through biological, social, or technological systems that can identify problems, do something about them, and then receive feedback to adjust themselves automatically. Wiener, a mathematician, developed the concept of cybernetics while working on anti-aircraft systems during World War II. Variations on this simple model of a system have been used extensively by systems theorists for many years, particularly around the development and use of management information systems, but we have not been able to locate anyone who used it before Wiener did in 1948.

FIGURE 1 • NORBERT WIENER'S MODEL OF AN ORGANIZATION AS AN
ADAPTIVE SYSTEM

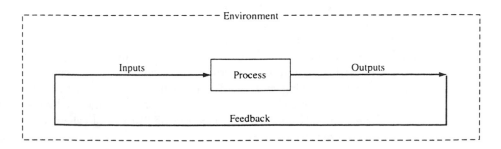

The search for order among complex variables has led to an extensive reliance on quantitative analytical methods and models. The systems approach is strongly cause-and-effect oriented (logical-positivist) in its philsophy and methods (Ott, 1989, Chapter 5). In these respects, systems theories have close ties to the scientific management approach of Frederick Winslow Taylor. Whereas Taylor used quantitative scientific methods to find "the one best way," the systems theorist uses quantitative scientific methods to identify cause-effect relationships and to find *optimal solutions*. In this sense, the conceptual approaches and purposes between the two perspectives are strikingly similar. Systems theories are often called *management sciences* or *administrative sciences*. (But be careful not to make the unpardonable error of calling them *scientific management*.)

Computers, models, and interdisciplinary teams of analysts are the basic "tools" of the systems perspective. Studies of organizations done by its members typically use the scientific method and quasi-experimental research techniques, or computer models. This quantitative orientation reflects the systems school's origins, the years immediately following World War II when the first serious attempts were made to apply mathematical and statistical probability models to organizational processes and decision making. Many of the early efforts started under the label of operations analysis, or operations research, in defense industry-related "think tanks" such as the RAND Corporation of Santa Monica, California. *Operations research* or *operations analysis* refers to the use of mathematical and scientific techniques to develop a quantitative basis for organizational decision making (Raiffa, 1968). During the subsequent decades, defense and aerospace programs provided the development and testing settings for many of the tools and techniques of operations research, including PERT, CPM, statistical inference, linear programming, gaming, Monte Carlo methods, and simulation.

Pioneering neoclassical theories provided important conceptual foundations for the systems approach. Herbert Simon and his associates contributed some of the most important of these (see Chapter II). Simon's visionary theories addressed *bounded rationality* and *satisficing* in organizational decision making (1957), and programmed and unprogrammed decisions (1960). With James March and others, Simon also made major contributions in the areas of cognitive limits on rationality and organizational innovation (1958). Indeed, it was Simon's further work in the areas of management decision making that led to his 1978 Nobel Prize for economics.

As the systems perspective ascended to the center stage of the field of organization theory during the later half of the 1960s, its focus on computers, information technology, and control systems spawned many heated debates between systems theorists and human relations-oriented organization theorists over philosophical issues such as computer domination of social structures, negative effects of centralized organizational decision making, and irresolvable conflicts between the individual freedom of organizational members and technology-based organizational confinement. Thus, for example, Norbert Wiener (1964), the "father" of cybernetics and a visionary systems-oriented scientist, wrote:

Render unto man the things which are man's and unto the computer the things which are the computer's. This would seem the intelligent policy to adopt when we employ men and computers together in common undertakings. It is a policy as far removed from that of the gadget worshipper as it is from the man who sees only blasphemy and the degradation of man in the use of any mechanical adjuvants whatever to thoughts. [An adjuvant is defined as something that serves to help or assist.]

William G. Scott's 1961 article, "Organization Theory: An Overview and an Appraisal," begins with an overview of how "modern" organization theory evolved from classical and neoclassical doctrine. We have reprinted here only the parts of the article that address the relationship between systems theory and organization theory, and that attempt to answer fundamentally important questions that are not addressed by classical or neoclassical theory: (1) What are the strategic parts of the system? (2) What is the nature of their mutual dependency? (3) What are the main processes in the system which link the parts together, and facilitate their adjustment to each other? and (4) What are the goals sought by systems?

In an a later article in this chapter, Fremont Kast and James Rosenzweig remind us of the importance of Scott's article. "The momentum of systems thinking was identified by Scott in 1961 when he described the relationship between general systems theory and organization theory. . . . Scott . . . helped us put into perspective the important writings of Herbert Simon, James March, Talcott Parsons, George Homans, E. Wight Bakke, Kenneth Boulding, and many others."

It is important to remember—and easy to forget—that there are *social* systems as well as *management* systems within the systems approach. The social systems theories have roots in the traditions and philosophies of social psychology, cultural anthropology, and sociology, as well as in the pioneering humanistically oriented philosophers of organization: including Elton Mayo (1933), Chester Barnard (1938), Roethlisberger and Dickson (1939), and Mary Parker Follett (1940).

Daniel Katz and Robert L. Kahn produced the first major statement on the applicability of social systems to organizations in their 1966 book *The Social Psychology of Organizations*. Katz and Kahn provided the intellectual basis for merging classical, neoclassical, human relations/behavioral, "modern" structural, and systems perspectives of organizations. Katz and Kahn balance these perspectives through their concept of organizations as open systems—systems that include organizations and their environments. Because organizations are open systems, they must continuously adapt to changing environmental factors, and managers must recognize that all organizational decisions and actions in turn influence their environments. Reprinted here is "Organizations and the System Concept," a chapter from *The Social Psychology of Organizations*, wherein Katz and Kahn conclude that the traditional closed system view of organizations has led to a failure to fully appreciate the interdependences and interactions between organizations and their environments. Katz and Kahn's concept of open systems has influenced the thinking of many organization theorists.

Classical organization theorists saw organizations as rational but closed systems that pursued the goal of economic efficiency. Because the systems were viewed as "closed" and not subject to influence from the external environment, major attention could be focused on such functions as planning and/or controlling. James D. Thompson, in his influential 1967 book *Organizations in Action*, classifies most organizations as open systems. Reprinted here are the first two chapters from his book, in which he suggests that the closed system approach may be realistic at the technical level of organizational operations. Thompson seeks to bridge the gap between open and closed systems by postulating that organizations "abhor uncertainty" and deal with uncertainty in the environment by creating specific elements designed to cope with the outside world, while other elements are able to focus on the rational nature of technical operations. The dominant technology used by an organization strongly influences its structure, activities, and evaluation/control processes.

In a 1972 *Academy of Management Journal* article, "General Systems Theory: Applications for Organization and Management," Fremont E. Kast and James E. Rosenzweig examine the "state of the art" of practical applications of systems theory. They attempt to assess the degree of success we have had in utilizing the "key concepts of general systems theory" in the development of "modern organization theory." After discussing some practical problems of applying systems theory to organizations, Kast and Rosenzweig observe that "many managers have used and will continue to use a systems approach and contingency views intuitively and implicitly"; thus, systems and contingency views are not new to most managers. The authors conclude with a call for ways to make systems views more usable by practicing managers.

Kast and Rosenzweig use the phrase "contingency views." Contingency theory is a "close cousin" of systems theories in which the effectiveness of an organizational action (for example, a decision) is viewed as dependent upon the relationship between the element in question and all other aspects of the system—at the particular moment. Everything is situational: there are no absolutes or universals. Thus, contingency views of organizations place high importance on rapid, accurate information systems. . . .

Population Ecology Theory

The theories that are known as population ecology of organizations, organizational ecology, ecological-evolutionary, and natural selection may warrant a separate chapter. However, their place in the field of organization theory is still the subject of heated controversy (Young, 1988; Hannan & Freeman, 1989a). Further, these theories represent logical extensions of systems and contingency theories (Grandori, 1987), and we find it most useful to consider them in conjunction with systems theory.

Theories of organizational ecology focus on the reasons for organizational diversity, formation, survival, and death. They seek to discover why there are so many kinds and sizes of organizations: "An ecology of organizations seeks to understand how social conditions affect the rates at which new organizations and new organizational forms arise, the rates at which organizations change forms, and the rates at which organizations and forms die out" (Hannan & Freeman, 1989b, p. 7). Population ecology theories are concerned with competition, selection, and survival of the fittest in populations (groupings) of organizations. They closely resemble Darwinian theories of evolution in that survival of an organization depends on its ability to acquire adequate supplies of critical resources. These theories are also interested in the distribution of organizational forms across environmental conditions and limitations on various organizational forms in different environments.

Population ecology theory of organizations assumes that natural selection processes operate among organizations. Organizations do not adapt to their changing environments by making decisions; instead, the environment selects among organizational forms based on:

- The magnitude of economies of specialization and scale in using a specialist *versus* generalist organizational form
- The trade-off costs of generalist organizations adapting to (coping with) environmental states *versus* the costs of errors resulting from maladaptation in specialist organizations

Thus, according to organizational ecology theories, organizational forms are selected naturally based on economies in production, organizational specialization, and change costs.

Organizational ecology theory is most applicable and useful

- When there is competition among the organizations in a population
- When there are many organizations in a population (so that natural selection can occur)
- Among newer rather than older organizations

The best known and most frequently cited work on natural selection or population ecology is Michael Hannan and John Freeman's 1977 *American Journal of Sociology* article "The Population Ecology of Organizations." Hannan and Freeman propose a model (or set of theories) for use in the study of organizational-environment relations. They assess the applicability and limitations of bioecological models to the study of organizational-environment relations. Populations of organizations—rather than individual organizations—are the appropriate units of analysis. The model incorporates an evolutionary explanation of the principle of isomorphism. They also suggest an organizational selection process based on competition theory and address dynamic considerations of excess capacity using fitness-set theory.

Organizational Economics

The field of organizational economics originated with a 1937 article by Ronald H. Coase, "The Nature of the Firm." Coase argued that the discipline of economics could not rely on price theory alone to explain behavior in and of firms. Although price theory often could adequately explain some resource allocation decisions, a second coordinating mechanism—hierarchy—also had to be considered. The concerns of organizational economics have expanded greatly since 1937. Two articles are reprinted here that discuss the essence of organizational economics and its core theory components: agency theory, the theory of property rights, and transaction cost theory. They are: "Theory of the Firm: Managerial Behavior, Agency Costs and Ownership Structure," by Michael C. Jensen and William H. Meckling (1976), and "The Ethereal Hand: Organizational Economics and Management Theory," by Lex Donaldson (1990).

"Agency theory" defines managers and other employees as "agents" of owners ("principals") who out of necessity must delegate some authority to agents. Price theory has been concerned with how to structure organizations for the free interplay of markets among agents and principals. "Why should not all economic activity be arranged as free contracts . . . ?" (Donaldson, 1990, p. 370) including the pricing structure needed to keep agents working in the best interests of principals. However, price theory falls short. "Since the interests of the principal and agent are inclined to diverge, the delegation of authority from the principal to the agent allows a degree of underfulfillment of the wishes of the principal by the agent" (Donaldson, 1990, p. 369).

There is good reason to believe that agents will not always act in the best interests of principals. Like everyone else, agents are utility maximizers who tend to act in *their own* best interests. Agency theory thus examines the combined use of price theory mechanisms (for example, incentives) and hierarchy mechanisms (for example, monitoring) that principals can use "to limit the aberrant activities of the agent" (Jensen & Meckling, 1976, p. 308).

The "theory of property rights" addresses the allocation of costs and rewards among the participants in an organization and, for example, how "claims on the assets and cash flows of the organization . . . can generally be sold without permission of the other contracting individuals" (p. 311). An organization is a form of legal fiction, a "multitude of complex relationships (i.e., contracts) between the legal fiction (the firm) and the owners of labor, material and capital inputs and the consumers of output" (Jensen & Meckling, 1976, p. 311).

The intellectual heritage of property rights theory can be traced to John Locke's *Two Treatises of Government* (1967) and, to a lesser extent, Jean-Jacques Rousseau's *The Social Contract* (1947). A more recent contributor to the theory is Richard Cyert and James March's seminal (1963) book, *A Behavioral Theory of the Firm*, in which organizations are described as coalitions of self-interested participants.

The final core element of organizational economics, "transaction cost theory," is interested in the costs of maintaining the principal-agent relationship and how to minimize them. Thus, Jensen and Meckling (p. 308) define "agency costs" as the sum of: (1) the monitoring expenditures paid by the principals, (2) the bonding expenditures paid by agents (to assure the principals that they will not harm the principals or, if they should, that the principals will be reimbursed), and (3) the residual loss (the costs to the principal of the "divergence between the agent's

decisions and those decisions which would maximize the welfare of the principal")
(Jensen & Meckling, 1976, p. 308).

Thus organizational economics deals with a universal problem of organizations:
how to induce managers and other employees to act in the best interests of those
who control ownership or, in the case of government agencies and nonprofit organizations, those who have the authority to control policy and resource allocation
decisions. The current wave of management theorists who advocate employee and
group empowerment approaches (Chapter IX) need to address the types of issues
that the organizational economists have been wrestling with since 1937.

REFERENCES

Barnard, C. I. (1938). *The functions of the executive*. Cambridge, MA: Harvard University
Press.

Barney, J. B. (1990). The debate between traditional management theory and organizational economics: Substantive differences or intergroup conflict? *Academy of Management Review, 15*(3), 382–393.

Barney, J. B., & Ouchi, W. G. (1986). *Organizational economics*. San Francisco: Jossey-
Bass.

Bertalanffy, L. von. (1951, December). General systems theory: A new approach to unity
of science. *Human Biology, 23*, 303–361.

Bertalanffy, L. von. (1968). *General systems theory: Foundations, development, applications*.
New York: George Braziller.

Blumenthal, S. C. (1969). *Management information systems*. Englewood Cliffs, NJ:
Prentice-Hall.

Boulding, K. E. (1956, April). General systems theory—The skeleton of science. *Management Science, 2, 3,* 197–208.

Carroll, G. R. (1987). *Publish and perish: The organizational ecology of newspaper industries*.
Greenwich, CT: JAI Press.

Carroll, G. R. (Ed.). (1988). *Ecological models of organizations*. Cambridge, MA: Ballinger.

Carzo, R., Jr., & Yanouzas, J. N. (1967). *Formal organizations: A systems approach*. Homewood, IL: Richard D. Irwin.

Coase, R. H. (1937). The nature of the firm. *Economica, New Series, IV,* 386–405.

Commons, J. R. (1934). *Institutional economics: Its place in political economy*. Madison, WI:
University of Wisconsin Press.

Cyert, R. M., & March, J. G. (1963). A behavioral theory of the firm. Englewood Cliffs,
NJ: Prentice-Hall.

Dearden, J. F., & McFarlan, F. W. (1966). *Management information systems*. Homewood,
IL: Richard D. Irwin.

Donaldson, L. (1990). The ethereal hand: Organizational economics and management
theory. *Academy of Management Review, 15*(3), 369–381.

Follett, M. P. (1940). *Dynamic administration: The collected papers of Mary Parker Follett*.
E. M. Fox & L. Urwick (Eds.). New York: Hippocrene Books.

Galbraith, J. (1973). *Designing complex organizations*. Reading, MA: Addison-Wesley.

Grandori, A. (1987). *Perspectives on organization theory.* Cambridge, MA: Ballinger.

Hannan, M. T., & Freeman, J. (1977). The population ecology of organizations. *American Journal of Sociology, 82,* 929–964.

Hannan, M. T., & Freeman, J. (1984). Where do organizational forms come from? *Sociological Forum, 1,* 50–72.

Hannan, M. T., & Freeman, J. (1989a). Setting the record straight on organizational ecology: Rebuttal to Young. *American Journal of Sociology, 95*(2), 425–438.

Hannan, M. T., & Freeman, J. (1989b). *Organizational ecology.* Cambridge, MA: Harvard University Press.

Jensen, M. C., & Meckling, W. H. (1976). Theory of the firm: Managerial behavior, agency costs, and ownership structure. *Journal of Financial Economics, 3,* 305–360.

Kast, F. E. & Rosenzweig, J. E. (1970). *Organization and management: A systems approach.* New York: McGraw-Hill.

Kast, F. E., & Rosenzweig, J. E. (1972, December). General systems theory: Applications for organization and management. *Academy of Management Journal,* 447–465.

Katz, D., & Kahn, R. L. (1966). *The social psychology of organizations.* New York: Wiley.

Locke, J. (1967). *Two treatises of government.* (Ed. by P. Laslett, 2d ed.) London: Cambridge University Press. (Original, 1690).

March, J. G., & Simon, H. A. (1958). *Organizations.* New York: Wiley.

Mayo, E. (1933). *The human problems of an industrial civilization.* New York: Viking Press.

Ott, J. S. (1989). *The organizational culture perspective.* Pacific Grove, CA: Brooks/Cole.

Raiffa, H. (1968). *Decision analysis.* Reading, MA: Addison-Wesley.

Roethlisberger, F. J., & Dickson, W. J. (1939). *Management and the worker.* Cambridge. MA: Harvard University Press.

Rousseau, J. J. (1947). The social contract. In E. Barker (Ed.), *Social contract* (pp. 167–307). London: Oxford University Press. (Original, 1762).

Scott, W. G. (1961, April). Organization theory: An overview and an appraisal. *Academy of Management Journal, 4,* 7–26.

Simon, H. A. (1957). *Administrative behavior* (2nd ed.). New York: Macmillan.

Simon, H. A. (1960). *The new science of management decisions.* New York: Harper & Row.

Singh, J., House, R. J., & Tucker, D. J. (1986). Organizational change and organizational mortality. *Administrative Science Quarterly, 31,* 587–611.

Thompson, J. D. (1967). *Organizations in action.* New York: McGraw-Hill.

Trist, E. (1977). A concept of organizational ecology. *Australian Journal of Management, 2,* 162–175.

Trist, E. (1983). Referent organizations and the development of inter-organizational domains. *Human Relations, 36*(3), 269–284.

Wiener, N. (1948). *Cybernetics.* Cambridge, MA: MIT Press.

Wiener, N. (1950). *The human use of human beings.* Boston: Houghton Mifflin.

Wiener, N. (1964). *God and Golem, inc.* Cambridge, MA: MIT Press.

Williamson, O. E. (1975). *Markets and hierarchies.* New York: Free Press.

Williamson, O. E., & Winter, S. G. (Eds.) (1991). *The nature of the firm: Origins, evolution, and development.* New York: Oxford University Press.

Young, R. C. (1988). Is population ecology a useful paradigm for the study of organizations? *American Journal of Sociology, 94*(1), 1–24.

23

Organization Theory: An Overview and an Appraisal

William G. Scott

* * *

MODERN ORGANIZATION THEORY

The distinctive qualities of modern organization theory are its conceptual-analytical base, its reliance on empirical research data and, above all, its integrating nature. These qualities are framed in a philosophy which accepts the premise that the only meaningful way to study organization is to study it as a system. As Henderson put it, the study of a system must rely on a method of analysis, ". . . involving the simultaneous variations of mutually dependent variables."[1] Human systems, of course, contain a huge number of dependent variables which defy the most complex simultaneous equations to solve.

Nevertheless, system analysis has its own peculiar point of view which aims to study organization in the way Henderson suggests. It treats organization as a system of mutually dependent variables. As a result, modern organization theory, which accepts system analysis, shifts the conceptual level of organization study above the classical and neoclassical theories. Modern organization theory asks a range of interrelated questions which are not seriously considered by the two other theories.

Key among these questions are: (1) What are the strategic parts of the system? (2) What is the nature of their mutual dependency? (3) What are the main processes in the system which link the parts together, and facilitate their adjustment to each other? (4) What are the goals sought by systems?[2]

Modern organization theory is in no way a unified body of thought. Each writer and researcher has his special emphasis when he considers the system. Perhaps the most evident unifying thread in the study of systems is the effort to look at the organization in its totality. Representative books in this field are March and Simon, *Organizations*,[3] and Haire's anthology, *Modern Organization Theory*.[4]

Instead of attempting a review of different writers' contributions to modern organization theory, it will be more useful to discuss the various ingredients involved in system analysis. They are the parts, the interactions, the processes, and the goals of systems.

[2]There is another question which cannot be treated in the scope of this paper. It asks, what research tools should be used for the study of the system?

[3]James G. March and Herbert A. Simon, *Organizations* (New York: John Wiley and Sons, 1958).

[1]Lawrence J. Henderson, *Pareto's General Sociology* (Cambridge: Harvard University Press, 1935), p. 13.

[4]Mason Haire, (editor) *Modern Organization Theory* (New York: John Wiley and Sons, 1959).

Source: William G. Scott, "Organization Theory: An Overview and an Appraisal," pp. 7–26, *Academy of Management Journal*, 4 (April 1961). Reprinted by permission.

The Parts of the System and Their Interdependency

The first basic part of the system is the *individual*, and the personality structure he brings to the organization. Elementary to an individual's personality are motives and attitudes which condition the range of expectancies he hopes to satisfy by participating in the system.

The second part of the system is the formal arrangement of functions, usually called the *formal organization*. The formal organization is the interrelated pattern of jobs which make up the structure of a system. Certain writers, like Argyris, see a fundamental conflict resulting from the demands made by the system, and the structure of the mature, normal personality. In any event, the individual has expectancies regarding the job he is to perform; and, conversely, the job makes demands on, or has expectancies relating to, the performance of the individual. Considerable attention has been given by writers in modern organization theory to incongruencies resulting from the interaction of organizational and individual demands.[5]

The third part in the organization system is the *informal organization*. Enough has been said already about the nature of this organization. But it must be noted that an interactional pattern exists between the individual and the informal group. This interactional arrangement can be conveniently discussed as the mutual modification of expectancies. The informal organization has demands which it makes on members in terms of anticipated forms of behavior, and the individual has expectancies of satisfaction he hopes to derive from association with people on the job. Both these sets of expectancies interact, resulting in the individual modifying his behavior to accord with the demands of the group, and the group, perhaps, modifying what it expects from an individual because of the impact of his personality on group norms.[6]

Much of what has been said about the various expectancy systems in an organization can also be treated using status and role concepts. Part of modern organization theory rests on research findings in social-psychology relative to reciprocal patterns of behavior stemming from role demands generated by both the formal and informal organizations, and role perceptions peculiar to the individual. Bakke's *fusion process* is largely concerned with the modification of role expectancies. The fusion process is a force, according to Bakke, which acts to weld divergent elements together for the preservation of organizational integrity.[7]

The fifth part of system analysis is the *physical setting* in which the job is performed. Although this element of the system may be implicit in what has been said already about the formal organization and its functions, it is well to separate it. In the physical surroundings of work, interactions are present in complex man-machine systems. The human "engineer" cannot approach the problems posed by such interrelationships in a purely technical, engineering fashion. As Haire says, these problems lie in the domain of the social theorist.[8] Attention must be centered on responses de-

[5]See Chris Argyris, *Personality and Organization* (New York: Harper and Brothers, 1957), esp. Chapters 2, 3, 7.

[6]For a larger treatment of this subject see: George C. Homans, *The Human Group* (New York: Harcourt, Brace and Company, 1950), Chapter 5.

[7]E. Wight Bakke, "Concept of the Social Organization," in *Modern Organization Theory*, Mason Haire (editor) (New York: John Wiley and Sons, 1959) pp. 60–61.

[8]Mason Haire, "Psychology and the Study of Business: Joint Behavioral Sciences," in *Social Science Research on Business: Product and Potential* (New York: Columbia University Press, 1959), pp. 53–59.

manded from a logically ordered production function, often with the view of minimizing the error in the system. From this standpoint, work cannot be effectively organized unless the psychological, social, and physiological characteristics of people participating in the work environment are considered. Machines and processes should be designed to fit certain generally observed psychological and physiological properties of men, rather than hiring men to fit machines. . . .

The Linking Processes

One can say, with a good deal of glibness, that all the parts mentioned above are interrelated. Although this observation is quite correct, it does not mean too much in terms of system theory unless some attempt is made to analyze the processes by which the interaction is achieved. Role theory is devoted to certain types of interactional processes. In addition, modern organization theorists point to three other linking activities which appear to be universal to human systems of organized behavior. These processes are communication, balance, and decision making.

(1) Communication is mentioned often in neoclassical theory, but the emphasis is on description of forms of communication activity, i.e., formal-informal, vertical-horizontal, line-staff. Communication, as a mechanism which links the segments of the system together, is overlooked by way of much considered analysis.

One aspect of modern organization theory is study of the communication network in the system. Communication is viewed as the method by which action is evoked from the parts of the system. Communication acts not only as stimuli resulting in action, but also as a control and coordination mechanism linking the decision centers in the system into a synchronized pattern. Deutsch points out that organizations are composed of parts which communicate with each other, receive messages from the outside world, and store information. Taken together, these communication functions of the parts comprise a configuration representing the total system.[9] More is to be said about communication later in the discussion of the cybernetic model.

(2) The concept of *balance* as a linking process involves a series of some rather complex ideas. Balance refers to an equilibrating mechanism whereby the various parts of the system are maintained in a harmoniously structured relationship to each other.

The necessity for the balance concept logically flows from the nature of systems themselves. It is impossible to conceive of an ordered relationship among the parts of a system without also introducing the idea of a stabilizing or an adapting mechanism.

Balance appears in two varieties—quasi-automatic and innovative. Both forms of balance act to insure system integrity in face of changing conditions, either internal or external to the system. The first form of balance, quasi-automatic, refers to what some think are "homeostatic" properties of systems. That is, systems seem to exhibit built-in propensities to maintain steady states.

If human organizations are open, self-maintaining systems, then control and regulatory processes are necessary. The issue hinges on the degree to which stabilizing processes in systems, when adapting to change, are automatic. March and Simon have an interesting answer to this problem, which in part is based on the type of change and the adjustment necessary to adapt to the

[9]Karl W. Deutsch "On Communication Models in the Social Sciences," *Public Opinion Quarterly*, 16 (1952), pp. 356–380.

change. System have programs of action which are put into effect when a change is perceived. If the change is relatively minor, and if the change comes within the purview of established programs of action, then it might be fairly confidently predicted that the adaptation made by the system will be quasi-automatic.[10]

The role of innovative, creative balancing efforts now needs to be examined. The need for innovation arises when adaptation to a change is outside the scope of existing programs designed for the purpose of keeping the system in balance. New programs have to be evolved in order for the system to maintain internal harmony.

New programs are created by trial and error search for feasible action alternatives to cope with a given change. But innovation is subject to the limitations and possibilities inherent in the quantity and variety of information present in a system at a particular time. New combinations of alternatives for innovative purposes depend on:

(a) the possible range of output of the system, or the capacity of the system to supply information.

(b) the range of available information in the memory of the system.

(c) the operating rules (program) governing the analysis and flow of information within the system.

(d) the ability of the system to "forget" previously learned solutions to change problems.[11] A system with too good a memory might narrow its behavioral choices to such an extent as to stifle innovation. In simpler language, old learned programs might be used to adapt

to change, when newly innovated programs are necessary.[12]

Much of what has been said about communication and balance brings to mind a cybernetic model in which both these processes have vital roles. Cybernetics has to do with feedback and control in all kinds of systems. Its purpose is to maintain system stability in the face of change. Cybernetics cannot be studied without considering communication networks, information flow, and some kind of balancing process aimed at preserving the integrity of the system.

Cybernetics directs attention to key questions regarding the system. These questions are: How are communication centers connected, and how are they maintained? Corollary to this question: what is the structure of the feedback system? Next, what information is stored in the organization, and at what points? And as a corollary: how accessible is this information to decision-making centers? Third, how conscious is the organization of the operation of its own parts? That is, to what extent do the policy centers receive control information with sufficient frequency and relevancy to create a real awareness of the operation of the segments of the system? Finally, what are the learning (innovating) capabilities of the system?[13]

Answers to the questions posed by cybernetics are crucial to understanding both the balancing and communication processes in systems.[14] Although cybernetics has been applied largely to

---

[10]March and Simon, *op. cit.*, pp. 139–140.

[11]Mervyn L. Cadwallader "The Cybernetic Analysis of Change in Complex Social Organization," *The American Journal of Sociology,* September 1959, p. 156.

[12]It is conceivable for innovative behavior to be programmed into the system.

[13]These are questions adapted from Deutsch, *op. cit.*, 368–370.

[14]Answers to these questions would require a comprehensive volume. One of the best approaches currently available is Stafford Beer, *Cybernetics and Management* (New York: John Wiley and Sons, 1959).

technical-engineering problems of automation, the model of feedback, control, and regulation in all systems has a good deal of generality. Cybernetics is a fruitful area which can be used to synthesize the processes of communication and balance.

(3) A wide spectrum of topics dealing with types of decisions in human systems makes up the core of analysis of another important process in organizations. Decision analysis is one of the major contributions of March and Simon in their book *Organizations*. The two major classes of decisions they discuss are decisions to produce and decisions to participate in the system.[15]

Decisions to produce are largely a result of an interaction between individual attitudes and the demands of organization. Motivation analysis becomes central to studying the nature and results of the interaction. Individual decisions to participate in the organization reflect on such issues as the relationship between organizational rewards versus the demands made by the organization. Participation decisions also focus attention on the reasons why individuals remain in or leave organizations.

March and Simon treat decisions as internal variables in an organization which depend on jobs, individual expectations and motivations, and organizational structure. Marschak[16] looks on the decision process as an independent variable upon which the survival of the organization is based. In this case, the organization is viewed as having, inherent to its structure, the ability to maximize survival requisites through its established decision processes.

[15]March and Simon, *op. cit.*, Chapters 3 and 4.

[16]Jacob Marschak, "Efficient and Viable Organizational Forms" in *Modern Organization Theory*, Mason Haire, editor (New York: John Wiley and Sons, 1959), pp. 307–320.

The Goals of Organization

Organization has three goals which may be either intermeshed or independent ends in themselves. They are growth, stability, and interaction. The last goal refers to organizations which exist primarily to provide a medium for association of its members with others. Interestingly enough these goals seem to apply to different forms of organization at varying levels of complexity, ranging from simple clockwork mechanisms to social systems.

These similarities in organizational purposes have been observed by a number of people, and a field of thought and research called general system theory has developed, dedicated to the task of discovering organizationed universals. The dream of general system theory is to create a science of organizational universals, or if you will, a universal science using common organizational elements found in all systems as a starting point.

Modern organization theory is on the periphery of general system theory. Both general system theory and modern organization theory studies:

(1) the parts (individuals) in aggregates, and the movement of individuals into and out of the system.

(2) the interaction of individuals with the environment found in the system.

(3) the interactions among individuals in the system.

(4) general growth and stability problems of systems.[17]

Modern organization theory and general system theory are similar in that they look at organization as an integrated whole. They differ, however, in terms of their generality. General system theory is concerned with every level of

[17]Kenneth E. Boulding, "General System Theory—The Skeleton of a Science," *Management Science*, April 1956, pp. 200–202.

system, whereas modern organization theory focuses primarily on human organization.

The question might be asked, what can the science of administration gain by the study of system levels other than human? Before attempting an answer, note should be made of what these other levels are. Boulding presents a convenient method of classification:

(1) The static structure—a level of framework, the anatomy of a system; for example, the structure of the universe.

(2) The simple dynamic system—the level of clockworks, predetermined necessary motions.

(3) The cybernetic system—the level of the thermostat, the system moves to maintain a given equilibrium through a process of self-regulation.

(4) The open system—level of self-maintaining systems, moves toward and includes living organisms.

(5) The genetic-societal system—level of cell society, characterized by a division of labor among cells.

(6) Animal systems—level of mobility, evidence of goal-directed behavior.

(7) Human systems—level of symbol interpretation and idea communication.

(8) Social system—level of human organization.

(9) Transcendental systems—level of ultimates and absolutes which exhibit systematic structure but are unknowable in essence.[18]

This approach to the study of systems by finding universals common at all levels of organization offers intriguing possibilities for administrative organization theory. A good deal of light could be thrown on social systems if structurally analogous elements could be found in the simpler types of systems. For ex-

ample, cybernetic systems have characteristics which seem to be similar to feedback, regulation, and control phenomena in human organizations. Thus, certain facets of cybernetic models could be generalized to human organization. Considerable danger, however, lies in poorly founded analogies. Superficial similarities between simpler system forms and social systems are apparent everywhere. Instinctually based ant societies, for example, do not yield particularly instructive lessons for understanding rationally conceived human organizations. Thus, care should be taken that analogies used to bridge system levels are not mere devices for literary enrichment. For analogies to have usefulness and validity, they must exhibit inherent structural similarities or implicitly identical operational principles.[19]

Modern organization theory leads, as it has been shown, almost inevitably into a discussion of general system theory. A science of organization universals has some strong advocates, particularly among biologists.[20] Organization theorists in administrative science cannot afford to overlook the contributions of

[18]*Ibid.*, pp. 202–205.

[19]Seidenberg, *op. cit.*, p. 136. The fruitful use of the type of analogies spoken of by Seidenberg is evident in the application of thermodynamic principles, particularly the entropy concept, to communication theory. See: Claude E. Shannon and Warren Weaver, *The Mathematical Theory of Communication* (Urbana: The University of Illinois Press, 1949). Further, the existence of a complete analogy between the operational behavior of thermodynamic systems, electrical communication systems, and biological systems has been noted by: Y. S. Touloukian, *The Concept of Entropy in Communication, Living Organisms, and Thermodynamics*, Research Bulletin 130, Purdue Engineering Experiment Station.

[20]For example see: Ludwig von Bertalanffy, *Problem of Life* (London: Watts and Company, 1952).

general system theory. Indeed, modern organization concepts could offer a great deal to those working with general system theory. But the ideas dealt with in the general theory are exceedingly elusive.

Speaking of the concept of equilibrium as a unifying element in all systems, Easton says, "It (equilibrium) leaves the impression that we have a useful general theory when in fact, lacking measurability, it is a mere pretence for knowledge."[21] The inability to quantify and measure universal organization elements undermines the success of pragmatic tests to which general system theory might be put.

Organization Theory: Quo Vadis?

Most sciences have a vision of the universe to which they are applied, and administrative science is not an exception. This universe is composed of parts. One purpose of science is to synthesize the parts into an organized conception of its field of study. As a science matures, its theorems about the configuration of its universe change. The direction of change in three sciences, physics, economics, and sociology, are noted briefly for comparison with the development of an administrative view of human organization.

The first comprehensive and empirically verifiable outlook of the physical universe was presented by Newton in his *Principia*. Classical physics, founded on Newton's work, constitutes a grand scheme in which a wide range of physical phenomena could be organized and predicted. Newtonian physics may rightfully be regarded as "macro" in nature, because its system of organization was concerned largely with gross events of which the movement of celestial bodies, waves, energy forms, and strain are examples. For years classical physics was supreme, being applied continuously to smaller and smaller classes of phenomena in the physical universe. Physicists at one time adopted the view that everything in their realm could be discovered by simply subdividing problems. Physics thus moved into the "micro" order.

But in the nineteenth century a revolution took place motivated largely because events were being noted which could not be explained adequately by the conceptual framework supplied by the classical school. The consequences of this revolution are brilliantly described by Eddington:

> From the point of view of philosophy of science the conception associated with entropy must I think be ranked as the great contribution of the nineteenth century to scientific thought. It marked a reaction from the view that everything to which science need pay attention is discovered by microscopic dissection of objects. It provided an alternative standpoint in which the centre of interest is shifted from the entities reached by the customary analysis (atoms, electric potentials, etc.) to qualities possessed by the system as a whole, which cannot be split up and located—a little bit here, and a little bit there. . . .
>
> We often think that when we have completed our study of *one* we know all about *two*, because "two" is "one and one." We forget that we have still to make a study of "and." Secondary physics is the study of "and"—that is to say, of organization.[22]

Although modern physics often deals in minute quantities and oscillations,

[21]David Easton, "Limits of the Equilibrium Model in Social Research," in *Profits and Problems of Homeostatic Models in the Behavioral Sciences*, Publication 1, Chicago Behavioral Sciences, 1953, p. 39.

[22]Sir Arthur Eddington, *The Nature of the Physical World* (Ann Arbor: The University of Michigan Press, 1958), pp 103–104.

the conception of the physicist is on the "macro" scale. He is concerned with the "and," or the organization of the world in which the events occur. These developments did not invalidate classical physics as to its usefulness for explaining a certain range of phenomena. But classical physics is no longer the undisputed law of the universe. It is a special case.

Early economic theory, and Adam Smith's *Wealth of Nations* comes to mind, examined economic problems in the macro order. The *Wealth of Nations* is mainly concerned with matters of national income and welfare. Later, the economics of the firm, micro-economics, dominated the theoretical scene in this science. And, finally, with Keynes' *The General Theory of Employment Interest and Money*, a systematic approach to the economic universe was re-introduced on the macro level.

The first era of the developing science of sociology was occupied by the great social "system builders." Comte, the so-called father of sociology, had a macro view of society in that his chief works are devoted to social reorganization. Comte was concerned with the interrelationships among social, political, religious, and educational institutions. As sociology progressed, the science of society compressed. Emphasis shifted from the macro approach of the pioneers to detailed, empirical study of small social units. The compression of sociological analysis was accompanied by study of social pathology or disorganization.

In general, physics, economics, and sociology appear to have two things in common. First, they offered a macro point of view as their initial systematic comprehension of their area of study. Second, as the science developed, attention fragmented into analysis of the parts of the organization, rather than attending to the system as a whole. This is the micro phase.

In physics and economics, discontent was evidenced by some scientists at the continual atomization of the universe. The reaction to the micro approach was a new theory or theories dealing with the total system, on the macro level again. This third phase of scientific development seems to be more evident in physics and economics than in sociology.

The reason for the "macro-micro-macro" order of scientific progress lies, perhaps, in the hypothesis that usually the things which strike man first are of great magnitude. The scientist attempts to discover order in the vastness. But after macro laws or models of systems are postulated, variations appear which demand analysis, not so much in terms of the entire system, but more in terms of the specific parts which make it up. Then, intense study of microcosm may result in new general laws, replacing the old models of organization. Or, the old and the new models may stand together, each explaining a different class of phenomenon. Or, the old and the new concepts of organization may be welded to produce a single creative synthesis.

Now, what does all this have to do with the problem of organization in administrative science? Organization concepts seem to have gone through the same order of development in this field as in the three just mentioned. It is evident that the classical theory of organization, particularly as in the work of Mooney and Reiley, is concerned with principles common to all organizations. It is a macro-organizational view. The classical approach to organization, however, dealt with the gross anatomical parts and processes of the formal organization. Like classical physics, the classical theory of organization is a special case. Neither are especially well equipped to account for variation from their established framework.

Many variations in the classical administrative model result from human behavior. The only way these variations could be understood was by a microscopic examination of particularized, situational aspects of human behavior. The mission of the neoclassical school thus is "micro-analysis."

It was observed earlier, that somewhere along the line the concept of the social system, which is the key to understanding the Hawthorne studies, faded into the background. Maybe the idea is so obvious that it was lost to the view of researchers and writers in human relations. In any event, the press of research in the microcosmic universes of the informal organization, morale and productivity, leadership, participation, and the like forced the notion of the social system into limbo. Now, with the advent of modern organization theory, the social system has been resurrected.

Modern organization theory appears to be concerned with Eddington's "and." This school claims that its operational hypothesis is based on a macro point of view; that is, the study of organization as a whole. This nobility of purpose should not obscure, however, certain difficulties faced by this field as it is presently constituted. Modern organization theory raises two questions which should be explored further. First, would it not be more accurate to speak of modern organization theor*ies?* Second, just how much of modern organization theory is modern?

The first question can be answered with a quick affirmative. Aside from the notion of the system, there are few, if any, other ideas of a unifying nature. Except for several important exceptions,[23] modern organization theorists

tend to pursue their pet points of view,[24] suggesting they are part of system theory, but not troubling to show by what mystical means they arrive at this conclusion.

The irony of it all is that a field dealing with systems has, indeed, little system. Modern organization theory needs a framework, and it needs an integration of issues into a common conception of organization. Admittedly, this is a large order. But it is curious not to find serious analytical treatment of subjects like cybernetics or general system theory in Haire's, *Modern Organizational Theory* which claims to be a representative example of work in this field. Beer has ample evidence in his book *Cybernetics and Management* that cybernetics, if imaginatively approached, provides a valuable conceptual base for the study of systems.

The second question suggests an ambiguous answer. Modern organization theory is in part a product of the past; system analysis is not a new idea. Further, modern organization theory relies for supporting data on microcosmic research studies, generally drawn from the journals of the last ten years. The newness of modern organization theory, perhaps, is its effort to synthesize recent research contributions of many fields into a system theory characterized by a reoriented conception of organization.

One might ask, but what is the modern theorist reorienting? A clue is found in the almost snobbish disdain assumed by some authors of the neo-classical human relations school, and particularly, the classical school. Re-evaluation of the classical school of organization is overdue. However, this does not mean that its contributions to organization theory

---

[23]For example: E. Wight Bakke, *op. cit.*, pp. 18–75.

[24]There is a large selection including decision theory, individual-organization interaction, motivation, vitality, stability, growth, and graph theory, to mention a few.

are irrelevant and should be overlooked in the rush to get on the "behavioral science bandwagon."

Haire announces that the papers appearing in *Modern Organization Theory* constitute, "the ragged leading edge of a wave of theoretical development."[25] Ragged, yes; but leading no! The papers appearing in this book do not represent a theoretical breakthrough in the concept of organization. Haire's collection is an interesting potpourri with several contributions of considerable significance. But readers should beware that they will not find vastly new insights into organizational behavior in this book, if they have kept up with the literature of the social sciences, and have dabbled to some extent in the esoteria of biological theories of growth, information theory, and mathematical model building. For those who have not maintained the pace, *Modern Organization Theory* serves the admirable purpose of bringing them up-to-date on a rather diversified number of subjects.

Some work in modern organization theory is pioneering, making its appraisal difficult and future uncertain. While the direction of this endeavor is unclear, one thing is patently true. Human behavior in organizations, and indeed, organization itself, cannot be adequately understood within the ground rules of classical and neo-classical doctrines. Appreciation of human organization requires a *creative* synthesis of massive amounts of empirical data, a high order of deductive reasoning, imaginative research studies, and a taste for individual and social val-

[25]Mason Haire, "General Issues," in Mason Haire (editor), *Modern Organization Theory* (New York: John Wiley and Sons, 1959), p. 2.

ues. Accomplishment of all these objectives, and the inclusion of them into a framework of the concept of the system, appears to be the goal of modern organization theory. The vitality of administrative science rests on the advances modern theorists make along this line.

Modern organization theory, 1960 style, is an amorphous aggregation of synthesizers and restaters, with a few extending leadership on the frontier. For the sake of these few, it is well to admonish that pouring old wine into new bottles may make the spirits cloudy. Unfortunately, modern organization theory has almost succeeded in achieving the status of a fad. Popularization and exploitation contributed to the disrepute into which human relations has fallen. It would be a great waste if modern organization theory yields to the same fate, particularly since both modern organization theory and human relations draw from the same promising source of inspiration—system analysis.

Modern organization theory needs tools of analysis and a conceptual framework uniquely its own, but it must also allow for the incorporation of relevant contributions of many fields. It may be that the framework will come from general system theory. New areas of research such as decision theory, information theory, and cybernetics also offer reasonable expectations of analytical and conceptual tools. Modern organization theory represents a frontier of research which has great significance for management. The potential is great, because it offers the opportunity for uniting what is valuable in classical theory with the social and natural sciences into a systematic and integrated conception of human organization.

24

Organizations and the System Concept

Daniel Katz & Robert L. Kahn

The aims of social science with respect to human organizations are like those of any other science with respect to the events and phenomena of its domain. The social scientist wishes to understand human organizations, to describe what is essential in their form, aspects, and functions. He wishes to explain their cycles of growth and decline, to predict their effects and effectiveness. Perhaps he wishes as well to test and apply such knowledge by introducing purposeful changes into organizations—by making them, for example, more benign, more responsive to human needs.

Such efforts are not solely the prerogative of social science, however; common sense approaches to understanding and altering organizations are ancient and perpetual. They tend, on the whole, to rely heavily on two assumptions: that the location and nature of an organization are given by its name; and that an organization is possessed of built-in goals—because such goals were implanted by founders, decreed by its present leaders, or because they emerged mysteriously as the purposes of the organizational system itself. These assumptions scarcely provide an adequate basis for the study of organizations and at times can be misleading and even fallacious. We propose, however, to make use of the information to which they point.

The first problem in understanding an organization or a social system is its location and identification. How do we know that we are dealing with an organization? What are its boundaries? What behavior belongs to the organization and what behavior lies outside it? Who are the individuals whose actions are to be studied and what segments of their behavior are to be included?

The fact that popular names exist to label social organizations is both a help and a hindrance. These popular labels represent the socially accepted stereotypes about organizations and do not specify their role structure, their psychological nature, or their boundaries. On the other hand, these names help in locating the area of behavior in which we are interested. Moreover, the fact that people both within and without an organization accept stereotypes about its nature and functioning is one determinant of its character.

The second key characteristic of the common sense approach to understanding an organization is to regard it simply as the epitome of the purposes of its designer, its leaders, or its key members. The teleology of this approach is again both a help and a hindrance. Since human purpose is deliberately built into organizations and is specifically recorded in the social compact, the bylaws, or other formal protocol of the undertaking, it would be inefficient not to utilize these sources of information. In the early

Source: Daniel Katz and Robert L. Kahn, *The Social Psychology of Organizations*, 14–29. Copyright © 1966 John Wiley & Sons, Inc. Reprinted by permission of John Wiley & Sons, Inc. Footnotes renumbered.

development of a group, many processes are generated which have little to do with its rational purpose, but over time there is a cumulative recognition of the devices for ordering group life and a deliberate use of these devices.

Apart from formal protocol, the primary mission of an organization as perceived by its leaders furnishes a highly informative set of clues for the researcher seeking to study organizational functioning. Nevertheless, the stated purposes of an organization as given by its by-laws or in the reports of its leaders can be misleading. Such statements of objectives may idealize, rationalize, distort, omit, or even conceal some essential aspects of the functioning of the organization. Nor is there always agreement about the mission of the organization among its leaders and members. The university president may describe the purpose of his institution as one of turning out national leaders; the academic dean sees it as imparting the cultural heritage of the past, the academic vice-president as enabling students to move toward self-actualization and development, the graduate dean as creating new knowledge, the dean of men as training youngsters in technical and professional skills which will enable them to earn their living, and the editor of the student newspaper as inculcating the conservative values which will preserve the status quo of an outmoded capitalistic society.

The fallacy here is one of equating the purposes or goals of organizations with the purposes and goals of individual members. The organization as a system has an output, a product or an outcome, but this is not necessarily identical with the individual purposes of group members. Though the founders of the organization and its key members do think in teleological terms about organization objectives, we should not accept such practical thinking, useful as it may be, in place of a theoretical set of constructs for purposes of scientific analysis. Social science, too frequently in the past, has been misled by such short-cuts and has equated popular phenomenology with scientific explanation.

In fact, the classic body of theory and thinking about organizations has assumed a teleology of this sort as the easiest way of identifying organizational structures and their functions. From this point of view an organization is a social device for efficiently accomplishing through group means some stated purpose; it is the equivalent of the blueprint for the design of the machine which is to be created for some practical objective. The essential difficulty with this purposive or design approach is that an organization characteristically includes more and less than is indicated by the design of its founder or the purpose of its leader. Some of the factors assumed in the design may be lacking or so distorted in operational practice as to be meaningless, while unforeseen embellishments dominate the organizational structure. Moreover, it is not always possible to ferret out the designer of the organization or to discover the intricacies of the design which he carried in his head. The attempt by Merton to deal with the latent function of the organization in contrast with its manifest function is one way of dealing with this problem.[1] The study of unanticipated consequences as well as anticipated consequences of organizational functioning is a similar way of handling the matter. Again, however, we are back to the purposes of the creator or leader, dealing with unanticipated consequences on the assumption that we can discover the consequences anticipated by him and can lump all other outcomes together as a kind of error variance.

It would be much better theoretically, however, to start with concepts which do not call for identifying the purposes of the designers and then correcting for them when they do not seem to be fulfilled. The theoretical concepts should begin with the input, output, and functioning of the organization as a system and not with the rational purposes of its leaders. We may want to utilize such purposive notions to lead us to sources of data or as subjects of special study, but not as our basic theoretical constructs for understanding organizations.

Our theoretical model for the understanding of organizations is that of an energic input-output system in which the energic return from the output reactivates the system. Social organizations are flagrantly open systems in that the input of energies and the conversion of output into further energic input consist of transactions between the organization and its environment.

All social systems, including organizations, consist of the patterned activities of a number of individuals. Moreover, these patterned activities are complementary or interdependent with respect to some common output or outcome; they are repeated, relatively enduring, and bounded in space and time. If the activity pattern occurs only once or at unpredictable intervals, we could not speak of an organization. The stability or recurrence of activities can be examined in relation to the *energic input* into the system, the *transformation of energies within the system*, and the *resulting product or energic output*. In a factory the raw materials and the human labor are the energic input, the patterned activities of production the transformation of energy, and the finished product the output. To maintain this patterned activity requires a continued renewal of the inflow of energy. This is guaranteed in social systems by the energic return from the product or outcome. Thus the outcome of the cycle of activities furnishes new energy for the initiation of a renewed cycle. The company which produces automobiles

sells them and by doing so obtains the means of securing new raw materials, compensating its labor force, and continuing the activity pattern.

In many organizations outcomes are converted into money and new energy is furnished through this mechanism. Money is a convenient way of handling energy units both on the output and input sides, and buying and selling represent one set of social rules for regulating the exchange of money. Indeed, these rules are so effective and so widespread that there is some danger of mistaking the business of buying and selling for the defining cycles of organization. It is a commonplace executive observation that businesses exist to make money, and the observation is usually allowed to go unchallenged. It is, however, a very limited statement about the purposes of business.

Some human organizations do not depend on the cycle of selling and buying to maintain themselves. Universities and public agencies depend rather on bequests and legislative appropriations, and in so-called voluntary organizations the output reenergizes the activity of organization members in a more direct fashion. Member activities and accomplishments are rewarding in themselves and tend therefore to be continued, without the mediation of the outside environment. A society of bird watchers can wander into the hills and engage in the rewarding activities of identifying birds for their mutual edification and enjoyment. Organizations thus differ on this important dimension of the source of energy renewal, with the great majority utilizing both intrinsic and extrinsic sources in varying degree. Most large-scale organizations are not as self-contained as small voluntary groups and are very dependent upon the social effects of their output for energy renewal.

Our two basic criteria for identifying social systems and determining their functions are (1) tracing the pattern of energy exchange or activity of people as it results in some output and (2) ascertaining how the output is translated into energy which reactivates the pattern. We shall refer to organizational functions or objectives not as the conscious purposes of group leaders or group members but as the outcomes which are the energic source for a maintenance of the same type of output.

This model of an energic input-output system is taken from the open system theory as promulgated by von Bertalanffy.[2] Theorists have pointed out the applicability of the system concepts of the natural sciences to the problems of social science. It is important, therefore, to examine in more detail the constructs of system theory and the characteristics of open systems.

System theory is basically concerned with problems of relationships, of structure, and of interdependence rather than with the constant attributes of objects. In general approach it resembles field theory except that its dynamics deal with temporal as well as spatial patterns. Older formulations of system constructs dealt with the closed systems of the physical sciences, in which relatively self-contained structures could be treated successfully as if they were independent of external forces. But living systems, whether biological organisms or social organizations, are acutely dependent upon their external environment and so must be conceived of as open systems.

Before the advent of open-system thinking, social scientists tended to take one of two approaches in dealing with social structures; they tended either (1) to regard them as closed systems to which the laws of physics applied or (2) to endow them with some vitalistic concept like entelechy. In the former

case they ignored the environmental forces affecting the organization and in the latter case they fell back upon some magical purposiveness to account for organizational functioning. Biological theorists, however, have rescued us from this trap by pointing out that the concept of the open system means that we neither have to follow the laws of traditional physics, nor in deserting them do we have to abandon science. The laws of Newtonian physics are correct generalizations but they are limited to closed systems. They do not apply in the same fashion to open systems which maintain themselves through constant commerce with their environment, i.e., a continuous inflow and outflow of energy through permeable boundaries.

One example of the operation of closed versus open systems can be seen in the concept of entropy and the second law of thermodynamics. According to the second law of thermodynamics a system moves toward equilibrium; it tends to run down, that is, its differentiated structures tend to move toward dissolution as the elements composing them become arranged in random disorder. For example, suppose that a bar of iron has been heated by the application of a blowtorch on one side. The arrangement of all the fast (heated) molecules on one side and all the slow molecules on the other is an unstable state, and over time the distribution of molecules becomes in effect random, with the resultant cooling of one side and heating of the other, so that all surfaces of the iron approach the same temperature. A similar process of heat exchange will also be going on between the iron bar and its environment, so that the bar will gradually approach the temperature of the room in which it is located, and in so doing will elevate somewhat the previous temperature of the room. More technically, entropy increases toward a maximum and equilib-

open systems

rium occurs as the physical system attains the state of the most probable distribution of its elements. In social systems, however, structures tend to become more elaborated rather than less differentiated. The rich may grow richer and the poor may grow poorer. The open system does not run down, because it can import energy from the world around it. Thus the operation of entropy is counteracted by the importation of energy and the living system is characterized by negative rather than positive entropy.

COMMON CHARACTERISTICS OF OPEN SYSTEMS

Though the various types of open systems have common characteristics by virtue of being open systems, they differ in other characteristics. If this were not the case, we would be able to obtain all our basic knowledge about social organizations through the study of a single cell.

The following nine characteristics seem to define all open systems.

1. Importation of Energy

Open systems import some form of energy from the external environment. The cell receives oxygen from the blood stream; the body similarly takes in oxygen from the air and food from the external world. The personality is dependent upon the external world for stimulation. Studies of sensory deprivation show that when a person is placed in a darkened soundproof room, where he has a minimal amount of visual and auditory stimulation, he develops hallucinations and other signs of mental stress.[3] Deprivation of social stimulation also can lead to mental disorganization.[4] Kohler's studies of the figural after-effects of continued stimulation show the dependence of perception upon its energic support from the external world.[5] Animals deprived of visual experience from birth for a pro-

longed period never fully recover their visual capacities.[6] In other words, the functioning personality is heavily dependent upon the continuous inflow of stimulation from the external environment. Similarly, social organizations must also draw renewed supplies of energy from other institutions, or people, or the material environment. No social structure is self-sufficient or self-contained.

2. The Through-Put

Open systems transform the energy available to them. The body converts starch and sugar into heat and action. The personality converts chemical and electrical forms of stimulation into sensory qualities, and information into thought patterns. The organization creates a new product, or processes materials, or trains people, or provides a service. These activities entail some reorganization of input. Some work gets done in the system.

3. The Output

Open systems export some products into the environment, whether it be the invention of an inquiring mind or a bridge constructed by an engineering firm. Even the biological organism exports physiological products such as carbon dioxide from the lungs which helps to maintain plants in the immediate environment.

4. Systems as Cycles of Events

The pattern of activities of the energy exchange has a cyclic character. The product exported into the environment furnishes the sources of energy for the repetition of the cycle of activities. The energy reinforcing the cycle of activities can derive from some exchange of the product in the external world or from the activity itself. In the former instance, the industrial concern utilizes raw materials and human labor to turn out a product which is marketed, and the monetary return is used to obtain more raw materials and labor to perpetuate the cycle of activities. In the latter instance, the voluntary organization can provide expressive satisfactions to its members so that the energy renewal comes directly from the organizational activity itself.

The problem of structure, or the relatedness of parts, can be observed directly in some physical arrangement of things where the larger unit is physically bounded and its subparts are also bounded within the larger structure. But how do we deal with social structures, where physical boundaries in this sense do not exist? It was the genius of F. H. Allport which contributed the answer, namely that the structure is to be found in an interrelated set of events which return upon themselves to complete and renew a cycle of activities.[7] It is events rather than things which are structured, so that social structure is a dynamic rather than a static concept. Activities are structured so that they comprise a unity in their completion or closure. A simple linear stimulus-response exchange between two people would not constitute social structure. To create structure, the responses of A would have to elicit B's reactions in such a manner that the responses of the latter would stimulate A to further responses. Of course the chain of events may involve many people, but their behavior can be characterized as showing structure only when there is some closure to the chain by a return to its point of origin with the probability that the chain of events will then be repeated. The repetition of the cycle does not have to involve the same set of phenotypical happenings. It may expand to include more subevents of exactly the same kind or it may involve similar activities directed toward the same outcomes. In the individual organism the eye may move in such a way as to have the point of light fall upon the center of the retina. As the point of light moves, the movements of the eye may also change but to complete the same cycle of activity, i.e., to focus upon the point of light.

A single cycle of events of a self-closing character gives us a simple form of structure. But such single cycles can also combine to give a larger structure of events or an event system. An event system may consist of a circle of smaller cycles or hoops, each one of which makes contact with several others. Cycles may also be tangential to one another from other types of subsystems. The basic method for the identification of social structures is to follow the energic chain of events from the input of energy through its transformation to the point of closure of the cycle.

5. Negative Entropy

To survive, open systems must move to arrest the entropic process; they must acquire negative entropy. The entropic process is a universal law of nature in which all forms of organization move toward disorganization or death. Complex physical systems move toward simple random distribution of their elements and biological organisms also run down and perish. The open system, however, by importing more energy from its environment than it expends, can store energy and can acquire negative entropy. There is then a general trend in an open system to maximize its ratio of imported to expended energy, to survive and even during periods of crisis to live on borrowed time. Prisoners in concentration camps on a starvation diet will carefully conserve any form of energy expenditure to make the limited food intake go as far as possible.[8] Social organizations will seek to improve their survival position and to acquire in their reserves a comfortable margin of operation.

The entropic process asserts itself in all biological systems as well as in closed physical systems. The energy replenishment of the biological organism is not of a qualitative character which can maintain indefinitely the complex organizational structure of living tissue. Social systems, however, are not anchored in the same physical constancies as biological organisms and so are capable of almost indefinite arresting of the entropic process. Nevertheless the number of organizations which go out of existence every year is large.

6. Information Input, Negative Feedback, and the Coding Process

The inputs into living systems consist not only of energic materials which become transformed or altered in the work that gets done. Inputs are also informative in character and furnish signals to the structure about the environment and about its own functioning in relation to the environment. Just as we recognize the distinction between cues and drives in individual psychology, so must we take account of information and energic inputs for all living systems.

The simplest type of information input found in all systems is negative feedback. Information feedback of a negative kind enables the system to correct its deviations from course. The working parts of the machine feed back information about the effects of their operation to some central mechanism or subsystem which acts on such information to keep the system on target. The thermostat which controls the temperature of the room is a simple example of a regulatory device which operates on the basis of negative feedback. The automated power plant would furnish more complex examples. Miller emphasizes the critical nature of negative feedback in his proposition: "When a system's negative feedback discontinues, its steady state vanishes, and at the same time its boundary disappears and the system terminates."[9] If there is no corrective device to get the system back on its course, it will expend too much energy or it will ingest too much energic input and no longer continue as a system.

The reception of inputs into a system is selective. Not all energic inputs are capable of being absorbed into every system. The digestive system of living creatures assimilates only those inputs to which it is adapted. Similarly, systems can react only to those information signals to which they are attuned. The general term for the selective mechanisms of a system by which incoming materials are rejected or accepted and translated for the structure is coding. Through the coding process, the "blooming, buzzing confusion" of the world is simplified into a few meaningful and simplified categories for a given system. The nature of the functions performed by the system determines its coding mechanisms, which in turn perpetuate this type of functioning.

7. The Steady State and Dynamic Homeostasis

The importation of energy to arrest entropy operates to maintain some constancy in energy exchange, so that open systems which survive are characterized by a steady state. A steady state is not motionless or a true equilibrium. There is a continuous inflow of energy from the external environment and a continuous export of the products of the system, but the character of the system, the ratio of the energy exchanges and the relations between parts, remains the same. The catabolic and anabolic processes of tissue breakdown and restoration within the body preserve a steady state so that the organism from time to time is not the identical organism it was but a highly similar organism. The steady state is seen in clear form in the homeostatic processes for the regulation of body temperature; external conditions of humidity and temperature may vary, but the temperature of the body remains the same. The endocrine glands are a regulatory mechanism for preserving an evenness of physiological functioning. The general principle here is that of Le Châtelier who maintains that any internal or external factor making for disruption of the system is countered by forces which restore the system as closely as possible to its previous state.[10] Krech and Crutchfield similarly hold, with respect to psychological organization, that cognitive structures will react to influences in such a way as to absorb them with minimal change to existing cognitive integration.[11]

The homeostatic principle does not apply literally to the functioning of all complex living systems, in that in counteracting entropy they move toward growth and expansion. This apparent contradiction can be resolved, however, if we recognize the complexity of the subsystems and their interaction in anticipating changes necessary for the maintenance of an overall steady state. Stagner has pointed out that the initial disturbance of a given tissue constancy within the biological organism will result in mobilization of energy to restore the balance, but that recurrent upsets will lead to actions to anticipate the disturbance:

> We eat before we experience intense hunger pangs. . . . energy mobilization for forestalling tactics must be explained in terms of a *cortical tension* which reflects the visceral-proprioceptive pattern of the original biological disequilibration. . . . *Dynamic homeostasis* involves the maintenance of tissue constancies by establishing a constant physical environment—by reducing the variability and disturbing ef-

fects of external stimulation. Thus the organism does not simply restore the prior equilibrium. A new, more complex and more comprehensive equilibrium is established.[12]

Though the tendency toward a steady state in its simplest form is homeostatic, as in the preservation of a constant body temperature, the basic principle is *the preservation of the character of the system*. The equilibrium which complex systems approach is often that of a quasi-stationary equilibrium, to use Lewin's concept.[13] An adjustment in one direction is countered by a movement in the opposite direction and both movements are approximate rather than precise in their compensatory nature. Thus a temporal chart of activity will show a series of ups and downs rather than a smooth curve.

In preserving the character of the system, moreover, the structure will tend to import more energy than is required for its output, as we have already noted in discussing negative entropy. To insure survival, systems will operate to acquire some margin of safety beyond the immediate level of existence. The body will store fat, the social organization will build up reserves, the society will increase its technological and cultural base. Miller has formulated the proposition that the rate of growth of a system— within certain ranges—is exponential if it exists in a medium which makes available unrestricted amounts of energy for input.[14]

In adapting to their environment, systems will attempt to cope with external forces by ingesting them or acquiring control over them. The physical boundedness of the single organism means that such attempts at control over the environment affect the behavioral system rather than the biological system of the individual. Social systems will move, however, towards incorporating within their boundaries the external resources essential to survival. Again the result is an expansion of the original system.

Thus, the steady state which at the simple level is one of homeostasis over time, at more complex levels becomes one of preserving the character of the system through growth and expansion. The basic type of system does not change directly as a consequence of expansion. The most common type of growth is a multiplication of the same type of cycles or subsystems—a change in quantity rather than in quality. Animal and plant species grow by multiplication. A social system adds more units of the same essential type as it already has. Haire has studied the ratio between the sizes of different subsystems in growing business organizations.[15] He found that though the number of people increased in both the production subsystem and the subsystem concerned with the external world, the ratio of the two groups remained constant. Qualitative change does occur, however, in two ways. In the first place, quantitative growth calls for supportive subsystems of a specialized character not necessary when the system was smaller. In the second place, there is a point where quantitative changes produce a qualitative difference in the functioning of a system. A small college which triples its size is no longer the same institution in terms of the relation between its administration and faculty, relations among the various academic departments, or the nature of its instruction.

In time, living systems exhibit a growth or expansion dynamic in which they maximize their basic character. They react to change or they anticipate change through growth which assimilates the new energic inputs to the nature of their structure. In terms of Lewin's quasi-stationary equilibrium the ups and downs of the adjustive process do not always result in a return to the old level. Under certain circumstances a solidification or freezing occurs during one of the adjustive cycles. A new base line level is thus established and successive movements fluctuate around this plateau which may be either above or below the previous plateau of operation.

8. Differentiation

Open systems move in the direction of differentiation and elaboration. Diffuse global patterns are replaced by more specialized functions. The sense organs and the nervous system evolved as highly differentiated structures from the primitive nervous tissues. The growth of the personality proceeds from primitive, crude organizations of mental functions to hierarchically structured and well-differentiated systems of beliefs and feelings. Social organizations move toward the multiplication and elaboration of roles with greater specialization of function. In the United States today medical specialists now outnumber the general practitioners.

One type of differentiated growth in systems is what von Bertalanffy terms progressive mechanization. It finds expression in the way in which a system achieves a steady state. The early method is a process which involves an interaction of various dynamic forces, whereas the later development entails the use of a regulatory feedback mechanism. He writes:

> It can be shown that the *primary* regulations in organic systems, that is, those which are most fundamental and primitive in embryonic development as well as in evolution, are of such nature of dynamic interaction. . . . Superimposed are those regulations which we may call *secondary*, and which are controlled by fixed arrangements, especially of the feedback type. This state of affairs is a consequence of a general principle of organization which may be called progressive mechanization.

At first, systems—biological, neurological, psychological or social—are governed by dynamic interaction of their components; later on, fixed arrangements and conditions of constraint are established which render the system and its parts more efficient, but also gradually diminish and eventually abolish its equipotentiality.[16]

9. Equifinality

Open systems are further characterized by the principle of equifinality, a principle suggested by von Bertalanffy in 1940.[17] According to this principle, a system can reach the same final state from differing initial conditions and by a variety of paths. The well-known biological experiments on the sea urchin show that a normal creature of that species can develop from a complete ovum, from each half of a divided ovum, or from the fusion product of two whole ova. As open systems move toward regulatory mechanisms to control their operations, the amount of equifinality may be reduced.

SOME CONSEQUENCES OF VIEWING ORGANIZATIONS AS OPEN SYSTEMS

[In a later chapter] we shall inquire into the specific implications of considering organizations as open systems and into the ways in which social organizations differ from other types of living systems. At this point, however, we should call attention to some of the misconceptions which arise both in theory and practice when social organizations are regarded as closed rather than open systems.

The major misconception is the failure to recognize fully that the organization is continually dependent upon inputs from the environment and that the inflow of materials and human energy is not a constant. The fact that organizations have built-in protective devices to maintain stability and that they are no-

toriously difficult to change in the direction of some reformer's desires should not obscure the realities of the dynamic interrelationships of any social structure with its social and natural environment. The very efforts of the organization to maintain a constant external environment produce changes in organizational structure. The reaction to changed inputs to mute their possible revolutionary implications also results in changes.

The typical models in organizational theorizing concentrate upon principles of internal functioning as if these problems were independent of changes in the environment and as if they did not affect the maintenance inputs of motivation and morale. Moves toward tighter integration and coordination are made to insure stability, when flexibility may be the more important requirement. Moreover, coordination and control become ends in themselves rather than means to an end. They are not seen in full perspective as adjusting the system to its environment but as desirable goals within a closed system. In fact, however, every attempt at coordination which is not functionally required may produce a host of new organizational problems.

One error which stems from this kind of misconception is the failure to recognize the equifinality of the open system, namely that there are more ways than one of producing a given outcome. In a closed physical system the same initial conditions must lead to the same final result. In open systems this is not true even at the biological level. It is much less true at the social level. Yet in practice we insist that there is one best way of assembling a gun for all recruits, one best way for the baseball player to hurl the ball in from the outfield and that we standardize and teach these best methods. Now it is true under certain conditions that there is one best way, but these conditions must first be established. The general principle, which characterizes all open systems, is that there does not have to be a single method for achieving an objective.

A second error lies in the notion that irregularities in the functioning of a system due to environmental influences are error variances and should be treated accordingly. According to this conception, they should be controlled out of studies of organizations. From the organization's own operations they should be excluded as irrelevant and should be guarded against. The decisions of officers to omit a consideration of external factors or to guard against such influences in a defensive fashion, as if they would go away if ignored, is an instance of this type of thinking. So is the now outmoded "public be damned" attitude of businessmen toward the clientele upon whose support they depend. Open system theory, on the other hand, would maintain that environmental influences are not sources of error variance but are integrally related to the functioning of a social system, and that we cannot understand a system without a constant study of the forces that impinge upon it.

Thinking of the organization as a closed system, moreover, results in a failure to develop the intelligence or feedback function of obtaining adequate information about the changes in environmental forces. It is remarkable how weak many industrial companies are in their market research departments when they are so dependent upon the market. The prediction can be hazarded that organizations in our society will increasingly move toward the improvements of the facilities for research in assessing environmental forces. The reason is that we are in the process of correcting our misconception of the organization as a closed system.

Emery and Trist have pointed out how current theorizing on organizations still reflects the older closed system conceptions. They write:

> In the realm of social theory, however, there has been something of a tendency to continue thinking in terms of a "closed" system, that is, to regard the enterprise as sufficiently independent to allow most of its problems to be analyzed with reference to its internal structure and without reference to its external environment. . . . In practice the system theorists in social science . . . did "tend to focus on the statics of social structure and to neglect the study of structural change." In an attempt to overcome this bias, Merton suggested that "the concept of strain, stress and tension on the structural level, provides an analytical approach to the study of dynamics and change." This concept has been widely accepted by system theorists but while it draws attention to sources of imbalance within an organization it does not conceptually reflect the mutual permeation of an organization and its environment that is the cause of such imbalance. It still retains the limiting perspectives of "closed system" theorizing. In the administrative field the same limitations may be seen in the otherwise invaluable contributions of Barnard and related writers.[18]

SUMMARY

The open-system approach to organizations is contrasted with common-sense approaches, which tend to accept popular names and stereotypes as basic organizational properties and to identify the purpose of an organization in terms of the goals of its founders and leaders.

The open-system approach, on the other hand, begins by identifying and mapping the repeated cycles of input, transformation, output, and renewed input which comprise the organizational pattern. This approach to organizations represents the adaptation of work in biology and in the physical sciences by von Bertalanffy and others.

Organizations as a special class of open systems have properties of their own, but they share other properties in common with all open systems. These include the importation of energy from the environment, the through-put or transformation of the imported energy into some product form which is characteristic of the system, the exporting of that product into the environment, and the reenergizing of the system from sources in the environment.

Open systems also share the characteristics of negative entropy, feedback, homeostasis, differentiation, and equifinality. The law of negative entropy states that systems survive and maintain their characteristic internal order only so long as they import from the environment more energy than they expend in the process of transformation and exportation. The feedback principle has to do with information input, which is a special kind of energic importation, a kind of signal to the system about environmental conditions and about the functioning of the system in relation to its environment. The feedback of such information enables the system to correct for its own malfunctioning or for changes in the environment, and thus to maintain a steady state or homeostasis. This is a dynamic rather than a static balance, however. Open systems are not at rest but tend toward differentiation and elaboration, both because of subsystem dynamics and because of the relationship between growth and survival. Finally, open systems are characterized by the principle of equifinality, which asserts that systems can reach the same final state from different initial conditions and by different paths of development.

Traditional organizational theories have tended to view the human organization as a closed system. This tendency has led to a disregard of differing organizational environments and the nature of organizational dependency on environment. It has led also to an overconcentration on principles of internal organizational functioning, with consequent failure to develop and understand the processes of feedback which are essential to survival.

NOTES

1. Merton, R. K. 1957. *Social theory and social structure*, rev. ed. New York: Free Press.

2. von Bertalanffy, L. 1956. General system theory. *General Systems*. Yearbook of the Society for the Advancement of General System Theory, *1*, 1–10.

3. Solomon, P., *et al.* (Eds.) 1961. *Sensory deprivation*. Cambridge, Mass: Harvard University Press.

4. Spitz, R. A. 1945. Hospitalism: an inquiry into the genesis of psychiatric conditions in early childhood. *Psychoanalytic Study of the Child*, *1*, 53–74.

5. Kohler, W., & H. Wallach. 1944. Figural after-effects: an investigation of visual processes. *Proceedings of the American Philosophical Society*, 88, 269–357. Also, Kohler, W., & D. Emery. 1947. Figural after-effects in the third dimension of visual space. *American Journal of Psychology*, 60, 159–201.

6. Melzack, R., & W. Thompson. 1956. Effects of early experience on social behavior. *Canadian Journal of Psychology*, 10, 82–90.

7. Allport, F. H. 1962. A structuronomic conception of behavior: individual and collective. I. Structural theory and the master problem of social psychology. *Journal of Abnormal and Social Psychology*, 64, 3–30.

8. Cohen, E. 1954. *Human behavior in the concentration camp*. London: Jonathan Cape.

9. Miller, J. G. 1955. Toward a general theory for the behavioral sciences. *American Psychologist*, 10, 513–531; quote from p. 529.

10. See Bradley, D. F., & M. Calvin. 1956. Behavior: imbalance in a network of chemical transformations. *General Systems*. Yearbook of the Society for the Advancement of General System Theory, *1*, 56–65.

11. Krech, D., & R. Crutchfield. 1948. *Theory and problems of social psychology*. New York: McGraw-Hill.

12. Stagner, R. 1951. Homeostasis as a unifying concept in personality theory. *Psychological Review, 58,* 5–17; quote from p. 5.

13. Lewin, K. 1947. Frontiers in group dynamics. *Human Relations, 1,* 5–41.

14. Miller, *op cit.*

15. Haire, M. 1959. Biological models and empirical histories of the growth of organizations. In M. Haire (Ed.), *Modern organization theory,* New York: Wiley, 272–306.

16. von Bertalanffy. 1956, *op cit,* p. 6.

17. von Bertalanffy, L. 1940. Der organismus als physikalisches system betrachtet. *Naturwissenschaften, 28,* 521 ff.

18. Emery, F. E., & E. L. Trist. 1960. Sociotechnical systems. In *Management sciences models and techniques.* Vol. 2, London: Pergamon Press; quote from p. 84.

25

Organizations in Action

James D. Thompson

STRATEGIES FOR STUDYING ORGANIZATIONS

Complex organizations—manufacturing firms, hospitals, schools, armies, community agencies—are ubiquitous in modern societies, but our understanding of them is limited and segmented.

The fact that impressive and sometimes frightening consequences flow from organizations suggests that some individuals have had considerable insight into these social instruments. But insight and private experiences may generate private understandings without producing a public body of knowledge adequate for the preparation of a next generation of administrators, for designing new styles of organizations for new purposes, for controlling organizations, or for appreciation of distinctive aspects of modern societies.

What we know or think we know about complex organizations is housed in a variety of fields or disciplines, and communication among them more nearly resembles a trickle than a torrent.[1] Although each of the several schools has its unique terminology and special heroes, Gouldner was able to discern two fundamental models underlying most of the literature.[2] He labeled these the "rational" and "natural-system" models of organizations, and these labels are indeed descriptive of the results.

To Gouldner's important distinction we wish to add the notion that the rational model results from a *closed-system strategy* for studying organizations, and that the natural-system model flows from an *open-system strategy*.

Closed-System Strategy

The Search for Certainty. If we wish to predict accurately the state a system will be in presently, it helps immensely to be dealing with a *determinate system*. As Ashby observes, fixing the present circumstances of a determinate system will determine the state it moves to next, and since such a system cannot go to two states at once, the transformation will be unique.[3]

Fixing the present circumstances requires, of course, that the variables and relationships involved by few enough for us to comprehend and that we have control over or can reliably predict all of the variables and relations. In other words, it requires that the system be closed or, if closure is not complete, that the outside forces acting on it be predictable.

Now if we have responsibility for the future states or performances of some system, we are likely to opt for a closed system. Bartlett's research on mental processes, comparing "adventurous thinking" with "thinking in closed systems," suggests that there are strong human tendencies to reduce various forms of knowledge to the closed-system variety, to rid them of all ultimate uncertainty.[4] If such tendencies appear in

Source: James D. Thompson, *Organizations in Action*, 3-24. Copyright © 1967 by McGraw-Hill, Inc. Used with permission of McGraw-Hill Book Company. References converted to footnotes.

puzzle-solving as well as in everyday situations, we would especially expect them to be emphasized when responsibility and high stakes are added. Since much of the literature about organizations has been generated as a by-product of the search for improved efficiency or performance, it is not surprising that it employs closed-system assumptions—employs a rational model—about organizations. Whether we consider *scientific management*,[5] *administrative management*,[6] or *bureaucracy*,[7] the ingredients of the organization are deliberately chosen for their necessary contribution to a goal, and the structures established are those deliberately intended to attain highest efficiency.

Three Schools in Caricature. Scientific management, focused primarily on manufacturing or similar production activities, clearly employs economic efficiency as its ultimate criterion, and seeks to maximize efficiency by planning procedures according to a technical logic, setting standards, and exercising controls to ensure conformity with standards and thereby with the technical logic. Scientific management achieves conceptual closure of the organization by assuming that goals are known, tasks are repetitive, output of the production process somehow disappears, and resources in uniform qualities are available.

Administrative-management literature focuses on structural relationships among production, personnel, supply, and other service units of the organization; and again employs as the ultimate criterion economic efficiency. Here efficiency is maximized by specializing tasks and grouping them into departments, fixing responsibility according to such principles as span of control or delegation, and controlling action to plans. Administrative management achieves closure by assuming that ultimately a master plan is known, against which spe-

cialization, departmentalization, and controls are determined. (That this master plan is elusive is shown by Simon.[8]) Administrative management also assumes that production tasks are known, that output disappears, and that resources are automatically available to the organization.

Bureaucracy also follows the pattern noted above, focusing on staffing and structure as means of handling clients and disposing of cases. Again the ultimate criterion is efficiency, and this time it is maximized by defining offices according to jurisdiction and place in a hierarchy, appointing experts to offices, establishing rules for categories of activity, categorizing cases or clients, and then motivating proper performance of expert officials by providing salaries and patterns for career advancement. [The extended implications of the assumptions made by bureaucratic theory are brought out by Merton's discussion of "bureaucratic personality"[9]] Bureaucratic theory also employs the closed system of logic. Weber saw three holes through which empirical reality might penetrate the logic, but in outlining his "pure type" he quickly plugged these holes. Policymakers, somewhere above the bureaucracy, could alter the goals, but the implications of this are set aside. Human components—the expert officeholders—might be more complicated than the model describes, but bureaucratic theory handles this by divorcing the individual's private life from his life as an officeholder through the use of rules, salary, and career. Finally, bureaucratic theory takes note of outsiders—clientele—but nullifies their effects by depersonalizing and categorizing clients.

It seems clear that the rational-model approach uses a closed-system strategy. It also seems clear that the developers of the several schools using the rational model have been primarily students of performance or efficiency, and only incidentally students of organizations. Having focused on control of the organization as a target, each employs a closed system of logic and conceptually closes the organization to coincide with that type of logic, for this elimination of uncertainty is the way to achieve determinateness. The rational model of an organization results in everything being functional—making a positive, indeed an optimum, contribution to the overall result. All resources are appropriate resources, and their allocation fits a master plan. All action is appropriate action, and its outcomes are predictable.

It is no accident that much of the literature on the management or administration of complex organization centers on the concepts of *planning* or *controlling*. Nor is it any accident that such views are dismissed by those using the open-system strategy.

Open-System Strategy

The Expectation of Uncertainty. If, instead of assuming closure, we assume that a system contains more variables than we can comprehend at one time, or that some of the variables are subject to influences we cannot control or predict, we must resort to a different sort of logic. We can, if we wish, assume that the system is determinate by nature, but that it is our incomplete understanding which forces us to expect surprise or the intrusion of certainty. In this case we can employ a natural-system model.

Approached as a natural system, the complex organization is a set of interdependent parts which together make up a whole because each contributes something and receives something from the whole, which in turn is interdependent with some larger environment. Survival of the system is taken to be the goal, and the parts and their relationships presumably are determined through evolutionary processes. Dysfunctions are conceivable, but it is assumed that an offending part will adjust to produce a net positive contribution or be disengaged, or else the system will degenerate.

Central to the natural-system approach is the concept of homeostasis, or self-stabilization, which spontaneously, or naturally, governs the necessary relationships among parts and activities and thereby keeps the system viable in the face of disturbances stemming from the environment.

Two Examples in Caricature. Study of the *informal organization* constitutes one example of research in complex organizations using the natural-system approach. Here attention is focused on variables which are not included in any of the rational models—sentiments, cliques, social controls via informal norms, status and status striving, and so on. It is clear that students of informal organization regard these variables not as random deviations or error, but as patterned, adaptive responses of human beings in problematic situations.[10] In this view the formal organization is a spontaneous and functional development, indeed a necessity, in complex organizations, permitting the system to adapt and survive.

A second version of the natural-system approach is more global but less crystallized under a label. This school views the organization as a unit in interaction with its environment, and its view was perhaps most forcefully expressed by Chester Barnard[11] and by the empirical studies of Selznick[12] and Clark.[13] This stream of work leads to the conclusion that organizations are not autonomous entities; instead, the best laid plans of managers have unintended consequences and are conditioned or upset by other social units—other complex organizations or publics—on whom the organization is dependent.

Again it is clear that in contrast to the rational-model approach, this research area focuses on variables not subject to complete control by the organization and hence not contained within a closed system of logic. It is also clear that students regard interdependence of organization and environment as inevitable or natural, and as adaptive or functional.

Choice or Compromise?

The literature about organizations, or at least much of it, seems to fall into one of the two categories, each of which at best tends to ignore the other and at worse denies the relevance of the other. The logics associated with each appear to be incompatible, for one avoids uncertainty to achieve determinateness, while the other assumes uncertainty and indeterminateness. Yet the phenomena treated by each approach, as distinct from the explanations of each, cannot be denied.

Viewed in the large, complex organizations are often effective instruments for achievement, and that achievement flows from planned, controlled action. In every sphere—educational, medical, industrial, commercial, or governmental—the quality or costs of goods or services may be challenged and questions may be raised about the equity of distribution within the society of the fruits of complex organizations. Still millions live each day on the assumption that a reasonable degree of purposeful, effective action will be forthcoming from the many complex organizations on which they depend. Planned action, not random behavior, supports our daily lives. Specialized, controlled, patterned action surround us.

There can be no question but that the rational model of organizations directs our attention to important phenomena—to important "truth" in the sense that complex organizations viewed in the large exhibit some of the patterns and results to which the rational model attends, but which the natural-system model tends to ignore. But it is equally evident that phenomena associated with the natural-system approach also exist in complex organizations. There is little room to doubt the universal emergence of the informal organization. The daily news about labor-management negotiations, interagency jurisdictional squabbles, collusive agreements, favoritism, breeches of contract, and so on, are impressive evidence that complex organizations are influenced in significant ways by elements of their environments, a phenomenon addressed by the natural-system approach but avoided by the rational. Yet most versions of the natural-system approach treat organizational purposes and achievements as peripheral matters.

It appears that each approach leads to some truth, but neither alone affords an adequate understanding of complex organizations. Gouldner calls for a synthesis of the two models, but does not provide the synthetic model.

Meanwhile, a serious and sustained elaboration of Barnard's work[14] has produced a newer tradition which evades the closed- versus open-system dilemma.

A Newer Tradition

What emerges from the Simon-March-Cyert stream of study is the organization as a problem-facing and problem-solving phenomenon. The focus is on organizational processes related to choice of courses of action in an environment which does not fully disclose the alternatives available or the consequences of those alternatives. In this view, the organization has limited capacity to gather and process information or to predict consequences of alternatives. To deal with situations of such great complexity, the organization must develop processes for *searching* and *learning*, as well as for *deciding*. The complexity, if fully faced, would overwhelm the organization, hence it must set limits to its definitions of situations; it must make decisions in *bounded rationality*.[15] This requirement involved replacing the maximum-efficiency criterion with one of satisfactory accomplishment, decision-making now involving *satisficing* rather than *maximizing*.[16]

These are highly significant notions, and it will become apparent that this book seeks to extend this "newer tradition." The assumptions it makes are consistent with the open-system strategy, for it holds that the processes going on within the organization are significantly affected by the complexity of the organization's environment. But this tradition also touches on matters important in the closed-system strategy; performance and deliberate decisions.

But despite what seem to be obvious advantages, the Simon-March-Cyert stream of work has not entirely replaced the more extreme strategies, and we need to ask why so many intelligent men and women in a position to make the same observations we have been making should continue to espouse patently incomplete views of complex organizations.

The Cutting Edge of Uncertainty. Part of the answer to that question undoubtedly lies in the fact that supporters of each strategy have had different purposes in mind, with open-system strategists attempting to understand organizations per se, and closed-system strategists interested in organizations mainly as vehicles for rational achievements. Yet this answer does not seem completely satisfactory, for these students could not have been entirely unaware of the challenges to their assumptions and beliefs.

We can suggest now that rather than reflecting weakness in those who use

them, the two strategies reflect something fundamental about the cultures surrounding complex organizations— the fact that our culture does not contain concepts for simultaneously thinking about rationality and indeterminateness. These appear to be incompatible concepts, and we have no ready way of thinking about something as half-closed, half-rational. One alternative, then, is the closed-system approach of ignoring uncertainty to see rationality; another is to ignore rational action in order to see spontaneous processes. The newer tradition with its focus on organizational coping with uncertainty is indeed a major advance. It is notable that a recent treatment by Crozier starts from the bureaucratic position but focuses on coping with uncertainty as its major topic.[17]

Yet in directing our attention to processes for meeting uncertainty, Simon, March, and Cyert may lead us to overlook the useful knowledge amassed by the older approaches. If the phenomena of rational models are indeed observable, we may want to incorporate some elements of those models; and if natural-system phenomena occur, we should also benefit from the relevant theories. For purposes of this volume, then, *we will conceive of complex organizations as open systems, hence indeterminate and faced with uncertainty, but at the same time as subject to criteria of rationality and hence needing determinateness and certainty.*

The Location of Problems

As a starting point, we will suggest that the phenomena associated with open- and closed-system strategies are not randomly distributed through complex organizations, but instead tend to be specialized by location. To introduce this notion we will start with Parsons' suggestion that organizations exhibit three distinct levels of responsibility and control—*technical, managerial,* and *institutional.*[18]

In this view, every formal organization contains a suborganization whose "problems" are focused around effective performance of the technical function—the conduct of classes by teachers, the processing of income tax returns and the handling of recalcitrants by the bureau, the processing of material and supervision of these operations in the case of physical production. The primary exigencies to which the technical suborganization is oriented are those imposed by the nature of the technical task, such as the materials, which must be processed and the kinds of cooperation of different people required to get the job done effectively.

The second level, the managerial, *services* the technical suborganization by (1) mediating between the technical suborganization and those who use its products—the customers, pupils, and so on—and (2) procuring the resources necessary for carrying out the technical functions. The managerial level *controls,* or administers, the technical suborganization (although Parsons notes that its control is not unilateral) by deciding such matters as the broad technical task which is to be performed, the scale of operations, employment and purchasing policy, and so on.

Finally, in the Parsons formulation, the organization which consists of both technical and managerial suborganizations is also part of a wider social system which is the source of the "meaning," or higher-level support which makes the implementation of the organization's goals possible. In terms of "formal" controls, an organization may be relatively independent; but in terms of the meaning of the functions performed by the organization and hence of its "rights" to command resources and to subject its customers to discipline, it is never wholly independent. This overall articulation of the organization and the institutional structure and agencies of the community is the function of the third, or institutional, level of the organization.

Parsons' distinction of the three levels becomes more significant when he points out that at each of the two points of articulation between them there is a *qualitative* break in the simple continuity of "line" authority because the functions at each level are qualitatively different. Those at the second level are not simply lower-order spellings-out of the top level functions. Moreover, the articulation of levels and functions rests on a two-way interaction, with each side, by withholding its important contribution, in a position to interfere with the functioning of the other and of the larger organization.

If we now reintroduce the conception of the complex organization as an open system subject to criteria of rationality, we are in a position to speculate about some dynamic properties of organizations. As we suggested, the logical model for achieving complete technical rationality uses a closed system of logic—closed by the elimination of uncertainty. In practice, it would seem, the more variables involved, the greater the likelihood of uncertainty, and it would therefore be advantageous for an organization subject to criteria of rationality to remove as much uncertainty as possible from its *technical core* by reducing the number of variables operating on it. Hence if both resource-acquisition and output-disposal problems—which are in part controlled by environmental elements and hence to a degree uncertain or problematic—can be removed from the technical core, the logic can be brought closer to closure, and the rationality, increased.

Uncertainty would appear to be greatest, at least potentially, at the other extreme, the institutional level. Here the organization deals largely with elements of the environment over which it has no formal authority or control. Instead, it is subjected to generalized norms, ranging from formally codified law to informal standards of good practice, to public authority, or to elements expressing the public interest.

At this extreme the closed system of logic is clearly inappropriate. The organization is open to influence by the environment (and vice versa) which can change independently of the actions of the organization. Here an open system of logic, permitting the intrusion of variables penetrating the organization from outside, and facing up to uncertainty, seems indispensable.

If the closed-system aspects of organizations are seen most clearly at the technical level, and the open-system qualities appear most vividly at the institutional level, it would suggest that a significant function of the managerial level is to mediate between the two extremes and the emphases they exhibit. If the organization must approach certainty at the technical level to satisfy its rationality criteria, but must remain flexible and adaptive to satisfy environmental requirements, we might expect the managerial level to mediate between them, ironing out some irregularities stemming from external sources, but also pressing the technical core for modifications as conditions alter. One exploration of this notion was offered in Thompson.[19]

Possible Sources of Variation. Following Parsons' reasoning leads to the expectation that differences in technical functions, or *technologies*, cause significant differences among organization, and since the three levels are interdependent, differences in technical functions should also make for differences at managerial and institutional levels of the

organization. Similarly, differences of the institutional structures in which organizations are imbedded should make for significant variations among organizations at all three levels.

Relating this back to the Simon-March-Cyert focus on organizational processes of searching, learning, and deciding, we can also suggest that while these adaptive processes may be generic, the ways in which they proceed may well vary with differences in technologies or in environments.

Recapitulation

Most of our beliefs about complex organizations follow from one or the other of two distinct strategies. The closed-system strategy seeks certainty by incorporating only those variables positively associated with goal achievement and subjecting them to a monolithic control network. The open-system strategy shifts attention from goal achievement to survival, and incorporates uncertainty by recognizing organizational interdependence with environment. A newer tradition enables us to conceive of the organization as an open system, indeterminate and faced with uncertainty, but subject to criteria of rationality and hence needing certainty.

With this conception the central problem for complex organizations is one of coping with uncertainty. As a point of departure, we suggest that organizations cope with uncertainty by creating certain parts specifically to deal with it, specializing other parts in operating under conditions of certainty or near certainty. In this case, articulation of these specialized parts becomes significant.

We also suggest that technologies and environments are major sources of uncertainty for organizations, and that differences in those dimensions will result in differences in organizations. To proceed, we now turn to a closer examination of the meaning of "rationality," in the context of complex organizations.

RATIONALITY IN ORGANIZATIONS

Instrumental action is rooted on the one hand in *desired outcomes* and on the other hand in *beliefs about cause/effect relationships*. Given a desire, the state of man's knowledge at any point in time dictates the kinds of variables required and the manner of their manipulation to bring that desire to fruition. To the extent that the activities thus dictated by man's beliefs are judged to produce the desired outcomes, we can speak of technology, or *technical rationality*.

Technical rationality can be evaluated by two criteria: instrumental and economic. The essence of the instrumental question is whether the specified actions do in fact produce the desired outcome, and the instrumentally perfect technology is one which inevitably achieves such results. The economic question in essence is whether the results are obtained with the least necessary expenditure of resources, and for this there is no absolute standard. Two different routes to the same desired outcome may be compared in terms of cost, or both may be compared with some abstract ideal, but in practical terms the evaluation of economy is relative to the state of man's knowledge at the time of evaluation.

We will give further consideration to the assessment of organizational action in a later chapter, but it is necessary to distinguish at this point between the instrumental and economic questions because present literature and organization gives considerable attention to the economic dimension of technology but hides the importance of the instrumental question, which in fact takes priority. The cost of doing something can be con-

sidered only after we know that the something can be done.

Complex organizations are built to operate technologies which are found to be impossible or impractical for individuals to operate. This does not mean, however, that technologies operated by complex organizations are instrumentally perfect. The instrumentally perfect technology would produce the desired outcome inevitably, and this perfection is approached in the case of continuous processing of chemicals or in mass manufacturing—for example, of automobiles. A less perfect technology will produce the desired outcome only part of the time; nevertheless, it may be incorporated into complex organizations, such as the mental hospital, because the desire for the possible outcome is intense enough to settle for possible rather than highly probable success. Sometimes the intensity of desire for certain kinds of outcomes, such as world peace, leads to the creation of complex organizations, such as the United Nations to operate patently imperfect technologies.

Variations in Technologies

Clearly, technology is an important variable in understanding the actions of complex organizations. In modern societies the variety of desired outcomes for which specific technologies are available seems infinite. A complete but simple typology of technologies which has found order in this variety would be quite helpful. Typologies are available for industrial production[20] and for mental therapy[21] but are not general enough to deal with the range of technologies found in complex organizations. Lacking such a typology, we will simply identify three varieties which are (1) widespread in modern society and (2) sufficiently different to illustrate the propositions we wish to develop.

The Long-linked Technology.[22] A long-linked technology involves serial interdependence in the sense that act Z can be performed only after successful completion of act Y, which in turn rests on act X, and so on. The original symbol of technical rationality, the mass production assembly line, is of this long-linked nature. It approaches instrumental perfection when it produces a single kind of standard product, repetitively and at a constant rate. Production of only one kind of product means that a single technology is required, and this in turn permits the use of clear-cut criteria for the selection of machines and tools, construction of work-flow arrangements, acquisition of raw materials, and selection of human operators. Repetition of the productive process provides experience as a means of eliminating imperfections in the technology; experience can lead to the modification of machines and provide the basis for scheduled preventive maintenance. Repetition means that human motions can also be examined, and through training and practice, energy losses and errors minimized. It is in this setting that the scientific-management movement has perhaps made its greatest contribution.

The constant rate of production means that, once adjusted, the proportion of resources involved can be standardized to the point where each contributes to its capacity; none need to be underemployed. This of course makes important contributions to the economic aspect of the technology.

The Mediating Technology. Various organizations have, as a primary function, the linking of clients or customers who are or wish to be interdependent. The commerical bank links depositors and borrowers. The insurance firm links those who would pool common risks. The telephone utility links those who would call and those who would be called. The post office provides a possible linkage of virtually every member of the modern society. The employment agency mediates the supply of labor and the demand for it.

Complexity in the mediating technology comes not from the necessity of having each activity geared to the requirements of the next but rather from the fact that the mediating technology requires operating in *standardized ways*, and *extensively*; e.g., with multiple clients or customers distributed in time and space.

The commercial bank must find and aggregate deposits from diverse depositors; but however diverse the depositors, the transaction must conform to standard terms and to uniform bookkeeping and accounting procedures. It must also find borrowers; but no matter how varied their needs or desires, loans must be made according to standardized criteria and on terms uniformly applied to the category appropriate to the particular borrower. Poor risks who receive favored treatment jeopardize bank solvency. Standardization permits the insurance organization to define categories of risk and hence to sort its customers or potential customers into appropriate aggregate categories; the insured who is not a qualified risk but is so defined upsets the probabilities on which insurance rests. The telephone company became viable only when the telephone became regarded as a necessity, and this did not occur until equipment was standardized to the point where it could be incorporated into one network. Standardization enables the employment agency to aggregate job applicants into categories which can be matched against standardized requests for employees.

Standardization makes possible the operation of the mediating technology over time and through space by assuring each segment of the organization that other segments are operating in compatible ways. It is in such situations that the bureaucratic techniques of categorization and impersonal application of rules have been most beneficial.[23]

The Intensive Technology. This third variety we label *intensive* to signify that a variety of techniques is drawn upon in order to achieve a change in some specific object; but the selection, combination, and order of application are determined by feedback from the object itself. When the object is human, this intensive technology is regarded as "therapeutic," but the same technical logic is found also in the construction industry[24] and in research where the objects of concern are nonhuman. . . .

The intensive technology is a custom technology. Its successful employment rests in part on the availability of all the capacities potentially needed, but equally on the appropriate custom combination of selected capacities as required by the individual case or project.

Boundaries of Technical Rationality. Technical rationality, as a system of cause/effect relationships which lead to a desired result, is an abstraction. It is instrumentally perfect when it becomes a closed system of logic. The closed system of logic contains all relevant variables, and only relevant variables. All other influences, or *exogenous variables*, are excluded; and the variables contained in the system vary only to the extent that the experimenter, the manager, or the computer determines they should.

When a technology is put to use, however, there must be not only desired outcomes and knowledge of relevant cause/effect relationships, but also power to control the empirical resources which correspond to the variables in the logical system. A closed system of action corresponding to a closed system of logic

would result in instrumental perfection in reality.

The mass production assembly operation and the continuous processing of chemicals are more nearly perfect, in application, than the other two varieties discussed above because they achieve a high degree of control over relevant variables and are relatively free from disturbing influences. Once started, most of the action involved in the long-linked technology is dictated by the internal logic of the technology itself. With the mediating technology, customers or clients intrude to make difficult the standardized activities required by the technology. And with the intensive technology, the specific case defines the component activities and their combination from the larger array of components contained in the abstract technology.

Since technical perfection seems more nearly approachable when the organization has control over all the elements involved,

> Proposition 2.1: Under norms of rationality, organizations seek to seal off their core technologies from environmental influences.

Organizational Rationality

When organizations seek to translate the abstractions called technologies into action, they immediately face problems for which the core technologies do not provide solutions.

Mass production manufacturing technologies are quite specific, *assuming* that certain inputs are provided and finished products are somehow removed from the premises before the productive process is clogged; but mass production technologies do not include variables which provide solutions to either the input- or output-disposal problems. The present technology of medicine may be rather specific if certain tests indicate an appendectomy is in order, if the condition of the patient meets certain criteria, and if certain medical staff, equipment, and medications are present. But medical technology contains no cause/effect statements about bringing sufferers to the attention of medical practitioners, or about the provision of the specified equipment, skills, and medications. The technology of education rests on abstract systems of belief about relationships among teachers, teaching materials, and pupils; but learning theories assume the presence of these variables and proceed from that point.

One or more technologies constitute the core of all purposive organizations. But this technical core is always an incomplete representation of what the organization must do to accomplish desired results. Technical rationality is a necessary component but never alone sufficient to provide *organizational rationality*, which involves acquiring the inputs which are taken for granted by the technology, and dispensing outputs which again are outside the scope of the core technology.

At a minimum, then, organizational rationality involves three major component activities, (1) input activities, (2) technological activities, and (3) output activities. Since these are interdependent, organizational rationality requires that they be appropriately geared to one another. The inputs acquired must be within the scope of the technology, and it must be within the capacity of the organization to dispose of the technological production.

Not only are these component activities interdependent, but both input and output activities are interdependent with environmental elements. Organizational rationality, therefore, never conforms to closed-system logic but demands the logic of an open system. Moreover, since the technological activities are embedded in and interdependent with activities which are open to the environment, the closed system can never be completely attained for the technological component. Yet we have offered the proposition that organizations subject to rationality norms seek to seal off their core technologies from environmental influences. How do we reconcile these two contentions?

Proposition 2.2: Under norms of rationality, organizations seek to buffer environmental influences by surrounding their technical cores with input and output components.

To maximize productivity of a manufacturing technology, the technical core must be able to operate as if the market will absorb the single kind of product at a continuous rate, and as if inputs flowed continuously, at a steady rate and with specified quality. Conceivably both sets of conditions could occur; realistically they do not. But organizations reveal a variety of devices for approximating these "as if" assumptions, with input and output components meeting fluctuating environments and converting them into steady conditions for the technological core.

Buffering on the input side is illustrated by the stockpiling of materials and supplies acquired in an irregular market, and their steady insertion into the production process. Preventive maintenance, whereby machines or equipment are repaired on a scheduled basis, thus minimizing surprise, is another example of buffering by the input component. The recruitment of dissimilar personnel and their conversion into reliable performers through training or indoctrination is another; it is most dramatically illustrated by basic training or boot camp in military organizations.[25]

Buffering on the output side of long-linked technologies usually takes the form of maintaining warehouse inventories and items in transit or in distributor inventories, which permits the technical core to produce at a constant rate, but distribution to fluctuate with market conditions.

Buffering on the input side is an appropriate and important device available to all types of organizations. Buffering on the output side is especially important for mass-manufacturing organizations, but is less feasible when the product is perishable or when the object is inextricably involved in the technological process, as in the therapeutic case.

Buffering of an unsteady environment obviously brings considerable advantages to the technical core, but it does so with costs to the organization. A classic problem in connection with buffering is how to maintain inventories, input or output, sufficient to meet all needs without recurring obsolescence as needs change. Operations research recently has made important contributions toward this problem of "run out versus obsolescence," both of which are costly.

Thus while a fully buffered technological core would enjoy the conditions for maximum technical rationality, organizational rationality may call for compromises between conditions for maximum technical efficiency and the energy required for buffering operations. In an unsteady environment, then, the organization under rationality norms must seek other devices for protecting its technical core.

Proposition 2.3: Under norms of rationality, organizations seek to smooth out input and output transactions.

Whereas buffering absorbs environmental fluctuations, smoothing or leveling involves attempts to reduce fluctuations in the environment. Utility firms—electric, gas, water, or telephone—may offer inducements to those who use their services during "trough"

periods, or charge premiums to those who contribute to "peaking." Retailing organizations faced with seasonal or other fluctuations in demand, may offer inducements in the form of special promotions or sales during slow periods. Transportation organizations such as airlines may offer special reduced fare rates on light days or during slow seasons.

Organizations pointed toward emergencies, such as fire departments, attempt to level the need for their services by activities designed to prevent emergencies, and by emphasis on the early detection so that demand is not allowed to grow to the point that would overtax the capacity of the organization. Hospitals accomplish some smoothing through the scheduling of nonemergency admissions.

Although action by the organization may thus reduce fluctuations in demand, complete smoothing of demand is seldom possible. But a core technology interrupted by constant fluctuation and change must settle for a low degree of technical rationality. What other services do organizations employ to protect core technologies?

Proposition 2.4: Under norms of rationality, organizations seek to anticipate and adapt to environmental changes which cannot be buffered or leveled.

If environmental fluctuations penetrate the organization and require the technical core to alter its activities, then environmental fluctuations are exogenous variables within the logic of technical rationality. To the extent that environmental fluctuations can be anticipated, however, they can be treated as *constraints* on the technical core within which a closed system of logic can be employed.

The manufacturing firm which can correctly forecast demand for a particular time period can thereby plan or schedule operations of its technical core at a steady rate during that period. Any changes in technical operations due to changes in the environment can be made at the end of the period on the basis of forecasts for the next period.

Organizations often learn that some environmental fluctuations are patterned, and in these cases forecasting and adjustment appear almost automatic. The post office knows, for example, that in large commercial centers large volumes of business mail are posted at the end of the business day, when secretaries leave offices. Recently the post office has attempted to buffer that load by promising rapid treatment of mail posted in special locations during morning hours. Its success in buffering is not known at this writing, but meanwhile the post office schedules its technical activities to meet known daily fluctuations. It can also anticipate heavy demand during November and December, thus allowing its input components lead time in acquiring additional resources.

Banks likewise learn that local conditions and customs result in peak loads at predictable times during the day and week, and can schedule their operations to meet these shifts.[26]

In cases such as these, organizations have amassed sufficient experience to know that fluctuations are patterned with a high degree of regularity or probability; but when environmental fluctuations are the result of combinations of more dynamic factors, anticipation may require something more than the simple projection of previous experience. It is in these situations that forecasting emerges as a specialized and elaborate activity, for which some of the emerging management-science or statistical-decision theories seem especially appropriate.

To the extent that environmental fluctuations are unanticipated they interfere with the orderly operation of the core technology and thereby reduce its performance. When such influences are anticipated and considered as constraints for a particular period of time, the technical core can operate as if it enjoyed a closed system.

Buffering, leveling, and adaptation to anticipated fluctuations are widely used devices for reducing the influence of the environment on the technological cores of organizations. Often they are effective, but there are occasions when these devices are not sufficient to ward off environmental penetration.

> Proposition 2.5: When buffering, leveling, and forecasting do not protect their technical cores from environmental fluctuations, organizations under norms of rationality resort to rationing.

Rationing is most easily seen in organizations pointed toward emergencies, such as hospitals. Even in nonemergency situations hospitals may ration beds to physicians by establishing priority systems for nonemergency admissions. In emergencies, such as community disasters, hospitals may ration pharmaceutical dosages or nursing services by dilution—by assigning a fixed number of nurses to a larger patient population. Mental hospitals, especially state mental hospitals, may ration technical services by employing primarily organic-treatment procedures—electroshock, drugs, insulin—which can be employed more economically than psychoanalytic or *milieu* therapies.[27] Teachers and case-workers in social welfare organizations may ration effort by accepting only a portion of those seeking service, or if not empowered to exercise such discretion, may concentrate their energies on the more challenging cases or on those which appear most likely to yield satisfactory outcomes.[28]

But rationing is not a device reserved for therapeutic organizations. The post office may assign priority to first-class mail, attending to lesser classes only when the priority task is completed. Manufacturers of suddenly popular items may ration allotments to wholesalers or dealers, and if inputs are scarce, may assign priorities to alternative uses of those resources. Libraries may ration book loans, acquisitions, and search efforts.[29]

Rationing is an unhappy solution, for its use signifies that the technology is not operating at its maximum. Yet some system of priorities for the allocation of capacity under adverse conditions is essential if a technology is to be instrumentally effective—if action is to be other than random.

The Logic of Organizational Rationality. Core technologies rest on closed systems of logic, but are invariably embedded in a larger organizational rationality which pins the technology to a time and place, and links it with the larger environment through input and output activities. Organizational rationality thus calls for an open-system logic, for when the organization is opened to environmental influences, some of the factors involved in organizational action become *constraints*; for some meaningful period of time they are not variables but fixed conditions to which the organization must adapt. Some of the factors become *contingencies*, which may or may not vary, but are not subject to arbitrary control by the organization.

Organizational rationality therefore is some result of (1) constraints which the organization must face, (2) contingencies which the organization must meet, and (3) variables which the organization can control.

Recapitulation

Perfection in technical rationality requires complete knowledge of cause/

effect relations plus control over all of the relevant variables, or closure. Therefore, under norms of rationality (Prop. 2.1), organizations seek to seal off their core technologies from environmental influences. Since complete closure is impossible (Prop.2.2), they seek to buffer environmental influences by surrounding their technical cores with input and output components.

Because buffering does not handle all variations in an unsteady environment, organizations seek to smooth input and output transactions (Prop. 2.3), and to anticipate and adapt to environmental changes which cannot be buffered or smoothed (Prop. 2.4), and finally, when buffering, leveling, and forecasting do not protect their technical cores from environmental fluctuations (Prop. 2.5), organizations resort to rationing.

These are maneuvering devices which provide the organization with some self-control despite interdependence with the environment. But if we are to gain understanding of such maneuvering, we must consider both the direction toward which maneuvering is designed and the nature of the environment in which maneuvering takes place.

NOTES

1. William R. Dill, "Desegregation or Integration? Comments about Contemporary Research in Organizations," in *New Perspectives in Organization Research*, eds. W. W. Cooper, Harold J. Leavitt, & Maynard W. Shelly II (New York: John Wiley & Sons, Inc., 1964). James G. March, "Introduction," in *Handbook of Organizations*, ed. James G. March (Chicago: Rand McNally, 1965).

2. Alvin W. Gouldner, "Organizational Analysis," in *Sociology Today*, eds. Robert K. Merton, Leonard Broom, and Leonard S. Cottrell, Jr. (New York: Basic Books, 1959).

3. W. Ross Ashby, *An Introduction to Cybernetics* (London: Chapman and Hall, Ltd., 1956).

4. Sir Frederic Bartlett, *Thinking: An Experimental and Social Study* (New York: Basic Books, 1958).

5. Frederick W. Taylor, *Scientific Management* (New York: Harper & Row, 1911).

6. Luther Gulick, & L. Urwick, eds., *Papers on the Science of Administration* (New York: Institute of Public Administration, 1937).

7. Max Weber, *The Theory of Social and Economic Organization*, ed. Talcott Parsons, trans. A. M. Henderson and Talcott Parsons (New York: Free Press, 1947).

8. Herbert A. Simon, *Administrative Behavior*, 2nd ed. (New York: Macmillan, 1957).

9. Robert K. Merton, "Bureaucratic Structure and Personality," in *Social Theory and Social Structure*, rev. ed., ed. Robert K. Merton (New York: Free Press, 1957).

10. Fritz L. Roethlisberger, & W. J. Dickson, *Management and the Worker* (Cambridge, Mass.: Harvard University Press, 1939).

11. Chester I. Barnard, *The Functions of the Executive* (Cambridge, Mass.: Harvard University Press, 1938).

12. Philip Selznick, *TVA and the Grass Roots* (Berkeley, Calif.: University of California Press, 1949).

13. Burton R. Clark, *Adult Education in Transition* (Berkeley, Calif.: University of California Press, 1956).

14. Herbert A. Simon, *Administrative Behavior*. James G. March, & Herbert A. Simon, *Organizations* (New York: Wiley, 1958). Richard M. Cyert, & James G. March, *A Behavioral Theory of the Firm* (Englewood Cliffs, N.J.: Prentice-Hall, 1963).

15. Herbert A. Simon, *Models of Man, Social and Rational* (New York: Wiley, 1957).

16. *Ibid.*

17. Michel Crozier, *The Bureaucratic Phenomenon* (Chicago: The University of Chicago Press, 1964).

18. Talcott Parsons, *Structure and Process in Modern Societies* (New York: Free Press, 1960).

19. James D. Thompson, "Decision-making, the Firm, and the Market, in *New Perspectives in Organization Research*, eds., W. W. Cooper et al. (New York: Wiley, 1964).

20. Joan Woodward, *Industrial Organization: Theory and Practice* (London: Oxford University Press, 1965).

21. Robert W. Hawkes, "Physical Psychiatric Rehabilitation Models Compared" (Paper presented at the Ohio Valley Sociological Society, 1962).

22. The notions in this section rest especially on conversations some years ago with Frederick L. Bates. For a different but somewhat parallel analysis of work flows, see Robert Dubin, "Stability of Human Organizations," in *Modern Organization Theory*, ed. Mason Haire (New York: Wiley, 1959).

23. Weber, *Theory of Organization*. Merton, *Social Theory and Structure*.

24. Arthur L. Stinchcombe, "Bureaucratic and Craft Administration of Production: A Comparative Study," *Administrative Science Quarterly* 4 (September 1959): 168-187.

25. Sanford M. Dornbusch, "The Military Academy as an Assimilating Institution," *Social Forces* 33 (May 1955): 316-321.

26. Chris Argyris, *Organization of a Bank* (New Haven, Conn.: Labor and Management Center, Yale University, 1954).

27. Ivan Belknap, *The Human Problems of a State Mental Hospital* (New York: McGraw-Hill, 1956).

28. Peter M. Blau, *The Dynamics of Bureaucracy* (Chicago: The University of Chicago Press, 1955).

29. Richard L. Meier, "Communications Overload," *Administrative Science Quarterly* 7 (March 1963): 521-544.

26
General Systems Theory: Applications for Organization and Management
Fremont E. Kast & James E. Rosenzweig

Biological and social scientists generally have embraced systems concepts. Many organization and management theorists seem anxious to identify with this movement and to contribute to the development of an approach which purports to offer the ultimate—the unification of all science into one grand conceptual model. Who possibly could resist? General systems theory seems to provide a relief from the limitations of more mechanistic approaches and a rationale for rejecting "principles" based on relatively "closed-system" thinking. This theory provides the paradigm for organization and management theorists to "crank into their systems model" all of the diverse knowledge from relevant underlying disciplines. It has become almost mandatory to have the word "system" in the title of recent articles and books (many of us have compromised and placed it only in the subtitle).[1] . . .

Even in the field of organization and management theory, systems views are not new. Chester Barnard used a basic systems framework.

> A cooperative system is a complex of physical, biological, personal, and social components which are in a specific systematic relationship by reason of the cooperation of two or more persons for at least one definite end. Such a system is evidently a subordinate unit of larger systems from one point of view; and itself embraces subsidiary systems—physical, biological, etc.—

from another point of view. One of the systems comprised within a cooperative system, the one which is implicit in the phrase "cooperation of two or more persons," is called an "organization" [3, p. 65].

And Barnard was influenced by the "systems views" of Vilfredo Pareto and Talcott Parsons. Certainly this quote (dressed up a bit to give the term "system" more emphasis) could be the introduction to a 1972 book on organizations. . . . The momentum of systems thinking was identified by Scott in 1961 when he described the relationship between general systems theory and organization theory.

> The distinctive qualities of modern organization theory are its conceptual-analytical base, its reliance on empirical research data, and above all, its integrating nature. These qualities are framed in a philosophy which accepts the premise that the only meaningful way to study organization is to study it as a system. . . . Modern organization theory and general system theory are similar in that they look at organization as an integrated whole [33, pp. 15–21].

Scott said explicitly what many in our field had been thinking and/or implying—he helped us put into perspective the important writings of Herbert Simon, James March, Talcott Parsons, George Homans, E. Wight Bakke, Kenneth Boulding, and many others.

Source: Fremont E. Kast and James E. Rosenzweig, "General Systems Theory: Applications for Organization and Management," *Academy of Management Journal* (December 1972): 447–465.

But how far have we really advanced over the past decade in applying general systems theory to organizations and their management? Is it still a "skeleton," or have we been able to "put some meat on the bones?" The systems approach has been touted because of its potential usefulness in understanding the complexities of "live" organizations. Has this approach really helped us in this endeavor or has it compounded confusion with chaos? Herbert Simon describes the challenge for the systems approach:

> In both science and engineering, the study of "systems" is an increasingly popular activity. Its popularity is more a response to a pressing need for synthesizing and analyzing complexity than it is to any large development of a body of knowledge and technique for dealing with complexity. If this popularity is to be more than a fad, necessity will have to mother invention and provide substance to go with the name [35, p. 114].

In this article we will explore the issue of whether we are providing substance for the term *systems approach* as it relates to the study of organizations and their management. There are many interesting historical and philosophical questions concerning the relationship between the mechanistic and organistic approaches and their applicability to the various fields of science, as well as other interesting digressions into the evolution of systems approaches. However, we will resist those temptations and plunge directly into a discussion of the key concepts of general systems theory, the way in which these ideas have been used by organization theorists, the limitations in their application, and some suggestions for the future.

KEY CONCEPTS OF GENERAL SYSTEMS THEORY

The key concepts of general systems theory have been set forth by many writers

[6, 7, 13, 17, 25, 28, 39] and have been used by many organization and management theorists [10, 14, 18, 19, 22, 23, 24, 32]. It is not our purpose here to elaborate on them in great detail because we anticipate that most readers will have been exposed to them in some depth. Figure 1 provides a very brief review of those characteristics of systems which seem to have wide acceptance. The review is far from complete. It is difficult to identify a "complete" list of characteristics derived from general systems theory; moreover, it is merely a first-order classification. There are many derived second- and third-order characteristics which could be considered. For example, James G. Miller sets forth 165 hypotheses, stemming from open systems theory, which might be applicable to two or more levels of systems [25]. He suggests that they are *general* systems theoretical hypotheses and qualifies them by suggesting that they are propositions applicable to general systems *behavior* theory and would thus exclude nonliving systems. He does not limit these propositions to individual organisms, but considers them appropriate for social systems as well. His hypotheses are related to such issues as structure, process, subsystems, information, growth, and integration. It is obviously impossible to discuss all of these hypotheses; we want only to indicate the extent to which many interesting propositions are being posed which might have relevance to many different types of systems. It will be a very long time (if ever) before most of these hypotheses are validated; however, we are surprised at how many of them can be agreed with intuitively, and we can see their possible verification in studies of social organizations. . . .

SOME DILEMMAS IN APPLYING GST TO ORGANIZATIONS

Why have writers embracing general systems theory as a basis for studying organi-

FIGURE 1 · KEY CONCEPTS OF GENERAL SYSTEMS THEORY

Subsystems or Components: A system by definition is composed of interrelated parts or elements. This is true for all systems—mechanical, biological, and social. Every system has at least two elements, and these elements are interconnected.

Holism, Synergism, Organicism, and Gestalt: The whole is not just the sum of the parts; the system itself can be explained only as a totality. Holism is the opposite of elementarism, which views the total as the sum of its individual parts.

Open Systems View: Systems can be considered in two ways: (1) closed or (2) open. Open systems exchange information, energy, or material with their environments. Biological and social systems are inherently open systems; mechanical systems may be open or closed. The concepts of open and closed systems are difficult to defend in the absolute. We prefer to think of open-closed as a dimension; that is, systems are relatively open or relatively closed.

Input-Transformation-Output Model: The open system can be viewed as a transformation model. In a dynamic relationship with its environment, it receives various inputs, transforms these inputs in some way, and exports outputs.

System Boundaries: It follows that systems have boundaries which separate them from their environments. The concept of boundaries helps us understand the distinction between open and closed systems. The relatively closed system has rigid, impenetrable boundaries; whereas the open system has permeable boundaries between itself and a broader suprasystem. Boundaries are relatively easily defined in physical and biological systems, but are very difficult to delineate in social systems, such as organizations.

Negative Entropy: Closed, physical systems are subject to the force of entropy which increases until eventually the entire system fails. The tendency toward maximum entropy is a movement to disorder, complete lack of resource transformation, and death. In a closed system, the change in entropy must always be positive; however, in open biological or social systems, entropy can be arrested and may even be transformed into negative entropy—a process of more complete organization and ability to transform resources—because the system imports resources from its environment.

Steady State, Dynamic Equilibrium, and Homeostasis: The concept of steady state is closely related to that of negative entropy. A closed system eventually must attain an equilibrium state with maximum entropy—death or disorganization. However, an open system may attain a state where the system remains in dynamic equilibrium through the continuous inflow of materials, energy, and information.

Feedback: The concept of feedback is important in understanding how a system maintains a steady state. Information concerning the outputs or the process of the system is fed back as an input into the system, perhaps leading to changes in the transformation process and/or future outputs. Feedback can be both positive and negative, although the field of cybernetics is based on negative feedback. Negative feedback is informational input which indicates that the system is deviating from a prescribed course and should readjust to a new steady state.

(continued)

FIGURE 1 • KEY CONCEPTS OF GENERAL SYSTEMS THEORY (continued)

Hierarchy: A basic concept in systems thinking is that of hierarchical relationships between systems. A system is composed of subsystems of a lower order and is also part of a suprasystem. Thus, there is a hierarchy of the components of the system.

Internal Elaboration: Closed systems move toward entropy and disorganization. In contrast, open systems appear to move in the direction of greater differentiation, elaboration, and a higher level of organization.

Multiple Goal-Seeking: Biological and social systems appear to have multiple goals or purposes. Social organizations seek multiple goals, if for no other reason than that they are composed of individuals and subunits with different values and objectives.

Equifinality of Open Systems: In mechanistic systems there is a direct cause and effect relationship between the initial conditions and the final state. Biological and social systems operate differently. Equifinality suggests that certain results may be achieved with different intial conditions and in different ways. This view suggests that social organizations can accomplish their objectives with diverse inputs and with varying internal activities (conversion processes).

zations had so much difficulty in following through? Part of this difficulty may stem from the newness of the paradigm and our inability to operationalize "all we think we know" about this approach. Or it may be because we know too little about the systems under investigation. Both of these possibilities will be covered later, but first we need to look at some of the more specific conceptual problems.

ORGANIZATIONS AS ORGANISMS

One of the basic contributions of general systems theory was the rejection of the traditional closed-system or mechanistic view of social organizations. But, did general systems theory free us from this constraint only to impose another, less obvious one? General systems theory grew out of the organismic views of von Bertalanffy and other biologists; thus, many of the characteristics are relevant to the living organism. It is conceptually easy to draw the analogy between living organisms and social organizations. "There is, after all, an intuitive similarity between the organization of the human body and the kinds of organizations men create. And so, undaunted by the failures of the human-social analogy through time, new theorists try afresh in each epoch" [2, p. 660]. General systems theory would have us accept this analogy between organism and social organization. Yet, we have a hard time swallowing it whole. Katz and Kahn warn us of the danger:

There has been no more pervasive, persistent, and futile fallacy handicapping the social sciences than the use of the physical model for the understanding of social structures. The biological metaphor, with its crude comparisons of the physical parts of the body to the parts of the social system, has been replaced by more subtle but equally misleading analogies between biological and social functioning. This figurative type of thinking ignores the essential difference between the socially contrived nature of social systems and the physical structure of the machine or the human organism. So long as writers are committed to a theoretical flamework based upon the physical model, they will miss the essential social-psychological facts of the highly variable, loosely articulated character of social systems [19, p. 31].

In spite of this warning, Katz and Kahn do embrace much of the general systems theory concepts which are based on the biological metaphor. We must be very cautious about trying to make this analogy too literal. We agree with Silverman who says, "It may, therefore, be necessary to drop the analogy between an organization and an organism: organizations may be systems but not necessarily *natural* systems" [34, p. 31].

Distinction between Organization and an Organization

General systems theory emphasizes that systems are organized—they are composed of interdependent components in some relationship. The social organization would then follow logically as just another system. But, we are perhaps being caught in circular thinking. It is true that all systems (physical, biological, and social) are by definition organized, but are all systems organizations? . . .

Why make an issue of this distinction? It seems to us that there is a vital matter involved. All systems may be considered to be organized, and more advanced systems may display differentiation in the activities of component parts—such as the specialization of human organs. However, all systems *do not* have purposeful entities. Can the heart or lungs be considered as purposeful entities in themselves or are they only components of the larger purposeful system, the human body? By contrast, the social organization is composed of two or more purposeful elements. "An organization

consists of elements that have and can exercise their own wills" [1, p. 669]. Organisms, the foundation stone of general systems theory, do not contain purposeful elements which exercise their own will. This distinction between the organism and the social organization is of importance. In much of general systems theory, the concern is primarily with the way in which the *organism* responds to environmentally generated inputs. Feedback concepts and the maintenance of a steady state are based on internal adaptations to environmental forces. (This is particularly true of cybernetic models.) But, what about those changes and adaptations which occur from *within* social organizations? Purposeful elements within the social organization may initiate activities and adaptations which are difficult to subsume under feedback and steady state concepts.

Open and Closed Systems

Another dilemma stemming from general systems theory is the tendency to dichotomize all systems as opened or closed. We have been led to think of physical systems as closed, subject to the laws of entropy, and to think of biological systems as open to their environment and, possibly, becoming negentropic. But applying this strict polarization to social organizations creates many difficulties. In fact, most social organizations and their subsystems are "partially open" and "partially closed." Open and closed are a matter of degree. Unfortunately, there seems to be a widely held view (often more implicit than explicit) that *open-system thinking is good and closed-system thinking is bad.* We have not become sufficiently sophisticated to recognize that both are appropriate under certain conditions. For example, one of the most useful conceptualizations set forth by Thompson is that the social organization *must seek* to use closed-system concepts (particularly at the technical core) to reduce uncertainty and to create more effective performance at this level.

Still Subsystems Thinking

Even though we preach a general systems approach, we often practice subsystems thinking. Each of the academic disciplines and each of us personally have limited perspective of the system we are studying. While proclaiming a broad systems viewpoint, we often dismiss variables outside our interest or competence as being irrelevant, and we only open our system to those inputs which we can handle with our disciplinary bag of tools. We are hampered because each of the academic disciplines has taken a narrow "partial systems view" and find comfort in the relative certainty which this creates. Of course, this is not a problem unique to modern organization theory. Under the more traditional process approach to the study of management, we were able to do an admirable job of delineating and discussing planning, organizing, and controlling as separate activities. We were much less successful in discussing them as integrated and interrelated activities.

How Does Our Knowledge Fit?

One of the major problems in utilizing general systems theory is that we know (or think we know) more about certain relationships than we can fit into a general systems model. For example, we are beginning to understand the two-variable relationship between technology and structure. But, when we introduce another variable, say psychosocial relationships, our models become too complex. Consequently, in order to discuss all the things we know about organizations, we depart from a systems approach. Perhaps it is because we know a great deal more about the elements or subsystems of an organization than we

do about the interrelationships and interactions between these subsystems. And, general systems theory forces us to consider those relationships about which we know the least—a true dilemma. So we continue to elaborate on those aspects of the organization which we know best—a partial systems view.

Failure to Delineate a Specific System

When the social sciences embraced general systems theory, the total system became the focus of attention and terminology tended toward vagueness. In the utilization of systems theory, we should be more precise in delineating the specific system under consideration. Failure to do this leads to much confusion. . . .

We need to be much more precise in delineating both the boundaries of the system under consideration and the level of our analysis. There is a tendency for current writers in organization theory to accept general systems theory and then to move indiscriminately across systems boundaries and between levels of systems without being very precise (and letting their readers in on what is occurring). James Miller suggests the need for clear delineation of levels in applying systems theory, "It is important to follow one procedural rule in systems theory in order to avoid confusion. Every discussion should begin with an identification of the level of reference, and the discourse should not change to another level without a specific statement that this is occurring" [25, p. 216]. Our field is replete with these confusions about systems levels. For example, when we use the term *organizational behavior* are we talking about the way the organization behaves as a system or are we talking about the behavior of the individual participants? By goals, do we mean the goals of the organization or the goals of the individuals within the organization? In using systems theory we must become more precise in our delineation of systems boundaries and systems levels if we are to prevent confusing conceptual ambiguity.

Recognition That Organizations Are "Contrived Systems"

We have a vague uneasiness that general systems theory truly does not recognize the "contrived" nature of social organizations. With its predominate emphasis on natural organisms, it may understate some characteristics which are vital for the social organization. Social organizations do not occur naturally in nature; they are contrived by man. They have structure; but it is the structure of events rather than of physical components, and it cannot be separated from the processes of the system. The fact that social organizations are contrived by human beings suggests that they can be established for an infinite variety of purposes and do not follow the same life-cycle patterns of birth, growth, maturity, and death as biological systems. As Katz and Kahn say:

> Social structures are essentially contrived systems. They are made of men and are imperfect systems. They can come apart at the seams overnight, but they can also outlast by centuries the biological organisms which originally created them. The cement which holds them together is essentially psychological rather than biological. Social systems are anchored in the attitudes, perceptions, beliefs, motivations, habits, and expectations of human beings [19, p. 33].

Recognizing that the social organization is contrived again cautions us against making an exact analogy between it and physical or biological systems.

Questions of Systems Effectiveness

General systems theory with its biological orientation would appear to have an evolutionary view of system effectiveness. That living system which best adapts to its environment prospers and survives. The primary measure of effectiveness is perpetuation of the organism's species. Teleological behavior is therefore directed toward survival. But, is survival the only criterion of effectiveness of the social system? It is probably an essential but not all-inclusive measure of effectiveness.

General systems theory emphasizes the organism's survival goal and does not fully relate to the question of the effectiveness of the system in its suprasystem—the environment. Parsonian functional-structural views provide a contrast. "The *raison d 'etre* of complex organizations, according to this analysis, is mainly to benefit the society in which they belong, and that society is, therefore, the appropriate frame of reference for the evaluation of organizational effectiveness" [41, p. 896].

But, this view seems to go to the opposite extreme from the survival view of general systems theory—the organization exists to serve the society. It seems to us that the truth lies somewhere between these two viewpoints. And it is likely that a systems viewpoint (modified from the species survival view of general systems theory) will be most appropriate. Yuchtman and Seashore suggest:

> The organization's success over a period of time in this competition for resources— i.e., its bargaining position in a given environment—is regarded as an expression of its overall effectiveness. Since the resources are of various kinds, and the competitive relationships are multiple, and since there is interchangeability among classes of resources, the assessment of organizational effectiveness must be in terms not of any single criterion but of an open-ended multidimensional set of criteria [41, p. 891].

This viewpoint suggests that questions of organizational effectiveness must be concerned with at least three levels of analysis. The level of the environment, the level of the social organization as a system, and the level of the subsystems (human participants) within the organization. Perhaps much of our confusion and ambiguity concerning organizational effectiveness stems from our failure to clearly delineate the level of our analysis and, even more important, our failure really to understand the relationships among these levels.

Our discussion of some of the problems associated with the application of general systems theory to the study of social organizations might suggest that we completely reject the appropriateness of this model. On the contrary, we see the systems approach as the new paradigm for the study of organizations; but, like all new concepts in the sciences, one which has to be applied, modified, and elaborated to make it as useful as possible.

SYSTEMS THEORY PROVIDES THE NEW PARADIGM

We hope the discussion of GST and organizations provides a realistic appraisal. We do not want to promote the value of the systems approach as a matter of faith; however, we do see systems theory as vital to the study of social organizations and as providing the major new paradigm for our field of study.

Thomas Kuhn provides an interesting interpretation of the nature of scientific revolution [20]. He suggests that major changes in all fields of science occur with the development of new conceptual schemes of "paradigms." These new paradigms do not just represent a step-by-step advancement in "normal" science (the science generally accepted and practiced) but, rather, a revolutionary

change in the way the scientific field is perceived by the practitioners. . . .

Systems theory does provide a new paradigm for the study of social organizations and their management. At this stage it is obviously crude and lacking in precision. In some ways it may not be much better than older paradigms which have been accepted and used for a long time (such as the management process approach). As in other fields of scientific endeavor, the new paradigm must be applied, clarified, elaborated, and made more precise. But, it does provide a fundamentally different view of the reality of social organizations and can serve as the basis for major advancements in our field.

We see many exciting examples of the utilization of the new systems paradigm in the field of organization and management. Several of these have been referred to earlier [7, 13, 19, 22, 23, 24, 31, 38], and there have been many others. Burns and Stalker made substantial use of systems views in setting forth their concepts of mechanistic and organic managerial systems [8]. Their studies of the characteristics of these two organization types lack precise definition to the variables and relationships, but their colleagues have used the systems approach to look at the relationship of organizations to their environment and also among the technical, structural, and behavioral characteristics within the organization [24]. Chamberlain used a system view in studying enterprises and their environment, which is substantially different from traditional microeconomics [9]. The emerging field of "environmental sciences" and "environmental administration" has found the systems paradigm vital.

Thus, the systems theory paradigm is being used extensively in the investigation of relationships between subsystems within organizations and in studying the environmental interfaces. But, it still has not advanced sufficiently to meet the needs. One of the major problems is that the practical need to deal with comprehensive systems of relationships is overrunning our ability to fully understand and predict these relationships. *We vitally need the systems paradigm but we are not sufficiently sophisticated to use it appropriately.* This is the dilemma. Do our current failures to fully utilize the systems paradigm suggest that we reject it and return to the older, more traditional, and time-tested paradigms? Or do we work with systems theory to make it more precise, to understand the relationships among subsystems, and to gather the informational inputs which are necessary to make the systems approach really work? We think the latter course offers the best opportunity.

Thus, we prefer to accept current limitations of systems theory, while working to reduce them and to develop more complete and sophisticated approaches for its application. We agree with Rapoport who says:

> The system approach to the study of man can be appreciated as an effort to restore meaning (in terms of intuitively grasped understanding of wholes) while adhering to the principles of *disciplined* generalizations and rigorous deduction. It is, in short, an attempt to make the study of man both scientific and meaningful [7, p. xxii].

We are sympathetic with the second part of Rapoport's comment, the need to apply the systems approach but to make disciplined generalizations and rigorous deductions. This is a vital necessity and yet a major current limitation. We do have some indication that progress (although very slow) is being made.

WHAT DO WE NEED NOW?

Everything is related to everything else—but how? General systems theory provides us with the macro paradigm for the study of social organizations. As Scott and others have pointed out, most sciences go through a macro-micromacro cycle or sequence of emphasis [33]. Traditional bureaucratic theory provided the first major macro view of organizations. Administrative management theorists concentrated on the development of macro "principles of management" which were applicable to all organizations. When these macro views seemed incomplete (unable to explain important phenomena), attention turned to the micro level—more detailed analysis of components or parts of the organization, thus the interest in human relations, technology, or structural dimensions.

The systems approach returns us to the macro level with a new paradigm. General systems theory emphasizes a very high level of abstraction. Phillips classifies it as a third-order study [29] that attempts to develop macro concepts appropriate for all types of biological, physical, and social systems.

In our view, we are now ready to move down a level of abstraction to consider second-order systems studies or mid-range concepts. These will be based on general systems theory but will be more concrete and will emphasize more specific characteristics and relationships in social organizations. They will operate within the broad paradigm of systems theory but at a less abstract level.

What should we call this new mid-range level of analysis? Various authors have referred to it as a "contingency view," a study of "patterns of relationships," or a search for "configurations among subsystems." Lorsch and Lawrence reflect this view:

> During the past few years there has been evident a new trend in the study of organizational phenomena. Underlying this new approach is the idea that the internal func-

tioning of organizations must be consistent with the demands of the organization task, technology, or external environment, and the needs of its members if organization is to be effective. Rather than searching for the panacea of the one best way to organize under all conditions, investigators have more and more tended to examine the functioning of organizations in relation to the needs of their particular members and the external pressures facing them. Basically, this approach seems to be leading to the development of a "contingency" theory of organization with the appropriate internal states and processes of the organization contingent upon external requirements and member needs [21, p. 1].

Numerous others have stressed a similar viewpoint. Thompson suggests that the essence of administration lies in understanding basic configurations which exist between the various subsystems and with the environment. "The basic function of administration appears to be co-alignment, not merely of people (in coalitions) but of institutionalized action—of technology and task environment into a viable domain, and of organizational design and structure appropriate to it" [38, p. 157].

Bringing these ideas together we can provide a more precise definition of the contingency view:

The contingency view of organizations and their management suggests that an organization is a system composed of subsystems and delineated by identifiable boundaries from its environmental suprasystem. The contingency view seeks to understand the interrelationships within and among subsystems as well as between the organization and its environment and to define patterns of relationships or configurations of variables. It emphasizes the multivariate nature of organizations and attempts to understand how organizations operate under varying conditions and in specific circumstances. Contingency views are ultimately directed toward suggesting organizational designs and managerial systems most appropriate for specific situations.

But, it is not enough to suggest that a "contingency view" based on systems concepts of organizations and their management is more appropriate than the simplistic "principles approach." If organization theory is to advance and make contributions to managerial practice, it must define more explicitly certain patterns of relationships between organizational variables. This is the major challenge facing our field. . . .

Various conceptual designs for the comparative study of organizations and their subsystems are emerging to help in the development of a contingency view. We do not want to impose our model as to what should be considered in looking for these patterns of relationships. However, the tentative matrix shown in Figure 2 suggests this approach. We have used as a starting point the two polar organization types which have been emphasized in the literature—closed/ stable/mechanistic and open/adaptive/ organic.

We will consider the environmental suprasystem and organizational subsystems (goals and values, technical, structural, psychosocial, and managerial) plus various dimensions or characteristics of each of these systems. By way of illustration we have indicated several specific subcategories under the Environmental Suprasystem as well as the Goals and Values subsystem. This process would have to be completed and extended to all of the subsystems. The next step would be the development of appropriate descriptive language (based on research and conceptualization) for each relevant characteristic across the continuum of organization types. For example, on the "stability" dimension for Goals and Values we would have High, Medium, and Low at appropriate places on

FIGURE 2 · MATRIX OF PATTERNS OF RELATIONSHIPS BETWEEN ORGANIZATION TYPES AND SYSTEMS VARIABLES

Organizational Supra- and Subsystems	Continuum of Organization Types	
	Closed/Stable/Mechanistic	Open/Adaptive/Organic
Environmental relation- ships		
General nature	Placid	Turbulent
Predictability	Certain, determinate	Uncertain, Indeterminate
Boundary relationships	Relatively closed; limited to few participants (sales, purchasing, etc); fixed and well-defined	Relatively open; many parti- cipants have external re- lationships; varied and not clearly defined
Goals and values		
Organizational goals in general	Efficient performance, sta- bility, maintenance	Effective problem-solving, innovation, growth
Goal set	Single, clear-cut	Multiple, determined by ne- cessity to satisfy a set of contraints
Stability	Stable	Unstable
Technical		
Structural		
Psychosocial		
Managerial		

the continuum. If the entire matrix were filled in, it is likely that we would begin to see discernible patterns of relation- ships among subsystems.

We do not expect this matrix to pro- vide *the* midrange model for everyone. It is highly doubtful that we will be able to follow through with the field work investigations necessary to fill in all the squares. Nevertheless, it does illustrate a possible approach for the translation of more abstract general systems theory into an appropriate midrange model which is relevant for organization theory and management practice. Frankly, we see this as a major long-term effort on the part of many researchers, investigating a wide variety of organizations. In spite of the difficulties involved in such research, the endeavor has practical significance. Sophistication in the study of organiza-

tions will come when we have a more complete understanding of organizations as total systems (configurations of subsys- tems) so that we can prescribe more ap- propriate organizational designs and managerial systems. Ultimately, organi- zation theory should serve as the founda- tion for more effective management practice.

APPLICATION OF SYSTEMS CONCEPTS TO MANAGEMENT PRACTICE

The study of organizations is an applied science because the resulting knowledge is relevant to problem-solving in on- going institutions. Contributions to or- ganization theory come from many sources. Deductive and inductive re- search in a variety of disciplines provide a theoretical base of propositions which are useful for understanding organizations and for managing them. Experience gained in management practice is also an important input to organization theory. In short, management is based on the body of knowledge generated by practical experience *and* eclectic scientific research concerning organizations. The body of knowledge developed through theory and research should be translatable into more effective organizational design and managerial practices.

Do systems concepts and contingency views provide a panacea for solving problems in organizations? The answer is an emphatic *no;* this approach does not provide "ten easy steps" to success in management. Such cookbook approaches, while seemingly applicable and easy to grasp, are usually shortsighted, narrow in perspective, and superficial—in short, unrealistic. Fundamental ideas, such as systems concepts and contingency views, are more difficult to comprehend. However, they facilitate more thorough understanding of complex situations and increase the likelihood of appropriate action.

It is important to recognize that many managers have used and will continue to use a systems approach and contingency views intuitively and implicitly. Without much knowledge of the underlying body of organization theory, they have an intuitive "sense of the situation," are flexible diagnosticians, and adjust their actions and decisions accordingly. Thus, systems concepts and contingency views are not new. However, if this approach to organization theory and management practice can be made more explicit, we can facilitate better management and more effective organizations.

Practicing managers in business firms, hospitals, and government agencies continue to function on a day-to-day basis. Therefore, they must use whatever theory is available, they cannot wait for the *ultimate* body of knowledge (there is none!). Practitioners should be included in the search for new knowledge because they control access to an essential ingredient—organizational data—and they are the ones who ultimately put the theory to the test. Mutual understanding among managers, teachers, and researchers will facilitate the development of a relevant body of knowledge.

Simultaneously with the refinement of the body of knowledge, a concerted effort should be directed toward applying what we do know. We need ways of making systems and contingency views more usable. Without oversimplification, we need some relevant guidelines for practicing managers.

The general tenor of the contingency view is somewhere between simplistic, specific principles and complex, vague notions. It is a midrange concept which recognizes the complexity involved in managing modern organizations but uses patterns of relationships and/or configurations of subsystems in order to facilitate improved practice. The art of management depends on a reasonable success rate for actions in a probabilistic environment. Our hope is that systems concepts and contingency views, while continually being refined by scientists/researchers/theorists, will also be made more applicable.

NOTE

1. An entire article could be devoted to a discussion of ingenious ways in which the term "systems approach" has been used in the literature pertinent to organization theory and management practice.

REFERENCES

1. Ackoff, Rusell L., "Towards a System of Systems Concepts," *Management Science* (July 1971).

2. Back, Kurt W., "Biological Models of Social Change," *American Sociological Review* (August 1971).

3. Barnard, Chester I., *The Functions of the Executive* (Cambridge, Mass.: Harvard University Press, 1938).

4. Berrien, F. Kenneth, *General and Social Systems* (New Brunswick, NJ: Rutgers University Press, 1968).

5. Blau, Peter M., "The Comparative Study of Organizations," *Industrial and Labor Relations Review* (April 1965).

6. Boulding, Kenneth E., "General Systems Theory: The Skeleton of Science," *Management Science* (April 1956).

7. Buckley, Walter, ed., *Modern Systems Research for the Behavioral Scientist* (Chicago: Aldine, 1968).

8. Burns, Tom, & G. M. Stalker, *The Management of Innovation* (London: Tavistock Publications, 1961).

9. Chamberlain, Neil W., *Enterprise and Environment: The Firm in Time and Place* (New York: McGraw-Hill, 1968).

10. Churchman, C. West, *The Systems Approach* (New York: Dell, 1968).

11. DeGreene, Kenyon, ed., *Systems Psychology* (New York: McGraw-Hill, 1970).

12. Deutsch, Karl W., "Toward a Cybernetic Model of Man and Society," in Walter Buckley, ed., *Modern Systems Research for the Behavioral Scientist* (Chicago: Aldine, 1968).

13. Easton, David, *A Systems Analysis of Political Life* (New York: Wiley, 1965).

14. Emery, F. E., & E. L. Trist, "Socio-technical Systems," in C. West Churchman and Michele Verhulst, eds., *Management Sciences: Models and Techniques* (New York: Pergamon Press, 1960).

15. Emshoff, James R., *Analysis of Behavioral Systems* (New York: Macmillan, 1971).

16. Gross, Bertram M., "The Coming General Systems Models of Social Systems," *Human Relations* (November 1967).

17. Hall, A. D., & R. E. Eagen, "Definition of System," *General Systems, Yearbook for the Society for the Advancement of General Systems Theory*, Vol. 1 (1956).

18. Kast, Fremont E., & James E. Rosenzweig, *Organization and Management Theory: A Systems Approach* (New York: McGraw-Hill, 1970).

19. Katz, Daniel, & Robert L. Kahn, *The Social Psychology of Organizations* (New York: Wiley, 1966).

20. Kuhn, Thomas S., *The Structure of Scientific Revolutions* (Chicago: University of Chicago Press, 1962).

21. Lorsch, Jay W., & Paul R. Lawrence, *Studies in Organizational Design* (Homewood, IL: Irwin-Dorsey, 1970).

22. Litterer, Joseph A., *Organizations: Structure and Behavior*, Vol. 1 (New York: Wiley, 1969).

23. ———, *Organizations: Systems, Control and Adaptation*, Vol. 2 (New York: Wiley, 1969).

24. Miller, E. J., & A. K. Rice, *Systems of Organizations* (London: Tavistock Publications, 1967).

25. Miller, James G., "Living Systems: Basic Concepts," *Behavioral Science* (July 1965).

26. Miller, Robert F., "The New Science of Administration in the USSR," *Administrative Science Quarterly* (September 1971).

27. Murray, Henry A., "Preparation for the Scaffold of a Comprehensive System," in Sigmund Koch, ed., *Psychology: A Study of a Science*, Vol. 3 (New York: McGraw-Hill, 1959).

28. Parsons, Talcott, *The Social System* (New York: Free Press, 1951).

29. Phillips, D.C., "Systems Theory—A Discredited Philosophy," in Peter P. Schoderbek, *Management Systems* (New York: Wiley, 1971).

30. Rapoport, Anatol, & William J. Horvath, "Thoughts on Organization Theory," in Walter Buckley, ed., *Modern Systems Research for the Behavioral Scientist* (Chicago: Aldine, 1968).

31. Rice, A. K., *The Modern University* (London: Tavistock Publications, 1970).

32. Schein, Edgar, *Organizational Psychology*, rev. ed. (Englewood Cliffs, NJ: Prentice-Hall, 1970).

33. Scott, William G., "Organization Theory: An Overview and an Appraisal," *Academy of Management Journal* (April 1961).

34. Silverman, David, *The Theory of Organizations* (New York: Basic Books, 1971).

35. Simon, Herbert A., "The Architecture of Complexity," in Joseph A. Litterer, *Organizations: Systems, Control and Adaptation*, Vol. 2 (New York: Wiley, 1969).

36. Springer, Michael, "Social Indicators, Reports, and Accounts: Toward the Management of Society," *The Annals of the American Academy of Political and Social Science* (March 1970).

37. Terreberry, Shirley, "The Evolution of Organizational Environments," *Administrative Science Quarterly* (March 1968).

38. Thompson, James D., *Organizations in Action* (New York: McGraw-Hill, 1967).

39. von Bertalanffy, Ludwig, *General System Theory* (New York: George Brazillet, 1968).

40. ———, "The Theory of Open Systems in Physics and Biology," *Science* (January 13, 1950).

41. Yuchtman, Ephraim, & Stanley E. Seashore, "A System Resource Approach to Organizational Effectiveness," *American Sociological Review* (December 1967).

27

The Population Ecology of Organizations*

Michael T. Hannan & John Freeman

I. INTRODUCTION

Analysis of the effects of environment on organizational structure has moved to a central place in organizations theory and research in recent years. This shift has opened a number of exciting possibilities. As yet nothing like the full promise of the shift has been realized. We believe that the lack of development is due in part to a failure to bring ecological models to bear on questions that are preeminently ecological. We argue for a reformulation of the problem in population ecology terms.

Although there is a wide variety of ecological perspectives, they all focus on selection. . . . The bulk of the literature on organizations subscribes to a different view, which we call the adaptation perspective.[1] According to the adaptation perspective, subunits of the organization, usually managers or dominant coalitions, scan the relevant environment for opportunities and threats, formulate strategic responses, and adjust organizational structure appropriately.

The adaptation perspective is seen most clearly in the literature on management. Contributors to it usually assume a hierarchy of authority and control that

locates decisions concerning the organization as a whole at the top. It follows, then, that organizations are affected by their environments according to the ways in which managers or leaders formulate strategies, make decisions, and implement them. Particularly successful managers are able either to buffer their organizations from environmental disturbances or to arrange smooth adjustments that require minimal disruption of organizational structure. . . .

Clearly, leaders of organizations do formulate strategies and organizations do adapt to environmental contingencies. As a result at least some of the relationship between structure and environment must reflect adaptive behavior or learning. But there is no reason to presume that the great structural variability among organizations reflects only or even primarily adaptation.

There are a number of obvious limitations on the ability of organizations to adapt. That is, there are a number of processes that generate structural inertia. The stronger the pressures, the lower the organizations' adaptive flexibility and the more likely that the logic of environmental selection is appropriate. As a consequence, the issue of structural inertia is central to the choice between adaptation and selection models. . . .

Inertial pressures arise from both internal structural arrangements and environmental constraints. A minimal list of the constraints arising from internal considerations follows.

* This research was supported in part by grants from the National Science Foundation (GS-32065) and the Spencer Foundation. Helpful comments were provided by Amos Hawley, François Nielsen, John Meyer, Marshall Meyer, Jeffrey Pfeffer, and Howard Aldrich.

Source: Michael T. Hannan and John Freeman, "The Population Ecology of Organizations," *American Journal of Sociology,* 82:5, pp. 929–964. Copyright © 1977 The University of Chicago. Reprinted with permission.

1. An organization's investment in plant, equipment, and specialized personnel constitutes assets that are not easily transferable to other tasks or functions. . . .

2. Organizational decision makers also face constraints on the information they receive. Much of what we know about the flow of information through organizational structures tells us that leaders do not obtain anything close to full information on activities within the organization and environmental contingencies facing the subunits.

3. Internal political constraints are even more important. When organizations alter structure, political equilibria are disturbed. As long as the pool of resources is fixed, structural change almost always involves redistribution of resources across subunits. Such redistribution upsets the prevailing system of exchange among subunits (or subunit leaders). So at least some subunits are likely to resist any proposed reorganization. Moreover, the benefits of structural reorganization are likely to be both generalized (designed to benefit the organization as a whole) and long-run. Any negative political response will tend to generate short-run costs that are high enough that organizational leaders will forego the planned reorganization. . . .

4. Finally, organizations face constraints generated by their own history. Once standards of procedure and the allocation of tasks and authority have become the subject of normative agreement, the costs of change are greatly increased. Normative agreements constrain adaptation in at least two ways. First, they provide a justification and an organizing principle for those elements that wish to resist reorganization (i.e., they can resist in terms of a shared principle). Second, normative agreements preclude the serious consideration of many alternative responses. For exam-

ple, few research-oriented universities seriously consider adapting to declining enrollments by eliminating the teaching function. To entertain this option would be to challenge central organizational norms.[2]

The external pressures toward inertia seem to be at least as strong. They include at least the following factors.

1. Legal and fiscal barriers to entry and exit from markets (broadly defined) are numerous. Discussions of organizational behavior typically emphasize barriers to entry (state licensed monopoly positions, etc.). Barriers to exit are equally interesting. There are an increasing number of instances in which political decisions prevent firms from abandoning certain activities. All such constraints on entry and exit limit the breadth of adaptation possibilities.

2. Internal constraints upon the availability of information are paralleled by external constraints. The acquisition of information about relevant environments is costly particularly in turbulent situations where the information is most essential. In addition, the type of specialists employed by the organization constrains both the nature of the information it is likely to obtain (see Granovetter 1973) and the kind of specialized information it can process and utilize.

3. Legitimacy constraints also emanate from the environment. Any legitimacy an organization has been able to generate constitutes an asset in manipulating the environment. To the extent that adaptation (e.g., eliminating undergraduate instruction in public universities) violates the legitimacy claims, it incurs considerable costs. So external legitimacy considerations also tend to limit adaptation.

4. Finally, there is the collective rationality problem. One of the most dif-

ficult issues in contemporary economics concerns general equilibria. If one can find an optimal strategy for some individual buyer or seller in a competitive market, it does not necessarily follow that there is a general equilibrium once all players start trading. More generally, it is difficult to establish that a strategy that is rational for a single decision maker will be rational if adopted by a large number of decision makers. . . . We should not presume that a course of action that is adaptive for a single organization facing some changing environment will be adaptive for many competing organizations adopting a similar strategy.

A number of these inertial pressures can be accommodated within the adaptation framework. But to do so greatly limits the scope of one's investigation. We argue that in order to deal with the various inertial pressures the adaptation perspective must be supplemented with a selection orientation.

We consider first two broad issues that are preliminary to ecological modeling. The first concerns appropriate units of analysis. Typical analyses of the relation of organizations to environments take the point of view of a single organization facing an environment. We argue for an explicit focus on populations of organizations. The second broad issue concerns the applicability of population ecology models to the study of human social organization. Our substantive proposal begins with Hawley's (1950, 1968) classic statement on human ecology. We seek to extend Hawley's work in two ways: by using explicit competition models to specify the process producing isomorphism between organizational structure and environmental demands, and by using niche theory to extend the problem to dynamic environments. We argue that Hawley's perspective, modified and extended in these ways, serves as a useful

starting point for population ecology theories of organizations.

II. POPULATION THINKING IN THE STUDY OF ORGANIZATION-ENVIRONMENT RELATIONS

. . . The comparison of unit choice facing the organizational analyst with that facing the bioecologist is instructive. To oversimplify somewhat, ecological analysis is conducted at three levels: individual, population, and community. Events at one level almost always have consequences at other levels. Despite this interdependence, population events cannot be reduced to individual events (since individuals do not reflect the full genetic variability of the population) and community events cannot be simply reduced to population events. Both the latter employ a population perspective which is not appropriate at the individual level.

The situation faced by the organizations analyst is more complex. Instead of three levels of analysis, he faces at least five: (1) members, (2) subunits, (3) individual organizations, (4) populations of organizations, and (5) communities of (populations of) organizations. Levels 3-5 can be seen as corresponding to the three levels discussed for general ecology, with the individual organization taking the place of the individual organism. The added complexity arises because organizations are more nearly decomposable into constituent parts than are organisms. Individual members and subunits may move from organization to organization in a manner which has no parallel in nonhuman organization.

Instances of theory and research dealing with the effects of environments on organizations are found at all five levels. . . . But, the most common focus is on the organization and its environment. In fact, this choice is so widespread that there appears to be a tacit understanding that individual organizations are the appropriate units for the study of organization-environment relations.

We argue for a parallel development of theory and research at the population (and, ultimately, the community) level. . . . Unfortunately, identifying a population of organizations is no simple matter. The ecological approach suggests that one focus on common fate with respect to environmental variations. Since all organizations are distinctive, no two are affected identically by any given exogenous shock. Nevertheless, we can identify classes of organizations which are relatively homogenous in terms of environmental vulnerability. . . .

If we are to follow the lead of population biologists, we must identify an analogue to the biologist's notion of species. Various species are defined ultimately in terms of genetic structure. As Monod (1971) indicates, it is useful to think of genetic content of any species as a blueprint. The blueprint contains the rules for transforming energy into structure. Consequently all of the adaptive capacity of a species is summarized in the blueprint. If we are to identify a species analogue for organizations, we must search for such blueprints. These will consist of rules or procedures for obtaining and acting upon inputs in order to produce an organizational product or response.

The type of blueprint one identifies depends on substantive concerns. . . . For us, an organizational form is a blueprint for organizational action, for transforming inputs into outputs. The blueprint can usually be inferred, albeit in somewhat different ways, by examining any of the following: (1) the formal structure of the organization in the narrow sense—tables of organization, written rules of operation, etc.; (2) the patterns of activity within the organization—what actually gets done by whom; or (3) the normative order—the ways of organizing that are defined as right and proper by both members and relevant sectors of the environment.

To complete the species analogue, we must search for qualitative differences among forms. It seems most likely that we will find such differences in the first and third areas listed above, formal structure and normative order. The latter offers particularly intriguing possibilities. Whenever the history of an organization, its politics, and its social structure are encoded in a normative claim (e.g., professionalization and collegial authority), one can use these claims to identify forms and define populations for research. . . .

Just as the organizational analyst must choose a unit of analysis, so must he choose a system for study. Given a systems definition, a population of organizations consists of all the organizations within a particular boundary that have a common form. . . . We suggest that a population ecology of organizations must seek to understand the distributions of organizations across environmental conditions and the limitations on organizational structures in different environments, and more generally seek to answer the question, Why are there so many kinds of organizations?

III. DISCONTINUITIES IN ECOLOGICAL ANALYSIS

Utilization of models from ecology in the study of organizations poses a number of analytic challenges involving differences between human and nonhuman organizations with regard to their essential ingredients. Consider, first, the nongenetic transmission of information. Biological analyses are greatly simplified by the fact that most useful information concerning adaptation to the environment (which information we call structure) is transmitted genetically. Genetic processes are so nearly invariant that extreme continuity in structure is the rule. . . . The extreme structural invariance of species greatly simplifies the problem of delimiting and identifying populations. . . . When a population with given properties increases its net reproduction rate following an environmental change, it follows that it is being selected for. . . .

Human social organization presumably reflects a greater degree of learning or adaptation. As a result it is more difficult to define fitness in a precise way. Under at least some conditions, organizations may undergo such extreme structural change that they shift from one form to another. As a result, extreme adaptation may give rise to observed changes that mimic selection. This is particularly problematic when the various organizational forms are similar on many dimensions. . . .

Many theorists have asserted that structural change attends growth; in other words, a single organization cannot grow indefinitely and still maintain its original form. For instance, a mouse could not possibly maintain the same proportion of body weight to skeletal structure while growing as big as a house. It would neither look like a mouse nor operate physiologically like a mouse. Boulding (1953) and Haire (1959) argue that the same is true for organizations. . . . If it is true that organizational form changes with size, selection mechanisms may indeed operate with regard to the size distribution. When big organizations prevail it may be useful to view this as a special case of selection, in which the movement from "small form" to "large form" is theoretically indistinguishable from the dissolution

("death") of small organizations and their replacement by (the "birth" of) large organizations. . . .

IV. THE PRINCIPLE OF ISOMORPHISM

In the best developed statement of the principles of human ecology, Hawley (1968) answers the question of why there are so many kinds of organizations. According to Hawley, the diversity of organizational forms is isomorphic to the diversity of environments. In each distinguishable environmental configuration one finds, in equilibrium, only that organizational form optimally adapted to the demands of the environment. Each unit experiences constraints which force it to resemble other units with the same set of constraints. . . .

While the proposition seems completely sound from an ecological perspective, it does not address a number of interesting considerations. There are at least two respects in which the isomorphism formulation must be modified and extended if it is to provide satisfactory answers to the question posed. The first modification concerns the mechanism or mechanisms responsible for equilibrium. In this respect, the principle of isomorphism must be supplemented by a criterion of selection and a competition theory. The second modification deals with the fact that the principle of isomorphism neither speaks to issues of optimum adaptation to changing environments nor recognizes that populations of organizations often face multiple environments which impose somewhat inconsistent demands. . . .

V. COMPETITION THEORY

. . . Optimization raises two issues: Who is optimizing, and what is being optimized? It is quite commonly held, as in the theory of the firm, that organizational decision makers optimize profit over sets of organizational actions. From a population ecology perspective, it is the environment which optimizes.[3] Whether or not individual organizations are consciously adapting, the environment selects out optimal combinations of organizations. So if there is a rationality involved, it is the "rationality" of natural selection. Organizational rationality and environmental rationality may coincide in the instance of firms in competitive markets. In this case, the optimal behavior of each firm is to maximize profit and the rule used by the environment (market, in this case) is to select out profit maximizers. . . .

A focus on selection invites an emphasis on competition. Organizational forms presumably fail to flourish in certain environmental circumstances because other forms successfully compete with them for essential resources. As long as the resources which sustain organizations are finite and populations have unlimited capacity to expand, competition must ensue.

Hawley (1950, pp. 201-3) following Durkheim (1947) among others, places a heavy emphasis on competition as a determinant of patterns of social organization. . . . In Hawley's model, competition processes typically involve four stages: (1) demand for resources exceeds supply; (2) competitors become more similar as standard conditions of competition bring forth a uniform response; (3) selection eliminates the weakest competitors; and (4) deposed competitors differentiate either territorially or functionally, yielding a more complex division of labor. . . .

The first step in constructing an ecological model of competition is to state the nature of the population growth process. At a minimum we wish the model to incorporate the idea that resources available at any moment for each form of organization are finite and fixed. . . . We also wish to incorporate the view that the rate at which units are added to populations of organizations depends on how much of the fixed capacity has already been exhausted. The greater the unexhausted capacity in an environment, the faster should be the rate of growth of populations of organizations. But the rate at which populations of organizations can expand into unused capacity varies among forms of organization. So there are two distinctive ecological considerations: the capacity of the environment to support forms of organization and the rate at which the populations grow (or decline) when the environmental support changes. . . .

One can show that when growth in population is constrained only by resource availability, the number of distinct resources sets an upper bound on diversity in the system.[4] Even more generally, the upper bound on diversity is equal to the number of distinct resources plus the number of additional constraints on growth (Levin 1970). . . .

The increasingly important role of the state in regulating economic and social action provides numerous opportunities for analyzing the impact of changes in constraint structures on the diversity of organizational forms. Consider the impact of licensing laws, minimum wage, health, and safety legislation, affirmative action, and other regulations on organizational action. When such regulations are applied to the full range of organizations in broad areas of activity they undoubtedly alter the size distributions of organizations. Most often they select out the smallest organizations. But it is not difficult to imagine situations in which medium-sized organizations (more precisely, those with some minimum level of complexity) would be more adversely affected. Besides altering size distributions, such regulations undoubtedly affect the diversity of organizational arrangements in other ways. Here one could analyze the impact of state action on the diversity of accounting systems within industries, curricula within universities, departmental structures within hospitals, etc. In each case it would be essential to determine whether the newly imposed constraint replaced lower level constraints, in which case diversity should decline, or whether the constraint cumulated with the existing constraints in which case organizational diversity would be likely to increase. . . .

When large-sized organizations emerge they pose a competitive threat to medium-sized but hardly any threat to small organizations. In fact, the rise of large organizations may increase the survival chances of small ones in a manner not anticipated in the classical model. When the large organizations enter, those in the middle of the size distribution are trapped. Whatever strategy they adopt to fight off the challenge of the larger form makes them more vulnerable in competition with small organizations and vice versa. That is, at least in a stable environment the two ends of the size distribution ought to outcompete the middle. . . .

VI. NICHE THEORY

. . . Intuition suggests that isomorphism holds as a good approximation only in stable environments. Faced with unstable environments, organizations ought to develop a generalist structure that is not optimally adapted to any single environmental configuration but is optimal over an entire set of configurations. In other words, we ought to find specialized organizations in stable and certain environments and generalist organizations in unstable and uncertain environments. Whether or not this simple proposition holds for social organiza-

tions, only empirical research will tell. However, a variety of population ecology models suggests that it is too simplistic. . . .

The concept of "niche," initially borrowed by biologists from early social science, plays a central role in ecological theory. . . . The (realized) niche of a population is defined as that area in constraint space (the space whose dimensions are levels of resources, etc.) in which the population outcompetes all other local populations. The niche, then, consists of all those combinations of resource levels at which the population can survive and reproduce itself.

Each population occupies a distinct niche. For present purposes it suffices to consider cases where pairs of populations differ with respect to a single environmental dimension, E, and are alike with respect to all others. Then relative competitive positions can be simply summarized as in Figure 1. As we have drawn this figure, one population, A, occupies a very broad niche, whereas the other, B, has concentrated its fitness, denoted W, on a very narrow band of environmental variation. This distinction, which is usually referred to as generalism versus specialism, is crucial to biological ecology and to a population ecology of organizations.

In essence, the distinction between specialism and generalism refers to whether a population of organizations flourishes because it maximizes its exploitation of the environment and accepts the risk of having that environment change or because it accepts a lower level of exploitation in return for greater security. Whether or not the equilibrium distribution of organizational forms is dominated by the specialist depends, as we will see, on the shape of the fitness sets and on properties of the environment.

Part of the efficiency resulting from specialism is derived from the lower re-

FIGURE 1 • FITNESS FUNCTIONS (NICHES) FOR SPECIALISTS
AND GENERALISTS

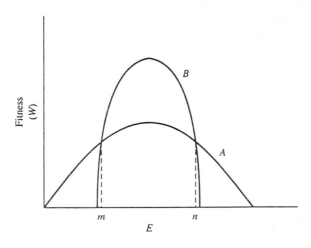

quirements for excess capacity. Given some uncertainty, most organizations maintain some excess capacity to insure the reliability of performance. In a rapidly changing environment, the definition of excess capacity is likely to change frequently. What is used today may become excess tomorrow, and what is excess today may be crucial tomorrow. . . .

The importance of excess capacity is not completely bound up with the issue of how much excess capacity will be maintained. It also involves the manner in which it is used. Organizations may insure reliable performance by creating specialized units, as Thompson (1967) suggests, or they may allocate excess capacity to organizational roles, by employing personnel with skills and abilities which exceed the routine requirements of their jobs. . . .

Excess capacity may also be allocated to the development and maintenance of procedural systems. When the certainty of a given environmental state is high, organizational operations should be routine, and coordination can be accomplished by formalized rules and the investment of resources in training incumbents to follow those formalized procedures. . . . However, when certainty is low, organizational operations are less routine. Under these circumstances, a greater allocation of resources to develop and maintain procedural systems is counterproductive and optimal organizational forms will allocate resources to less formalized systems capable of more innovative responses (e.g., committees and teams). In this case, excess capacity is represented by the increased time it takes such structures to make decisions and by increased coordination costs.

The point here is that populations of organizational forms will be selected for or against depending upon the amount of excess capacity they maintain and how they allocate it. . . . Under a given set of environmental circumstances the fundamental ecological question is: which forms thrive and which forms disappear.

Generalism may be observed in a population of organizations, then, either in its reliance upon a wide variety of resources simultaneously or in its maintenance of excess capacity at any given time. This excess capacity allows such organizations to change in order to take advantage of resources which become more readily available. Corporations which maintain an unusually large proportion of their total assets in fluid form ("slack," in terms of theory of the firm; Penrose 1959; Cyert and March 1963) are generalizing. In either case, generalism is costly. Under stable environmental circumstances, generalists will be outcompeted by specialists. And at any given point in time, a static analysis will reveal excess capacity. An implication—shifting our focus to individual generalists—is that outside agents will often mistake excess capacity for waste. . . .

Variation is fine-grained when typical durations in states are short relative to the lifetime of organizations. Otherwise, the environment is said to be coarse-grained. Demand for products or services is often characterized by fine-grained variation whereas changes in legal structures are more typically coarse-grained.

The essential difference between two types of environmental variation is the cost of suboptimal strategies. The problem of ecological adaptation can be considered a game of chance in which the population chooses a strategy (specialism or generalism) and then the environment chooses an outcome (by, say, flipping a coin). If the environment "comes up" in a state favorable to the organizational form, it prospers; otherwise, it declines. However, if the variation is fine-grained (durations are short), each population of organizations experiences a great many trials and environment is experienced as an average. When variation is coarse-grained, however, the period of decline stemming from a wrong choice may exceed the organizational

capacity to sustain itself under unfavorable conditions. . . .

Consider first the cases in which the environment is stable (i.e., $p = 1$). Not surprisingly, specialism is optimal. The results for unstable environments diverge. When the fitness set is convex (i.e., the demands of the different environmental states are similar and/or complementary), generalism is optimal. But when the environmental demands differ (and the fitness set is concave), specialism is optimal. This is not as strange a result as it first appears. When the environment changes rapidly among quite different states, the cost of generalism is high. Since the demands in different states are dissimilar, considerable structural management is required of generalists. But since the environment changes rapidly, these organizations will spend most of their time and energies adjusting structure. It is apparently better under such conditions to adopt a specialized structure and "ride out" the adverse environments.

The case of coarse-grained environments is somewhat more complex. Our intuitive understanding is that since the duration of an environmental state is long, maladaptation ought to be given greater weight. That is, the costs of maladaptation greatly outweigh any advantage incurred by the correct choice. . . .

The combination of coarse-grained environmental variation and concave fitness sets raises a further possibility. The optimal adaptation in the face of environmental uncertainty possesses fairly low levels of fitness in either state. It seems clear that there must be a better solution. . . .

Coarse-grained and uncertain variation favors a distinct form of generalism: polymorphism. We do not have to search very far to find an analogous outcome. Organizations may federate in such a way that supraorganizations consisting of heterogeneous collections of specialist organizations pool resources. When the environment is uncertain and coarse-grained and subunits difficult to set up and tear down, the costs of maintaining the unwieldy structure imposed by federation may be more than offset by the fact that at least a portion of the amalgamated organization will do well no matter what the state of the environment. In terms of the model suggested above there are no other situations in which such federated organizations have a competitive advantage. And even in this case, the only time during which they have such an advantage is when coarse-grained variation is uncertain. . . .

Much more can be said concerning applications of niche theory to organization-environment relations. We have focused on a simple version highlighting the interplay between competition and environmental variation in the determination of optimal adaptive structure in order to show that the principle of isomorphism needs considerable expansion to deal with multiple environmental outcomes and their associated uncertainty. The literature in ecology to which we have made reference is growing exponentially at the moment and new results and models are appearing monthly. The products of these developments provide students of organizations with a rich potential for the study of organization-environment relations. . . .

VII. DISCUSSION

Our aim in this paper has been to move toward an application of modern population ecology theory to the study of organization-environment relations. For us, the central question is, why are there so many kinds of organizations? Phrasing the question in this way opens the possibility of applying a rich variety of formal models to the analysis of the effects of environmental variations on organizational structure.

We begin with Hawley's classic formulation of human ecology. However, we recognize that ecological theory has progressed enormously since sociologists last systematically applied ideas from bioecology to social organization. Nonetheless, Hawley's theoretical perspective remains a very useful point of departure. In particular we concentrate on the principle of isomorphism. This principle asserts that there is a one-to-one correspondence between structural elements of social organization and those units that mediate flows of essential resources into the system. It explains the variations in organizational forms in equilibrium. But any observed isomorphism can arise from purposeful adaptation of organizations to the common constraints they face or because nonisomorphic organizations are selected against. Surely both processes are a work in most social systems. We believe that the organizations literature has emphasized the former to the exclusion of the latter.

We suspect that careful empirical research will reveal that for wide classes of organizations there are very strong inertial pressures on structure arising both from internal arrangements (e.g., internal politics) and the environment (e.g., public legitimation of organizational activity). To claim otherwise is to ignore the most obvious feature of organizational life. Failing churches do not become retail stores; nor do firms transform themselves into churches. Even within broad areas of organizational action, such as higher education and labor union activity, there appear to be substantial obstacles to fundamental structural change. Research is needed on this issue. . . .

We suggest that the concrete implication of generalism for organizations is the accumulation and retention of varieties of excess capacity. To retain the flexibility of structure required for adaptation to different environmental outcomes requires that some capacities be held in reserve and not committed to action. Generalists will always be outperformed by specialists who, with the same levels of resources, happen to have hit upon their optimal environment. Consequently, in any cross-section the generalists will appear inefficient because excess capacity will often be judged waste. Nonetheless, organizational slack is a pervasive feature of many types of organizations. The question then arises: what types of environments favor generalists? Answering this question comprehensively takes one a long way toward understanding the dynamic of organization-environment relations. . . .

We have identified some of the leading conceptual and methodological obstacles to applying population ecology models to the study of organization-environment relations. We pointed to differences between human and nonhuman social organization in terms of mechanisms of structural invariance and structural change, associated problems of delimiting populations of organizations, and difficulties in defining fitness for populations of expandable units. In each case we have merely sketched the issues and proposed short-run simplifications which would facilitate the application of existing models. Clearly, each issue deserves careful scrutiny. . . .

We doubt that many readers will dispute the contention that failure rates are high for new and/or small organizations. However, much of the sociological literature and virtually all of the critical literature on large organizations tacitly accepts the view that such organizations are not subject to strong selection pressures. While we do not yet have the empirical data to judge this hypothesis,

we can make several comments. First, we do not dispute that the largest organizations individually and collectively exercise strong dominance over most of the organizations that constitute their environments. But it does not follow from the observation that such organizations are strong in any one period that they will be strong in every period. Thus, it is interesting to know how firmly embedded are the largest and most powerful organizations. Consider the so-called Fortune 500, the largest publicly owned industrial firms in the United States. We contrasted the lists for 1955 and 1975 (adjusting for pure name changes). Of those on the list in 1955, only 268 (53.6%) were still listed in 1975. One hundred twenty-two had disappeared through merger, 109 had slipped off the "500," and one (a firm specializing in Cuban sugar!) had been liquidated. The number whose relative sales growth caused them to be dropped from the list is quite impressive in that the large number of mergers had opened many slots on the list. So we see that, whereas actual liquidation was rare for the largest industrial firms in the United States over a 20-year period, there was a good deal of volatility with regard to position in this pseudodominance structure because of both mergers and slipping sales.[5]

Second, the choice of time perspective is important. Even the largest and most powerful organizations fail to survive over long periods. For example, of the thousands of firms in business in the United States during the Revolution, only 13 survive as autonomous firms and seven as recognizable divisions of firms (*Nation's Business* 1976). Presumably one needs a longer time perspective to study the population ecology of the largest and most dominant organizations.

Third, studying small organizations is not such a bad idea. The sociological literature has concentrated on the largest organizations for obvious design reasons. But, if inertial pressures on certain aspects of structure are strong enough, intense selection among small organizations may greatly constrain the variety observable among large organizations. At least some elements of structure change with size (as we argued in Section III) and the pressure toward inertia should not be overemphasized. Nonetheless we see much value in studies of the organizational life cycle that would inform us as to which aspects of structure get locked in during which phases of the cycle. For example, we conjecture that a critical period is that during which the organization grows beyond the control of a single owner/manager. At this time the manner in which authority is delegated, if at all, seems likely to have a lasting impact on organizational structure. This is the period during which an organization becomes less an extension of one or a few dominant individuals and more an organization per se with a life of its own. If the selection pressures at this point are as intense as anecdotal evidence suggests they are, selection models will prove very useful in accounting for the varieties of forms among the whole range of organizations. . . .

Fourth, we must consider what one anonymous reader, caught up in the spirit of our paper, called the anti-eugenic actions of the state in saving firms such as Lockheed from failure. This is a dramatic instance of the way in which large dominant organizations can create linkages with other large and powerful ones so as to reduce selection pressures. If such moves are effective, they alter the pattern of selection. In our view the selection pressure is bumped up to a higher level. So instead of individual organizations failing, entire networks fail. The general consequence of a large number of linkages of this sort is an increase

in the instability of the entire system (Simon 1962, 1973; May 1973), and therefore we should see boom and bust cycles of organizational outcomes. Selection models retain relevance, then, even when the systems of organizations are tightly coupled (see Hannan 1976).

Finally, some readers of earlier drafts have (some approvingly, some disapprovingly) treated our arguments as metaphoric. This is not what we intend. In a fundamental sense all theoretical activity involves metaphoric activity (although admittedly the term "analogue" comes closer than does "metaphor"). The use of metaphors or analogues enters into the formulation of "if . . . then" statements. For example, certain molecular genetic models draw an analogy between DNA surfaces and crystal structures. The latter have simple well-behaved geometric structures amenable to strong topological (mathematical) analysis. No one argues that DNA proteins are crystals; but to the extent that their surfaces have certain crystal-like properties, the mathematical model used to analyze crystals will shed light on the genetic structure. This is, as we understand it, the general strategy of model building. . . .

Instead of applying biological laws to human social organization, we advocate the application of population ecology theories. As we have indicated at a number of points, these theories are quite general and must be modified for any concrete application (sociological *or* biological). Our purpose has been twofold. First, we sketched some of the alterations in perspective required if population ecology theories are to be applied to the study of organizations. Second, we wished to stimulate a reopening of the lines of communication between sociology and ecology. It is ironic that Hawley's (1944, p. 399) diagnosis of some 30 years ago remains apt today: "Probably most of the difficulties which beset human ecology may be traced to the isolation of the subject from the mainstream of ecological thought."

NOTES

1. There is a subtle relationship between selection and adaptation. Adaptive learning for individuals usually consists of selection among behavioral responses. Adaptation for a population involves selection among types of members. More generally, processes involving selection can usually be recast at a higher level of analysis as adaptation processes. However, once the unit of analysis is chosen there is no ambiguity in distinguishing selection from adaptation. Organizations often adapt to environmental conditions in concert and this suggests a systems effect. Though few theorists would deny the existence of such systems effects, most do not make them a subject of central concern. It is important to notice that, from the point of view embraced by sociologists whose interests focus on the broader social system, selection in favor of organizations with one set of properties to the disfavor of those with others is often an adaptive process. Societies and communities which consist in part of formal organizations adapt partly through processes that adjust the mixture of various kinds of organizations found within them. Whereas a complete theory of organization and environment would have to consider both adaptation and selection, recognizing that they are complementary processes, our purpose here is to show what can be learned from studying selection alone (see Aldrich and Pfeffer [1976] for a synthetic review of the literature fcusing on these different perspectives).

2. Meyer's (1970) discussion of an organization's charter adds further support to the argument that normative agreements arrived at early in an organization's history constrain greatly the organization's range of adaptation to environmental constraints.

3. In biological applications, one assumes that power (in the physical sense) is optimized by natural selection in accordance with the so-called Darwin-Lotka law. For the case of human social organization, one might argue that selection optimizes the utilization of a specific set of resources including but not restricted to the power and the time of members.

4. A more precise statement of the theorem is that no stable equilibrium exists for a system of M competitors and $N < M$ resources (MacArthur and Levins 1964).

5. From at least some perspectives, mergers can be viewed as changes in form. This will almost certainly be the case when the organizations merged have very different structures. These data also indicate a strong selective advantage for a conglomerate form of industrial organization.

REFERENCES

Aldrich, Howard E., & Jeffrey Pfeffer. 1976. "Environments of Organizations." *Annual Review of Sociology* 2: 79–105.

Aldrich, Howard E., & Albert J. Reiss. 1976. "Continuities in the Study of Ecological Succession: Changes in the Race Composition of Neighborhoods and Their Businesses." *American Journal of Sociology* 81 (January): 846–866.

Blau, Peter M. 1972. "Interdependence and Hierarchy in Organizations." *Social Science Research* 1 (April): 1–24.

Blau, Peter M., & Richard A. Schoenherr. 1971. *The Structure of Organizations.* New York: Basic.

Blau, Peter M., & W. Richard Scott. 1962. *Formal Organizations.* San Francisco: Chandler.

Bolton, J. E. 1971. *Small Firms.* Report of the Committee of Inquiry on Small Firms. London: Her Majesty's Stationery Office.

Boulding, Kenneth. 1953. "Toward a General Theory of Growth." *Canadian Journal of Economics and Political Science* 19: 326–340.

Burns, Tom, & G. M. Stalker. 1961. *The Management of Innovation.* London: Tavistock.

Caplow, Theodore. 1957. "Organizational Size." *Administrative Science Quarterly* 1(March): 484–505.

Churchill, Betty C. 1955. "Age and Life Expectancy of Business Firms." *Survey of Current Business* 35 (December): 15–19.

Crozier, Michel. 1964. *The Bureaucratic Phenomenon.* Chicago: University of Chicago Press.

Cyert, Richard M., & James G. March. 1963. *A Behavioral Theory of the Firm.* Englewood Cliffs, N.J.: Prentice-Hall.

Downs, Anthony. 1967. *Inside Bureaucracy.* Boston: Little, Brown.

Durkheim, E. 1947. *The Division of Labor in Society*. Translated by G. Simpson. Glencoe, Ill.: Free Press.

Elton, C. 1927. *Animal Ecology*. London: Sidgwick & Jackson.

Freeman, John. 1975. "The Unit Problem in Organizational Research." Presented at the annual meeting of the American Sociological Association, San Francisco.

Freeman, John , & Jack Brittain. 1977. "Union Merger Processes and Industrial Environments." *Industrial Relations*, in press.

Friedman, Milton. 1953. *Essays on Positive Economics*. Chicago: University of Chicago Press.

Gause, G. F. 1934. *The Struggle for Existence*. Baltimore: Williams & Wilkins.

Graicunas, V. A. 1933. "Relationship in Organizations." *Bulletin of the International Management Institute* (March), pp. 183–187.

Granovetter, Mark S. 1973. "The Strength of Weak Ties." *American Journal of Sociology* 78 (May): 1360–1380.

Haire, Mason. 1959. "Biological Models and Empirical Histories of the Growth of Organizations." Pp. 272–306 in *Modern Organization Theory*, edited by Mason Haire. New York: Wiley.

Hannan, Michael T. 1975. "The Dynamics of Ethnic Boundaries." Unpublished.

———. 1976. "Modeling Stability and Complexity in Networks of Organizations." Presented at the annual meeting of the American Sociological Association, New York.

Hannan, Michael T. & John Freeman. 1974. "Environment and the Structure of Organizations." Presented at the annual meeting of the American Sociological Association, Montreal.

Hawley, Amos H. 1944. "Ecology and Human Ecology." *Social Forces* 22 (May): 398-405.

———. 1950. *Human Ecology: A Theory of Community Structure*. New York: Ronald.

———. 1968. "Human Ecology." Pp. 328-337 in *International Encyclopedia of the Social Sciences*, edited by David L. Sills. New York: Macmillan.

Hollander, Edward O., ed. 1967. *The Future of Small Business*. New York: Praeger.

Hummon, Norman P., Patrick Doreian, & Klaus Teuter. 1975. "A Structural Control Model of Organizational Change." *American Sociological Review* 40 (December): 812–824.

Hutchinson, G. Evelyn. 1957. "Concluding Remarks." *Cold Spring Harbor Symposium on Quantitative Biology* 22:415–427.

———. 1959. "Homage to Santa Rosalia, or Why Are There So Many Kinds of Animals?" *American Naturalist* 93: 145–159.

Levin, Simon A. 1970. "Community Equilibrium and Stability: An Extension of the Competitive Exclusion Principle." *American Naturalist* 104 (September-October): 413–423.

Levine, Sol & Paul E. White. 1961. "Exchange as a Framework for the Study of Interorganizational Relationships." *Administrative Science Quarterly* 5 (March): 583–601.

Levins, Richard. 1962. "Theory of Fitness in a Heterogeneous Environment. I. The Fitness Set and Adaptive Function." *American Naturalist* 96 (November-December): 361–378.

———. 1968. *Evolution in Changing Environments*. Princeton, N.J.: Princeton University Press.

MacArthur, Robert H. 1972. *Geographical Ecology: Patterns in the Distribution of Species*. Princeton, N.J.: Princeton University Press.

MacArthur, Robert H., & Richard Levins. 1964. "Competition, Habitat Selection and Character Displacement in Patchy Environment." *Proceedings of the National Academy of Sciences* 51: 1207–1210.

March, James G., & Herbert Simon. 1958. *Organizations*. New York: Wiley.

Marschak, Jacob, & Roy Radner. 1972. *Economic Theory of Teams*. New Haven, Conn.: Yale University Press.

May, Robert M. 1973. *Stability and Complexity in Model Ecosystems*. Princeton, N.J.: Princeton University Press.

Meyer, John W. 1970. "The Charter: Conditions of Diffuse Socialization in Schools." Pp. 564–578 in *Social Processes and Social Structures*, edited by W. Richard Scott. New York: Holt, Rinehart & Winston.

Monod, Jacques. 1971. *Chance and Necessity*. New York: Vintage.

Nation's Business. 1976. "America's Oldest Companies." 64 (July): 36–37.

Nielsen, François, & Michael T. Hannan. 1977. "The Expansion of National Educational Systems: Tests of a Population Ecology Model." *American Sociological Review*, in press.

Parsons, Talcott. 1956. "Suggestions for a Sociological Approach to the Theory of Organizations, I." *Administrative Science Quarterly* 1 (March): 63–85.

Penrose, Edith T. 1959. *The Theory of the Growth of the Firm*. New York: Wiley.

Selznick, Philip. 1957. *Leadership in Administration*. New York: Row, Peterson.

Simon, Herbert A. 1962. "The Architecture of Complexity." *Proceedings of the American Philosophical Society* 106 (December): 467–482.

———. 1973. "The Organization of Complex Systems." Pp. 1-28 in *Hierarchy Theory: The Challenge of Complex Systems*, edited by H. Patee. New York: Braziller.

Simon, Herbert A., & C. P. Bonini. 1958. "The Size Distribution of Business Firms." *American Economic Review* 48 (September): 607–617.

Stinchcombe, Arthur L. 1959. "Bureaucratic and Craft Administration of Production." *Administrative Science Quarterly* 4 (June): 168–187.

———. 1965. "Social Structure and Organizations." Pp. 153-193 in *Handbook of Organiza-*

tions, edited by James G. March. Chicago: Rand McNally.

Templeton, Alan R., & Edward A. Rothman. 1974. "Evolution in Heterogenous Environments." *American Naturalist* 108 (July-August): 409–428.

Thompson, James D. 1967. *Organizations in Action*. New York: McGraw-Hill.

Turk, Herman. 1970. "Interorganizational Networks in Urban Society: Initial Perspectives and Comparative Research." *American Sociological Review* 35 (February): 1–19.

Whittaker, Robert N., & Simon Levin, eds. 1976. *Niche: Theory and Application*. Stroudsberg, Pa.: Dowden, Hutchinson & Ross.

Winter, Sidney G., Jr. 1964. "Economic 'Natural Selection' and the Theory of the Firm." *Yale Economic Essays* 4:224–272.

Zald, Mayer. 1970. "Political Economy: A Framework for Analysis." Pp. 221-261 in *Power in Organizations*, edited by M. N. Zald. Nashville, Tenn.: Vanderbilt University Press.

28

Theory of the Firm: Managerial Behavior, Agency Costs and Ownership Structure

Michael C. Jensen & William H. Meckling

1. INTRODUCTION AND SUMMARY

1.1. Motivation of the Paper: In this paper we draw on recent progress in the theory of (1) property rights, (2) agency, and (3) finance to develop a theory of ownership structure[1] for the firm. In addition to tying together elements of the theory of each of these three areas, our analysis casts new light on and has implications for a variety of issues in the professional and popular literature such as the definition of the firm, the "separation of ownership and control," the "social responsibility" of business, the definition of a "corporate objective function," the determination of an optimal capital structure, the specification of the content of credit agreements, the theory of organizations, and the supply side of the completeness of markets problem.

Our theory helps explain:

1. why an entrepreneur or manager in a firm which has a mixed financial

---

[1] We do not use the term "capital structure" because that term usually denotes the relative quantities of bonds, equity, warrants, trade credit, etc., which represent the liabilities of a firm. Our theory implies there is another important dimension to this problem—namely the relative amounts of ownership claims held by insiders (management) and outsiders (investors with no direct role in the management of the firm).

structure (containing both debt and outside equity claims) will choose a set of activities for the firm such that the total value of the firm is less than it would be if he were the sole owner and why this result is independent of whether the firm operates in monopolistic or competitive product or factor markets;

2. why his failure to maximize the value of the firm is perfectly consistent with efficiency;

3. why the sale of common stock is a viable source of capital even though managers do not literally maximize the value of the firm;

4. why debt was relied upon as a source of capital before debt financing offered any tax advantage relative to equity;

5. why preferred stock would be issued;

6. why accounting reports would be provided voluntarily to creditors and stockholders, and why independent auditors would be engaged by management to testify to the accuracy and correctness of such reports;

7. why lenders often place restrictions on the activities of firms to whom they lend, and why firms would themselves be led to suggest the imposition of such restrictions;

8. why some industries are characterized by owner-operated firms whose sole outside source of capital is borrowing;

9. why highly regulated industries such as public utilities or banks will have

Source: "Theory of the Firm: Managerial Behavior, Agency Costs and Ownership Structure," by Michael C. Jensen and William H. Meckling in *Journal of Financial Economics* 3 (1976) 305–360. Reprinted by permission.

higher debt equity ratios for equivalent levels of risk than the average non-regulated firm;

10. why security analysis can be socially productive even if it does not increase portfolio returns to investors.

1.2. Theory of the Firm: An Empty Box? While the literature of economics is replete with references to the "theory of the firm," the material generally subsumed under that heading is not a theory of the firm but actually a theory of markets in which firms are important actors. The firm is a "black box" operated so as to meet the relevant marginal conditions with respect to inputs and outputs, thereby maximizing profits, or more accurately, present value. Except for a few recent and tentative steps, however, we have no theory which explains how the conflicting objectives of the individual participants are brought into equilibrium so as to yield this result. The limitations of this black box view of the firm have been cited by Adam Smith and Alfred Marshall, among others. More recently, popular and professional debates over the "social responsibility" of corporations, the separation of ownership and control, and the rash of reviews of the literature on the "theory of the firm" have evidenced continuing concern with these issues.[2]

A number of major attempts have been made during recent years to construct a theory of the firm by substituting other models for profit or value maximization; each attempt motivated by a conviction that the latter is inadequate to explain managerial behavior in large corporations.[3] Some of these reformula-

tion attempts have rejected the fundamental principle of maximizing behavior as well as rejecting the more specific profit maximizing model. We retain the notion of maximizing behavior on the part of all individuals in the analysis to follow.[4]

1.3. Property Rights. An independent stream of research with important implications for the theory of the firm has been stimulated by the pioneering work of Coase, and extended by Alchian, Demsetz and others.[5] A comprehensive survey of this literature is given by Furubotn and Pejovich (1972). While the focus of this research has been "property rights,"[6] the subject matter encompassed is far broader than that term suggests. What is important for the prob-

these and other contributions are given by Machlup (1961) and Alchian (1965).

Simon (1955) developed a model of human choice incorporating information (search) and computational costs which also has important implications for the behavior of managers. Unfortunately, Simon's work has often been misinterpreted as a denial of maximizing behavior, and misused, especially in the marketing and behavioral science literature. His later use of the term "satisficing"[Simon (1959)] has undoubtedly contributed to this confusion because it suggests rejection of maximizing behavior rather than maximization subject to costs of information and of decision making.

[4] See Meckling (1976) for a discussion of the fundamental importance of the assumption of resourceful, evaluative, maximizing behavior on the part of individuals in the development of theory. Klein (1976) takes an approach similar to the one we embark on in this paper in his review of the theory of the firm and the law.

[5] See Coase (1937, 1959, 1960), Alchian (1965, 1968), Alchian and Kessel (1962), Demsetz (1967), Alchian and Demsetz (1972), Mortsen and Downs (1965), Silver and Auster (1969), and McManus (1975).

[6] Property rights are of course human rights, i.e., rights which are possessed by human beings. The introduction of the wholly false distinction between property rights and human rights in many policy discussions is surely one of the all time great semantic flim flams.

[2] Reviews of this literature are given by Peterson (1965), Alchian (1965, 1968), Machlup (1967), Shubik (1970), Cyert and Hedrick (1972), Branch (1973), Preston (1975).

[3] See Williamson (1964, 1970, 1975), Marris (1964), Baumol (1959), Penrose (1958), and Cyert and March (1963). Thorough reviews of

lems addressed here is that specification of individual rights determines how costs and rewards will be allocated among the participants in any organization. Since the specification of rights is generally effected through contracting (implicit as well as explicit), individual behavior in organizations, including the behavior of managers, will depend upon the nature of these contracts. We focus in this paper on the behavioral implications of the property rights specified in the contracts between the owners and managers of the firm.

1.4. Agency Costs. Many problems associated with the inadequcy of the current theory of the firm can also be viewed as special cases of the theory of agency relationships in which there is a growing literature.[7] This literature has developed independently of the property rights literature even though the problems with which it is concerned are similar; the approaches are in fact highly complementary to each other.

We define an agency relationship as a contract under which one or more persons (the principal(s)) engage another person (the agent) to perform some service on their behalf which involves delegating some decision-making authority to the agent. If both parties to the relationship are utility maximizers there is good reason to believe that the agent will not always act in the best interests of the principal. The *principal* can limit divergences from his interest by establishing appropriate incentives for the agent and by incurring monitoring costs designed to limit the aberrant activities of the agent. In addition in some situations it will pay the *agent* to expend resources (bonding costs) to guarantee that he will not take certain actions which would harm the principal or to

ensure that the principal will be compensated if he does take such actions. However, it is generally impossible for the principal or the agent at zero cost to ensure that the agent will make optimal decisions from the principal's viewpoint. In most agency relationships the principal and the agent will incur positive monitoring and bonding costs (nonpecuniary as well as pecuniary), and in addition there will be some divergence between the agent's decisions[8] and those decisions which would maximize the welfare of the principal. The dollar equivalent of the reduction in welfare experienced by the principal due to this divergence is also a cost of the agency relationship, and we refer to this latter cost as the "residual loss." We define *agency costs* as the sum of:

1. the monitoring expenditures by the principal,[9]
2. the bonding expenditures by the agent,
3. the residual loss.

Note also that agency costs arise in any situation involving cooperative effort (such as the co-authoring of this paper) by two or more people even though there is no clear cut principal–agent relationship. Viewed in this light it is clear that our definition of agency costs and their importance to the theory of the firm bears a close relationship to the problem of shirking and monitoring of team production which Alchian and Demsetz (1972) raise in their paper on the theory of the firm.

Since the relationship between the stockholders and manager of a corpora-

---

[7] Cf. Berhold (1971), Ross (1973, 1974a), Wilson (1968, 1969), and Heckerman (1975).

[8] Given the optimal monitoring and bonding activities by the principal and agent.

[9] As it is used in this paper the term monitoring includes more than just measuring or observing the behavior of the agnet. It includes efforts on the part of the principal to "control" the behavior of the agent through budget restrictions, compensation policies, operating rules etc.

tion fits the definition of a pure agency relationship it should be no surprise to discover that the issues associated with the "separation of ownership and control" in the modern diffuse ownership corporation are intimately associated with the general problem of agency. We show below that an explanation of why and how the agency costs generated by the corporate form are born leads to a theory of the ownership (or capital) structure of the firm.

Before moving on, however, it is worthwhile to point out the generality of the agency problem. The problem of inducing an "agent" to behave as if he were maximizing the "principal's" welfare is quite general. It exists in all organizations and in all cooperative efforts—at every level of management in firms,[10] in universities, in mutual companies, in cooperatives, in governmental authorities and bureaus, in unions, and in relationships normally classified as agency relationships such as are common in the performing arts and the market for real

---

[10] As we show below the existence of positive monitoring and bonding costs will result in the manager of a corporation possessing control over some resources which he can allocate (within certain constraints) to satisfy his own preferences. However, to the extent that he must obtain the cooperation of others in order to carry out his tasks (such as divisional vice presidents) and to the extent that he cannot control their behavior perfectly and costlessly they will be able to appropriate some of these resources for their own ends. In short, there are agency costs generated at every level of the organization. Unfortunately, the analysis of these more general oganizational issues is even more difficult than that of the "ownership and control" issue because the nature of the contractual obligations and rights of the parties are much more varied and generally not as well specified in explicit contractual arrangements. Nevertheless, they exist and we believe that extensions of our analysis in these directions show promise of producing insights into a viable theory of organization.

estate. The development of theories to explain the form which agency costs take in each of these situations (where the contractual relations differ significantly), and how and why they are born will lead to a rich theory of organizations which is now lacking in economics and the social sciences generally. We confine our attention in this paper to only a small part of this general problem—the analysis of agency costs generated by the contractual arrangements between the owners and top management of the corporation.

Our approach to the agency problem here differs fundamentally from most of the existing literature. That literature focuses almost exclusively on the normative aspects of the agency relationship; that is how to structure the contractual relation (including compensation incentives) between the principal and agent to provide appropriate incentives for the agent to make choices which will maximize the principal's welfare given that uncertainty and imperfect monitoring exist. We focus almost entirely on the positive aspects of the theory. That is, we assume individuals solve these normative problems and given that only stocks and bonds can be issued as claims, we investigate the incentives faced by each of the parties and the elements entering into the determination of the equilibrium contractual form characterizing the relationship between the manager (i.e., agent) of the firm and the outside equity and debt holders (i.e., principals).

1.5. Some General Comments on the Definition of the Firm. Ronald Coase (1937) in his seminal paper on "The Nature of the Firm" pointed out that economics had no positive theory to determine the bounds of the firm. He characterized the bounds of the firm as that range of exchanges over which the market system was suppressed and resource allocation was accomplished instead by authority and direction. He focused on the cost of using markets to effect contracts and exchanges and argued that activities would be included within the firm whenever the costs of using markets were greater than the costs of using direct authority. Alchian and Demsetz (1972) object to the notion that activities within the firm are governed by authority, and correctly emphasize the role of contracts as a vehicle for voluntary exchange. They emphasize the role of monitoring in situations in which there is joint input or team production.[11] We sympathize with the importance they attach to monitoring, but we believe the emphasis which Alchian–Demsetz place on joint input production is too narrow and therefore misleading. Contractual relations are the essence of the firm, not only with employees but with suppliers, customers, creditors, etc. The problem of agency costs and monitoring exists for all of these contracts, independent of whether there is joint production in their sense; i.e., joint production can explain only a small fraction of the behavior of individuals associated with a firm. A detailed examination of these issues is left to another paper.

It is important to recognize that most organizations are simply *legal fictions*[12] *which serve as a nexus for a set of contracting relationships among individuals*. This includes firms, non-profit institutions such as universities, hospitals and foundations, mutual organizations such as mutual savings banks and insurance companies and co-operatives, some private clubs, and even governmental bodies such as cities, states and the Federal government, government enterprises such as TVA, the Post Office, transit systems, etc.

The private corporation or firm is simply one form of *legal fiction which serves as a nexus for contracting relationships and which is also characterized by the existence of divisible residual claims on the assets and cash flows of the organization which can generally be sold without permisison of the other contracting individuals*. While this definition of the firm has little substantive content, emphasizing the essential contractual nature of firms and other organizations focuses attention on a crucial set of questions—why particular sets of contractual relations arise for various types of organizations, what the consequences of these contractual relations are, and how they are affected by changes exogenous to the organization. Viewed this way, it makes little or no sense to try to distinguish those things which are "inside" the firm (or any other organization) from those things that are "outside" of it. There is in a very real sense only a multitude of complex relationships (i.e., contracts) between the legal fiction (the firm) and the owners of labor, material and capital inputs and the consumers of output.[13]

[11] They define the classical capitalist firm as a contractual organization of inputs in which there is "(a) joint input production, (b) several input owners, (c) one party who is common to all the contracts of the joint inputs, (d) who has rights to renegotiate any input's contract independently of contracts with other input owners, (e) who holds the residual claim, and (f) who has the right to sell his contractual residual status."

[12] By legal fiction we mean the artificial construct under the law which allows certain organizations to be treated as individuals.

[13] For example, we ordinarily think of a product as leaving the firm at the time it is sold, but implicitly or explicitly such sales generally carry with them continuing contracts between the firm and the buyer. If the product does not perform as expected the buyer often can and does have a right to satisfaction. Explicit evidence that such implicit contracts do exist is the practice we occasionally observe of specific provision that all sales are final."

Viewing the firm as the nexus of a set of contracting relationships among individuals also serves to make it clear that the personalization of the firm implied by asking questions such as "what should be the objective function of the firm", or "does the firm have a social responsibility" is seriously misleading. *The firm is not an individual.* It is a legal fiction which serves as a focus for a complex process in which the conflicting objectives of individuals (some of whom may "represent" other oganizations) are brought into equilibrium within a framework of contractual relations. In this sense the "behavior " of the firm is like the behavior of a market; i.e., the outcome of a complex equilibrium process. We seldom fall into the trap of characterizing the wheat or stock market as an individual, but we often make this error by thinking about organizations as if they were persons with motivations and intentions.[14] . . .

[14] This view of the firm points up the important role which the legal system and the law play in social organizations, especially, the organization of economic activity. Statutory laws set bounds on the kinds of contracts into which individuals and organizations may enter without risking criminal prosecution. The police powers of the state are available and used to enforce performance of contacts or to enforce the collection of damages for non-performance. The courts adjudicate conflicts between contracting parties and establish precedents which form the body of common law. All of these government activities affect both the kinds of contracts executed and the extent to which contracting is relied upon. This in turn determines the usefulness, productivity, profitablity and viability of various forms of organization. Moreover, new laws as well as court decisions often can and do change the rights of contracting parties ex post, and they can and do serve as a vehicle for redistribution of wealth. An analysis of some of the implications of these facts is contained in Jensen and Meckling (1976) and we shall not pursue them here.

2. THE AGENCY COSTS OF OUTSIDE EQUITY

2.1. Overview. . . . If a wholly owned firm is managed by the owner, he will make operating decisions which maximize his utility. These decisions will involve not only the benefits he derives from pecuniary returns but also the utility generated by various non-pecuniary aspects of his entrepreneurial activities such as the physical appointments of the office, the attractiveness of the secretarial staff, the level of employee discipline, the kind and amount of charitable contributions, personal relations ("love," "respect," etc.) with employees, a larger than optimal computer to play with, purchase of production inputs from friends, etc. The optimum mix (in the absence of taxes) of the various pecuniary and non-pecuniary benefits is achieved when the marginal utility derived from an additional dollar of expenditure (measured net of any productive effects) is equal for each nonpecuniary item and equal to the marginal utility derived from an additional dollar of after tax purchasing power (wealth).

If the owner-manager sells equity claims on the corporation which are identical to his (i.e., share proportionately in the profits of the firm and have limited liability) agency costs will be generated by the divergence between his interest and those of the outside shareholders, since he will then bear only a fraction of the costs of any non-pecuniary benefits he takes out in maximizing his own utility. If the manager owns only 95 percent of the stock, he will expend resources to the point where the marginal utility derived from a dollar's expenditure of the firm's resources on such items equals the marginal utility of an additional 95 cents in general purchasing power (i.e., *his* share of the wealth reduction) and not one dollar. Such activities, on his part, can be limited (but probably not eliminated) by the expenditure of resources on monitoring activities by the outside stockholders. But as we show below, the owner will bear the entire wealth effects of these expected costs so long as the equity market anticipates these effects. Prospective minority shareholders will realize that the owner–manager's interests will diverge somewhat from theirs, hence the price which they will pay for shares will reflect the monitoring costs and the effect of the divergence between the manager's interest and theirs. Nevertheless, ignoring for the moment the possibility of borrowing against his wealth, the owner will find it desirable to bear these costs as long as the welfare increment he experiences from converting his claims on the firm into general purchasing power[15] is large enough to offset them.

As the owner-manager's fraction of the equity falls, his fractional claim on the outcomes falls and this will tend to encourage him to appropriate larger amounts of the corporate resources in the form of perquisites. This also makes it desirable for the minority shareholders to expend more resources in monitoring his behavior. Thus, the wealth costs to the owner of obtaining additional cash in the equity markets rise as his fractional ownership falls.

We shall continue to characterize the agency conflict between the owner–manager and outside shareholders as deriving from the manager's tendency to

[15] For use in consumption, for the diversification of his wealth, or more importantly, for the financing of "profitable" projects which he could not otherwise finance out of his personal wealth. We deal with these issues below after having developed some of the elementary analytical tools necessary to their solution.

appropriate perquisites out of the firm's resources for his own consumption. However, we do not mean to leave the impression that this is the only or even the most important source of conflict. Indeed, it is likely that the most important conflict arises from the fact that as the manager's ownership claim falls, his incentive to devote significant effort to creative activities such as searching out new profitable ventures falls. He may in fact avoid such ventures simply because it requires too much trouble or effort on his part to manage or to learn about new technologies. Avoidance of these personal costs and the anxieties that go with them also represent a source of on-the-job utility to him and it can result in the value of the firm being substantially lower than it otherwise could be. . . .

7. CONCLUSIONS

The publicly held business corporation is an awesome social invention. Millions of individuals voluntarily entrust billions of dollars, francs, pesos, etc., of personal wealth to the care of managers on the basis of a complex set of contracting relationships which delineate the rights of the parties involved. The growth in the use of the corporate form as well as the growth in market value of established corporations suggests that at least, up to the present, creditors and investors have by and large not been disappointed with the results, despite the agency costs inherent in the corporate form.

Agency costs are as real as any other costs. The level of agency costs depends among other things on statutory and common law and human ingenuity in devising contracts. Both the law and the sophistication of contracts relevant to the modern corporation are the products of a historical process in which there were strong incentives for individuals to minimize agency costs. Moreover, there were alternative organizational forms available, and opportunities to invent new ones. Whatever its shortcomings, the corporation has thus far survived the market test against potential alternatives.

REFERENCES

Alchian, A. A., 1965, The basis of some recent advances in the theory of management of the firm, Journal of Industrial Economics, Nov., 30–44.

Alchian, A. A., 1968, Corporate management and property rights, in: Economic policy and the regulation of securities (American Enterprise Institute, Washington, DC).

Alchian, A. A., and H. Demsetz, 1972, Production, information costs, and economic organization, American Economic Review LXII, no. 5, 777–795.

Alchian, A. A. and R. A. Kessel, 1962, Competition, monopoly and the pursuit of pecuniary gain, in: Aspects of labor economics (National Bureau of Economic Research, Princeton, NJ).

Baumol, W. J., 1959, Business behavior, value and growth (Macmillan, New York).

Berhold, M., 1971, A theory of linear profit sharing incentives, Quarterly Journal of Economics LXXXV, Aug., 460–482.

Branch, B., 1973, Corporate objectives and market performance, Financial Management, Summer, 24–29.

Coase, R. H., 1937, The nature of the firm, Economica, New Series, IV, 386–405. Reprinted in: Readings in price theory (Irwin, Homewood, IL) 331–351.

Coase, R. H., 1959, The Federal Communications Commission, Journal of Law and Economics II, Oct., 1–40.

Coase, R. H., 1960, The problem of social cost, Journal of Law and Economics III, Oct., 1–44.

Coase, R. H., 1964, Discussion, American Economic Review LIV, no. 3, 194–197.

Cyert, R. M., and C. L. Hedrick, 1972, Theory of the firm: Past, present and future; An interpretation, Journal of Economic Literature X, June, 398–412.

Cyert, R. M. and J. G. March, 1963, A behavioral theory of the firm (Prentice Hall, Englewood Cliffs, NJ).

Demsetz, H., 1967, Toward a theory of property rights, American Economic Review LVII, May, 347–359.

Furubotn, E. G. and S. Pejovich, 1972, Property rights and economic theory: A survey of recent literature, Journal of Economic Literature X, Dec., 1137–1162.

Heckerman, D. G., 1975, Motivating managers to make investment decisions, Journal of Financial Economics 2, no. 3, 273–292.

Jensen, M. C. and W. H. Meckling, 1976, Can the corporation survive? Center for Research in Government Policy and Business Working Paper no. PPS 76–4 (University of Rochester, Rochester, NY).

Klein, W. A., 1976, Legal and eocnomic perspectives on the firm, unpublished manuscript (University of California, Los Angeles, CA).

Machlup, F., 1967, Theories of the firm: Marginalist, behavioral, managerial, American Economic Review, March, 1–33.

Marris, R., 1964, The economic theory of managerial capitalism (Free Press of Glencoe, Glencoe, IL).

Mason, E. S., 1959, The corporation in modern society (Harvard University Press, Cambridge MA).

McManus, J. C., 1975, The costs of alternative economic organizations, Canadian Journal of Economics VIII, Aug., 334–350.

Meckling, W. H., 1976, Values and the choice of the model of the individual in the social sciences, Schweizerische Zeitschrift für Volkswirtschaft und Statistik, Dec.

Monsen, R. J. and A. Downs, 1965, A theory of large managerial firms, Journal of Political Economy, June, 221–236.

Penrose, E., 1958, The theory of the growth of the firm (Wiley, New York).

Preston, L. E., 1975, Corporation and society: The search for a paradigm, Journal of Economic Literature XIII, June, 434–453.

Ross, S. A., 1973, The economic theory of agency: The principals problems, American Economic Review LXII, May, 134–139.

Ross, S. A., 1974a, The economic theory of agency and the principle of similarity, in: M. D. Balch et al., eds., Essays on economic behavior under uncertainty (North-Holland, Amsterdam).

Shubik, M., 1970, A curmudgeon's guide to microeconomics, Journal of Economic Literature VIII, June, 405–434.

Silver, M. and R. Auster, 1969, Entrepreneurship, profit and limits on firm size, Journal of Business 42, July, 277–281.

Simon, H. A., 1955, A behavioral model of rational choice, Quarterly Journal of Eocnomics 69, 99–118.

Simon, H. A., 1959, Theories of decision making in economics and behavioral science, American Economic Review, June, 253–283.

Williamson, O. E., 1964, The economics of discretionary behavior: Managerial objectives in a theory of the firm (Prentice-Hall, Englewood Cliffs, NJ).

Williamson, O. E., 1970, Corporate control and business behavior (Prentice-Hall, Englewood Cliffs, NJ).

Williamson, O. E., 1975, Markets and hierarchies: Analysis and antitrust implications (The Free Press, New York).

Wilson, R., 1968, On the theory of syndicates, Econometrica 36, Jan., 119–132.

Wilson, R., 1969, La decision: Agregation et dynamique des orders de preference, Extrait (Editions du Centre National de la Recherche Scientifique, Paris) 288–307.

29

The Ethereal Hand: Organizational Economics and Management Theory

Lex Donaldson

A new theoretical paradigm has entered the field of management. The new arrival hails from economics and has been called *organizational economics* (Barney & Ouchi, 1986). The new theory has two major components: agency theory and transaction cost economics. The arrival of a new paradigm in management poses questions for established theories in the area. Such questions encompass the nature of the new theory relative to preexisting theories and the nature of the distinctive contribution potentially offered by the new paradigm. These, in turn, generate certain challenges for the field as a whole. This article will discuss the nature and potentiality of organizational economics in order to identify key issues and problems and to point the way toward a path for their resolution. Above all, the present remarks are not those of an expert in organizational economics. Rather, they are observations about the organizational economics phenomenon made by a structural contingency theorist and, therefore, they come from a follower of more established thought-ways within management theory, one who has wrestled elsewhere with the relationship between structural contingency theory and other new organizational theory paradigms (Donaldson, 1985a).

ORGANIZATIONAL ECONOMICS AND MANAGEMENT

Organizational economics is composed of agency theory and transaction cost economics (Barney & Ouchi, 1986). Agency theory holds that many social relationships can be usefully understood as involving two parties: a principal and an agent. The agent performs certain actions on behalf of the principal, who necessarily must delegate some authority to the agent (Jensen & Meckling, 1976). Since the interests of the principal and agent are inclined to diverge, the delegation of authority from the principal to the agent allows a degree of underfulfillment of the wishes of the principal by the agent, which is termed *agency loss*. Agency theory specifies the mechanisms that will be used to try to minimize agency loss in order to maintain an efficient principal-agent relationship (Jensen & Meckling, 1976; Pratt & Zeckhauser, 1985). Transaction cost economics likewise deals with the problem of one economic actor not giving full value to another in an economic exchange (Williamson, 1985). Transaction cost economics provides an analysis of the conditions under which such problems will exist, and specifies mecha-

Source: Lex Donaldson, "The Ethereal Hand: Organizational Economics and Management Theory," pp. 369–81, *Academy of Management Review*, 15(3) 1990. Reprinted by permission.

nisms whereby the transaction can be structured to minimize such transaction costs. If the transacting parties are each firms, the analysis is extended to issues of vertical integration, joint venturing, and like specifications of the boundaries of the firm (Williamson, 1985).

The disciplinary roots of organizational economics go back into economics, though in the case of agency theory there was some early discussion of these issues in political science (Mitnick, 1975). Economists have been much concerned with how society can be most satisfactorily structured through the free interplay of agents in the marketplace. Indeed, the classic statement of economic theory by Adam Smith (1937) is a critique of the absolutist monarchical state. To this day, economics continues to have as one of its principal agendas and achievements criticism of governmental regulation and policy and advocacy of a free market economy. When such economic theory is extended to the firm, especially the large-scale bureaucratic firm, the firm is liable to be perceived as a state in miniature, thereby advancing the usual critique. For traditional economic analysis, a firm is composed of capital, labor, and an entrepreneur. There is no mention of tiers of management and administrative staff. In economics the question often develops as to why in an ideal economy any firm would exist above the size and complexity of the entrepreneurial small business. Why should not all economic activity be arranged as free contracts between entrepreneurial owners of small businesses, responding to the signaling system of prices in the market? This is a scenario with no place for administration through the visible hand of management, that is, through the management hierarchy (Chandler, 1977). If transac-

tion cost economics enters into the economic discussion, it can be argued that for exchanges that are different from spot market transactions, exchange may be more efficiently achieved within a single firm through coordination by a managerial hierarchy (Coase, 1937). Thus, transaction cost economics contributes to economics the idea, alien within that discipline, that management plays a positive role in the economy.

The transaction cost argument is based on the difficulties in certain exchanges of obtaining credible commitments, that is, the difficulty of one party being assured that the other party will in fact deliver at a future time the performance that is promised in spirit in the contract (Williamson, 1985). These difficulties originate because of the opportunities for one party to gain its interests to the detriment of the other, in particular through deceit. In much of the organizational economics literature, be it agency theory or transaction cost theory in variant, the deceitful, shirking economic actors are managers, either (in agency theory) as individual agents opposite their principals, the owners of the firms, or (in transaction cost theory) as the management team of one firm acting guilefully vis-à-vis a second management team. Therefore, the organizational economics model of management is peculiarly two-edged. In transaction cost theory, managers are necessary in a market economy because they cannot be trusted. The opportunism of one group of managers, say in a supplier firm, opposite a second group of managers, say in the purchaser firm, necessitates vertical integration, whereby the two managerial groups are governed by a third group, their superordinate level of management. In agency theory, principal-agency problems arise in part from the separation of ownership from control in the large modern corporation with its dispersed shareholders. Management has developed as a social institution within free market capitalism because of the limitations of free market relations (i.e., in a large firm the size is too great to allow direct rule by the entrepreneurs). Management becomes necessary when market mechanisms and disciplines fail. Thus, because of the economic roots of organizational economics there is a deep ambivalence in its view of management. This ambivalence presents both a rapprochement between economics and management theory and a problem for the ready absorption of organizational economics within management theory.

METHODOLOGICAL INDIVIDUALISM

The economic roots of organizational economics lead to a further characteristic. Economics generally is beholden to the social science doctrine known as methodological individualism. This doctrine states that social phenomena, and in this case economic phenomena, should be analyzed as arising from conscious actions of individuals. There is a disinclination to treat action as located within levels of analysis larger than the individual, particularly at the unit of analysis of the corporate organization. Yet much management theory has been conceived as propositions about organizations, for example, how corporate strategy leads to corporate structure (Chandler, 1962), how corporate planning affects corporate profitability (Lorange & Vancil, 1977), and so on. In general, organizations are conceived as systems that have purposes, structures, and outputs which interact with the other organizational systems in their environment. Although systems-level analysis is widely accepted in manage-

ment theory, economics, under the influence of methodological individualism, finds this systems talk to be dubious. In this way of thinking, economists join with other critics from sociology and psychology (see Donaldson, 1985a). Organizational economics, especially in agency theory mode, would wish to analyze organizational systems in terms of their constituent individual actors, that is, in terms of the rational economic "man" (and woman). In particular, agency theory focuses on the interests pursued by each actor and how the interest of one actor may conflict with the interest of another (i.e., the conflict of interest between principal and agent). Agency theory is a theory of interest, of motivation, and of compliance. By contrast, much systems-level analysis considers the willingness of constituent actors to cooperate toward organizational goals as unproblematic. The question for this more macroscopic analysis becomes how to structure the team of willing cooperators to overcome the technical difficulties of achieving adequate integration through optimal structures, systems, planning mechanisms, and so on (e.g., Chandler, 1962; Galbraith, 1973). Thus, organizational economics is aligned with management theories from psychology, sociology, and politics that treat human motivation, inducement, and compliance as distinct from theories of organization structure, strategy, and planning (which treat appropriate designs for a team in which the willing compliance of members is unproblematic). Agency theory is therefore part of a wider movement out of sociology and politics to reassert the struggle between individuals as a critical agenda for social science in contradiction to the tradition of structural-functionalist systems analysis (Burrell & Morgan, 1979). This tension between individualistic and systemic modes of analysis poses a problem of how to adequately integrate the two levels within management theory.

NARROW MODEL OF HUMAN BEHAVIOR

The focus on individual motivation, and its economistic character, raises a further point about the relationship between organizational economics and management theory. Organizational economics draws upon the rational economic model of man (and woman). This is a model of persons pursuing their self-interests and maximizing their personal felicific calculus. Typically, such organizational economic actors seek personal wealth, status, leisure, or the like (Jensen & Meckling, 1976; Williamson, 1985). Accordingly, their behavior as potentially shirking or opportunistic agents can be curbed by vigilant monitoring, together with incentive schemes based around money, promotion, negative sanctions, and the like. This is a model of the Theory X variety of man (McGregor, 1960). Students of human behavior have identified a much larger range of human motives, including needs for achievement, responsibility, and recognition, as well as altruism, belief, respect for authority, and the intrinsic motivation of an inherently satisfying task (Wood & Bandura, 1989). In addition, psychologists and sociologists point out that human behavior is often produced without conscious thought, that is, through habit, emotion, taken-for-granted custom, conditioned reflex, unconditioned reflex, posthypnotic suggestion, and unconscious desires. Although these variegated causations of human behavior are not all as equally salient to the analysis of organizational behavior as is calculation with regard to positive and negative rewards, nevertheless, the account of human motivation offered by organizational eco-

nomics is a narrow one relative to preexisting motivation theory in organization behavior. This poses a problem of synthesis for management theory between traditional organizational behavior on the one hand and the newer organizational economics on the other. Traditionally, human motivation has been viewed as neither wholly Theory X nor wholly Theory Y but as some more complex and contingent admixture of the two (Miner, 1980; Schein, 1970). . . .

NEGATIVE MORAL EVALUATIONS

One aspect of the new economistic language of organizational economics is its evaluative tone. Accordingly, the manager is viewed as an individual who has the inherent propensity to *shirk*, to be *opportunistic*, to maximize his or her self-interest, to act with *guile*, and to behave in ways that constitute a *moral hazard* (Williamson, 1985). Such terms normally carry negative evaluations in our society. Indeed, organizational economists insist that the term *moral hazard* is correct because the behaviors are precisely ones that attract moral odium (Alchian & Woodward, 1988). If managerial behavior can actually be classified as this type, these descriptions are truthful, and many people might say that the negative evaluations were deserved. However, there is a major problem concerning how much of managerial behavior is this type (empirically) and to what frequency and severity. Further, because organizational economics lacks descriptions of managerial behavior that are more benign in nature (e.g., as altruistic, loyal, driven by high ethical standards, or motivated by intrinsic job satisfaction), it is not easy to identify less pernicious managerial behavior according to the terminology of organizational economic analysis. Organizational economics creates a theoretical scenario in which managers act opportunistically, and any other type of behavior falls outside of the theory (Jensen & Meckling, 1976; Williamson, 1975). Thus, there is created and reiterated a fable in which managerial acts are antiorganizational or antisocial (Barney & Ouchi, 1986; Pratt & Zeckhauser, 1985; Williamson, 1985). Further, because such behavior is assumed in the fundamental axioms, rather than treated contingently or empirically, all managers are presumed to act in this fashion whenever they are in certain situations as specflied by the theory. This is guilt by axiom.

The strong evaluative characteristic of organizational economics poses problems for management theory. Some management theorists may find organizational economics repellent, being both overly generalized and cynical. Other management academics may fear that the organizational economics perspective will corrode collaboration between academic institutions and practitioners, who may take some exception to the way they have been characterized.

Therefore, organizational economics poses some problems for management theory and management theorists regarding its relationship with previous work, the integration of management theory, and its realism, oversimplification, validity, and evaluative coloration. Nonetheless, proponents of any new theoretical approach can fairly claim that they should be given the opportunity to show the contribution that it can make. The development of the future body of knowledge cannot be predicted (Popper, 1945) and, therefore, the potential contribution of organizational economics cannot be known a priori; this will become clearer only as the research paradigm or program runs its course. Although Arrow (1985) commented on the strictly limited achievements of

agency theory to date, he nevertheless endorsed the continuation of the program. Moreover, to the degree that managers in reality act in the way specified in organizational economics, then management theory should accurately record this, out of respect for the truth.

To gain some orientation and perspective about the issues raised thus far and as a precursor to possible directions for their resolutions, a conceptual overview is offered in Figure 1. This overview arrays the issues in two dimensions. The vertical axis describes the focus of the theory, that is, the more traditional (structuralist theory) focus on structuring for the coordination of team players versus the focus on conflict of interest in organizational economics theory. The horizontal axis describes the nature of the theory, that is, whether it is positive or normative. Because the question of theory focus has been discussed previously, the issue of the nature of theory will be examined next.

NORMATIVE OR POSITIVE THEORY

Theories in social science can be classified as positive (purely explanatory) or normative (for making prescriptions). The agency theory literature has been described by Pratt and Zeckhauser (1985) as containing both positive and normative writings. Much of the foundational organizational economics literature as contributed by economists is positive in character. Such agency theory analyses explain why institutions are as they are (Pratt & Zeckhauser, 1985). These theories explain how problems of endemic mistrust, cheating, and the like can be avoided through the placement of social organizational mechanisms. Thus, the shirking, opportunism, and so on for which the agents have a propensity do not have to occur; they can be held in

FIGURE 1 • KEY DISTINCTIONS BETWEEN ORGANIZATIONAL
ECONOMIC AND ORGANIZATIONAL STRUCTURAL THEORIES

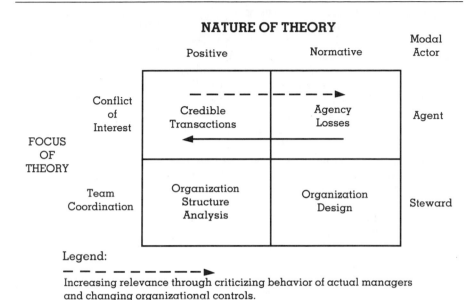

NATURE OF THEORY

Modal
Actor

Positive   Normative

Conflict
of   Credible   Agency
Interest   Transactions   Losses   Agent

FOCUS
OF
THEORY

Team   Organization   Organization
Coordination   Structure   Design   Steward
        Analysis

Legend:

- - - - - - - - ►

Increasing relevance through criticizing behavior of actual managers
and changing organizational controls.

◄————————

Increasing relevance through appreciating institutions and resisting
reforms.

place by institutional structures. Such organizational economics offers a deeper appreciation of the wisdom of present organizational arrangements. Much of this is intriguing, offers potentially rich insights (see Pratt & Zeckhauser, 1985), and is a type of theoretical illumination not presently found in either conventional theory on organizations or organizational behavior. However, these justifications of the status quo, quite apart from the strictures of social critics (Clegg & Dunkerley, 1980; Perrow, 1986), tend not to satisfy management scholars who would wish to offer managers advice about changing organizations in order to attain better performance or to fulfill other objectives. . . .

As described in Figure 1, theories of organizational economics that focus upon conflict of interest and that are positive by nature dwell on what might be termed the *credible transaction* (top left-hand quadrant) and its deeper appreciation. The normative aspect of such theories (top right-hand quadrant) is the theory of opportunistic agency loss, which is held to actually occur and to be reducible to a degree through proper implementation of agency theory–derived prescriptions (e.g., monitoring and sanctioning). There is some present tendency for organizational economics to be utilized to contribute to management theory by moving from the top left-hand box to the top right hand box. The opposite program would be for organizational economics within management theory to move in the reverse direction, from the top right-hand box to the top left-hand box, and in so doing become more like the original eocnomic variant of organizational economics. Moving vertically downward in Figure 1, the focus of theory changes from conflict of interest to team coordination. In its positive aspect, for example, regarding the structural facets of coordination, this is the theory of organization structure, such as structural contingency theory (e.g., Lawrence & Lorsch, 1967). In its normative aspect this becomes the theory of organization design (e.g., Galbraith, 1973).

Regarding the potential of the positive approach (i.e., top left-hand box of Figure 1), organizational economics has contributed to the understanding of organizational structures in terms of M-form divisions, corporate governance structures, and so on (Williamson, 1985). . . .

Again, vertical disintegration at present among some large insurance organizations, whereby the investment function has become a separate company that accepts clients other than those of the original parent company, is amenable to analysis in terms of transaction cost theory. Increasing competition and performance require more emphasis on expertise and performance by investment managers and, hence, employment contracts that feature high and variable rewards and short-horizon contracts—because investment managers are placed on higher risk-reward schedules. These features differ from the lower and less variable salaries and lifetime employment contracts typical of regular insurance organizations. The difference in expertise and employment contracts curtails the traditional practice of rotating personnel in and out of the investment function. The result is two separate employment contracting situations for both the investment and noninvestment functions. More credible commitments can be made with employees if each or-

ganization is a separate entity able to contract in a homogeneous manner with its own personnel. . . .

An Application— Corporate Governance

As a way of bringing some of these theoretical and metatheoretical issues into focus let us briefly consider one substantive area in which agency theory has been applied. Corporate governance is the structure whereby managers at the organizational apex are controlled through the board of directors, its associated structures, executive incentive, and other schemes of monitoring and bonding. As agency theory and transaction cost theory have become popularized, so too has the view that managerial tendencies toward self-interested opportunism at the expense of the interests of the shareholding owners need to be checked by strong governance structures (Williamson, 1985). This is especially descriptive of the modern large corporation where mangement has become separated from ownership and ownership is widely diffused among a multitude of shareholders (Jensen & Meckling, 1976). Some effective governance structures for the control of managers include a board of directors who are predominantly outsiders with no personal relationship with management, a chairperson of the board who is not an executive manager of the company, a chief executive officer whose personal interest is aligned with shareholders through stock ownership or a bonus compensation plan that is linked to shareholder wealth, and so on. The agency theory perspective is critical of governance structures that lack such institutional features, for example, a board of directors that is dominated by executives, the board chairperson who is also the chief executive officer, or the chief executive officer who has little or no personal shareholding in the corporation or who is paid a straight salary without any element of bonus compensation linked to the fate of shareholders' wealth. Kesner and Dalton (1986) have contributed a particularly persuasive critique of the weak governance structures that are pervasive among U.S. corporations. In it they enumerate many different forms of institutional weakness. Empirical research (Rechner & Dalton, 1991) has produced evidence that lower financial performance results when the chairperson of the board is also the CEO; this is compared to the situation in which the two roles have separate incumbents—as agency theory would predict.

A countervailing view, called *stewardship theory*, has developed about corporate governance (Donaldson & Davis, 1989). This holds that there is no conflict of interest between managers and owners and that the desideratum of governance structure is to find an organizational structure that allows coordination to be achieved most effectively. Consequently, managers are team players, and the optimal structure is one that authorizes them to act, given that they will act in the best interests of owners. Managers are not opportunistic agents, according to this theory, but good stewards (Donaldson & Davis, 1989). Whereas agency theory is derived from the economic model of man (i.e., Theory X), stewardship theory is derived from the Theory Y stream of organization behavior research (McGregor, 1960). In particular, when the chairperson and the CEO are the same person, the command becomes unified, removing role ambiguities and conflicts that could otherwise arise where power is shared. In this way, the combination of these roles is predicted to lead to higher corporate financial performance. Some empirical evidence in support of this proposition has been found (Donaldson & Davis, 1989).

Additionally, according to stewardship theory, there would be benefits in having a preponderance of executive directors among the board because this adds to the available expertise, allows ventilation of points of contention within management, and provides a status reward for the executives. There is empirical evidence that a predominance of insiders on the board of directors is associated with higher corporate financial performance (Sullivan, 1988) and leads to higher corporate financial performance (Rechner & Dalton, 1988).

Thus, the corporate governance topic has been addressed here in terms of two rival theories, agency theory from organizational economics and stewardship theory from organizational behavior research that organizational economics tends to overlook. One task for future research is to establish the empirical validity of each of these theories. Moreover, it is possible that each theory may be valid within its own domain. For instance, stewardship theory may prove correct as long as the coalition (Cyert & March, 1963) between managers and owners persists and is perceived by managers as persisting. Under conditions where the existing coalition between managers and owners is called into question, such as by a takeover threat, the interests of each party start to diverge; this is when agency theory may prove correct. Evidence of this latter position is provided in the study by Kosnik (1987) in which several agency theory propositions received empirical support for corporations that were subject to takeover threats and greenmail. Additional tasks for future theory construction would be to specify the theoretical domains would be to specify the theoretical domains of agency theory and stewardship theory and to identify the contingency factors that demarcate each.

However, organizational economics may be sufficiently flexible that it can act as the covering law for propositions about corporate governance quite opposite to those that are usually imputed. A particularly flexible argument from agency theory is that managerial agents are confined from acting opportunistically by fear of loss of their reputation and, therefore, may not act opportunistically even in the absence of more formal mechanisms for monitoring and bonding. By extension, a CEO who is also a board chairperson, and thus lacks the formal discipline of an independent hierarchical superordinate, may nevertheless be effectively constrained from acting opportunistically out of fear of loss of reputation. Because the CEO is also the board chairperson, it is less credible for the CEO to blame the board and its chair for interference or lack of decision in circumstances where returns to shareholders are suboptimal.

Unambiguous authority over the corporation implies unambiguous responsibility for failure. Again, by extension, in a situation where the majority of board members are executives, any failings of the corporation in returns to shareholders fall more directly on those executives in terms of blame and loss of reputation. Also, there is a more formal mechanism that goes beyond mere reputation; that is, when the CEO and other senior executives are prominent on the board, the legal liability of board directors to shareholders will fall more squarely upon their shoulders. Indemnification insurance provided for board members by the corporation will reduce the immediate material loss from successful prosecutions, but the loss of reputation will remain, and this is nontrivial even in situations where the courts side with the board members. Thus, through the reputational loss argument, an agency theory basis might be established; from this base

the proposition can be derived that company performance will be enhanced by combining the roles of the board chairperson and the CEO and by having executives compose a majority of the board.

The fluidity of agency theory suggests something of its power, but it also suggests something of its limitations. Any theory that is capable of subsuming a wide range of mutually contradictory propositions is not falsifiable (Popper, 1945).

A more exact specification of the theory in the future by agency theorists may render the theory more exclusive and thus falsifiable. Agency theory in its present form has the potential to survive unvanquished for a long time as a broad master theory—perhaps containing many antithetic and schismatic subtheories.

The stewardship theory also may reveal a potentiality to resist falsification and to more broadly encompass seemingly antithetic propositions. For example, consider the agency theory findings of Kosnik (1987) that corporations are more likely to pay greenmail, thereby resisting takeover and reducing shareholder wealth to the benefit of securing the tenure of incumbent management, where the board of directors is less independent from corporate management (e.g., through family ties). On the face of it, in the absence of an independent board to discipline management on behalf of shareholders, managers are paying greenmail out of the pockets of the shareholders in order to secure their continued tenure as a managerial oligarchy, and thereby to continue to act opportunistically relative to shareholders in many other ways. However, a stewardship theory reinterpretation of these empirical findings would be that incumbent management uses its ties with board members to resist paying greenmail and to resist takeover out of the commitment of management to the company. Incumbent management perceives that a takeover by a corporate raider would lead not only to replacement of key executive personnel but also to drastic restructuring, involving perhaps both the breakup of the corporation and ruinous levels of higher debt. Incumbent management may perceive that takeovers by corporate raiders are not in the best interests of the corporation and the long-run interests of shareholders. Such incumbent managers may also believe that their greater experience and expertise in the management of their corporation in their industry will lead to better long-term corporate performance than management by a team that is new to the corporation and industry. The objective connections between the experience of the top management team and performance and between enforced restructuring and performance might be different than those contained in these perceptions. Nevertheless, incumbent top management might genuinely perceive themselves as acting in the best interests of shareholders and, therefore, not opportunistically or guilefully.

In sum, both agency theory and stewardship theory show some capacity for accommodating seemingly antithetic propositions and, therefore, seem to resist attempts at falsification. This is characteristic of theories at a high level of abstraction. There is the need for a more fundamental analysis of agency and stewardship theories aimed at eliciting their integral components and distinguishing one from the other as well as identifying their underlying theoretical commonalities.

CONCLUSIONS

Organizational economics follows from economics as a way of theorizing a neglected category within economics, namely management. Transaction cost economics gives a positive role to management while nevertheless painting managers in bleak terms. Both transaction cost theory and agency theory depict managers as inherently tending to act in opportunistic, self-serving, guileful, and lazy ways—at cost to their employers. These frameworks lack concepts for acknowledging a more positive view of managerial motives and behavior. This makes the relationship between organizational economics and traditional management theory—as well as the relationship between management academics and managers—problematic. Nevertheless, the future contribution to management theory by organizational economics can only be known through its prosecution.

The future development of organizational economics raises several issues. First is the relationship between the simple account of human motivation offered by organizational economics and the richer account offered in organization behavior (where Theory X is combined with Theory Y). Second is the relationship between the methodological individualist focus on motivation and interest and the system theoretic focus on the structure of the team for effective coordination. Together, these two issues raise challenges of integration and synthesis. A third issue is whether organizational economics within management theory will concentrate primarily on the development of positive theory or normative theory. Normative theories that yield prescriptions for organizational change will fit a customary research agenda within the study of management, but they will entail a less customary denigration of some managers as shirkers and the like. In contrast, positive theories will obviate the critique of managers, making managerial organizational economics more like the original organizational economics (which offers an appreciation of the institutional status quo and a critique of reform programs). The potentiality of positive organizational economics was briefly explored through an analysis of the origins of matrix organization structures and vertical disintegration in the insurance industry by reference to the attainment of credible commitments.

A more conventional application of agency theory was illustrated in the corporate governance field. Agency theory views were contrasted with those from the antithetic stewardship theory. The discussion served to note the flexibility of both theories in that both could accommodate research findings that on the surface appeared to be contradictory. Such flexibility emphasizes the need for further theoretical analysis.

Organizational economics developed from economics as a way to give a role to management within the market. It thus allowed a role for the visible hand of management within a milieu mainly directed by the invisible hand. However, the visible hand turned out to be a twisted and grasping hand, encased within a smooth velvet glove. Meanwhile, the market for ideas produced management theory—the ethereal hand of management. The question now is whether the visible hand of managment will reach out and warmly shake the ethereal hand of management, or push it away.

REFERENCES

Alchian, A., & Woodward, S. (1988) The firm is dead: Long live the firm [Review of Oliver Williamson's *The Economic Institutions of Capitalism*]. *Journal of Economic Literature*, 26, 65–79.

Arrow, K. J. (1985) The economics of agency. In J. W. Pratt & R. J. Zeckhauser (Eds.), *Principals and agents: The structure of business* (pp. 37–51). Boston: Harvard Business School Press.

Barney, J. B., & Ouchi, W. G. (1986) *Organizational economics*. San Francisco: Jossey-Bass.

Burrell, G., & Morgan, G. (1979) *Sociological paradigms and organizational analysis*. London: Heinemann.

Chalmers, A. F. (1982) *What is this thing called science?* (2nd ed.). Queensland: University of Queensland Press.

Chandler, A. D. (1962) *Strategy and structure: Chapters in the history of American industrial enterprise*. Cambridge, MA: MIT Press.

Chandler, A. D. (1977) *The visible hand: The managerial revolution in American business*. Cambridge, MA: Belknap Press.

Clegg, S., & Dunkerley, D. (1980) *Organization, class and control*. London: Routledge & Kegan Paul.

Coase, R. (1937) The nature of the firm. *Economica*, 4, 386–405.

Corey, E. R., & Star, S. H. (1971) Lockheed Aircraft Corporation: Lockheed-Georgia Company. In E. R. Corey & S. H. Star (Eds.), *Organizational strategy: A marketing approach* (pp. 61–107). Boston, MA: Division of Research, Graduate School of Business Administration, Harvard University.

Cyert, R. M., & March, J. G. (1963) *A behavioral theory of the firm*. Englewood Cliffs, NJ: Prentice-Hall.

Davis, S. M., & Lawrence, P. R. (1977) *Matrix*. Reading, MA: Addison-Wesley.

Donaldson, L. (1985a) *In defence of organisation theory: A reply to the critics*. Cambridge: Cambridge Unviersity Press.

Donaldson, L. (1985b) Organization design and the life cycles of products. *Journal of Management Studies*, 22, 25–37.

Donaldson, L., & Davis, J. H. (1989, August) *CEO governance and shareholder returns: Agency theory or stewardship theory*. Paper presented at the meeting of the Academy of Management, Washington, DC.

Egelhoff, W. G. (1988) *Organizing the multinational enterprise: An information-processing perspective*. Cambridge, MA: Ballinger.

Friedman, M. (1953) The methodology of positive economics. In M. Friedman (Ed.), *Essays in positive economics* (pp. 23–47). Chicago: University of Chicago Press.

Galbraith, J. R. (1973) *Designing organizations*. Reading, MA: Addison-Wesley.

Jensen, M. C., & Meckling, W. H. (1976) Theory of the firm: Managerial behavior, agency costs, and ownership structure. *Journal of Financial Economics, 3(4)*, 305–360.

Kesner, I. F., & Dalton, D. R. (1986) Boards of directors and the checks and (im)balances of corporate governance. *Business Horizons* (5), 17–23.

Kesner, I., & Dalton, D. R. (1989, August) *The role of shareholders and the board of directors in the corporate governance process.* Paper presented at the meeting of the Academy of Management, Washington, DC.

Kosnik, R. D. (1987) Greenmail: A study of board performance in corporate governance. *Administrative Science Quarterly, 32*, 163–185.

Lawrence, P. R., & Lorsch, J. W. (1967) *Organization and environment: Managing differentiation and integration.* Boston: Division of Research, Graduate School of Business Administration, Harvard University.

Lorange, P., & Vancil, R. F. (Eds.) (1977) *Strategic planning systems.* Englewood Cliffs, NJ: Prentice-Hall.

McGregor, D. (1960) *The human side of enterprise.* New York: McGraw-Hill.

Miner, J. B. (1980) *Theories of organizational behaviour.* Hinsdale, IL: Dryden Press.

Mitnick, B. (1975, Winter) The theory of agency: The policing "paradox" and regulatory behavior. *Public Choice, 24*, 27–42.

Perrow, C. (1986) *Complex organizations: A critical essay* (3rd ed.). Glenview, IL: Scott, Foresman.

Popper, K. R. (1945). *The open society and its enemies.* London: Routledge & Kegan Paul.

Pratt, J. W., & Zeckhauser, R. J. (1985) *Principals and agents: The structure of business.* Boston: Harvard Business School Press.

Rechner, P. L., & Dalton, D. R. (1988, August) *Board composition and organizational performance: A longitudinal assessment.* Paper presented at the meeting of the Academy of Management, Anaheim, CA.

Rechner, P. L., & Dalton, D. R. (1991, February) CEO duality and organizational performance: A longitudinal analysis. *Strategic Management Journal, 12*, 155–160.

Schein, E. (1970) *Organizational psychology* (2nd ed.). Englewood Cliffs, NJ: Prentice-Hall.

Smith, A. (1937) *An inquiry into the nature and causes of the wealth of nations.* New York: Modern Library.

Sullivan, M. K. (1988, August) *Outsider versus insider boards revisited: A new look at performance and board composition.* Paper presented at the meeting of the Academy of Management, Anaheim, CA.

Williamson, O. E. (1975) *Markets and hierarchies.* New York: Free Press.

Williamson, O. E. (1985) *The economic institutions of capitalism.* New York: Free Press.

Wood, R., & Bandura, A. (1989) Social cognitive theory of organizational management. *Academy of Management Review, 14*, 361–384.

CHAPTER VI

Power and Politics Organization Theory

The neatest thing about power is that we all understand it. We may have first discovered power as children when our mothers said, "Don't do that!" And we learn about power in organizations as soon as we go to school. Most of us have a pretty good intuitive grasp of the basic concepts of organizational power by the time we reach the third grade. So, the newest thing about power in organizations is not our understanding of it, but rather our intellectualizing about it.

Ordinary people—as well as scholars—have hesitated to talk about power. First, for many, power is not a subject for polite conversation. We have often equated power with force, brutality, unethical behavior, manipulation, connivance, and subjugation. Rosabeth Moss Kanter (1979) contends that "power is America's last dirty word. It is easier to talk about money—and much easier to talk about sex—than it is to talk about power." Second, many of the important writings from the power school are quite recent, and the theoretical grounding of the school is not as advanced as it is in the classical, "modern" structural, and systems schools. For both of the above reasons, fewer people have been exposed to analyses of organizational power. So, it will be useful to start our introduction to the power and politics school by contrasting some of its basic assumptions with those of its immediate predecessors, the "modern" structural and systems schools.

In both the "modern" structural and the systems schools of organization theory, organizations are assumed to be institutions whose primary purpose is to accomplish established goals. Those goals are set by people in positions of formal authority. In these two schools, the primary questions for organization theory involve how best to design and manage organizations to achieve their declared purposes effectively and efficiently. The personal preferences of organizational members are restrained by systems of formal rules, authority, and by norms of rational behavior (see Chapters IV and V for more complete discussions).

The power school rejects these assumptions about organizations as being naive, unrealistic, and therefore of minimal practical value. Instead, organizations are viewed as complex systems of individuals and coalitions, each having its own interests, beliefs, values, preferences, perspectives, and perceptions. The coalitions continuously compete with each other for scarce organizational resources. Conflict is inevitable. Influence—and the power and political activities through which influence is acquired and maintained—is the primary "weapon" for use in competition and conflicts. Thus, power, politics, and influence are critically important and permanent facts of organizational life.

Only rarely are organizational goals established by those in positions of formal authority. Goals result from ongoing maneuvering and bargaining among individuals and coalitions. Coalitions tend to be transitory: They shift with issues and often cross vertical and horizontal organizational boundaries. (For example, they may include people at several levels in the organizational hierarchy and from different product, functional, and/or geographical divisions or departments.) Thus, organizational goals change with shifts in the balance of power among coalitions. J. V. Baldridge (1971) found that organizations had many conflicting goals, and different sets of goals take priority as the balance of power changes among coalitions—as different coalitions gain and use enough power to control them. Why are organizational goals so important in the theory of organizational power and politics? Because they provide the "official" rationale and the legitimacy for resource allocation decisions.

Power relations are permanent features of organizations primarily because specialization and the division of labor result in the creation of many small, interdependent organization units with varying degrees of importance. The units compete with each other for scarce resources—as well as with the transitory coalitions. As James D. Thompson points out in *Organizations in Action* (1967), a lack of balance in the interdependence among units sets the stage for the use of power relations. Jeffery Pfeffer emphasizes this point in his Preface to *Power in Organizations* (1981): "Those persons and those units that have the responsibility for performing the more critical tasks in the organization have a natural advantage in developing and exercising power in the organization. . . . Power is first and foremost a structural phenomenon, and should be understood as such."

The "modern" structural school of organization theory places high importance on "legitimate authority" (authority that flows down through the organizational hierarchy) and formal rules (promulgated and enforced by those in authority) to ensure that organizational behavior is directed toward the attainment of established organizational goals. Structuralists tend to define power as synonymous with authority. In contrast, John Kotter (1985) argues that in today's organizational world, there is an increasing gap between the power one needs to get the job done and the power that automatically comes with the job (authority). The power and politics school views authority as only one of the many available sources of organizational power, and power is aimed in *all* directions—not just down through the hierarchy. For example, Robert W. Allen and Lyman W. Porter divide their 1983 book of readings on *Organizational Influence Processes* into three parts: downward influence (authority), lateral influence, and upward influence.

Other forms of power and influence often prevail over authority-based power. Several of this chapter's selections identify different sources of power in organizations, so we list only a few here as examples: control over scarce resources (for example, office space, discretionary funds, current and accurate information, and time and skill to work on projects), easy access to others who are perceived as having power (for example, important customers or clients, members of the board of directors, or someone else with formal authority or who controls scarce resources), a central place in a potent coalition, ability to "work the organizational rules" (knowing how to get things done or to prevent others from getting things done), and credibility (for example, that one's word can be trusted).

By now you should be wondering just what power, politics, and influence are. Many definitions have been proposed, and Jeffrey Pfeffer explores the advantages and limitations of some of the better ones in his chapter on "Understanding the Role of Power in Decision Making" from his 1981 book *Power in Organizations,* which is reprinted here. We like the following definition of power, which is a blending of definitions proposed by Gerald Salancik and Jeffrey Pfeffer (1977), and Robert Allen and Lyman Porter (1983): "Power is the ability to get things done the way one wants them done; it is the latent ability to influence people." This definition offers several advantages for understanding organizations. First, it emphasizes the relativity of power. As Pfeffer points out, "power is context or relationship specific. A person is not 'powerful' or 'powerless' in general, but only with respect to other social actors in a specific social relationship."

Second, the phrase "the way one wants them done" is a potent reminder that conflict and the use of power often are over the choice of methods, means, approaches, and/or "turf." They are not limited to battles about outcomes. This point is important because power is primarily a structural phenomenon—a consequence of the division of labor and specialization. For example, competing organizational coalitions often form around professions: hospital nurses versus paramedics, sociologists versus mathematicians in a college of liberal arts, business school—educated staff specialists versus generalists from the "school of hard knocks" in a production unit, or social workers versus educators in a center for incarcerated youth. Organizational conflicts among people representing different professions, educational backgrounds, genders, and ages frequently do not involve goals. They center on questions about the "right" of a profession, academic discipline, or sex or age group to exercise its perception of its "professional rights," to control the way things will be done, or to protect its "turf" and status. Why is this point important? Because it reemphasizes that organizational behavior and decisions frequently are not "rational"—as the word is used by the "modern" structural school and the systems school, meaning "directed toward the accomplishment of established organizational goals." Thus, this definition of power highlights a fundamental reason why the power and politics school rejects the basic assumptions of the "modern" structural school and the systems school as being naive and unrealistic, and considers those theories of organization to be of minimal value.

Jeffrey Pfeffer's chapter "Understanding the Role of Power in Decision Making," provides an excellent synopsis of the power and politics perspective on organizations. We have placed it first among this chapter's selections in order to provide the reader with a macroperspective on the school. His basic theme is that power and politics are fundamental concepts for understanding behavior in organizations.

He defines the concepts of power, authority, and organizational politics, and he identifies the "place of power" in the literature of organization theory.

"The Bases of Social Power," by John R. P. French, Jr., and Bertram Raven (1959), reprinted here, starts from the premise that power and influence involve relations between at least two agents (they limit their definition of agents to individuals), and theorizes that the reaction of the *recipient agent* is the more useful focus for explaining the phenomena of social influence and power. The core of French and Raven's piece, however, is their identification of five bases or sources of social power: reward power, the perception of coercive power, legitimate power (organizational authority), referent power (through association with others who possess power), and expert power (power of knowledge or ability).

French and Raven examine the effects of power derived from the five different bases on *attraction* (the recipient's sentiment toward the agent who uses power) and *resistance* to the use of power. Their investigations show that the use of power from the different bases has different consequences. For example, coercive power typically decreases attraction and causes high resistance, whereas reward power increases attraction and creates minimal levels of resistance. In what amounts to one of the earliest looks at ethical limits on the use of power, they conclude that "the more legitimate the coercion (is perceived to be) the less it will produce resistance and decreased attraction."

"Leadership in an Organized Anarchy" (reprinted here) is the concluding chapter from Michael Cohen and James March's 1974 general report prepared for The Carnegie Commission on Higher Education. It was published in book form as *Leadership and Ambiguity: The American College President*. The overall study was conducted in response to the almost continual crises, demonstrations, and fiscal deterioration of many colleges and universities in the United States in the late 1960s and early 1970s. During these turbulent years, university presidents lost much of their power; the role of university president that historically had been a blend of mediation and authoritative functions became predominantly mediative.

Through an extensive series of interviews conducted on and around campuses, Cohen and March found that universities have "uncertain goals, a familiar but unclear technology, and inadequate knowledge about who is attending to what." Thus, they introduced the phrase *organized anarchies* to communicate why American universities are distinctive organizational forms with unique leadership needs and problems: Most notably, the major characteristic of a presidency is ambiguity. Further, "presidents discover that they have less power than is believed, that their power to accomplish things depends heavily on what they want to accomplish, that the acceptance of authority is not automatic, that the necessary details of organizational life confuse power . . . , and that their colleagues seem to delight in complaining simultaneously about presidential weakness and presidential willfulness." *Ambiguity of power* is one of four important ambiguities of anarchy facing university presidents: The others are ambiguity of *purpose*, *experience*, and *success*. Cohen and March propose "elementary tactics of administrative action"—effective tactics for leading in an organized anarchy—that reflect the assumptions and strategies of power and politics organization theory. They also stress the importance of *sensible foolishness:* "The contribution of a college president may often be measured by his capability for sustaining that creative interaction of foolishness and rationality."

In her 1979 *Harvard Business Review* article "Power Failure in Management Circuits," which is reprinted here, Rosabeth Moss Kanter argues that executive and managerial power is a necessary ingredient for moving organizations toward their goals. "Power can mean efficacy and capacity" for organizations. The ability of managers to lead effectively cannot be predicted by studying their styles or traits; it requires knowledge of a leader's real power sources. Kanter identifies three groups of positions within organizations that are particularly susceptible to powerlessness: first-line supervisors, staff professionals, and top executives. However, she carefully distinguishes between "power" and "dominance, control, and oppression." Her primary concern is that at higher organizational levels, the power to "punish, to prevent, to sell off, to reduce, to fire, all without appropriate concern for consequences" grows, but the power needed for positive accomplishments does not. Managers who perceive themselves as being powerless and who think their subordinates are discounting them tend to use more dominating or punishing forms of influence. Thus, in large organizations, powerlessness (or perceived powerlessness) can be a more substantive problem than possession of power. By empowering others, leaders actually can acquire more "productive power"—the power needed to accomplish organizational goals. "Power Failure in Management Circuits" also contains an embedded subarticle on the particular problems that power poses for women managers.

Henry Mintzberg describes his 1983 book *Power in and Around Organizations* as a discussion of a theory of organizational power. Organizational behavior is viewed as a power game. The "players" are "influencers" with varying personal needs, who attempt to control organizational decisions and actions. "Thus, to understand the behavior of the organization, it is necessary to understand which influencers are present, what needs each seeks to fulfill in the organization, and how each is able to exercise power to fulfill them." His chapter "The Power Game and the Players," which is reprinted here, focuses on the "influencers"—who they are and where their power comes from. Eleven groups of possible influencers are listed: five are in the "external coalition" and six in the "internal coalition." The external coalition consists of the owners, "associates" (suppliers, clients, trading partners, and competitors), employee associations (unions and professional associations), the organization's various publics (at large), and the corporate directors (which includes representatives from the other four groups in the external coalition and also some internal influencers). The internal coalition is comprised of six groups of influencers: the chief executive officer, operators (the organization's "producers"), line managers, analysts (staff specialists), and the support staff. The final "actor" in Mintzberg's internal coalition is the ideology of the organization—"the set of beliefs shared by its internal influencers that distinguishes it from other organizations." Factors like organizational ideology actually are more representative of our final school of organization theory, the organizational culture school, which is discussed in the next chapter.

REFERENCES

Allen, R. W., & Porter, L. W. (1983). *Organizational influence processes.* Glenview IL: Scott, Foresman.

Baldridge, J. V. (1971). *Power and conflict in the university.* New York: Wiley.

Cohen, A. R., & Bradford, D. L. (1990). *Influence without authority.* New York: Wiley.

Cummings, L. L., & Staw, B. M. (Eds.). (1981). *Research in organizational behavior* (Vol. 3). Greenwich, CT: JAI Press.

Cobb, A. T., & Margulies, N. (1981). Organization development: A political perspective. *Academy of Management Review,* 6(1), 49–59.

Cohen, M. D., & March, J. G. (1974). *Leadership and ambiguity: The American college president.* New York: McGraw-Hill.

Cyert, R. M., & March, J. G. (1963). *A behavioral theory of the firm.* Englewood Cliffs, NJ: Prentice-Hall.

French, W. L., & Bell, C. H., Jr. (1984). *Organization development* (3d ed.). Englewood Cliffs, NJ: Prentice-Hall.

Jay, A. (1967). *Management and Machiavelli.* New York: Holt, Rinehart & Winston.

Kanter, R. M. (1977). *Men and women of the corporation.* New York: Basic Books.

Kanter, R. M. (July-August 1979). Power failure in management circuits. *Harvard Business Review,* 57, 65–75.

Kaufman, H. (March 1964). Organization theory and political theory. *American Political Science Review,* 58, 5–14.

Korda, M. (1975). *Power! How to get it, how to use it.* New York: Random House.

Kotter, J. P. (July-August 1977). Power, dependence, and effective management. *Harvard Business Review,* 55, 125–136.

Kotter, J. P. (1985). *Power and influence: Beyond formal authority.* New York: Free Press.

Mechanic, D. (December 1962). Sources of power of lower participants in complex organizations. *Administrative Science Quarterly,* 7, 3, 349–364.

Mintzberg, H. (1983). *Power in and around organizations.* Englewood cliffs, NJ: Prentice-Hall.

Ott, J. S. (Ed.), (1996). *Classic readings in organizational behavior.* (2d. ed.) Belmont, CA: Wadsworth.

Pfeffer, J. (1981). *Power in organizations.* Boston: Pitman.

Pfeffer, J. (1992). *Managing with power: Politics and influence in organizations.* Boston: Harvard Business School Press.

Porter, L. W., Allen, R. W., & Angle, H. L (1981). The politics of upward influence in organizations. In L. L. Cummings & B. M. Staw (Eds.), *Research in Organizational Behavior,* Vol. 3 (pp. 408–422). Greenwich, CT: JAI Press.

Salancik, G. R., & Pfeffer, J. (1977). Who gets power—and how they hold on to it: A strategic-contingency model of power. *Organizational Dynamics,* 5, 2–21.

Siu, R. G. H. (1979). *The craft of power.* New York: Wiley.

Thompson, J. D. (1967). *Organizations in action.* New York: McGraw-Hill.

Tushman, M. L. (April 1977). A political approach to organizations: A review and rationale. *The Academy of Management Review, 2,* 206–216.

Yates, D., Jr. (1985). *The politics of management.* San Francisco: Jossey-Bass.

Zaleznik, A., & Kets De Vries, M. F. R. (1985). *Power and the corporate mind.* Chicago: Bonus Books.

30
Understanding the Role of Power in Decision Making
Jeffrey Pfeffer

More than 40 years ago Harold Lasswell (1936) defined politics as the study of who gets what, when, and how. Certainly, who gets what, when, and how, are issues of fundamental importance in understanding formal organizations. Nevertheless, organizational politics and organizational power are both topics which are made conspicuous by their absence in management and organization theory literature (Allen, et al., 1979). Why?

It is certainly not because the terms *power* and *politics* are concepts used infrequently in everyday conversation. Both are often used to explain events in the world around us. Richard Nixon's behavior while in the presidency has been ascribed to a need for power. Budget allocations among various federal programs are described as being the result of politics. Success in obtaining a promotion may be attributed to an individual's ability to play office politics. The fact that certain business functions (such as finance) or occupational specialities (such as law) are frequently important in organizations is taken to reflect the power of those functions or occupations. There are few events that are not ascribed to the effects of power and politics. As Dahl (1957: 201) noted, "The concept of power is as ancient and ubiquitous as any that social theory can boast." . . .

Power has been neglected for several reasons. First, the concept of power is itself problematic in much of the social science literature. In the second place, while power is something it is not everything. There are other competing perspectives for understanding organizational decision making. These perspectives are frequently persuasive, if for no other reason than that they conform more closely to socially held values of rationality and effectiveness. And third, the concept of power is troublesome to the socialization of managers and the practice of management because of its implications and connotations. . . .

THE CONCEPT OF POWER

The very pervasiveness of the concept of power, referred to in the earlier quote from Robert Dahl, is itself a cause for concern about the utility of the concept in assisting us to understand behavior in organizations. Bierstedt (1950: 730) noted that the more things a term could be applied to the less precise was its meaning. Dahl (1957: 210) wrote, ". . . a Thing to which people attach many labels with subtly or grossly different meanings in many different cultures and times is probably not a Thing at all but many Things." March (1966) has suggested that in being used to explain almost everything, the concept of power can become almost a tautology, used to explain that which cannot be explained

Source: Jeffrey Pfeffer, *Power in Organizations* (Marshfield, Mass.: Pitman Publishing, 1981), 1–32. Reprinted by permission of the publisher.

by other ideas, and incapable of being disproved as an explanation for actions and outcomes. . . .

It is generally agreed that power characterized relationships among social actors. A given social actor, by which we mean an individual, subunit, or organization, has more power with respect to some social actors and less power with respect to others. Thus, power is context or relationship specific. A person is not "powerful" or "powerless" in general, but only with respect to other social actors in a specific social relationship. To say, for example, that the legal department in a specific firm is powerful, implies power with respect to other departments within that firm during a specific period of time. That same legal department may not be at all powerful with respect to its interactions with the firm's outside counsel, various federal and state regulatory agencies, and so forth. And, the power of the department can and probably will change over time. . . .

Most studies of power in organizations have focused on hierarchical power, the power of supervisors, or bosses over employees. The vertical, hierarchical dimension of power is important in understanding social life, but it is not the only dimension of power. As Perrow (1970: 59) wrote, "It is my impression that for all the discussion and research regarding power in organizations, the preoccupation with interpersonal power has led us to neglect one of the most obvious aspects of this subject: in complex organizations, tasks are divided up between a few major departments or subunits, and all of these subunits are not likely to be equally powerful." Implicit in this statement is the recognition that power is, first of all, a structural phenomenon, created by the division of labor and departmentation that characterize the specific organization or set of organizations being investigated. It is this more structural

approach to power that constitutes the focus of this book, although at times we will consider what individual characteristics affect the exercise of structurally determined power.

It should be evident why power is somewhat tricky to measure and operationalize. In order to assess power, one must be able to estimate (a) what would have happened in the absence of the exercise of power; (b) the intentions of the actor attempting to exercise power; and (c) the effect of actions taken by that actor on the probability that what was desired would in fact be likely to occur. . . . It should be recognized that the definition and assessment of power are both controversial and problematic.

THE CONCEPT OF AUTHORITY

It is important to distinguish between power and authority. In any social setting, there are certain beliefs and practices that come to be accepted within that setting. The acceptance of these practices and values, which can include the distribution of influence within the social setting, binds together those within the setting, through their common perspective. Activities which are accepted and expected within a context are then said to be legitimate within that context. The distribution of power within a social setting can also become legitimate over time, so that those within the setting expect and value a certain pattern of influence. When power is so legitimated, it is denoted as authority. Weber (1947) emphasized the critical role of legitimacy in the exercise of power. By transforming power into authority, the exercise of influence is transformed in a subtle but important way. In social situations, the exercise of power typically has costs. Enforcing one's way over others requires the expenditure of resources, the making of commitments, and a level of effort which can be undertaken only when the issues at hand are relatively important. On the other hand, the exercise of authority, power which has become legitimated, is expected and desired in the social context. Thus, the exercise of authority, far from diminishing through use, may actually serve to enhance the amount of authority subsequently possessed.

Dornbusch and Scott (1975), in their book on evaluation in organizations, made a similar point with respect to the evaluation process. They noted that in formal organizations, some people have the right to set criteria, to sample output, and to apply the criteria to the output that is sampled. Persons with such authority or evaluation rights are expected to engage in these authorized activities, and, instead of being punished for doing so, are punished when they fail to do so.

The transformation of power into authority is an important process, for it speaks to the issue of the institutionalization of social control. As such, we will return to this issue when political strategies are considered and when we take up the topic of institutionalized power. For the moment, it is sufficient to note that within formal organizations, norms and expectations develop that make the exercise of influence expected and accepted. Thus, social control of one's behavior by others becomes an expected part of organizational life. Rather than seeing the exercise of influence within organizations as a contest of strength or force, power, once it is transformed through legitimation into authority, is not resisted. At that point, it no longer depends on the resources or determinants that may have produced the power in the first place.

The transformation of power into authority can be seen most clearly in the relationship between supervisors and subordinates in work organizations. As Mechanic (1962) noted, lower level organizational members have, in reality, a great amount of power. If they refused to accept and accede to the instructions provided by higher level managers, those managers would have difficulty carrying out sanctions and operating the organization. Furthermore, the lower level participants have power that comes from specialized knowledge about the work process and access to information that higher level managers may not have. Thus, Mechanic (1962) argued, what is interesting is not that subordinates accept the instructions of managers because of the greater power possessed by the managers. Rather, it is interesting that in spite of the considerable degree of power possessed by lower level employees, these employees seldom attempt to exercise their power or to resist the instructions of their managers. . . .

When social understanding and social consensus develops to accept, ratify, and even prefer the distribution of power, then the power becomes legitimated and becomes authority. Authority is maintained not only by the resources or sanctions that produced the power, but also by the social pressures and social norms that sanction the power distribution and which define it as normal and acceptable. Such social acceptance and social approval adds stability to the situation and makes the exercise of power easier and more effective. Legitimation, of course, occurs in a specific social context, and what is legitimate in one setting may be illegitimate in another. The degree and kind of supervisor-subordinate control exercised in U.S. organizations, for instance, may be perceived as illegitimate in the organizations of countries where there is more worker self-management and industrial democracy. Legitimation of power is thus ultimately problematic and far from inevitable. The examination of the conditions under which power and social control become legitimated and transformed into authority is an important undertaking in trying to understand the governance and control of organizations.

DEFINITION OF ORGANIZATIONAL POLITICS

The task of defining the term organizational politics is as difficult as that of defining power. The problem is to distinguish between political activity and organizational or administrative activity in general. As in the case of power, if politics refers to all forms of administrative or managerial action, then the term becomes meaningless because it includes every behavior.

From Lasswell's (1936) definition of politics as who gets what, when, and how, and from Wildavsky's (1979) descriptions of the politics of the budgetary process, the inference is that politics involves how differing preferences are resolved in conflicts over the allocation of scarce resources. Thus, politics involves activities which attempt to influence decisions over critical issues that are not readily resolved through the introduction of new data and in which there are differing points of view. For our purposes, organizational politics will be defined as:

> Organizational politics involves those activities taken within organizations to acquire, develop, and use power and other resources to obtain one's preferred outcomes in a situation in which there is uncertainty or dissensus about choices.

If power is a force, a store of potential influence through which events can be affected, politics involves those activities or behaviors through which power is developed and used in organizational settings. Power is a property of the system at rest; politics is the study of power in action. An individual, subunit, or de-

partment may have power within an organizational context at some period of time; politics involves the exercise of power to get something accomplished, as well as those activities which are undertaken to expand the power already possessed or the scope over which it can be exercised. This definition is similar to that provided by Allen, et al. (1979: 77): "Organizational politics involve intentional acts of influence to enhance or protect the self-interest of individuals or groups."

From the definition of power, it is clear that political activity is activity which is undertaken to overcome some resistance or opposition. Without opposition or contest within the organization, there is neither the need nor the expectation that one would observe political activity. And, because political activity is focused around the acquisition and use of power, it can be distinguished from activity involved in making decisions which uses rational or bureaucratic procedures. In both rational and bureaucratic models of choice, there is no place for and no presumed effect of political activity. Decisions are made to best achieve the organization's goals, either by relying on the best information and options that have been uncovered, or by using rules and procedures which have evolved in the organization. Political activity, by contrast, implies the conscious effort to muster and use force to overcome opposition in a choice situation. . . .

THE PLACE OF POWER IN ORGANIZATION THEORY LITERATURE

. . . Examination of the major textbooks now current in the field will indicate that the subject of power is either not mentioned at all in the subject index or, if it is, it receives short shrift in terms of the number of pages devoted to it. When the subject of power is found in the index, it is frequently associated with a discussion of the individual bases of power (e.g., French and Raven, 1968) or the need for power. Size, technology, and environment all receive much more time and attention, even in those books with a presumably more sociological perspective. And, in specialized books dealing with topics such as organization design or organization development, power typically receives no mention at all, even though it is a particularly critical variable for some of these more specialized concerns. . . .

A likely explanation for the neglect of power in the management and organizational behavior literature is found by considering the role of management writing in the management process, and the position of a topic such as power as implied by the various functions served by management writing. The argument to be developed is relatively straightforward: management writing serves a variety of functions; in virtually all of these functions there is a strong component of ideology and values; topics such as power and politics are basically incompatible with the values and ideology being developed; therefore, it is reasonable, if not theoretically useful, to ignore topics which detract from the functions being served by the writing, and this includes tending to ignore or to downplay the topics of power and politics.

To ask what functions are served by management writing, we can begin by asking who reads management books. . . .

In the case of students, there is little doubt that one of the important functions of business education is socialization. This statement reflects both the more general importance of socialization in the educational process, and the specific prominence of socialization with respect to certain occupations and professions. It is not in just the fields of medicine and law that socialization plays an important part of the educational process. Although less frequently empirically examined, there are important considerations of socialization in the education of young, aspiring managers (e.g., Schein, 1968). Socialization involves the inculcation of norms and values that are central to the profession and that are, not incidentally, useful to the organizations in which the professionals are going to work. There is no norm so central to the existing practice and ideology of management as the norm of rationality. . . . Rationality and rational choice models focus attention on the development of technologies to more effectively achieve a goal or set of goals, such as profit or efficiency. Concern is directed toward the development of alternatives, the development of sophisticated techniques for evaluating the alternatives, their possible consequences, and the assembling of information that facilitates the evaluation of performance along these specified dimensions. . . .

To socialize students into a view of business that emphasizes power and politics would not only make the compliance to organizational authority and the acceptance of decision outcomes and procedures problematic, but also it might cause recruitment problems into the profession. It is certainly much more noble to think of oneself as developing skills toward the more efficient allocation and use of resources—implicitly for the greater good of society as a whole—than to think of oneself as engaged with other organizational participants in a political struggle over values, preferences, and definitions of technology. Technical rationality, as a component of the managerial task, provides legitimation and meaning for one's career, fulfilling a function similar to healing the sick for doctors, or serving the nation's system of laws and justice for attorneys.

For . . . practicing managers, as well as for the student, the ideology of rationality and efficiency provides an explanation for career progress, or lack thereof, that is much more likely to lead to the acceptance of one's position rather than an attempt at making a radical change. . . .

In this way, the ideology of efficiency and rationality provides comforting explanations for practicing managers who find the progress of their careers blocked or less than what they might like, or feel a general sense of malaise about their work and their future. The invisible hands of marginal productivity and human capital have put them where they deserve to be. If power is to be considered at all, it is in terms of individually-oriented political strategies (e.g., Korda, 1975), which provide the managers with the illusion that, with a few handy hints, they can improve their lot in the organization. Explanations which focus on structural variables, as most of the explanations for power and politics developed here do, are less popular, as they provide no easy palliatives and imply a need for much more fundamental change in terms of affecting decision outcomes.

For the third set of readers of the management literature, the general public, the emphasis on rationality and efficiency and the deemphasis on power and politics, assures them that the vast power and wealth controlled by organizations is, indeed, being effectively and legitimately employed. In this sense, organization theory and economic theory frequently find themselves fulfilling similar roles in explaining the status quo in terms which both justify and legitimate it. . . .

The ideology of functional rationality—decision making oriented toward the improvement of efficiency or performance—provides a legitimation of formal organizations, for the general public as well as for those working within specific organizations. Bureaucracies are, as Perrow (1972) argued, tremendous stores of resources and energy, both human and financial. Bureaucracies also represent concentrations of energy on a scale seldom seen in the history of the world. The legitimation and justification of these concentrations of power are clearly facilitated by theories arguing that efficiency, productivity, and effectiveness are the dominant dynamics underlying the operation of organizations.

To maintain that organizations are less than totally interested in efficiency, effectiveness or market performance is to suggest that it is legitimate to raise questions concerning the appropriateness of the concentration of power and energy they represent and makes it possible to introduce political concerns into the issues of corporate governance. The introduction of these concerns makes the present control arrangements less certain and permanent and would be resisted by all of those who benefit from the status quo.

The argument, then, is that the very literature of management and organizational behavior (as well, we might add, of much of economics, though that is a topic worthy of separate development) is itself political (Edelman, 1964), and causes support to be generated and opposition to be reduced as various conceptions of organizations are created and maintained in part through their very repetition. In this literature, efficiency-enhancing or profit-increasing behavior are not being taken as hypotheses about motivation and causes for action, but rather as accepted facts. Then, a theory is developed which is both consistent with these assumptions and finds excuses for why so much variation in actual decisions and behaviors is missed. . . .

Models of organizations which emphasize power and politics have their own political problems. It is important for those analyzing organizations to be able to figure out the kind of analytical framework that can be most usefully employed to diagnose the particular organization of interest. Kaplan's (1964) parable of the hammer is relevant. Because one has a hammer, one tends to use it on everything and for every task. Similarly, there is a tendency to take a noncontingent approach to the analysis of organizations, and to see them all as rational, bureaucratic, or political. Just as it is difficult to play football with baseball equipment, it is difficult to diagnose or effectively operate in an organization unless its dominant paradigm or mode of operation is understood. Furthermore, in order to evaluate the validity of a political approach to organizational analysis, there must be some alternatives with which to compare the model. For both of these reasons—to place the political model in a broader context of competing perspectives on organizational decision making and to raise issues relevant to diagnosing the form of system one is dealing with—we will describe the major contending models of organizational decision making.

RATIONAL CHOICE MODELS

The model of rational choice is prominent in the social choice literature. It is not only prescribed as being the best way to make choices in organizations, but frequently claims to be descriptive of actual choice processes as well. The rational model presumes that events are "purposive choices of consistent actors" (Allison, 1971: 11). It is important to recognize, therefore, that the rational model presumes and assumes that "be-

havior reflects purpose or intention" (Allison, 1971: 13). Behavior is not accidental, random, or rationalized after the fact; rather, purpose is presumed to pre-exist and behavior is guided by that purpose. With respect to understanding organizations or other social collectivities, the rational model further presumes that there is a unified purpose or set of preferences characterizing the entity taking the action. As Allison (1971: 28-29) has noted:

> What rationality adds to the concept of purpose is *consistency*: consistency among goals and objectives relative to a particular action; consistency in the application of principles in order to select the optimal alternative (emphasis in original).

The rational choice model presumes that there are goals and objectives that characterize organizations. As Friedland (1974) has noted, rationality cannot be defined apart from the existence of a set of goals. Thus, all rational choice models start with the assumption of a goal or consistent goal set. In the case of subjective expected utility maximization models (Edwards, 1954), the goals are called utilities for various outcomes, associated with the pleasure or pain producing properties of the outcomes. In the language of economics and management science, the goals are called the objectives or objective function to be maximized. Occasionally, goals are called preferences, referring to the states of the world the social actor prefers. Rational choice models require that these goals be consistent (March, 1976: 70).

Given a consistent set of goals, the next element in theories of rational choice is a set of decision-making alternatives to be chosen. Alternatives are presumed to be differentiable one from the other, so that each is uniquely identified. Such alternatives are produced by a search process. Until Simon (1957) introduced the concept of satisficing, it was generally assumed that search was costless and that large numbers of alternatives would be considered. Simon's contribution was to introduce the concept of bounded rationality, which held that persons had both limited capacities to process information and limited resources to devote to search activities. Thus a search for alternatives would be conducted only until a satisfactory alternative was uncovered. The concept of satisfaction was defined in terms of the social actor's level of aspiration (March and Simon, 1958).

Be they many or few, once a set of alternatives are uncovered, the next step in the rational decision-making process involves the assessment of the likely outcomes or consequences of the various possible courses of action. If there is risk or uncertainty involved, then estimates of the probability of the occurrence of various consequences would be used in making statements about the values of the consequences of different choices. At this stage in the decision process, it is assumed that consequences can be fully and completely anticipated, albeit with some degree of uncertainty. In other words, everything that can possibly occur as a result of the decision is presumably specified, though which of the various possibilities will actually occur may be subject to chance.

Then, a rational choice involves selecting that course of action or that alternative which maximizes the social actor's likelihood of attaining the highest value for achievement of the preferences or goals in the objective function. . . .

It is clear that in analyzing choice processes in organizations or other social collectives, the assumption of consistency and unity in the goals, information and decision processes is problematic. However, one of the advantages of the rational model is that it permits prediction of behavior with complete certainty and specificity if one knows (or assumes one knows) the goals of the other organization. Allison (1971: 13), in reviewing foreign policy analysis, has argued that this advantage is one important reason that "most contemporary analysts . . . proceed *predominantly* . . . in terms of this framework when trying to explain international events." The rational choice model facilitates the prediction of what the other social actor will do, assuming various goals; turning the model around, various goals can be inferred (though scarcely unambiguously) from the behavior of the other actor. It is inevitably the case that "an imaginative analyst can construct an account of value-maximizing choice for an action or set of actions performed" (Allison, 1971: 35). . . .

BUREAUCRATIC MODELS OF DECISION MAKING

The rational model of choice implies the need for some substantial information processing requirements in organizational decision making. These may be unrealistic or unattainable in some cases, and organizations may operate using standard operating procedures and rules rather than engaging in rational decision making on a continuous basis. The bureaucratic model of organizations substitutes procedural rationality for substantive rationality (Simon, 1979); rather than having choices made to maximize values, choices are made according to rules and processes which have been adaptive and effective in the past.

The best explication of what is meant by bureaucratically-rational decision processes can be found in March and Simon (1958) and Cyert and March (1963). In this framework, goals are viewed as systems of constraints (Simon,

1964) which decisions must satisfy. Because of bounded rationality, search is limited and stops as soon as a satisfactory alternative is found. Uncertainty tends to be avoided in that, rather than making comprehensive assessments of risk and probabilities, decisions are made with relatively short time horizons. Conflict among different alternatives or points of view is never fully resolved, and priorities and objectives are attended to sequentially, first, for instance, worrying about profit, then about market share, then personnel problems, and so forth. Throughout this process, organizations learn and adapt, and their learning and knowledge takes the form of rules of action or standard operating procedures, repertoires of behavior which are activated in certain situations and which provide a program, a set of behaviors for organizational participants, that serve as a guide to action and choice.

Seen from this perspective, decisions are viewed "less as deliberate choices and more as *outputs* or large organizations functioning according to standard patterns of behavior" (Allison, 1971: 67). It is presumed that "most of the behavior is determined by previously established procedures" (Allison, 1971: 79). The model of organizations as bureaucratically rational presumes less conscious foresight and less clearly defined preferences and information. Both rely on habitual ways of doing things and the results of past actions, and constrain how the organization proceeds to operate in the future. Decisions are not made as much as they evolve from the policies, procedures, and rules which constitute the organization and its memory. . . .

DISTINGUISHING BUREAUCRATIC ORGANIZATIONS

Distinguishing between the bureaucratic and political models of oganization may be somewhat more difficult. After all, if the distribution of power is stable in the organization, which is a reasonable assumption, particularly over relatively short time periods, and if power and politics determine organizational decisions, then organizational choices will be relatively stable over time. But, this stability is also characteristic of the use of precedent in decision making, which is one of the hallmarks of bureaucratic organizations. One way of distinguishing, then, would involve looking at the correlates of the incremental changes in decisions and allocations made within the organization. While both models might be consistent with the use of precedent for the bulk of the decisions, there are some implicit differences in how incremental resources will be allocated. In bureaucratic organizations, changes in resource allocation patterns should either follow a proportional basis, be based on some standard measure of operations and performance, or reflect an attempt to shift the resources to better achieve the goals and values of the organization. By contrast, political models of organizations would suggest that power would best predict changes and shifts in decisions and allocations. . . .

DECISION PROCESS MODELS

Although they exist within much the same tradition as the bureaucratic model of organizations, decision process models differ in that they presume even less rationality and more randomness in organizational functioning. As power models depart from bureaucratic rationality by removing the assumption of consistent, overall organizational objectives and shared beliefs about technology, decision process models depart even further by removing the presumption of predefined, known preferences held by the various social actors. Decision process models posit that there are no overall organizational goals being maximized through choice, and no powerful actors with defined preferences who possess resources through which they seek to obtain those preferences. Stava (1976: 209) described decision process models as follows:

> In *decision process theories* it is presumed that policy is the outcome of a choice made by one or several decision-makers. Which choice is made is determined by the situation in which the decision-maker finds himself. This situation is, in turn, largely caused by the processes preceding the choice. It is impossible, then, to predict policies without knowing the details of the preceding processes.

March (1966: 180) argued that in such decision process models, although one might posit that the various actors have preferences and varying amounts of power, the concept of power does not add much to the prediction of behavior and choice in such systems.

More recently, March (1978) and others (e.g., Weick, 1969) have questioned whether or not the concept of preferences makes sense at any level of analysis, individual or organizational. One of the arguments raised is that instead of preferences guiding choice, choice may determine preferences. In other words, one only knows what one likes after it has been experienced; or, as Weick has argued, one only knows what one has done after he or she has done it, since the meaning of action is retrospective and follows the action rather than preceeds it. In this framework, goals are seen as the products of sense making activities which are carried on after the action has occurred to explain that action or rationalize it. The action itself is presumed to be the result of habit, custom, or the influence of other social actors in the environment.

One example of a decision process model of social choice is the garbage can model (Cohen, March, and Olsen, 1972). The basic idea of the model is that decision points are opportunities into which various problems and solutions are dumped by organizational participants. "In a garbage can situation, a decision is an outcome of an interpretation of several relatively independent 'streams' within an organization" (Cohen, March, and Olsen, 1976: 26). The streams consist of problems, solutions (which are somebody's product), participants, and choice opportunities. The decision process models developed by March and his colleagues emphasize the problematic nature of participation by various social actors in choices. They note that systems are frequently so overloaded with problems, solutions, and decision opportunities that any given social actor will attend to only certain decisions. . . .

The garbage can model emerged largely from a study of universities and university presidents (Cohen and March, 1974). Universities were characterized as organized anarchies, and garbage can decision process models were believed to be particularly appropriate in such contexts, although the assertion is also made that elements of these models are found in most organizations. . . . The theory holds further that problems move autonomously among choice opportunities in search for a choice process in which the problem can be resolved" (Weiner, 1976: 243). Decision making is viewed as an activity which absorbs the energy of those available, works on problems, and comes up with solutions which are determined in large measure by a random stream of events.

DISTINGUISHING ORGANIZED ANARCHIES

The key concept used in diagnosing whether or not the organization is an organized anarchy which can best be understood by using decision process organizational models is that of intention. Not only are there presumed to be no overarching organizational goals, but presumably intention is problematic even at the level of subunits and groups within the organization. Action occurs, but it is not primarily motivated by conscious choice and planning. Although not made explicit, there should be relatively little consistency or consensus over behavior in an organized anarchy. Events should unfold in ways predictable only by considering the process, and not through consideration of value maximization, precedent, power, or force. . . .

POLITICAL MODELS OF ORGANIZATIONS

One criticism that has been leveled against rational choice models is that they fail to take into account the diversity of interests and goals within organizations. March (1962) described business firms as political coalitions. The coalitional view of organizations was developed by Cyert and March (1963) in their description of organizational decision making. In bureaucratic theories of organizations, the presumption is that through control devices such as rewards based on job performance or seniority, rules that ensure fair and standardized treatment for all, and careers within the organization, the operation of self-interest can be virtually eliminated as an influence on organizational decision making. Economic or incentive theories of organizations argue that through the payment of wage, particularly when compensation is made contingent on performance, individuals hired into the organization come to accept the organization's goals. Political models of organizations assume that these control devices, as well as others such as socialization, are not wholly effective in

producing a coherent and unified set of goals or definitions of technology. Rather, as Baldridge (1971: 25) has argued, political models view organizations as pluralistic and divided into various interests, subunits, and subcultures. Conflict is viewed as normal or at least customary in political organizations. Action does not presuppose some overarching intention. Rather, action results "from games among players who perceive quite different faces of an issue and who differ markedly in the actions they prefer" (Allison, 1971: 175). Because action results from bargaining and compromise, the resulting decision seldom perfectly reflects the preferences of any group or subunit within the organization.

Political models of choice further presume that when preferences conflict, the power of the various social actors determines the outcome of the decision process. Power models hypothesize that those interests, subunits, or individuals within the organization who possess the greatest power, will receive the greatest rewards from the interplay of organizational politics. In such models, power "is an intervening variable between an initial condition, defined largely in terms of the individual components of the system, and a terminal state, defined largely in terms of the system as a whole" (March, 1966: 168–169). Power is used to overcome the resistance of others and obtain one's way in the organization.

To understand organizational choices using a political model, it is necessary to understand who participates in decision making, what determines each player's stand on the issues, what determines each actor's relative power, and how the decision process arrives at a decision; in other words, how the various preferences become combined (majority rule; unanimity; ⅔ vote; etc.) (Allison, 1971: 164). A change in any one of these aspects—relative power, the rules of decision making, or preferences—can lead to a change in the predicted organizational decision.

DISTINGUISHING POLITICAL MODELS OF ORGANIZATIONS

. . . Power models can be distinguished from rational models if it can be demonstrated that either no overarching organizational goal exists or even if such a goal does exist, decisions are made which are inconsistent with maximizing the attainment of the goal. Power can be distinguished from chance or organized anarchy models by demonstrating that actors in organizations have preferences and intentions which are consistent across decision issues and which they attempt to have implemented. Further evidence for political models would come from finding that measures of power in social systems, rather than goals, precedent, or chance, bring about decision outcomes. Indeed, the ability to measure and operationalize power is critical both for diagnosing political systems and for testing political models of organizations.

SUMMARY

One of the points of Allison's (1971) analysis of the Cuban missile crisis is that it is not necessary to choose between analytical frameworks. Each may be partly true in a particular situation, and one can obtain a better understanding of the organization by trying to use all of the models rather than by choosing among them. This point is different than saying that some organizations are characterized more by the political model and others by the rational model. Allison's argument is that insight can be gained from the application of all the frameworks in the same situation. This

statement is true, but only within limits. At some point, the various perspectives will begin to make different predictions about what will occur, and will generate different recommendations concerning the strategy and tactics to be followed. At that point, the participant will need to decide where to place his or her bets. . . .

In Figure 1, the four decision models described in this chapter are briefly summarized along eight relevant dimensions. The ability to perfectly distinguish between the models, using a single dimension in a particular situation, is likely to be limited. However, by considering the dimensions in combination and by using comparative frames of reference, it becomes feasible to assess the extent to which the organization in question is operating according to one or the other of the models.

It is evident from the title of this book what my view is concerning the relative applicability of the four models of organizational decision making. Circumstances of bureaucratically rational decision making occur only in certain conditions on an infrequent basis. As Thompson and Tuden (1959) have argued, consensus on both goals and technology, or the connections between actions and consequences, are necessary in order for computational forms of decision making to be employed. Where them is disagreement over goals, compromise is used; when there is disagreement over technology, judgment is employed; and when there is disagreement about both, Thompson and Tuden characterize the decision situation as one requiring inspiration. In the case of judgment, compromise, and inspiration, it is the relative power of the various social actors that provides both the sufficient and necessary way of resolving the decision.

FIGURE 1 • OVERVIEW OF FOUR ORGANIZATIONAL
DECISION-MAKING MODELS

	Model			
Dimension	Rational	Bureaucratic	Decision Process/ Organized Anarchy	Political Power
Goals, preferences	Consistent within and across social actors	Reasonably consistent	Unclear, ambiguous, may be constructed ex post to rationalize action	Consistent within social actors; inconsistent, pluralistic within the organization
Power and control	Centralized	Less centralized with greater reliance on rules	Very decentralized, anarchic	Shifting coalitions and interest groups
Decision process	Orderly, substantively rational	Procedural rationality embodied in programs and standard operating procedures	Ad hoc	Disorderly, characterized by push and pull of interests
Rules and norms	Norm of optimization	Precedent, tradition	Segmented and episodic participation in decisions	Free play of market forces; conflict is legitimate and expected
Information and computational requirements	Extensive and systematic	Reduced by the use of rules and procedures	Haphazard collection and use of information	Information used and withheld strategically
Beliefs about action-consequence relationships	Known at least to a probability distribution	Consensually shared acceptance of routines	Unclear, ambiguous technology	Disagreements about technology
Decisions	Follow from value-maximizing choice	Follow from programs and routines	Not linked to intention; result of intersection of persons, solutions, problems	Result of bargaining and interplay among interests
Ideology	Efficiency and effectiveness	Stability, fairness, predictability	Playfulness, loose coupling, randomness	Struggle, conflict, winners and losers

Furthermore, if intention is not always a guiding force in the taking of action and if preferences are not always clear or consistent, then there are at least some participants in organizations who know what they want and have the social power to get it. The randomness implied by the decision process model of organizations is inconsistent with the observation that in organizational decision making, some actors seem to usually get the garbage, while others manage to get the can.

Standard operating procedures, rules, and behavior repertoires clearly exist and are important in organizations. Much organizational decision making involves issues that are neither important nor contested, and in such cases, standard operating procedures are sufficient to get the decisions made in an inexpensive fashion. However, it is necessary to be aware that these various rules, norms, and procedures have in themselves implications for the distribution of power and authority in organizations and for how contested decisions should be resolved. The rules and processes themselves become important focal points for the exercise of power. They are not always neutral and not always substantively rational. Sometimes they are part and parcel of the political contest that occurs within organizations.

One of the reasons why power and politics characterize so many organizations is because of what some of my students have dubbed the Law of Political Entropy: given the opportunity, an organization will tend to seek and maintain a political character. The argument is that once politics are introduced into a situation, it is very difficult to restore rationality. Once consensus is lost, once disagreements about preferences, technology, and management philosophy emerge, it is very hard to restore the kind of shared perspective and solidarity which is necessary to operate under the rational model. If rationality is indeed this fragile, and if the Law of Political Entropy is correct, then over time one would expect to see more and more organizations characterized by the political model.

REFERENCES

Allen, R. W., Madison, D. L., Porter, L. W., Renwick, P. A., & Mayes, B. T. (1979). Organizational politics: Tactics and characteristics of its actors. *California Management Review, 22*, 77–83.

Allison, G. T. (1971). *Essence of decision.* Boston: Little, Brown.

Baldridge, J. V. (1971). *Power and conflict in the university.* New York: Wiley.

Baritz, J. H. (1960). *The servants of power.* Middletown, CT: Wesleyan University Press.

Bierstedt, R. (1950). An analysis of social power. *American Sociological Review, 15,* 730–738.

Blau, P. M. (1964). *Exchange and power in social life.* New York: Wiley.

———, and Schoenherr, R. A. (1971). *The structure of organizations.* New York: Basic Books.

Burns, T., & Stalker, G. M. (1961). *The management of innovation.* London: Tavistock.

Carey, A. (1967). The Hawthorne studies: A radical criticism. *American Sociological Review, 32,* 403–416.

Cartwright, D. (1979). Contemporary social psychology in historical perspective. *Social Psychology Quarterly, 42,* 82–93.

Cohen, M.D., & March, J. G. (1974). *Leadership and ambiguity: The American college president.* New York: McGraw-Hill.

———, & Olsen, J. P. (1972). A garbage can model of organizational choice. *Administrative Science Quarterly, 17:* 1–25.

———. (1976). People, problems, solutions, and the ambiguity of relevance. In J. G. March and J. P. Olsen, (Eds.), *Ambiguity and choice in organizations* (pp. 24–37). Bergen, Norway: Universitetsforlaget.

Crecine, J. P. (1967). A computer simulation model of municipal budgeting. *Management Science, 13:* 786–815.

Crozier, M. (1964). *The bureaucratic phenomenon*. Chicago: University of Chicago Press.

Cyert, R. M., & March, J. G. (1963). *A behavioral theory of the firm*. Englewood Cliffs, NJ: Prentice-Hall.

Dahl, R. A. (1957). The concept of power. *Behavioral Science, 2,* 201–215.

Davis, O. A., Dempster, M. A. H., & Wildavsky, A. (1966). A theory of the budgeting process. *American Political Science Review, 60:* 529–547.

Dornbusch, S. M., & Scott, W. R. (1975). *Evaluation and the exercise of authority: A theory of control applied to diverse organizations*. San Francisco, CA: Jossey-Bass.

Edelman, M. (1964). *The symbolic uses of politics*. Urbana, IL: University of Illinois Press.

Edwards, W. (1954). The theory of decision making. *Psychological Bulletin, 51:* 380–417.

Emerson, R. M. (1962). Power-dependence relations. *American Sociological Review, 27,* 31–41.

French, J. R. P., Jr., & Raven, B. (1968). The bases of social power. In D. Cartwright & A. Zander (Eds.), *Group dynamics* (3rd ed.). (pp. 259–269). New York: Harper & Row.

Friedland, E. I. (1974). *Introduction to the concept of rationality in political science*. Morristown, NJ: General Learning Press.

Galbraith, J. R. (1973). *Designing complex organizations*. Reading, MA: Addison-Wesley.

Gerwin, D. (1969). A process model of budgeting in a public school system. *Management Science, 15:* 338–361.

Kaplan A. (1964). *The conduct of inquiry*. Scranton, PA: Chandler.

Karpik, L. (1978). Organizations, institutions and history. In Lucien Karpik (Ed.), *Organization and environment: Theory, issues and reality* (pp. 15–68). Newbury Park, CA: Sage.

Korda, M. (1975). *Power*. New York: Ballantine Books.

Lasswell, H. D. (1936). *Politics: Who gets what, when, how*. New York: McGraw-Hill.

Lawrence, P. R., & Lorsch, J. W. (1967). *Organization and environment*. Boston: Graduate School of Business Administration, Harvard University.

March, J. G. (1962). The business firm as a political coalition. *Journal of Politics, 24,* 662–678.

———. (1966). The power of power. In D. Easton (Ed.), *Varieties of political theory* (pp. 39–70). Englewood Cliffs, NJ: Prentice-Hall.

———. (1976). The technology of foolishness. In J. G. March and J. P. Olsen, (Eds.), *Ambiguity and choice in organizations* (pp. 69–81). Bergen, Norway: Universitetsforlaget.

———. (1978). Bounded rationality, ambiguity, and the engineering of choice. *Bell Journal of Economics, 9,* 587–608.

———, & Simon, H. A. (1958). *Organizations*. New York: John Wiley.

Mayes, B. T., & Allen, R. W. (1977). Toward a definition of organizational politics. *Academy of Management Review, 2,* 672–678.

Mechanic, D. (1962). Sources of power of lower participants in complex organizations. *Administrative Science Quarterly, 7,* 349–364.

Nehrbass, R. G. (1979). Ideology and the decline of management theory. *Academy of Management Review, 4,* 427–431.

Nord, W. R. (1974). The failure of current applied behavioral science: A Marxian perspective. *Journal of Applied Behavioral Science, 10,* 557–578.

Pennings, J. M. (1975). The relevance of the structural-contingency model for organizational effectiveness. *Administrative Science Quarterly, 20,* 393–410.

Perrow, C. (1961). The analysis of goals in complex organizations. *American Sociological Review, 26,* 859–866.

———. (1970). Departmental power and perspectives in industrial firms. In M. N. Zald (Ed.), *Power in organizations* (pp. 59–89). Nashville: Vanderbilt University Press.

———. (1972). *Complex organizations: A critical essay*. Glenview, IL: Scott, Foresman.

Pfeffer, J. (1978a). The micropolitics of organizations. In M. W. Meyer and Assoc., (Eds.), *Environments and organizations* (pp. 29–50). San Francisco: CA: Jossey-Bass.

Pfeffer, J., & Salancik, G. R. (1974). Organizational decision making as a political process: The case of a university budget. *Administrative Science Quarterly, 19,* 135–151.

———. (1978). *The external control of organizations: A resource dependence perspective*. New York: Harper & Row.

———, & Leblebici, H. (1976). The effect of uncertainty on the use of social influence in organizational decision making. *Administrative Science Quarterly, 21,* 227–245.

Pondy, L. R. (1969). Effects of size, complexity, and ownership on administrative intensity. *Administrative Science Quarterly, 14,* 47–60.

Pugh, D. S. (1966). Modern organization theory. *Psychological Bulletin, 66,* 235–251.

Salancik, G. R., & Pfeffer, J. (1974). The bases and use of power in organizational decision making: The case of a university. *Administrative Science Quarterly, 19,* 453–473.

———. (1977b). Who gets power—and how they hold on to it: A strategic-contingency model of power. *Organizational Dynamics, 5,* 3–21.

Schein, E. H. (1968). Organizational socialization and the profession of management. *Industrial Management Review, 9,* 1–16.

Simon, H. A. (1957). *Models of man.* New York: Wiley.

———. (1964). On the concept of organizational goal. *Administrative Science Quarterly, 9:* 1–22.

———. (1979). Rational decision making in business organizations. *American Economic Review, 69:* 493–513.

Stava, P. (1976). Constraints on the politics of public choice. In *Ambiguity and choice in organizations,* James G. March and Johan P. Olsen, pp. 206–224. Bergen, Norway: Universitetsforlaget.

Thompson, J. D. (1967). *Organizations in action.* New York: McGraw-Hill.

———, and Tuden, A. (1959). Strategies, structures, and processes of organizational decision. In J. D. Thompson, P. B. Hammond, R. W. Hawkes, B. H. Junker, and A. Tuden, (Eds.), *Comparative studies in administration* (pp. 195–216). Pittsburgh: University of Pittsburgh Press.

Weber, M. (1947). *The theory of social and economic organization.* New York: Free Press.

Weick, K. E. (1969). *The social psychology of organizing.* Reading, MA: Addison-Wesley.

Weiner, S. S. (1976). Participation, deadlines, and choice. In J. G. March and J. P. Olsen, (Eds.), *Ambiguity and choice in organizations* (pp. 225–250). Bergen, Norway: Universitetsforlaget.

Wildavsky, A. (1979). *The politics of the budgeting process.* (3rd ed.). Boston: Little, Brown.

———, and Hammond, A. (1965). Comprehensive versus incremental budgeting in the department of agriculture. *Administrative Science Quarterly, 10:* 321–346.

Williamson, O. E. (1975). *Markets and hierarchies: Analysis and antitrust implications.* New York: Free Press.

Woodward, J. (1965). *Industrial organization: Theory and practice.* London: Oxford University Press.

Zald, M. N. (1965). Who shall rule? A political analysis of succession in a large welfare organization. *Pacific Sociological Review, 8,* 52–60.

31

The Bases of Social Power

John R. P. French, Jr., & Bertram Raven

The processes of power are pervasive, complex, and often disguised in our society. Accordingly one finds in political science, in sociology, and in social psychology a variety of distinctions among different types of social power or among qualitatively different processes of social influence (1, 6, 14, 20, 23, 29, 30, 38, 41). Our main purpose is to identify the major types of power and to define them systematically so that we may compare them according to the changes which they produce and the other effects which accompany the use of power. The phenomena of power and influence involve a dyadic relation between two agents which may be viewed from two points of view: (a) What determines the behavior of the agent who exerts power? (b) What determines the reactions of the recipient of this behavior? We take this second point of view and formulate our theory in terms of the life space of P, the person upon whom the power is exerted. In this way we hope to define basic concepts of power which will be adequate to explain many of the phenomena of social influence, including some which have been described in other less genotypic terms. . . .

POWER, INFLUENCE, AND CHANGE

Psychological Change

Since we shall define power in terms of influence, and influence in terms of psychological change, we begin with a discussion of change. We want to define change at a level of generality which includes changes in behavior, opinions, attitudes, goals, needs, values and all other aspects of the person's psychological field. We shall use the word "system" to refer to any such part of the life space.[1] Following Lewin (26, p. 305) the state of a system at time 1 will be noted $s_1(a)$.

Psychological change is defined as any alteration of the state of some system a over time. The amount of change is measured by the size of the difference between the states of the system a at time 1 and at time 2: $ch(a) = s_2(a) - s_1(a)$.

Change in any psychological system may be conceptualized in terms of psychological forces. But it is important to note that the change must be coordinated to the resultant force of all the forces operating at the moment. Change in an opinion, for example, may be determined jointly by a driving force induced by another person, a restraining force corresponding to anchorage in a group opinion, and an own force stemming from the person's needs.

Social Influence

Our theory of social influence and power is limited to influence on the person, P, produced by a social agent, O, where O

[1] The word "system" is here used to refer to a whole or to a part of the whole.

Source: John R. P. French, Jr., and Bertram Raven, "The Bases of Social Power," in *Studies in Social Power*, edited by Dorwin P. Cartwright (Ann Arbor, MI: Institute for Social Research, The University of Michigan, 1959), pp. 150–167. Reprinted by permission of the publisher.

can be either another person, a role, a norm, a group or a part of a group. We do not consider social influence exerted on a group.

The influence of O on system *a* in the life space of P is defined as the resultant force on system *a* which has its source in an act of O. This resultant force induced by O consists of two components: a force to change the system in the direction induced by O and an opposing resistance set up by the same act of O.

By this definition the influence of O does not include P's own forces nor the forces induced by other social agents. Accordingly the "influence" of O must be clearly distinguished from O's "control" of P. O may be able to induce strong forces on P to carry out an activity (i.e., O exerts strong influence on P); but if the opposing forces induced by another person or by P's own needs are stronger, then P will locomote in an opposite direction (i.e., O does not have control over P). Thus psychological change in P can be taken as an operational definition of the social influence of O on P only when the effects of other forces have been eliminated.

Commonly social influence takes place through an intentional act on the part of O. However, we do not want to limit our definition of "act" to such conscious behavior. Indeed, influence might result from the passive presence of O, with no evidence of speech or overt movement. A policeman's standing on a corner may be considered an act of an agent for the speeding motorist. Such acts of the inducing agent will vary in strength, for O may not always utilize all of his power. The policeman, for example, may merely stand and watch or act more strongly by blowing his whistle at the motorist.

The influence exerted by an act need not be in the direction intended by O. The direction of the resultant force on P will depend on the relative magnitude of the induced force set up by the act of O and the resisting force in the opposite direction which is generated by that same act. In cases where O intends to influence P in a given direction, a resultant force in the same direction may be termed positive influence whereas a resultant force in the opposite direction may be termed negative influence. . . .

Social Power

The strength of power of O/P in some system *a* is defined as the maximum potential ability of O to influence P in *a*.

By this definition influence is kinetic power, just as power is potential influence. It is assumed that O is capable of various acts which, because of some more or less enduring relation to P, are able to exert influence on P.[2] O's power is measured by his maximum possible influence, though he may often choose to exert less than his full power.

An equivalent definition of power may be stated in terms of the resultant of two forces set up by the act of O: one in the direction of O's influence attempt and another resisting force in the opposite direction. Power is the maximum resultant of these two forces:

$$\text{Power of O/P(a)} = (f_{a,x} - f_{\overline{a,x}})^{\max}$$

where the source of both forces is an act of O.

Thus the power of O with respect to system *a* of P is equal to the maximum

[2] The concept of power has the conceptual property of *potentiality*; but it seems useful to restrict this potential influence to more or less enduring power relations between O and P by excluding from the definition of power those cases where the potential influence is so momentary or so changing that it cannot be predicted from the existing relationship. Power is a useful concept for describing social structure only if it has a certain stability over time; it is useless if every momentary social stimulus is viewed as actualizing social power.

resultant force of two forces set up by any possible act of O: (a) the force which O can set up on the system *a* to change in the direction x, (b) the resisting force,[3] in the opposite direction. Whenever the first component force is greater than the second, positive power exists; but if the second component force is greater than the first, then O has negative power over P.

For certain purposes it is convenient to define the range of power as the set of all systems within which O has power of strength greater than zero. A husband may have a broad range of power over his wife, but a narrow range of power over his employer. We shall use the term "magnitude of power" to denote the summation of O's power over P in all systems of his range.

The Dependence of s(a) on O.

We assume that any change in the state of a system is produced by a change in some factor upon which it is functionally dependent. The state of an opinion, for example, may change because of a change either in some internal factor such as a need or in some external factor such as the arguments of O. Likewise the maintenance of the same state of a system is produced by the stability or lack of change in the internal and external factors. In general, then, psychological change and stability can be conceptualized in terms of dynamic dependence. Our interest is focused on the special case of dependence on an external agent, O (31).

In many cases the initial state of the system has the character of a quasistationary equilibrium with a central force field around $s_1(a)$ (26, p. 106). In such cases we may derive a tendency toward retrogression to the original state as soon as the force induced by O is removed.[4] . . .

Consider the example of three separated employees who have been working at the same steady level of production despite normal, small fluctuations in the work environment. The supervisor orders each to increase his production, and the level of each goes up from 100 to 115 pieces per day. After a week of producing at the new rate of 115 pieces per day, the supervisor is removed for a week. The production of employee A immediately returns to 100 but B and C return to only 110 pieces per day. Other things being equal, we can infer that A's new rate was completely dependent on his supervisor whereas the new rate of B and C was dependent on the supervisor only to the extent of 5 pieces. Let us further assume that when the supervisor returned, the production of B and of C returned to 115 without further orders from the supervisor. Now another month goes by during which B and C maintain a steady 115 pieces per day. However, there is a difference between them: B's level of production still depends on O to the extent of 5 pieces whereas C has come to rely on his own sense of obligation to obey the order of his legitimate supervisor rather than on the supervisor's external pressure for the maintenance of his 115 pieces per day. Accordingly, the next time the supervisor departs, B's production again drops to 110 but C's remains at 115 pieces per

[3] We define resistance to an attempted induction as a force in the opposite direction which is set up by the same act of O. It must be distinguished from opposition which is defined as existing opposing forces which do not have their source in the same act of O. For example, a boy might resist his mother's order to eat spinach because of the manner of the induction attempt, and at the same time he might oppose it because he didn't like spinach.

[4] Miller (33) assumes that all living systems have this character. However, it may be that some systems in the life space do not have this elasticity.

day. In cases like employee B, the degree of dependence is contingent on the perceived probability that O will observe the state of the system and note P's conformity (5, 6, 11, 12, 23). The level of observability will in turn depend on both the nature of the system (e.g., the difference between a covert opinion and overt behavior) and on the environmental barriers to observation (e.g., O is too far away from P). . . .

THE BASES OF POWER

By the basis of power we mean the relationship between O and P which is the source of that power. It is rare that we can say with certainty that a given empirical case of power is limited to one source. Normally, the relation between O and P will be characterized by several qualitatively different variables which are bases of power. . . . Although there are undoubtedly many possible bases of power which may be distinguished, we shall here define five which seem especially common and important. These five bases of O's power are: (1) reward power, based on P's perception that O has the ability to mediate rewards for him; (2) coercive power, based on P's perception that O has the ability to mediate punishments for him; (3) legitimate power, based on the perception by P that O has a legitimate right to prescribe behavior for him; (4) referent power, based on P's identification with O; (5) expert power, based on the perception that O has some special knowledge or expertness. . . .

Reward Power

Reward power is defined as power whose basis is the ability to reward. The strength of the reward power of O/P increases with the magnitude of the rewards which P perceives that O can mediate for him. Reward power depends on O's ability to administer positive va-

lences and to remove or decrease negative valences. The strength of reward power also depends upon the probability that O can mediate the reward, as perceived by P. A common example of reward power is the addition of a piecework rate in the factory as an incentive to increase production.

The new state of the system induced by a promise of reward (for example the factory worker's increased level of production) will be highly dependent on O. Since O mediates the reward, he controls the probability that P will receive it. Thus P's new rate of production will be dependent on his subjective probability that O will reward him for conformity minus his subjective probability that O will reward him even if he returns to his old level. Both probabilities will be greatly affected by the level of observability of P's behavior. . . .

The utilization of actual rewards (instead of promises) by O will tend over time to increase the attraction of P toward O and therefore the referent power of O over P. As we shall note later, such referent power will permit O to induce changes which are relatively independent. Neither rewards nor promises will arouse resistance in P, provided P considers it legitimate for O to offer rewards.

The range of reward power is specific to those regions within which O can reward P for conforming. The use of rewards to change systems within the range of reward power tends to increase reward power by increasing the probability attached to future promises. However, unsuccessful attempts to exert reward power outside the range of power would tend to decrease the power; for example if O offers to reward P for performing an impossible act, this will reduce for P the probability of receiving future rewards promised by O.

Coercive Power

Coercive power is similar to reward power in that it also involves O's ability to manipulate the attainment of valences. Coercive power of O/P stems from the expectation on the part of P that he will be punished by O if he fails to conform to the influence attempt. Thus negative valences will exist in given regions of P's life space, corresponding to the threatened punishment by O. The strength of coercive power depends on the magnitude of the negative valence of the threatened punishment multiplied by the perceived probability that P can avoid the punishment by conformity, i.e., the probability of punishment for nonconformity minus the probability of punishment for conformity (11). Just as an offer of a piece-rate bonus in a factory can serve as a basis for reward power, so the ability to fire a worker if he falls below a given level of production will result in coercive power.

Coercive power leads to dependent change also; and the degree of dependence varies with the level of observability of P's conformity. An excellent illustration of coercive power leading to dependent change is provided by a clothes presser in a factory observed by Coch and French (3). As her efficiency rating climbed above average for the group the other workers began to "scapegoat" her. That the resulting plateau in her production was not independent of the group was evident once she was removed from the presence of the other workers. Her production immediately climbed to new heights.[5] . . .

The distinction between these two types of power is important because the

dynamics are different. The concept of "sanctions" sometimes lumps the two together despite their opposite effects. While reward power may eventually result in an independent system, the effects of coercive power will continue to be dependent. Reward power will tend to increase the attraction of P toward O; coercive power will decrease this attraction (11,12). The valence of the region of behavior will become more negative, acquiring some negative valence from the threatened punishment. The negative valence of punishment would also spread to other regions of the life space. Lewin (25) has pointed out this distinction between the effects of rewards and punishment. In the case of threatened punishment, there will be a resultant force on P to leave the field entirely. Thus, to achieve conformity, O must not only place a strong negative valence in certain regions through threat of punishment, but O must also introduce restraining forces, or other strong valences, so as to prevent P from withdrawing completely from O's range of coercive power. Otherwise the probability of receiving the punishment, if P does not conform, will be too low to be effective.

Legitimate Power

. . . There has been considerable investigation and speculation about socially prescribed behavior, particularly that which is specific to a given role or position. Linton (29) distinguishes group norms according to whether they are universals for everyone in the culture, alternatives (the individual having a choice as to whether or not to accept them), or specialties (specific to given positions). Whether we speak of internalized norms, role prescriptions and expectations (34), or internalized pressures (15), the fact remains that each individual sees certain regions toward which he should locomote, some regions toward which he should not locomote, and some

---

[5] Though the primary influence of coercive power is dependent, it often produces secondary changes which are independent. Brainwashing, for example, utilizes coercive power to produce many primary changes in the life space of the prisoner, but these dependent changes can lead to identification with the aggressor and hence to secondary changes in ideology which are independent.

regions toward which he may locomote if they are generally attractive for him. This applies to specific behaviors in which he may, should, or should not engage; it applies to certain attitudes or beliefs which he may, should, or should not hold. The feeling of "oughtness' may be an internalization from his parents, from his teachers, from his religion, or may have been logically developed from some idiosyncratic system of ethics. He will speak of such behaviors with expressions like "should," "ought to," or "has a right to." In many cases, the original source of the requirement is not recalled.

Though we have oversimplified such evaluations of behavior with a positive-neutral-negative trichotomy, the evaluation of behaviors by the person is really more one of degree. This dimension of evaluation, we shall call "legitimacy." Conceptually, we may think of legitimacy as a valence in a region which is induced by some internalized norm or value. This value has the same conceptual property as power, namely an ability to induce force fields (26, p. 40–41). . . .

Legitimate power of O/P is here defined as that power which stems from internalized values in P which dictate that O has a legitimate right to influence P and that P has an obligation to accept this influence. We note that legitimate power is very similar to the notion of legitimacy of authority which has long been explored by sociologists, particularly by Weber (42), and more recently by Goldhammer and Shils (14). However, legitimate power is not always a role relation: P may accept an induction from O simply because he had previously promised to help O and he values his word too much to break the promise. In all cases, the notion of legitimacy involves some sort of code or standard, accepted by the individual, by virtue of which the external agent can assert his

power. We shall attempt to describe a few of these values here.

Bases for Legitimate Power. Cultural values constitute one common basis for the legitimate power of one individual over another. O has characteristics which are specified by the culture as giving him the right to prescribe behavior for P, who may not have these characteristics. These bases, which Weber (42) has called the authority of the "eternal yesterday," include such things as age, intelligence, caste, and physical characteristics. In some cultures, the aged are granted the right to prescribe behavior for others in practically all behavior areas. In most cultures, there are certain areas of behavior in which a person of one sex is granted the right to prescribe behavior for the other sex.

Acceptance of the social structure is another basis for legitimate power. If P accepts as right the social structure of his group, organization, or society, especially the social structure involving a hierarchy of authority, P will accept the legitimate authority of O who occupies a superior office in the hierarchy. Thus legitimate power in a formal organization is largely a relationship between offices rather than between persons. And the acceptance of an office as *right* is a basis for legitimate power—a judge has a right to levy fines, a foreman should assign work, a priest is justified in prescribing religious beliefs, and it is the management's prerogative to make certain decisions (10). However, legitimate power also involves the perceived right of the person to hold the office.

Designation by a legitimizing agent is a third basis for legitimate power. An influencer O may be seen as legitimate in prescribing behavior for P because he has been granted such power by a legitimizing agent whom P accepts. Thus a department head may accept the authority of his vice-president in a certain area because that authority has been specifically delegated by the president. An election is perhaps the most common example of a group's serving to legitimize the authority of one individual or office for other individuals in the group. The success of such legitimizing depends upon the acceptance of the legitimizing agent and procedure. In this case it depends ultimately on certain democratic values concerning election procedures. The election process is one of legitimizing a person's right to an office which already has a legitimate range of power associated with it.

Range of Legitimate Power of O/P. The areas in which legitimate power may be exercised are generally specified along with the designation of that power. A job description, for example, usually specifies supervisory activities and also designates the person to whom the job holder is responsible for the duties described. Some bases for legitimate authority carry with them a very broad range. Culturally derived bases for legitimate power are often especially broad. It is not uncommon to find cultures in which a member of a given caste can legitimately prescribe behavior for all members of lower castes in practically all regions. More common, however, are instances of legitimate power where the range is specifically and narrowly prescribed. A sergeant in the army is given a specific set of regions within which he can legitimately prescribe behavior for his men.

The attempted use of legitimate power which is outside of the range of legitimate power will decrease the legitimate power of the authority figure. Such use of power which is not legitimate will also decrease the attractiveness of O (11, 12, 36).

Legitimate Power and Influence. The new state of the system which results from legitimate power usually has high dependence on O though it may become independent. Here, however, the degree of dependence is not related to the level of observability. Since legitimate power is based on P's values, the source of the forces induced by O include both these internal values and O. O's induction serves to activate the values and to relate them to the system which is influenced, but thereafter the new state of the system may become directly dependent on the values with no mediation by O. Accordingly this new state will be relatively stable and consistent across varying environmental situations since P's values are more stable than his psychological environment. . . .

Referent Power

The referent power of O/P has its basis in the identification of P with O. By identification, we mean a feeling of oneness of P with O, or a desire for such an identity. If O is a person toward whom P is highly attracted, P will have a feeling of membership or a desire to join. If P is already closely associated with O he will want to maintain this relationship (39, 41). P's identification with O can be established or maintained if P behaves, believes, and perceives as O does. Accordingly O has the ability to influence P, even though P may be unaware of this referent power. A verbalization of such power by P might be, "I am like O, and therefore I shall behave or believe as O does," or "I want to be like O, and I will be more like O if I behave or believe as O does." The stronger the identification of P with O the greater the referent power of O/P. . . .

We must try to distinguish between referent power and other types of power which might be operative at the same time. If a member is attracted to a group and he conforms to its norms only because he fears ridicule or expulsion from the group for nonconformity, we would call this coercive power. On the other hand if he conforms in order to obtain praise for conformity, it is a case of reward power. . . . Conformity with majority opinion is sometimes based on a respect for the collective wisdom of the group, in which case it is expert power. It is important to distinguish these phenomena, all grouped together elsewhere as "pressures toward uniformity," since the type of change which occurs will be different for different bases of power.

The concepts of "reference group" (40) and "prestige suggestion" may be treated as instances of referent power. In this case, O, the prestigeful person or group, is valued by P; because P desires to be associated or identified with O, he will assume attitudes or beliefs held by O. Similarly a negative reference group which O dislikes and evaluates negatively may exert negative influence on P as a result of negative referent power.

It has been demonstrated that the power which we designate as referent power is especially great when P is attracted to O (2, 7, 8, 9, 13, 23, 30). In our terms, this would mean that the greater the attraction, the greater the identification, and consequently the greater the referent power. In some cases, attraction or prestige may have a specific basis, and the range of referent power will be limited accordingly: a group of campers may have great referent power over a member regarding campcraft, but considerably less effect on other regions (30). However, we hypothesize that the greater the attraction of P toward O, the broader the range of referent power of O/P. . . .

Expert Power

The strength of the expert power of O/P varies with the extent of the knowledge or perception which P attibutes to O within a given area. Probably P evaluates O's expertness in relation to his own knowledge as well as against an absolute standard. In any case expert power results in primary social influence on P's cognitive structure and probably not on other types of systems. Of course changes in the cognitive structure can change the direction of forces and hence of locomotion, but such a change of behavior is secondary social influence. Expert power has been demonstrated experimentally (8, 33). Accepting an attorney's advice in legal matters is a common example of expert influence; but there are many instances based on much less knowledge, such as the acceptance by a stranger of directions given by a native villager.

Expert power, where O need not be a member of P's group, is called "informational power" by Deutsch and Gerard (4). This type of expert power must be distinguished from influence based on the content of communication as described by Hovland et al. (17, 18, 23, 24). The influence of the content of a communication upon an opinion is presumably a secondary influence produced after the *primary* influence (i. e., the acceptance of the information). Since power is here defined in terms of the primary changes, the influence of the content on a related opinion is not a case of expert power as we have defined it, but the initial acceptance of the validity of the content does seem to be based on expert power or referent power. . . .

The range of expert power, we assume, is more delimited than that of referent power. Not only is it restricted to cognitive systems but the expert is seen as having superior knowledge or ability in very specific areas, and his power will be limited to these areas, though some "halo effect" might occur. Recently, some of our renowned physical scientists have found quite painfully that their expert power in physical sciences does not extend to regions involving international politics. Indeed, there is some evidence that the attempted exertion of expert power outside of the range of expert power will reduce that expert power. An undermining of confidence seems to take place.

SUMMARY

We have distinguished five types of power: referent power, expert power, reward power, coercive power, and legitimate power. These distinctions led to the following hypotheses.

1. For all five types, the stronger the basis of power the greater the power.
2. For any type of power the size of the range may vary greatly, but in general referent power will have the broadest range.
3. Any attempt to utilize power out-side the range of power will tend to reduce the power.
4. A new state of a system produced by reward power or coercive power will be highly dependent on O, and the more observable P's conformity the more dependent the state. For the other three types of power, the new state is usually dependent, at least in the beginning, but in any case the level of observability has no effect on the degree of dependence.
5. Coercion results in decreased attraction of P toward O and high resistance; reward power results in increased attraction and low resistance.
6. The more legitimate the coercion the less it will produce resistance and decreased attraction.

REFERENCES

1. Asch, S. E. *Social psychology.* New York: Prentice-Hall, 1952.
2. Back, K. W. Influence through social communication. *J. abnorm. soc. Psychol.*, 1951, **46**, 9–23.
3. Coch, L., & French, J. R. P., Jr. Overcoming resistance to change. *Hum. Relat.*, 1948, **1**, 512–32.
4. Deutsch, M., & Gerard, H. B. A study of normative and informational influences upon individual judgment. *J. abnorm. soc. Psychol.*, 1955, **51**, 629–36.
5. Dittes, J. E., & Kelley, H. H. Effects of different conditions of acceptance upon conformity to group norms. *J. abnorm. soc. Psychol.*, 1956, **53**, 100–107.
6. Festinger, L. An analysis of compliant behavior. In Sherif, M., & Wilson, M. O., (Eds.). *Group relations at the crossroads.* New York: Harper, 1953, 232–56.
7. Festinger, L. Informal social communication. *Psychol. Rev.*, 1950, **57**, 271–82.
8. Festinger, L., Gerard, H. B., Hymovitch, B., Kelley, H. H., & Raven, B. H. The influence process in the presence of extreme deviates. *Hum. Relat.*, 1952, **5**, 327–346.
9. Festinger, L., Schachter, S., & Back, K. The operation of group standards. In Cartwright, D., & Zander, A. *Group dynamics: research and theory.* Evanston: Row, Peterson, 1953, 204–23.
10. French, J. R. P., Jr., Israel, Joachim & Ås, Dagfinn. "Arbeidernes medvirkning i industribedriften. En eksperimentell undersøkelse." Institute for Social Research, Oslo, Norway, 1957.
11. French, J. R. P., Jr., Levinger, G., & Morrison, H. W. The legitimacy of coercive power. In preparation.
12. French, J. R. P., Jr., & Raven, B. H. An experiment in legitimate and coercive power. In preparation.
13. Gerard, H. B. The anchorage of opinions in face-to-face groups. *Hum. Relat.*, 1954, **7**, 313–325.
14. Goldhammer, H., & Shils, E. A. Types of power and status. *Amer. J. Sociol.*, 1939, **45**, 171–178.
15. Herbst, P. G. Analysis and measurement of a situation. *Hum. Relat.*, 1953, **2**, 113–140.
16. Hochbaum, G. M. Self-confidence and reactions to group pressures. *Amer. soc. Rev.*, 1954, **19**, 678–687.
17. Hovland, C. I., Lumsdaine, A. A., & Sheffield, F. D. *Experiments on mass communication.* Princeton: Princeton Univer. Press, 1949.
18. Hovland, C. I., & Weiss, W. The influence of source credibility on communication effectiveness. *Publ. Opin. Quart.*, 1951, **15**, 635–650.

19. Jackson, J. M., & Saltzstein, H. D. The effect of person-group relationships on conformity processes. *J. abnorm. soc. Psychol.*, 1958, **57**, 17–24.

20. Jahoda, M. Psychological issues in civil liberties. *Amer. Psychologist*, 1956, **11**, 234–240.

21. Katz, D., & Schank, R. L. *Social psychology.* New York: Wiley, 1938.

22. Kelley, H. H., & Volkart, E. H. The resistance to change of group-anchored attitudes. *Amer. soc. Rev.*, 1952, **17**, 453–465.

23. Kelman, H. Three processes of acceptance of social influence: compliance, identification and internalization. Paper read at the meetings of the American Psychological Association, August 1956.

24. Kelman, H., & Hovland, C. I. "Reinstatement" of the communicator in delayed measurement of opinion change. *J. abnorm. soc. Psychol.*, 1953, **48**, 327–335.

25. Lewin, K. *Dynamic theory of personality.* New York: McGraw-Hill, 1935, 114–170.

26. Lewin, K. *Field theory in social science.* New York: Harper, 1951.

27. Lewin, K., Lippitt, R., & White, R. K. Patterns of aggressive behavior in experimentally created social climates. *J. soc. Psychol.*, 1939, **10**, 271–301.

28. Lasswell, H. D., & Kaplan, A. *Power and society: A framework for political inquiry.* New Haven: Yale Univer. Press, 1950.

29. Linton, R. *The cultural background of personality.* New York: Appleton-Century-Crofts, 1945.

30. Lippitt, R., Polansky, N., Redl, F., & Rosen, S. The dynamics of power. *Hum. Relat.*, 1952, **5**, 37–64.

31. March, J. G. An introduction to the theory and measurement of influence. *Amer. polit. Sci. Rev.*, 1955, **49**, 431–451.

32. Miller, J. G. Toward a general theory for the behavioral sciences. *Amer. Psychologist*, 1955, **10**, 513–531.

33. Moore, H. T. The comparative influence of majority and expert opinion. *Amer. J. Psychol.*, 1921, **32**, 16–20.

34. Newcomb, T. M. *Social psychology.* New York: Dryden, 1950.

35. Raven, B. H. The effect of group pressures on opinion, perception, and communication. Unpublished doctoral dissertation, University of Michigan, 1953.

36. Raven, B. H., & French, J. R. P., Jr. Group support, legitimate power, and social influence. *J. Person.*, 1958, **26**, 400–409.

37. Rommetveit, R. *Social norms and roles.* Minneapolis: Univer. Minnesota Press, 1953.

38. Russell, B. *Power: A new social analysis.* New York: Norton, 1938.

39. Stotland, E., Zander, A., Burnstein, E.,Wolfe, D., & Natsoulas, T. Studies on the effects of identification. University of Michigan, Institute for Social Research. Forthcoming.

40. Swanson, G. E., Newcomb, T. M., & Hartley, E. L. *Readings in social psychology.* New York: Henry Holt, 1952.

41. Torrance, E. P., & Mason, R. Instructor effort to influence: an experimental evaluation of six approaches. Paper presented at USAF-NRC Symposium on Personnel, Training, and Human Engineering. Washington, D.C., 1956.

42. Weber, M. *The theory of social and economic organization.* Oxford: Oxford Univer. Press, 1947.

32
Leadership in an Organized Anarchy
Michael D. Cohen & James G. March

THE AMBIGUITIES
OF ANARCHY

The college president faces four fundamental ambiguities. The first is the ambiguity of *purpose*. In what terms can action be justified? What are the goals of the organization? The second is the ambiguity of *power*. How powerful is the president? What can he accomplish? The third is the ambiguity of *experience*. What is to be learned from the events of the presidency? The fourth is the ambiguity of *success*. When is a president successful? How does he assess his pleasures?

These ambiguities are fundamental to college presidents because they strike at the heart of the usual interpretations of leadership. When purpose is ambiguous, ordinary theories of decisionmaking and intelligence become problematic. When power is ambiguous, ordinary theories of social order and control become problematic. When experience is ambiguous, ordinary theories of learning and adaptation become problematic. When success is ambiguous, ordinary theories of motivation and personal pleasure become problematic. . . .

The Ambiguity of Purpose

Efforts to generate normative statements of the goals of a university tend to produce goals that are either meaningless or dubious. They fail one or more of the following reasonable tests. First, is the goal clear? Can one define some specific procedure for measuring the degree of goal achievement? Second, is it problematic? Is there some possibility that the organization will accomplish the goal? Is there some chance that it will fail? Third, is it accepted? Do most significant groups in the university agree on the goal statement? For the most part, the level of generality that facilitates acceptance destroys the problematic nature or clarity of the goal. The level of specificity that permits measurement destroys acceptance. . . .

Efforts to specify a set of consciously shared, consistent objectives within a university or to infer such a set of objectives from the activities or actions of the university have regularly revealed signs of inconsistency. To expose inconsistencies is not to resolve them, however. There are only modest signs that universities or other organized anarchies respond to a revelation of ambiguity of purpose by reducing the ambiguity. These are organizational systems without clear objectives; and the processes by which their objectives are established and legitimized are not extraordinarily sensitive to inconsistency. In fact, for many purposes the ambiguity of purpose is produced by our insistence on treating purpose as a necessary property of a good university. The strains arise from trying to impose a model of action as flowing

Source: Michael D. Cohen and James G. March, *Leadership and Ambiguity: The American College President*, pp. 195–229. Copyright 1974 Carnegie Foundation for the Advancement of Teaching. Reprinted by permission.

from intent on organizations that act in another way.

College presidents live within a normative context that presumes purpose and within an organizational context that denies it. They serve on commissions to define and redefine the objectives of higher education. They organize convocations to examine the goals of the college. They write introductory statements to the college catalog. They accept the presumption that intelligent leadership presupposes the rational pursuit of goals. Simultaneously, they are aware that the process of choice in the college depends little on statements of shared direction. They recognize the flow of actions as an ecology of games (Long, 1958), each with its own rules. They accept the observation that the world is not like the model.

The Ambiguity of Power

Power is a simple idea, pervasive in its appeal to observers of social events. Like *intelligence* or *motivation* or *utility*, however, it tends to be misleadingly simple and prone to tautology. A person has power if he gets things done; if he has power, he can get things done. . . .

As a shorthand casual expression for variations in the potential of different positions in the organization, *power* has some utility. The college president has more potential for moving the college than most people, probably more potential than any one other person. Nevertheless, presidents discover that they have less power than is believed, that their power to accomplish things depends heavily on what they want to accomplish, that the use of formal authority is not automatic, that the necessary details of organizational life confuse power (which is somewhat different from diffusing it), and that their colleagues seem to delight in complaining simulta-

neously about presidential weakness and presidential willfulness.

The ambiguity of power, like the ambiguity of purpose, is focused on the president. Presidents share in and contribute to the confusion. They enjoy the perquisites and prestige of the office. They enjoy its excitement, at least when things go well. They announce important events. They appear at important symbolic functions. They report to people. They accept and thrive on their own importance. It would be remarkable if they did not. Presidents even occasionally recite that "the buck stops here" with a finality that suggests the cliché is an observation about power and authority rather than the proclamation of administrative style and ideology.

At the same time, presidents solicit an understanding of the limits to their control. They regret the tendency of students, legislators, and community leaders to assume that a president has the power to do whatever he chooses simply because he is president. They plead the countervailing power of other groups in the college or the notable complexities of causality in large organizations. . . .

The confusion disturbs the president, but it also serves him. Ambiguity of power leads to a parallel ambiguity of responsibility. The allocation of credit and blame for the events of organizational life becomes—as it often does in political and social systems—a matter for argument. The "facts" of responsibility are badly confounded by the confusions of anarchy; and the conventional myth of hierarchical executive responsibility is undermined by the countermyth of the nonhierarchical nature of colleges and universities. Presidents negotiate with their audiences on the interpretations of their power. As a result, during the recent years of campus troubles, many college presidents sought to emphasize the limitations of presidential control. During the more glorious days of conspicuous success, they solicited a recognition of their responsibility for events. . . .

The Ambiguity of Experience

College presidents attempt to learn from their experience. They observe the consequences of actions and infer the structure of the world from those observations. They use the resulting inferences in attempts to improve their future actions.

Consider the following very simple learning paradigm:

1. At a certain point in time a president is presented with a set of well-defined, discrete action alternatives.
2. At any point in time he has a certain probability of choosing any particular alternative (and a certainty of choosing one of them).
3. The president observes the outcome that apparently follows his choice and assesses the outcome in terms of his goals.
4. If the outcome is consistent with his goals, the president increases his probability of choosing that alternative in the future; if not, he decreases the probability.

Although actual presidential learning certainly involves more complicated inferences, such a paradigm captures much of the ordinary adaptation of an intelligent man to the information gained from experience.

The process produces considerable learning. The subjective experience is one of adapting from experience and improving behavior on the basis of feedback. If the world with which the president is dealing is relatively simple and relatively stable, and if his experience is relatively frequent, he can expect to improve over time (assuming he has some appropriate criterion for testing the consistency of outcomes with goals). As we have suggested earlier, however, the world in which the president lives has two conspicuous properties that make experience ambiguous even where goals are clear. First, the world is relatively complex. Outcomes depend heavily on factors other than the president's action. These factors are uncontrolled and, in large part, unobserved. Second, relative to the rate at which the president gathers experimental data, the world changes rapidly. These properties produce considerable potential for false learning. . . .

College presidents probably have greater confidence in their interpretations of college life, college administration, and their general environment than is warranted. The inferences they have made from experience are likely to be wrong. Their confidence in their learning is likely to have been reinforced by the social support they receive from the people around them and by social expectations about the presidential role. As a result, they tend to be unaware of the extent to which the ambiguities they feel with respect to purpose and power are matched by similar ambiguities with respect to the meaning of the ordinary events of presidential life.

The Ambiguity of Success

Administrative success is generally recognized in one of two ways. First, by promotion: An administrator knows that he has been successful by virtue of a promotion to a better job. He assesses his success on the current job by the opportunities he has or expects to have to leave it. Second, by widely accepted, operational measures of organizational output: a business executive values his own performance in terms of a profit-and-loss statement of his operations.

Problems with these indicators of success are generic to high-level administrative positions. Offers of promotion become less likely as the job improves and the administrator's age advances. The criteria by which success is judged become less precise in measurement, less stable over time, and less widely shared. The administrator discovers that a wide assortment of factors outside his control are capable of overwhelming the impact of any actions he may take.

In the case of the college president all three problems are accentuated. As we have seen earlier, few college presidents are promoted out of the presidency. There are job offers, and most presidents ultimately accept one; but the best opportunity the typical president can expect is an invitation to accept a decent version of administrative semiretirement. The criteria of success in academic administration are sometimes moderately clear (e.g., growth, quiet on campus, improvement in the quality of students and faculty), but the relatively precise measures of college health tend neither to be stable over time nor to be critically sensitive to presidential action. . . .

One basic response to the ambiguities of success is to find pleasure in the process of presidential life. A reasonable man will seek reminders of his relevance and success. Where those reminders are hard to find in terms of socially validated outcomes unambiguously due to one's actions, they may be sought in the interactions of organizational life. George Reedy (1970) made a similar observation about a different presidency: "Those who seek to lighten the burdens of the presidency by easing the workload do no occupant of that office a favor. The 'workload'—especially the ceremonial work load—are the only events of a president's day which make life endurable."

LEADER RESPONSE TO ANARCHY

The ambiguities that college presidents face describe the life of any formal leader

of any organized anarchy. The metaphors of leadership and our traditions of personalizing history (even the minor histories of collegiate institutions) confuse the issues of leadership by ignoring the basic ambiguity of leadership life. We require a plausible basic perspective for the leader of a loosely coupled, ambiguous organization.

Such a perspective begins with humility. It is probably a mistake for a college president to imagine that what he does in office affects significantly either the long-run position of the institution or his reputation as a president. So long as he does not violate some rather obvious restrictions on his behavior, his reputation and his term of office are more likely to be affected by broad social events or by the unpredictable viscissitudes of official responsibility than by his actions. . . .

In this respect the president's life does not differ markedly from that of most of us. A leadership role, however, is distinguished by the numerous temptations to self-importance that it provides. Presidents easily come to believe that they can continue in office forever if they are only clever or perceptive or responsive enough. They easily come to exaggerate the significance of their daily actions for the college as well as for themselves. They easily come to see each day as an opportunity to build support in their constituencies for the next "election.". . .

The ambiguities of leadership in an organized anarchy require a leadership posture that is somewhat different from that implicit in most discussions of the college presidency. In particular, we believe that a college president is, on the whole, better advised to think of himself as trying to do good than as trying to satisfy a political or bureaucratic audience; better advised to define his role in terms of the modest part he can play in making the college slightly better in the long run than in terms of satisfying current residents or solving current problems. He requires an enthusiam for a Tolstoyan view of history and for the freedom of individual action that such a view entails. Since the world is absurd, the president's primary responsibility is to virtue.

Presidents occupy a minor part in the lives of a small number of people. They have some power, but little magic. They can act with a fair degree of confidence that if they make a mistake, it will not matter much. They can be allowed the heresy of believing that pleasure is consistent with virtue.

The Elementary Tactics of Administrative Action

The tactics of administrative action in an organized anarchy are somewhat different from the tactics of action in a situation characterized by clearer goals, better specified technology, and more persistent participation. Nevertheless, we can examine how a leader with a purpose can operate within an organization that is without one. . . .

As we will indicate later in this chapter, a conception of leadership that merely assumes that the college president should act to accomplish what he wants to accomplish is too narrow. A major part of his responsibility is to lead the organization to a changing and more complex view of itself by treating goals as only partly knowable. Nevertheless, the problems of inducing a college to do what one wants it to do are clearly worthy of attention. If presidents and others are to function effectively within the college, they need to recognize the ways in which the character of the college as a system for exercising problems, making decisions, and certifying status conditions their attempts to influence the outcome of any decision.

We can identify five major properties of decision making in organized anarchies that are of substantial importance to the tactics of accomplishing things in colleges and universities:

1. Most issues most of the time have *low salience* for most people. The decisions to be made within the organization secure only partial and erratic attention from participants in the organization. A major share of the attention devoted to a particular issue is tied less to the content of the issue than to its symbolic significance for individual and group esteem.

2. The total system has *high inertia*. Anything that requires a coordinated effort of the organization in order to start is unlikely to be started. Anything that requires a coordinated effort of the organization in order to be stopped is unlikely to be stopped.

3. Any decision can become a *garbage can* for almost any problem. The issues discussed in the context of any particular decision depend less on the decision or problems involved than on the timing of their joint arrivals and the existence of alternative arenas for exercising problems.

4. The processes of choice are easily subject to *overload*. When the load on the system builds up relative to its capacities for exercising and resolving problems, the decision outcomes in the organization tend to become increasingly separated from the formal process of decision.

5. The organization has a *weak information base*. Information about past events or past decisions is often not retained. When retained, it is often difficult to retrieve. Information about current activities is scant.

These properties are conspicuous and ubiquitous. They represent some important ways in which all organizations sometimes, and an organization like a university often, present opportunities for tactical action that in a modest way strengthen the hand of the participant who attends them. We suggest eight basic tactical rules for use by those who seek to influence the course of decisions in universities or colleges.

Rule 1: Spend Time. The kinds of decision-making situations and organizations we have described suffer from a shortage of decision-making energy. Energy is a scarce resource. If one is in a position to devote time to the decision-making activities within the organization, he has a considerable claim on the system. Most organizations develop ways of absorbing the decision-making energy provided by sharply deviant participants; but within moderate boundaries, a person who is willing to spend time finds himself in a strong position for at least three significant reasons:

- By providing a scarce resource (energy), he lays the basis for a claim. If he is willing to spend time, he can expect more tolerant consideration of the problems he considers important. One of the most common organizational responses to a proposal from a participant is the request that he head a committee to do something about it. This behavior is an acknowledgement both of the energy-poor situation and of the price the organization pays for participation. That price is often that the organization must allow the participant some significant control over the definition of problems to be considered relevant.[1]
- By spending time on the homework for a decision, he becomes a major information source in an information-poor world. At the limit, the information provided need have no particular evidential validity. Consider, for example, the common assertions in college decision-making processes about what some constituency (e.g., board of trustees, legislature, student body, ethnic group) is "thinking." The assertions are rarely based on defensible evidence,

but they tend to become organizational facts by virtue of the shortage of serious information. More generally, reality for a decision is specified by those willing to spend the time required to collect the small amounts of information available, to review the factual assertions of others, and to disseminate their findings.

- By investing more of his time in organizational concerns, he increases his chance of being present when something important to him is considered. A participant who wishes to pursue other matters (e.g., study, research, family, the problems of the outside world) reduces the number of occasions for decision making to which he can afford to attend. A participant who can spend time can be involved in more arenas. Since it is often difficult to anticipate when and where a particular issue will be involved (and thus to limit one's attention to key times and domains), the simple frequency of availability is relatively important.

Rule 2: Persist. It is a mistake to assume that if a particular proposal has been rejected by an organization today, it will be rejected tomorrow. Different sets of people and concerns will be reflected each time a problem is considered or a proposal discussed. We noted earlier the ways in which the flow of participants leads to a flow of organizational concerns.[2] The specific combination of sentiments and people that is associated with a specific choice opportunity is partly fortuitous, and Fortune may be more considerate another day.

For the same reason, it is a mistake to assume that today's victory will be implemented automatically tomorrow. The distinction between decision making and decision implementation is usually a false one. Decisions are not "made" once and for all. Rather they happen as a result of a series of episodes involving different people in different settings, and they may be unmade or modified by subsequent episodes. The participant who spends much time celebrating his victory ordinarily can expect to find the victory short-lived. The loser who spends his time weeping rather than reintroducing his ideas will persistently have something to weep about. The loser who persists in a variety of contexts is frequently rewarded.

Rule 3: Exchange Status for Substance. As we have indicated, the specific substantive issues in a college, or similar organization, typically have low salience for participants. A quite typical situation is one in which significant numbers of participants and groups of participants care less about the specific substantive outcome than they do about the implications of that outcome for their own sense of self-esteem and the social recognition of their importance. Such an ordering of things is neither surprising nor normatively unattractive. It would be a strange world indeed if the mostly minor issues of university governance, for example, became more important to most people than personal and group esteem.

A college president, too, is likely to become substantially concerned with the formal acknowledgment of office. Since it is awkward for him to establish definitively that he is substantively important, the president tends to join other participants in seeking symbolic confirmation of his significance.

The esteem trap is understandable but unfortunate. College presidents who can forgo at least some of the pleasures of self-importance in order to trade status for substance are in a strong position. Since leaders receive credit for many things over which they have little control and to which they contribute little, they should find it possible to accomplish some of the things they want by allowing others to savor the victories, enjoy the pleasures of involvement, and receive the profits of public importance.

Rule 4: Facilitate Opposition Participation. The high inertia of organizations and the heavy dependence of organizational events on processes outside of the control of the organization make organizational power ambiguous. Presidents sense their lack of control despite their position of authority, status, and concern. Most people who participate in university decision making sense a disappointment with the limited control their position provides.

Persons outside the formal ranks of authority tend to see authority as providing more control. Their aspirations for change tend to be substantially greater than the aspirations for change held by persons with formal authority. One obvious solution is to facilitate participation in decision making. Genuine authoritative participation will reduce the aspirations of oppositional leaders. In an organization characterized by high inertia and low salience it is unwise to allow beliefs about the feasibility of planned action to outrun reality. From this point of view, public accountability, participant observation, and other techniques for extending the range of legitimate participation in the decision-making processes of the organization are essential means of keeping the aspirations of occasional actors within bounds. Since most people most of the time do not participate much, their aspirations for what can be done have a tendency to drift away from reality. On the whole, the direct involvement of dissident groups in the decision-making process is a more effective depressant of exaggerated aspirations than is a lecture by the president.

Rule 5: Overload the System. As we have suggested, the style of decision making changes when the load exceeds the capabilities of the system. Since we are talking about energy-poor organizations, accomplishing overload is not hard. In practical terms, this means having a large repertoire of projects for organizational action; it means making substantial claims on resources for the analysis of problems, discussion of issues, and political negotiation.

Within an organized anarchy it is a mistake to become absolutely committed to any one project. There are innumerable ways in which the processes we have described will confound the cleverest behavior with respect to any single proposal, however imaginative or subjectively important. What such processes cannot do is cope with large numbers of projects. Someone with the habit of producing many proposals, without absolute commitment to any one, may lose any one of them (and it is hard to predict a priori which one), but cannot be stopped on everything. . . .

Rule 6: Provide Garbage Cans. One of the complications in accomplishing something in a garbage can decision-making process is the tendency for any particular project to become intertwined with a variety of other issues simply because those issues exist at the time the project is before the organization. A proposal for curricular reform becomes an arena for a concern for social justice. A proposal for construction of a building becomes an arena for concerns about environmental quality. A proposal for bicycle paths becomes an arena for discussion of sexual inequality.

It is pointless to try to react to such problems by attempting to enforce rules of relevance. Such rules are, in any event, highly arbitrary. Even if they were not, it would still be difficult to persuade a person that his problem (however important) could not be discussed because it is not relevant to the current agenda. The appropriate tactical response is to provide garbage cans into which wide varieties of problems can be dumped. The more conspicuous the can, the more

garbage it will attract away from other projects.

The prime procedure for making a garbage can attractive is to give it precedence and conspicuousness. On a grand scale, discussions of overall organizational objectives or overall organizational long-term plans are classic first-quality cans. They are general enough to accommodate anything. They are socially defined as being important. They attract enough different kinds of issues to reinforce their importance. An activist will push for discussions of grand plans (in part) in order to draw the garbage away from the concrete day-to-day arenas of his concrete objectives.

On a smaller scale, the first item on a meeting agenda is an obvious garbage can. It receives much of the status allocation concerns that are a part of meetings. It is possible that any item on an agenda will attract an assortment of things currently concerning individuals in the group; but the first item is more vulnerable than others. As a result, projects of serious substantive concern should normally be placed somewhat later, after the important matters of individual and group esteem have been settled, most of the individual performances have been completed, and most of the enthusiasm for abstract argument has waned.

The garbage can tactic has long-term effects that may be important. Although in the short run the major consequence is to remove problems from the arena of short-term concrete proposals, the separation of problem discussion from decision making means that general organizational attitudes develop outside the context of immediate decisions. The exercise of problems and the discussion of plans contribute to building of the climate within which the organization will operate in the future. . . .

Rule 7: Manage Unobtrusively. If you put a man in a boat and tell him to plot a course, he can take one of three views of his task. He can float with the currents and winds, letting them take him wherever they wish; he can select a destination and try to use full power to go directly to it regardless of the current or winds; or he can select a destination and use his rudder and sails to let the currents and wind eventually take him where *he* wants to go. On the whole, we think conscious university leadership is properly seen in the third light. . . .

Unobtrusive management uses interventions of greater impact than visibilty. Such actions generally have two key attributes: (1) They affect many parts of the system slightly rather than a few parts in a major way. The effect on any one part of the system is small enough so that either no one really notices or no one finds it sensible to organize significantly against the intervention. (2) Once activated, they stay activated without further organizational attention. Their deactivation requires positive organizational action. . . .

Major bureaucratic interventions lie in the ordinary systems of accounting and managerial controls. Such devices are often condemned in academic circles as both dreary and inhibiting. Their beauty lies in the way in which they extend throughout the system and in the high degree of arbitrariness they exhibit. For example, . . .

Universities and colleges have official facts (accounting facts) with respect to student activities, faculty activities, and space utilization. In recent years such accounting facts have increased in importance as colleges and universities struggled first with the baby boom and now with fiscal adversity. These official facts enter into reports and filter into decisions made throughout the system. As a typical simple example, consider the impact of changing the accounting for faculty teaching load from number

of courses to student credit hours taught. Or, consider the impact of separating in accounting reports the teaching of language (number of students, cost of faculty) from the teaching literature in that language at a typical American university. . . .

Rule 8: Interpret History. In an organization in which most issues have low salience, and information about events in the system is poorly maintained, definitions of what is happening and what has happened become important tactical instruments. If people in the organization cared more about what happened (or is happening), the constraints on the tactic would be great. Histories would be challenged and carefully monitored. If people in the organization accepted more openly the idea that much of the decision-making process is a status-certifying rather than a choice-making system, there would be less dependence on historical interpretation. The actual situation, however, provides a tactically optimal situation. On the one hand, the genuine interest in keeping a good record of what happened (in substantive rather than status terms) is minimal. On the other hand, the belief in the relevance of history, or the legitimacy of history as a basis for current action, is fairly strong.

Minutes should be written long enough after the event as to legitimize the reality of forgetfulness. They should be written in such a way as to lay the basis for subsequent independent action—in the name of the collective action. In general, participants in the organization should be assisted in their desire to have unambiguous actions taken today derived from the ambiguous decisions of yesterday with a minimum of pain to their images of organizational rationality and a minimum of claims on their time. The model of consistency is maintained by a creative resolution of uncertainty about the past. . . .

THE TECHNOLOGY OF FOOLISHNESS

The tactics for moving an organization when objectives are clear represent important parts of the repertoire of an organizational leader.[3] Standard prescriptions properly honor intention, choice, and action; and college presidents often have things they want to accomplish. Nevertheless, a college president may sometimes want to confront the realities of ambiguity more directly and reconsider the standard dicta of leadership. He may want to examine particularly the place of purpose in intelligent behavior and the role of foolishness in leadership.

Choice and Rationality

The concept of choice as a focus for interpreting and guiding human behavior has rarely had an easy time in the realm of ideas. It is beset by theological disputations over free will, by the dilemmas of absurdism, by the doubts of psychological behaviorism, and by the claims of historical, economic, social, and demographic determinism. Nevertheless, the idea that humans make choices has proved robust enough to become a matter of faith in important segments of contemporary Western civilization. It is a faith that is professed by virtually all theories of social policy making.

The major tenets of this faith run something like this:

> Human beings make choices. Choices are properly made by evaluating alternatives in terms of goals and on the basis of information currently available. The alternative that is most attractive in terms of the goals is chosen. By using the technology of choice, we can improve the quality of the search for alternatives, the quality of

information, and the quality of the analysis used to evaluate alternatives. Although actual choice may fall short of this ideal in various ways, it is an attractive model of how choices should be made by individuals, organizations, and social systems. . . .

Our cultural ideas of intelligence and our theories of choice display a substantial resemblance. In particular, they share three conspicuous interrelated ideas:

The first idea is the *preexistence of purpose*. We find it natural to base an interpretation of human-choice behavior on a presumption of human purpose. We have, in fact, invented one of the most elaborate terminologies in the professional literature: "values," "needs," "wants," "goods," "tastes," "preferences," "utility," "objectives," "goals," "aspirations," "drives." All of these reflect a strong tendency to believe that a useful interpretation of human behavior involves defining a set of objectives that (1) are prior attributes of the system, and (2) make the observed behavior in some sense intelligent vis-à-vis those objectives. . . .

The second idea is the *necessity of consistency*. We have come to recognize consistency both as an important property of human behavior and as a prerequisite for normative models of choice. Dissonance theory, balance theory, theories of congruency in attitudes, statuses, and performances have all served to remind us of the possibilities for interpreting human behavior in terms of the consistency requirements of a limited-capacity, information-processing system.

At the same time, consistency is a cultural and theoretical virtue. Action should be consistent with belief. Actions taken by different parts of an organization should be consistent with each other. Individual and organizational activities are seen as connected with each other in terms of their consequences for some consistent set of purposes. In an organization, the structural manifestation of consistency is the hierarchy with its obligations of coordination and control. In the individual, the structural manifestation is a set of values that generates a consistent preference ordering.

The third idea is the *primacy of rationality*. By rationality we mean a procedure for deciding what is correct behavior by relating consequences systematically to objectives. By placing primary emphasis on rational techniques, we have implicitly rejected—or seriously impaired—two other procedures for choice: (1) the processes of intuition, through which people do things without fully understanding why; and (2) the processes of tradition and faith, through which people do things because that is the way they are done. . . .

These ideas are obviously deeply embedded in the culture. Their roots extend into ideas that have conditioned much of modern Western history and interpretations of that history. Their general acceptance is probably highly correlated with the permeation of rationalism and individualism into the style of thinking within the culture. The ideas are even more obviously embedded in modern theories of choice. It is fundamental to those theories that thinking should precede action; that action should serve a purpose; that purpose should be defined in terms of a consistent set of preexistent goals; and that choice should be based on a consistent theory of the relation between action and its consequences. . . .

The Problem of Goals

The tools of intelligence as they are fashioned in modern theories of choice are necessary to any reasonable behavior in contemporary society. It is inconceivable that we would fail to continue their development, refinement, and exten-

sion. As might be expected, however, a theory and ideology of choice built on the ideas outlined above is deficient in some obvious, elementary ways, most conspicuously in the treatment of human goals.

Goals are thrust upon the intelligent man. We ask that he act in the name of goals. We ask that he keep his goals consistent. We ask that his actions be oriented to his goals. We ask that a social system amalgamate individual goals into a collective goal. But we do not concern ourselves with the origin of goals. Theories of individual, organizational, and social choice assume actors with preexistent values. . . .

We know how to advise a society, an organization, or an individual if we are first given a consistent set of preferences. Under some conditions, we can suggest how to make decisions if the preferences are consistent only up to the point of specifying a series of independent constraints on the choice. But what about a normative theory of goal-finding behavior? What do we say when our client tells us that he is not sure his present set of values is the set of values in terms of which he wants to act? . . .

Within the context of normative theory of choice as it exists, the answer we give is: First determine the values, then act. The advice is frequently useful. Moreover, we have developed ways in which we can use conventional techniques for decision analysis to help discover value premises and to expose value inconsistencies. These techniques involve testing the decision implications of some successive approximations to a set of preferences. The object is to find a consistent set of preferences with implications that are acceptable to the person or organization making the decisions. Variations on such techniques are used routinely in operations research, as well as in personal counseling and analysis. . . .

Perhaps we should explore a somewhat different approach to the normative question of how we ought to behave when our value premises are not yet (and never will be) fully determined. Suppose we treat action as a way of creating interesting goals at the same time as we treat goals as a way of justifying action. It is an intuitively plausible and simple idea, but one that is not immediately within the domain of standard normative theories of intelligent choice.

Interesting people and interesting organizations construct complicated theories of themselves. To do this, they need to supplement the technology of reason with a technology of foolishness. Individuals and organizations sometimes need ways of doing things for which they have no good reason. They need to act before they think. . . .

Play and Reason

Even if we know which of several foolish things we want to do, we still need a mechanism for allowing us to do it. How do we escape the logic of our reason?

Here we are closer to understanding what we need. It is playfulness. Playfulness is the deliberate, temporary relaxation of rules in order to explore the possibilities of alternative rules. When we are playful, we challenge the necessity of consistency. In effect, we announce—in advance—our rejection of the usual objections to behavior that does not fit the standard model of intelligence.

Playfulness allows experimentation at the same time that it acknowledges reason. It accepts an obligation that at some point either the playful behavior will be stopped or it will be integrated into the structure of intelligence in some way

that makes sense. The suspension of the rules is temporary. . . .

Playfulness is a natural outgrowth of our standard view of reason. A strict insistence on purpose, consistency, and rationality limits our ability to find new purposes. Play relaxes that insistence to allow us to act "unintelligently" or "irrationally" or "foolishly" to explore alternative ideas of purposes and alternative concepts of behavioral consistency. And it does this while maintaining our basic commitment to intelligence.

Although play and reason are in this way functional complements, they are often behavioral competitors. They are alternative styles and alternative orientations to the same situation. There is no guarantee that the styles will be equally well developed, that all individuals, organizations, or societies will be equally adept in both styles; or that all cultures will be sufficiently encouraging to both.

Our design problem is either to specify the best mix of styles or, failing that, to assure that most people and most organizations most of the time use an alternation of strategies rather than persevering in either one. It is a difficult problem. The optimization problem looks extremely complex on the face of it, and the learning situations that will produce alternation in behavior appear to be somewhat less common than those that produce perseverance.

Consider, for example, the difficulty of sustaining playfulness as a style within contemporary American society. Individuals who are good at consistent rationality are rewarded early and heavily. We define consistent rationality as intelligence, and the educational rewards of society are associated strongly with it. Social norms press in the same direction, particularly for men. "Changing one's mind" is viewed as feminine and undesirable. Politicians and other leaders will go to enormous lengths to avoid admitting an inconsistency. Many demands of modern organizational life reinforce the same rational abilities and preferences for a style of unchanging purposes.

The result is that many of the most influential and best-educated citizens have experienced a powerful overlearning with respect to rationality. They are exceptionally good at maintaining consistent pictures of themselves, of relating action to purposes. They are exceptionally poor at a playful attitude toward their own beliefs, toward the logic of consistency, or toward the way they see things as being connected in the world. The dictates of manliness, forcefulness, independence, and intelligence are intolerant of playful urges if they arise. The playful urges that arise are weak ones, scarcely discernible in the behavior of most businessmen, mayors, or college presidents.

The picture is probably overdrawn, but we believe that the implications are not. Reason and intelligence have had the unnecessary consequence of inhibiting the development of purpose into more complicated forms of consistency. To move away from that position, we need to find some ways of helping individuals and organizations to experiment with doing things for which they have no good reason, to be playful with their conceptions of themselves. We suggest five things as a small beginning:

First, we can treat *goals as hypotheses*. Conventional theories of decision making allow us to entertain doubts about almost everything except the thing about which we frequently have the greatest doubt—our objectives. Suppose we define the decision-making process as a time for the sequential testing of hypotheses about goals. If we can experiment with alternative goals, we stand some chance of discovering complicated and interesting combinations of good values that none of us previously imagined.

Second, we can treat *intuition as real*. We do not know what intuition is or even if it is any one thing. Perhaps it is simply an excuse for doing something we cannot justify in terms of present values or for refusing to follow the logic of our own beliefs. Perhaps it is an inexplicable way of consulting that part of our intelligence and knowledge of the world that is not organized in a way anticipated by standard theories of choice. In either case, intuition permits us to see some possible actions that are outside our present scheme for justifying behavior.

Third, we can treat *hypocrisy as a transition*. Hypocrisy is an inconsistency between expressed values and behavior. Negative attitudes about hypocrisy stem mainly from a general onus against inconsistency and from a sentiment against combining the pleasures of vice with the appearance of virtue. It seems to us that a bad man with good intentions may be a man experimenting with the possibility of becoming good. Somehow it seems more sensible to encourage the experimentation than to insult it.

Fourth, we can treat *memory as an enemy*. The rules of consistency and rationality require a technology of memory. For most purposes, good memories make good choices. But the ability to forget or overlook is also useful. If you do not know what you did yesterday or what other people in the organization are doing today, you can act within the system of reason and still do things that are foolish.

Fifth, we can treat *experience as a theory*. Learning can be viewed as a series of conclusions based on concepts of action and consequences that we have invented. Experience can be changed retrospectively. By changing our interpretive concepts now, we modify what we learned earlier. Thus we expose the possibility of experimenting with alternative histories. The usual strictures against "self-deception" in experience need occasionally to be tempered with an awareness of the extent to which all experience is an interpretation subject to conscious revision. Personal histories and national histories need to be rewritten continuously as a base for the retrospective learning of new self-conceptions.

If we knew more about the normative theory of acting before thinking, we could say more intelligent things about the functions of management and leadership when organizations or societies do not know what they are doing. Consider, for example, the following general implications.

First, we need to reexamine the functions of management decision making. One of the primary ways in which the goals of an organization are developed is by interpreting the decisions it makes, and one feature of good managerial decisions is that they lead to the development of more interesting value premises for the organization. As a result, decisions should not be seen as flowing directly or strictly from a preexistent set of objectives. College presidents who make decisions might well view that function somewhat less as a process of deduction or a process of political negotiation, and somewhat more as a process of gently upsetting preconceptions of what the organization is doing.

Second, we need a modified view of planning. Planning can often be more effective as an interpretation of past decisions than as a program for future ones. It can be used as a part of the efforts of the organization to develop a new consistent theory of itself that incorporates the mix of recent actions into a moderately comprehensive structure of goals. Procedures for interpreting the meaning of most past events are familiar

to the memoirs of retired generals, prime ministers, business leaders, and movie stars. They suffer from the company they keep. In an organization that wants to continue to develop new objectives, a manager needs to be tolerant of the idea that he will discover the meaning of yesterday's action in the experiences and interpretations of today.

Third, we need to reconsider evaluation. As nearly as we can determine, there is nothing in a formal theory of evaluation that requires that criteria be specified in advance. In particular, the evaluation of social experiments need not be in terms of the degree to which they have fulfilled our prior expectations. Rather we can examine what they did in terms of what we now believe to be important. The prior specification of criteria and the prior specification of evaluational procedures that depend on such criteria are common presumptions that inhibit the serendipitous discovery of new criteria. Experience should be used explicitly as an occasion for evaluating our values as well as our actions.

Fourth, we need a reconsideration of social accountability. Individual preferences and social action need to be consistent in some way. But the process of pursuing consistency is one in which both the preferences and the actions change over time. Imagination in social policy formation involves systematically adapting to and influencing preference. It would be unfortunate if our theories of social action encouraged leaders to ignore their responsibilities for anticipating public preferences through action and for providing social experiences that modify individual expectations.

Fifth, we need to accept playfulness in social organizations. The design of organizations should attend to the problems of maintaining both playfulness and reason as aspects of intelligent choice. Since much of the literature on social design is concerned with strengthening the rationality of decision making, managers are likely to overlook the importance of play. This is partly a matter of making the individuals within an organization more playful by encouraging the attitudes and skills of inconsistency. It is also a matter of making organizational structure and organizational procedures more playful. Organizations can be playful even when the participants in them are not. The managerial devices for maintaining consistency can be varied. We encourage organizational play by insisting on some temporary relief from control, coordination, and communication.

Presidents and Foolishness

Contemporary theories of decision making and the technology of reason have considerably strengthened our capabilities for effective social action. The conversion of the simple ideas of choice into an extensive technology is a major achievement. It is, however, an achievement that has reinforced some biases in the underlying models of choice in individuals and groups. In particular, it has reinforced the uncritical acceptance of a static interpretation of human goals.

There is little magic in the world, and foolishness in people and organizations is one of the many things that fail to produce miracles. Under certain conditions, it is one of several ways in which some of the problems of our current theories of intelligence can be overcome. It may be a good way, for it preserves the virtues of consistency while stimulating change. If we had a good technology of foolishness, it might (in combination with the technology of reason) help in a small way to develop the unusual combinations of attitudes and behaviors that describe the interesting people, interesting organizations, and interesting societies of the world. The contribution of a college president may often be measured by his capacity for sustaining that creative interaction of foolishness and rationality.

NOTES

1. For a discussion of this point in the context of public school decision making, see Stephen Weiner (1972).

2. For a discussion of the same phenomenon in a business setting, see R. M. Cyert and J. G. March (1963).

3. These ideas have been the basis for extended conversation with a number of friends. We want to acknowledge particularly the help of Lance Bennett, Patricia Nelson Bennett, Michael Butler, Søren Christensen, Michel Crozier, Claude Faucheux, James R. Glenn, Jr., Cudmund Hernes, Helga Hernes, Jean Carter Lave, Harold J. Leavitt, Henry M. Levin, Leslie Lincoln, André Massart, John Miller, Johan Olsen, Richard C. Snyder, Alexander Szalai, Eugene J. Webb, and Gail Whitacre.

REFERENCES

Cyert, Richard M., & James G. March: *A Behavioral Theory of the Firm*, Prentice-Hall, Inc., Englewood Cliffs, N.J., 1963.

Long, Norton A.: "The Local Community as an Ecology of Games," *American Journal of Sociology*, vol. 44, pp. 251–261, 1958.

Reedy, George E.: *The Twilight of the Presidency*, The World Publishing Company, New York, 1970.

Weiner, Stephen S.: "Educational Decisions in an Organized Anarchy," Ph.D. dissertation, Stanford University, Stanford, Calif., 1972.

33
Power Failure in Management Circuits
Rosabeth Moss Kanter

Power is America's last dirty word. It is easier to talk about money—and much easier to talk about sex—than it is to talk about power. People who have it deny it; people who want it do not want to appear to hunger for it; and people who engage in its machinations do so secretly.

Yet, because it turns out to be a critical element in effective managerial behavior, power should come out from undercover. Having searched for years for those styles or skills that would identify capable organization leaders, many analysts, like myself, are rejecting individual traits or situational appropriateness as key and finding the sources of a leader's real power.

Access to resources and information and the ability to act quickly make it possible to accomplish more and to pass on more resources and information to subordinates. For this reason, people tend to prefer bosses with "clout." When employees perceive their manager as influential upward and outward, their status is enhanced by association and they generally have high morale and feel less critical or resistent to their boss.[1] More powerful leaders are also more likely to delegate (they are too busy to do it all themselves), to reward talent, and to build a team that places subordinates in significant positions.

Powerlessness, in contrast, tends to breed bossiness rather than true leadership. In large organizations, at least, it is powerlessness that often creates ineffective, desultory management and petty, dictatorial, rules-minded managerial styles. Accountability without power—responsibility for results without the resources to get them—creates frustration and failure. People who see themselves as weak and powerless and find their subordinates resisting or discounting them tend to use more punishing forms of influence. If organizational power can "ennoble," then, recent research shows, organizational powerlessness can (with apologies to Lord Acton) "corrupt."[2]

So perhaps power, in the organization at least, does not deserve such a bad reputation. Rather than connoting only dominance, control, and oppression, *power* can mean efficacy and capacity—something managers and executives need to move the organization toward its goals. Power in organizations is analogous in simple terms to physical power: it is the ability to mobilize resources (human and material) to get things done. The true sign of power, then, is accomplishment—not fear, terror, or tyranny. Where power is "on," the system can be productive; where the power is "off," the system bogs down. . . .

WHERE DOES POWER COME FROM?

The effectiveness that power brings evolves from two kinds of capacities:

first, access to the resources, information, and support necessary to carry out a task; and, second, ability to get cooperation in doing what is necessary. (Figure 1 identifies some symbols of an individual manager's power.) . . .

We can regard the uniquely organizational sources of power as consisting of three "lines":

1. Lines of Supply. Influence outward, over the environment, means that managers have the capacity to bring in the things that their own organizational domain needs—materials, money, resources to distribute as rewards, and perhaps even prestige.

2. Lines of Information. To be effective, managers need to be "in the know" in both the formal and the informal sense.

3. Lines of Support. In a formal framework, a manager's job parameters need to allow for nonordinary action, for a show of discretion or exercise of judgment. Thus managers need to know that they can assume innovative, risk-taking activities without having to go through the stifling multi-layered approval process. And, informally, managers need the backing of other important figures in the organization whose tacit approval becomes another resource they bring to their own work unit as well as a sign of the manager's being "in."

Note that productive power has to do with *connections* with other parts of a system. Such systemic aspects of power derive from two sources—job activities and political alliances:

1. Power is most easily accumulated when one has a job that is designed and located to allow *discretion* (nonroutinized action permitting flexible, adaptive, and creative contributions), *recognition* (visibility and notice), and *relevance* (being central to pressing organizational problems).

2. Power also comes when one has relatively close contact with *sponsors* (higher-level people who confer approval, prestige, or backing), *peer networks* (circles of acquaintanceship that provide reputation and information, the grapevine often being faster than formal communication channels), and *subordinates* (who can be developed to relieve managers of some of their burdens and to represent the manager's point of view).

When managers are in powerful situations, it is easier for them to accomplish more. Because the tools are there, they are likely to be highly motivated and, in turn, to be able to motivate subordinates. Their activities are more likely to be on target and to net them successes. They can flexibly interpret or shape policy to meet the needs of particular areas, emer-

---

FIGURE 1 • SOME COMMON SYMBOLS OF A MANAGER'S
ORGANIZATIONAL POWER (INFLUENCE UPWARD AND OUTWARD)

To What Extent a Manager Can—

Intercede favorably on behalf of someone in trouble with the organization.
Get a desirable placement for a talented subordinate.
Get approval for expenditures beyond the budget.
Get above-average salary increases for subordinates.
Get items on the agenda at policy meetings.
Get fast access to top decision makers.
Get regular, frequent access to top decision makers.
Get early information about decisions and policy shifts.

gent situations, or sudden environmental shifts. They gain the respect and cooperation that attributed power brings. Subordinates' talents are resources rather than threats. And, because powerful managers have so many lines of connection and thus are oriented outward, they tend to let go of control downward, developing more independently functioning lieutenants.

The powerless live in a different world. Lacking the supplies, information, or support to make things happen easily, they may turn instead to the ultimate weapon of those who lack productive power—oppressive power: holding others back and punishing with whatever threats they can muster.

Figure 2 summarizes some of the major ways in which variables in the organization and in job design contribute to either power or powerlessness.

POSITIONS OF POWERLESSNESS

Understanding what it takes to have power and recognizing the classic behavior of the powerless can immediately help managers make sense out of a number of familiar organizational problems that are usually attributed to inadequate people:

The ineffectiveness of first-line supervisors.

The petty interest protection and conservatism of staff professionals.

The crises of leadership at the top.

Instead of blaming the individuals involved in organizational problems, let us look at the positions people occupy. . . .

FIRST-LINE SUPERVISORS

Because an employee's most important work relationship is with his or her su-

FIGURE 2 · WAYS ORGANIZATIONAL FACTORS CONTRIBUTE TO POWER OR POWERLESSNESS

Factors	Generates Power When Factor Is	Generates Powerlessness When Factor Is
Rules inherent in the job	few	many
Predecessors in the job	few	many
Established routines	few	many
Task variety	high	low
Rewards for reliability/predictability	few	many
Rewards for unusual performance/innovation	many	few
Flexibility around use of people	high	low
Approvals needed for nonroutine decisions	few	many
Physical location	central	distant
Publicity about job activities	high	low
Relation of tasks to current problem areas	central	peripheral
Focus of tasks	outside work unit	inside work unit
Interpersonal contact in the job	high	low
Contact with senior officials	high	low
Participation in programs, conferences, meetings	high	low
Participation in problem-solving task forces	high	low
Advancement prospects of subordinates	high	low

pervisor, when many of them talk about "the company," they mean their immediate boss. Thus a supervisor's behavior is an important determinant of the average employee's relationship to work and is in itself a critical link in the production chain.

Yet I know of no U.S. corporate management entirely satisfied with the performance of its supervisors. Most see them as supervising too closely and not training their people. In one manufacturing company where direct laborers were asked on a survey how they learned their job, on a list of seven possibilities "from my supervisor" ranked next to last. (Only company training programs ranked worse.) Also, it is said that supervisors do not translate company policies into practice—for instance, that they do not carry out the right of every employee to frequent performance reviews or to career counseling.

In court cases charging race or sex discrimination, first-line supervisors are frequently cited as the "discriminating official."[3] And, in studies of innovative work redesign and quality of work life projects, they often appear as the implied villains; they are the ones who are said to undermine the program or interfere with its effectiveness. In short, they are often seen as "not sufficiently managerial." . . .

A large part of the problem lies in the position itself—one that almost universally creates powerlessness.

First-line supervisors are "people in the middle," and that has been seen as the source of many of their problems.[4] But by recognizing that first-line supervisors are caught between higher management and workers, we only begin to skim the surface of the problem. There is practically no other organizational category as subject to powerlessness.

First, these supervisors may be at a virtual dead end in their careers. Even

in companies where the job used to be a stepping stone to higher-level management jobs, it is now common practice to bring in MBAs from the outside for those positions. Thus moving from the ranks of direct labor into supervision may mean, essentially, getting "stuck" rather than moving upward. Because employees do not perceive supervisors as eventually joining the leadership circles of the organization, they may see them as lacking the high-level contacts needed to have clout. Indeed, sometimes turnover among supervisors is so high that workers feel they can outwait—and outwit—any boss.

Second, although they lack clout, with little in the way of support from above, supervisors are forced to administer programs or explain policies that they have no hand in shaping. In one company, as part of a new personnel program supervisors were required to conduct counseling interviews with employees. But supervisors were not trained to do this and were given no incentives to get involved. Counseling was just another obligation. Then managers suddenly encouraged the workers to bypass their supervisors or to put pressure on them. The personnel staff brought them together and told them to demand such interviews as a basic right. If supervisors had not felt powerless before, they did after that squeeze from below, engineered from above.

The people they supervise can also make life hard for them in numerous ways. This often happens when a supervisor has himself or herself risen up from the ranks. Peers that have not made it are resentful or derisive of their former colleague, whom they now see as trying to lord it over them. Often it is easy for workers to break the rules and let a lot of things slip.

Yet first-line supervisors are frequently judged according to rules and regulations while being limited by other regulations in what disciplinary actions they can take. They often lack the resources to influence or reward people; after all, workers are guaranteed their pay and benefits by someone other than their supervisors. Supervisors cannot easily control events; rather, they must react to them. . . .

It is not surprising, then, that supervisors frequently manifest symptoms of powerlessness: overly close supervision, rules-mindedness, and a tendency to do the job themselves rather than to train their people (since job skills may be one of the few remaining things they feel good about). Perhaps this is why they sometimes stand as roadblocks between their subordinates and the higher reaches of the company.

Women Managers Experience Special Power Failures

The traditional problems of women in management are illustrative of how formal and informal practices can combine to engender powerlessness. Historically, women in management have found their opportunities in more routine, low-profile jobs. In staff positions, where they serve in support capacities to line managers but have no line responsibilities of their own, or in supervisory jobs managing "stuck" subordinates, they are not in a position either to take the kinds of risks that build credibility or to develop their own team by pushing bright subordinates.

Such jobs, which have few favors to trade, tend to keep women out of the mainstream of the organization. This lack of clout, coupled with the greater difficulty anyone who is "different" has in getting into the information and support networks, has meant that merely by organizational situation women in management have been more likely than men to be rendered structurally powerless. This is one reason those women who have achieved power have often had family connections that put them in the mainstream of the organization's social circles.

A disproportionate number of women managers are found among first-line supervisors or staff professionals; and they, like men in those circumstances, are likely to be organizationally powerless. But the behavior of other managers can contribute to the powerlessness of women in management in a number of less obvious ways.

One way other managers can make a woman powerless is by patronizingly overprotecting her: putting her in "a safe job," not giving her enough to do to prove herself, and not suggesting her for high-risk, visible assignments. This protectiveness is sometimes born of "good" intentions to give her every chance to succeed (why stack the deck against her?). Out of managerial concerns, out of awareness that a woman may be up against situations that men simply do not have to face, some very well-meaning managers protect their female managers ("It's a jungle, so why send her into it?").

Overprotectiveness can also mask a manager's fear of association with a woman should she fail. One senior bank official at a level below vice president told me about his concerns with respect to a high-performing, financially experienced woman reporting to him. Despite *his* overwhelmingly positive

(continued)

work experiences with her, he was still afraid to recommend her for other assignments because he felt it was a personal risk. "What if other managers are not as accepting of women as I am?" he asked. "I know I'd be sticking my neck out; they would take her more because of my endorsement than her qualifications. And what if she doesn't make it? My judgment will be on the line."

Overprotection is relatively benign compared with rendering a person powerless by providing obvious signs of lack of managerial support. For example, allowing someone supposedly in authority to be bypassed easily means that no one else has to take him or her seriously. If a woman's immediate supervisor or other managers listen willingly to criticism of her and show they are concerned every time a negative comment comes up and that they assume she must be at fault, then they are helping to undercut her. If managers let other people know that they have concerns about this person or that they are testing her to see how she does, then they are inviting other people to look for signs of inadequacy or failure.

Furthermore, people assume they can afford to bypass women because they "must be uninformed" or "don't know the ropes." Even though women may be respected for their competence or expertise, they are not necessarily seen as being informed beyond the technical requirements of the job. There may be a grain of historical truth in this. Many women come to senior management positions as "outsiders" rather than up through the usual channels.

Also, because until very recently men have not felt comfortable seeing women as businesspeople (business clubs have traditionally excluded women), they have tended to seek each other out for informal socializing. Anyone, male or female, seen as organizationally naive and lacking sources of "inside dope" will find his or her own lines of information limited.

Finally, even when women are able to achieve some power on their own, they have not necessarily been able to translate such personal credibility into an organizational power base. To create a network of supporters out of individual clout requires that a person pass on and share power, that subordinates and peers be empowered by virtue of their connection with that person. Traditionally, neither men nor women have seen women as capable of sponsoring others, even though they may be capable of achieving and succeeding on their own. Women have been viewed as the *recipients of sponsorship rather than as the sponsors themselves.* . . .

Viewing managers in terms of power and powerlessness helps explain two familiar stereotypes about women and leadership in organizations: that no one wants a woman boss (although studies show that anyone who has ever had a woman boss is likely to have had a positive experience), and that the reason no one wants a woman boss is that women are "too controlling, rules-minded, and petty."

The first stereotype simply makes clear that power is important to leadership. Underneath the preference for men is the assumption that, given the current distribution of people in organizational leadership positions, men are more likely than women to be in positions to achieve power and, therefore, to share

(continued)

their power with others. Similarly, the "bossy woman boss" stereotype is a perfect picture of powerlessness. All of those traits are just as characteristic of men who are powerless, but women are slightly more likely, because of circumstances I have mentioned, to find themselves powerless than are men. Women with power in the organization are just as effective—and preferred— as men.

Recent interviews conducted with about 600 bank managers show that, when a woman exhibits the petty traits of powerlessness, people assume that she does so "because she is a woman." A striking difference is that, when a man engages in the same behavior, people assume the behavior is a matter of his own individual style and characteristics and do not conclude that it reflects on the suitability of men for management.

Staff Professionals

Also working under conditions that can lead to organizational powerlessness are the staff specialists. As advisers behind the scenes, staff people must sell their programs and bargain for resources, but unless they get themselves entrenched in organizational power networks, they have little in the way of favors to exchange. They are seen as useful adjuncts to the primary tasks of the organization but inessential in a day-to-day operating sense. This disenfranchisement occurs particularly when staff jobs consist of easily routinized administrative functions which are out of the mainstream of the currently relevant areas and involve little innovative decision making.

Furthermore, in some organizations, unless they have had previous line experience, staff people tend to be limited in the number of jobs into which they can move. Specialists' ladders are often very short, and professionals are just as likely to get "stuck" in such jobs as people are in less prestigious clerical or factory positions.

Staff people, unlike those who are being groomed for important line positions, may be hired because of a special expertise or particular background. But management rarely pays any attention to developing them into more general organizational resources. Lacking growth prospects themselves and working alone or in very small teams, they are not in a position to develop others or pass on power to them. They miss out on an important way that power can be accumulated. . . .

Staff people tend to act out their powerlessness by becoming turf-minded. They create islands within the organization. They set themselves up as the only ones who can control professional standards and judge their own work. They create sometimes false distinctions between themselves as experts (no one else could possibly do what they do) and lay people, and this continues to keep them out of the mainstream.

One form such distinctions take is a combination of disdain when line managers attempt to act in areas the professionals think are their preserve and of subtle refusal to support the managers' efforts. Or staff groups battle with each other for control of new "problem areas," with the result that no one really handles the issue at all. To cope with their essential powerlessness, staff groups may try to evaluate their own status and draw boundaries between themselves and others.

When staff jobs are treated as final resting places for people who have reached their level of competence in the organization—a good shelf on which to dump managers who are too old to go anywhere but too young to retire—then staff groups can also become pockets of conservatism, resistant to change. Their own exclusion from the risk-taking action may make them resist *anyone's* innovative proposals. In the past, personnel departments, for example, have sometimes been the last in their organization to know about innovations in human resource development or to be interested in applying them.

Top Executives

Despite the great resources and responsibilities concentrated at the top of an organization, leaders can be powerless for reasons that are not very different from those that affect staff and supervisors: lack of supplies, information, and support.

We have faith in leaders because of their ability to make things happen in the larger world, to create possibilities for everyone else, and to attract resources to the organization. These are their supplies. But influence outward—the source of much credibility downward—can diminish as environments change, setting terms and conditions out of the control of the leaders. Regardless of top management's grand plans for the organization, the environment presses. At the very least, things going on outside the organization can deflect a leader's attention and drain energy. And more detrimental, decisions made elsewhere can have severe consequences for the organization and affect top management's sense of power and thus its operating style inside. . . .

As powerlessness in lower levels of organizations can manifest itself in overly routinized jobs where performance measures are oriented to rules and absence of change, so it can at upper levels as well. Routine work often drives out nonroutine work. Accomplishment becomes a question of nailing down details. Short-term results provide immediate gratifications and satisfy stockholders or other constituencies with limited interests.

It takes a powerful leader to be willing to risk short-term deprivations in order to bring about desired long-term outcomes. Much as first-line supervisors are tempted to focus on daily adherence to rules, leaders are tempted to focus on short-term fluctuations and lose sight of long-term objectives. The dynamics of such a situation are self-reinforcing. The more the long-term goals go unattended, the more a leader feels powerless and the greater the scramble to prove that he or she is in control of daily events at least. The more he is involved in the organization as a short-term Mr. Fix-it, the more out of control of long-term objectives he is, and the more ultimately powerless he is likely to be.

Credibility for the top executives often comes from doing the extraordinary: exercising discretion, creating, inventing, planning, and acting in nonroutine ways. But since routine problems look easier and more manageable, require less change and consent on the part of anyone else, and lend themselves to instant solutions that can make any leader look good temporarily, leaders may avoid the risk by taking over what their subordinates should be doing. Ultimately, a leader may succeed in getting all the trivial problems dumped on his or her desk. This can establish expectations even for leaders attempting more challenging tasks. When Warren Bennis was president of the University of Cincinnati, a professor called him when the heat was down in a classroom. In writing about this incident, Bennis commented,

"I suppose he expected me to grab a wrench and fix it."[5]

People at the top need to insulate themselves from the routine operations of the organization in order to develop and exercise power. But this very insulation can lead to another source of powerlessness—lack of information. In one multinational corporation, top executives who are sealed off in a large, distant office, flattered and virtually babied by aides, are frustrated by their distance from the real action.[6]

At the top, the concern for secrecy and privacy is mixed with real loneliness. In one bank, organization members were so accustomed to never seeing the top leaders that when a new senior vice president went to the branch offices to look around, they had suspicion, even fear, about his intentions.

Thus leaders who are cut out of an organization's information networks understand neither what is really going on at lower levels nor that their isolation may be having negative effects. All too often top executives design "beneficial" new employee programs or declare a new humanitarian policy (e.g., "Participatory management is now our style") only to find the policy ignored or mistrusted because it is perceived as coming from uncaring bosses.

The information gap has more serious consequences when executives are so insulated from the rest of the organization or from other decision makers that, as Nixon so dramatically did, they fail to see their own impending downfall. Such insulation is partly a matter of organizational position and, in some cases, of executive style.

For example, leaders may create closed inner circles consisting of "doppelgängers," people just like themselves, who are their principal sources of organizational information and tell them only what they want to know. The reasons for the distortions are varied: key aides want to relieve the leader of burdens, they think just like the leader, they want to protect their own positions of power, or the familiar "kill the messenger" syndrome makes people close to top executives reluctant to be the bearers of bad news.

Finally, just as supervisors and lower-level managers need their supporters in order to be and feel powerful, so do top executives. But for them sponsorship may not be so much a matter of individual endorsement as an issue of support by larger sources of legitimacy in the society. For top executives the problem is not to fit in among peers; rather, the question is whether the public at large and other organization members perceive a common interest which they see the executives as promoting. . . .

When common purpose is lost, the system's own politics may reduce the capacity of those at the top to act. Just as managing decline seems to create a much more passive and reactive stance than managing growth, so does mediating among conflicting interests. When what is happening outside and inside their organizations is out of control, many people at the top turn into decline managers and dispute mediators. Neither is a particularly empowering role.

Thus when top executives lose their own lines of supply, lines of information, and lines of support, they too suffer from a kind of powerlessness. The temptation for them then is to pull in every shred of power they can and to decrease the power available to other people to act. Innovation loses out in favor of control. Limits rather than targets are set. Financial goals are met by reducing "overhead" (people) rather than by giving people the tools and discretion to increase their own productive capacity. Dictatorial statements come down from the top, spreading the mentality of powerlessness farther until the whole organization becomes sluggish and people concentrate on protecting what they can. . . .

TO EXPAND POWER, SHARE IT

In no case am I saying that people in the three hierarchical levels described are always powerless, but they are susceptible to common conditions that can contribute to powerlessness. Figure 3 summarizes the most common symptoms of powerlessness for each level and some typical sources of that behavior. . . .

The absence of ways to prevent individual and social harm causes the polity to feel it must surround people in power with constraints, regulations, and laws that limit the arbitrary use of their authority. But if oppressive power corrupts, then so does the absence of productive power. In large organizations, powerlessness can be a bigger problem than power. . . .

Organizational power can grow, in part, by being shared. We do not yet know enough about new organizational forms to say whether productive power is infinitely expandable or where we reach the point of diminishing returns. But we do know that sharing power is different from giving or throwing it away. Delegation does not mean abdication.

Some basic lessons could be translated from the field of economics to the realm

FIGURE 3 · COMMON SYMPTOMS AND SOURCES OF POWERLESSNESS FOR THREE KEY ORGANIZATIONAL POSITIONS

Position	Symptoms	Sources
First-line supervisors	Close, rules-minded supervision	Routine, rules-minded jobs with little control over lines of supply
	Tendency to do things oneself, blocking of subordinates' development and information	Limited lines of information
	Resistant, underproducing subordinates	Limited advancement or involvement prospects for oneself/subordinates
Staff professionals	Turf protection, information control	Routine tasks seen as peripheral to "real tasks" of line organization
	Retreat into professionalism	Block careers
	Conservative resistance to change	Easy replacement by outside experts
Top executives	Focus on internal cutting, short-term results, "punishing"	Uncontrollable lines of supply because of environmental changes
	Dictatorial top-down communications	Limited or blocked lines of information about lower levels of organization
	Retreat to comfort of like-minded lieutenants	Diminished lines of support because of challenges to legitimacy (e.g., from the public or special interest groups)

of organizations and management. Capital investment in plants and equipment is not the only key to productivity. The productive capacity of nations, like organizations, grows if the skill base is upgraded. People with the tools, information, and support to make more informed decisions and act more quickly can often accomplish more. By empowering others, a leader does not decrease his power; instead he may increase it—especially if the whole organization performs better. . . .

Also, if the powerless bosses could be encouraged to share some of the power they do have, their power would grow. Yet, of course, only those leaders who feel secure about their own power outward—their lines of supply, information, and support—can see empowering subordinates as a gain rather than as a loss. The two sides of power (getting it and giving it) are closely connected.

There are important lessons here for both subordinates and those who want to change organizations, whether executives or change agents. Instead of resisting or criticizing a powerless boss, which only increases the boss's feeling of powerlessness and need to control, subordinates instead might concentrate on helping the boss become more powerful. Managers might make pockets of ineffectiveness in the organization more productive not by training or replacing individuals but by structural solutions such as opening supply and support lines.

Similarly, organizational change agents who make a new program or policy to succeed should make sure that the change itself does not render any other level of the organization powerless. In making changes, it is wise to make sure that the key people in the level or two directly above and in neighboring functions are sufficiently involved, informed, and taken into account, so that the program can be used to build their own sense

of power also. If such involvement is impossible, then it is better to move these people out of the territory altogether than to leave behind a group from whom some power has been removed and who might resist and undercut the program.

In part, of course, spreading power means educating people to this new definition of it. But words alone will not make the difference; managers will need the real experience of a new way of managing. . . .

Naturally, people need to have power before thay can learn to share it. Exhorting managers to change their leadership styles is rarely useful by itself. In one large plant of a major electronics company, first-line production supervisors were the source of numerous complaints from managers who saw them as major roadblocks to overall plant productivity and as insufficiently skilled supervisors. So the plant personnel staff undertook two pilot programs to increase the supervisor's effectiveness. The first program was based on a traditional competency and training model aimed at teaching the specific skills of successful supervisors. The second program, in contrast, was designed to empower the supervisors by directly affecting their flexibility, access to resources, connections with higher-level officials, and control over working conditions. . . .

One might wonder why more organizations do not adopt such empowering strategies. There are standard answers: that giving up control is threatening to people who have fought for every shred of it; that people do not want to share power with those they look down on; that managers fear losing their own place and special privileges in the system; that "predictability" often rates higher than "flexibility" as an organizational value; and so forth.

But I would also put skepticism about employee abilities high on the list. Many modern bureaucratic systems are designed to minimize dependence on individual intelligence by making routine as many decisions as possible. So it often comes as a genuine surprise to top executives that people doing the more routine jobs could, indeed, make sophisticated decisions or use resources entrusted to them in intelligent ways. . . .

NOTES

1. Donald C. Pelz, "Influence: A Key to Effective Leadership in the First-Line Supervisor," *Personnel*, November 1952, p. 209.

2. See my book, *Men and Women of the Corporation* (New York: Basic Books, 1977), pp. 164–205; and David Kipnis, *The Powerholders* (Chicago: University of Chicago Press, 1976).

3. William E. Fulmer, "Supervisory Selection: The Acid Test of Affirmative Action," *Personnel*, November-December 1976, p. 40.

4. See my chapter (coauthor, Barry A. Stein), "Life in the Middle: Getting In, Getting Up, and Getting Along," in *Life in Organizations*, eds. Rosabeth M. Kanter and Barry A. Stein (New York: Basic Books, 1979).

5. Warren Bennis, *The Unconscious Conspiracy: Why Leaders Can't Lead* (New York: AMACOM, 1976).

6. See my chapter, "How the Top Is Different," in *Life in Organizations*.

34
The Power Game and the Players
Henry Mintzberg

The core of this book is devoted to the discussion of a theory of organizational power. It is built on the premise that organizational behavior is a power game in which various players, called *influencers*, seek to control the organization's decisions and actions. The organization first comes into being when an initial group of influencers join together to pursue a common mission. Other influencers are subsequently attracted to the organization as a vehicle for satisfying some of their needs. Since the needs of influencers vary, each tries to use his or her own levers of power—*means or systems of influence*—to control decisions and actions. How they succeed determines what configuration of organizational power emerges. Thus, to understand the behavior of the organization, it is necessary to understand which influencers are present, what needs each seeks to fulfill in the organization, and how each is able to exercise power to fulfill them.

Of course, much more than power determines what an organization does. But our perspective in this book is that power is what matters, and that, if you like, everyone exhibits a lust for power (an assumption, by the way, that I do not personally favor, but that proves useful for the purposes of this book). When our conclusions here are coupled with those of the first book in this series, *The Structuring of Organizations* (Mintzberg 1979a,

which will subsequently be referred to as the *Structuring book*), a more complete picture of the behavior of organizations emerges.

THE EXERCISE OF POWER

Hirschman (1970) notes in a small but provocative book entitled *Exit, Voice, and Loyalty,* that the participant in any system has three basic options:

To stay and contribute as expected, which Hirschman calls *loyalty* (in the vernacular, "Shut up and deal")

To leave, which Hirschman calls *exit* ("Take my marbles and go")

To stay and try to change the system, which Hirschman refers to as *voice* ("I'd rather fight than switch")

Should he or she choose voice, the participant becomes what we call an influencer.[1] Those who exit—such as the client who stops buying or the employee who seeks work elsewhere—cease to be influencers, while those who choose loyalty over voice—the client who buys without question at the going rate, the employees who do whatever they are told quietly—choose not to participate as active influencers (other than to support implicitly the existing power structure).

To resort to voice, rather than exit, is for the customer or member to make an attempt at changing the practices, policies, and outputs of the firm from which one buys or of the organization to which one belongs. Voice is here defined as any attempt at all to change, rather than to escape from, an objectionable state of affairs . . . (Hirschman 1970, p. 30)[2]

For those who stay and fight, what gives power to their voice? Essentially the influencer requires (1) some source or basis of power, coupled with (2) the expenditure of energy in a (3) politically skillful way when necessary. These are the three basic conditions for the exercise of power. In Allison's concise words, "Power . . . is an elusive blend of . . . bargaining advantages, skill and will in using bargaining advantages . . ." (1971, p. 168).

The General Bases of Power

In the most basic sense, the power of the individual in or over the organization reflects some *dependency* that is has— some gap in its own power as a system, in Crozier's view, an "uncertainty" that the organization faces (Crozier 1964; also Crozier and Friedberg 1977). This is especially true of three of the five bases of power we describe here.[3] Three prime bases of power are control of (1) a resource, (2) a technical skill, or (3) a body of knowledge, any one critical to the organization. For example, a monopolist may control the raw material supply to an organization, while an expert may control the repair of important and highly complex machinery. To serve as a basis of power, a resource, skill or body of knowledge must first of all be *essential* to the functioning of the organization. Second, it must be *concentrated*, in short supply or else in the hands of one person or a small number of people who cooperate to some extent. And third it must be *nonsubstitutable*, in other words irreplaceable. These three characteristics create the dependency—the organization needs something, and it can get it only from the few people who have it.

A fourth general basis of power stems from legal prerogatives—exclusive rights or privileges to impose choices. Society, through its governments and judicial system, creates a whole set of legal prerogatives which grant power—*formal power*—to various influencers. In the first place governments reserve for themselves the power to authorize the creation of the organization and thereafter impose regulations of various sorts on it. They also vest owners and/or the directors of the organization with certain powers, usually including the right to hire and fire the top executives. And these executives, in turn, usually have the power to hire and perhaps fire the rest of the employees, and to issue orders to them, tempered by other legal prerogatives which grant power to employees and their associations.

The fifth general basis of power derives from access to those who can rely on the other four. That access may be personal. For example, the spouses and friends of government regulators and of chief executives have power by virtue of having the ear of those who exercise legal prerogatives. The control of an important constituency which itself has influence—the customers who buy or the accountants who control the costs—can also be an important basis for power. Likewise power flows to those who can sway other influencers through the mass media—newspaper editors, TV commentators, and the like.

Sometimes access stems from favors traded: Friends and partners grant each other influence over their respective activities. In this case, power stems not from dependency but from *reciprocity*, the gaining of power in one sphere by the giving up of power in another. As we shall see in many examples in this book, the organizational power game is characterized as much by reciprocal as by dependency—onesided, or "asymmetrical"—relationships.[4]

Will and Skill

But having a basis for power is not enough. The individual must act in order to become an influencer, he or she must expend energy, use the basis for power. When the basis is formal, little effort would seem to be required to use it. But many a government has passed legislation that has never been respected, in many cases because it did not bother to establish an agency strong enough to enforce it. Likewise managers often find that their power to give orders means little when not backed up by the effort to ensure that these are in fact carried out. On the other hand, when the basis of power is informal, much effort would seem to be required to use it. If orders cannot be given, battles will have to be won. Yet here too, sometimes the reverse is true. In universities, for example, power often flows to those who take the trouble to serve on the committees. As two researchers noted in one study: "Since few people were involved and those who were involved wandered in and out, someone who was willing to spend time being present could often become influential" (March and Romelaer 1976, p. 272). In the game of power, it is often the squeaky wheel that gets the grease.

In effect, the requirement that energy be expected to achieve outcomes, and the fact that those with the important bases of power have only so much personal energy to expend, means that power gets distributed more widely than our discussions of the bases of power would suggest. Thus, one article shows how the attendants in a mental hospital, at the bottom of the formal hierarchy, could block policy initiatives from the top because collectively they were willing and able to exert far more effort than

could the administrators and doctors (Scheff 1961). What this means is that influencers pick and choose their issues, concentrating their efforts on the ones most important to them, and, of course, those they think they can win. Thus Patchen (1974) finds that each influencer stakes out those areas that affect him or her most, deferring elsewhere to other influencers.

Finally, the influencer must not only have some basis for power and expend some energy, but often he or she must also do it in a clever manner, with political skill. Much informal and even formal power backed by great effort has come to naught because of political ineptness. Managers, by exploiting those over whom they have formal power, have often provoked resistance and even mutiny; experts regularly lose reasonable issues in meetings because they fail to marshall adequate support. Political skill means the ability to use the bases of power effectively—to convince those to whom one has access, to use one's resources, information, and technical skills to their fullest in bargaining, to exercise formal power with a sensitivity to the feelings of others, to know where to concentrate one's energies, to sense what is possible, to organize the necessary alliances.

Related to political skill is a set of intrinsic leadership characteristics—charm, physical strength, attractiveness, what Kipnis calls "personal resources" (1974, p. 88). *Charisma* is the label for that mystical quality that attracts followers to an individual. Some people become powerful simply because others support them; the followers pledge loyalty to a single voice.

Thus power derives from some basis for it is coupled with the efforts and the abilities to use the basis. We shall assume this in the rest of the book, and look more concretely at the channels through which power is exercised, what we call the *means* and *the systems of influence*— the specific instruments influencers are able to use to effect outcomes.

THE CAST OF PLAYERS IN ORDER OF APPEARANCE

Who are these influencers to whom we have referred? We can first distinguish *internal* from *external* influencers. The internal influencers are the full-time employees who use voice, those people charged with making the decision and taking the actions on a permanent, regular basis; it is they who determine the outcomes, which express the goals pursued by the organization. The external influencers are nonemployees who use their bases of influence to try to affect the behavior of the employees.[5] The first two sections of our theory, on the elements of power, describe respectively the *External Coalition*, formed by the external influencers, and the *Internal Coalition*, formed by the internal influencers.

(As the word *coalition* was retained in this book only after a good deal of consideration, it is worth explaining here why it was chosen. In general, an attempt was made to avoid jargon whenever it was felt to be possible—for example, employing "chief executive officer" instead of "peak coordinator." "Coalition" proved to be a necessary exception. Because there are no common labels— popular or otherwise—to distinguish the power in from that around the organization, one had to be selected. But why *coalition*? Because it seems to fit best, even though it may be misleading to the reader at first. The word *coalition* is normally used for a group of people who band together to win some issue. As the Hickson research team at the University of Bradford notes, it has the connotation of "engineered agreements and alliances" (Astley et al. 1980, p. 21). Osten-

sibly, we are not using the word in this sense, at least not at first. We use it more in the sense that Cyert and March (1963) introduced it, as a set of people who bargain among themselves to determine a certain distribution of organizational power. But as we proceed in our discussion, the reader will find the two meanings growing increasingly similar. For one thing, in the External or Internal Coalition, the various influencers band together around or within the same organization to satisfy their needs. They do form some sort of "coalition." As Hickson et al. note in an earlier publication, "it is their coalition of interests that sustains (or destroys) [the] organization" (1976, p. 9).[6] More importantly, we shall see that the external and internal influencers each typically form rather stable systems of power, usually focussed in nature. These become semipermanent means to distribute benefits, and so resemble coalitions in the usual meaning of the term.

Our power play includes ten groups of possible influencers, listed below in order of appearance. The first four are found in the External Coalition:

- First are the *owners*, who hold the legal title to the organization. Some of them perhaps conceived the idea of founding the organization in the first place and served as brokers to bring the initial influencers together.
- Second are the *associates*, the suppliers of the organization's input resources, the clients for its output products and services, as well as its trading partners and competitors. It should be noted that only those associates who resort to voice—for example, who engage in contacts of other than a purely economic nature—are counted as influencers in the External Coalition.
- Third are the *employee associations*, that is, unions and professional associations. Again these are included as influencers to the extent that they seek to influence the organization in other than purely eco-

nomic ways, that is, to use voice to affect decisions and actions directly. Such employee associations see themselves as representatives of more than simple suppliers of labor resources. Note that employee associations are themselves considered *external* influencers, even though they represent people who can be internal influencers. Acting collectively, through their representatives, the employees choose to exert their influence on the organization from outside of its regular decision-making and action-taking channels, much as do owners and clients. (Singly, or even collectively but in different ways, the employees can of course bring their influence to bear directly on these processes, as internal influencers. Later we shall in fact see that it is typically their impotence in the Internal Coalition that causes them to act collectively in the External Coalition.)

- A fourth category comprises the organization's various *publics*, groups representing special or general interests of the public at large. We can divide these into three: (1) such general groups as families, opinion leaders, and the like; (2) special interest groups such as conservation movements or local community institutions; and (3) government in all of its forms— national, regional, local, departments and ministries, regulatory agencies, and so on.
- Another group of influencers, which is really made up of representatives from among the other four, as well as from the internal influencers, are the *directors* of the organization. These constitute a kind of "formal coalition." This group stands at the interface of the External and Internal Coalitions, but because it meets only intermittently, . . . it is treated as part of the External Coalition.

The Internal Coalition comprises six groups of influencers:

- First is the top or general management of the organization, Papandreou's peak coordinator. We shall refer to this by the single individual at the top of the hierarchy of authority, in standard American terminology, the *chief executive officer*, or CEO.[7]
- Second are the *operators*, those workers who actually produce the products and ser-

vices, or who provide the direct support to them, such as the machine operators in the manufacturing plant or the doctors and nurses in the hospital.
- Third are the managers who stand in the hierarchy of line authority from the CEO down to the first-line supervisors to whom the operators formally report. We shall refer to these simply as the *line managers*.
- Fourth are the *analysts of the technostructure*, those staff specialists who concern themselves with the design and operation of the systems for planning and for formal control, people such as work study analysts, cost accountants, and long-range planners.
- Fifth is the *support staff*, comprising those staff specialists who provide indirect support to the operators and the rest of the organization, in a business firm, for example, the mailroom staff, the chef in the cafeteria, the researchers, the public relation officers, and the legal counsel.[8]
- Finally, there is an eleventh actor in the organizational power system, one that is technically inanimate but in fact shows every indication of having a life of its own, namely the *ideology* of the organization— the set of beliefs shared by its internal influencers that distinguishes it from other organizations.

Figure 1 shows the position of each of these eleven groups schematically. The Internal Coalition is shown in the center, with the Chief Executive Officer at the top, followed, according to the formal hierarchy of authority, by the line managers and then the operators. (In some parts of the discussion, we shall accept these notions of formal authority, in others, we shall not. For now, we retain them.) Shown at either side to represent their roles as staff members are the analysts and the support staff. Above the CEO is shown the board of directors to which the CEO formally reports. And emanating from the organization is a kind of aura to represent its ideology. Surrounding all this are the various groups of the External Coalition. The owners are shown closest to the top of

FIGURE 1 · THE CAST OF PLAYERS

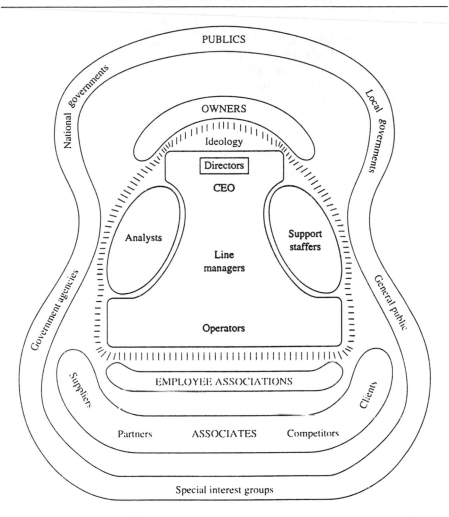

the hierarchy, and to the board of directors, where they are often inclined to exert their influence. The associates are shown surrounding the operating core where the operators work, the suppliers on the left (input) side and the clients on the right (output) side, with the partners and competitors in between. The employee associations are shown closest to the operators, whom they represent, while the various publics are shown to form a ring around the entire power system, in effect influencing every part of it. Thus the organization of Figure 1 can be seen to exist in a complex field of influencer forces.

Each of these eleven groups of players in the organizational power game will be discussed in turn, together with the means of influence they have at their disposal. We assume in this discussion that each is driven by the needs inherent in the roles they play. For example, owners will be described as owners, not as fathers, or Episcopalians, or power-hungry devils. People are of course driven by a variety of needs—by intrinsic values such as the need for control or autonomy, or in Maslow's (1954) needs hierarchy theory, by physiological, safety, love, esteem, and self-actualization needs; by the values instilled in them as children or developed later through socialization and various identifications; by the need to exploit fully whatever skills and abilities they happen to have; by their desire to avoid repetition of painful experiences or to repeat successful ones; by opportunism, the drive to exploit whatever opportunities happen to present themselves. All of these needs contribute to the makeup of each influencer and lead to an infinite variety of behaviors. All are, therefore, important to understand. But they are beyond the scope of this book. Here we focus on those behaviors that are dictated strictly by role. We assume throughout that each group discussed above is driven to gain power in or over the organization—in other words, is an influencer; our discussion then focuses on what ends each seeks to attain, what means or systems of influence each has at its disposal, and how much power each tends to end up with by virtue of the role it plays in the power coalition to which it happens to belong. This is the point of departure for the discussion of our theory.

NOTES

1. Some writers call the influencer a "stakeholder" since he or she maintains a stake in the organization the way a shareholder maintains shares. Other use the term "claimant," in that he or she has a claim on the organization's benefits. Both these terms, however, would include those who express loyalty as well as voice.

2. There are some interesting linkages among these three options, as Hirschman points out.

Exit is sometimes a last resort for frustrated voice, or in the case of a strike (temporary exit), a means to supplement voice. The effect of exit can be "galvanizing" when voice is the norm, or vice versa, as in the case of Ralph Nader who showed consumers how to use voice instead of exit against the automobile companies (p. 125). Of course, an inability to exit forces the disgruntled individual to turn to voice. Hirschman also makes the intriguing point that exit belongs to the study of economics, voice to that of political science. In economic theory, the customer or employee dissatisfied with one firm is supposed to shift to another: ". . . one either exits or one does not; it is impersonal" (p. 15). In contrast, voice is "a far more 'messy' concept because it can be graduated, all the way from hint grumbling to violent protest . . . voice is political action par excellence" (p. 16). But students of political science also have a "blind spot": ". . . exit has often been branded as *criminal*, for it has been labelled desertion, defection, and treason" (p. 17).

3. Related discussions of bases of power can be found in Allison (1971), Crozier and Friedberg (1977), Jacobs (1974), Kipnis (1974), Mechanic (1962), and Pfeffer and Salancik (1978).

4. French and Raven's (1959) five categories of power, as perhaps the most widely quoted typology of power, should be related to these five bases of power. Their "reward" and "coercive" power are used formally by those with legal prerogatives and may be used informally by those who control critical resources, skills, or knowledge (for example, to coerce by holding these back). Their "legitimate" power corresponds most closely to our legal prerogatives and their "expert" power to our critical skills and knowledge. Their fifth category, "referent" power, is discussed below in our section on political skill.

5. As we shall soon see, there are some circumstances in which external influencers can impose decisions directly on the organization, and others in which full-time employees acting in concert through their associations behave as external influencers by trying to affect the behavior of the senior managers. As Pfeffer and Salancik (1978, p. 30) point out, actors can be part of the organization as well as its environment. Nevertheless, the distinction between full-time employees—those individuals with an intensive and regular commitment to the organization—and others will

prove to be a useful and important one in all that follows.

6. It might be noted that the Hickson group in the1980 publication cited earlier (as Astley et al.) decided to replace the word *coalition* by *constellation*. That was tried in this book, but dropped as not having quite the right ring to it.

7. An alternate term which appears frequently in the more recent literature is *dominant coalition*. But we have no wish to prejudice the discussion of the power of one of our groups of influencers by the choice of its title.

8. For a more elaborate description of each of these five groups as well as clarification of the differences between technocratic and support staff and of line and staff in general, see Chapter 2 of the *Structuring* book [Mintzberg, 1979a].

REFERENCES

Allison, G. T. (1971). *Essence of decision: Explaining the Cuban missile crisis.* Boston: Little, Brown. Copyright © 1971 by Graham T. Allison. Reprinted by permission of the publisher.

Astley, W. G., Axelsson, R., Butler, R. J., Hickson, D. J., & Wilson, D. C. (1980). Decision making: Theory III. Working Paper, University of Bradford Management Centre. Used with permission.

Crozier, M. (1964). *The bureaucratic phenomenon.* Chicago: University of Chicago Press. Used with permission.

————. (1974). Why is France blocked? In H. J. Leavitt, L. Pinfield, & E. J. Webb (Eds.). *Organizations of the future: Interaction with the external environment.* New York: Praeger. Used with permission.

————, & Friedberg, E. (1977). *L'acteur et le système.* Paris: Editions du Seuil.

Cyert, R. M., & March, J. G. (1963). *A behavioral theory of the firm.* Englewood Cliffs, NJ: Prentice-Hall.

French, J. R. P., Jr., & Raven, B. (1959). The bases of social power. In D. Cartwright (Ed.). *Studies in social power* (pp. 150–167). Ann Arbor: Institute for Social Research, University of Michigan.

Hickson, D. J., Butler, R. J., Axelsson, R., & Wilson, D. (1976). Decisive coalitions. Paper presented to International Conference on Coordination and Control of Group and Organizational Performance, Munich, West Germany.

Hirschman, A. O. (1970). *Exit, voice, and loyalty: Responses to decline in firms, organizations, and states.* Cambridge, MA: Harvard University Press.

Jacobs, D. (1974). Dependency and vulnerability: An exchange approach to the control of organizations. *Administrative Science Quarterly,* 45–59.

Kipnis, D. (1974). The powerholder. In J. T. Tedeschi (Ed.), *Perspectives on social power* (pp. 82–122). Chicago: Aldine.

March, J. G., & Romelaer, P. J. (1976). Position and presence in the drift of decisions. In J. G. March & J. P. Olsen (Eds.), *Ambiguity and choice in organizations.* Bergen, Norway: Universitetsforlaget.

Maslow, A. H. (1954). *Motivation and personality.* New York: Harper & Row.

Mechanic, D. (1962). Sources of power of lower participants in complex organizations. *Administrative Science Quarterly,* 349–364.

Mintzberg, H. (1979a). *The structuring of organizations: A synthesis of the research.* Englewood Cliffs, NJ: Prentice-Hall.

Patchen, M. (1974). The locus and basis of influence on organizational decisions. *Organizational Behavior and Human Performance,* 195–221.

Pfeffer, N., and Salancik, G. R. (1978). *The external control of organizations: A resource dependence perspective.* New York: Harper & Row.

Scheff, T. J. (1961). Control over policy by attendants in a mental hospital. *Journal of Health and Human Behavior,* 93–105.

CHAPTER VII

Organizational Culture and Sense-Making

Organizational culture is the culture that exists in an organization, something akin to a societal culture. It is comprised of many intangible things such as values, beliefs, assumptions, perceptions, behavioral norms, artifacts, and patterns of behavior. It is the unseen and unobservable force that is always behind the organizational activities that *can* be seen and observed. According to Kilmann and others (1985), organizational culture is a social energy that moves people to act. "Culture is to the organization what personality is to the individual—a hidden, yet unifying theme that provides meaning, direction, and mobilization."

Secondly, organizational culture is an emerging set of organization theories with its own assumptions about organizational realities and relationships. It is yet another way of viewing, thinking about, studying, and trying to understand organizations. Like power and politics organization theory, the organizational culture perspective represents a counterculture within organization theory. Its assumptions, units of analysis, research methods, and approaches are very different from those of the dominant, rational, "modern" structural and systems theories. The organizational culture perspective challenges the basic views of the "modern" structural and systems perspectives about, for example, how organizations make decisions and how and why organizations—and people in organizations—act as they do.

In both the "modern" structural and the systems theories of organization, organizations are assumed to be utilitarian instutitions whose primary purpose is to accomplish established goals. Those goals are set by people in positions of formal authority. The primary questions for organization theory thus involve how best to design and manage organizations to achieve their declared purposes effectively and efficiently. The personal preferences of organizational members are restrained by systems of formal rules, authority, and by norms of rational behavior. In a 1982 *Phi Delta Kappan* article, Karl Weick argues that four organizational conditions must exist in order for basic assumptions of the structuralists and systemists to be valid:

1. A self-correcting system of interdependent people
2. Consensus on objectives and methods
3. Coordination achieved through sharing information
4. Predictable organizational problems and solutions

But, unfortunately, Weick is forced to conclude that these conditions seldom—if ever—exist in modern organizations.

Consequently, the organizational culture perspective rejects the assumptions of the "modern" structural and systems theories. Instead, it assumes that many organizational behaviors and decisions are almost predetermined by the patterns of basic assumptions that are held by members of an organization. Those patterns of assumptions continue to exist and to influence behaviors because they repeatedly lead people to make decisions that "worked in the past" for the organization. With repeated use, the assumptions slowly drop out of peoples' consciousness but continue to influence organizational decisions and behaviors, even when the organization's environment changes. They become the underlying, unquestioned, but virtually forgotten reasons for "the way we do things here"—even when the ways are no longer appropriate. They are so basic, so pervasive, and so totally accepted as "the truth" that no one thinks about or remembers them.

Thus, a strong organizational culture literally controls organizational behavior: For example, an organizational culture can block an organization from making changes that are needed to adapt to a changing environment. From the organizational culture perspective, the personal preferences of organizational members are not restrained by systems of formal rules, authority, and by norms of rational behavior. Instead, they are controlled by cultural norms, values, beliefs and assumptions. In order to understand or predict how an organization will behave under varying circumstances, one must know and understand the organization's patterns of basic assumptions—its organizational culture.

Every organizational culture is different, for several reasons. First, what has "worked" repeatedly for one organization may not for another, so the basic assumptions differ. Second, an organization's culture is partially shaped by many factors including, for example, the societal culture in which it resides; its technologies, markets, and competition; and the personality of its founder(s) or dominant early leaders. Some organizational cultures are more distinctive than others; some organizations have strong, unified, pervasive cultures, whereas others have weaker cultures; some organizational cultures are quite pervasive, whereas others may have many *subcultures* existing in different functional or geographical areas (Ott, 1989, Chapter 4).

Knowledge of an organization's structure, information systems, strategic planning processes, markets, technology, goals, and so forth, will give clues about an organization's culture, but not accurately or reliably. As a consequence, an organization's behavior can not be understood or predicted by studying its structural or systems elements; its organizational culture must be studied. And, the quantitative quasi-experimental research methods used by the "modern" structural and systems schools *cannot* identify or measure unconscious, virtually forgotten basic assumptions. Van Maanen, Dabbs, and Faulkner, in their 1982 book *Varieties of Qualitative Research*, describe a growing wave of disenchantment with the use of quantitative quasi-experimental research methods for studying organizations, mainly because these methods have produced very little useful knowledge about organizations over the last twenty years. Yet, quantitative research using quasi-experimental designs, control groups, computers, multivariate analyses, heuristic models, and the like are the essential "tools"of the systems and "modern" structural schools. More and more, the organizational culture school (and the power and politics school) are turning to qualitative research methods like ethnography and participant observation.

Earlier, we said that organizational culture represents a counterculture within the field of organization theory. The reasons should be becoming evident. The organizational culture perspective believes that the "modern" structural and systems schools of organization theory are using the wrong tools (or "lenses") to look at the wrong organizational elements in their attempts to understand and predict organizational behavior. In other words, they are wasting their time.

It takes courage to challenge the basic views of a mainstream school in any profession or academic discipline. Yet this is just what the organizational culture and the power and politics perspectives are doing when they advocate such radically different ways of looking at and working with organizations. For example, from the organizational culture perspective, AT&T's basic problems since deregulation and court-ordered splintering of the Bell System are not in its structure, information systems, or people. Rather, they rest in an organizational culture that no longer is appropriate for AT&T's deregulated world. The long-standing AT&T culture had been centered on assumptions about (1) the value of technical superiority, (2) AT&T's possession of technical superiority, and thus (3) AT&T's rightful dominance in the telephone and telecommunications market. Therefore, working to improve things like AT&T's goals, structure, differentiation and integration processes, strategic plans, and information systems will not solve AT&T's monumental problems. The solution requires changing an ingrained organizational culture: changing basic *unconscious* assumptions about what makes for success in a competitive telephone and communications market.

Lee Iacocca faced a similar problem (but different in its content) when he took over leadership of the Chrysler Corporation. Chrysler was a "loser"—in just about every way—in the eyes of employees, potential employees, investors, car dealers, financers, suppliers, and car buyers. It was simply *assumed* that Chrysler could not compete head-on. Iacocca had to change not only an organizational culture, but also *everybody's perception* of that culture. Chrysler needed and got in Iacocca what Warren Bennis (1984) and Tichy and Ulrich (1984) have called a "transformational leader," one who could totally transform an imbedded organizational culture by creating a new vision of and for the organization, and successfully selling that vision—by rallying commitment and loyalty to make the vision become a reality.

In Chapter VI, we said that much of the important writing from the power theories of organization is quite recent and its theoretical grounding is not as well developed as, for example, it is in the classical, "modern" structural, and systems theories. Most of the research and writing from the organizational culture perspective is even more recent. Thus, the organizational culture perspective suffers from the problems and limitations of youthfulness. Although phrases like *organizational culture* and *culture of a factory* can be found in a few books on management written as early as the 1950s (for example, Elliott Jaques' 1951 book *The Changing Culture of a Factory* and William H. Whyte, Jr.'s, 1956 book about conformity in business, *The Organization Man*), few students of management or organizations paid much attention to the nature and content of organizational culture until the late 1970s. (The few who did were mostly proponents of organization development [Ott, 1996, Chapter VII].)

During the 1960s and early 1970s, several books on organizational and professional socialization processes received wide attention. As useful as these earlier works were, they *assumed* the presence of organizational or professional cultures and proceeded to examine issues involving the match between individuals and cultures. Some of the more widely read of these were the 1961 book *Boys in White* by Becker, Geer, Hughes, and Strauss, which chronicled the processes used to socialize medical students into the medical profession; Herbert Kaufman's 1960 study of how the United States Forest Service developed the "will and capacity to conform" among its remotely stationed rangers in *The Forest Ranger;* Ritti and Funkhouser's 1977 humorous-but-serious look at *The Ropes to Skip and the Ropes to Know;* John Van Maanen's articles on "Police Socialization" (1975) and "Breaking in: Socialization to Work" (1976). During this period, Edgar H. Schein contributed significantly to the knowledge about both organizational and professional socialization processes in numerous writings including, for example, "How to Break in the College Graduate" (1964), "Organizational Socialization and the Profession of Management" (1968), and *Career Dynamics: Matching Individual and Organizational Needs* (1978). Once again, however, these earlier writings did not address important questions such as how cultures are formed or changed, how cultures affect leadership, or the relationship between culture and strategic planning (establishing organizational directions); rather, they focused on the process of socializing employees into existing organizational cultures and the impacts of existing cultures on organizational members.

A different orientation to cultures in organizations started to appear in the organization theory literature during the late 1970s. This orientation is known as the symbolic frame, symbolic management, or organizational symbolism. Bolman and Deal (1991) identify the basic tenets of symbolic management as follows:

1. The meaning or the interpretation of what is happening in organizations is more important than what actually is happening.
2. Ambiguity and uncertainty, which are prevalent in most organizations, preclude rational problem solving and decision-making processes.
3. People use symbols to reduce ambiguity and to gain a sense of direction when they are faced with uncertainty.

In their 1967 book, *The Social Construction of Reality*, Peter Berger and Thomas Luckman define meanings as "socially constructed realities." In other words, things are not real in and of themselves; the perceptions of them are, in fact, reality. As

W. I. Thomas said (1923), "If people believe things are real, they are real in their consequences." According to the organizational culture perspective, meanings (realities) are established by and among the people in organizations—by the organizational culture. Experimenters have shown that there is a strong relation between culturally determined values and the perception of symbols. People will distort their perceptions of symbols according to the need for what is symbolized (Davis, 1963). Thus, organizational symbolism is an integral part of the organizational culture perspective.

The turning point for the organizational culture/symbolic management perspective arrived in 1981 or 1982. Almost overnight, organizational culture became a very hot topic in books, journals, and periodicals aimed at management practitioners and academicians, including Thomas Peters and Robert Waterman, Jr.'s, 1982 best-seller *In Search of Excellence* (and its sequels); Terrence Deal and Allan Kennedy's 1982 book *Corporate Cultures; Fortune* Magazine's 1983 story on "The Corporate Culture Vultures"; *Business Week's* May 14, 1984 cover story "Changing a Corporate Culture." The first comprehensive, theoretically based, integrative writing on organizational culture did not appear until 1984 and 1985. Products of these two years include Thomas Sergiovanni and John Corbally's heady reader *Leadership and Organization Culture* (1984); Edgar Schein's pioneering *Organizational Culture and Leadership* (1985); Vijay Sathe's *Culture and Related Corporate Realitites* (1985); and the first of Ralph Kilmann's series of books built from interactive conference papers, *Gaining Control of the Corporate Culture* (1985).

"Total Quality Management" (TQM) has thrust organizational culture onto the front pages of the management and organizational literature in the 1990s (see Chapter IX). Several professional management and behavioral sciences journals now carry articles regularly on a variety of issues that reflect the organizational culture and symbolic management perspective. And, books with important insights continue to roll off the publishers' presses: For example, *Developing Corporate Character* by Alan Wilkins (1989); *Organisational Cultures in Theory and Practice* by Pedersen and Sørensen (1989); *Organizational Climate and Culture* edited by Schneider (1990); *Corporate Culture and Organizational Effectiveness* by Dennison (1990); *Cultural Knowledge in Organizations*, by Sackman (1991); and Trice and Beyer (1993) *The Cultures of Work Organizations*.

The first selection reprinted here is Edgar H. Schein's chapter from his 1985 book *Organizational Culture and Leadership* titled "Defining Organizational Culture." In it, Schein proposes a "formal definition" of organizational culture that has gained wide acceptance. His definition is a model of three levels of culture, which is particularly useful for sorting through myriad methodological and substantive problems associated with identifying an organizational culture.

Schein also takes a unique stand on behalf of using a "clinical" rather than an "ethnographic" perspective for gaining knowledge about an organization's culture. He argues that an ethnographer seeks to understand an organizational culture for "intellectual and scientific" reasons, and organization members "have no particular stake in the intellectual issues that may have motivated the study." Thus, the ethnographer must work to obtain cooperation. In contrast, when clients call in an "outsider" (consultant) to help solve problems, "the nature of the psychological contract between client and helper is completely different from that between researcher and subject, leading to a different kind of relationship between them, the revelation of different kinds of data, and the use of different criteria for when enough has been 'understood' to terminate the inquiry."

The organizational culture perspective provides useful insights into the mental processes new employees use as they struggle to cope or "make sense" of their new environment. Meryl Reis Louis's 1980 article that is included here, "Surprise and Sense Making: What Newcomers Experience in Entering Unfamiliar Organizational Settings," begins with a model of the "entry experience" that incorporates the features of change, contrast and surprise. Louis proposes that sense-making by newcomers usually must rely on inadequate sources of information, which can lead them astray.

The practical implications of Louis's model are readily evident. "Decisions [of newcomers] to stay in or leave organizations and feelings of commitment or alienation would appear to follow from sense made by newcomers of early job experiences." Thus, "it is important that [newcomers] have information available for amending internal cognitive maps and for attaching meaning to such surprises as may arise during early job experiences." (Karl Weick's article, "Technology as Equivoque: Sensemaking in New Technologies," which is in Chapter IX, applies the sense-making theme to the problem of coping with technological change.)

Gareth Morgan's 1986 book, *Images of Organization* (parts of which are reprinted here), uses the metaphor as yet another approach to sense-making in organizations— "complex and paradoxical phenomena that can be understood in many different ways." The metaphor provides an analytical method for "highlighting certain interpretations [as] it tends to force others into a background role." In addition to aiding in understanding organizations, metaphors offer insights for changing them. "The way we 'read' organizations influences how we produce them. Images and metaphors are not just interpretive constructs. . . . They are central to the process of *imaginization* through which people enact or 'write' the character of organizational life."

Morgan's theme, "the way we 'read' organizations influences how we produce them," paves the way for Joan Acker's contribution to this chapter, "Gendering Organization Theory" (1992). Feminist organization theorists argue that long-standing male control of organizations has been accompanied and maintained by male perspectives of organization theory. Thus it is through male lenses that we *see* and analyze organizations. At least four sets of gendered processes perpetuate this male reality of organizations: (1) gender divisions that produce gender patterning of jobs, (2) creation of symbols and images, (3) interactions characterized by dominance and subordination, and (4) "the internal mental work of individuals as they consciously construct their understandings of the organization's gendered structure of work and opportunity and the demands for gender-appropriate behaviors and attitudes."

Ordinary activities in organizations are not gender-neutral. They perpetuate the "gendered substructure within the organization itself and within the wider society"—as well as in organization theory. Morgan reinforces this contention when he asserts that "our images and metaphors are not just interpretive constructs . . . they are central to the process of *imaginization* through which people enact or 'write' the character of organizational life."

This chapter on organizational culture concludes with "Changing Organizational Cultures," from Harrison Trice and Janice Beyer's 1993 book, *The Cultures of Work Organizations.* The core of the Trice and Beyer entry is a set of eight "prescriptive aphorisms" or "specific considerations in changing [organizational] cultures":

- capitalize on propitious moments;
- combine caution with optimism;
- understand resistance to culture change;
- change many elements, but maintain some continuity;
- recognize the importance of implementation;
- select, modify, and create appropriate cultural forms;
- modify socialization tactics; and
- find and cultivate innovative leadership.

Trice and Beyer's selection serves as a transition to Chapter VIII, "Organizational Culture Reform Movements." Whereas Chapter VII concentrates on organizational culture and sense making, Chapter VIII explores theories of organization which assume that organizational cultures need to be changed. Altered organizational culture is simply the starting point for reshaping organizations to be more flexible, responsive, and customer-driven. Trice and Beyer remind us that changing an organizational culture is not a task to be taken lightly.

REFERENCES

Acker, J. (1992). Gendering organizational theory. In A. J. Mills & P. Tancred (Eds.), *Gendering organizational analysis* (248–260). Newbury Park, CA: Sage.

Becker, H. S., Geer, B., Hughes, E. C., & Strauss, A. L. (1961). *The boys in white: Student culture in medical school.* Chicago: University of Chicago Press.

Bennis, W. G. (1984). Transformative power and leadership. In T. J. Sergiovanni & J. E. Corbally (Eds.), *Leadership and organizational culture* (pp. 64–71). Urbana, IL: University of Illinois Press.

Berger, P. L., & Luckman, T. (1967). *The social construction of reality.* Garden City, NY: Doubleday Anchor.

Bergquist, W. H. (1992). *The four cultures of the academy.* San Francisco: Jossey-Bass.

Bolman, L. G. & Deal, T. D. (1991). *Reframing organizations: Artistry, choice, and leadership.* San Francisco: Jossey-Bass.

Business Week (May 14, 1984). Changing a corporate culture: Can J&J move from band-aids to high tech?, pp. 130–138.

Clark, B. R. (1970). *The distinctive college: Antioch, Reed & Swarthmore.* Chicago: Aldine.

Davis, J. C. (1963). *Human nature in politics: The dynamics of political behavior.* New York; Wiley.

Deal, T. E., & Kennedy, A. A. (1982). *Corporate cultures.* Reading, MA: Addison-Wesley.

Dennison, D. R. (1990). *Corporate culture and organizational effectiveness.* New York: Wiley.

Fortune (October 17, 1983). The corporate culture vultures, pp. 66–71.

Gannon, M. J. (1994). *Understanding global cultures: Metaphorical journeys through 17 countries.* Thousand Oaks, CA: Sage.

Graves, D. (1986). *Corporate culture: Diagnosis and change.* New York: St. Martin's Press.

Handy, C. (1989). *The age of unreason.* Boston: Harvard Business School Press.

Helgesen, S. (1990). *The female advantage: Women's ways of leadership.* New York: Doubleday/Currency.

Hummel, R. P. (January/February 1991). Stories managers tell: Why they are as valid as science. *Public Administration Review, 51,* 31–41.

Hunt, J. G., Hosking, D. M., Schriesheim, C. A., & Stewart, R. (Eds.). *Leaders and managers.* New York: Pergamon.

Ingersoll, V. H., & Adams, G. B. (1992). *The tacit organization.* Greenwich, CT: JAI Press.

Jaques, E. (1951). *The changing culture of a factory.* London: Tavistock Institute.

Jones, M. O., Moore, M. D., & Snyder, R. C. (Eds.). (1988). *Inside organizations: Understanding the human dimension.* Newbury Park, CA: Sage.

Kaufman, H. (1960). *The forest ranger.* Baltimore, MD: The Johns Hopkins Press.

Kilmann, R. H., Saxton, M. J., Serpa, R., & Associates (Eds.) (1985). *Gaining control of the corporate culture.* San Francisco: Jossey-Bass.

Kotkin, J. (1992). *Tribes: How race, religion, and identity determine success in the new global economy.* New York: Random House.

Louis, M. R. (June 1980). Surprise and sense making: What newcomers experience in entering unfamiliar organizational settings. *Administrative Science Quarterly, 25* 226–251.

Louis, M. R. (1983). Organizations as culture-bearing milieux. In L. R. Pondy, P. J. Frost, G. Morgan, & T. C. Dandridge (Eds.). *Organizational symbolism* (pp. 39–54). Greenwich, CT: JAI Press.

Martin, J. (1992). *Cultures in organizations: Three perspectives.* New York: Oxford University Press.

Morgan, G. (1986). *Images of organization.* Beverly Hills, CA: Sage.

Neuhauser, P. C. (1993). *Corporate legends and lore: The power of storytelling as a management tool.* New York: McGraw-Hill.

Ott, J. S. (1989). *The organizational culture perspective.* Belmont, CA: Wadsworth.

Ott, J. S. (Ed.). (1996). *Classic readings in organizational behavior* (2d ed.) Belmont, CA: Wadsworth.

Ouchi, W. G. (1981). *Theory Z.* Reading, MA: Addison-Wesley.

Pascale, R. T., & Athos, A. G. (1981). *The art of Japanese management*. New York: Simon & Schuster.

Pedersen, J. S., & Sørensen, J. S. (1989). *Organisational cultures in theory and practice*. Aldershot, UK: Gower.

Peters, T. J. (Autumn 1978). Symbols, patterns, and settings: An optimistic case for getting things done. *Organizational Dynamics*, 3–23.

Peters, T. J., & Waterman, R. H., Jr. (1982). *In search of excellence*. New York: Harper & Row.

Pondy, L. R., Frost, P. J., Morgan, G., & Dandridge, T. C. (Eds.). (1983). *Organizational symbolism*. Greenwich, CT: JAI Press.

Quinn, R. E., & Cameron, K. S. (Eds.). (1988). *Paradox and transformation: Toward a theory of change in organization and management*. Cambridge, MA: Ballinger.

Ritti, R. R., & Funkhouser, G. R. (1977). *The ropes to skip and the ropes to know*. New York: Wiley.

Sackman, S. A. (1991). *Cultural knowledge in organizations: Exploring the collective mind*. Newbury Park, CA: Sage.

Sathe, V. (1985). *Culture and related corporate realities*. Homewood, IL: Richard D. Irwin.

Schein, E. H. (1964). How to break in the college graduate. *Harvard Business Review, 42*, 68–76.

Schein, E. H. (1968). Organizational socialization and the profession of management. *Industrial Management Review, 9*, 1–15.

Schein, E. H. (1978). *Career dynamics: Matching individual and organizational needs*. Reading, MA: Addison-Wesley.

Schein, E. H. (1985). *Organizational culture and leadership*. San Francisco: Jossey-Bass.

Schneider, B. (Ed.) (1990). *Organizational climate and culture*. San Francisco: Jossey-Bass.

Sergiovanni, T. J. (1984). Cultural and competing perspectives in administrative theory and practice. In T. J. Sergiovanni & J. F. Corbally (Eds.), *Leadership and organizational culture: New perspectives on administrative theory and practice* (pp. 1–11). Urbana, IL: University of Illinois Press.

Sergiovanni, T. J., & Corbally, J. E. (Eds.). (1984). *Leadership and organizational culture*. Urbana, IL: University of Illinois Press.

Siehl, C., & Martin, J. (1984). The role of symbolic management: How can managers effectively transmit organizational culture? In J. G. Hunt, D. M. Hosking, C. A. Schriesheim, & R. Stewart (Eds.), *Leaders and Managers* (pp. 227–239). New York: Pergamon.

Simon, H. A. (1969). *The sciences of the artificial*. Cambridge, MA: MIT Press.

Smircich, L. (1983). Organizations as shared meanings. In L. R. Pondy, P. J. Frost, G. Morgan, & T. C. Dandridge (Eds.), *Organizational symbolism* (pp. 55–65). Greenwich, CT: JAI Press.

Thomas, W. I. (1923). *The unadjusted girl*. New York: Harper Torchbooks, 1967.

Tichy, N. M., & Ulrich, D. O. (Fall 1984). The leadership challenge—A call for the transformational leader. *Sloan Management Review, 26*(1), 59–68.

Trice, H. M. (1993). *Occupational subcultures in the workplace*. Ithaca, NY: ILR Press.

Trice, H. M., & Beyer, J. M. (1993). *The cultures of work organizations*. Englewood Cliffs, NJ: Prentice Hall.

Van Maanen, J. (1975). Police socialization. *Adminsitrative Science Quarterly, 20*, 207–228.

Van Maanen, J. (1976). Breaking in: Socialization to work. in R. Dubin (Ed.), *Handbook of work, organization and society* (pp. 67–130). Chicago: Rand McNally.

Van Maanen, J. (Ed.) (1979, 1983). *Qualitative methodology*. Newbury Park, CA: Sage.

Van Maanen, J., Dabbs, J. M., Jr., & Faulkner, R. R. (Eds.). (1982). *Varieties of qualitative research*. Newbury Park, CA: Sage.

Weick, K. E. (June 1982). Administering education in loosely coupled schools. *Phi Delta Kappan*, 673–676.

Weick, K. E. (1995). *Sensemaking in Organizations*. Thousand Oaks, CA: Sage.

Whyte, W. H., Jr. (1956). *The organization man*. New York: Simon & Schuster.

Wilkins, A. L. (1989). *Developing corporate character: How to successfully change an organization without destroying it*. San Francisco: Jossey-Bass.

35
Defining Organizational Culture
Edgar H. Schein

are necessary 'q created by the leader

Most of us—whether students, employees, managers, researchers, or consultants—live in organizations and have to deal with them. Yet we continue to find it amazingly difficult to understand and justify much of what we observe and experience in our organizational life. Too much seems to be "bureaucratic," or "political," or just plain "irrational." People in positions of authority, especially our immediate bosses, often frustrate us or act incomprehensibly, and those we consider the "leaders" of our organizations often disappoint us and fail to meet our aspirations. The fields of organizational psychology and sociology have developed a variety of useful concepts for understanding individual behavior in organizations and the ways in which organizations structure themselves. But the dynamic of why and how they grow, change, sometimes fail, and—perhaps most important of all—do things that don't seem to make any sense continues to elude us.

The concept of organizational culture holds promise for illuminating this difficult area. I will try to show that a deeper understanding of cultural issues in organizations is necessary not only to decipher what goes on in them but, even more important, to identify what may be the priority issues for leaders and leadership. Organizational cultures are created by leaders, and one of the most decisive functions of leadership may well be the creation, the management, and—

if and when that may become necessary—the destruction of culture. Culture and leadership, when one examines them closely, are two sides of the same coin, and neither can really be understood by itself. In fact, there is a possibility—underemphasized in leadership research—that the *only thing of real importance that leaders do is to create and manage culture* and that the unique talent of leaders is their ability to work with culture. If the concept of leadership as distinguished from management and administration is to have any value, we must recognize the centrality of this culture management function in the leadership concept.

But before we examine closely the tie to leadership, we must fully understand the concept of organizational culture. I would like to begin with two examples from my own consulting experience. In the first case (Company A), I was called in to help a management group improve its communication, interpersonal relationships, and decision making. After sitting in on a number of meetings, I observed, among other things, high levels of interrupting, confrontation, and debate; excessive emotionality about proposed courses of action; great frustration over the difficulty of getting a point of view across; and a sense that every member of the group wanted to win all the time. Over a period of several months, I made many suggestions about better listening, less interrupting, more

Source: Edgar H. Schein, *Organizational Culture and Leadership* (San Francisco, CA: Jossey-Bass, 1985), 1–22. Reprinted by permission of the publisher.

orderly processing of the agenda, the potential negative effects of high emotionality and conflict, and the need to reduce the frustration level. The group members said that the suggestions were helpful, and they modified certain aspects of their procedure, such as lengthening some of their meetings. However, the basic pattern did not change, no matter what kind of intervention I attempted. I could not understand why my efforts to improve the group's problem-solving process were not more successful.

In the second case (Company B), I was asked, as part of a broader consultation project, to help create a climate for innovation in an organization that felt a need to become more flexible in order to respond to its increasingly dynamic business environment. The organization consisted of many different business units, functional groups, and geographical groups. As I got to know more about these units and their problems, I observed that some very innovative things were going on in many places in the company. I wrote several memos describing these innovations, added other ideas from my own experience, and gave the memos to my contact person in the company, hoping that he would distribute them to other managers who might benefit from the ideas. I also gave the memos to those managers with whom I had direct contact. After some months I discovered that whoever got my memo thought it was helpful and on target, but rarely, if ever, did the memo get past the person to whom I gave it. I suggested meetings of managers from different units to stimulate lateral communication, but found no support at all for such meetings. No matter what I did, I could not seem to get information flowing, especially laterally across divisional, functional, or geographical boundaries. Yet everyone agreed in principle that innovation would be stimulated by more lateral communication and encouraged me to keep on helping.

I did not really understand what happened in either of these cases until I began to examine my own assumptions about how things should work in these organizations and began to test whether my assumptions fitted those operating in my client systems. This step of examining the shared assumptions in the client system takes one into "cultural" analysis and will be the focus from here on. Such analysis is, of course, common when we think of ethnic or national cultures, but insufficient attention has been paid to the possibility that groups and organizations within a society also develop cultures that affect in a major way how the members think, feel, and act. Unless we learn to analyze such organizational cultures accurately, we cannot really understand why organizations do some of the things they do and why leaders have some of the difficulties that they have. The concept of organizational culture is especially relevant to gaining an understanding of the mysterious and seemingly irrational things that go on in human systems. And culture *must* be understood if one is to get along at all, as tourists in foreign lands and new employees in organizations often discover to their dismay.

But a concept is not helpful if we misuse it or fail to understand it. My primary purpose . . . therefore, is to explain the concept of organizational culture, show how it can best be applied, and relate it to leadership. . . .

Underlying these several purposes is a chronic fear I have that both students of culture and those consultants and managers who deal with culture in a more pragmatic way continue to misunderstand its real nature and significance. In both the popular and the academic literature, I continue to see simplistic, cavalier statements about culture, which not only confuse matters but positively mislead the reader and promise things that probably cannot be delivered. For example, all the recent writings about improving organizational effectiveness through creating "strong" and "appropriate" cultures continue to proliferate the possibly quite *incorrect* assumption that culture can be changed to suit our purposes. Suppose we find that culture can only "evolve" and that groups with "inappropriate" or "weak" cultures simply will not survive. The desire to change culture may become tantamount to destroying the group and creating a new one, which will build or evolve a new culture. Leaders do at times have to do this, but under what conditions is it possible or practical? Are we aware that we may be suggesting something very drastic when we say "Let's Change the culture"?

So throughout . . . I will be hammering away at the idea that culture is a *deep* phenomenon, that culture is *complex* and difficult to understand, but that the effort to understand it is worthwhile because much of the mysterious and the irrational in organizations suddenly becomes clear when we do understand it.

A FORMAL DEFINITION OF ORGANIZATIONAL CULTURE

The word "culture" has many meanings and connotations. When we combine it with another commonly used word, "organization," we are almost certain to have conceptual and semantic confusion. In talking about organizational culture with colleagues and members of organizations, I often find that we agree "it" exists and is important in its effects but that we have completely different ideas of what the "it" is. I have also had colleagues tell me pointedly that they do *not* use the concept of culture in their work, but when I ask them what it is they do *not* use, they cannot define "it" clearly. Therefore, before launching into

the reasons for studying "it," I must give a clear definition of what I will mean by "it."

. . . I will argue that the term "culture" should be reserved for the deeper level of *basic assumptions* and *beliefs* that are shared by members of an organization, that operate unconsciously, and that define in a basic "taken-for-granted" fashion an organization's view of itself and its environment. These assumptions and beliefs are *learned* responses to a group's problems of *survival* in its external environment and its problems of *internal integration*. They come to be taken for granted because they solve those problems repeatedly and reliably. This deeper level of assumptions is to be distinguished from the "artifacts" and "values" that are manifestations or surface levels of the culture but not the essence of the culture (Schein, 1981a, 1983, 1984; Dyer, 1982).

But this definition immediately brings us to a problem. What do we mean by the word "group" or "organization," which, by implication, is the locale of a given culture (Louis, 1983)? Organizations are not easy to define in time and space. They are themselves open systems in constant interaction with their many environments, and they consist of many subgroups, occupational units, hierarchical layers, and geographically dispersed segments. If we are to locate a given organization's culture, where do we look, and how general a concept are we looking for?

Culture should be viewed as a property of an independently defined stable social unit. That is, if one can demonstrate that a given set of people have shared a significant number of important experiences in the process of solving external and internal problems, one can assume that such common experiences have led them, over time, to a shared view of the world around them and their place in it.

There has to have been enough shared experience to have led to a shared view, and this shared view has to have worked for long enough to have come to be taken for granted and to have dropped out of awareness. Culture, in this sense, is a *learned product of group experience* and is, therefore, to be found only where there is a definable group with a significant history.

Whether or not a given company has a single culture in addition to various subcultures then becomes an empirical question to be answered by locating stable groups within that company and determining what their shared experience has been, as well as determining the shared experiences of the members of the total organization. One may well find that there are several cultures operating within the larger social unit called the company or the organization: a managerial culture, various occupationally based cultures in functional units, group cultures based on geographical proximity, worker cultures based on shared hierarchical experiences, and so on. The organization as a whole may be found to have an overall culture if that whole organization has a significant shared history, but we cannot assume the existence of such a culture ahead of time.

This concept of culture is rooted more in theories of group dynamics and group growth than in anthropological theories of how large cultures evolve. When we study organizations, we do not have to decipher a completely strange language or set of customs and mores. Rather, our problem is to distinguish—within a broader host culture—the unique features of a particular social unit in which we are interested. This social unit often will have a history that can be deciphered, and the key actors in the formation of that culture can often be studied, so that we are not limited, as the anthropologist is often limited, by the lack of historical data.

Because we are looking at evolving social units within a larger host culture, we also can take advantage of learning theories and develop a dynamic concept of organizational culture. Culture is learned, evolves with new experiences, and can be changed if one understands the dynamics of the learning process. If one is concerned about managing or changing culture, one must look to what we know about the learning and unlearning of complex beliefs and assumptions that underlie social behavior.

The word "culture" can be applied to any size of social unit that has had the opportunity to learn and stabilize its view of itself and the environment around it—its basic assumptions. At the broadest level, we have *civilizations* and refer to Western or Eastern cultures; at the next level down, we have *countries* with sufficient ethnic commonality that we speak of American culture or Mexican culture. But we recognize immediately that within a country we also have various *ethnic groups* to which we attribute different cultures. Even more specific is the level of *occupation, profession,* or *occupational community*. If such groups can be defined as stable units with a shared history of experience, they will have developed their own cultures. Finally, we get to the level of analysis that is the focus of this book—*organizations*. Within organizations we will find subunits that can be referred to as groups, and such groups may develop group cultures.

To summarize, at any of these structural levels, I will mean by "culture": *a pattern of basic assumptions—invented, discovered, or developed by a given group as it learns to cope with its problems of external adaptation and internal integration—that has worked well enough to be considered valid and, therefore, to be taught*

to new members as the correct way to perceive, think, and feel in relation to those
problems.

Because such assumptions have
worked repeatedly, they are likely to be
taken for granted and to have dropped
out of awareness. Note that the definition does not include overt behavior patterns. I believe that overt behavior is
always determined both by the cultural
predisposition (the assumptions, perceptions, thoughts, and feelings that are patterned) and by the situational contingencies that arise from the external
environment. Behavioral regularities
could thus be as much a reflection of
the environment as of the culture and
should, therefore, not be a prime basis for
defining the culture. Or, to put it another
way, when we observe behavior regularities, we do not know whether we are
dealing with a cultural artifact or not.
Only after we have discovered the
deeper layers that I am defining as the
culture can we specify what is and what
is not an artifact that reflects the culture.

LEVELS OF CULTURE

Throughout the previous discussion, I
have referred to various cultural "elements," such as the physical layout of an
organization's offices, rules of interaction
that are taught to newcomers, basic values that come to be seen as the organization's ideology or philosophy, and the
underlying conceptual categories and assumptions that enable people to communicate and to interpret everyday occur-
rences. As Figure 1 shows, I distinguish
among these elements by treating basic
assumptions as the essence—what culture really is—and by treating values and
behaviors as observed manifestations of
the cultural essence. In a sense these are
"levels" of the culture, and they need to
be carefully distinguished to avoid conceptual confusion.

Level 1: Artifacts. The most visible
level of the culture is its artifacts and
creations—its constructed physical and
social environment. At this level one
can look at physical space, the technological output of the group, its written
and spoken language, artistic productions, and the overt behavior of its members. Since the insiders of the culture
are not necessarily aware of their own
artifacts, one cannot always ask about
them, but one can always observe them
for oneself.

Every facet of a group's life produces
artifacts, creating the problem of classification. In reading cultural descriptions,
one often notes that different observers
choose to report on different sorts of artifacts, leading to noncomparable descriptions. Anthropologists have developed
classification systems, but these tend to
be so vast and detailed that cultural essence becomes difficult to discern.

Moreover, whereas it is easy to observe artifacts—even subtle ones, such
as the way in which status is demonstrated by members—the difficult part is
figuring out what the artifacts mean, how
they interrelate, what deeper patterns, if
any, they reflect. What has been called
the "semiotic" approach to cultural analysis (Spradley, 1979; Frake, 1964; Barley,
1983; Manning, 1979; Van Maanen,
1977) deals with this problem by collect-
ing enough data on how people communicate to enable one to understand, from
the point of view of the insider, what
meanings are to be attached to the visible behavior. If the anthropologist lives
in the cultural environment long
enough, the meanings gradually become clear.

If one wants to achieve this level of
understanding more quickly, one can attempt to analyze the central values that
provide the day-to-day operating principles by which the members of the culture
guide their behavior.

FIGURE 1 • LEVELS OF CULTURE AND THEIR INTERACTION

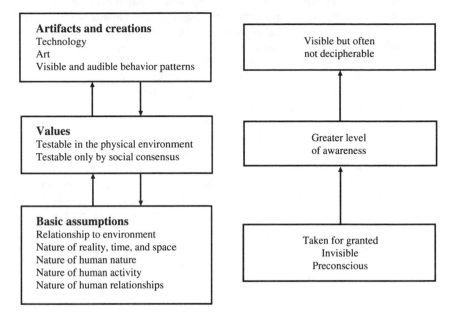

Source: Adapted from Schein, 1980. p. 4.

Level 2: Values. In a sense all cultural learning ultimately reflects someone's original values, their sense of what "ought" to be, as distinct from what is. When a group faces a new task, issue, or problem, the first solution proposed to deal with it can only have the status of a value because there is not as yet a shared basis for determining what is factual and real. Someone in the group, usually the founder, has convictions about the nature of reality and how to deal with it, and will propose a solution based on those convictions. That individual may regard the proposed solution as a belief or principle based on facts, but the group cannot feel that same degree of conviction until it has collectively shared in successful problem solution. For example, in a young business if sales begin to decline, the leader may say "We must increase advertising" because of his* *belief* that "advertising always increases sales." The group, never having experienced this situation before, will hear that assertion as a statement of the leader's *values:* "He thinks that one should always advertise more when one is in trouble." What the leader initially proposes, therefore, cannot have any status other than a value to be questioned, debated, and challenged.

If the solution works, and the group has a shared perception of that success, the value gradually starts a process of *cognitive transformation* into a belief and, ultimately, an assumption. If this transformation process occurs—and it will

* The author uses *his* and *he* for reasons of convenience and acknowledges the inequity of the traditional use of masculine pronouns.

occur only if the proposed solution continues to work, thus implying that it is in some larger sense "correct" and must reflect an accurate picture of reality—group members will tend to forget that the values were therefore debated and confronted. As the values begin to be taken for granted, they gradually become beliefs and assumptions and drop out of consciousness, just as habits become unconscious and automatic. Thus, if increased advertising consistently results in increased sales, the group begins to believe that the leader is "right" and has an understanding of how the world really works.

Not all values undergo such transformation. First of all, the solution based on a given value may not work reliably. Only those values that are susceptible of physical or social validation, and that continue to work reliably in solving the group's problems, will become transformed into assumptions. Second, certain value domains, those dealing with the less controllable elements of the environment or with aesthetic matters, may not be testable at all. In such cases consensus through social validation is still possible, but it is not automatic. By social validation I mean that values about how people should relate to each other, exercise power, define what is beautiful, and so on, can be validated by the experience that they reduce uncertainty and anxiety. A group can learn that the holding of certain beliefs and assumptions is necessary as a basis for maintaining the group.

Many values remain conscious and are explicitly articulated because they serve the normative or moral function of guiding members of the group in how to deal with certain key situations. For example, if a company states explicitly in its charter and other public documents that it

strongly values people, it may be doing so because it wants everyone to operate by that value, even without any historical experience that such a value actually improves its performance in its environment. A set of values that become embodied in an ideology or organizational philosophy thus can serve as a guide and as a way of dealing with the uncertainty of intrinsically uncontrollable or difficult events. Such values will predict much of the behavior that can be observed at the artifactual level. But if those values are not based on prior cultural learning, they may also come to be seen only as what Argyris and Schön (1978) have called "espoused values," which predict well enough what people will *say* in a variety of situations but which may be out of line with what they will actually *do* in situations where those values should be operating. Thus, the company may *say* that it values people, but its record in that regard may contradict what it says.

If the espoused values are reasonably congruent with the underlying assumptions, then the articulation of those values into a philosophy of operating can be helpful in bringing the group together, serving as a source of identity and core mission (Ouchi, 1981; Pascale and Athos, 1981; Peters and Waterman, 1982). But in analyzing values one must discriminate carefully between those that are congruent with underlying assumptions and those that are, in effect, either rationalizations or aspirations for the future.

If we can spell out the major espoused values of an organization, have we then described and understood its culture? And how do we know whether we have *really* understood it? The answer often lies in our own feelings as observers and analysts. Even after we have listed and articulated the major values of an organization, we still may feel that we are dealing only with a list that does not quite hang together. Often such lists of values are not patterned, sometimes they are even mutually contradictory, sometimes they are incongruent with observed behavior. Large areas of behavior are often left unexplained, leaving us with a feeling that we understood a piece of the culture but still do not have the culture as such in hand. To get at that deeper level of understanding, to decipher the pattern, to predict future behavior correctly, we have to understand more fully the category of "basic assumptions."

Level 3: Basic Underlying Assumptions. When a solution to a problem works repeatedly, it comes to be taken for granted. What was once a hypothesis, supported by only a hunch or a value, comes gradually to be treated as a reality. We come to believe that nature really works this way. Basic assumptions, in this sense, are different from what some anthropologists call "dominant value orientations" (Kluckhohn and Strodtbeck, 1961) in that such dominant orientations reflect the *preferred* solutions among several basic alternatives, but all the alternatives are still visible in the culture, and any given member of the culture could, from time to time, behave according to variant as well as dominant orientations. Basic assumptions, in the sense in which I want to define that concept, have become so taken for granted that one finds little variation within a cultural unit. In fact, if a basic assumption is strongly held in a group, members would find behavior based on any other premise inconceivable. For example, in a group whose basic assumption is that the individual's rights supercede those of the group, members would find it inconceivable that they should commit suicide or in some other way sacrifice themselves to the group even if they had dishonored the group. In a company in a capitalist country, it is inconceivable that one might sell products at a financial loss or that it does not matter whether a product works.

What I am calling basic assumptions are congruent with what Argyris has identified as "theories-in-use," the implicit assumptions that actually guide behavior, that tell group members how to perceive, think about, and feel about things (Argyris, 1976; Argyris and Schön, 1974). Basic assumptions, like theories-in-use, tend to be nonconfrontable and nondebatable. To relearn in the area of "theories-in-use," to resurrect, reexamine, and possibly change basic assumptions—a process that Argyris and others have called "double-loop learning"—is intrinsically difficult because assumptions are, by definition, not confrontable or debatable.

Clearly, such unconscious assumptions can distort data. If we assume, on the basis of past experience or education, that other people will take advantage of us whenever they have an opportunity (essentially what McGregor, 1960, meant by his "Theory X"), we expect to be taken advantage of and then interpret the behavior of others in a way that coincides with those expectations. We observe people sitting idly at their desk and perceive them as loafing rather than thinking out an important problem; we perceive absence from work as shirking rather than doing work at home. In contrast, if we assume . . . that everyone is highly motivated and competent (McGregor's "Theory Y"), we will act in accordance with that assumption. Thus, if someone . . . is absent or seems to be idle, the managers ask themselves what has happened to their job assignment process, not what is wrong with the individual. The person is still seen as motivated, but the environment is perceived as somehow turning him or her off. Managerial energy then goes into redesigning the work or the environment to enable the person to become productive once again.

Unconscious assumptions sometimes lead to "Catch 22" situations, as illustrated by a common problem experienced by American supervisors in some other cultures. A manager who comes from an American pragmatic tradition assumes and takes it for granted that solving a problem always has the highest priority. When that manager encounters a subordinate who comes from a different cultural tradition, in which good relationships and protecting the superior's "face" are assumed to have top priority, the following scenario can easily result.

The manager proposes a solution to a given problem. The subordinate knows that the solution will not work, but his unconscious assumption requires that he remain silent because to tell the boss that the proposed solution is wrong is a threat to the boss's face. It would not even occur to the subordinate to do anything other than remain silent or even reassure the boss that they should go ahead and take the action.

The action is taken, the results are negative, and the boss, somewhat surprised and puzzled, asks the subordinate what he would have done. When the subordinate reports that he would have done something different, the boss quite legitimately asks why the subordinate did not speak up sooner. This question puts the subordinate into an impossible bind because the answer itself is a threat to the boss's face. He cannot possibly explain his behavior without committing the very sin he is trying to avoid in the first place—namely, embarrassing the boss. He might even lie at this point and argue that what the boss did was right and only bad luck or uncontrollable circumstances prevented it from succeeding.

From the point of view of the subordinate, the boss's behavior is incomprehensible because it shows lack of self-pride, possibly causing the subordinate to lose respect for that boss. To the boss the subordinate's behavior is equally incomprehensible. He cannot develop any sensible explanation of his subordinate's behavior that is not cynically colored by the assumption that the subordinate at some level just does not care about effective performance and therefore must be gotten rid of. It never occurs to the boss that another assumption—such as "One never embarrasses a superior"—is operating and that, to the subordinate, that assumption is even more powerful than "One gets the job done."

In this instance probably only a third party or some cross-cultural education could help to find common ground whereby both parties could bring their implicit assumptions to the surface. And even after they have surfaced, such assumptions would still operate, forcing the boss and the subordinate to invent a new communication mechanism that would permit each to remain congruent with his culture—for example, agreeing that, before any decision is made and before the boss has stuck his neck out, the subordinate will be asked for suggestions and for factual data that would not be face threatening.

I have dwelled on this long example to illustrate the potency of implicit, unconscious assumptions and to show that such assumptions often deal with fundamental aspects of the culture. But such assumptions are hard to locate. If we examine carefully an organization's artifacts and values, we can try to infer the underlying assumptions that tie things together. Such assumptions can usually be brought to the surface in interviews if both the interviewer and the interviewee are committed to trying to piece together the cultural pattern. But this requires detective work and commitment, not because people are reluctant to surface their assumptions but because they are so taken for granted. Yet when we do surface them, the cultural pattern suddenly clarifies and we begin to feel we really understand what is going on and why.

ETHNOGRAPHIC VERSUS CLINICAL PERSPECTIVE

In reviewing my own "data base," the sources of my own knowledge about organizational culture, I have found it necessary to distinguish the perspective of the *ethnographer* from that of the *clinician*. The ethnographer obtains concrete data in order to understand the culture he is interested in, presumably for intellectual and scientific reasons. Though the ethnographer must be faithful to the observed and experienced data, he brings to the situation a set of concepts or models that motivated the research in the first place. The group members studied are often willing to participate but usually have no particular stake in the intellectual issues that may have motivated the study.

In contrast, a "clinical perspective" is one where the group members are clients who have their own interests as the prime motivator for the involvement of the "outsider," often labeled "consultant" or "therapist" in this context. In the typical ethnographic situation, the researcher must obtain the cooperation of the subjects; in the clinical situation, the client must get the cooperation of the helper/consultant. The psychological contract between client and helper is completely different from that between researcher and subject, leading to a different kind of relationship between them, the revelation of different kinds of data, and the use of different criteria

for when enough has been "understood" to terminate the inquiry.

Clients call in helpers when they are frustrated, anxious, unhappy, threatened, or thwarted; when their rational, logical approaches to things do not work. Inevitably, then, the clinical view brings one to the topic of the "irrational" in organizations. I have found . . . that one of the simplest ways of understanding the seemingly irrational is to relate such phenomena to culture, because culture often explains things that otherwise seem mysterious, silly, or "irrational."

Consultants also bring with them their models and concepts for obtaining and analyzing information, but the function of those models is to provide insight into how the client can be *helped*. In order to provide help, the consultant must "understand" at some level. Some theories, in fact, argue that only by attempting to change a system (that is, giving help) does one demonstrate any real level of understanding (Lewin, 1952; Schein, 1980). For me this criterion has always been the relevant one for "validating" my understanding, even though that understanding often is incomplete, since the clinical relationship does not automatically license the helper to inquire into areas the client may not wish to pursue or considers irrelevant. On the other hand, the level of understanding is likely to be deeper and more dynamic.

The point of spelling all of this out now is to let the reader know that my data base is a clinical one, not an ethnographic one. I have not been a participant-observer in organizations other than the ones I had membership in, but in being a consultant I have spent long periods of time in client organizations. I believe that this clinical perspective provides a useful counterpoint to the pure ethnographic perspective; because the clinician learns things that are different from what an ethnographer learns. Clients are motivated to reveal certain things when they are paying for help that may not come out if they are only "willing" to be studied.

So this kind of inquiry leads, I believe, to a "deeper" analysis of culture as a phenomenon—deeper in the sense of its impact on individual members of the organization. This perspective also leads inevitably to a more dynamic view of how things work, how culture begins, evolves, changes, and sometimes disintegrates. And, as we will see, this perspective throws into high relief what leaders and other change agents can or cannot do to change culture deliberately.

REFERENCES

Argyris, C. (1976). *Increasing leadership effectiveness*. New York: Wiley-Interscience.

Argyris, C., & Schön, D. A. (1974). *Theory in practice: Increasing professional effectiveness*. San Francisco: Jossey-Bass.

Argyris, C., & Schön D. A. (1978). *Organizational learning*. Reading, MA: Addison-Wesley Publishing.

Barley, S. R. (1983). Semiotics and the study of occupational and organizational cultures. *Administrative Science Quarterly, 28*, 393–413.

Deal, T. E., & Kennedy, A. A. (1982). *Corporate cultures*. Reading, MA: Addison-Wesley Publishing.

Dyer, W. G., Jr. (1982). Culture in organizations. A case study and analysis. Unpublished paper, Sloan School of Management, MIT.

Frake, C. O. (1964). Notes on queries in ethnography. *American Anthropologist, 66*, 132–145.

Goffman, E. (1959). *The presentation of self in everyday life*. New York: Doubleday.

Goffman, E. (1967). *Interaction ritual*. Hawthorne, NY: Aldine.

Homans, G. (1950). *The human group*. New York: Harcourt Brace Jovanovich.

Kluckhohn, F. R., & Strodtbeck, F. L. (1961). *Variations in value orientations*. New York: Harper & Row.

Lewin, K. (1952). Group decision and social change. In G. E. Swanson, T. N. Newcomb, & E. L. Hartley (Eds.), *Readings in Social Psychology* (rev. ed.). New York: Holt, Rinehart & Winston.

Louis, M. R. (1983). Organizations as culture bearing milieux. In L. R. Pondy & others (Eds.), *Organizational symbolism*. Greenwich, CT: JAI Press.

McGregor, D. M. (1960). *The human side of enterprise*. New York: McGraw-Hill.

Manning, P. (1979). Metaphors of the field: Varieties of organizational discourse. *Administrative Science Quarterly, 24*, 660–671.

Ouchi, W. G. (1981). *Theory Z*. Reading, MA: Addison-Wesley.

Pascale, R. T., & Athos, A. G. (1981). *The art of Japanese management*. New York: Simon & Schuster.

Peters, T. J., & Waterman, R. H., Jr. (1982). *In search of excellence*. New York: Harper & Row.

Ritti, R. R., & Funkhouser, G. R. (1982). *The ropes to skip and the ropes to know*. Columbus, OH: Grid.

Schein, E. H. (1968). Organizational socialization and the profession of management. *Industrial Management Review, 9*, 1–15.

Schein, E. H. (1978). *Career dynamics: Matching individual and organizational needs*. Reading, MA: Addison-Wesley.

Schein, E. H. (1980). *Organizational psychology* (3rd ed.). Englewood Cliffs, NJ: Prentice-Hall. (First published 1965, 2nd ed. 1970.)

Schein, E. H. (1981a). Does Japanese management style have a message for American managers? *Sloan Management Review, 23*, 55–68.

Schein, E. H. (Summer 1983). The role of the founder in creating organizational culture. *Organizational Dynamics*, pp. 13–28.

Schein, E. H. (1984). Coming to a new awareness of organizational culture. *Sloan Management Review, 25*, 3–16.

Spradley, J. P. (1979). *The ethnographic interview*. New York: Holt, Rinehart & Winston.

Tagiuri, R., & Litwin, G. H. (Eds.). (1968). *Organizational climate: Exploration of a concept*. Boston: Division of Research, Harvard Graduate School of Business.

Van Maanen, J. (1976). Breaking in: Socialization to work. In R. Dubin (Ed.), *Handbook of work, organization and society*. Chicago: Rand McNally.

Van Maanen, J. (1977). Experiencing organizations. In J. Van Maanen (Ed.), *Organizational careers: Some new perspectives*. New York: Wiley.

Van Maanen, J. (1979b). The self, the situation, and the rules of interpersonal relations. In W. Bennis & others, *Essays in interpersonal dynamics*. Pacific Grove, CA: Brooks/Cole.

36

Surprise and Sense Making: What Newcomers Experience in Entering Unfamiliar Organizational Settings

Meryl Reis Louis

The purpose of this article is to identify crucial gaps in current approaches to organizational entry and to develop a perspective that fills the gaps. The new perspective proposes that an appreciation of what newcomers typically experience during the transition period and how they cope with their experiences is fundamental to designing entry practices that facilitate newcomers' adaptation in the new setting. . . .

A MODEL OF THE NEWCOMER EXPERIENCE

In order to understand the processes by which newcomers cope with entry and socialization experiences, we must first understand that experience. In the following pages we identify some key features of the newcomer experience and outline a model for understanding the processes of newcomers' coping, or sense making. It is proposed that change, contrast, and surprise constitute major features of the entry experience. Although all refer to differences associated with entering new settings, they focus on separate types of differences.

Entry Experiences

Change. "Change" is defined here as an objective difference in a major feature between the new and old settings. It is the newness of the "changed to" situation that requires adjustment by the individual. The more elements that are different in the new situation as compared with the previous situation, the more the newcomer potentially has to cope with. This is true even though differences represent improvements over the previous situation. Defined more elaborately, change is publicly noted and knowable; that is, there is recordable evidence of a difference. Evidence includes new location, addresses, telephone numbers, title, salary, job description, organizational affiliation, prerequisites, etc. Such evidence exists in advance of the transition. In fact, changes themselves are knowable in advance.

With the start of a new job, the individual experiences a change in role and often in professional identity, from student to financial analyst, for instance. Such role changes are often accompanied by changes in status. Similarly, there are often major differences in basic working conditions. Discretion in scheduling time, opportunities for feedback, and peer interaction may be very different at work versus in school, in field sales versus marketing research or management.

Source: Meryl Reis Louis, "Surprise and Sense Making: What Newcomers Experience in Entering Unfamiliar Organizational Settings," *Administrative Science Quarterly*, Volume 25-2 (June 1980) pp. 226–251. Reprinted by permission.

Schein (1971a) has stated that an individual entering or organization crosses three boundaries: functional, hierarchical, and inclusionary. Together, the boundaries represent three more dimensions of change for newcomers. The newcomer takes on a set of tasks within a functional area (e.g., marketing, finance) and must learn how they are to be accomplished. The newcomer also acquires a position in the hierarchy, implying supervisory authority over subordinates and reporting responsibility to a superior.

A more informal but no less crucial boundary is the inclusionary one, which refers to one's position in the informal information and influence networks. Influence and information access from the previous situation can seldom be transferred into the new situation. As a result, newcomers usually hold peripheral rather than central positions in the inclusionary network. Over time they may develop access and influence bases, but initially they are usually "on the outside." Based on this view of change, we can generally expect a transition from school to a first full-time, career-related job to be accompanied by more changes and, therefore, more to cope with than a transition from one work organization to another, especially when the new job is similar to the previous one.

Contrast. The second feature of the entry experience is *contrast*, which is personally, rather than publicly, noticed and is not, for the most part, knowable in advance. Contrast, an effect described by gestalt psychologists (Koffka, 1935; Kohler, 1947), involves the emergence within a perceptual field of "figure," or noticed features, against ground, or general background. Particular features emerge when individuals experience new settings. Which features emerge as figure is, in part, determined by features of previously experienced settings. Both differences between settings and charac-

teristics within (new) settings contribute to the selection of features experienced as figure. For example, how people dress in the new setting may or may not be noticed or experienced as a contrast by the newcomer, depending in part on whether dress differs between new and old settings. The presence of a difference in dress is a necessary but not sufficient precondition for the noticing of a contrast. Similarly, the absence of windows may or may not emerge through the contrast effect as a distinguishing feature of the new setting, depending on the individual and the full set of potential contrasts in the situation. Contrast is, therefore, person-specific rather than indigenous to the organizational transition. That is to say, for two people undergoing the same change, (e.g., leaving Stanford and entering Merrill Lynch), different contrasts will emerge.

A special case of contrast is associated with the process of letting go of old roles, which often seems to continue well into the socialization process. The prolonged letting go in organizational entry seems to differ markedly from the situation in tribal rites of passage and total institution inductions, as described earlier. In typical entry situations no newcomer transition ritual erases all trace of the old role before the new role is taken on. Instead, newcomers voluntarily undertake the role change, change only one of the many roles they simultaneously hold, and carry into the new role memories of experiences in old roles. The first time the newcomer is involved in almost any activity in the new role (e.g., a professor uses the computer or library or has a manuscript typed at the new university), the memory of the corresponding activity in one or more old roles may be brought to mind. The process is similar, though on a less emotionally charged scale, to the event-anniversary phenomenon that occurs in adjusting to the death of a loved one. As experiences from prior roles are recalled, contrasts are generated, and a variety of subprocesses may be triggered. For instance, the newcome may evaluate aspects of the new role using old-role experiences as anchors on internal comparison scales. Or the newcomer may try to incorporate aspects of the old into the new role or resist the new role in favor of the old role.

Based on the natural limits of human capabilities for perceptual processing (Miller, 1956), we surmise that there may be some maximum number of contrasts to which individuals can attend simultaneously. In addition, it appears that for individuals in new situations, some minimum number of the contrasts emerge. The contrasts represent subjective differences between new and old settings by which newcomers characterize and otherwise define the new situation.

Surprise. The third feature of the entry experience is surprise, which represents a difference between an individual's anticipations and subsequent experiences in the new setting. Surprise also encompasses one's affective reactions to any differences, including contrasts and changes. Surprise may be positive (e.g., delight at finding that your office window overlooks a garden) and/or negative (e.g., disappointment at finding that your office window can not be opened). The subject of anticipation and, therefore, surprise may be the job, the organization, or self. Anticipations may be conscious, tacit, or emergent; either overmet or undermet anticipations can produce surprise. Figure 1 summarizes several forms of surprise in relation to three dimensions for understanding organizational entry phenomena. It is presented to illustrate some typical sources and forms of surprise and is not intended to be inclusive.

Several forms of surprise often arise during the encounter stage and require adaptation on the part of the newcomer. Only the first three can be traced directly to Figure 1. The first form of surprise occurs when conscious expectations about the job are not fulfilled in the newcomer's early job experiences. Unmet expectations, as typically used, refers to undermet conscious job expectations, shown as the shaded area in Figure 1.

FIGURE 1 · VARIETIES OF SURPRISE

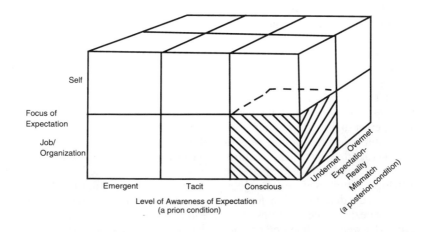

A second form of surprise that may occur during encounter arises when expectations (both conscious and unconscious) about oneself are unmet. Choice of the new organization is often based on assumptions about one's own skills, values, needs, etc. During encounter, errors in assumptions sometimes emerge, and the newcomer must cope with the recognition that he or she is different from his or her previous perceptions of self. For example: "1 chose this job because it offered a great deal of freedom; now I realize I really don't want so much freedom."

A third form of surprise arises when unconscious job expectations are unmet or when features of the job are unanticipated. Job aspects not previously considered important stand out as important because their presence or absence is experienced as undesirable. As one newcomer said, "I had no idea how important windows were to me until I'd spent a week in a staff room without any." This is an example both of inadequacy in anticipations producing surprise and a contrast, indicating a typical overlap between the two features.

A fourth form of surprise arises from difficulties in accurately forecasting internal reactions to a particular new experience. "What will happen" (the external events) may be accurately anticipated, whereas "how it will feel" (the internal experience of external events) may not be accurately assessed by the individual. How new experiences will feel, as opposed to how the individual expected them to feel, is difficult to anticipate and often surprising. The difference is analogous to the distinction that can be drawn between "knowing about" in a cognitive sense and being "acquainted with" in an experiential sense. "I knew I'd have to put in a lot of overtime, but I had no idea how bad I'd feel after a month of 65-hour weeks, how

tired I'd be all the time." In this example, the facts were available to the individual and were accepted; what was inaccurately anticipated and, therefore, surprising was how it would "actually feel," the subjective experience. The individual in this example might interpret his experience as, "I don't have as much energy as I thought," a form of unmet expectation about self.

A fifth form of surprise comes from the cultural assumptions that newcomers make. Surprise results when the newcomer relies on cultural assumptions brought from previous settings as operating guides in the new setting, and they fail. Van Maanen (1977a: 20) describes the situation as follows:

> . . . a newcomer assumes that he knows what the organization is about, assumes others in the setting have the same idea, and practically never bothers to check out these two assumptions. What occurs upon experience is that the neophyte receives a surprise of sorts . . . in which he discovers that significant others . . . do not share his assumptions. The newcomer must then reorient himself relative to others . . . through a cognitive revision of his previously taken-for-granted assumptions.

Since cultures differ between organizations, a cognitive framework for expressing and interpreting meanings in a particular culture must be developed in and for the specific culture in which it will be used.

A final point about surprise is necessary. Both pleasant and unpleasant surprises require adaptation. However, traditional formulations of unmet expectations implicitly treat only undermet expectations or unpleasant surprises. In the future, it will be important to include both overmet and undermet expectations in considering surprises that contribute to newcomers' entry experiences.

The picture of the newcomer experience developed here suggests that the strategy of enhancing the realism only of conscious pre-entry job expectations is not adequate. Similarly, strategies to ensure that conscious pre-entry job expectations are not underfulfilled (unmet) in early job experiences are also not sufficient. Ultimately both views seek to aid newcomers by reducing the extent of their unmet expectations. Both implicitly deny the near inevitability of the myriad unanticipated and even unanticipatable changes, contrasts, and surprises attendant on entering substantially different organizational settings. Unmet conscious job expectations constitute merely one subset of surprise.

It is proposed that appreciation of changes, contrasts, and surprises characteristic of newcomers' entry experiences is essential in designing organizational structures that facilitate newcomer transitions. In essence, they constitute a part of the experiential landscape of individuals during the encounter stage of organizational socialization.

Sense Making

The Role of Conscious Thought in Coping. In order to understand how individuals in organizational settings cope with entry experiences, particularly surprises, we must first ask how people anywhere cope with normal, everyday situations that are not surprising. In familiar, nonsurprising situations, individuals seem to operate in a kind of loosely preprogrammed, nonconscious way, guided by cognitive scripts. A cognitive script, as defined by Abelson (1976: 33) is ". . . a coherent sequence of events expected by the individual. . . ." Several constructs are similar in idea to the cognitive script, among them schema (Bartlett, 1932: Weick, 1979), habitualization (Berger and Luckman, 1966), and "trustworthy recipes for thinking-as-usual" (Schutz, 1964: 95). What each of the constructs suggests is that con-

scious thought is not a very large part of our everyday mode of operating. We may drive to work, greet our colleagues, and sit in meetings with about the same deliberateness with which we brush our teeth. In fact, Taylor and Fiske (1978) suggest that most of our everyday decisions are made "off the top of our heads." In acting that is guided by cognitive scripts, conscious thought is minimal.

If that is the case, then it is necessary to know under what conditions coping is guided by thought or cognition rather than by preprogrammed scripts. One possibility is that conscious thought is provoked when the individual senses something "out of the ordinary." A number of writers have suggested that possibility, including James (1890), Dewey (1933), Mills (1940), Lewin (1951), Schutz (1964), and Langer (1978). Schutz (1964: 105), for example, states:

> If we encounter in our experience something previously unknown and which therefore stands out of the ordinary order of our knowledge, we begin a process of inquiry.

Mills (1940: 905) expressed his view as follows:

> . . . men live in immediate acts of experience and their attentions are directed outside themselves until acts are in some way frustrated. It is then that awareness of self and of motive occur.

More recently, Langer (1978: 58) developed a set of conditions under which thinking occurs. She proposed that conscious thinking is necessary when the outcomes of our acts are inconsistent with anticipated outcomes or when scripted behavior is effortful or interrupted. Abelson (1976) and Langer (1978) also treat behavior in novel situations as unscripted and, therefore, guided by thinking. However, it is clear that people do not always recognize when situations are novel and act, or rather think, accordingly (Schutz, 1964; Van Maanen, 1977a).

Scripts provide the individual with predictions of event sequences and outcomes. Implicitly, reasons for outcomes, that is, prospective explanations, are supplied. As long as the predicted outcomes occur, thinking is not necessary. However, when predicted outcomes do not occur, the individual's cognitive consistency is threatened (Festinger, 1957; Abelson et al., 1968). The discrepancy between predicted and actual outcomes, that is, between anticipations and experience, produces a state of tension which acts as a quasi-need, in Lewin's (1951) terms, unbalancing the equilibrium of the individual's psychological field. The quasi-need is for a return to equilibrium. Hence, when scripts fail, the individual must develop explanations for why the actual outcomes occurred and why the predicted outcomes did not. The retrospective explanations help to resolve tension states by restoring equilibrium, although in a new configuration. Retrospective explanations are produced through a particular thinking process that we call sense making. The explanatory products of sense making have been studied under such labels as accounts (Scott and Lyman, 1968) and attributions (Ross, 1977). Accounts are ". . . statements made to explain untoward behavior and bridge the gap between actions and expectations" (Scott and Lyman, 1968: 46). They provide reasons for outcomes, and for discrepancies.

In attribution research, individuals have been viewed as naive scientists, who make sense of events on the basis of available information (Ross, 1977). Researchers have identified rules and biases that guide naive scientists in attributing causes to events and properties to causes (Jones and Davis, 1965; Kelley, 1967; Jones et al., 1972). They have also characterized types of attributions and examined attribution patterns produced in response to different outcomes (Weiner, 1974). Attributions about anticipated outcomes that actually occurred are examined; attributions about anticipated outcomes that did not occur are overlooked. Similarly, inadequate attention has been given to the question of when attributions are made (Kelley, 1976). Instead, this research seems to have assumed that people are always making attributions (and, hence, are engaged in thinking) and that attributions prospectively guide, as well as retrospectively explain, events (Taylor and Fiske, 1978). Attribution research has not adequately considered either the cognitive processes through which attributions are created or the social and institutional conditions in which attributions are employed (Kelley, 1976).

On the other hand, Weick (1977, 1979) has examined cognitive processes in organizational settings. He suggested that an analysis of cognition in organizations ought to address the question of what provokes cognition in organizations (1979: 71). What we suggest here is that one kind of event that provokes cognition is surprise and that surprise seems to be an inevitable part of the experience of entering (in the sense of joining) an unfamiliar organizational setting.

How Individuals Cope with Surprise. Recently a model describing the processes by which individuals detect and interpret surprises was developed (Louis, 1978). It suggests that sense making can be viewed as a recurring cycle comprised of a sequence of events occurring over time. The cycle begins as individuals form unconscious and conscious anticipations and assumptions, which serve as predictions about future events. Subsequently, individuals experience events that may be discrepant from predictions. Discrepant events, or surprises, trigger a need for explanation, or post-diction, and, correspondingly, for a process through which interpretations of discrepancies are developed. Interpretation, or meaning, is attributed to surprises. Based on the attributed meanings, any necessary behavioral responses to the immediate situation are selected. Also based on attributed meanings, understandings of actors, actions, and settings are updated and predictions about future experiences in the setting are revised. The updated anticipations and revised assumptions are analogous to alterations in cognitive scripts.

The cycle as described focuses on the more rational elements in sense making. It is meant to represent general stages in understanding one's experience, rather than the literal process by which all individuals respond to each experience. It is crucial to note that meaning is assigned to surprise as an output of the sense-making process, rather than arising concurrently with the perception or detection of differences.

In making sense, or attributing meaning to surprise, individuals rely on a number of inputs. Their past experiences with similar situations and surprises help them in coping with current situations. Individuals are also guided by their more general personal characteristics, including predispositions to attribute causality to self, others, fate, etc. (e.g., the locus of control [Rotter, 1966] and anomie [McClosky and Schaar, 1963]), as well as their orienting purposes in the situation and in general. Another input that shapes how sense is made of surprise is the individual's set of cultural assumptions or interpretive schemes, that is, internalizations of context-specific dictionaries of meaning, which ". . . structure routine interpretations and conduct within an institutional area" (Berger and Luckmann, 1966: 138). In addition, information and interpretations from oth-

ers in the situation contribute to the sense-making process. Figure 2 summarizes the model and presents it in relation to the features of entry experiences described earlier in the section.

What Newcomers Need. In order to assess the special needs of newcomers during sense making, we compare their situation in general with that of insiders. The experiences of newcomers differ in three important ways from those of insiders. First, insiders normally know what to expect in and of the situation. For the most part, little is surprising or needs to be made sense of. Second, when surprises do arise (e.g., not getting an expected raise), the insider usually has sufficient history in the setting to interpret them more accurately or to make sense based on relevant knowledge of the immediate situation. An insider probably knows, for instance, whether the denied raise is due to company-wide budget cuts or is related to the job performance and whether it is an indication of how the future may unfold or a temporary situation. Third, when surprises arise and sense making is necessary, the insider usually has other insiders with whom to compare perceptions and interpretations.

The comparison of newcomers' and insiders' experiences suggests that two types of input to sense making shown in Figure 2 may be problematic for newcomers: local interpretation schemes and others' interpretations. Concerning local interpretation schemes, newcomers probably do not have adequate history in the setting to appreciate as fully as insiders might why and how surprises have arisen. With time and experience in the new setting, they may come to understand how to interpret the actions of superiors and others and what meanings to attach to events and outcomes in the work setting. According to Berger and Luckmann (1966), during the early

FIGURE 2 • SENSE MAKING IN ORGANIZATIONAL ENTRY

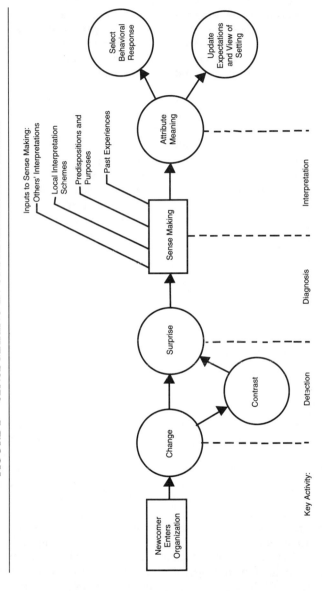

stages in a new setting, newcomers internalize context-specific dictionaries of meaning used by members of the setting. At the outset, however, newcomers typically are unfamiliar with these interpretation schemes of the new setting. And, as we saw earlier, they are usually unaware of *both* their need to understand context-specific meaning dictionaries, or interpretation schemes, and the fact that they are unfamiliar with them (Van Maanen, 1977a).

As a result, newcomers often attach meanings to action, events, and surprises in the new setting using interpretation schemes developed through their experiences in other settings. Based on these, inappropriate and dysfunctional interpretations may be produced. For example, what it means to "take initiative" or "put in a hard day's work" in a school situation may be quite different from its meaning in a work setting. In essence, this constitutes a variation on the kind of surprise that arises when tacit job-related expectations are unmet. Newcomers may also attribute permanence or stability to temporary situations, or vice versa (Weiner, 1974). Or, newcomers may see themselves as the source or cause of events when external factors are responsible for outcomes (Weiner, 1974). Similarly, one's understanding of why a superior responds in a particularly harsh manner may be inadequate. Overpersonalized attributions may result in the absence of knowledge about how that superior typically behaves toward other subordinates or without relevant background information, for instance, about the superior's recent divorce, lack of promotion, or reduction in scope of authority and responsibility.

The dysfunctional effects of such interpretational errors can be seen by tracing how the responses chosen are influenced by the meanings attributed in situations. In a series of studies by

Weiner (1974), subjects attributing events to stable causes changed behavior more often than did subjects attributing events to unstable or temporary causes (e.g., the boss is always like this, or the boss is going through a rough, but temporary, period). In laboratory experiments, shifts in subjects' affect were more likely to result from personal, or internal, attributions than from external attributions (e.g., the boss doesn't like me, or the boss treats everyone harshly). Although further work is needed to assess the extent to which Weiner's findings hold in organizational settings, it seems obvious that individuals select responses to events at least in part on the basis of the meaning they attach to them. Decisions to stay in or leave organizations and feelings of commitment or alienation would appear to follow from sense made by newcomers of early job experiences.

The second type of input to make sense making problematic for newcomers is information and interpretations from others in the situation. In comparison to the situation of insiders, newcomers probably have not developed relationships with others in the setting with whom they could test their perceptions and interpretations. Since reality testing is seen as an important input to sense making, it seems particularly important for newcomers to have insiders who might serve as sounding boards and guide them to important background information for assigning meaning to events and surprises. Insiders are seen as a potentially rich source of assistance to newcomers in diagnosing and interpreting the myriad surprises that may arise during their transitions into new settings. Insiders are already "on board"; presumably, they are equipped with richer historical and current interpretive perspectives than the newcomer alone possesses. Information may also come through insider-newcomer relationships, averting and/or precipitating surprises. These relationships might also facilitate the newcomer's acquisition of the context-specific meaning dictionary or interpretation scheme.

The framework presented here suggests that sense made of surprises by newcomers may be inadequate in the absence of relevant information about organizational, interpersonal, and personal histories. Inputs to sense making from sources in the organization balance the inputs provided by the newcomer (i.e., past experiences, personal predispositions, and interpretive schemes from old settings), which are likely to be inadequate in the new setting. Until newcomers develop accurate internal maps of the new setting, until they appreciate local meanings, it is important that they have information available for amending internal cognitive maps and for attaching meaning to such surprises as may arise during early job experiences.

Research Implications

Theoretical and empirical implications of the perspective developed here for each of the two literatures concerned with organizational entry are briefly outlined below. First, the perspective provides a theoretical framework for understanding which aspects or dimensions of socialization are critical and why. It suggests that socialization practices that facilitate sense making and, in the process, encourage appreciation of the local culture and acquisition of a setting-specific interpretation scheme ultimately facilitate adaptation to the new setting and progress through the stages of socialization. Practices that facilitate sense making provide the newcomer with relevant and reliable information. Specific information is made available in response to newcomers' needs, rather than in advance, according to what is considered to be organizationally efficient. The in-

formation comes from someone who knows and is willing and able to share with the newcomer a particular part of "how things operate around here." Other newcomers do not have this information, and written orientation material usually does not give it. The perspective leads us to expect that "in-response" socialization practices facilitate sense making and adaptation far more effectively than "in-advance" practices. And similarly, practices in which insiders, rather than other newcomers, are the newcomers' primary/associates and informal socializing agents should facilitate adaptation. . . .

The surprise and sense-making perspective bears on recruit turnover research in a number of ways. We saw that the turnover approach to organizational entry focused on newcomers' conscious pre-entry expectations about the job. Yet the perspective proposed here suggests that surprise may arise from tacit and even emergent anticipations and assumptions, as well as from conscious expectations. It also suggests that expectations are not formed once and for all before entering the new setting, but evolve and are periodically revised as a result of sense made of surprises. Further, it indicates that assumptions about oneself (e.g., what I can and want to do) may lead to surprises that have at least as much impact as expectations about the job. On the basis of the variety of sources and types of surprise typically experienced in entering organizations, we suggest that the narrow view of unmet expectations adopted in earlier research should be broadened in future research. In addition, the separate effects of initial and disconfirmed expectations and overmet as well as undermet expectations should be assessed. Future research is also needed to explore the underlying psychological processes by which expectations, and surprise in general, affect individuals. Toward that end, the sense-making model presented here provides a theoretical outline of some basic processes by which surprise precipitates sense making and through which individuals select responses to surprise. . . .

Another area in which future research is needed is the transition from the old role itself, the leavetaking aspect of changing roles. How do newcomers in modern organizations let go of old roles as they take on new ones? Two alternative explanations of the letting-go process have been suggested here. In the *tabula rasa* process initiates are stripped of old roles before taking on new roles. In the event-anniversary process, letting go occurs gradually as experiences in the new role trigger recall of complementary experiences in old roles. The relative merit of each as an explanation of letting go during organizational entry is a question for future research.

Finally, further work is needed on surprise and sense making. Specific subprocesses within the sense-making cycle have not been adequately articulated. Perceptual and cognitive processes overlap from the detection to the interpretation of surprise. How do the processes interface? In terms of surprise, what personal and situational factors influence the newcomer's "novelty" threshold? Why do some people seem to thrive on novelty, whereas others seem burdened and surprised by almost any novel experience?

Practical Implications

Previous research has favored strategies for managing newcomers' entry into work organizations that provide individuals with more accurate (realistic) initial expectations, through a Realistic Job Preview. In contrast, strategies developed from the new perspective take as given the near inevitability that new-comers will experience some unmet expectations and, more generally, surprise in entering unfamiliar organizational settings. Strategies based on the present framework would aim to intervene in the newcomer's cycle as sense is made of surprise, rather than merely attempting to prevent one form of surprise, the unmet conscious pre-entry job expectation. . . .

Another potential aid for newcomers is the appraisal process. Timely formal and informal feedback from superiors to newcomers about their performance may reduce the stress-producing uncertainty of "not knowing how you're doing," and replace possibly inaccurate self-appraisals with data from superiors, which guide the newcomer's subsequent assessments of equity in the situation. An early appraisal could provide newcomers with an understanding of the process and criteria of performance evaluation. With such first-hand knowlege, the newcomer can be expected to make more reality-based self-assessments; in addition, he or she is better equipped to interpret other events related to evaluation, a crucial area in the newcomer's early organizational life. An early appraisal could be treated as a collaborative sense-making session, in which the superior helps the newcomer try on a portion of an important insider's interpretive scheme.

Finally, there are implications for newcomers themselves and for those who help prepare them to select and enter organizations. It would be beneficial for newcomers to enter organizations with an understanding of the nature of entry experiences: why it is likely that they may experience surprises during the socialization period; why they, as newcomers, are relatively ill-equipped to make accurate sense of surprises arising during early job experiences; and how they might proactively seek information from insiders at work to supplement their own inadequate internal interpretive schemes. Toward that end, college curricula and placement activities could, as a matter of course, provide students with a preview of typial entry experiences and ways to manage them.

The implications for research and practice are based on the assumption that newcomers are ill-equipped to make sense of the myriad surprises that potentially accompany entry into an unfamiliar organization. It has been proposed that entry practices that enhance newcomers' understandings of their experiences in and of new organizational settings will facilitate newcomers' adaptation. Socialization practices should be developed that help provide newcomers with insiders' situation-specific interpretations and setting-specific interpretive schemes. The insiders' view can supplement and balance natural inadequacies in newcomers' sense-making tendencies and can hasten the development of more adequate long-term self-sufficient functioning. Furthermore, it is likely that supplementing newcomers' sense making will facilitate accuracy in newcomers' interpretations of their immediate experiences, on the basis of which individuals choose affective and behavioral responses to early experiences on the job and in the organization.

REFERENCES

Abelson, Robert. (1976). "Script processing in attitude formation and decision making." In John S. Carroll and John W. Payne (eds.), Cognition and Social Behavior: 33–46. Hillsdale, N.J.: Lawrence Erlbaum.

Abelson, Robert P., Elliot Aronson, William J. McGuire, Theodore M. Newcomb, Milton J. Rosenberg, and Percy H. Tannenbaum (1968). Theories of Cognitive Consistency: A Sourcebook. Chicago: Rand McNally.

Anderson, Rolph E. (1973). "Consumer dissatisfaction: The effect of disconfirmed expec-

tancy on perceived product performance." Journal of Marketing Research, 10: 38–44.

Argyris, Chris (1964). Integrating the Individual and the Organization. New York: John Wiley.

Bartlett, F. C. (1932). Remembering. Cambridge: Cambridge University Press.

Becker, Howard S., and Anselm L. Strauss. (1956). "Careers, personality, and adult socialization." American Journal of Sociology, 62: 253–263.

Berger, Peter, and Thomas Luckmann (1956). The Social Construction of Reality: A Treatise in the Sociology of Knowledge. New York: Anchor Books.

Berlew, David E., and Douglas T. Hall. (1966). "The socialization of managers: Effects of expectations on performance." Administrative Science Quarterly, 11: 207–223.

Bluedorn, Allen C. (1978). "A taxonomy of turnover." Academy of Management Review, 3: 647–650.

Bray, D., R. Campbell, and D. Grant (1974). Formative Years in Business: A Long-Term AT&T Study of Managerial Lives. New York: Wiley.

Brim, Orville G., Jr. (1966). "Socialization through the life cycle." In Orville G. Brim, Jr. and Stanton Wheeler (eds.), Socialization after Childhood: Two Essays, 1–49. New York: Wiley.

——— (1968). "Adult socialization." In John A. Clausen (ed.), Socialization and Society: 182–226. Boston: Little, Brown.

Bruner, Jerome S., ed. (1973). Beyond the Information Given: Studies in the Psychology of Knowing. New York: Norton.

Carlsmith, J. Merrill, and Elliot Aronson (1963). "Some hedonic consequences of the confirmation and disconfirmation of expectancies." Journal of Abnormal and Social Psychology, 66: 151–156.

Cicourel, Aaron V. (1974). Cognitive Sociology: Language and Meaning in Social Interaction. New York: Free Press.

Dandridge, Thomas C. (1979). "Major corporate anniversary celebrations as means of intraorganizational communication." Presentation to the Academy of Management meetings, Atlanta, August.

Dewey, John (1933). How We Think: A Restatement of the Relation of Reflective Thinking to the Educative Process. Lexington, MA: Heath.

Dunnette, Marvin D., Richard D. Arvey, and Paul A. Banas (1973). "Why do they leave?" Personnel, 50: 25–39.

Feldman, Daniel Charles (1976). "A contingency theory of socialization." Administrative Science Quarterly, 21: 433–452.

Festinger, Leon (1957). A Theory of Cognitive Dissonance. Stanford, CA: Stanford University Press.

Gagné, R. M. (1965). The Conditions for Learning. New York: Holt, Rinehart and Winston.

Garnst, Frederick C., and Edward Noerbeck, eds. (1976). Ideas of Culture: Sources and Uses. New York: Holt, Rinehart and Winston.

Geertz, Clifford (1973). The Interpretation of Cultures. New York: Basic Books.

Glaser, Barney G., and Anselm L. Strauss (1971). Status Passage. Chicago: Aldine.

Goodenough, Ward H. (1964). Explorations in Cultural Anthropology. New York: McGraw-Hill.

Hall, Douglas T. (1976). Careers in Organizations. Pacific Palisades, CA: Goodyear.

———— (1979). "Socialization processes in latter years: Adult development in organizations." Presentation to the Academy of Management meetings, Atlanta, August.

Hand, Herbert H., Rodger W. Griffeth, and William H. Mobley (1977). "Military enlistment, reenlistment, an withdrawal research: A critical review of the literature." Columbia, SC: Center for Management and Organizational Research, University of South Carolina, Office of Naval Research, Technical Report No. 3 (ONR: TR3), ADA048955, April.

Hughes, Everett C. (1958). Men and Their Work. Glencoe, IL: Free Press.

Ilgen, Daniel R. (1975). "The psychological impact of realistic job previews." Technical Report No. 2, Department of Psychological Sciences, Purdue University, August.

Ilgen, Daniel R., and Bernard L. Dugoni (1977). "Initial orientation to the organization: The impact on psychological processes associated with the adjustment of new employees." Presentation to the Academy of Management meetins, Kissimmee, FL, August.

Ilgen, Daniel R., Cynthia D. Fisher, and M. Susan Taylor (1979). "Consequences of individual feedback on behavior in organizations." Journal of Applied Psychology, 4: 349–371.

James, William (1890). Principles of Psychology. New York: Holt.

Jones, E. E., and K. E. Davis (1965). "From acts to dispositions: The attribution process in person perceptions." In L. Berkowitz (ed.), Advances in Experimental Social Psychology, 2: 219–266.

Jones, E. E., D. E. Kanouse, H. H. Kelley, R. E. Nisbett, S. Valins, and B. Weiner, eds. (1972). Attribution: Perceiving the Causes of Behavior. Morristown, NJ: General Learning Press.

Katzell, Mildred Engberg (1968). "Expectations and dropouts in schools of nursing." Journal of Applied Psychology, 52: 154–157.

Kelley, Harold H. (1967). "Attribution theory in social psychology." In D. Levine (ed.), Nebraska Symposium on Motivation. Lincoln, NB: University of Nebrasks Press, 15: 192–238.

———— (1976). "Recent researcyh in causal attribution." Address to Western Psychological Association, Los Angeles, April 10.

Koffka, Kurt (1935). Principles of Gestalt Psychology. New York: Harcourt Brace.

Kohler, Wolfgang (1947). Gestalt Psychology. New York: Mentor.

Kotter, John Paul (1973). "The psychological contract: Managing the joining-up process." California Management Review, 15: 91–99.

Kuhn, Thomas S. (1970). The Structure of Scientific Revolutions. Chicago: Unviersity of Chicago Press.

Langer, Ellen J. (1978). "Rethinking the role of thought in social interactions." In John H. Harvey, William Ickes, Robert F. Kidd (eds.), New Directions in Attribution Research, 2: 35–58.

Latham, Gary P., and Gary A. Yukl (1975). "A review of research on the application of goal setting in organizations." Academy of Management Journal, 18: 824–845.

Leifer, Richard (1979). "Mythology as an organizational variable." Unpublished paper, Department of Management, University of Massachusetts.

Lewin, Kurt (1951). Field Theory in Social Science. Dorwin Cartwright, ed. New York: Harper and Row.

Locke, E. A. (1968). "Toward a theory of task motivation and incentives." Organizational Behavior and Human Performance, 3: 157–189.

Louis, Meryl Reis (1978). "How MBA graduates cope with early job experiences: An expectation/attribution approach." Unpublished dissertation, Graduate School of Management, University of California-Los Angeles.

McClosky, Herber, and John H. Schaar (1963). "Psychological dimensions of anomy." American Sociological Review, 30: 14–40.

McHugh, Peter (1968). Defining the Situation: The Organization of Meaning in Social Interaction. Indianapolis: Bobbs-Merrill.

Mead, Goerge Herbert (1964). On Social Psychology. Anselm Strauss, ed. Chicago: University of Chicago Press.

Merton, Robert (1957). Social Theory and Social Structure. Glencoe, IL: Free Press.

Miller, George A. (1956). "The magical number seven, plus or minus two: Some limits on our capacity for processing on our capacity for processing information." Psychological Review, 63: 81–96.

Mills, C. Wright (1940). "Situated actions and vocabularies of motive." American Sociological Review, 5: 904–913.

Mitroff, Ian I., and Ralph Kilmann (1976). "On organizational stories: An approach to the design and analysis of organizations through myths and stories." In Ralph H. Kilmann, Louis R. Pondy, and Donald P. Slevin (eds.), The Management of Organization Design: Strategies and Implementation: 189–208. New York: Elsevier.

Mobley, W. H., H. H. Hand, B. M. Meglino, and R. W. Griffeth (1979a). "Review and conceptual analaysis of the employee turnover process." Psychological Bulletin, 85: 493–522.

Mobley, William H., Herbert H. Hand, Robert L. Baker, and Bruce M. Meglino (1979b). "Conceptual and empirical analysis of military recruit training attrition." Journal of Applied Psychology, 64: 10–18.

Mobley, William H., and Bruce M. Meglino (1979). "Toward further understanding of the employee turnover process." Presentation to the Academy of Management meetings, Atlanta, August.

Mowday, Richard T. (1979). "Reconciling expectations with job experiences: Some thoughts on the role of unmet expectations in the turnover process." Unpublished paper, Graduate School of Management, University of Oregon.

Muchinsky, Paul M., and Mark L. Tuttle (1979). "Employee turnover: An empirical and methodological assessment." Journal of Vocational Behavior, 14: 43–77.

Oliver, Richard L. (1977). "Effect of expectation and disconfirmation on post exposure product evaluations: An alternative interpretation." Journal of Applied Psychology, 62: 480–486.

Ouchi, William G., and Alfred M. Jaeger (1978). "Type Z organization: Stability in the midst of mobility." Academy of Management Review, 3: 305–314.

Porter, Lyman W., and Richard M. Steers (1973). "Organizational, work, and personal factors in employee turnover and absenteeism." Psychological Bulletin, 80: 151–176.

Price, James L. (1977). The Study of Turnover. Ames. IA: Iowa State University Press.

Reilly, Richard R., Mary L. Tenopyr, and Steven M. Sperling (1979). "Effects of job previews on job acceptance and survival of telephone operator candidates." Journal of Applied Psychology, 64: 218–220.

Ritti, R. Richard, and G. Ray Funkhouser (1977). The Ropes to Skip and the Ropes to Know. Columbus, OH: Grid.

Ross, Ian C., and Alvin Zander (1957). "Need satisfaction and employee turnover." Personnel Psychology, 10: 327–338.

Ross, Lee (1977). "The intuitive psychologist and his shortcomings: Distortions in the attribution process." In L. Berkowitz (eds.), Advances in Experimental Social Psychology, 10: 173–220.

Rotter, Julian B. (1966). "Generalized expectations for internal versus external control of reinforcement." Psychological Monographs: General and Applied, 80, No. 1.

Schein, Edgar H. (1962). "Problems of the first year at work: Report of the first career panel re-union." School of Industrial Management, Massachusetts Institute of Technology, September, No. 03-62.

——— (1965). Organizational Psychology. Englewood Cliffs, NJ: Prentice-Hall.

——— (1968). "Organizational socialization and the profession of management." Industrial Management Review, 9: 1–16.

——— (1971a). "The individual, the organization, and the career: A conceptual scheme." Journal of Applied Behavioral Science, 7: 401–426.

——— (1971b). "Occupational socialization in the professions: The case of the role innovator." Journal of Psychiatric Research, 8: 521–530.

——— (1978). Career Dynamics: Matching Individual and Organizational Needs. Reading, MA: Addison-Wesley.

——— (1979). "Personal change through interpersonal relationships." In Warren Bennis, John Van Maanen, Edgar H. Schein, Fred I. Steele (eds.), Essays in Interpersonal Dynamics: 129–162. Homewood, IL: Dorsey Press.

Schutz, Alfred (1964). Collected Papers II: Studies in Social Theory. Arvid Brodersen, ed. The Hague: Martinus Nijhoff.

Scott, Marvin B., and Stanford M. Lyman (1968). "Accounts." American Sociological Review, 33: 46–62.

Sherif, Muzafer, and Carl I. Hovland (1961). Social Judgment: Assimilation and Contrast Effects in Communication and Attitude Change. New Haven: Yale University Press.

Tannenbaum, Robert (1976). "Some matters of life and death." OD Practitioner, 8: 1–7.

Taylor, Shelley E., and Susan T. Fiske (1978). "Salience, attention and attribution: Top of the head phenomena." In L. Berkowitz (ed.), Advances in Experimental Social Psychology, 11: 249–288.

Turner, Victor W. (1969). The Ritual Process. Chicago: Aldine.

Van Gennep, Arnold (1960). The Rites of Passage. London: Routledge and Kegan Paul.

Van Maanen, John (1976). "Breaking in: Socialization to work." In Robert Dubin (ed.), Handbook of Work, Organization, and Society: 67–130. Chicago: Rand McNally.

——— (1977a). "Experiencing organization: Notes on the meaning of careers and socialization." In John Van Maanen (ed.), Organizational Careers: Some New Perspectives: 15–45. New York: Wiley.

——— (1977b). Organizational Careers: Some New Perspectives. New York: Wiley.

Van Maanen, John, and Edgar H. Schein (1979). "Toward a theory of organizational socialization." In Barry M. Staw (ed.), Research in Organizational Behavior, 1: 209–264.

Vroom, Victor, and Edward L. Deci (1971). "The stability of post-decision dissonance: A follow-up study of the job attitudes of business school graduates." Organizational Behavior and Human Performance, 6: 36–49.

Wanous, John P. (1976). "Organizational entry: From naive expectations to realistic beliefs." Journal of Applied Psychology, 61: 22–29.

——— (1977). "Organization entry: Newcomers moving from outside to inside." Psychological Bulletin, 84: 601–618.

——— (1978). "Realistic job previews: Can a procedure to reduce turnover also influence the relationship between abilities and performance?" Personnel Psychology, 31: 249–258.

——— (1979). "Socialization processes at organizational contact: Organizational entry reconceptualized." Presentation to the Academy of Management meetings, Atlanta, August.

——— (1980). Organizational Entry. Reading, MA: Addison-Wesley.

Ward, Lewis B., and Anthony G. Athos (1972). Student Expectations of Corporate Life: Implications for Management Recruiting. Boston: Division of Research, Harvard University.

Weick, Karl E. (1977). "Enactment processes in organizations." In Barry M. Staw and Gerald R. Salancik (eds.), New Directions in Organizational Behavior: 267–300. Chicago: St. Clair.

——— (1979). "Cognitive processes in organizations." In Barry M. Staw (ed.), Research in Organizational Behavior, 1: 41–74.

Weiner, Bernard (1974). Achievement Motivation and Attribution Theory. Morristown, NJ: General Learning Press.

Weiss, Howard M. (1978). "Social learning of work values in organizations." Journal of Applied Psychology, 63: 711–718.

Wheeler, Stanton (1966). "The structure of formally organized socialization settings." In Orville G. Brim, Jr., and Stanton Wheeler (eds.), Socialization after Childhood: Two Essays: 51–116. New York: Wiley.

Wilkins, Alan L. (1979). "Organizational history, legends, and control." Unpublished paper, Department of Organizational Behavior, Brigham Young University.

Wilkins, Alan L., and Joanne Martin (1979). "Organizational legends." Unpublished paper, Graduate School of Business, Stanford University.

37
Images of Organization
Gareth Morgan

INTRODUCTION

Effective managers and professionals in all walks of life, whether they be business executives, public administrators, organizational consultants, politicians, or trade unionists, have to become skilled in the art of "reading" the situations that they are attempting to organize or manage.

This skill usually develops as an intuitive process, learned through experience and natural ability. Though at times a person may actually declare that he or she needs to "read what's happening at X," or to "get a handle on Y," the process of reading and rereading often occurs at an almost subconscious level. For this reason it is often believed that effective managers and problem solvers are born rather than made, and have a kind of magical power to understand and transform the situations that they encounter.

If we take a closer look at the processes used, however, we find that this kind of mystique and power is often based on an ability to develop deep appreciations of the situations being addressed. Skilled readers develop the knack of reading situations with various scenarios in mind, and of forging actions that seem appropriate to the readings thus obtained.

They have a capacity to remain open and flexible, suspending immediate judgments whenever possible, until a more comprehensive view of the situation emerges. They are aware of the fact that new insights often arise as one reads a situation from "new angles," and that a wide and varied reading can create a wide and varied range of action possibilities. Less effective managers and problem solvers, on the other hand, seem to interpret everything from a fixed standpoint. As a result, they frequently hit blocks that they can't get around; their actions and behaviors are often rigid and inflexible and a source of conflict. When problems and differences of opinion arise, they usually have no alternative but to hammer at issues in the same old way and to create consensus by convincing others to "buy into" their particular view of the situation.

There is a close relationship between this process of reading organizational life and the process known as organizational analysis. The formal analysis and diagnosis of organizations, like the process of reading, always rests in applying some kind of theory to the situation being considered. For theories, like readings, are interpretations of reality. We theorize about or "read" situations as we attempt to formulate images and explanations that help us to make sense of their fundamental nature. And an effective analysis, like an effective reading, rests in being able to do this in ways that take account

Source: "Introduction" and "Imagination," pp. 11–17 and 339–44 in *Images of Organization*, by Gareth Morgan. Copyright © 1986. Reprinted by permission of Sage Publications, Inc.

of rival theories or explanations, rather than being committed to a fixed and unshakable point of view.

This book explores and develops the art of reading and understanding organizations. . . .

The basic premise on which the book builds is that our theories and explanations of organizational life are based on metaphors that lead us to see and understand organizations in distinctive yet partial ways. Metaphor is often just regarded as a device for embellishing discourse, but its significance is much greater than this. For the use of metaphor implies *a way of thinking* and *a way of seeing* that pervade how we understand our world generally. For example, research in a wide variety of fields has demonstrated that metaphor exerts a formative influence on science, on our language and on how we think, as well as on how we express ourselves on a day-to-day basis.

We use metaphor whenever we attempt to understand one element of experience in terms of another. Thus, metaphor proceeds through implicit or explicit assertions that A *is* (or is like) B. When we say "the man is a lion," we use the image of a lion to draw attention to the lionlike aspects of the man. The metaphor frames our understanding of the man in a distinctive yet partial way.

One of the interesting aspects of metaphor rests in the fact that it always produces this kind of one-sided insight. In highlighting certain interpretations it tends to force others into a background role. Thus in drawing attention to the lionlike bravery, strength, or ferocity of the man, the metaphor glosses the fact that the same person may well also be a chauvinist pig, a devil, a saint, a bore, or a recluse. Our ability to achieve a comprehensive "reading" of the man depends on an ability to see how these different aspects of the person may coexist in a complementary or even a paradoxical way.

It is easy to see how this kind of thinking has relevance for understanding organization and management. For organizations are complex and paradoxical phenomena that can be understood in many different ways. Many of our taken-for-granted ideas about organizations are metaphorical, even though we may not recognize them as such. For example, we frequently talk about organizations *as if* they were machines designed to achieve predetermined goals and objectives, and which should operate smoothly and efficiently. And as a result of this kind of thinking we often attempt to organize and manage them in a mechanistic way, forcing their human qualities into a background role.

By using different metaphors to understand the complex and paradoxical character of organizational life, we are able to manage and design organizations in ways that we may not have thought possible before. The following chapters illustrate how this can be done by exploring the implications of different metaphors for thinking about the nature of organization. While some of the metaphors tap familiar ways of thinking, others develop insights and perspectives that will be rather new. . . .

The metaphors discussed have been selected to illustrate a broad range of ideas and perspectives, but, of course, by no means exhaust the possibilities. This is why it is important to understand that the mode of analysis developed here rests in *a way of thinking* rather than in the mechanistic application of a small set of clearly defined analytical frameworks. While the book focuses on a number of key metaphors that have relevance for understanding a wide range of organizational situations, there are others that can produce their own special insight.

Effective organizational analysis must always remain open to this possibility.

We live in a world that is becoming increasingly complex. Unfortunately, our styles of thinking rarely match this complexity. We often end up persuading ourselves that everything is more simple than it actually is, dealing with complexity by presuming that it does not really exist. This is very evident in the way fad and fashion dominate approaches to organizational analysis and problem-solving, an interest in one type of solution or set of techniques quickly giving way to another.

The approach to organizational analysis developed in this book stands against this general trend, in the belief that organizations are generally complex, ambiguous, and paradoxical. The real challenge is to learn to deal with this complexity. The method of analysis offered here points to a way in which we can begin to take up this challenge by relying on the most valuable asset we have: our capacity for critical thinking. I believe that by building on the use of metaphor—which is basic to our way of thinking generally—we have a means of enhancing our capacity for creative yet disciplined thought, in a way that allows us to grasp and deal with the many-sided character of organizational life. And in doing so, I believe that we can find new ways of organizing and new ways of approaching and solving organizational problems.

IMAGINIZATION: A DIRECTION FOR THE FUTURE

Organizations are many things at once! . . . I believe that some of the most fundamental problems that we face stem from the fact that the complexity and sophistication of our thinking do not match the complexity and sophisti-

cation of the realities with which we have to deal. This seems to be true in the world of organization as well as in social life more generally. The result is that our actions are often simplistic, and at times downright harmful. I have written this book in an attempt to make some small contribution to our understanding of the way we oversimplify, and to identify a possible means through which we might begin to develop a capacity for doing a little better than we do now.

My overall approach has been to foster a kind of critical thinking that encourages us to understand and grasp the multiple meanings of situations and to confront and manage contradiction and paradox, rather than to pretend that they do not exist. I have chosen to do this through metaphor, which I believe is central to the way we organize and understand our world. But one does not have to accept this thesis. The much more important general point is that our ways of seeing the world are always bounded ones, and that much can be learned by appreciating the partial nature of our understandings and how they can be broadened. I have used metaphors to show how we can frame and reframe our understanding of the same situation, in the belief that new kinds of understanding can emerge from the process.

When we look at our world with our two eyes we get a different view from that gained by using each eye independently. Each eye sees the same reality in a different way, and when working together, the two combine to produce yet another way. Try it and see. I believe that the same process occurs when we learn to interpret the world through different metaphors. The process of framing and reframing itself produces a qualitatively different kind of understanding that parallels the quality of binocular vision. As we try and understand phenomena like organizations as machines, organisms, cultures, political systems, instruments of domination, and so on, a new depth of insight emerges. The way of seeing itself transforms our understanding of the nature of the phenomenon.

On Elephants and Organizations

At first sight, much of what I have tried to say has a great deal in common with the old Indian tale of the six blind men and the elephant. The first man feels a tusk, claiming the animal to be like a spear. The second, feeling the elephant's side, proclaims that it is more like a wall. Feeling a leg, the third describes it as a tree; and a fourth, feeling the elephant's trunk, is inclined to think it like a snake. The fifth, who has seized the elephant's ear, thinks it remarkably like a fan; and the sixth, grabbing the tail, says it is much more like a rope. Their understandings would be even further complicated, as Peter Vaill has noted, if the elephant were set in motion. For the man clinging to the elephant's leg would experience an elliptical forward motion. The man holding the tail would be whipped in random fashion, while the others would be jerked and jolted, and perhaps splashed and splattered with water and manure. The elephant's motion would probably destroy all their previous understandings and further complicate the task of arriving at a consensus.

There can be little doubt that, as with the blind men, our actual experiences of organizations are often different and hence we make sense of our experiences in different ways. Thus a person in a dingy factory may find obvious credibility in the idea that organizations are instruments of domination, while a manager in a comfortable office may be more enthusiastic about understanding the organization as a kind of organism faced with the problem of survival, or as a pattern of culture and subculture.

However, the parallels with the Indian tale break down in some important ways. First, as we look at the plight of the blind men we do so with the privilege of sight. We know that they are dealing with an elephant, and that if they were able to get together and share their experiences they might arrive at a much better consensus with regard to what the elephant is really like. However, the problem of understanding organization is more difficult in that we do not really know what organizations are, in the sense of having a single authoritative position from which they can be viewed. While many writers on organization attempt to offer such a position—for example, by defining organizations as groups of people who come together in pursuit of common goals—the reality is that to an extent we are *all* blind men and women groping to understand the nature of the beast. While we may be able to share our different experiences and even come to some consensus, we will never achieve that degree of certainty that is implicitly communicated in the Indian tale by the idea that it is they who are blind and we who have sight.

Stated in more conventional terms, there is a difference between the full and rich reality of an organization, and the knowledge that we are able to gain about that organization. We can know organizations only through our experience of them. We can use metaphors and theories to grasp and express this knowledge and experience, and to share our understandings, but we can never be sure that we are absolutely right. I believe we must always recognize this basic uncertainty.

A second important difference between the moral of the Indian tale and the problem of understanding organizations is that the very same aspect of organization can be many different things at the same time. Thus different ideas about organization do not stem just from the fact that like the blind men we are grasping different aspects of the beast, but because different dimensions are always intertwined. For example, a bureaucratic organization is simultaneously machinelike, a cultural and political phenomenon, an expression of unconscious preoccupations and concerns, an unfolded aspect of a deeper logic of social change, and so on. It *is* all these things at one and the same time. We can try to decompose organization into sets of related variables: structural, technical, political, cultural, human, and so forth; but we must remember that this does not really do justice to the nature of the phenomenon. For the structural and technical dimensions of an organization are simultaneously human, political, and cultural. The division between the different dimensions is in our minds rather than in the phenomenon.

To illustrate this point, I would like to take one of my favorite examples. The authoritarian owner of a small organization, concerned about his negative impact on employee morale and his general loss of control, has just returned from a course on human-resource management. He genuinely feels that he has had "a conversion experience" and wants to change his style of management to be more people-oriented. In an attempt to build closer and better relations with the workforce he decides to visit one of his factories. On the shop floor he makes a point of shaking hands with each employee. They are naturally surprised and don't quite know what to make of the situation, because "the boss" has always kept a clear distance and ruled with an iron hand.

Clearly, numerous different meanings are latent in the very same phenomenon—the handshake. The handshake is a symbolic gesture, an expression of a human-relations approach to management, possibly the beginning of a different and more democratic kind of political relationship within the firm, but also possibly the beginning of a new kind of employee control. The handshake embodies potentially contradictory meanings, e.g., of friendship, people-centeredness, manipulation, and control, just as the rationality of an organization can simultaneously have political and exploitative dimensions.

In trying to understand an organizational situation we have to be able to cope with these different and potentially paradoxical meanings, identifying them through some form of decomposition while retaining a sense of their interrelationship and essential integration.

This has obvious implications for . . . making us aware of the dangers of theories that overcompartmentalize or decompose our understanding of organizations. I have emphasized that one of my main goals has been to develop *a way of thinking* that can cope with ambiguity and paradox. We must avoid the pitfalls of the blind-men syndrome. In using metaphors or other frames of reference to unravel the complexities of organizational life we can see certain metaphors fitting certain situations better than others (e.g., organization X is more machinelike than organization Y, department A is more holographic than department B, group C has a team-based culture while D is more adversarial), but we must always remember that aspects of every metaphor may be found in every situation.

The analytical scheme that I have developed is thus best understood as a sensitizing or interpretive process rather than as a model or static framework. Good analysis rests not just in spotting "what metaphor fits where" or "which metaphor fits best," but in using metaphor to unravel multiple patterns of significance and their interrelations. I believe that the best intuitive readings made by managers and other organizational members have the same quality. These individuals are open to the kind of nuance that stems from an appreciation that any given situation can be many different things at once.

Imaginization: Organization as a Way of Thinking

Images and metaphors are not only interpretive constructs or ways of seeing; they also provide frame-works for action. Their use creates insights that often allow us to act in ways that we may not have thought possible before. I have tried to bring out this point in various ways, for example by demonstrating how the use of different metaphors can lead to different ways of organizing and managing, and in discussing the prescriptive functions of my approach to organizational analysis.

I now want to be more forthright in my position on the close links between thought and action and suggest that we could well begin to think about organization in a broader and more open way by using the word *imaginization* to provide us with a much more empowering view of the basic phenomenon. . . .

The word organization derives from the Greek *organon*, meaning tool or instrument. It is thus hardly surprising that the concept of organization is usually loaded with mechanical or instrumental significance. In coining the word *imaginization* my intention is to break free of this mechanical meaning by symbolizing the close link between images and actions. Organization is always shaped by underlying images and ideas; we organize as we imaginize; and it is always possible to imaginize in many different ways.

When we think about organization in this manner we are provided with a constant reminder that we are involved in a creative process where new images and ideas can create new actions. In the field of architecture new kinds of buildings have arisen from major revisions in the concepts underlying the building process. For example, the assumption that sturdy buildings depend on a satisfactory pattern of stress *compression* confines the architect to producing traditional structures. The idea that buildings can be held in place through appropriate patterns of *tension* gives rise to freer-flowing forms held in place by wires and buttresses. I believe that we can create similar revolutions in the way we organize by being aware that we are always engaged in *imaginization*.

Rather than just interpreting the way organizations are, this book also seeks to show how we can change the way they are. In recognizing the close links between thought and action in organizational life, we recognize that the way we "read organizations influences how we produce them. Images and metaphors are not just interpretive constructs used in the task of analysis. They are central to the process of *imaginization* through which people enact or "write" the character of organizational life.

38
Gendering Organizational Theory

Joan Acker

Although early critical analyses of organizational theory (e.g., Acker and Van Houten 1974; Kanter 1977a) led to few immediate further efforts, feminist examination of organizational theory has developed rapidly in the last few years (Ferguson 1984; Calás and Smircich 1989a, 1989b; Hearn and Parkin 1983, 1987; Burrell 1984, 1987; Mills 1988b; Hearn et al. 1989; Acker 1990; Martin 1990a, 1990b). The authors of these critiques are responding to and helping to create the conditions for a fundamental reworking of organizational theories to account for the persistence of male advantage in male organizations and to lay a base for new critical and gendered theories of organizations that can better answer questions about how we humans come to organize our activities as we do in contemporary societies.

The conditions for a new critique began with the rapid proliferation of studies about women and work, conceptualized in theoretical terms of prefeminist social science. For example, studies of women's economic and occupational inequality, sex segregation, and the wage gap document the extent of the problems but give us no convincing explanations for their persistence or for the apparently endless reorganization of gender and permutations of male power. Similarly, the extensive literature on women and management documents difficulties and dif-

ferences but provides no adequate theory of gendered power imbalance. The need for new theory was implicit in the inadequacies of old theory.

Developments within feminist theory also provide foundations for a new criticism of organizational theory. . . .

THINKING ABOUT GENDER

Gender refers to patterned, socially produced, distinctions between female and male, feminine and masculine. Gender is not something that people are, in some inherent sense, although we may consciously think of ourselves in this way. Rather, for the individual and the collective, it is a daily accomplishment (West and Zimmerman 1987) that occurs in the course of participation in work organizations as well as in many other locations and relations.

. . . Gender, as patterned differences, usually involves the subordination of women, either concretely or symbolically, and, as Joan Scott (1986) points out, gender is a pervasive symbol of power.

The term *gendered processes* "means that advantage and disadvantage, exploitation and control, action and emotion, meaning and identity, are patterned through and in terms of a distinction between male and female, masculine and feminine" (Acker 1990:

Source: "Gendering Organizational Theory," by Joan Acker from *Gendering Organizational Analysis*, pp. 248–260. Copyright © 1992. Reprinted by permission of Sage Publications, Inc.

146; see also Scott 1986; Harding 1986; Connell 1987; Flax 1990). Gendered processes are concrete activities, what people do and say, and how they think about these activities, for thinking is also an activity. The daily construction, and sometimes deconstruction, of gender occurs within material and ideological constraints that set the limits of possibility. For example, the boundaries of sex segregation, themselves continually constructed and reconstructed, limit the actions of particular women and men at particular times. Gendered processes do not occur outside other social processes but are integral parts of these processes—for example, class and race relations—which cannot be fully understood without a comprehension of gender (Connell 1987). At the same time, class and race processes are integral to gender relations. The links between class and race domination and gender are ubiquitous. For example, at the top of the typical Southern California high-tech firm stands the rational, aggressive, controlling white man (occasionally a woman but one who has learned how to operate in the class/gender structure), while at the very bottom there are often women of color working on a production line where they have little control over any aspect of their working lives (Fernandez Kelly and Garcia 1988). Examining how the organization was started and is controlled by these particular men and how these particular women came to be the production workers leads us back into the class/gender/race relations of that time and place. Similarly, if we look at the work processes and organizational controls that keep the firm going, we will see the intertwining of gender, race, and class.

Gendered processes and practices may be open and overt, as when managers choose only men or only women for certain positions or when sexual jokes deni-

grating women are part of the work culture. On the other hand, gender may be deeply hidden in organizational processes and decisions that appear to have nothing to do with gender. For example, deregulation and internationalization of banking has altered the gender structure of banks in both Sweden (Acker 1991) and Britain (Morgan and Knights 1991). In Sweden, these changes contributed to a growing wage gap between women and men, as women remained in low-wage branch banking and men, chosen more often for the growing international banking departments, were rewarded with disproportionate salary increases. In Britain, deregulation, and the resulting increase in competitiveness in the industry, was an important cause of reorganization in one bank that gave women new tasks at the expense of some men but still protected the privileges of men in traditional managerial positions. To understand the persistence of gender patterns, even as external changes cause internal organizational restructuring, I think we should consider the gender substructure of organizations and the ways that gender is used as an organizational resource, topics discussed below.

ELEMENTS IN A THEORY OF GENDERED ORGANIZATIONS

Gendered Processes

Gendered organizations can be described in terms of four sets of processes that are components of the same reality, although, for purposes of description, they can be seen as analytically distinct. As outlined above, gendering may occur in gender-explicit or gender-neutral practices; it occurs through concrete organizational activities; and its processes usually have class and racial implications as well. Sexuality, in its diverse forms and meanings, is implicated in each of these processes of gendering organizations.

The first set of processes is the production of gender divisions. Ordinary organizational practices produce the gender patterning of jobs, wages, and hierarchies, power, and subordination (e.g., Kanter 1977a). Managers make conscious decisions that re-create and sometimes alter these patterns (Cohn 1985); unions, where they exist, often collude, whether intentionally or not. For example, while employers can no longer, by law, advertise for female workers for some jobs and male workers for others, many still perceive women as suited for certain work and men as suited for other work. These perceptions help to shape decisions. The introduction of new technology may offer the possibility for the reduction of gender divisions but most often results in a reorganization, not an elimination, of male predominance (e.g., Cockburn 1983, 1985). The depth and character of gender divisions vary dramatically from one society to another and from one time to another. In Britain, for example, when women first began to enter clerical work, separate offices were often set up so that women and men would not have to meet on the job, thus avoiding the possibility of sexual encounters and resulting in extreme gender segregation (Cohn 1985). Whatever the variation, there is overwhelming evidence that hierarchies are gendered and that gender and sexuality have a central role in the reproduction of hierarchy.

Gendering also involves the creation of symbols, images, and forms of consciousness that explicate, justify, and, more rarely, oppose gender divisions. Complex organizations are one of the main locations of the production of such images and forms of consciousness in our societies. Television, films, and advertising are obvious examples, but all organizations are sites of symbolic production.

Gender images, always containing implications of sexuality, infuse organizational structure. The top manager or business leader is always strong, decisive, rational, and forceful—and often seductive (Calás and Smircich 1989b). The organization itself is often defined through metaphors of masculinity of a certain sort. Today, organizations are lean, mean, aggressive, goal oriented, efficient, and competitive but rarely empathetic, supportive, kind, and caring. Organizational participants actively create these images in their efforts to construct organizational cultures that contribute to competitive success.

The third set of processes that reproduce gendered organizations are interactions between individuals, women and men, women and women, men and men, in the multiplicity of forms that enact dominance and subordination and create alliances and exclusions. In these interactions, at various levels of hierarchy, policies that create divisions are developed and images of gender are created and affirmed. Sexuality is involved here, too, in overt or hidden ways; links between dominance and sexuality shape interaction and help to maintain hierarchies favoring men (Pringle 1989). Interactions may be between supervisors and subordinates, between coworkers, or between workers and customers, clients, or other outsiders. Interactions are part of the concrete work of organization, and the production of gender is often "inside" the activities that constitute the organization itself.

The fourth dimension of gendering of organizations is the internal mental work of individuals as they consciously construct their understandings of the organization's gendered structure of work and opportunity and the demands for gender-appropriate behaviors and attitudes (e.g., Pringle 1989; Cockburn 1991). This includes creating the correct gendered persona and hiding unacceptable aspects of one's life, such as homosexuality. As Pringle (1989: 176) says, "Sexual games are integral to the play of power at work, and success for women depends on how they negotiate their sexuality." Such internal work helps to reproduce divisions and images even as it ensures individual survival.

Gender and Sexuality as Organizational Resources

Gender, sexuality, and bodies can be thought of as organizational resources, primarily available to management but also used by individuals and groups of workers. Simultaneously, however, gender, sexuality, and bodies are problems for management. Solutions to these problems become resources for control. Both female and male bodies have physical needs on the job. Management often controls lunch and toilet breaks as well as physical movement around the workplace as integral elements in furthering productivity. Numbers of researchers, from Crozier on (Acker and Van Houten 1974), have observed that women workers are more tightly controlled in these ways than men workers. Higher-level employees are often rewarded with fewer bodily constraints and special privileges in regard to physical needs—for example, the executive washroom and dining room.

Reproduction and sexuality are often objects of and resources for control. As Burrell (1984: 98) argues, "Individual organizations inaugurate mechanisms for the control of sexuality at a very early stage in their development." Reproduction and sexuality may disrupt ongoing work and seriously undermine the orderly and rational pursuit of organizational goals. Women's bodies, sexuality, and procreative abilities are used as grounds for exclusion or objectification. On the other hand, men's sexuality dom-

inates most workplaces and reinforces their organizational power (Collinson and Collinson 1989). In addition, talk about sex and male sexual superiority helps construct solidarity and cooperation from the bottom to the top of many organizations, thus promoting organizational stability and control.

Gender is also a resource in organizational change. Hacker (1979) showed how technological transformation at ATT in the 1970s was facilitated by moving women into formerly male jobs slated to be eliminated. Today, in the drive for organizational "flexibility," managements often consciously create part-time jobs, low paid and dead end, to be filled by women (see, e.g., Cockburn 1991). It is gender, and often race, that makes women ideal employees. These are only examples from a multiplicity of processes that suggest the possibilities for research about gender and sexuality in organizational control and change.

The Gendered Substructure of Organization

The more or less obvious manifestations of gender in organizational processes outlined above are built upon, and in turn help to reproduce, a gendered substructure of organization. The gendered substructure lies in the spatial and temporal arrangements of work, in the rules prescribing workplace behavior, and in the relations linking workplaces to living places. These practices and relations, encoded in arrangements and rules, are supported by assumptions that work is separate from the rest of life and that it has first claim on the worker. Many people, particularly women, have difficulty making their daily lives fit these expectations and assumptions. As a consequence, today, there are two types of workers, those, mostly men, who, it is assumed, can adhere to organizational rules, arrangements, and assumptions, and those, mostly women, who, it is assumed, cannot, because of other obligations to family and reproduction.

Organizations depend upon this division, for, in a free market economy, in contrast to a slave economy, they could not exist without some outside organization of reproduction to take care of supplying workers. In this sense, the gender substructure of organization is linked to the family and reproduction. This relationship is not simply a functional link. It is embedded in and re-created daily in ordinary organizational activities, most of which do not appear on the surface to be gendered. In the exploration of some of these processes, it is possible to see how integral to modern organization this gendered substructure is, and how relatively inaccessible to change it remains.

I began this discussion by considering some of the problems posed by the gendered nature of existing, ostensibly gender-neutral, organizational theory and processes. Feminist critics of traditional theory now widely recognize that this body of theory is gendered, that it implicitly assumes that managers and workers are male, with male-stereotypic powers, attitudes, and obligations (e.g., Acker 1990; Calás and Smircich 1992; Mills 1989).

What is problematic is the discontinuity, even contradiction, between organizational realities obviously structured around gender and ways of thinking and talking about these same realities as though they were gender neutral. What activities or practices produce the facade of gender neutrality and maintain this disjuncture between organizational life and theory? These questions can provide a point of entry into the underlying processes that maintain gender divisions, images, interactions, and identities.

This analytic strategy is based on Dorothy Smith's *The Conceptual Practices of Power* (1990) in which she argues that concepts that feminists may see as misrepresenting reality—here the concept of gender-neutral structure—indicate something about the socal relations they represent. That is, such concepts are not "wrong." On the contrary, they are constructed out of the working knowledge of those who manage and control, thus they say something about processes of power, including the suppression of knowledge about gender. While it is important to "deconstruct"these concepts, revealing hidden meanings, we can, in addition, investigate the concrete activities that produce them.

The break between a gendered reality and gender-neutral thought is maintained, I believe, through the impersonal, objectifying practices of organizing, managing, and controlling large organizations. As Smith (1987) argues, these processes are increasingly textually mediated. Bureaucratic rules and written guides for organizational processes have been around for a long time, but their proliferation continues as rationalization of production and management expands on a global scale. The fact that much of this is now built into computer programs may mystify the process but only increases objectification and the appearance of gender neutrality. The continuing replication of the assumption of gender neutrality is part of the production of texts that can apply to workers, work processes, production, and management as general phenomena. Thus gender neutrality, the suppression of knowledge about gender, is embedded in organizational control processes.

This work of re-creating gender neutrality as part of the construction of general phenomena that can be organized and controlled through the application of documentary processes is evident in job evaluation,[1] a textual tool used by management to rationalize wage setting and the construction of organizational hierarchies. Other managerial processes produce assumptions of gender neutrality, but job evaluation provides a particularly good example because it is widely used in every industrial country (International Labour Office 1986).

Job evaluators use documents, or instruments, that describe general aspects of jobs, such as knowledge, skill, complexity, and responsibility,to assess the "value" of particular, concrete jobs in comparison with other particular, concrete jobs. The content of the documents and the way evaluators discuss and interpret them in the course of the job evaluation process provide an illustration of how concrete organizational activities reproduce the assumption of gender neutrality (Acker 1989, 1990).

Job evaluation, as most experts will tell you, evaluates jobs, not the people who do the jobs. Job evaluation consultants and trainers admonish evaluators to consider only the requirements of the job, not the gender or other characteristics of the incumbent. The tasks, skill requirements, and responsibilities of a job can be reliably described and assessed, while people who fill the jobs vary in their knowledge and commitment. Jobs can be rationalized and standardized; people cannot. A job exists separate from those who fill it, as a position in the hierarchy of an organizational chart. It is a reified, objectified category. But the abstract job must contain the assumption of an abstract worker if it is to be more than a set of tasks written on a piece of paper. Such a worker has no obligations outside the demands of the job, which is a bounded, abstract entity. To fit such demands, the abstract worker does not eat, urinate, or procreate, for these activities are not part of the job. Indeed, the abstract worker has no body and thus no gender. Jobs and hierarchies are represented as gender neutral, and every time such a job eval-

uation system is used, the notion of gender-neutral structure and the behavior based on that notion are re-created within the organization. Gender-neutral organizational theories reflect this gender-neutral rendering of organizational reality.

Real jobs and real workers are, of course, deeply gendered and embodied. The abstract worker transformed into a concrete worker turns out to be a man whose work is his life and whose wife takes care of everything else. Thus the concept of a job is gendered, in spite of its presentation as gender neutral, because only a male worker can begin to meet its implicit demands. Hidden within the concept of a job are assumptions about separations between the public and private spheres and the gendered organization of reproduction and production. Reproduction itself, procreation, sexuality, and caring for children, the ill, and the aged, unless transferred to the public sphere, are outside job and organizational boundaries. Too much involvement in such activities makes a person unsuitable for the organization. Women do not fit the assumptions about the abstract worker. Thus they are less than ideal organization participants, best placed in particular jobs that separate them from "real" workers.

The exclusion of reproduction is, as I argue above, linked to the ideology of the gender-neutral, abstract worker who has no body and no feelings, along with no gender. This abstraction facilitates the idea that the organization and its goals come first before the reproductive needs of individuals and society, such as, for example, the need to preserve and restore the natural environment. The concept of the abstract worker, completely devoted to the job, also supports the idea that strong commitment to the organization over and above commitment to family and community are necessary and normal. . . . As a consequence, management can more easily make the tough decisions, such as those to close factories while opposing all efforts to protect actual, concrete bodies and minds through plant closure legislation.

The theory and practice of gender neutrality covers up, obscures, the underlying gender structure, allowing practices that perpetuate it to continue even as efforts to reduce gender inequality are also under way (e.g., Cockburn 1991). The textual tools of management, as they are employed in everyday organizational life, not only help to create and then obscure gender structures that disadvantage women but are also part of complex processes that daily re-create the subordination of reproduction to production and justify the privileging of production over all other human necessities.

The gender-neutral character of the job and the worker, central to organizational processes and theories discussed above, depends upon the assumption that the worker has no body. This disembodied worker is a manifestation of the universal "citizen" or "individual" fundamental to ideas of democracy and contract. As Carole Pateman (1986: 8) points out, the most fundamental abstraction in the concept of liberal individualism is "the abstraction of the 'individual' from the body. In order for the individual to appear in liberal theory as a universal figure, who represents anyone and everyone, the individual must be disembodied." If the individual had bodily form, it would be clear that he represents one gender and one sex rather than a universal being. The universal individual is "constructed from a male body so that his identity is always masculine" (Pateman 1988: 223). Even with the full rights of citizens, women stand in an ambiguous relation to this universal

individual. In a similar way, the concept of the universal worker, so common in talk about work organizations, "excludes and marginalizes women who cannot, almost by definition, achieve the qualities of a real worker because to do so is to become like a man" (Acker 1990: 150).

SUMMARY AND CONCLUSIONS

A gendered organization theory should produce better answers to questions about both the organization of production and the reproduction of organization (Burrell and Hearn 1989). I have suggested one strategy for developing such a theory, starting with an inventory of gendered processes that necessarily include manifestations of sexuality. In any concrete organization, these processes occur in complex interrelations. Gendered processes are often resources in organizational control and transformation. Underlying these processes, and intimately connected to them, is a gendered substructure of organization that links the more surface gender arrangements with the gender relations in other parts of the society. Ostensibly gender neutral, everyday activities of organizing and managing large organizations reproduce the gendered substructure within the organization itself and within the wider society. I think that this is the most important part of the process to comprehend, because it is hidden within abstract, objectifying, textually mediated relations and is difficult to make visible. The fiction of the universal worker obscures the gendered effects of these ostensibly gender-neutral processes and helps to banish gender from theorizing about the fundamental character of complex organizations. Gender, sexuality, reproduction, and emotionality of women are outside organizational boundaries, continually and actively consigned to that social space by ongoing organizational practices. Complex organizations play an important role, therefore, in defining gender and women's disadvantage for the whole society.

What are the practical implications of analyses, such as mine, in which ordinary organizational practices and thinking about those practices are grounded in the prior exclusion of women? The implications are not a return to an imaginary, utopian past where production is small scale and reproduction and production are fully integrated in daily life. Nor are the implications an Orwellian future where sexuality, procreation, and child raising would be integrated in superorganizations where all of life is paternalistically regulated.

Instead, we might think about alternative possibilities, some short term and others long term. Short-term, new strategies to transform parts of large organizations from the inside are possible.[2] One way to do this is to take control of, or at least to influence and use, the textual tools of management. This is what comparable worth activists aim to do, as they attempt to affect the construction and use of job evaluation instruments to increase the value placed on women's jobs. Comparable worth experience shows that this is difficult and time consuming but not impossible (Acker 1989; Blum 1991). Many other practices could be similarly altered, but union organization controlled by women is the essential condition for doing such things. In the meantime, individual women can become experts in using and manipulating organizational texts; superior knowledge of rules and procedures can often facilitate change. . . .

Long-term strategies will have to challenge the privileging of the "economy" over life and raise questions about the rationality of such things as organizational and work commitment . . . as well as the legitimacy of organizations' claims for the priority of their goals over other broader goals. The gendered structure of organizations will only be completely changed with a fundamental reorganization of both production and reproduction. The long term is very long term and impossible to specify, but this should not lead us to abandon the search for other ways of organizing complex collective human activities.

NOTES

1. The following discussion of job evaluation is based on Acker (1989).

2. This has been suggested by Beatrice Halsaa, Hildur Ve, and Cynthia Cockburn, who are proposing an international feminist activist/researcher conference on the topic.

REFERENCES

Acker, J. 1980. "Women and Stratification: A Review of Recent Literature." *Contemporary Sociology* 9:25–34.

———. 1988. "Class, Gender, and the Relations of Distribution." *Signs: Journal of Women in Culture and Society* 13:473–97.

———. 1989. *Doing Comparable Worth: Gender, Class and Pay Equity*. Philadelphia: Temple University Press.

———. 1990. "Hierarchies, Jobs, Bodies: A Theory of Gendered Organizations." *Gender & Society* 4:139–58.

———. 1991. "Thinking About Wages: The Gendered Wage Gap in Swedish Banks." *Gender & Society* 5:390–407.

Acker, J., and D. R. Van Houten. 1974. "Differential Recruitment and Control: The Sex Structuring of Organizations." *Administrative Science Quarterly* 19(2):152–63.

Blum, L. M. 1991. *Between Feminism and Labor: The Significance of the Comparable Worth Movement*. Berkeley: University of California Press.

Burrell, G. 1980. "Radical Organization Theory." In *The International Yearbook of Organization Studies 1979*, edited by D. Dunkerley and G. Salaman. London: Routledge & Kegan Paul.

———. 1984. "Sex and Organizational Analysis." *Organization Studies* 5(2):97–118.

———. 1987. "No Accounting for Sexuality." *Accounting, Organizations, and Society* 12:89–101.

Burrell, G., and J. Hearn. 1989. "The Sexuality of Organization." In *The Sexuality of Organization*, edited by J. Hearn, D. L. Sheppard, P. Tancred-Sheriff, and G. Burrell. London: Sage.

Butler, J. 1990. *Gender Trouble: Feminism and the Subversion of Identity*. New York: Routledge.

Calás M. B., and L. Smircich. 1989a. "Voicing Seduction to Silence Leadership." Paper presented at the Fourth International Conference on Organizational Symbolism and Corporate Culture, Fountainbleau, France.

———. 1989b. "Using the 'F' Word: Feminist Theories and the Social Consequences of Organizational Research." Pp. 355–59. in *Academy of Management Best Papers Proceedings*. Washington, DC: Academy of Management.

———. 1992. "Re-writing Gender into Organization Theorizing: Directions from Feminist Perspectives." In *Re-thinking Organization: New Directions in Organizational Research and Analysis*, edited by M. I. Reed and M. D. Hughes. London: Sage.

Cockburn, C. 1981. "The Material of Male Power." *Feminist Review* 9:51.

———. 1983. *Brothers: Male Dominance and Technological Change*. London: Pluto.

———. 1985. *Machinery of Dominance*. London: Pluto.

———. 1991. *In the Way of Women: Men's Resistance to Sex Equality in Organizations*. Ithaca: ILR Press.

Cohn, S. 1985. *The Process of Occupational Sex-Typing*. Philadelphia: Temple University Press.

Collinson, D. L., and M. Collinson. 1989. "Sexuality in the Workplace: The Domination of Men's Sexuality." In *The Sexuality of Organization*, edited by J. Hearn, D. L. Sheppard, P. Tancred-Sheriff, and G. Burrell, London: Sage.

Connell, R. W. 1987. *Gender and Power*. Standford, CA: Stanford University Press.

Czarniawska-Joerges, B. 1991. "Gender, Power, Organizations: An Interruptive Interpretation." Paper presented at the New Theory in Organizations Conference at Keele, England.

Ferguson, K. E. 1984. *The Feminist Case Against Bureaucracy*. Philadelphia: Temple University Press.

———. 1988. "Knowledge, Politics and Personhood." Presented at the conference, The Feminine in Public Administration and Policy, Washington, DC, May 7.

Fernandez Kelly, M. P., and A. M. Garcia. 1988. "Invisible Amidst the Glitter: Hispanic Women in the Southern California Electronics Industry." In *The Worth of Women's work*, edited by A. Statham, E. M. Miller, and H. O. Mauksch: Albany: SUNY Press.

Flax, J. 1987. "Postmodernism and Gender Relations in Feminist Theory." *Signs: Journal of Women in Culture and Society* 12:621–43.

———. 1990. *Thinking Fragments: Psychoanalysis, Feminism, and Postmodernism in the Contemporary West*. Berkeley: University of California Press.

Foucault, M. 1972. *The Archeology of Knowledge*. New York: Pantheon.

———. 1979. *The History of Sexuality*. Vol. 1. London: Allen Lane.

Hacker, S. L. 1979. "Sex Stratification, Technology and Organizational Change: A Longitudinal Case Study of AT&T." *Social Problems* 26:539–57.

Harding, S. 1986. *The Science Question in Feminism*. Ithaca, NY: Cornell University Press.

Hearn, J., and P. W. Parkin. 1983. "Gender and Organizations: A Selective Review and a Critique of a Neglected Area." *Organization Studies* 4(3):219–42.

———. 1987. *'Sex' at 'Work': The Power and Paradox of Organizational Sexuality*. Brighton: Wheatsheaf.

———. 1991. "Women, Men and Leadership: A Critical Review of Assumptions, Practices and Changes in the Industrialized Nations." In *Women in Management Worldwide*. 2nd ed., edited by N. J. Adler and D. Izraeli. New York: M. E. Sharpe.

Hearn, J., D., Sheppard, P. Tancred-Sheriff, and G. Burrell, eds. 1989. *The Sexuality of Organization*. London: Sage.

Hill-Collins, P. 1989. "The Social Construction of Black Feminist Thought." *Signs: Journal of Women in Culture and Society* 14:745–73.

———. 1990. *Black Feminist Thought: Knowledge, Consciousness, the Politics of Empowerment*. Boston: Unwin Hyman.

International Labour Office. 1986. *Job Evaluation*. Geneva: Author.

Kanter, R. M. 1977a. *Men and Women of the Corporation*. New York: Basic Books.

———. 1977b. "Some Effects of Proportions of Group Life: Skewed Sex-Ratios and Responses to Token Women." *American Journal of Sociology* 82:965–90.

MacKinnon, C. 1979. *Sexual Harassment of Working Women*. New Haven, CT: Yale University Press.

———. 1982. "Feminism, Marxism, Method and the State: An Agenda for Theory." *Signs: Journal of Women in Culture and Society* 7:515–44.

Martin, J. 1988. "The Suppression of Gender Conflict in Organizations: Deconstructing the Fissure Between Public and Private." Paper presented at the Academy of Management Meeting, Anaheim, CA, August.

———. 1990a. "Deconstructing Organizational Taboos: The Suppression of Gender Conflict in Organizations." *Organizational Science* 1:1–21.

———. 1990b. "Re-reading Weber: Searching for Feminist Alternatives to Bureaucracy." Paper presented at the annual meeting of the Academy of Management, San Francisco.

———. 1990c. "Organizational Taboos: The Suppression of Gender Conflict in Organizations." *Organization Science* 1:334–59.

Mills, A. J. 1988a. "Organizational Acculturation and Gender Discrimination." Pp. 1–22 in *Canadian Issues, Vol. 11, Women and the Workplace*, edited by P. K. Kresl. Montreal: Association of Canadian Studies/International Council for Canadian Studies.

———. 1988b. "Organization, Gender and Culture." *Organization Studies* 9(3):351–69.

———. 1989. "Gender, Sexuality and Organization Theory." In *The Sexuality of Organization*, edited by J. Hearn, D. L. Sheppard, P. Tancred-Sheriff, and G. Burrell. London: Sage.

Morgan, G. and D. Knights. 1991. "Gendering Jobs: Corporate Strategy, Managerial Control and the Dynamics of Job Segregation." *Work, Employment & Society* 5:181–200.

Pateman, C. 1981. "The Concept of Equality." In *A Just Society? Essays on Equity in Australia*, edited by P. N. Troy. Sydney: George Allen and Unwin.

———. 1986. "Introduction: The Theoretical Subversiveness of Feminism." In *Feminist Challenges*, edited by C. Pateman and E. Gross. Winchester, MA: Allen & Unwin.

———. 1988. *The Sexual Contract*. Cambridge, MA: Polity.

Pringle, R. 1989. "Bureaucracy, Rationality and Sexuality: The Case of Secretaries." In *The Sexuality of Organization*, edited by J. Hearn, D. L. Sheppard, P. Tancred-Sheriff, and G. Burrell. London: Sage.

Scott, J. 1986. "Gender: A Useful Category of Historical Analysis." *American Historical Review* 91:1053–75.

Smith, D. 1975. "Analysis of Ideological Structures and How Women Are Excluded: Considerations for Academic Women." *Canadian Review of Sociology and Anthropology* 12:353–69.

———. 1977. "Women, the Family and Corporate Capitalism." In *Women in Canada*. Rev. ed., edited by M. Stephenson. Don Mills, Ontario: General Publishing.

———. 1987. *The Everyday World as Problematic: A Feminist Sociology*. Toronto: University of Toronto Press.

———. 1990. *The Conceptual Practices of Power: A Feminist Sociology of Knowledge*. Toronto: University of Toronto Press.

West, C., and D. H. Zimmerman. 1987. "Doing Gender." *Gender & Society* 1: 125–51.

39
Changing Organizational Cultures
Harrison M. Trice & Janice M. Beyer

Because it entails introducing something new and substantially different from what prevails in existing cultures, cultural innovation is bound to be more difficult than cultural maintenance. Managers who want to change existing cultures need to find ways to incorporate new elements into prevalent ideologies and cultural forms. Managers who want to create cultures need to figure out how to develop and inculcate distinctive sets of ideologies and cultural forms that will fit their circumstances and membership. Whether changing or creating cultures, managers inevitably need to replace some of existing ideologies, symbols, and customs with new ones. Even in new organizations, members do not arrive without cultural baggage from their pasts.

The underlying duality of creation and destruction that is required by innovation is often downplayed by those who preach it. But when innovation occurs, some things replace or displace others. . . . People often resist such changes. They have good reasons to. It is realistic for people to expect that any change will bring some losses as well as possible gains. Often the losses are more certain than the gains. The successful management of the processes of culture change or creation thus often entails convincing people that likely gains outweigh the losses. . . .

WAYS OF THINKING ABOUT CULTURE CHANGE

A Definition of Culture Change
Discussing culture change can be very confusing unless we define what we mean by change. . . . Cultures are dynamic entities; they naturally give rise to all kinds of incremental changes. Furthermore, . . . attempts to maintain a culture inevitably involve some adjustments in ideologies and cultural forms that could be considered changes. Neither of these forms of change, however, are what most experts and managers mean when they refer to culture change. Most mean something more deliberate, drastic, and profound than incremental changes or cultural adjustments. We will reserve the term *culture change* to refer to planned, more encompassing, and more substantial kinds of changes than those which arise spontaneously within cultures or as a part of conscious efforts to keep an existing culture vital. Culture change involves a break with the past; cultural continuity is noticeably disrupted. It is an inherently disequilibriating process.

Considering what culture change is not is one way to begin the search for a definition. One observer concluded that ". . . a few examples of new practices here and there throughout an organization do not represent 'culture change';

Source: Trice/Beyer, *The Cultures of Work Organizations,* © 1993, pp. 393–428. Reprinted by permission of Prentice-Hall, Inc., Englewood Cliffs, N.J.

they need to be woven into the entire fabric of the system" (Kanter 1984, p. 196). Thus, culture change amounts to more than a reduction in litter and vandalism, the promotion of executive health, or the turnaround of an unprofitable two-year history. On the positive side, other analysts suggest culture change is marked by

> . . . real changes in the behavior of people throughout the organization. In a technical sense we mean people in the organization identifying with new role-model heroes . . . telling different stories to one another . . . spending their time differently on a day-to-day basis . . . asking different questions and carrying out different work rituals. (Deal and Kennedy 1982, p. 158).

Like the description of culture change that opened this chapter, these analyses make it clear that culture change in organizations is not an easy process; rather it is a difficult, complicated, and demanding effort that may not succeed. It involves not one change, but many changes in many cultural elements so that ". . . *together* [they] reflect a new pattern of values, norms, and expectations" (Kanter 1984, p. 196). Such concerted, widespread changes don't happen spontaneously. Rather they are planned and consciously carried out—usually at the instigation of top management.

Because it involves such wholesale change, culture change is a relatively drawn out and slow process. The popular press during the 1980s seemed to suggest the possibility that new "designer cultures" could be produced quickly. More cautious thinking has challenged such facile promises, but they have not entirely disappeared. Most experts now agree that culture change usually takes several years to accomplish.

Types of Culture Change
Accounts describe at least three different types of culture change efforts in organi-

zations. Some of these efforts seek to bring about massive changes in whole organizations with as much speed as possible. Others are just as radical, but are confined to only parts of an organization. Still others involve many smaller changes that are spread out over years and decades. The descriptions seem to fall into three basic types: (1) revolutionary and comprehensive efforts to change the cultures of entire organizations; (2) efforts confined largely to changing specific subcultures or subunits within organizations; and (3) efforts that are gradual and incremental, but nevertheless cumulate in a comprehensive reshaping of an entire organization's culture. The changes made at the post office in the 1970s . . . exemplify the first type—revolutionary, comprehensive culture change. Efforts that transformed the L-1011 plant at Lockheed, . . . which will be described later in this chapter exemplify the second type—culture change limited to subcultures or subunits. The last type is exemplified by Cadbury, Limited, the British chocolate confectionery company that continuously and self-consciously modified its culture over a period of almost thirty years to fit its changing environment (Child and Smith 1987). . . .

Assessing Amounts of Change
If culture change is viewed as an ongoing process, and not a discrete event or outcome, it becomes easier to disaggregate different aspects of the process. Change processes can be described along four dimensions that help to clarify the amount of change involved in a planned culture change. These dimensions . . . are the pervasiveness, magnitude, innovativeness, and duration of a change process (Beyer and Trice 1978, pp. 18–20). By analyzing an envisioned change in terms of these dimensions, managers will

have a better understanding of the amounts of change they are taking on.

The *pervasiveness* of an envisioned culture change is the proportion of the activities in an organization that will be affected by it. This proportion is determined by at least two factors: how many members are expected to change their cultural understandings and behaviors, and how frequently these changes will call upon them to behave differently in doing their work. . . .

The *magnitude* of a change involves the distance between old understandings and behaviors and the new ones members are expected to adopt. Will organizational members see the new desired ideologies and values as close to ones they already hold or as very different and distant from them? Are some existing ideologies and values now so incompatible with the desired culture that members must stop subscribing to them and put others in their place? In effect, must parts of the existing cultures be destroyed or just displaced somewhat? Looking at the behavioral side, how much replacement or displacement of programs and activities that act as cultural forms is involved? How much will the status quo be disturbed in regard to time allocations, status, power, and other resources?

Innovativeness refers to the degee to which the ideas and behaviors required by a desired culture are unprecedented or have some similarity to what already happened somewhere. If a desired culture is similar to that used by other groups or organizations, managers and members can adapt what others have learned about how such a culture works. In particular, they can perhaps imitate some of the cultural forms that help to communicate and affirm such a culture.[1]

If it is not similar, originality will be required to devise cultural forms with novel content. Also relevant is whether some groups inside the organization already have a subculture similar to the desired culture. If any internal examples exist, managers and other members can learn something from them. But if a totally new and radical culture is envisioned, managers and members must invent new networks of ideologies and values to give it substance. They may also have to invent variations of cultural forms no one has ever tried before. . . .

Duration refers to how long a change effort is likely to take and how permanent the change will be. While all radical organizationwide culture changes take years, some are more protracted than others. We would expect that culture change in organizations with poor performance or rapidly changing environments would proceed more rapidly than that in other organizations. While management usually intends cultural changes to persist over the foreseeable future, some cultures are temporary— either because they deal with temporary circumstances that are clearly recognized as such, or because they grow up in temporary organizations. . . .

Because the four dimensions of change are conceptually distinct, we should not expect any given change to be either high or low on all dimensions. In assessing amounts of culture change, managers will want to especially con-

---

[1] The imitation of Japanese quality circles provides a well-known example of such cultural borrowing. U.S. users did not invent this cultural form; therefore it was not a totally new cultural innovation. However, the first U.S. users of quality circles did confront a more innovative change than later users because the first users had to figure out how to adapt this cultural form to the U.S. culture. The hazards of borrowing cultural forms are also evident from this example. Most observers agree that quality circles have had only modest success in the United States and have not been successfully grafted onto U.S. organizational cultures (Lawler and Mohrman 1987, Shea 1986).

sider the magnitude and innovativeness of a change; together these dimensions indicate how much the envisioned changes represent a break with the past. If magnitude is high and innovativeness is low or medium, managers are facing a culture change effort. If innovativeness is high, managers may need to create a new culture, especially if the change will also be pervasive. This is what General Motors chose to do in founding the Saturn Corporation. Saturn represents GM's attempt to build cars in what is a radically new way for that company and its employees. If both magnitude and innovativeness are low, managers are dealing with cultural maintenance rather than innovation. The pervasiveness of an envisioned change indicates how comprehensive it will be. High pervasiveness indicates that the whole organization must be persuaded to change; low pervasiveness indicates that the change effort can be targeted to certain subunits or groups. Table 1 combines the three types of change discussed in the last section with the four dimensions just discussed. The table shows that different dimensions of change are key indicators of the types of culture change described in the literature. While other combina-

tions of dimensions are possible, these appear to be the most common.

The third type of culture change is the least discontinuous of the three. The culture breaks that occur are numerous, but each is moderate in magnitude. Also, this type of change tends to seek pervasive changes—ones intended to affect virtually all employees to some degree. Because the cultural reshapmg occurs gradually, through many changes that accumulate and are internalized over time, this type of change may be easiest to implement and most enduring.

SPECIFIC CONSIDERATIONS IN CHANGING CULTURES

Capitalize on Propitious Moments

Culture change is best initiated at propitious moments, when some obvious problem, opportunity, or change in circumstances makes change seem desirable. . . . By the time that John Egan and his new management team took over at Jaguar, performance was so poor that another cultural change could be readily justified. Many analyses of all kinds of social changes point to the pres-

TABLE 1 • TYPES AND DIMENSIONS OF CULTURE CHANGE

Types of Culture Change	Placement on Dimensions
1. Revolutionary, comprehensive	Pervasiveness: high Magnitude: high Innovativeness: variable Duration: variable
2. Subunit or subculture	Pervasiveness: low Magnitude: moderate to high Innovativeness: variable Duration: variable
3. Cumulative comprehensive reshaping	Pervasiveness: high Magnitude: moderate Innovativeness: moderate Duration: high

ence of accumulated excesses or deficiencies of the past social order as triggers to cultural revolutions (Lundberg 1985b; Miller and Friesen 1980; Meyer 1982b; Kuhn 1970).

Managers should be cautious not only about whether culture change is appropriate and really needed . . . but also about whether they can persuade members and outside constituents that a culture change is justified. They should not assume that because the need for change seems obvious to them it is obvious to others. Proponents of culture change often need to dramatize the circumstances that call for change to various stakeholders in order to win their support and cooperation. This may require sharing some bad news about the organization that management is reluctant to disclose lest it reflect badly on their performance. Fortunately, any problems that have accumulated can often be blamed on environmental change of some sort (Salancik and Meindl 1984). . . .

Combine Caution with Optimism

Once they have decided to embark on a cultural change effort, managers need to create an optimistic outlook on what the change effort will bring. While cultures are undoubtedly difficult to change (Uttal 1983; Barley and Louis 1983; Beyer 1981; Martin and Siehl 1983), managers must have confidence that they can succeed or they will likely communicate their doubts to others. A thorough understanding of the various leverage points they have available to them should help to create such confidence. It will also help if they realize that cultures inevitably change anyway, and that it is natural for them as managers to attempt to channel and initiate such change (Jones 1984). Consistency and persistence in their efforts is absolutely essential in conveying optimism and confidence.

One way to resolve doubts about whether an organization's culture can be changed is to realize that the truth lies roughly halfway between extreme views on the subject. Recall that some analysts claim it is practically impossible to change cultures deliberately. According to this argument, cultures are too elusive and hidden to be accurately described, managed, or changed (Uttal 1983). Other analyses, however, imply that cultures can be readily manipulated, suggesting that managers can use direct, intentional actions to change their cultures (Peters and Waterman 1982; Deal and Kennedy 1982; Kilmann 1982). A consensus seems to be emerging that the middle ground between these two viewpoints is realistic. Thus, both caution and optimism are warranted. . . .

Understand Resistance to Culture Change

. . . Research on organizational change of all kinds has documented many reasons that people resist change. Table 2 gives a fairly comprehensive listing of common sources of such resistance. All of them may come into play in culture change efforts. . . .

Change Many Elements, But Maintain Some Continuity

One way to honor the past and maintain continuity is to identify the principles that will remain constant "in the midst of turbulence, both internal and external" (Wilkins 1989, p. 56). Hewlett-Packard, for example, has been forced by its growth to develop large corporate structures that require increased coordination between far-flung operations. Despite these changed conditions, HP management has made substantial efforts to continue the "HP way"—an em-

TABLE 2 · COMMON SOURCES OF RESISTANCE TO CHANGE

At *the individual level:*
  Fear of the unknown
  Self-interest
  Selective attention and retention
  Habit
  Dependence
  Need for security
At *the organization or group level:*
  Threats to power and influence
  Lack of trust
  Different perceptions and goals
  Social disruption
  Resource limitations
  Fixed investments
  Interorganizational agreements

SOURCE: Adapted from Hellriegel, Slocum, and Woodman 1986; and Daft and Steers, 1986.

phasis on decentralized operations, autonomous management, and the promotion of employee welfare. By increasing the number of meetings and coordinating efforts among division general managers, HP has been able to maintain division autonomy. "By focusing upon what will remain unchanged, and showing that these commitments will be kept inviolate, the company has apparently been able to significantly improve coordination between divisions" (Wilkins 1989, p. 57). . . .

Of course, changing organizational cultures requires not one change, but many changes in many different cultural elements. In particular, change efforts must encompass both ideologies and the accumulated cultural forms that express them. It is not easy to keep cultural practices and associated meanings consistent with each other and with new ideologies as changes occur. Since ideologies lie at the core of culture, change efforts must be aimed directly at changing "the experiences people have and what they learn from them so that assumptions and core values are altered" (Wilkins and Patterson 1985, p. 289). Detailed studies of cultural change at Jaguar and at a British merchant bank showed that attempts to alter cultures by attending only to cultural beliefs have little success. "Those efforts which are directed towards the essence of . . . values, *as well as* the logics, languages, metaphors or status patterns in which they are embodied promise greater return" (Whipp, Rosenfeld, and Pettigrew 1989, p. 581 [emphasis added]). . . .

Recognize the Importance of Implementation

An informal survey of management consultants found that over 90 percent of American companies have been unable to carry out changes in corporate strategies (Kiechel 1979). This astonishing figure dramatizes the fact that many adopted changes are never successfully implemented. Initial acceptance and enthusiasm are insufficient to carry change forward. Many carefully adopted changes are subsequently abandoned.

Every stage of any change process carries the hazard of omission, abandonment, or return to an earlier stage. A simplified three-stage model of a change process begins with adoption—the decision to make some change. The next stage is implementation—the actions required to put the change in place. The last stage is institutionalization—the persistent incorporation of the change into the daily routines and cultures of the organization (Beyer and Trice 1978). While these stages may overlap, especially in culture change efforts, the model is useful in showing that how thoroughly and well a logically prior stage is executed is likely to affect the next stage. In particular, it suggests that the institutionalization of a culture change effort depends heavily on how well it is implemented. . . .

The kinds of strategies that can be employed to diffuse a cultural innovation are well illustrated by what happened when Blount set out to change the U.S. Post Office (Biggart, 1977). His implementation strategies employed extensive communications and training. Because unhappy mailers frequently complained to members of Congress, the new United States Postal Service (USPS) created a consumer advocate position in an effort to funnel complaints away from Congress. It also established an Office of Advertising to propagate its new image of autonomy from outsiders and from Congress. At the same time, it dispatched top level executives on media tours to hold briefings in all regions of the country. Finally, training of supervisors focused upon learning new businesslike attitudes and unlearning old practices of relating to employees, customers, and work itself. A large training institute was established in Bethesda, Maryland with a 75-member faculty of specialists

in training, development, and technical areas. They trained approximately 20,000 supervisors a year. Also, members of this faculty often went to major post offices and conducted on-site training in decision making directed explicitly at reducing the accumulated emphasis on authoritarianism in the organization.

Despite the many avenues Blount used to implement culture change, critics of the post office see considerable cultural persistence. Many feel the post office has not entirely shed its old ways and that its competitors are still more efficient and businesslike. But it is hard to deny that the post office has changed. What critics see are residues of the old culture. It is unrealistic to expect a complete disappearance of an existing culture without total destruction of the group or organization involved or dispersal of its members. Even then, members will carry much of what they learned in that culture with them as they enter new organizations or join new groups. All culture change is partial; it cannot reasonably be expected to achieve total eradication of a prior culture. Even when envisioned changes are pervasive and of great magnitude, culture change usually amounts to some degree of modification of a culture. Changes that entail innovative responses—unprecedented and genuinely unfamiliar understandings and behaviors—are likely to result in the most radical cultural change.

Select, Modify, and Create Appropriate Cultural Forms

Numerous scholars have suggested that cultural change comes about by managers' employing symbols, rituals, languages, and stories to modify cultural meanings. Some argue that the manipulation of symbols is the "very stuff" of managerial behavior (Peters 1978, p. 10; Schein 1985). The actions of managers can also symbolically legitimate changes in the culture (Pfeffer 1981a; Jones 1984). Their calendar and phone behavior, the apportionment of their time, and their control of settings are powerful symbolic tools managers can use to change organizational cultures. The presence or absence of top managers, the location of meetings, who attends, what types of questions managers ask—all of these act as "mundane tools" that can be consciously "packaged and managed" (Peters 1978, p. 10). Other scholars advise that managers should "be seen as spending a lot of time on matters visibly related to the values they preach" (Deal and Kennedy 1982, p. 169).

Metaphors can also be effective vehicles for change (Krefting and Frost 1985, p. 155). By changing or eliminating long-standing metaphors that depict an old organizational ideology, a culture can be moved toward change. For example, the elimination of the family metaphor "Ma Bell" signaled that AT&T was modifying its protective ideology relative to employees and customers. A new symbol was chosen for the new culture—a globe girdled by electronic communications. Long-standing metaphors can be hard to eradicate, however. As pointed out earlier, the press still regularly refers to the regional companies spun off from AT&T more than ten years ago as Baby Bells.

Devising and promulgating new myths has also been advocated as a particularly effective way to change cultures (Boje, Fedor, and Rowland 1982). Through myths, managers can invent new explanations for the way things are. They can also change existing myths in various ways (Hedberg 1981, p. 12). Ruling myths can be undermined when the actions they support fail to materialize. New leaders and new political coalitions can then discredit old myths as the doubts about them spread. Also, competing myths from outside the organization can be introduced to challenge the old myths.

Although rites and ceremonials can also act as levers for change (Moore and Myerhoff 1977), change is clearly not their usual purpose. They usually maintain and celebrate current, traditional ideologies (Trice and Beyer 1985). For this reason it seems unrealistic to expect that rites composed entirely of forms that express new ideologies will seem appropriate and appealing to members of a culture. Instead, new messages can be combined with accepted, ongoing cultural elements. Either existing rites can be modified to incorporate new values, or entirely new rites that consciously combine elements of the old and the new can be established. . . .

While rites of passage are usually used to maintain the continuity of cultures, there is no inherent reason why they cannot be used to instill new ideologies and values. . . .

Other possibilities for resocializing members include rites of passage to mark any changes of status of existing members and rites of enhancement that reward those behaviors most in accord with desired ideologies. The latter are likely to be most effective when they reinforce behaviors already instilled in some employees through rites of passage. Of course, all of the other culture forms can also be used to support and facilitate cultural change. Uniforms can be changed, new jargon created, new stories circulated, new songs written, and so on. Readers have probably seen some of these uses and can readily think of ideas for others.

In general, it seems that establishing rites of creation and transition, and new rites of passage and enhancement for individuals may be the best way to begin cultural change efforts. Both newcomers and current employees can learn about and be indoctrinated into new understandings with demanding training that readies members for the changes that will be required.

Rites of degradation logically complete this cluster of rites, but probably should ordinarily not follow until members have had a chance to learn the new expectations. Even when a jolt would be desirable to signal that quick change is imperative, and rites of degradation look like a logical starting point, early use may make members of the organization feel that those degraded are being treated unfairly. If firings must take place, it may be better to delay and then gloss over them as quickly as possible (Gooding 1972) while getting on to positive celebrations of new culture. . . .

Modify Socialization Tactics

Because the primary way that people learn their cultures is through the socialization processes they experience (Van Maanen 1973), if these processes are changed, an organization's cultures will begin to change. We have already discussed the crucial role that cultural forms, especially rites, play in socializing new members and resocializing old ones during a planned culture change. Rites of passage are, of course, the cultural form most directly aimed at socializing people into new roles. One reason that they tend to function to ensure cultural continuity rather than change is that they are often structured as institutionalized tactics, which tend to produce custodial role orientations. In work organizations, rites of passage often consist of collective, formal training of a fixed duration that prepares a group of recruits for one of a sequence of established statuses. They may also employ experienced members of the culture to communicate expectations and provide role models, and often endeavor to divest recruits of past identities. It is easy to see how socialization structured in this way is likely to produce cultural continuity.

However, it is far from clear that changing all of these tactics is advisable to further planned culture change. More individualized tactics may produce more innovative role orientations by individual members but are too random and dissimilar in their effects across individuals to be very helpful in instilling desired cultural beliefs and values uniformly throughout an organization. Rather, persons who experience individualized tactics are freer to develop their own ideas about how to carry out their roles. If management already has a set of new cultural ideologies, values, and norms it wishes to instill throughout an organization, some of the institutionalized tactics are still appropriate because a relatively uniform response to socialization is desirable. Collective and formal tactics of a fixed duration can be used to impart new cultural substance in addition to those elements of the old culture that are desirable to retain. . . .

Although we have focused on the socialization of newcomers, most of the considerations discussed also apply to socialization of present members for new roles and responsibilities or their general resocialization into a desired new culture. Members cannot be expected to change their convictions without some organized presentation and discussion of the new ideas they are expected to internalize. General resocialization efforts usually begin at the top levels of large organizations and work downwards, for it seems unrealistic to expect lower level managers and employees to subscribe to values different from those evidenced by their superiors' behaviors and decisions.

Find and Cultivate Innovative Leadership

Probably the most important quality of an innovative cultural leader is that he or she be able to convince members of the organization to follow new visions. "Members are unlikely to give up whatever security they derive from existing cultures and follow a leader in new directions unless that leader exudes self-confidence, has strong convictions, a dominant personality, and can preach the new vision with drama and eloquence" (Trice and Beyer 1991, p. 163). . . .

Managers who seek to change an existing culture often have to find ways to discredit and destroy parts of the old culture. One way to do so is to remove prominent persons representing those aspects of the old culture. Their removal has both symbolic and practical consequences. It communicates to other members that certain values and beliefs are no longer acceptable. It also typically eliminates powerful persons who might generate resistance to the new culture. As already mentioned, there are some dangers, however, that firing prominent members of the old culture may cause widespread resentment. Some new CEOs, like Blount in the U.S. Postal Service, used incentives to persuade old-guard members to retire. Others force out those who oppose their managerial ideologies with rites of degradation. They assemble evidence to discredit those they want to dismiss, make it public, and then fire them. . . .

SUMMARY

Cultural innovation involves the duality of creation and destruction. Whether old cultures are being changed or new cultures are being created in new organizations, members will need to replace or displace ideologies and customary behaviors they bring from past roles and experiences in different cultures. There is, however, a range of degrees of creation and destruction—of displacements and innovations—involved in what people caught up in them experience as "changes." Because cultures inevitably change incrementally and people within them adjust their behaviors and beliefs in various ways, discussing cultural innovation and change can be confusing if we do not draw a line somewhere to separate substantial changes from minor fluctuations and adjustments. Also, managers need to be clear about which they are attempting because substantial change and minor adjustments in cultures involve different issues and require different behaviors.

Culture change involves a noticeable break with the past; it also inevitably involves changes in both ideologies and cultural forms. Three types of cultural change have been identified: (1) relatively fast, revolutionary, comprehensive change; (2) subunit or subcultural change; and (3) a more gradual cumulative but comprehensive reshaping of a culture. Each of these types has a characteristic pattern along four dimensions of change processes: pervasiveness, magnitude, innovativeness, and duration. . . .

REFERENCES

Barley Stephen R., and Meryl Louis (1983). Many in one: Organizations as multicultural entities. Paper presented at the annual meeting of the Academy of Management, August 14–17, Dallas, Tex.

Beyer, Janice M. (1981). Ideologies, values and decison-making in organizations. Pp. 166–97 in Nystrom, Paul, and William H. Starbuck (eds.) *Handbook of Organizational Design*, vol. 2. London: Oxford University Press.

Beyer, Janice M., and Harrison M. Trice (1978). *Implementing Change: Alcoholism Programs in Work Organizations*. New York: Free Press.

Biggart, Nicole W. (1977). The creative-destructive process of organizational change: The case of the post office. *Administrative Science Quarterly*, 22: 410–26.

Boje, David M., Donald B. Fedor, and Kendrith M. Rowland (1982). Mythmaking: A qualitative step in OD interventions. *Journal of Applied Behavioral Science*, 18: 17–28.

Child, John, and Chris Smith (1987). The context and process of organizational transformation—Cadbury Limited in its sector. *Journal of Management Studies*, 24(November): 565–93.

Daft, Richard L., and Richard M. Steers (1986). *Organizations: A Micro/Macro Approach*. Glenview, Ill.: Scott, Foresman.

Deal, Terrence E., and Allan A. Kennedy (1982). *Corporate Cultures: The Rites and Rituals of Corporate Life*. Reading, Mass.: Addison-Wesley.

Gooding, Judson (1972). The art of firing an executive. *Fortune*, October, Pp. 22–30.

Hedberg, Bo (1981). How organizations learn and unlearn. Pp. 3–27 in Nystrom, Paul C., and William H. Starbuck (eds.) *Handbook of Organizational Design*. London: Oxford University Press.

Hellriegel, Don, John W. Slocum, Jr., and Richard W. Woodman (1986). *Organizational Behavior*, 4th ed. New York: West Publishing Co.

Jones, Michael O. (1984). Corporate natives confer on culture. *The American Folklore Society Newsletter*, 13(October): 6, 8.

Kanter, Rosabeth M. (1984). Managing transitions in organizational culture: The case of participative management at Honeywell. Pp. 195–217 in Kimberly, John R., and Robert Quinn (eds.) *New Futures: The Challenges of Managing Corporate Transitions*. Homewood, Ill.: Dow Jones-Irwin.

Kiechel, Walter (1979). Playing the rules of the corporate strategy game. *Fortune*, September, 24, Pp. 110–15.

Kilmann, Ralph H. (1982). Getting control of the corporate culture. *Managing*, 3: 11–17.

Krefting, Linda A., and Peter J. Frost (1985). Untangling webs, surfing waves, and wildcatting: A multiple-metaphor perspective on

managing organizational cultures. Pp. 155–68 in Frost, Pester, et al. (eds.) *Organizational Culture*. Beverly Hills, Calif.: Sage Publications, Inc.

Kuhn, Thomas (1970). *The Structure of Scientific Revolutions*. Chicago: University of Chicago Press.

Lawler, Edward E., and Susan A. Mohrman (1987). Quality circles: After the honeymoon. *Organizational Dynamics*, 15(Spring): 42–54.

Lundberg, Craig C. (1985b). How should organizational culture be studied? Pp. 197–200 in Frost, Peter J., et al. (eds.) *Organizational Culture*. Beverly Hills, Calif.: Sage Publications, Inc.

Martin, Joanne, and Caren Siehl (1983). Organizational culture and counterculture: An uneasy symbiosis. *Organizational Dynamics*, 12(2): 52–65.

Meyer, Alan D. (1982b). How ideologies supplant formal structures and shape responses to environments. *Journal of Management Studies*, 19(1): 45–61.

Miller, Danny and Peter H. Friesen (1980). Momentum and revolution in organizational adaptation. *Academy of Management Journal*, 23(4): 591–614.

Moore, Sally F., and Barbara G. Myerhoff (1977). Secular ritual: Forms and Meaning. Pp. 3–25 in Moore, Sally F., and Barbara G. Myerhoff (eds.) *Secular Ritual*. Assen, Amsterdam, The Netherlands: Van Gorcum.

Peters, Thomas J. (1978). Symbols, patterns, and settings. *Organizational Dynamics*, 7: 3–23.

Peters, Thomas J., and Robert H. Waterman (1982). *In Search of Excellence: Lessons from America's Best Run Companies*. New York: Harper & Row, Pub.

Pfeffer, Jeffrey (1977). The ambiguity of leadership. *Academy of Management Review*, 2(1): 104–12.

——— (1981a). Management as symbolic action: The creation and maintenance of organizational paradigms. *Research in Organizational Behavior*, 3: 1–52.

Salancik, Gerald R., and J. R. Meindl (1984). Corporate attributions as strategic illusions of management control. *Administrative Science Quarterly*, 29: 238–54.

Schein, Edgar H. (1985). *Organizational Culture and Leadership*. San Francisco: Jossey-Bass.

Shea, Gregory P. (1986). Quality circles: The danger of bottled change. *Sloan Management Review*, Spring: 33–46.

Trice, Harrison M., and Janice M. Beyer (1985). Using six organizational rites to change cultures. Pp. 370–99 in Kilmann, Ralph H., Mary J. Saxton, and Roy Serpa (eds.) *Gaining Control of the Corporate Culture*. San Francisco: Jossey-Bass Publishers.

——— (1991). Cultural leadership in organizations. *Organization Science*, 2(2): 149–69.

Uttal, Bro (1983). The corporate culture vultures. *Fortune*, October, 17, Pp. 66–72.

Van Maanen, John (1973). Observations on the making of policemen. *Human Organization*, 32(Winter): 407–17.

Whipp, Richard, Robert Rosenfeld, and Andrew Pettigrew (1989). Culture and Competitiveness: Evidence from two mature U.K. Industries. *Journal of Management Studies*, 26(November): 561–85.

Wilkins, Alan L. (1989). *Developing Corporate Character: How to Successfully Change an Organization without Destroying It*. San Francisco: Jossey-Bass.

Wilkins, Alan L., and Kerry J. Patterson (1985). You can't get there from here: What will make culture-change projects fail. Pp. 262–91 in Kilmann, Ralph H., and Associates (eds.) *Gaining Control of the Corporate Culture*. San Francisco: Jossey-Bass.

CHAPTER VIII

The Organizational Culture Reform Movements

This chapter is a concession to readers and reviewers who have repeatedly asked us to include articles that are representative of the current trends in management and organization. The "reform movements" that are represented here share a common theme—the centrality of organizational culture. Organizational cultures that reflect the values of bigness, hierarchy, rigidity, and rules must be replaced with cultures in which flexibility, responsiveness, individual and group empowerment, and customer service are valued.

THE CONTEXT

These organizational culture reform movements of the 1980s and early 1990s share two features: (1) their origination out of the fear that accompanied widespread realization in the late 1970s that U.S. companies had lost their competitiveness, and (2) their commitment to increasing organizational effectiveness, competitiveness, flexibility, and responsiveness by changing organizational cultures. "Command-and-control" cultures must be replaced with cultures that encourage and support widespread use of employee participation and empowerment approaches, individually and in work teams.

The recognition that American industry was losing—or had already lost—its competitiveness (and the fear that accompanied the realization) began late in the decade of the 1970s as globalism became a reality. Where once U.S. firms had competed mostly with each other, they now were forced to compete in global markets against worthy competitors. The competitive marketplace had become a worldwide economic playing field on which all competitors were not bound by the same rules. Of equal concern, however, was the mounting evidence that U.S. productivity was not increasing and in some industries was actually decreasing.

Declining productivity in the U.S. coincided with noticeable productivity gains in many industrialized nations, particularly in Japan but also in West Germany and France. Overwhelming evidence pointed to the loss of U.S. position in the global marketplace. By the late 1980s, fifty-three of the top one hundred corporations in the world were Japanese. Japan had become the largest creditor nation in the world, while the U.S. was the largest debtor nation. "The rate of growth in U.S. productivity from 1973 to 1986 ranked last among developed nations, growing at a mere 0.49 in gross domestic product per employee. In the same period of time, Japan's growth was six times as fast" (Lindsay, Curtis & Manning, 1989, p. 80).

Thus the problem for U.S. industries was twofold. The decline in the U.S. competitive position resulted from an absolute failure to increase productivity as well as an even larger relative decline in comparison with other industrialized nations (Ingle, 1987). The U.S. faced a competitiveness crisis, and the general public was becoming aware that unless the current trend was reversed, it could result in a lower standard of living for all Americans (American Productivity & Quality Center, 1988).

THE ORIGINS OF THE CULTURE REFORM MOVEMENTS

Although the organizational culture reform movements have taken different shapes, jargon, and directions in the 1980s and 1990s, the origins of all of them can be traced back to Dr. W. Edwards Deming's 1950 invited trip to Japan. Deming succeeded in convincing a number of Japanese executives to adopt his approach to statistical quality control. Joseph Juran, who emphasizes the "management" part of "quality," followed Deming to Japan in 1954. In turn, Val Feigenbaum followed Juran with "total quality control" (TQC), a management approach that required all employees to participate in quality improvement activities—from the chair of the board to hourly workers, from suppliers to customers, and the community.

By 1975, Japan had developed into the world leader in quality and productivity. In contrast, "quality teachings" were mostly ignored in the U.S. "Deming's popularity in Japan was in contrast to an almost total ignorance about him in the United States. . . . Deming remained in the quality wilderness of America for a whole generation" (Bhote, 1994, p. 156).

The specific event that triggered the "total quality movement" in the United States was a June 24, 1980, NBC television documentary, "If Japan Can . . . Why Can't We?" The program documented Deming's experience and successes in Japan. The response was overwhelming. Within months, hundreds of major U.S. corporations and government agencies had scrambled aboard the quality bandwagon (Al-Khalaf, 1994). Quality circles—voluntary work groups that cut across organizational layers and boundaries to analyze and recommend solutions to organizational problems—appeared everywhere as if by magic.

THE CULTURE REFORM MOVEMENTS

The most important of the organizational culture reform movements that followed the early work by Deming, Juran, and Feigenbaum with Japanese industries and the NBC documentary, include:

- Total Quality Management (TQM): (Crosby, 1979, 1984; Deming, 1986, 1993; Joiner, 1994; Juran, 1992; Walton, 1986);
- Japanese Management: (Ouchi, 1981; Pascale & Athos, 1981);
- The Search for Excellence: (Peters & Waterman, 1982; Peters, 1987);

- Socio-technical Systems or Quality of Work Life (QWL): (Weisbord, 1991);
- Learning Organizations: (Senge, 1990);
- Reinventing Government: (Gore, 1993; Osborne & Gaebler, 1992); and
- Reengineering, Process Reengineering, or Business Reengineering: (Hammer & Champy, 1993).

Virtually all of these reform movements have sought to increase organizational productivity, flexibility, responsiveness, and customer service by re-shaping organizational cultures (see Chapter VII). Most—but not all of them—advocate the empowerment of individual employees and work groups. Employees and work teams are granted autonomy and discretion to make decisions. Work teams coordinate tasks and discipline their own members. Policies, procedures, and layers of hierarchy are eliminated. Accountability to bosses is replaced by accountability to customers or clients. Data-based information systems provide the information needed to coordinate and correct actions in real time (see Chapter IX.). Levels of middle managers and supervisors are eliminated because they are not needed, do not add value, cost too much, and get in the way of empowered workers.

Four of the most important and popular examples of the culture reform movement's literature are included in this chapter: William Ouchi's "The Z Organization," Peters and Waterman's *In Search of Excellence*, Peter Senge's *The Fifth Discipline*, and Osborne & Gaebler's *Reinventing Government*. In addition, a selection from Hammer and Champy's 1993 book, *Reengineering the Corporation*, is reproduced in Chapter IX, "Postmodernism and the Information Age." And, for the most inquisitive, excerpts from Weisbord's "socio-technical systems" are included in the second edition of Steven Ott's companion to this volume, *Classic Readings in Organizational Behavior* (1996).

We start our exploration of the substance of the reform movements, though, with the "driving force"—W. Edwards Deming's Total Quality Management

Total Quality Management (TQM)

In 1991, the United States Government Accounting Office defined "quality management" as:

> A leadership philosophy that demands a relentless pursuit of quality and the stamina for continuous improvement in all aspects of operations: product, service, processes, and communications. The major components of quality management are leadership, a customer focus, continuous improvement, employee empowerment, and management by fact (pp. 41–42).

For most people who are familiar with TQM, though, Deming's now-famous 14 points of management represent its essence. Thus, instead of reproducing an article here by Deming, we introduce Deming's "theory of TQM" by listing and elaborating briefly on his 14 points of management (Al-Khalaf, 1994. Adapted from Deming, 1986, pp. 24–92).

1. *Create constancy of purpose for improvement of product and service.* If organizations are to survive, they must allocate resources for long-term planning research and education, and for the constant improvement of the design of their products and services.

2. *Adopt the new philosophy.* Government regulations that represent obstacles to competitiveness must be revised. Transformation of companies is needed.

3. *Cease dependence on mass inspections.* Quality needs to be designed and built into the processes to prevent defects rather than attempting to detect them after they have occurred.

4. *End the practice of awarding business on the basis of price tag alone.* Lowest bids lead to low quality. Organizations should establish long-term relationships with single suppliers.

5. *Improve constantly and forever the system of production and service.* Management and employees must search continuously for ways to improve quality and productivity.

6. *Institute training.* Training at all organizational levels is a necessity, not an option.

7. *Adopt and institute leadership.* Management's job is to lead, not to supervise. Leaders should eliminate barriers that prevent people from doing the job well and from learning new methods.

8. *Drive out fear.* Unless employees feel secure enough to express ideas and ask questions, they will do things the wrong way or not do them at all.

9. *Break down barriers between staff areas.* Working in teams will solve problems and thus improve quality and productivity.

10. *Eliminate slogans, exhortations, and targets for the work force.* Problems with quality and productivity are caused by the *system*—not by individuals. Posters and slogans generate frustration and resentment.

11. *Eliminate numerical quotas for the work force and numerical goals for people in management.* In order to meet quotas, people produce defective products. Instead, management must take decisive steps to replace work standards, rates, and piece work with intelligent leadership.

12. *Remove barriers that rob people of pride of workmanship.* Deming views individual performance appraisals as one of the greatest of the barriers to pride of achievement.

13. *Encourage education and self-improvement for everyone.* Education should never end, for people at all levels of the organization.

14. *Take action to accomplish the transformation.* Top management and employee commitment is required

Japanese Management

The titles of the "Japanese Management" movement's two best-selling books reflect the fears of declining competitiveness and the economic challenge from the Pacific

Rim: *Theory Z: How American Business Can Meet the Japanese Challenge* (Ouchi, 1981), and *The Art of Japanese Management: Applications for American Executives* (Pascale and Athos, 1981).

In 1980, William Ouchi turned his attention to a key practical question: Could Japanese management methods (as introduced by Deming and Juran) be utilized in the United States? At the time, most scholars and businessmen were convinced that they could not. The differences between the cultures of Japan and the United States were too great. Ouchi's "objective became to separate the culturally specific principles from those universally applicable to economic organizations" (1981, p. viii). Ouchi began from the premise that organizations are social beings. "The Z Organization," which is reprinted in this chapter, describes the style and substance of companies that have achieved a high state of consistency in their organizational cultures. "In the sense that Z organizations are more like clans than markets or bureaucracies, they foster close interchange between work and social life." While acknowledging the differences between the United States and Japan, Ouchi contends that "social organizations are incompatible with formality, distance, and contractualism. They proceed smoothly only with intimacy, subtlety, and trust."

The Search for Excellence

Tom Peters and Bob Waterman—like Bill Ouchi—were driven by the twin swords of declining American corporate productivity and the rising overall excellence of Japanese companies, products, services, and quality. These quotations from *In Search of Excellence: Lessons from America's Best-Run Companies* reflect their concern with Japan but also their optimism that the U.S. could compete with Japanese corporations:

> There is good news from America. Good management practice today is not resident only in Japan (p. xxiii).

> Finally, it dawned on us that we did not have to look all the way to Japan for models with which to attack the corporate malaise that has us in its viselike grip (p. xx).

> What really fascinated us as we began to pursue our survey of corporate excellence was that. . . . these [excellent U.S.] companies had cultures as strong as any Japanese organization (pp. xix, xx).

While Deming built his quality movement on 14 points of management, the foundations of the Peters and Waterman movement are "eight attributes of management excellence";

- A Bias for Action
- Close to the Customer
- Autonomy and Entrepreneurship
- Productivity Through People
- Hands-On, Value-Driven
- Stick to the Knitting

- Simple Form, Lean Staff
- Simultaneous Loose-Tight Properties

Peters and Waterman describe "Simultaneous Loose-Tight Properties" (a chapter from *In Search of Excellence* that is reprinted here) as a summary point of the other seven. "It is in essence the co-existence of firm central direction and maximum individual autonomy. . . . Organizations that live by the loose-tight principle are on the one hand rigidly controlled, yet at the same time allow (indeed, insist on) autonomy, entrepreneurship, and innovation from the rank and file." The "auras" of Deming, TQM, and Ouchi are readily evident in this reading, but the approach and style of Peters and Waterman are uniquely their own. Their message to managers (Tom Peters' in particular) remains a powerful force in the 1990s.

Learning Organizations

Peter Senge's 1990 book, *The Fifth Discipline*, has rivaled *In Search of Excellence* in influence with management practitioners and academicians alike. For Senge, change *is* learning, and learning *is* change—for people and organizations. Thus, it is possible for organizations to learn to change because "deep down, we are all learners." Senge's purpose in *The Fifth Discipline* is "to destroy the illusion that the world is created of separate, unrelated forces. When we give up this illusion—we can then build 'learning organizations,' organizations where people continually expand their capacity to create the results they truly desire, where new and expansive patterns of thinking are nurtured, where collective aspiration is set free, and where people are continually learning how to learn together" (Senge, 1990, p. 3). To do so, managers must learn to detect seven organizational "learning disabilities" and how to use five "disciplines" as antidotes to them.

In a chapter from *The Fifth Discipline*, "A Shift of Mind," (reprinted here), Senge argues that five new "component technologies" are gradually converging that will collectively permit the emergence of learning organizations. He labels these component technologies the "five disciplines":

- *systems thinking*—"systems" of the variety described by Douglas Kiel and William Bergquist (see Chapter IX)
- *personal mastery*—people approaching life and work "as an artist would approach a work of art" (p. 7)
- *mental models*—deeply ingrained assumptions or mental images "that influence how we understand the world and how we take action" (p. 8)
- *building shared vision*—"when there is a genuine vision . . . people excel and learn, not because they are told to, but because they want to" (p. 9)
- *team learning*—team members engaging in true dialogue with their assumptions suspended

A true learning organization employs all five of the disciplines in a never-ending quest to expand its capacity to create its future. "Systems thinking" is the fifth discipline—the integrative discipline that fuses the others into a coherent body of theory and practice. Learning organizations are organizations that are able to move past mere survival learning to engage in generative learning—"learning that enhances our capacity to create" (p. 14).

Reinventing Government

Whereas Ouchi, Peters and Waterman, and Senge focused on private industry, David Osborne and Ted Gaebler elected to take on the public bureaucracy in *Reinventing government: How the entrepreneurial spirit is transforming the public sector* (1992). Their concept is straightforward. Governments that are tall, sluggish, over-centralized, and preoccupied with rules and regulations don't work well. We designed public agencies to protect against politicians and bureaucrats gaining too much power or misusing public money. "In making it difficult to steal the public's money, we made it virtually impossible to *manage* the public's money. . . . In attempting to control virtually everything, we became so obsessed with dictating *how* things should be done—regulating the process, controlling the inputs—that we ignored the outcomes, the *results*." Osborne and Gaebler argue for the emergence of "entrepreneurial government," government that can—and must—compete with for-profit businesses, nonprofit agencies, and other units of government. "We must turn bureaucratic institutions into entrepreneurial institutions, ready to kill off obsolete initiatives, willing to do more with less, eager to absorb new ideas."

It seems as though all of the culture reform movements of the 1980s and 1990s have their lists of essential points. Osborne and Gaebler list 10 "principles" of reinvention:

1. *Catalytic Government:* Steering Rather Than Rowing
2. *Community-Owned Government:* Empowering Rather Than Serving
3. *Competitive Government:* Injecting Competition into Service Delivery
4. *Mission-Driven Government:* Transforming Rule-Driven Organizations
5. *Results-Oriented Government:* Funding Outcomes, Not Inputs
6. *Customer-Driven Government:* Meeting the Needs of the Customer, Not the Bureaucracy
7. *Enterprising Government:* Earning Rather Than Spending
8. *Anticipatory Government:* Prevention Rather Than Cure
9. *Decentralized Government:* From Hierarchy to Participation and Teamwork
10. *Market-Oriented Government:* Leveraging Change Through the Market

Osborne and Gaebler—and the culture reform movements more generally—are having a pronounced and visible effect on national, state, and local governments. On September 7, 1993, Vice President Al Gore and the National Performance Review released a report that had taken six months of study: "From Red Tape to Results: Creating a Government That Works Better and Costs Less." It is better known as *The Gore Report on Reinventing Government*. Thus, the organizational culture reform movement is the intellectual force that undergirds current efforts to transform the federal government.

Reengineering

The "message" of reengineering is that all large organizations must undertake a radical reinvention of what they do, how they do it, and how they are structured. There is no room for incremental improvement—for small and cautious steps. Organizations need to quit asking, "how can we do things faster?" or "how can we do our current work at the lowest cost?" The question needs to be, "why do we do what we do—at all?" In *Reengineering the Corporation* (1993), Michael Hammer and James Champy claim that business reengineering "is to the next revolution of business what the specialization of labor was to the last" (p. 2). It is the process of asking: "If I were re-creating this company today, given what I know and given current technology, what would it look like?" (p. 31). More formally, reengineering is "the fundamental rethinking and radical redesign of business processes to achieve dramatic improvements in critical, contemporary measures of performance, such as cost, quality, service, and speed" (p. 32). Thus, reengineering is the search for new models for organizing work: it is a new beginning that requires a cultural reform (see "The Enabling Role of Information Technology," by Hammer and Champy, in Chapter IX).

REFERENCES

Al-Khalaf, A. (1994). *Factors that affect the success and failure of TQM implementation in small U.S. cities.* Doctoral dissertation, Graduate School of Public and International Affairs, University of Pittsburgh: University Microfilms.

American Productivity & Quality Center. (1988). Results of a national survey: American people aware of competitiveness problem. *The Letter, APQC, 8* (September), 1–9.

Bhote, K. R. (Spring 1994). Dr. W. Edwards Deming: A prophet with belated honor in his own country. *National Productivity Review, 13,* 153–159.

Crosby, P. B. (1979). *Quality is free.* New York: McGraw-Hill.

Crosby, P. B. (1984). *Quality without tears.* New York: McGraw-Hill.

Deming, W. E. (1986). *Out of the crisis.* Cambridge, MA: MIT Press.

Deming, W. E. (1993). *The new economics.* Cambridge, MA: MIT Press.

Gore, A. (1993). *The Gore report on reinventing government.* New York: Times Books.

Hammer, M. & Champy, J. (1993). *Reengineering the corporation.* New York: Harper-Business.

Ingle, S. (1987). Training. *The Journal for Quality and Participation, 10* (December), 4–6.

Joiner, B. L. (1994). *Fourth generation management.* New York: McGraw-Hill.

Juran, J. M. (1992). *Juran on quality by design.* New York: Free Press.

Lindsay, W. M., Curtis, R. K., & Manning, G. E. (1989). A participative management primer. *The Journal for Quality and Participation, 12* (June), 78–84.

Mroczkowski, T. (1984/1985). Productivity and quality improvement at GE's Video Products Division: The cultural change component. *National Productivity Review, 4* (Winter), 15–23.

Nadler, D. A., Gerstein, M. S., & Shaw, R. B. (Eds.) (1992). *Organizational architecture: Designs for changing organizations*. San Francisco: Jossey-Bass.

Osborne D., & Gaebler, T. (1992). *Reinventing government*. Reading, MA: Addison-Wesley.

Ott, J. S. (Ed.). (1996). *Classic readings in organizational behavior* (2d. ed.). Belmont, CA: Wadsworth.

Ouchi, W. G. (1981). *Theory Z: How American business can meet the Japanese challenge*. Reading, MA: Addison-Wesley.

Pascale, R. T., & Athos, Anthony G. (1981). *The art of Japanese management*. New York: Simon & Schuster.

Peters, T. J. (1987). *Thriving on chaos*. New York: Knopf.

Peters, T. J., & Waterman, R. H., Jr. (1982). *In search of excellence: Lessons from America's best-run companies*. New York: Harper & Row.

Senge, P. M. (1990). *The fifth discipline: The art and practice of the learning organization*. New York: Doubleday Currency.

U. S. General Accounting Office (GAO). (1991). *Management practices: U. S. companies improve performance through quality efforts*. Washington, DC, GAO/OCG-94-1.

Walton, M. (1986). *The Deming management method*. New York: Putnam.

Weisbord, M. R. (1991). *Productive workplaces: Organizing and managing for dignity, meaning, and community*. San Francisco: Jossey-Bass.

40
The Z Organization
William G. Ouchi

Each Type Z company has its own distinctiveness—the United States military has a flavor quite different from IBM or Eastman Kodak. Yet all display features that strongly resemble Japanese firms. Like their Japanese counterparts, Type Z companies tend to have long-term employment, often for a lifetime, although the lifetime relationship is not formally stated. The long-term relationship often stems from the intricate nature of the business; commonly, it requires lots of learning-by-doing. Companies, therefore, want to retain employees, having invested in their training to perform well in that one unique setting. Employees tend to stay with the company, since many of their skills are specific to that one firm with the result that they could not readily find equally remunerative nor challenging work elsewhere. These task characteristics that produce the life-long employment relationship also produce a relatively slow process of evaluation and promotion. Here we observe one important adaptation of the Japanese form. Type Z companies do not wait ten years to evaluate and promote: any Western firm that did so would not retain many of its talented employees. Thus such firms frequently provide the sorts of explicit performance interviews that are commonplace. However, promotions are slower in coming. . . .

Career paths in Type Z companies display much of the "wandering around" across functions and offices that typifies the Japanese firm. This effectively produces more company-specific skills that work toward intimate coordination between steps in the design, manufacturing, and distribution process. An employee who engages in such "non-professional" development takes the risk that the end skills will be largely non-marketable to other companies. Therefore, long-term employment ties into career development in a critical way.

Typically Type Z companies are replete with the paraphernalia of modern information and accounting systems, formal planning, management by objectives, and all of the other formal, explicit mechanisms of control. . . . Yet in Z companies these mechanisms are tended to carefully for their information, but rarely dominate in major decisions. By contrast, managers in big companies, hospitals, and government agencies often complain about feeling powerless to exercise their judgement in the face of quantitative analysis, computer models, and numbers, numbers, numbers. Western management seems to be characterized for the most part by an ethos which roughly runs as follows: rational is better than non-rational, objective is more nearly rational than subjective, quantitative is more objective than non-quantitative, and thus quantitative analysis is preferred over judgements based on wisdom, experience, and subtlety. Some observers, such as Professor Harold

Source: William G. Ouchi, *Theory Z: How American Business Can Meet the Japanese Challenge*, pp. 71–94. © 1981 by Addison-Wesley Publishing Company, Inc. Reprinted by permission of the publisher.

Leavitt of Stanford University, have written that the penchant for the explicit and the measurable has gone well beyond reasonable limits, and that a return to the subtle and the subjective is in order.[1]

In a Type Z company, the explicit and the implicit seem to exist in a state of balance. While decisions weigh the complete analysis of facts, they are also shaped by serious attention to questions of whether or not this decision is "suitable," whether it "fits" the company. A company that isolates sub-specialities is hardly capable of achieving such fine-grained forms of understanding. Perhaps the underlying cause is the loss of the ability for disparate departments within a single organization to communicate effectively with one another. They communicate in the sparse, inadequate language of numbers, because numbers are the only language all can understand in a reasonably symmetrical fashion. Let us consider one example.

A MATTER OF COMPANY STYLE

One of the more dramatic new businesses to develop during the decade of the 1970s was the digital watch industry. At the outset, the digital or electronic watch presented a mystery to everyone in the business. The old, main-line watch firms such as Timex and Bulova were suspicious of the new semiconductor technology which replaced the mainspring and the tuning fork. The semiconductor firms that knew this technology supplied parts to other companies and did not know the business of selling goods to the individual consumer. I watched the reaction of two of these semiconductor firms to a new business opportunity. . . .

[1] See Harold J. Leavitt, *Managerial Psychology*, 4th ed. (Chicago: University of Chicago, 1978).

The digital watch seemed from the first to hold out the promise of a huge new industry. This new watch, which was more accurate, more reliable, and cheaper than the conventional timepiece, held the promise of replacing almost all timepieces in the Western world. Company A performed a careful analysis of the potential market, estimating the number of digital watches that could be sold at various prices, the cost of manufacturing and distributing these watches to retail outlets, and thus the potential profits to be earned by the firm. Company A, already a supplier of the central electronic component, possessed the necessary technical skill. The executives of the company knew that the business of selling consumer goods was unfamiliar to them, but they felt that they could develop the necessary knowledge. Following their analysis of the situation, they proceeded to go out and buy a company that manufactured watch cases, another that manufactured wrist bands for watches, and within weeks after their go-ahead decision, were in the watch business. Starting from zero, Company A rapidly gained a major share of the watch business and, eighteen months after the decision, was a major factor in the new industry and earned large profits on digital watches.

The executives of Company Z also recognized the opportunities in digital watches; they too manufactured the key electronic component that is the heart of the digital watch. Their analyses of the market promised very great rewards should they enter the business. But at Company Z, the numbers never dominate. The top executives at the firm asked whether this business really fit their "style." They saw the anticipated profits but wondered whether this would be a one-shot success or whether the company could continue to be an innovator and a leader in the watch business in the years to come. Most importantly, entering the watch business seemed to conflict with the company's philosophy. In Company Z, talking about the company philosophy is not considered soft-headed, wishful, or unrealistic. Rather, the company consists of a set of managers who see clearly that their capacity to achieve close cooperation depends in part on their agreeing on a central set of objectives and ways of doing business. These agreements comprise their philosophy of business, a broad statement that contemplates the proper relationship of the business to its employees, its owners, its customers, and to the public-at-large. This general statement must be interpreted to have meaning for any specific situation, and it is therefore important that managers be sufficiently familiar with the underlying corporate culture so that they can interpret the philosophy in ways which produce cooperation rather than conflict. One element of the philosophy concerns the kinds of products the company should manufacture, and that statement seemed clearly to exclude a product like the digital watch. On that basis, it seemed, the philosophy outweighed the financial analysis, and the watch project should have ended there.

But it didn't. A second major element of this corporation's philosophy had to do with preserving the freedom of employees to pursue projects they felt would be fruitful. In particular, the freedom of a unit manager to set goals and pursue them to their conclusion is cherished. In this case, a young general manager with a proven record of success wanted to take the company into the watch business. The top executives of the company disagreed with his judgement but were unwilling to sacrifice the manager's freedom. Two very central values conflicted in their implications for action. What was striking about this case was that values, not market share or profitability, lay

at the heart of the conflict in Company Z.

Let me not seem to imply that Company Z is unconcerned with profitability. The record is clear. Company Z is among the fastest-growing, most profitable of major American firms. Every manager knows that projects survive only as long as they produce profits well above what other companies demand. But at Company Z, profits are regarded not as an end in itself nor as the method of "keeping score" in the competitive process. Rather, profits are the reward to the firm if it continues to provide true value to its customers, to help its employees to grow, and to behave responsibly as a corporate citizen. Many of us have heard these words and are by now cynical about that kind of a public face which frequently shields a far less attractive internal reality. One of the distinctive features of Company Z is that these values are not a sham, not cosmetic, but they are practiced as the standard by which decisions are made. Again, the process is not faultless. Some managers within the firm are skeptical about the wisdom of these values and about the firm's true commitment to them, but by and large, the culture is intact and operating effectively.

Why a philosophy of management when firms in a free enterprise economy are supposed to seek profits only? In a large organization, it is impossible to determine over the period of a few months or a year whether a business segment is profitable or not. Suppose that you become the manager in charge of a new division created to enter the digital watch market. You buy the electronics from another division, you share salespersons with other divisions, you draw on a central engineering staff to design and maintain both your product and your manufacturing process, you rely heavily on the good name of the company to promote your product, and you staff your new operation with skilled managers and technicians who are products of the company's training programs. How much should you be charged for each of these inputs to your business? No one can know. Someone, inevitably, will come up with some numbers, sometimes referred to as "transfer prices" and other times referred to as "magic numbers," and these numbers will be used to calculate your costs in order to subtract those from your sales revenues so that a profit can be measured. Everyone, however, knows that the stated profits are a very inexact measure of your true profits, and that your true profits are unknowable.

Suppose that your company is in fact run by a strict profitability standard. If you are being undercharged for the central engineering services, then you will use as much engineering as you can, thereby taking that service away from some other use in the company. If another division manager asks to borrow three of your experienced staff, you may deny this request or send three not very skilled persons instead, since another's success is not reflected in your profits. In many ways, large and small, the inexact measurement of value will result in an explicit, formal mechanism that yields low coordination, low productivity, and high frustration.

Organizational life is a life of interdependence, of relying upon others. It is also a life of ambiguity. Armen Alchian and Harold Demsetz, two distinguished economists at UCLA, have argued that where teamwork is involved the measurement of individual performance will inevitably be ambiguous. Knowing this, and understanding the extreme complexity of interdependence in their business, the top management of Company Z has determined that explicit measures not be the final arbiter of decision making. They feel that if most of the top managers agree on what the company ought to be trying to do and how, in general, it ought to go about that set of tasks, then they will be able to rely on their mutual trust and goodwill to reach decisions far superior to anything that a formal system of control could provide.

They furthermore understand that the informal, implicit mechanisms of control cannot succeed alone. They can develop only under the conditions of stable employment, slow evaluation and promotion, and low career specialization. Even with those aids, however, the subtle and the implicit must be supported with the crutch of formal control and analysis in a large, multiproduct, multinational, multi-technology organization in which a complete agreement on values and beliefs can never be fully realized.

In the end, Company Z authorized the general manager to enter a relatively small and specialized segment of the digital watch market. He had the opportunity to "grow" his new venture if it succeeded, but the initial venture was small enough that its failure would not jeopardize the health of the company overall. Three years after the initial decisions by both companies, the picture was quite different. Following a dramatic surge in sales and profits, Company A had encountered stiff competition from other firms who were more experienced than they in this industry. Eighteen months after their initial success, they had taken severe losses and had sold their watch business to a competitor. They were, once again, back to zero in watches. Company Z also experienced an early success with its more limited digital watch venture, and after the initial success they, too, experienced stiff competition and a decline in profits. Rather than sell off the business, however, they slowly de-emphasized it, continuing to service the watches that they already had sold and, perhaps, maintaining the skeletal business as a valuable lesson from which future managers could learn.

A MATTER OF COMPANY SUBSTANCE

In Type Z organizations, as we have seen, the decision-making process is typically a consensual, participative one. Social scientists have described this as a democratic (as opposed to autocratic or apathetic) process in which many people are drawn into the shaping of important decisions. This participative process is one of the mechanisms that provides for the broad dissemination of information and of values within the organization, and it also serves the symbolic role of signaling in an unmistakable way the cooperative intent of the firm. Many of the values central to a corporate culture are difficult to test or to display. Some do not come into play more than once every few years, when a crisis appears (for example, the commitment to long-term employment, which is tested only during a recession), while others, such as the commitment to behave unselfishly, are difficult to observe. These values and beliefs must be expressed in concrete ways if they are to be understood and believed by new employees, particularly since new employees arrive with the expectation that all companies are basically the same: they are not to be trusted, not to be believed. Consensual decision making both provides the direct values of information and value sharing and at the same time openly signals the commitment of the organization to those values. When people get together in one room to discuss a problem or to make a decision, that meeting is often noticed and even talked about: it is a highly visible form of commitment to working together. Typically, Type Z organizations

devote a great deal of energy, to developing the interpersonal skills necessary to effective group decision making, perhaps in part for this symbolic reason.

In Type Z companies, the decision making may be collective, but the ultimate responsibility for decision still resides in one individual. It is doubtful that Westerners could ever tolerate the collective form of responsibility that characterizes Japanese organizations. This maintenance of the sense of individual responsibility remains critical to Western society but it also creates much tension in the Type Z organization. When a group engages in consensual decision making, members are effectively being asked to place their fate to some extent in the hands of others. Not a common fate but a set of individual fates is being dealt with. Each person will come from the meeting with the responsibility for some individual targets set collectively by the group. The consensual process, as defined by Professor Edgar Schein of M.I.T., is one in which members of the group may be asked to accept responsibility for a decision that they do not prefer, but that the group, in an open and complete discussion, has settled upon.[2] This combination of collective decision making with individual responsibility demands an atmosphere of trust. Only under a strong assumption that all hold basically compatible goals and that no one is engaged in self-serving behavior will individuals accept personal responsibility for a group decision and make enthusiastic attempts to get the job done.

The wholistic orientation of Type Z companies is in many ways similar to that found in the Japanese form but with some important differences. The similarity has to do with orientation of superior

[2] See Edgar Schein, *Process Consultation* (Reading, Mass.: Addison-Wesley, 1969).

to subordinates and of employees at all levels to their co-workers. Type Z companies generally show broad concern for the welfare of subordinates and of co-workers as a natural part of a working relationship. Relationships between people tend to be informal and to emphasize that whole people deal with one another at work, rather than just managers with workers and clerks with machinists. This wholistic orientation, a central feature of the organization, inevitably maintains a strong egalitarian atmosphere that is a feature of all Type Z organizations.

If people deal with one another in segmented ways, as one role to another rather than as one human being to another, then these dehumanized relationships easily become authoritarian. Feelings of superiority and inferiority prevail in relationships narrowly defined and constrained to "my" duties as department head and "your" duties as worker. That attitude, out of step in a democratic society, implies class distinctions. The subordinate will inevitably be alienated both from the superior who takes such an attitude and from the company that he or she represents. The superior is often relieved of some of the anxiety and stress that come with having to respond to the needs of others, whether those are superiors, subordinates, or peers. Most of us cannot block off the requests or complaints of superiors and peers, but if we become impersonal and formal and thus distant from the needs of subordinates, that gives one less thing to worry about. Of course we recognize that feeling as being improper, unfair, and unproductive, but short-term pressures will often beckon in that direction.

An organization that maintains a wholistic orientation and forces employees at all levels to deal with one another as complete human beings creates a condition in which de-personalization is im-possible, autocracy is unlikely, and open communication, trust, and commitment are common. In one Type Z company with which I am familiar, each plant in the company holds a monthly "beer bust" at the end of a working day. Beer and snacks are consumed, neither in large quantities, and informal games and skits are frequently offered. Any manager who regularly fails to take part in the beer bust will fail to achieve success and continued promotion. Is this an example of "politics at work," of "it's who you know, not what you know," or is it simply a holdover from earlier days?

The beer bust, as I interpret it, is similar to the cocktails after work shared by bosses and subordinates in Japan. Both have the same group of people who work together each day now cast in different roles. The hierarchy of work, somewhat relaxed in this setting, gives people the opportunity to interact more as equals, or at least without the familiar hierarchical roles. Technicians can express their willingness to regard foremen as regular people rather than as superiors to be suspected. Managers show subordinates their acceptance of them as equals, as whole human beings. In this particular company with the beer bust, managers must be willing to engage in frivolous games and skits in which their obvious lack of skill and their embarrassment bring them down to earth both in their own eyes and in the eyes of their subordinates.

Very few of us are superior to our fellow workers in every way. As long as we cling to our organizational roles, we can maintain the fiction that we are indeed superior in every way. But if we engage these people in social intercourse, the fiction is dispelled. The natural force of organizational hierarchy promotes a segmented relationship and a hierarchical attitude. A wholistic relationship provides a counterbalance that encourages a more egalitarian attitude.

Egalitarianism is a central feature of Type Z organizations. Egalitarianism implies that each person can apply discretion and can work autonomously without close supervision, because they are to be trusted. Again, trust underscores the belief that goals correspond, that neither person is out to harm the other. This feature, perhaps more than any other, accounts for the high levels of commitment, of loyalty, and of productivity in Japanese firms and in Type Z organizations. . . .

The central importance of trust is revealed in a study of utopian societies by Rosabeth Moss Kanter.[3] Kanter described the Amana (refrigerators), the Oneida (tableware), and other utopian communities that succeeded as commercial enterprises. In these communities one of the key values was egalitarianism—equality of influence and of power. Consistent with this value, all explicit forms of supervision and of direction were forgone. Now the problem was how to ensure a high level of discipline and hard work without hierarchical supervision and monitoring of production. The chief danger was of self-interest in the form of laziness, shirking, and selfishness at work. Such behavior could not readily be corrected without hierarchy, and other means had to be found to limit such tendencies. The answer was to develop a complete unity of goals between individuals and the community such that an autonomous individual would naturally seek to work hard, cooperate, and benefit the community. In order to accomplish this complete socialization, utopian communities engaged in a variety of practices that had the objective of developing common goals. Open sex

or complete celibacy, the most dramatic of these, both have characterized all successful utopian communes in the United States. From Kanter's point of view, open sex and complete celibacy are functionally equivalent: each prevents the formation of loyalties to another individual and so preserves the loyalty of all to the community. Open sex allows no free choice of partners but rather a strict assignment of older men to younger women and older women to younger men. As soon as partners begin to show preference for one another in this system, they are reassigned. The example illustrates both the great difficulty of achieving complete goal integration in a Western society and the central importance of selfless goals in non-hierarchical organizations.

Type Z organizations, unlike utopian communities, do employ hierarchical modes of control, and thus do not rely entirely upon goal congruence among employees for order. Nevertheless, they do rely extensively upon symbolic means to promote an attitude of egalitarianism and of mutual trust, and they do so in part by encouraging a wholistic relation between employees. Self-direction replaces hierarchical direction to a great extent which enhances commitment, loyalty, and motivation.

Argyris challenged managers to integrate individuals into organizations, not to create alienating, hostile, and impersonally bureaucratic places of work. In a real sense, the Type Z organization comes close to realizing that ideal. It is a consent culture, a community of equals who cooperate with one another to reach common goals. Rather than relying exclusively upon hierarchy and monitoring to direct behavior, it relies also upon commitment and trust.

THE THEORY BEHIND THE THEORY Z ORGANIZATION

The difference between a hierarchy—or bureaucracy—and Type Z is that Z

[3] See Rosabeth Moss Kanter, *Commitment and Community* (Cambridge: Harvard University Press, 1972).

organizations have achieved a high state of consistency in their internal culture. They are most aptly described as clans in that they are intimate associations of people engaged in economic activity but tied together through a variety of bonds.[4] *Clans* are distinct from *hierarchies*, and from *markets*, which are the other two fundamental social mechanisms through which transactions between individuals can be governed. In a market, there will be competitive bidding for, say, an engineer's services as well as for a weaver's baskets. Each will know the true value of their products according to the terms the market sets. In a bureaucracy, however, workers lack any clear sense of the value of their services. No competitive bidding sets the yearly wage for an engineering vice-president, for example. Since each job is unique, companies instead rely upon the hierarchy to evaluate performance and to estimate the amount that an employee is worth. The hierarchy succeeds only to the extent that we trust it to yield equitable outcomes, just as the marketplace succeeds only because we grant legitimacy to it. As long as the vice-president regards the president as a fair and well-informed person who will arrive at a fair appraisal of his performance, the contented employee will let the hierarchy operate unobstructed. However, mistrust will bring about prespecified contractual protections such as those written when selling some service to an outside firm. The writ-

[4] Here and elsewhere . . . I refer to industrial clans. The meaning of *clan* I derive from the use by the sociologist Emile Durkheim. In this usage, a disorganized aggregation of individuals is a *horde*, the smallest organized unit is a *band*, and a clan is a group of bands. A clan is an intimate association of individuals who are connected to each other through a variety of ties. The members of a clan may or may not share blood relations. Here I refer to an intimate group of industrial workers who know one another well but who typically do not share blood relations.

ing and enforcement of that contract will vastly increase the costs of managing the vice-president.

More common is the example of the hourly employee who learns, over time, that the corporate hierarchy cannot be trusted to provide equitable treatment and insists upon union representation and contractual specification of rights. The employee pays additional costs in the form of union dues, the company pays additional costs in the form of more industrial relations staff, and everyone pays more costs in the form of less cooperation, less productivity, and less wealth to be shared. Thus the success of a hierarchy, or bureaucracy, can be costly. But whatever the financial cost, these protective mechanisms take over when individual contribution can be equitably assessed only through the somewhat more subtle form of bureaucratic surveillance.

By comparison clans succeed when teamwork and change render individual performance almost totally ambiguous. At these times long-term commitment, supported by agreement on goals and operating methods, is necessary to achieve an equitable balance. Individual performance and reward can be judged equitably only over a period of several years, thus relationships must be long-term and trust must be great.

In a market each individual is in effect asked to pursue selfish interests. Because the market mechanism will exactly measure the contribution of each person to the common good, each person can be compensated exactly for personal contributions. If one chooses not to contribute anything, then one is not compensated and equity is achieved.

In a clan, each individual is also effectively told to do just what that person wants. In this case, however, the socialization of all to a common goal is so complete and the capacity of the system to measure the subtleties of contributions over the long run is so exact that individuals will naturally seek to do that which is in the common good. Thus the monk, the marine, or the Japanese auto worker who appears to have arrived at a selfless state is, in fact, achieving selfish ends quite thoroughly. Both of these governance mechanisms realize human potential and maximize human freedom because they do not constrain behavior.

Only the bureaucratic mechanism explicitly says to individuals, "Do not do what you want, do what we tell you to do because we pay you for it." The bureaucratic mechanism alone produces alienation, anomie, and a lowered sense of autonomy. This is the reason that the employees of Z companies report a higher sense of personal autonomy and freedom than do the employees of Type A companies. Feelings of autonomy and freedom make the employees in Japanese firms work with so much more enthusiasm than their counterparts in many Western firms.

In the sense that Z organizations are more like clans than markets or bureaucracies, they foster close interchange between work and social life. Consider this example: Chinese-American entrepreneurs appear in greater numbers than would be expected, based on their fraction of the population as a whole. For many years, the explanation offered by social scientists was that by contrast black Americans were systematically denied access to banks and other sources of capital necessary to start a small business, whereas Asian-Americans had better access to these capital markets. As a number of studies have shown, however, both blacks and asians find the same difficulties in raising capital for businesses.[5] Yet Asian-Americans brought with them from their homelands the tradition

[5] See Ivan H. Light, *Ethnic Enterprise in America* (Berkeley: University of California Press, 1972).

of informal revolving-credit societies, the *Tanomoshi* for the Japanese-Americans and the *Hui* for the Chinese-Americans. A *Tanomoshi* or *Hui* typically consists of about one dozen individuals, each one wanting to own his own service station, a one-truck hauling service, or other such small businesses. Once each month, the group gathers at one member's home for dinner, and each person brings with him a prespecified sum of money, perhaps $1,000. The host of the evening keeps the whole sum— say, $12,000—which he then uses to buy a second truck or open his service station. The group meets in this fashion for twelve successive months until each person has put in $12,000 and has taken out $12,000. In this manner, people who would have great difficulty saving the whole sum of $12,000 are able to raise capital.

The process on closer scrutiny has some unusual properties. First, the earlier recipients of the pot effectively pay a lower interest rate than do the later recipients. The first host has the use of $11,000 of other people's money for one month without interest, then $10,000 (as he adds his $1,000 to the second dinner), and so on. By comparison the last host has to put $11,000 dollars into the pot, money that he could have left in the bank to draw interest, before he receives his pot. Surely this is an inequitable process, yet it persists. The second interesting property is that no contracts are signed, no collateral is offered, even though the late borrowers willingly turn over large sums of money to others with no assurance that they will be paid. They have no evidence of even having made a loan that would stand up in a court of law, should there be a default.

Japanese-Americans' membership in a *Tanomoshi* is limited strictly by the geographical regions of birth in Japan, and by the region in Japan from which one's ancestors came. Among the Chinese-Americans, membership in a *Hui* is limited to those within the kinship network. Thus one can only be born into a *Tanomoshi* or a *Hui*, and one can never escape from the network of familiar, communal, social, religious, and economic ties that bind those groups together. If a member should fail to make good on his obligations, members of his family would certainly take up his obligation or else pay the very high price of having all branches of the family shut out of the economic and social network of the community. This ethnically bound community thus obviates the need for contracts or collateral to protect a loan. But what about the unfair difference in the implicit interest rates paid by the early versus late borrowers? We can understand this phenomenon in two ways. First, we note that these short-run inequities are made up in the long run. Because each adult in these ethnic communities typically participates in a large number of *Huis* or *Tanomoshis* over his lifetime, at times simultaneously participating in two or more. Many opportunities arise to repay past debts by taking a later position in the chain. In addition, a debt incurred to one person may be repaid to that person's son or brother, who in turn has the capacity to repay the initial creditor through one of a thousand favors. What is critical is that there be a communal memory—much like that of the corporate memory in Theory Z—and that the community have a stable membership. The effects of this memory mechanism are far-reaching. Depending on his behavior as a borrower and lender, an individual may or may not be invited to participate in various other groups and may be included in or left out of religious and social activities that could affect the marital prospects of his children, the economic prospects of his business, and

so on. In fact the more valuable his *Tanomoshi* membership, the higher the price he can command in the form of sought-after affiliations. Although the individuals in a *Hui* or *Tanomoshi* do not share complete goal congruence, they are at once largely committed to a congruent set of goals which have to do with maintaining the social structure of the community, and they are also subject to the long-run evaluation of an ethnically bound marketplace.

These clans also work largely on the basis of trust. Marcel Mauss, a French anthropologist, has noted that the willingness to be in someone's debt is an important signal of trust.[6] For instance, in most societies it is considered rude to rush over to repay a neighbor for a favor just received. To do so implies lack of trust in that neighbor and a fear that the neighbor may abuse your obligation by asking in return something you find particularly difficult or distasteful. Thus, the leaving of many debts between people amounts to evidence of their trust of one another, and the evidence of trust in turn serves as the oil that lubricates future social transactions.

The point is that organizations are social organisms and, like any other social creations, are profoundly shaped by the social environment in which they exist. As we will see, the Type Z organization succeeds only under social conditions that support lifetime employment. The *Hui* and the *Tanomoshi* succeed in the United States only because the Chinese and Japanese immigrants found themselves living together in ethnic ghettoes.

DIFFICULTIES IN TRANSLATION

Despite its remarkable properties, the clan form in industry possesses a few po-

---

[6] See Marcel Mauss, *The Gift* (New York: W. W. Norton, 1967).

tentially disabling weaknesses. A clan always tends to develop xenophobia, a fear of outsiders. In the words of the president of one major Type Z company: "We simply can't bring in an outsider at top levels. We've tried it, but the others won't accept him. I consider that to be one of our biggest problems." In other ways, too, the Type Z resists deviance in all forms. Because the glue that holds it together is consistency of belief rather than application of hierarchy, it tends indiscriminately to reject all inconsistency. The trouble is that it is difficult, perhaps impossible, to discriminate in advance between a deviant idea that is useful and adaptive and one that is simply stupid and immoral. Companies such as IBM, General Motors, and Xerox, in which innovation is critical, typically segregate their researchers and those who come up with new product ideas, sometimes locating them on the opposite end of the continent from headquarters in order to shield them from the sometimes oppressive corporate culture. What happens, of course, is that those scientists indeed become deviant from the main-line culture, develop lots of different ideas, and then discover that the headquarters decision-makers reject their ideas as being too deviant.

In a Type Z organization, changing people's behavior by changing a measure of performance or by changing the profit calculation is an impossibility: The only way to influence behavior is to change the culture. A culture changes slowly because its values reach deeply and integrate into a consistent network of beliefs that tends to maintain the status quo. Therefore, a Type Z organization runs the risk of becoming an industrial dinosaur, unable to react quickly enough to a major shift in the environment. Where operating changes are involved, Type Z organizations tend to be unusually adaptive. A better way to accomplish some

task can be adopted without having to rewrite a book of rules specifying job descriptions and without worrying about whether this change will hurt the current way of measuring our performance. This is one of the greatest strengths of the Japanese firm. Japanese companies in the United States are fast becoming legendary for their capacity to quickly adopt changes in procedure, unencumbered by bureaucratic paraphernalia. However, the coordination in this system is provided by adherence to an underlying set of values that are deeply held and closely followed. If adaptation required a change in those values, then Type Z organizations would be at a severe disadvantage. . . .

Every Type Z organization that I know experiences some loss of professionalism.[7] Whether it is a financial analyst, a salesperson, a personnel specialist, or an engineer, a Type Z company manifests a lower level of professionalism. I systematically interviewed everyone at the level of vice-president and above at two high-technology companies, one a pure Type A and one a pure Type Z (or as nearly pure as possible). I also interviewed a random selection of employees in each company. At Company A, each person was introduced to me with pride as being, ". . . the top public relations man in the industry," or ". . . the most innovative electrical engineer, the holder of twenty patents on circuit design," or ". . . the personnel manager who set the pattern for industry in per-

[7] I have developed this work in collaboration with Jerry B. Johnson. For a complete description of the initial study, see W. G. Ouchi and Jerry B. Johnson, "Types of Organizational Control and Their Relationship to Emotional Well-Being," Administrative Science Quarterly, Vol. 23 (June 1978). We were assisted in this work by Alan Wilkins, David Gibson, Alice Kaplan, and Raymond Price, to whom I am grateful.

formance appraisal." At Company Z, by comparison, the emphasis was on how the individuals comprised a working team, with little mention of specialized skills, although great emphasis was placed on the company's practice of hiring only the most skilled and able young people and then developing them. The offices of Company A managers were typically filled with shelves of books and journals, and people would often offer me an article that they had written on their speciality. At Company Z people read fewer journals, wrote fewer articles, and attended fewer professional meetings. At the extreme, Type Z companies will express the "not-invented-here" mentality: "We have most of the top people in the field right here, so why should I go talk to anyone else?" The trouble, of course, comes if the company starts to slip. They will not know it, since they have no external point of comparison.

With respect to sex and race, Type Z companies have a tendency to be sexist and racist. This is another paradox, because while Type Z companies typically work much harder and care much more about offering equality of opportunity to minorities, in some ways they have much greater obstacles to overcome than do Type A companies. As I visited the managers in the high technology Type A, I was struck by the ethnic diversity among the upper levels of management: Spanish-Americans, Asian-Americans, Hungarian-Americans, and Anglo-Saxon-Americans. At Company A, new promotion opportunity is simply awarded to that candidate who has had the best "bottom line" for the past few periods. Whether that manager is obnoxious or strange, succeeds by abusing his employees or by encouraging them, doesn't matter. The only thing that counts is the bottom line, and thus a diverse group of people make it to the top. How well they are able to work with one another once at the top is another question.

At Company Z the cast of top managers is so homogeneous that one member of my research team characterized the dominant culture as "Boy Scout Macho." That is, the top management is wholesome, disciplined, hard-working, and honest, but unremittingly white, male, and middle class. Company Z has affirmative action goals at the top of its list and devotes great time and expense to recruiting, training, and developing women and ethnic minorities. Why is it nonetheless typical of "Boy Scout Macho"? Imagine that you are a general manager at Company Z. In your division you have an opening for a new manager in charge of marketing. Both a white male engineer and a female Mexican-American are completely qualified for the promotion. The difference between them is past experience. You have evaluated forty or fifty white male engineers in the past, you have worked with them day in and day out for twenty years, and you know how to calibrate them, how to read their subtle instincts, values, and beliefs. You are quite certain that you have correctly evaluated this white male engineer as being fully qualified for the job of marketing manager. But how about the female Mexican-American? How many of them have you evaluated or worked with at this level? She is probably the first. You cannot be sure that what you regard as initiative is truly that; you cannot be sure that the signs you see of ambition, of maturity, or of integrity are what they seem to be. It takes time and experience to learn to read subtleties in one who is culturally different, and because subtleties are everything in the Type Z organization, you cannot be confident that you have correctly appraised this candidate, and she is therefore at a considerable disadvantage, since no one in his right mind will choose an uncertainty over a certainty.

Probably no form of organization is more sexist or racist than the Japanese corporation. They do not intentionally shut out those who are different nor do they consider male Japanese to be superior. Their organizations simply operate as culturally homogeneous social systems that have very weak explicit or hierarchical monitoring properties and thus can withstand no internal cultural diversity. To the extent that women or ethnic minorities (caucasians or Koreans, for example) are culturally different, they cannot succeed in Japan. The Japanese firm in the United States has a considerably greater tolerance for heterogeneity and thus can operate successfully with white people and women in high positions, but the tendency toward sameness is still present. The Type Z organization is still more open to heterogeneity, but it too requires a high level of homogeneity. Perhaps the other extreme, the cultural opposite of the Japanese firm in Japan, is the United States federal bureaucracy.

In a sense the federal bureaucracy is a microcosm of our society. Here our values of equality of opportunity for all people are crystallized, if not always realized. Much the same is true of state and local government agencies, but let us consider the federal agencies for a moment. Equality of opportunity and of treatment is taken far more seriously in the federal agencies than in almost any private sector organizations. What this means is that the government must promulgate a series of bureaucratic rules that should ordinarily prevent, insofar as humanly possible, the application of capricious or unfair standards that will harm women and ethnic minorities. Unfortunately, this set of bureaucratic rules must be geared to catch the lowest common denominator. That is, they cannot leave any rule ambiguous, to be decided on the discretion of an individual manager, since that leaves open the possibility of the manager arriving at a discriminatory interpretation. Thus the bureaucratic rules are not only explicit and inflexible but also constraining and impersonal. This thoroughgoing bureaucratization rests on the assumption that bureaucrats cannot be trusted to share the society's egalitarian goals nor to enact an egalitarian form of organization. Thus they are directed not to use their discretion and judgement. If we place a priceless value on equality in our public institutions, then we will pay any price to keep them democratic.

The price that we pay, of course, is in inefficiency, inflexibility, indolence, and impersonality. All too often a federal bureau will fail to do that which makes sense because common sense does not fit the rules. All too often bureaucrats, trained not to allow personal values to intrude on decisions, will treat us, their customers, in an unfeeling manner. All too often the machinery of government will respond slowly and inefficiently with poor coordination between agencies, because they have learned not to trust one another, not to rely on subtlety, not to develop intimacy.

Social organizations are incompatible with formality, distance, and contractualism. They proceed smoothly only with intimacy, subtlety, and trust. But these conditions can develop only over a long period of cultural homogenization during which the people of a nation become accustomed to one another and come to espouse a common body of values and beliefs. In a nation as young and as heterogeneous as ours, that level of cultural agreement is yet some distance away. The United States is not Japan. We are not a homogeneous body of people. Our institutions cannot operate in a wholly synchronized manner. On the other hand, we cannot allow our institutions to become so thoroughly unfeeling and unthinking that they make work and social intercourse unbearable for all of us most of the time. We must find those organizational innovations which can permit a balance between freedom and integration, which go beyond our current interpretation of individualism.

41

In Search of Excellence: Simultaneous Loose-Tight Properties

Thomas J. Peters & Robert H. Waterman, Jr.

Simultaneous loose-tight properties, . . . is in essence the co-existence of firm central direction and maximum individual autonomy—what we have called "having one's cake and eating it too." Organizations that live by the loose-tight principle are on the one hand rigidly controlled, yet at the same time allow (indeed, insist on) autonomy, entrepreneurship, and innovation from the rank and file. They do this literally through "faith"—through value systems, which . . . most managers avoid like the plague. They do it also through painstaking attention to detail, to getting the "itty-bitty, teeny-tiny things" right, as Alabama's inimitable football coach, Bear Bryant, stresses.

Loose-tight? Most businessmen's eyes glaze over when the talk turns to value systems, culture, and the like. Yet ours light up: we recall ex-chairman Bill Blackie of Caterpillar talking about Cat's commitment to "Forty-eight-hour parts service anywhere in the world." We are drawn back to a minus 60° chill factor day in Minneapolis–St. Paul, where 3 M's Tait Elder talked to us about the "irrational champions" running around 3M. And we see Rene McPherson speaking to a class at Stanford. He is animated. The class asks him for the magic prescriptions with which he mastered productivity problems at Dana. He

sticks his hands out in front of him, palms upright, and says, "You just keep pushing. You just keep pushing. I made every mistake that could be made. But I just kept pushing." You suspect he is serious: that really *is* all there was to it.

You think of Tom Watson, Sr., coming in after a hard day of selling pianos to farmers, and reporting to his headquarters in Painted Post, New York. And you think of what he became and why. You picture J. Willard Marriott, Sr., at that first food stand in Washington, D.C. And you see him now, at eighty-two, still worrying about a single lobby's cleanliness, although his food stand is a $2 billion enterprise. You picture Eddie Carlson working as a page boy at a Western International Hotel, the Benjamin Franklin in 1929, and marvel at the legend he has become.

Carlson doesn't blush when he talks about values. Neither did Watson—he said that values are really all there is. They lived by their values, these men—Marriott, Ray Kroc, Bill Hewlett and Dave Packard, Levi Strauss, James Cash Penney, Robert Wood Johnson. And they meticulously applied them within their organizations. They *believed* in the customer. They *believed* in granting autonomy; room to perform. They *believed* in open doors, in quality. But they were stern disciplinarians, every one. They

Source: "Simultaneous Loose-Tight Properties," pp. 318–25, from *In Search of Excellence: Lessons from America's Best-Run Companies*, by Thomas J. Peters and Robert H. Waterman, Jr. Copyright © 1982 by Thomas J. Peters, and Robert H. Waterman, Jr. Reprinted by permission of HarperCollins Publishers, Inc.

gave plenty of rope, but they accepted the chance that some of their minions would hang themselves. Loose-tight is about rope. Yet in the last analysis, it's really about culture. Now, culture is the "softest" stuff around. Who trusts its leading analysts—anthropologists and sociologists—after all? Businessmen surely don't. Yet culture is the hardest stuff around, as well. Violate the lofty phrase, "IBM Means Service," and you are out of a job, the company's job security program to the contrary notwithstanding. Digital is crazy (soft). Digital is anarchic (soft). "People at Digital don't know who they work for," says a colleague. But they do know quality: the products they turn out work (hard). So "Soft is hard."

Patrick Haggerty says the only reason that OST (hard) works at Texas Instruments is because of TI's "innovative culture" (soft). Lew Lehr, 3M's chairman, goes around telling tales of people who have failed monumentally—but gone on, after decades of trying, to become vice presidents of the company. He's describing the loose-tight, soft-hard properties of the 3M culture.

We have talked about lots of soft traits, lots of loose traits. We have mentioned clubby, campus-like environments, flexible organizational structures (hiving off new divisions, temporary habit-breaking devices, regular reorganizations), volunteers, zealous champions, maximized autonomy for individuals, teams and divisions, regular and extensive experimentation, feedback emphasizing the positive, and strong social networks. All of these traits focus on the positive, the excitement of trying things out in a slightly disorderly (loose) fashion.

But at the same time, a remarkably tight—culturally driven/controlled set of properties marks the excellent companies. Most have rigidly shared values. The action focus, including experimen-

tation itself, emphasizes extremely regular communication and very quick feedback; nothing gets very far out of line. Concise paperwork and the focus on realism are yet other, nonaversive ways of exerting extremely tight control. If you have only three numbers to live by, you may be sure they are all well checked out. A predominant discipline or two is in itself another crucial measure of tightness. The fact that the vast majority of the management group at 3M consists of chemical engineers, at Fluor of mechanical engineers, is another vital assurance of realism, a form of tight control.

Intriguingly, the focus on the outside, the external perspective, the attention to the customer, is one of the tightest properties of all. In the excellent companies, it is perhaps the most stringent means of self-discipline. If one is really paying attention to what the customer is saying, being blown in the wind by the customer's demands, one may be sure he is sailing a tight ship. And then there is the peer pressure: weekly Rallies at Tupperware, Dana's twice-annual Hell Weeks. Although this is not control via massive forms and incalculable numbers of variables, it is the toughest control of all. As McPherson said, it's easy to fool the boss, but you can't fool your peers. These are the apparent contradictions that turn out in practice not to be contradictions at all.

Take the quality versus cost trade-off, for example, or small versus big (i.e., effectiveness versus efficiency). They turn out in the excellent companies not to be trade-offs at all. There is a story about a GM foundry manager who led a remarkable economic turnaround; he painted the grimy interior of his foundry white, insisting that he would pay attention to quality (and housekeeping, safety), and that cost would follow. As he pointed out: "To begin with, if you are making it with good quality, you don't have to make everything twice." There is nothing like quality. It is the most important word used in these companies. Quality leads to a focus on innovativeness—to doing the best one can for every customer on every product; hence it is a goad to productivity, automatic excitement, an external focus. The drive to make "the best" affects virtually every function of the organization.

In the same way, the efficiency/effectiveness contradiction dissolves into thin air. Things of quality are produced by craftsmen, generally requiring small-scale enterprise, we are told. Activities that achieve cost efficiencies, on the other hand, are reputedly best done in large facilities, to achieve economies of scale. Except that that is not the way it works in the excellent companies. In the excellent companies, small *in almost every case* is beautiful. The small facility turns out to be the most efficient; its turned-on, motivated, highly productive worker, in communication (and competition) with his peers, outproduces the worker in the big facilities time and again. It holds for plants, for project teams, for divisions—for the entire company. So we find that in this most vital area, there really is no conflict. Small, quality, excitement, autonomy—and efficiency—are all words that belong on the same side of the coin. Cost and efficiency, over the long run, *follow* from the emphasis on quality, service, innovativeness, result sharing, participation, excitement, and an external problem-solving focus that is tailored to the customer. The revenue line does come first. But once the ball gets rolling, cost control and innovation effectiveness become fully achievable, parallel goals.

Surprisingly, the execution versus autonomy contradiction becomes a paradox, too. Indeed, one can appreciate this paradox almost anywhere. Studies in the classroom, for example, suggest that effective classes are the ones in which discipline is sure: students are expected to come to class on time; homework is regularly turned in and graded. On the other hand, those same classrooms as a general rule emphasize positive feedback, posting good reports, praise, and coaching by the teacher. Similarly, when we look at McDonald's or virtually any of the excellent companies, we find that *autonomy is a product of discipline. The discipline (a few shared values) provides the framework. It gives people confidence (to experiment, for instance) stemming from stable expectations about what really counts.*

Thus a set of shared values and rules about discipline, details, and execution can provide the framework in which practical autonomy takes place routinely. Regular experimentation takes place at 3M in a large measure because of all the tight things that surround it—extraordinarily regular communication (nothing gets far out of line), the shared values that result from the common denominator of the engineering degree, the consensus on customer problem solving that comes from a top management virtually all of whom started as down-the-line salesmen.

3M is, indeed, the tightest organization we have seen, tighter by far, in our opinion, than ITT under Geneen. At ITT, there were countless rules and variables to be measured and filed. But the dominant theme there was gamesmanship—beating the system, pulling end runs, joining together with other line officers to avoid the infamous staff "flying squads." Too much overbearing discipline of the wrong kind will kill autonomy. But the more rigid discipline, the discipline based on a small number of shared values that marks a 3M, an HP, a J&J, or a McDonald's, in fact, induces practical autonomy and experimentation throughout the organization and beyond.

The nature of the rules is crucial here. The "rules" in the excellent companies have a positive cast. They deal with quality, service, innovation, and experimentation. Their focus is on building, expanding, the opposite of restraining; whereas most companies concentrate on controlling, limiting, constraint. We don't seem to understand that rules can reinforce positive traits as well as discourage negative ones, and that the former kind are far more effective.

Even the external versus internal contradiction is resolved in the excellent companies. Quite simply, these companies are simultaneously externally focused and internally focused—externally in that they are truly driven by their desire to provide service, quality, and innovative problem solving in support of their customers; internally in that quality control, for example, is put on the back of the individual line worker, not primarily in the lap of the quality control department. Service standards likewise are substantially self-monitored. The organization thrives on internal competition. And it thrives on intense communication, on the family feeling, on open door policies, on informality, on fluidity and flexibility, on nonpolitical shifts of resources. This constitutes the crucial internal focus: the focus on people.

The skill with which the excellent companies develop their people recalls that grim conflict . . . our basic need for security versus the need to stick out, the "essential tension" that the psychoanalyst Ernest Becker described. Once again the paradox, as it is dealt with in the excellent companies, holds. By offering meaning as well as money, they give their employees a mission as well as a sense of feeling great. Every man becomes a pioneer, an experimenter, a leader. The institution provides guiding belief and creates a sense of excitement, a sense of being a part of the best, a sense of producing something of quality that is generally valued. And in this way it draws out the best—from Ken Ohmae's "worker at the frontier" as from Kyoto Ceramic chairman Kazuo Inamori's "fifty percent man." The *average* worker in these companies is expected to contribute, to add ideas, to innovate in service to the customer and in producing quality products. In short, each individual—like the 9,000 leaders of PIP teams at Texas Instruments—is expected to stand out and contribute, to be distinctive. At the same time he is part of something great: Caterpillar, IBM, 3M, Disney Productions.

Finally, the last of our paradoxes involves the short-term versus long-term "trade-off." Again, we found there was no conflict at all. We found that the excellent companies are not really "long-term thinkers." They don't have better five-year plans. Indeed, the formal plans at the excellent companies are often marked by little detail, or don't exist at all (recall the complete absence of corporate level planners in many of them).

But there is a value set—and it is a value set for all seasons. (Remember the content areas: quality, innovativeness, informality, customer service, people.) However, it is executed by attention to mundane, nitty-gritty details. Every minute, every hour, every day is an opportunity to act in support of overarching themes.

We will conclude with one strange contradiction that may really hold. We call it the smart-dumb rule. Many of today's managers—MBA-trained and the like—may be a little bit too smart for their own good. The smart ones are the ones who shift direction all the time, based upon the latest output from the expected value equation. The ones who juggle hundred-variable models with facility; the ones who design complicated incentive systems; the ones who wire up matrix structures. The ones who have 200-page strategic plans and 500-page market requirement documents that are but step one in product development exercises.

Our "dumber" friends are different. They just don't understand why every product can't be of the highest quality. They just don't understand why every customer can't get personalized service, even in the potato chip business. They are personally affronted . . . when a bottle of beer goes sour. They can't understand why a regular flow of new products isn't possible, or why a worker can't contribute a suggestion every couple of weeks. Simple-minded fellows, really; simplistic even. Yes, simplistic has a negative connotation. But the people who lead the excellent companies *are* a bit simplistic. They are seemingly unjustified in what they believe the worker is capable of doing. They are seemingly unjustified in believing that every product can be of the highest quality. They are seemingly unjustified in believing that

service can be maintained at a high standard for virtually every customer, whether in Missoula, Montana, or Manhattan. They are seemingly unjustified in believing that virtually every worker can contribute suggestions regularly. It is simplistic. But it may be the true key to inducing astonishing contributions from tens of thousands of people.

Of course, what one is simplistic about is vitally important. It's a focus on the external, on service, on quality, on people, on informality, those value content words we noted. And those may very well be things—the only things—worth being simplistic about. Remember the executive James Brian Quinn interviewed: he said that it was important for his people to want to be "the best" at something. He doesn't really care very much what.

But so many can't see it. There are always practical, justifiable, inevitable, sensible, and sane reasons to compromise on any of these variables. Only those simplistic people—like Watson, Hewlett, Packard, Kroc, Mars, Olsen, McPherson, Marriott, Procter, Gamble, Johnson—stayed simplistic. And their companies have remained remarkably successful.

42

The Fifth Discipline: A Shift of Mind

Peter M. Senge

SEEING THE WORLD ANEW

There is something in all of us that loves to put together a puzzle, that loves to see the image of the whole emerge. The beauty of a person, or a flower, or a poem lies in seeing all of it. It is interesting that the words "whole" and "health" come from the same root (the Old English *hal,* as in "hale and hearty"). So it should come as no surprise that the unhealthiness of our world today is in direct proportion to our inability to see it as a whole.

Systems thinking is a discipline for seeing wholes. It is a framework for seeing interrelationships rather than things, for seeing patterns of change rather than static "snapshots." It is a set of general principles—distilled over the course of the twentieth century, spanning fields as diverse as the physical and social sciences, engineering, and management. It is also a set of specific tools and techniques, originating in two threads: in "feedback" concepts of cybernetics and in "servo-mechanism" engineering theory dating back to the nineteenth century. During the last thirty years, these tools have been applied to understand a wide range of corporate, urban, regional, economic, political, ecological, and even physiological systems.[1] And systems thinking is a sensibility—for the subtle interconnectedness that gives living systems their unique character.

Today, systems thinking is needed more than ever because we are becoming overwhelmed by complexity. Perhaps for the first time in history, humankind has the capacity to create far more information than anyone can absorb, to foster far greater interdependency than anyone can manage, and to accelerate change far faster than anyone's ability to keep pace. Certainly the scale of complexity is without precedent. All around us are examples of "systemic breakdowns"—problems such as global warming, ozone depletion, the international drug trade, and the U.S. trade and budget deficits—problems that have no simple local cause. Similarly, organizations break down, despite individual brilliance and innovative products, because they are unable to pull their diverse functions and talents into a productive whole.

Complexity can easily undermine confidence and responsibility—as in the frequent refrain, "It's all too complex for me," or "There's nothing I can do. It's the system." Systems thinking is the antidote to this sense of helplessness that many feel as we enter the "age of interdependence." Systems thinking is a discipline for seeing the "structures" that underlie complex situations, and for discerning high from low leverage change. That is, by seeing wholes we learn how to foster health. To do so, systems thinking offers a language that begins by restructuring how we think.

I call systems thinking the fifth discipline because it is the conceptual cornerstone that underlies all of the five learning disciplines . . . All are concerned with a shift of mind from seeing parts to seeing wholes, from seeing people as helpless reactors to seeing them as active participants in shaping their reality, from reacting to the present to creating the future. Without systems thinking, there is neither the incentive nor the means to integrate the learning disciplines once they have come into practice. As the fifth discipline, systems thinking is the cornerstone of how learning organizations think about their world. . . .

Sophisticated tools of forecasting and business analysis, as well as elegant strategic plans, usually fail to produce dramatic breakthroughs in managing a business. They are all designed to handle the sort of complexity in which there are many variables: *detail complexity. But there are two types of complexity.* The second type is *dynamic complexity*, situations where cause and effect are subtle, and where the effects over time of interventions are not obvious. Conventional forecasting, planning, and analysis methods are not equipped to deal with dynamic complexity. Mixing many ingredients in a stew involves detail complexity, as does following a complex set of instructions to assemble a machine, or taking inventory in a discount retail store. But none of these situations is especially complex dynamically.

When the same action has dramatically different effects in the short run and the long, there is dynamic complexity. When an action has one set of consequences locally and a very different set of consequences in another part of the system, there is dynamic complexity. When obvious interventions produce nonobvious consequences, there is dynamic complexity. A gyroscope is a dynamically complex machine: If you push

downward on one edge, it moves to the left; if you push another edge to the left, it moves upward. Yet, how trivially simple is a gyroscope when compared with the complex dynamics of an enterprise, where it takes days to produce something, weeks to develop a new marketing promotion, months to hire and train new people, and years to develop new products, nurture management talent, and build a reputation for quality—and all of these processes interact continually.

The real leverage in most management situations lies in understanding dynamic complexity, not detail complexity. Balancing market growth and capacity expansion is a dynamic problem. Developing a profitable mix of price, product (or service) quality, design, and availability that make a strong market position is a dynamic problem. Improving quality, lowering total costs, and satisfying customers in a sustainable manner is a dynamic problem.

Unfortunately, most "systems analyses" focus on detail complexity not dynamic complexity. Simulations with thousands of variables and complex arrays of details can actually distract us from seeing patterns and major interrelationships. In fact, sadly, for most people "systems thinking" means "fighting complexity with complexity," devising increasingly "complex" (we should really say "detailed") solutions to increasingly "complex" problems. In fact, this is the antithesis of real systems thinking. . . .

The essence of the discipline of systems thinking lies in a shift of mind:

- seeing interrelationships rather than linear cause-effect chains, and
- seeing processes of change rather than snapshots

The practice of systems thinking starts with understanding a simple concept called "feedback" that shows how actions can reinforce or counteract (balance) each other. *It builds to learning to recognize types of "structures" that recur again and again:* the arms race is a generic or archetypal pattern of escalation, at its heart no different from turf warfare between two street gangs, the demise of a marriage, or the advertising battles of two consumer goods companies fighting for market share. Eventually, systems thinking forms a rich language for describing a vast array of interrelationships and patterns of change. Ultimately, *it simplifies life* by helping us see the deeper patterns lying behind the events and the details. . . .

SEEING CIRCLES OF CAUSALITY[2]

Reality is made up of circles but we see straight lines. Herein lie the beginnings of our limitation as systems thinkers.

One of the reasons for this fragmentation in our thinking stems from our language. Language shapes perception. What we *see* depends on what we are prepared to see. Western languages, with their subject-verb-object structure, are biased toward a linear view.[3] If we want to see systemwide interrelationships, we need a language of interrelationships, a language made up of circles. Without such a language, our habitual ways of seeing the world produce fragmented views and counterproductive actions—as it has done for decision makers in the arms race. Such a language is important in facing dynamically complex issues and strategic choices, especially when individuals, teams, and organizations need to see beyond events and into the forces that shape change.

To illustrate the rudiments of the new language, consider a very simple system—filling a glass of water. You might think, "That's not a system—it's too simple." But think again.

From the linear viewpoint, we say, "I am filling a glass of water." . . .

But, in fact, as we fill the glass, we are watching the water level rise. We monitor the "gap" between the level and our goal, the "desired water level." As the water approaches the desired level, we adjust the faucet position to slow the flow of water, until it is turned off when the glass is full. In fact, when we fill a glass of water we operate in a "water-regulation" system involving five variables: our desired water level, the glass's current water level, the gap between the two, the faucet position, and the water flow. These variables are organized in a circle or loop of cause-effect relationships which is called a "feedback process." The process operates continuously to bring the water level to its desired level.

People get confused about "feedback" because we often use the word in a somewhat different way—to gather opinions about an act we have undertaken. "Give me some feedback on the brewery decision," you might say. "What did you think of the way I handled it?" In that context, "positive feedback" means encouraging remarks and "negative feedback" means bad news. But in systems thinking, feedback is a broader concept. It means any reciprocal flow of influence. In systems thinking it is an axiom that every influence is both *cause* and *effect*. Nothing is ever influenced in just one direction. . . .

Though simple in concept, the feedback loop overturns deeply ingrained ideas—such as causality. In everyday English we say, "I am filling the glass of water" without thinking very deeply about the real meaning of the statement. It implies a one-way causality—"I am causing the water level to rise." More precisely, "My hand on the faucet is controlling the rate of flow of water into the glass." Clearly, this statement describes only half of the feedback process: the linkages from "faucet position" to "flow of water" to "water level."

But it would be just as true to describe only the other "half" of the process: "The level of water in the glass is controlling my hand."

Both statements are equally incomplete. The more complete statement of causality is that my intent to fill a glass of water creates a system that causes water to flow in when the level is low, then shuts the flow off when the glass is full. In other words, the structure causes the behavior. This distinction is important because seeing only individual actions and missing the structure underlying the actions . . . lies at the root of our powerlessness in complex situations.

In fact, all causal attributions made in everyday English are highly suspect! Most are embedded in linear ways of seeing. They are at best partially accurate, inherently biased toward describing portions of reciprocal processes, not the entire processes.

Another idea overturned by the feedback perspective is anthropocentrism— or seeing ourselves as the center of activities. The simple description, "I am filling the glass of water," suggests a world of human actors standing at the center of activity, operating on an inanimate reality. *From the systems perspective, the human actor is part of the feedback process, not standing apart from it. This represents a profound shift in awareness.* It allows us to see how we are continually both influenced by and influencing our reality. It is the shift in awareness so ardently advocated by ecologists in their cries that we see ourselves as part of nature, not separate from nature. It is the shift in awareness recognized by many (but not all) of the world's great philosophical

systems—for example, the *Bhagavad Gita's* chastisement:

> All actions are wrought by the qualities of nature only. The self, deluded by egoism, thinketh: "I am the doer."[4]

In addition, the feedback concept complicates the ethical issue of responsibility. In the arms race, who is responsible? From each side's linear view, responsibility clearly lies with the other side: "It is their aggressive actions, and their nationalistic intent, that are causing us to respond by building our arms." A linear view always suggests a simple locus of responsibility. When things go wrong, this is seen as blame— "he, she, it did it"—or guilt—"I did it." At a deep level, there is no difference between blame and guilt, for both spring from linear perceptions. From the linear view, we are always looking for someone or something that must be responsible—they can even be directed toward hidden agents within ourselves. When my son was four years old, he used to say, "My stomach won't let me eat it," when turning down his vegetables. We may chuckle, but is his assignment of responsibility really different from the adult who says, "My neuroses keep me from trusting people."

In mastering systems thinking, we give up the assumption that there must be an individual, or individual agent, responsible. The feedback perspective suggests that *everyone shares responsibility for problems generated by a system.* That doesn't necessarily imply that everyone involved can exert equal leverage in changing the system. But it does imply that the search for scapegoats—a particularly alluring pastime in individualistic cultures such as ours in the United States—is a blind alley.

Finally, the feedback concept illuminates the limitations of our language. When we try to describe in words even a very simple system, such as filling the water glass, it gets very awkward: "When I fill a glass of water, there is a feedback process that causes me to adjust the faucet position, which adjusts the water flow and feeds back to alter the water position. The goal of the process is to make the water level rise to my desired level." This is precisely why a new language for describing systems is needed. If it is this awkward to describe a system as simple as filling a water glass, *imagine our difficulties using everyday English to describe the multiple feedback processes in an organization.*

All this takes some getting used to. We are steeped in a linear language for describing our experience. We find simple statements about causality and responsibility familiar and comfortable. It is not that they must be given up, anymore than you give up English to learn French. There are many situations where simple linear descriptions suffice and looking for feedback processes would be a waste of time. But not when dealing with problems of dynamic complexity.

REINFORCING AND BALANCING FEEDBACK AND DELAYS: THE BUILDING BLOCKS OF SYSTEMS THINKING

There are two distinct types of feedback processes: reinforcing and balancing. *Reinforcing* (or amplifying) feedback processes are the engines of growth. Whenever you are in a situation where things are growing, you can be sure that reinforcing feedback is at work. Reinforcing feedback can also generate accelerating decline—a pattern of decline where small drops amplify themselves into larger and larger drops, such as the decline in bank assets when there is a financial panic.

Balancing (or stabilizing) feedback operates whenever there is a goal-oriented behavior. If the goal is to be not moving,

then balancing feedback will act the way the brakes in a car do. If the goal is to be moving at sixty miles per hour, then balancing feedback will cause you to accelerate to sixty but no faster. The "goal" can be an explicit target, as when a firm seeks a desired market share, or it can be implicit, such as a bad habit, which despite disavowing, we stick to nevertheless.

In addition, many feedback processes contain "*delays*," interruptions in the flow of influence which make the consequences of actions occur gradually.

All ideas in the language of systems thinking are built up from these elements, just as English sentences are built up from nouns and verbs. Once we have learned the building blocks, we can begin constructing stories: the systems archetypes . . .

REINFORCING FEEDBACK: DISCOVERING HOW SMALL CHANGES CAN GROW

If you are in a reinforcing feedback system, you may be blind to how small actions can grow into large consequences—for better or for worse. Seeing the system often allows you to influence how it works.

For example, managers frequently fail to appreciate the extent to which their own expectations influence subordinates' performance. If I see a person as having high potential, I give him special attention to develop that potential. When he flowers, I feel that my original assessment was correct and I help him still further. Conversely, those I regard as having lower potential languish in disregard and inattention, perform in a disinterested manner, and further justify, in my mind, the lack of attention I give them.

Psychologist Robert Merton first identified this phenomenon as the "self-fulfilling prophecy."[5] It is also known as the "Pygmalion effect," after the famous George Bernard Shaw play (later to become *My Fair Lady*). Shaw in turn had taken his title from Pygmalion, a character in Greek and Roman mythology, who believed so strongly in the beauty of the statue he had carved that it came to life. . . .

In *reinforcing processes* such as the Pygmalion effect, a small change builds on itself. Whatever movement occurs is amplifed, producing more movement in the same direction. A small action snowballs, with more and more and still more of the same, resembling compounding interest. Some reinforcing (amplifying) processes are "vicious cycles," in which things start off badly and grow worse. The "gas crisis" was a classic example. Word that gasoline was becoming scarce set off a spate of trips to the local service station, to fill up. Once people started seeing lines of cars, they were convinced that the crisis was here. Panic and hoarding then set in. Before long, everyone was "topping off" their tanks when they were only one-quarter empty, lest they be caught when the pumps went dry. A run on a bank is another example, as are escalation structures such as the arms race or price wars.

But there's nothing inherently bad about reinforcing loops. There are also "virtuous cycles"—processes that reinforce in desired directions. For instance, physical exercise can lead to a reinforcing spiral; you feel better, thus you exercise more, thus you're rewarded by feeling better and exercise still more. The arms race run in reverse, if it can be sustained, makes another virtuous circle. The growth of any new product involves reinforcing spirals. For example, many products grow from "word of mouth." Word of mouth about a product can reinforce a snowballing sense of good feeling (as occurred with the Volkswagen Beetle

and more recent Japanese imports) as satisfied customers tell others who then become satisfied customers, who tell still others. . . .

The behavior that results from a reinforcing loop is either accelerating growth or accelerating decline. . . .

Positive word of mouth produced rapidly rising sales of Volkswagens during the 1950s, and videocassette recorders during the 1980s. A bank run produces an accelerating decline in a bank's deposits.

Folk wisdom speaks of reinforcing loops in terms such as "snowball effect," "bandwagon effect," or "vicious circle," and in phrases describing particular systems: "the rich get richer and the poor get poorer." In business, we know that "momentum is everything," in building confidence in a new product or within a fledgling organization. We also know about reinforcing spirals running the wrong way. The rats are jumping ship" suggests a situation where, as soon as a few people lose confidence, their defection will cause others to defect in a vicious spiral of eroding confidence. Word of mouth can easily work in reverse, and (as occurred with contaminated over-the-counter drugs) produce marketplace disaster.

Both good news and bad news reinforcing loops accelerate so quickly that they often take people by surprise. A French schoolchildren's jingle illustrates the process. First there is just one lily pad in a corner of a pond. But every day the number of lily pads doubles. It takes thirty days to fill the pond, but for the first twenty-eight days, no one even notices. Suddenly, on the twenty-ninth day, the pond is half full of lily pads and the villagers become concerned. But by this time there is little that can be done. The next day their worst fears come true. That's why environmental dangers are so worrisome, especially those that follow reinforcing patterns (as many environmentalists fear occurs with such pollutants as CFCs). By the time the problem is noticed, it may be too late. Extinctions of species often follow patterns of slow, gradually accelerating decline over long time periods, then rapid demise. So do extinctions of corporations.

But pure accelerating growth or decline rarely continues unchecked in nature, because reinforcing processes rarely occur in isolation. Eventually, limits are encountered—which can slow growth, stop it, divert it, or even reverse it. Even the lily pads stop growing when the limit of the pond's perimeter is encountered. These limits are one form of *balancing feedback*, which, after reinforcing processes, is the second basic element of systems thinking.

BALANCING PROCESSES: DISCOVERING THE SOURCES OF STABILITY AND RESISTANCE

If you are in a balancing system, you are in a system that is seeking stability. If the system's goal is one you like, you will be happy. If it is not, you will find all your efforts to change matters frustrated—until you can either change the goal or weaken its influence.

Nature loves a balance—but many times, human decision makers act contrary to these balances, and pay the price. For example, managers under budget pressure often cut back staff to lower costs, but eventually discover that their remaining staff is now overworked, and their costs have not gone down at all—because the remaining work has been farmed out to consultants, or because overtime has made up the difference. The reason that costs don't stay down is that *the system has its own agenda.* There is an implicit goal, unspoken but very real—the amount of work that is expected to get done.

In a balancing (stabilizing) system, there is a self-correction that attempts to maintain some goal or target. Filling the glass of water is a balancing process with the goal of a full glass. Hiring new employees is a balancing process with the goal of having a target work force size or rate of growth. Steering a car and staying upright on a bicycle are also examples of balancing processes, where the goal is heading in a desired direction.

Balancing feedback processes are everywhere. They underlie all goal-oriented behavior. Complex organisms such as the human body contain thousands of balancing feedback processes that maintain temperature and balance, heal our wounds, adjust our eyesight to the amount of light, and alert us to threat. A biologist would say that all of these processes are the mechanisms by which our body achieves *homeostasis*—its ability to maintain conditions for survival in a changing environment. Balancing feedback prompts us to eat when we need food, and to sleep when we need rest, or . . . to put on a sweater when we are cold.

As in all balancing processes, the crucial element—our body temperature—gradually adjusts itself toward its desired level.

Organizations and societies resemble complex organisms because they too have myriad balancing feedback processes. In corporations, the production and materials ordering process is constantly adjusting in response to changes in incoming orders; short-term (discounts) and long-term (list) prices adjust in response to changes in demand or competitors' prices; and borrowing adjusts with changes in cash balances or financing needs.

Planning creates longer-term balancing processes. A human resource plan might establish long-term growth targets in head count and in skill profile of the work force to match anticipated needs. Market research and R&D plans shape new product development and investments in people, technologies, and capital plant to build competitive advantage.

What makes balancing processes so difficult in management is that the goals are often implicit, and no one recognizes that the balancing process exists at all. I recall a good friend who tried, fruitlessly, to reduce burnout among professionals in his rapidly growing training business. He wrote memos, shortened working hours, even closed and locked offices earlier—all attempts to get people to stop overworking. But all these actions were offset—people ignored the memos, disobeyed the shortened hours, and took their work home with them when the offices were locked. Why? Because an unwritten norm in the organization stated that the *real* heros, the people who really cared and who got ahead in the organization, worked seventy hours a week—a norm that my friend had established himself by his own prodigious energy and long hours.

To understand how an organism works we must understand its balancing processes—those that are explicit *and* implicit. We could master long lists of body parts, organs, bones, veins, and blood vessels and yet we would not understand how the body functions—until we understand how the neuromuscular system maintains balance, or how the cardiovascular system maintains blood pressure and oxygen levels. This is why many attempts to redesign social systems fail. The state-controlled economy fails because it severs the multiple self-correcting processes that operate in a free market system.[6] This is why corporate mergers often fail. . . .

Though simple in concept, balancing processes can generate surprising and problematic behavior if they go undetected.

In general, balancing loops are more difficult to see than reinforcing loops because it often *looks* like nothing is happening. There's no dramatic growth of sales and marketing expenditures, or nuclear arms, or lily pads. Instead, the balancing process maintains the status quo, even when all participants want change. The feeling, as Lewis Carroll's Queen of Hearts put it, of needing "all the running you can do to keep in the same place," is a clue that a balancing loop may exist nearby.

Leaders who attempt organizational change often find themselves unwittingly caught in balancing processes. To the leaders, it looks as though their efforts are clashing with sudden resistance that seems to come from nowhere. In fact, as my friend found when he tried to reduce burnout, the resistance is a response by the system, trying to maintain an implicit system goal. Until this goal is recognized, the change effort is doomed to failure. So long as the leader continues to be the "model," his work habits will set the norm. Either he must change his habits, or establish new and different models.

Whenever there is "resistance to change," you can count on there being one or more "hidden" balancing processes. Resistance to change is neither capricious nor mysterious. It almost always arises from threats to traditional norms and ways of doing things. Often these norms are woven into the fabric of established power relationships. The norm is entrenched because the distribution of authority and control is entrenched. Rather than pushing harder to overcome resistance to change, artful leaders discern the source of the resistance. They focus directly on the implicit norms and power relationships within which the norms are embedded.

DELAYS: WHEN THINGS HAPPEN . . . EVENTUALLY

As we've seen, systems seem to have minds of their own. Nowhere is this more evident than in delays—interruptions between your actions and their consequences. Delays can make you badly overshoot your mark, or they can have a positive effect if you recognize them and work with them. . . .

Delays, when the effect of one variable on another takes time, constitute the third basic building block for a systems language. Virtually all feedback processes have some form of delay. But often the delays are either unrecognized or not well understood. This can result in "overshoot," going further than needed to achieve a desired result. The delay between eating and feeling full has been the nemesis of many a happy diner; we don't yet feel full when we should stop eating, so we keep going until we are overstuffed. The delay between starting a new construction project and its completion results in overbuilding real estate markets and an eventual shake-out. . . .

Unrecognized delays can also lead to instability and breakdown, especially when they are long. Adjusting the shower temperature, for instance, is far more difficult when there is a ten-second delay before the water temperature adjusts, then when the delay takes only a second or two.

During that ten seconds after you turn up the heat, the water remains cold. You receive no response to your action; so you *perceive* that your act has had no effect. You respond by continuing to turn up the heat. When the hot water finally arrives, a 190-degree water gusher erupts from the faucet. You jump out and turn it back; and, after another delay, it's frigid again. On and on you go, through the balancing loop process. Each cycle of adjustments compensates somewhat for the cycle before. . . .

The more aggressive you are in your behavior—the more drastically you turn the knobs—the longer it will take to reach the right temperature. That's one of the lessons of balancing loops with delays: that aggressive action often produces exactly the opposite of what is intended. It produces instability and oscillation, instead of moving you more quickly toward your goal.

Delays are no less problematic in reinforcing loops. In the arms race example, each side perceives itself as gaining advantage from expanding its arsenal because of the delay in the other side's response. This delay can be as long as five years because of the time required to gather intelligence on the other side's weaponry, and to design and deploy new weapons. It is this temporary perceived advantage that keeps the escalation process going. If each side were able to respond instantly to buildups of its adversary, incentives to keep building would be nil.

The systems viewpoint is generally oriented toward the long-term view. That's why delays and feedback loops are so important. In the short term, you can often ignore them; they're inconsequential. They only come back to haunt you in the long term.

Reinforcing feedback, balancing feedback, and delays are all fairly simple. They come into their own as building blocks for the "systems archetypes"—more elaborate structures that recur in our personal and work lives again and again.

NOTES

1. A comprehensive summary of the "cybernetic" and "servo-mechanism" schools of thought in the social sciences can be found in George Richardson, *Feedback Thought in*

Social Science and Systems Theory (Philadelphia: University of Pennsylvania Press), 1990.

2. The principles and tools of systems thinking have emerged from diverse roots in physics, engineering, biology, and mathematics. The particular tools presented in this chapter come from the "system dynamics" approach pioneered by Jay Forrester at MIT. See, for example, *Industrial Dynamics* (Cambridge, Mass.: MIT Press), 1961; *Urban Dynamics* (Cambridge, Mass.: MIT Press), 1969; and "The Counterintuitive Behavior of Social Systems," *Technology Review* (January 1971), 52–68. This particular section owes a special debt to Donella Meadows, whose earlier article "Whole Earth Models and Systems," *Co-Evolution Quarterly* (Summer 1982), 98–108 provided the model and the inspiration for its development.

3. By contrast, many "Eastern" languages such as Chinese and Japanese do not build up from subject-verb-object linear sequences. David Crystal, *The Cambridge Encyclopedia of Language* (New York: Cambridge University Press), 1987.

4. The *Bhagavad-Gita*, or "The Lord's Song," translated by Annie Besant, reprinted in Robert O. Ballou, *The Bible of the World* (New York: Viking), 1939.

5. Robert K. Merton, "The Self-Fulfilling Prophecy," in Robert K. Merton, editor, *Social Theory and Social Structure* (New York: Free Press), 1968.

6. This does not suggest that free-market forces are sufficient for all forms of balance and control needed in modern societies—delays, inadequate information, unrealistic expectations, and distortions such as monopoly power also reduce efficiency of "free markets."

43
Reinventing Government: Introduction
David Osborne & Ted Gaebler

As the 1980s drew to a close, *Time* magazine asked on its cover: "Is Government Dead?"

As the 1990s unfold, the answer—to many Americans—appears to be yes.

Our public schools are the worst in the developed world. Our health care system is out of control. Our courts and prisons are so overcrowded that convicted felons walk free. And many of our proudest cities and states are virtually bankrupt.

Confidence in government has fallen to record lows. By the late 1980s, only 5 percent of Americans surveyed said they would choose government service as their preferred career.[1] Only 13 percent of top federal employees said they would recommend a career in public service.[2] Nearly three out of four Americans said they believed Washington delivered less value for the dollar than it had 10 years earlier.[3]

And then, in 1990, the bottom fell out. It was as if all our governments had hit the wall, at the same time. Our states struggled with multibillion-dollar deficits. Our cities laid off thousands of employees. Our federal deficit ballooned toward $350 billion.

Since the tax revolt first swept the nation in 1978, the American people have demanded, in election after election and on issue after issue, more performance for less money. And yet, during the recession of 1990 and 1991, their leaders debated the same old options: fewer services or higher taxes.

Today, public fury alternates with apathy. We watch breathlessly as Eastern Europe and the Soviet republics overthrow the deadening hand of bureaucracy and oppression. But at home we feel impotent. Our cities succumb to mounting crime and poverty, our states are handcuffed by staggering deficits, and Washington drifts through it all like 30 square miles bounded by reality.

Yet there is hope. Slowly, quietly, far from the public spotlight, new kinds of public institutions are emerging. They are lean, decentralized, and innovative. They are flexible, adaptable, quick to learn new ways when conditions change. They use competition, customer choice, and other nonbureaucratic mechanisms to get things done as creatively and effectively as possible. And they are our future.

Visalia, California, is the prototypical American community. A leafy oasis of 75,000 people in California's hot, dry San Joaquin Valley, it is the county seat of rural, conservative Tulare County. It is an All-American city: the streets are clean, the lawns are mowed, the Rotary Clubs are full.

In 1978, Proposition 13 cut Visalia's tax base by 25 percent. With financing from one final bond issue that slipped

Source: Reinventing Government: How the Entrepreneurial Spirit is Transforming the Public Sector (pp 1–24), © 1992 by David Osborne and Ted Gaebler. Reprinted by permission of Addison-Wesley Publishing Company, Inc.

through on the same day as Proposition 13, the school district managed to build a new high school. But as the years went by, it could never scrape together the money to put in a swimming pool.

One hot Thursday in August 1984, a parks and recreation employee got a call from a friend in Los Angeles, who told him that the Olympic committee was selling its training pool. The employee immediately called the school district, and two days later he and an assistant superintendent flew down to take a look. They liked what they saw: an all-aluminum, Olympic-size pool that would likely survive an earthquake. To buy one new, they would have spent at least $800,000; they could buy this one slightly used and put it in the ground for half that amount.

Like any other government agency, the school district needed at least two weeks to advertise the question, hold a board meeting, and get approval for a special appropriation. But on Monday, the parks and recreation employee got a second call. Two colleges wanted the pool, and they were racing each other to get the nonrefundable $60,000 deposit together. So he got in his car and took a check down that afternoon.

How could a third-level parks and recreation employee get a check for $60,000, with no action by the city council and no special appropriation? The answer is simple. Visalia had adopted a radically new budget system, which allowed managers to respond quickly as circumstances changed. Called the Expenditure Control Budget, it made two simple changes. First, it eliminated all line items within departmental budgets—freeing managers to move resources around as needs shifted. Second, it allowed departments to keep what they didn't spend from one year to the next, so they could shift unused funds to new priorities.

Normal government budgets encourage managers to waste money. If they don't spend their entire budget by the end of the fiscal year, three things happen: they lose the money they have saved; they get less next year; and the budget director scolds them for requesting too much last year. Hence the time-honored government rush to spend all funds by the end of the fiscal year. By allowing departments to keep their savings, Visalia not only eliminated this rush, but encouraged managers to save money. The idea was to get them thinking like owners: "If this were my money, would I spend it this way?"

Under the new budget system, Visalia's Parks and Recreation Department had managed to save $60,000 toward a new pool. Arne Croce, an assistant city manager who had worked on the problem, knew that both the school district and the city council wanted a pool. Between them, he was sure, they could find $400,000. (They ended up raising nearly half the money with a community fundraising drive.) Because Visalia regularly engaged in strategic planning, Croce also understood the city's priorities and values—he knew, for instance, that the council and manager valued entrepreneurial behavior. Although the Olympic pool was a totally unexpected opportunity, he had no qualms about seizing it. "It's something you'd find in private enterprise," said the admiring school superintendent. "You don't have the bureaucracy you have to deal with in most governments." . . .

In Visalia, even the man in charge of street sweeping changed his thinking. For years, Ernie Vierra had had the streets swept every three weeks. Quietly, under the guise of equipment problems, he tried four weeks, then five. When he hit six the complaints rolled in, so he eventually settled on four. He did the same thing with the grass in the parks.

Visalia's Police Department pioneered a lease-purchase program for squad cars that was quickly copied by two dozen other cities. The shop that repaired Visalia's vehicles cut its energy consumption by 30 percent. By 1985, with other California governments still crying poor in the wake of Proposition 13, Visalia had $20 million in cash squirreled away—almost as much as its entire annual operating budget. (Ironically, by freezing property taxes, Proposition 13 made it impossible for Visalia to lower its rates.)

The philosophy embodied by the new budget—a philosophy city leaders dubbed "public entrepreneurial management"—permeated the organization. Managers talked of "profit centers," "enterprise budgets," "the CEO," and the "board of directors." They gave bonuses of up to $1,000 per person to reward outstanding group effort. And they encouraged employees to help the city save or earn money by allowing them to take home 15 percent of the savings or earnings their innovations generated in their first year—with no ceiling on the amount.

When Visalia's leaders decided the city needed more cultural life, the convention director coventured with private promoters to bring in headliner acts, limiting their risk by putting up half the capital and taking half the profits. When a citizens' task force found a dearth of affordable housing, the city helped create a private, nonprofit organization, loaned it $100,000, and sold it 13 acres of excess city land. Fifteen months later, 89 families—with incomes ranging from $9,000 to $18,000 a year—moved into their own single-family homes. The planning department officials assigned to work on the project gave up their summer vacations to bring it in on time. But they didn't mind. "We've got one of the most exciting jobs in the city," one of them said. "It's like owning your own business—you spend the amount of time necessary to get the job done."

East Harlem is not the prototypical American community. It is one of the poorest communities in America. Single mothers head more than half of its families; 35 percent of its residents are on public assistance; median income is $8,300.[4] Dilapidated public schools—their windows covered by protective grilles—coexist with crack houses. East Harlem is precisely the sort of community in which public schools normally fail. Yet it has some of the most successful public schools in America.

New York City has 32 school districts. Twenty years ago, Community School District 4, in East Harlem, was at the bottom of the barrel: thirty-second out of 32 in test scores. Only 15 percent of its students—*15 of every 100*—read at grade level. Attendance rates were pathetic.[5]

"It was totally out of control," says Michael Friedman, now director of a junior high called the Bridge School:

> The year before I started the Bridge School was probably the worst year of my life. The schools were chaotic, they were overcrowded. There was a lot of violence, gangs roaming the streets. It was sink or swim as a classroom teacher. They closed the door: "That's your class, do what you can. "And it seemed like nobody could or would try to do anything about it. You had a lot of people who had been there a long time, and they were just punching that clock.

In 1974, out of sheer desperation, then superintendent Anthony Alvarado, an assistant principal named John Falco, and several teachers decided they had to get the "incorrigible, recalcitrant, aggressive kids"[6] out of the schools, so others could learn. They created an alternative junior high for troubled students.

The task was so daunting that Alvarado told Falco and his teachers to do whatever it took to get results. They created a very nontraditional school, which worked. Two other alternative schools opened that year were also successful, so they tried several more. Soon teachers began proposing others: the East Harlem Career Academy, the Academy of Environmental Sciences, the Isaac Newton School of Science and Mathematics, a traditional school in which children wore uniforms. Each provided a basic core of instruction in math, English, and social sciences, but each also had its own special focus.

Before long, parents and students in District 4 found themselves with a variety of choices. But they could choose only within the "zone" where they lived, and there were only so many spots in the alternative schools. "We had created alternative schools to create good learning environments," says Falco, "but we couldn't let everyone into them. So there was a lot of pressure from parents. It just made sense to go further." In 1983, the district converted all its junior high schools to schools of choice, doing away with assignment by zone. By 1990, District 4 boasted 21 junior high schools, plus six alternative grade schools.[7]

Under the new system, schools were no longer synonymous with buildings; many buildings housed three or four schools, one on each floor. (All told, there were 52 schools in 20 buildings.) Schools were small—from 50 to 300 students—and education was personal. "Kids need to be dealt with personally," says Falco, who now administers the choice program. "The downsizing of the schools has been a tremendous plus."

Alvarado also decentralized authority: he let teachers manage their own schools. Principals still administered school buildings, but actual schools were run by "directors"—most of whom also taught—and their teachers. If a teacher wanted to create a new school, or move to an alternative school, Alvarado usually said yes. This simple change released tremendous energy. "There are teachers who were burned out—they were going nowhere," says Falco. "We put them in an alternative setting, and they flowered."

Before long, the junior highs were competing for students. Teachers and directors began paying close attention to how many applicants ranked their schools number one each spring. And district leaders began closing schools that were not attracting enough students, or replacing their directors and staff. "If you're not operating a program that kids want to come to, you're out of business," says Falco. "You just can't rest on your laurels. You have to continually strive for ways to meet the needs of these kids." Successful schools, on the other hand, were allowed to grow until they hit an upper limit of about 300. At that point, district leaders encouraged their directors to clone them, if space was available for another school.

Ed Rodriguez, principal of one of the last junior highs to become a school of choice, was not eager to compete. But he found the competition a powerful motivator:

> Now that we absolutely have to attract youngsters to our building, we have to really take a long, hard look at ourselves and determine—Are we good enough? Are we going to be competitive enough? We replaced the idea that we're going to be here forever with the idea that we are here with a purpose, and that purpose has to be maximized. The mission, the dream of the school, has to be in everyone's mind and everyone's heart. The level of performance has to increase.[8]

Just as important as competition and a sense of mission is the ownership students and teachers feel for their schools.

Rather than being assigned to a school and offered a cookie-cutter education, they are allowed to choose the style of education they prefer. They can choose traditional schools or open classrooms; schools with mentor programs or those that use heavy tutoring; reading institutes for those behind grade level or advanced schools for gifted students; photography programs or computer programs; experiential education or even a school run in cooperation with the Big Apple Circus.

"When a child chooses the school, there's ownership in that choice," says Robert Nadel, assistant director of a junior high called the Creative Learning Center. "There's also ownership on the part of the parent and ownership on the part of the teachers." That ownership translates into student attitudes very different from those created when a child is simply assigned to a building. "What you own," says Sy Fliegel, the choice system's first director, "you treat better."[9]

The results of District 4's experiment have been startling. Reading scores are up sharply: in 1973, 15 percent of junior high students read at grade level; by 1988, 64 percent did.[10] Writing skills have improved: in 1988, state tests found that 75 percent of the district's eighth-graders were competent writers.[11] And the percentage of District 4 graduates accepted to New York's four elite public high schools, such as Bronx Science and Brooklyn Technical, has shot up. In the mid-1970s, fewer than 10 of District 4's graduates were admitted to these schools each year. By 1987, 139 were—10 percent of District 4's graduates, almost double the rate for the rest of New York City. Another 180 attended a second tier of selective public high schools. And 36 went to selective private schools, including Andover and the Hill School. All told, more than a quarter of District 4's graduates earned places in outstanding high schools—schools that were virtually off limits 15 years before.[12]

District 4 is smack in the middle of one of America's most renowned ghettos. Yet it has a waiting list of teachers who want to work there.[13] Perhaps the most telling statistic is this: out of 14,000 students in District 4, close to 1,000 come in from outside the district. "On any given day, I receive at least four or five calls from parents requesting admission from outside the district," says Falco. "I just have to turn them away."[14]

Bob Stone works in America's archetypal bureaucracy, the Department of Defense. As deputy assistant secretary of defense for installations, he has at least theoretical authority over 600 bases and facilities, which house 4.5 million people and consume $100 billion a year. Soon after he was promoted to the job, in 1981, Stone visited an air base in Sicily. "We have 2,000 airmen there, and they're out in the middle of nowhere," he says:

No families, no towns. They are an hour and a half drive over a horrible mountain road from a Sicilian city of 20,000—and when you get there there's not much to do. So most of our bases have bowling alleys, and we built a bowling alley at this base. I visited them two or three weeks after the bowling center opened. They took me in and they started showing me plans—they're going to take out this wall and add six more lanes over there. I thought, "Gee, you've been open for a couple of weeks, and you're going to tear the place apart and expand it? Why is that?"

"Well," they told me, "there's this rule that says, if you have 2,000 troops, you're allowed to construct eight lanes." [You can get a waiver to build more—but only after you can prove you need them.] I got the book and that is what it says: 1,000 troops, four lanes; 2,000 troops, eight lanes. And it's true if you're in the wilds of Sicily, with no families, or in the northern part of Greenland, where you can't even go outdoors for most of the year.

The rule book Stone refers to covered 400 pages. The rules governing the operation of military housing covered 800 pages. Personnel rules for civilian employees covered another 8,800 pages. "My guess is that *a third* of the defense budget goes into the friction of following bad regulations—doing work that doesn't have to be done," Stone says. Engineers in New Mexico write reports to convince people in Washington that their roofs leak. Soldiers trek halfway across their bases to the base chemist when the shelf life of a can of spray paint expires, to have it certified for another year. The Department of Defense (DOD) pays extra for special paint, but because it takes longer to establish its specifications than it takes companies to improve their paint, DOD employees pay a premium for paint that is inferior to paint available at their local store.

"This kind of rule has two costs," Stone says. "One is, we've got people wasting time. But the biggest cost—and the reason I say it's a third of the defense budget—is it's a message broadcast to everybody that works around this stuff that it's a crazy outfit. 'You're dumb. We don't trust you. Don't try to apply your common sense.'"

Stone cut the rules governing military base construction from 400 pages down to 4, those governing housing from 800 to 40. Then he decided to go farther. In an experiment straight out of *In Search of Excellence*, he decided to turn one base, called a Model Installation, free from these rules and regulations. If the commander would commit to radically improving his installation, Stone would do his best to get any rules that were standing in his way waived. The principle was simple: let the base commander run the base his way, rather than Washington's

way. A corollary was also important: if he saved money in the process, he didn't have to give it back. He could keep it to spend on whatever he felt was most important.

Forty commanders volunteered for the experiment. In the first two years, they submitted more than 8,000 requests for waivers or changes in regulations. Stone can tell stories about them for hours. In the air force, for instance, airmen use complex electronic test kits to check Minuteman missiles. When a kit fails, they send it to Hill Air Force Base in Utah for repair. Meanwhile, the missile is put off alert—typically for 10 days. An airman at Whiteman Air Force Base got approval to fix the test kits himself— and suddenly Whiteman didn't have a Minuteman missile off alert for more than three hours.

Throughout Defense, people buy by the book. Stone holds up a simple steam trap, which costs $100. "When it leaks," he says, "it leaks $50 a week worth of steam. The lesson is, when it leaks, replace it quick. But it takes us a year to replace it, because we have a system that wants to make sure we get the very best buy on this $100 item, and maybe by waiting a year we can buy the item for $2 less. In the meantime, we've lost $3,000 worth of steam." Under the Model Installations program, commanders requested authority to buy things on their own. An entire army command requested permission to let craftsmen decide for themselves when spray paint cans should be thrown away, rather than taking them to the base chemist. Five air force bases received permission to manage their own construction, rather than paying the Corps of Engineers to do it. Shaken by the threat of competition, the corps adopted a new goal: to be "leaders in customer care."[15]

The Model Installations experiment was so successful that in March 1986,

Deputy Secretary of Defense William Howard Taft IV directed that it be applied to all defense installations. Stone and his staff then developed a budget experiment modeled on Visalia's system. Normal installation budgets, first drawn up *three years in advance*, include hundreds of specific line items. The Unified Budget Test allowed commanders to ignore the line items and shift resources as needs changed.

In its first year, the test revealed that 7 to 10 percent of the funding locked into line items was in the wrong account, and that when commanders could move it around, they could significantly increase the performance of their troops. The army compared the results at its two participating bases with normal bases and concluded that in just one year, the Unified Budget increased performance by 3 percent. The long-term impact would no doubt be greater. According to Stone and his colleagues, "Senior leaders in the Services have estimated that if all the unnecessary constraints on their money were removed, they could accomplish their missions with up to 10 percent less money." But in a $100 billion installations budget, even 3 percent is $3 billion.[16]

Visalia, East Harlem, and the Defense Department are not alone. Look almost anywhere in America, and you will see similar success stories. We believe these organizations represent the future.

Our thesis is simple: The kind of governments that developed during the industrial era, with their sluggish, centralized bureaucracies, their preoccupation with rules and regulations, and their hierarchical chains of command, no longer work very well. They accomplished great things in their time, but somewhere along the line they got away from us. They became bloated, wasteful, ineffective. And when the world began to change, they failed to change with it.

Hierarchical, centralized bureaucracies designed in the 1930s or 1940s simply do not function well in the rapidly changing, information-rich, knowledge-intensive society and economy of the 1990s. They are like luxury ocean liners in an age of supersonic jets: big, cumbersome, expensive, and extremely difficult to turn around. Gradually, new kinds of public institutions are taking their place.

Government is hardly leading the parade; similar transformations are taking place throughout American society. American corporations have spent the last decade making revolutionary changes: decentralizing authority, flattening hierarchies, focusing on quality, getting close to their customers—all in an effort to remain competitive in the new global marketplace. Our voluntary, nonprofit organizations are alive with new initiatives. New "partnerships" blossom overnight—between business and education, between for-profits and nonprofits, between public sector and private. It is as if virtually all institutions in American life were struggling at once to adapt to some massive sea change—striving to become more flexible, more innovative, and more entrepreneurial.

THE BANKRUPTCY OF BUREAUCRACY

It is hard to imagine today, but 100 years ago the word *bureaucracy* meant something positive. It connoted a rational, efficient method of organization—something to take the place of the arbitrary exercise of power by authoritarian regimes. Bureaucracies brought the same logic to government work that the assembly line brought to the factory. With their hierarchical authority and functional specialization, they made possible the efficient undertaking of large, complex tasks. Max Weber, the great German sociologist, described them using words no modern American would dream of applying:

> The decisive reason for the advance of bureaucratic organization has always been its purely technical superiority over any other form of organization. . . .
>
> Precision, speed, unambiguity, . . . reduction of friction and of material and personal costs—these are raised to the optimum point in the strictly bureaucratic administration.[17]

In the United States, the emergence of bureaucratic government was given a particular twist by its turn-of-the-century setting. A century ago, our cities were growing at breakneck speed, bulging with immigrants come to labor in the factories thrown up by our industrial revolution. Boss Tweed and his contemporaries ran these cities like personal fiefdoms: In exchange for immigrant votes, they dispensed jobs, favors, and informal services. With one hand they robbed the public blind; with the other they made sure those who delivered blocs of loyal votes were amply rewarded. Meanwhile, they ignored many of the new problems of industrial America— its slums, its sweatshops, its desperate need for a new infrastructure of sewers and water and public transit.

Young Progressives like Theodore Roosevelt, Woodrow Wilson, and Louis Brandeis watched the machines until they could stomach it no more. In the 1890s, they went to war. Over the next 30 years, the Progressive movement transformed government in America. To end the use of government jobs as patronage, the Progressives created civil service systems, with written exams, lockstep pay scales, and protection from arbitrary hiring or dismissal. To keep major construction projects like bridges and tunnels out of the reach of politicians, they created independent public authorities. To limit the power of political bosses, they split up management func-

tions, took appointments to important offices away from mayors and governors, created separately elected clerks, judges, even sheriffs. To keep the administration of public services untainted by the influence of politicians, they created a profession of city managers—professionals, insulated from politics, who would run the bureaucracy in an efficient, businesslike manner.

Thanks to Boss Tweed and his contemporaries, in other words, American society embarked on a gigantic effort to *control* what went on inside government—to keep the politicians and bureaucrats from doing anything that might endanger the public interest or purse. This cleaned up many of our governments, but in solving one set of problems it created another. In making it difficult to steal the public's money, we made it virtually impossible to *manage* the public's money. In adopting written tests scored to the third decimal point to hire our clerks and police officers and fire fighters, we built mediocrity into our work force. In making it impossible to fire people who did not perform, we turned mediocrity into deadwood. In attempting to control virtually everything, we became so obsessed with dictating *how* things should be done—regulating the process, controlling the inputs— that we ignored the outcomes, the *results*.

The product was government with a distinct ethos: slow, inefficient, impersonal. This is the mental image the word *government* invokes today; it is what most Americans assume to be the very essence of government. Even government buildings constructed during the industrial era reflect this ethos: they are immense structures, with high ceilings, large hallways, and ornate architecture, all designed to impress upon the visitor the impersonal authority and immovable weight of the institution.[18]

For a long time, the bureaucratic model worked—not because it was efficient, but because it solved the basic problems people wanted solved. It provided security—from unemployment, during old age. It provided stability, a particularly important quality after the Depression. It provided a basic sense of fairness and equity. (Bureaucracies, as Weber pointed out, are designed to treat everyone alike.) It provided jobs. And it delivered the basic, no-frills, one-size-fits-all services people needed and expected during the industrial era: roads, highways, sewers, schools.

During times of intense crisis—the Depression and two world wars—the bureaucratic model worked superbly. In crisis, when goals were clear and widely shared, when tasks were relatively straightforward, and when virtually everyone was willing to pitch in for the cause, the top-down, command-and-control mentality got things done. The results spoke for themselves, and most Americans fell in step. By the 1950s, as William H. Whyte wrote, we had become a nation of "organization men."

But the bureaucratic model developed in conditions very different from those we experience today. It developed in a slower-paced society, when change proceeded at a leisurely gait. It developed in an age of hierarchy, when only those at the top of the pyramid had enough information to make informed decisions. It developed in a society of people who worked with their hands, not their minds. It developed in a time of mass markets, when most Americans had similar wants and needs. And it developed when we had strong geographic communities—tightly knit neighborhoods and towns.

Today all that has been swept away. We live in an era of breathtaking change. We live in a global marketplace, which puts enormous competitive pressure on our economic institutions. We live in an information society, in which people get access to information almost as fast as their leaders do. We live in a knowledge-based economy, in which educated workers bridle at commands and demand autonomy. We live in an age of niche markets, in which customers have become accustomed to high quality and extensive choice.

In this environment, bureaucratic institutions developed during the industrial era—public *and* private—increasingly fail us.

Today's environment demands institutions that are extremely flexible and adaptable. It demands institutions that deliver high-quality goods and services, squeezing ever more bang out of every buck. It demands institutions that are responsive to their customers, offering choices of nonstandardized services; that lead by persuasion and incentives rather than commands; that give their employees a sense of meaning and control, even ownership. It demands institutions that *empower* citizens rather than simply *serving* them.

Bureaucratic institutions still work in some circumstances. If the environment is stable, the task is relatively simple, every customer wants the same service, and the quality of performance is not critical, a traditional public bureaucracy can do the job. Social security still works. Local government agencies that provide libraries and parks and recreational facilities still work, to a degree.

But most government institutions perform increasingly complex tasks, in competitive, rapidly changing environments, with customers who want quality and choice. These new realities have made life very difficult for our public institutions—for our public education system, for our public health care programs, for our public housing authorities, for virtually every large, bureaucratic program created by American governments before 1970. It was no accident that during the 1970s we lost a war, lost faith in our national leaders, endured repeated economic problems, and experienced a tax revolt. In the years since, the clash between old and new has only intensified. The result has been a period of enormous stress in American government.

In some ways, this is a symptom of progress—of the disruptive clash that occurs when new realities run headlong into old institutions. Our information technologies and our knowledge economy give us opportunities to do things we never dreamed possible 50 years ago. But to seize these opportunities, we must pick up the wreckage of our industrial-era institutions and rebuild. "It is the first step of wisdom," Alfred North Whitehead once wrote, "to recognize that the major advances in civilization are processes which all but wreck the society in which they occur."[19]

THE EMERGENCE OF ENTREPRENEURIAL GOVERNMENT

The first governments to respond to these new realities were local governments—in large part because they hit the wall first. On June 6, 1978, the voters of California passed Proposition 13, which cut local property taxes in half. Fed by the dual fires of inflation and dissatisfaction with public services, the tax revolt spread quickly. In 1980, Ronald Reagan took it national—and by 1982, state and local governments had lost nearly one of every four federal dollars they received in 1978.[20] During the 1982 recession, the deepest since the Depression, state governments began to hit the wall.

Under intense fiscal pressure, state and local leaders had no choice but to change the way they did business. Mayors and governors embraced "public-private partnerships" and developed "alternative" ways to deliver services. Cities fostered competition between service providers and invented new budget systems. Public managers began to speak of "enterprise management," "learning organizations," and "self-reliant cities." States began to restructure their most expensive public systems: education, health care, and welfare.

Phoenix, Arizona, put its Public Works Department in head-to-head competition with private companies for contracts to handle garbage collection, street repair, and other services. St. Paul, Minnesota, created half a dozen private, nonprofit corporations to redevelop the city. Orlando, Florida, created so many profit centers that its earnings outstripped its tax revenues. The Housing Authority of Louisville, Kentucky, began surveying its customers—15,000 residents of public housing—and encouraging them to manage their own developments. It even *sold* one development, with 100 units, to tenants.

The Michigan Department of Commerce adopted a new slogan: "Customer Service Is Our Reason for Being." It surveyed its customers, hired a customer service chief, created classes for employees in customer orientation, and set up an ombudsman with a toll-free telephone line for small businesses. Several of the department's 10 Action Teams embraced Total Quality Management, the management philosophy espoused by W. Edwards Deming.

Minnesota let parents and students choose their public schools—as in East Harlem—and six other states quickly followed suit. South Carolina developed performance incentives under which schools and teachers competed for funds to try new ideas, principals and teachers who achieved superior results got incentive pay, and schools whose students made large improvements in basic skills and attendance got extra money.[21] In the program's first three years, statewide attendance increased, teacher morale shot up faster than in any other state, and Scholastic Aptitude Test scores rose 3.6 percent, one of the largest gains in the country.

Indianapolis Mayor William Hudnut described the phenomenon as well as anyone. "In government," he said in a 1986 speech, "the routine tendency is to protect turf, to resist change, to build empires, to enlarge one's sphere of control, to protect projects and programs regardless of whether or not they are any longer needed." In contrast, the "entrepreneurial" government "searches for more efficient and effective ways of managing:

It is willing to abandon old programs and methods. It is innovative and imaginative and creative. It takes risks. It turns city functions into money makers rather than budget-busters. It eschews traditional alternatives that offer only life-support systems. It works with the private sector. It employs solid business sense. It privatizes. It creates enterprises and revenue generating operations. It is market oriented. It focuses on performance measurement. It rewards merit. It says "Let's make this work," and it is unafraid to dream the great dream.[22]

. . . It is difficult for the average citizen, who must rely on the mass media to interpret events, to make heads or tails of these changes. Their substance is all but invisible, in part because they take place outside the glare of publicity that shines on Washington. They also stubbornly refuse to fit into the traditional liberal versus conservative categories through which the media views the world. Because most reporters are asked to provide instant analysis, they have little choice but to fall back on the tried and true lenses of past practice. And because their standard formula relies on conflict to sell a story, they look for heroes and villains rather than innovation and change. In the process, they inevitably miss much that is new and significant. To paraphrase author Neil Postman, American society hurtles into the future with its eyes fixed firmly on rearview mirror.[23]

Over the past five years, as we have journeyed through the landscape of governmental change, we have sought constantly to understand the underlying trends. We have asked ourselves: What do these innovative, entrepreneurial organizations have in common? What incentives have they changed, to create such different behavior? What have they done which, if other governments did the same, would make entrepreneurship the norm and bureaucracy the exception?

The common threads were not hard to find. Most entrepreneurial governments promote *competition* between service providers. They *empower* citizens by pushing control out of the bureaucracy, into the community. They measure the performance of their agencies, focusing not on inputs but on *outcomes*. They are driven by their goals—their *missions*—not by their rules and regulations. They redefine their clients as *customers* and offer them choices—between schools, between training programs, between housing options. They *prevent* problems before they emerge, rather than simply offering services afterward. They put their energies into *earning* money, not simply spending it. They *decentralize* authority, embracing participatory management. They prefer *market* mechanisms to bureaucratic mechanisms. And they focus not simply on providing public services, but on *catalyzing* all sectors—public, private, and voluntary—

into action to solve their community's problems.

We believe that these ten principles . . . are the fundamental principles behind this new form of government we see emerging: the spokes that hold together this new wheel. Together they form a coherent whole, a new model of government. They will not solve all of our problems. But if the experience of organizations that have embraced them is any guide, they will solve the major problems we experience with bureaucratic government.

WHY GOVERNMENT CAN'T BE "RUN LIKE A BUSINESS"

Many people, who believe government should simply be "run like a business," may assume this is what we mean. It is not.

Government and business are fundamentally different institutions. Business leaders are driven by the profit motive; government leaders are driven by the desire to get reelected. Businesses get most of their money from their customers; governments get most of their money from taxpayers. Businesses are usually driven by competition; governments usually use monopolies.

Differences such as these create fundamentally different incentives in the public sector. For example, in government the ultimate test for managers is not whether they produce a product or profit—it is whether they please the elected politicians. Because politicians tend to be driven by interest groups, public managers—unlike their private counterparts—must factor interest groups into every equation.

Governments also extract their income primarily through taxation, whereas businesses earn their income when customers buy products or services of their own free will. This is one reason

why the public focuses so intensely on the cost of government services, exercising a constant impulse to *control*—to dictate how much the bureaucrats spend on every item, so they cannot possibly waste, misuse, or steal the taxpayers' money.

All these factors combine to produce an environment in which public employees view risks and rewards very differently than do private employees. "In government all of the incentive is in the direction of not making mistakes," explains Lou Winnick of the Ford Foundation. "You can have 99 successes and nobody notices, and one mistake and you're dead."[24] Standard business methods to motivate employees don't work very well in this kind of environment.

There are many other differences. Government is democratic and open; hence it moves more slowly than business, whose managers can make quick decisions behind closed doors. Government's fundamental mission is to "do good," not to make money; hence cost-benefit calculations in business turn into moral absolutes in the public sector. Government must often serve everyone equally, regardless of their ability to pay or their demand for a service; hence it cannot achieve the same market efficiencies as business. One could write an entire book about the differences between business and government. Indeed, James Q. Wilson, the eminent political scientist, already has. It is called *Bureaucracy: What Government Agencies Do and Why They Do It*.

These differences add up to one conclusion: government cannot be run like a business. There are certainly many similarities. Indeed, we believe that our ten principles underlie success for *any* institution in today's world—public, private, or nonprofit. And we have learned a great deal from business management theorists such as Peter Drucker, W. Edwards Deming, Tom Peters, and Robert Waterman. But in government, business theory is not enough. . . .

The fact that government cannot be run just like a business does not mean it cannot become more *entrepreneurial,* of course. Any institution, public or private, can be entrepreneurial, just as any institution, public or private, can be bureaucratic. Few Americans would really want government to act just like a business—making quick decisions behind closed doors for private profit. If it did, democracy would be the first casualty. But most Americans would like government to be less bureaucratic. There is a vast continuum between bureaucratic behavior and entrepreneurial behavior, and government can surely shift its position on that spectrum.

A THIRD CHOICE

Most of our leaders still tell us that there are only two ways out of our repeated public crises: we can raise taxes, or we can cut spending. For almost two decades, we have asked for a third choice. We do not want less education, fewer roads, less health care. Nor do we want higher taxes. We want better education, better roads, and better health care, for the same tax dollar.

Unfortunately, we do not know how to get what we want. Most of our leaders assume that the only way to cut spending is to eliminate programs, agencies, and employees. Ronald Reagan talked as if we could simply go into the bureaucracy with a scalpel and cut out pockets of waste, fraud, and abuse.

But waste in government does not come tied up in neat packages. It is marbled throughout our bureaucracies. It is embedded in the very way we do business. It is employees on idle, working at half speed—or barely working at all. It is people working hard at tasks that aren't

worth doing, following regulations that should never have been written, filling out forms that should never have been printed. It is the *$100 billion* a year that Bob Stone estimates the Department of Defense wastes with its foolish overregulation.

Waste in government is staggering, but we cannot get at it by wading through budgets and cutting line items. As one observer put it, our governments are like fat people who must lose weight. They need to eat less and exercise more; instead, when money is tight they cut off a few fingers and toes.

To melt the fat, we must change the basic incentives that drive our governments. We must turn bureaucratic institutions into entrepreneurial institutions, ready to kill off obsolete initiatives, willing to do more with less, eager to absorb new ideas. . . .

But our fundamental problem today is not too much government or too little government. We have debated that issue endlessly since the tax revolt of 1978, and it has not solved our problems. Our fundamental problem is that we have *the wrong kind of government*. We do not need more government or less government, we need *better* government. To be more precise, we need better *governance*.

Governance is the process by which we collectively solve our problems and meet our society's needs. Government is the instrument we use. The instrument is outdated, and the process of reinvention has begun. We do not need another New Deal, nor another Reagan Revolution. We need an American *perestroika*.

NOTES

1. "By the late 1980s, only five percent . . . ": Derek Bok, "Why Graduates Are Shunning Public-Service Careers," *Sacramento Bee,* June 26, 1988, p. 1.

2. "Only 13 percent of top federal employees . . . ": Susan B. Garland et al., "Beltway

Brain Drain: Why Civil Servants Are Making Tracks," *Business Week,* January 23, 1989, pp. 60–61. The survey cited was conducted by the federal General Accounting Office (GAO).

3. "Nearly three out of four Americans . . . ": Laurence I. Barrett, "Giving the Public What It Wants," *Time,* October 23, 1989, p. 34. From a Time/CNN poll, conducted October 9–10, 1989, by Yankelovich Clancy Shulman. The exact percentage was 73 percent.

4. "Single mothers head . . . median income is $8,300": Raymond J. Domanico, *Education Policy Paper Number 1: Model for Choice; A Report on Manhattan's District 4* (New York: Manhattan Institute for Policy Research, June 1989), p. 3.

5. "Twenty years ago . . . " and "Only 15 percent . . . ": Ibid., p. 10.

6. "Incorrigible, recalcitrant, aggressive kids": John Falco, interview with authors.

7. "By 1990, District 4 boasted . . . ": Ibid.

8. Ed Rodriguez quotation: From his remarks, at "Choosing Better Schools: Regional Strategy Meetings on Choice in Education," an East Harlem conference sponsored by the U.S. Department of Education, October 17, 1989.

9. Sy Fliegel quotation: Quoted in Robert Merrow, "Schools of Choice: More Talk Than Action," in *Public Schools By Choice,* ed. Joe Nathan (St. Paul, Minn.: Institute for Learning and Teaching, 1989), p. 118.

10. "Reading scores are up sharply . . . ": Personal communication, District 4. See also Domanico, *Education Policy Paper Number 1,* p. 10. In 1989 the reading test manufacturer renormed the test to reflect heightened reading achievement nationwide and the percentage of children in New York City schools who read at grade level dropped below 50 percent. Using these new national norms, 43.1 percent of District 4 students read at grade level in May of 1991.

11. "Writing skills have improved . . . ": Mary Ann Raywid, "The Mounting Case for Schools of Choice," in *Public Schools by Choice,* p. 27.

12. Statistics on admittance to selective public and private schools: John Falco, interview with authors, and Domanico, *Education Policy Paper Number 1,* pp. 15–17.

13. "Yet it has a waiting list . . . ": Joe Nathan, "Prime Examples of School-Choice Plans," *Wall Street Journal,* April 20, 1989.

14. "Perhaps the most telling statistic . . . ": John Falco, interview with authors.

15. "In an experiment straight out of *In Search of Excellence* . . . ": See Thomas J. Peters and Robert H. Waterman, Jr., *In Search of Excellence* (New York: Warner Books, 1982), pp. 146–47.

For more information on the Model Installations program, see *Model Installations and the Graduate Program: A DoD Report to the President's Blue Ribbon Commission on Defense Management,* May 16, 1986, available from the Office of the Deputy Assistant Secretary of Defense for Installations.

16. Data on the Unified Budget Test: *The Unified Budget Test* (Washington, D.C.: Deputy Secretary of Defense [Installations], March 1988).

17. Weber quotation: H. H. Gerth and C. Wright Mills, eds., *From Max Weber: Essays in Sociology* (New York: Oxford University Press, 1958), p. 214.

18. For a fascinating study of government buildings, see Charles T. Goodsell, *The Social Meaning of Civic Space: Studying Political Authority Through Architecture* (Lawrence: University Press of Kansas, 1988).

19. Alfred North Whitehead quotation: Quoted in William Van Dusen Wishard, "What in the World Is Going On?" *Vital Speeches,* March 1, 1990, pp. 311–317.

20. " . . . by 1982, state and local governments had lost . . . ": According to Table 21 in *Significant Features of Fiscal Federalism,* vol. 2: *Revenues and Expenditures* (Washington, D.C.: Advisory Commission on Intergovernmental Relations, 1990), p. 21, federal grants to state and local governments totaled $77.9 billion in 1978 and $88.2 billion in 1982. Expressed in 1978 dollars, the 1982 figure would have been $59.6 billion. This is a reduction of $18.3 billion, or 23.5 percent, between 1978 and 1982.

21. South Carolina's education reforms: Gary Putka, "South Carolina's Broad School Reform Includes Incentives or Punishment Based on Performance," *Wall Street Journal,* July 12, 1988, p. 62, and Terry Peterson, "Five Years and a Quantum Leap," *Entrepreneurial Economy Review* (December–January 1989), published by the Corporation for Enterprise Development, Washington, D.C.

22. William Hudnut quotation: Quoted in Marjorie George, "Can a City Be Run Like a Business?" *San Antonio* (December 1986): 22–29.

23. Neil Postman paraphrase: From Neil Postman, *Teaching As a Subversive Activity* (New York: Dell, 1987).

24. Lou Winnick quotation: From "The Cleveland Conference on Fiscal Constraints/ Constructive Responses/Action Steps," report on a conference held in Cleveland, April 21–23, 1982, sponsored by the Cleveland Foundation and the Hubert H. Humphrey Institute of Public Affairs, University of Minnesota. Available from Ted Kolderie, Center for Policy Studies, Minneapolis.

CHAPTER IX

Postmodernism and the Information Age

Large organizations today are living on the edge of a new era, on the boundary between order and chaos. In this context, however, "chaos" is not synonymous with "anarchy." Instead, it refers to a pervasive condition of unpredictability and complexity. We are incapable of controlling things and events when we are in chaos, not necessarily because they are "out of control" or have fallen into complete disorganization, but because cause-and-effect relationships are not known or do not exist. If we don't understand causal relationships, we don't know what to do to "correct" or "fix" whatever needs to be remedied.

The chaos and uncertainty of this approaching postmodern era has been accompanied by—and accelerated by—rapidly advancing information technology, particularly information networks. In the space of only a very few years, information technology has evolved from mainframes to personal computers (PCs), modems, networked PCs, local area networks (LANs), remote bulletin boards (RBBs), information networks, and Internet—the "information superhighway," cyber-space, and virtual reality. Unfortunately, as information is able to move more rapidly, so also is misinformation—misleading information, garbled information, and errors.

Despite this abundance of information, we are frequently discovering that we do not understand cause-and-effect relationships—relationships that we *thought* we understood, sometimes for decades. Traditional technical systems can't deal with chaos and uncertainty. Thus, managers in postmodern organizations are abandoning their "modern era" reliance on technical systems—turning instead to information technology to help them into the postmodern era.

We have been experiencing technological advancement, however, almost since time began. Is something different happening now? The answer is a resounding *yes*. "There is a class of technology that is qualitatively different from previous ones and for which new dimensions may be necessary. . . . At the cognitive level, understanding and operating programmable technology requires different reasoning skills than does mechanical technology" (Sproull & Goodman, 1990, p. 256). We are creating "technical systems with machines that are programmable and methods that are mechanical. Thus, the technology may be fundamentally new, but the technical systems are not . . . . these hybrid technical systems must represent an unstable state. Their performance is often disappointing, if not life-threatening" (pp. 257, 258).

Karl Weick's distinction between "technology" and "and technical system" is useful. (See his selection, "Information as Equivoque," in this chapter.) In essence, Weick defines a "technical system" as a specific set of hardware and software systems that produces a desired outcome. Technical systems—that are products of the "modern era"—are designed to accomplish desired purposes using known information and existing technology. "Technology," on the other hand, refers to the "knowledge of cause-and-effect relationships embedded in machines and methods. The knowledge may be certain or probabilistic. It may be codified in formal systems or in folk wisdom" (Sproull & Goodman, 1990, p. 254).

Information—and information technology—can extend human mental capability. We are not certain, though, what effects information technology will have on interpersonal relations, working teams, and thus organizations as we know them. Emerging forms of communication technology already are spanning time and space. Information networks that tap into (and simultaneously update) real-time data bases are providing empowered, self-managing work teams with the information they need to schedule and coordinate their own tasks as well as discipline their own members. Layer upon layer of supervisors and middle managers are not needed and are being eliminated (see Chapter VIII).

Information networks in the postmodern era are raising vexing questions that tax existing theories of organization. With a technology that spans time and space, what is an organization? What are the boundaries of an organization? What is in and what is out? "As we apply such concepts as structuration and population ecology [see Chapter V] . . . new understandings can be generated and the concepts themselves may be revised" (Goodman & Sproull, 1990, pp. xii, xiii).

Technology and postmodernism also raise questions about the experience of people who work in—or around—organizations. Will Warren Bennis's (1966) prediction finally come true—will bureaucratic organizations as we know them disappear because they are unable to adapt to rapidly changing environments? Will working at home and "telecommuting" become the norm? Will Charles Handy (1989) be right: organizations will resemble "donuts" and "shamrocks"? If so, how will people satisfy their social needs? Can trusting relations be established through relationships that exist only on the information highway in cyberspace? Can "virtual realities" and holograms created by information technology satisfy needs for affiliation and association? Who is an organizational member and who is not? Will it make any difference? The questions posed above about the meaning of *organizational boundaries* and *organization*, are not hypothetical.

Old familiar machine analogies of organization simply do not apply in the postmodern era. We can't turn back to the models that were introduced in Chapter I. Prigogine and Stengers (1984), for example, suggest that "fire" is a more appropriate analogy for organizational processes in the postmodern era for two reasons. First, fire is a "second-order" change process. And, it is irreversible.

The process of change in organizations often operates like fire. We blurt out organizational truths in moments of frustration or anger and can never cover them up again. We tentatively consider a change in organizational structure, but the word gets out and we are soon stuck with the change whether we like it or not. Equilibrium has been disturbed, chaos often follows, and we ourselves are not the same as we were before. Time moves in one direction and cannot be reversed (Bergquist, 1993, p. 5).

Second, fire is ephemeral. "It is all process and not much substance. . . . Organizational processes (like fires) are elusive. They are hard to measure and even harder to document in terms of their ultimate impact on an organization" (Bergquist, 1993, p. 5).

The evolution from technical systems (in modern organizations) to information technology (in postmodern organizations), is more than an evolutionary step. The texture of the relationships between individuals, their work, and their organization is changed irreversibly. They cannot revert to a prior state. In the "Preface" to *In the Age of the Smart Machine* (1988), Shoshana Zuboff describes this irreversible change in the texture of work relationships on the occasion of her first introduction to the application of advanced information technology to clerical work.

> Visiting the bank's offices, I witnessed a sight that would eventually become so familiar as to defy notice—an entire floor of people seated at their partitioned workstations, staring into the screens of desktop terminals. . . . Many [of these] people voiced distress, describing their work as "floating in space" or "lost behind the screen." They complained that they were no longer able to see or touch their work (p. xii).
>
> The material alterations in their means of production were manifested in transformations at intimate levels of experience—assumptions about knowledge and power, their beliefs about work and the meaning they derived from it, the content and rhythm of their social exchanges, and the ordinary mental and physical disciplines to which they accommodated in their daily lives. I saw that a world of sensibilities and expectations was being irretrievably displaced by a new world (p. xiii).

Organizations today must wrestle with complex dilemmas about participating in the information age and maintaining their boundaries. If they decide not to participate, they risk missing out on information and thus important opportunities. On the other hand, if they decide to participate "in this relatively anarchic frontier of social interactions, it could also expose internal organizational information to the problems of external players anxious to disrupt or divert their organizational actions." Consequently, "linking up may be unavoidable to stay competitive or relevant but it may also install dangerous exposure to external competitors" or render a government agency unable to perform its regulatory functions (Demchak, 1994, p. 8). Demchak asks vexing boundary questions that are faced by government agencies that will be expected to regulate other organizations (p. 8). For example:

- What will be required for public "cybercrats" to operate in the world of "cyberorgs" without being disrupted or disruptive?
- Do public agencies need to run the networks, or can they be effective by simply dipping in occasionally to check on the flows and pools of key information and other transactions?

- How will public agencies in a cyberspaced nation meet the public needs for accountable, effective, equitable, efficient governance?

Zuboff (1988) coined the term "informate" to highlight a duality that is central to the issues and dilemmas we are raising in this chapter. Technology can be used to automate operations using the same logic that was in place before the automating was initiated. This use of technology, to "automate," enables a task to be performed with more control and predictability than when it was performed by humans. Automation, then, is a logical, evolutionary extension of the work begun by Federick Winslow Taylor and his associates early in the twentieth century (see Chapter I, "Classical Organization Theory.") On the other hand:

> The same technology simultaneously generates information about the underlying productive and administrative processes through which an organization accomplishes its work. It provides a deeper level of transparency to activities that had been either partially or completely opaque. In this way information technology supersedes the traditional logic of automation. . . . Activities, events, and objects are translated into and made visible by information when a technology *informates* as well as *automates* (Zuboff, 1988, pp. 9,10).

Although "automating" represented an information technology revolution in the 1960s, it does not now. The organizational implications of automation are incorporated in and explained adequately by the systems theories of organization (see Chapter V).

In contrast, "informating" is concerned with "radical changes as it alters the intrinsic character of work. . . . It also poses fundamentally new choices for our organizational futures, and the ways in which labor and management respond to these new choices will finally determine whether our era becomes a time for radical change or a return to the familiar patterns and pitfalls of the traditional workplace" (Zuboff, 1988, p. 11).

The readings that we have included in this chapter raise a broad spectrum of issues about information technology, postmodern organizations, and the mental ability of humans in organizations to make sense in the face of complexity. The first reading, "The Limits of Hierarchy in an Informated Organization," is a chapter from Zuboff's book, *In the Age of the Smart Machine*. Zuboff examines a series of crucial choices that management makes at the time it decides to automate: Will it automate only, or will it also design the organization and information systems to informate? "Are we all going to be working for a smart machine, or will we have smart people around the machine?" The difference is a matter of strategic choice that depends upon management's commitment to learning. "Learning requires a learning environment if it is to be nurtured as a core organizational process. . . . A learning environment would encourage questions and dialogue. It would assume shared knowledge and collegial relationships." (See also the reading by Peter Senge in Chapter VIII).

Informating requires the adoption of new concepts of authority for management as well as a redistribution of authority. "The explication of meaning that is so central to the development of intellective skill requires that people become their own authorities." Authority, thus, is derived from the process of creating and articulating meaning. It does not reside in an individual, position, function, or level of a hierarchy.

"The informating process sets knowledge and authority on a collision course. In the absence of a strategy to synthesize their force, neither can emerge a clear victor, but neither can emerge unscathed." The information age thus requires us to critically revisit our notions of systems, power, authority, accountability, and the role of people in organizations. An organization that automates is locked into the predictability and control system logic of the modern era. An organization that informates has the potential to adapt to the changes and uncertainties of the postmodern era.

Karl Weick's 1990 selection, "Technology as Equivoque: Sensemaking in New Technologies," could have fit comfortably in Chapter VII, "Organizational Culture and Sensemaking." We decided to include it here instead because it both fits well and advances Zuboff's prescriptions for management. Weick carefully examines "perceived realities" and "sensemaking," cognitive processes that are used by people who are struggling to adapt to complexity and uncertainty. Whereas technologies in the modern era were deterministic and predictable, employees and managers alike now work in environments where important events are unpredictable and chaotic.

"An *equivoque* is something that admits of several possible or plausible interpretations and therefore can be esoteric, subject to misunderstandings, uncertain, complex, and recondite"—the types of issues and questions that are becoming increasingly characteristic of organizational life in the postmodern era. As organizational processes become more automated, continuous, and invisible to people who are responsible for them, they become more difficult (or impossible) to understand by analysis. "These equivocal properties of organizations can be grasped more readily if analysts talk about structuration rather than structure, affect rather than analysis, dynamic interactive complexity rather than static interactive complexity, and premise control rather than behavioral control."

Information technology produces complex equivocality, that requires us to "grapple with a key issue in technology—namely, how to apply perceptual perspectives to a material world. . . . New technologies are paradoxical, as well as equivocal. These descriptions . . . speak to the core issues we need to resolve if we want to understand technologies in which mental representation plays a central role in operation."

Bill Bergquist's (1993) selection that is reprinted here, "Postmodern Thought in a Nutshell: Where Art and Science Come Together," is the most understandable introduction to the complexities (and the jargon) of "postmodernism" that we have been able to locate. "In many ways, postmodernism is a fad—and is at the same time about fads. Even though postmodernism is characterized by superficial, facile, and often internally contradictory analyses, it must not be dismissed, for these analyses offer insightful and valuable (even essential) perspectives on and criticisms of an emerging era." Bergquist identifies and explicates four themes of postmodernism:

1. *Objectivism Versus Constructivism:* "Objectivism"—which predominated in the modern era—is "rational." It assumes that there is an objective reality that can be discovered. "Constructivism," which is a postmodern phenomenon, "believe[s] that we construct our own social realities. . . . There are no universal truths or principles, nor are there any global models of justice or order. . . . Ways of knowing may themselves change over time and in differing situations."

2. *Language Is Itself Reality:* Language, and the use of verbal symbols and signs, is more than a means for communicating information about reality. It is (at least a part of) reality. "The language being used to describe . . . elusive and changing reality is itself a major source of this social construction."

3. *Globalization and Segmentalism:* "According to the postmodernists, our world is becoming progressively more global, while at the same time becoming progressively more segmented and differentiated." At the same time that information technology is allowing us to know more about our commonalties with people around the world, we seem to have lost our sense of community and organization. Thus perhaps we live in an era of "contradiction between globalism and localism in many aspects of our daily lives."

4. *Fragmented and Inconsistent Images:* "Postmodernists are enthralled with the superficial and the trendy." Virtual reality machines "convey the sense of depth, yet like holographic devices, they actually replicate only the surface, never the depth of the experience. We are tricked into believing that we have experienced depth or virtual reality when in fact we have seen only the surface."

These four themes represent the central realities of a fragmented and inconsistent postmodern world. "The modern manager sees systems as the ultimate tool for making sense out of chaos. The postmodern manager sees chaos as what is to be managed and systems, though very useful, as merely one aspect of the chaotic environment. To the postmodern manager chaos is not bad. It is what is."

In "Nonlinear Dynamical Analysis: Assessing Systems Concepts in a Government Agency" (1993, which is reprinted here), L. Douglas Kiel examines what government administrators can learn from chaos theory. He argues that nonlinear dynamics, or chaos theory, can be applied to public agencies because human organizations are nonlinear systems. "In linear systems, the relationships between relevant variables remain stable over time. . . . Linear systems respond to changes in their parameters, or to external shocks, in a proportionate and consistent manner . . . Nonlinear systems are typified by a potential for dynamic relationships between variables during the life of the system. As these relationships change, the temporal behavior of the system may change from smooth to unstable and even to seeming randomness, referred to as chaos." Management is expected to maintain order within the chaos, particularly so in government organizations.

Kiel describes a "quantitative and graphical perspective" of managed equilibrium in a government organization. "This perspective allows the analyst to examine organizational work as if it were some biological or chemical system examined on an oscilloscope. This approach interjects time into organizational analyses allowing the observer to view the oscillation and rhythms of organizational work." Thus, Kiel presents an analytical approach for organizational adaptation to turbulence and uncertainty—to chaos.

The final reading, "The Enabling Role of Information Technology," is from Michael Hammer and James Champy's (1993) book, *Reengineering the Corporation: A Manifesto for Business Revolution*, one of the most popular of the organizational culture reform movements. (See Chapter VIII.) *Reengineering the Corporation* argues that American corporations—indeed all large organizations—must radically reinvent how they are structured and work. "The alternative is for corporate America to close its doors and go out of business." There is no middle ground.

Hammer and Champy echo the ideas about information technology and organizations that we have encountered from Demchak, Zuboff, Weick, and Bergquist. "A company that cannot change the way it thinks about information technology cannot reengineer. A company that equates technology with automation cannot reengineer. . . . Modern state of the art information technology is part of the reengineering effort, an *essential enabler* . . . since it *permits* companies to reengineer." Organizations in a postmodern era need managers who think inductively— people who have "the ability to first recognize a powerful solution and then seek the problems it might solve, problems the company probably doesn't even know that it has."

Companies commit a fundamental error when they try to find uses for technology that fit current functions and processes. Instead, they need to develop applications for functions that do not exist. Peoples' needs and aspirations are limited by their understanding of what is possible. "Breakthrough technology makes feasible activities and actions of which people have not yet dreamed."

Information technology has the potential to be positively disruptive—to allow people to think inductively by "breaking rules" that limit how we conduct work. For example:

> *Old Rule:* Only experts can perform complex work.
> *Disruptive Technology:* Expert systems.
> *New Rule:* A generalist can do the work of an expert.

And:

> *Old Rule:* Businesses must choose between centralization and decentralization.
> *Disruptive Technology:* Telecommunications networks.
> *New Rule:* Businesses can simultaneously reap the benefits of centralization and decentralization.

Organizations must "stay on top of new technology" and work continuously to learn how to use it imaginatively. "Companies need to make technology exploitation one of their core competencies if they are to succeed in a period of ongoing technological change. . . . Our view is that if you can buy a technology, it is not new." Thus, technology that is used inductively rather than deductively is a necessary enabler of organizational adaptation.

REFERENCES

Anderson, W. (1990). *Reality isn't what it used to be*. San Francisco: Harper San Francisco.

Bateson, G. (1979). *Mind and nature: A necessary unity*. New York: Dutton.

Benedikt, M. (Ed.). (1992). *Cyberspace: First steps* (2d. ed.). Cambridge, MA: MIT Press.

Bennis, W. G. (1966). *Changing organizations*. New York: McGraw-Hill.

Bergquist, W. (1993). *The postmodern organization: Mastering the art of irreversible change*. San Francisco: Jossey-Bass.

Bernstein, R. J. (1992). *The new constellation: The ethical-political horizons of modernity/postmodernity*. Cambridge, MA: MIT Press.

Briggs, J., & Peat, F. D. (1989). *Turbulent mirror*. New York: HarperCollins.

Clegg, S. (1990). *Modern organizations: Organizational studies in the postmodern world*. Newbury Park, CA: Sage.

Demchak, C. C. (November 1994). Cyberspace and emergent body politic: Tough issues, murky structures and unknowns of the "net-polis." *Policy Currents: Newsletter of the Public Policy Section of the American Political Science Association*, 4, 1, 6–9.

Fox, C. J., & Miller, H. T. (1995). *Postmodern public administration: Toward discourse*. Thousand Oaks, CA: Sage.

Giddens, A. (1984). *The consequences of modernity*. Stanford, CA: Stanford University Press.

Gleick, J. (1987). *Chaos: Making a new science*. New York: Viking.

Goodman, P. S., & Sproull, L. S. (Eds.). (1990). *Technology and organizations*. San Francisco: Jossey-Bass.

Hammer, M., & Champy, J. (1993). *Reengineering the corporation: A manifesto for business revolution*. New York: HarperBusiness.

Handy, C. (1989). *The age of unreason*. Boston: Harvard Business School Press.

Hayles, N. I. (Ed.). (1991). *Chaos and order: Complex dynamics in literature and science*. Chicago: University of Chicago Press.

Herbert, N. (1987). *Quantum reality: Beyond the new physics*. Garden City, NY: Anchor.

Hoesterey, I. (Ed.). (1991). *Zeitgeist in Babel: The post-modernist controversy*. Bloomington: Indiana University Press.

Kellert, S. H. (1993). *In the wake of chaos: Unpredictable order in dynamical systems*. Chicago: University of Chicago Press.

Kiel, L. D. (1993). Nonlinear dynamical analysis: Assessing systems concepts in a government agency. *Public Administration Review*, 53, 143–153.

Keil, L. D. (1995). *Managing chaos and complexity in government.* San Francisco: Jossey-Bass.

Loye, D., & Eisler, R. (1987). Chaos and transformation: Implications of nonequilibrium theory for social science and society. *Behavioral Science, 32,* 53–65.

Lyotard, J. (1984). *The postmodern condition.* Minneapolis: University of Minnesota Press.

Powell, W. W. (1990). Neither market nor hierarchy: Network forms of organization. *Research in Organizational Behavior, 12,* 295–336.

Prigogine, I., & Stengers, I. (1984). *Order out of chaos.* New York: Bantam.

Rheingold, H. (1993). *The virtual community.* Reading, MA: Addison-Wesley.

Sproull, L. S., & Goodman, P. S. (1990). "Technology and organizations: Integration and opportunities." In P. S. Goodman & L. S. Sproull (Eds.), *Technology and organizations* (pp. 254–265). San Francisco: Jossey-Bass.

Thompson, J. M. T., & Stewart, H. B. (1986). *Nonlinear dynamics and chaos.* New York: Wiley.

Villa, D. R. (1992). "Postmodernism and the public sphere." *American Political Science Review, 86,* 712–721.

Weick, K. E. (1990). "Technology as equivoque: Sensemaking in new technologies." In P. S. Goodman & L. S. Sproull (Eds.), *Technology and organizations* (pp. 1–44). San Francisco: Jossey-Bass.

Wheatley, M. (1992). *Leadership and the new science.* San Francisco: Berrett-Koehler.

Zuboff, S. (1988). *In the age of the smart machine: The future of work and power.* New York: Basic Books.

44

In the Age of the Smart Machine: The Limits of Hierarchy in an Informated Organization

Shoshana Zuboff

WHO WILL HARVEST?

. . . A technology that informates can have a corrosive effect on the hierarchical organization of work, but its transformative power finally depends upon a series of crucial managerial choices. When the plant manager asks, "Are we all going to be working for a smart machine, or will we have smart people around the machine?" he portrays two divergent scenarios. In the former, the line that separates workers from managers is sharply drawn. Workers are treated as laboring bodies, though in fact there is less that their bodies can contribute in effort or skill. As workers become more resentful and dependent, managers react by sinking more resources into automation. In the alternative scenario, both groups work together to forge the terms of a new covenant, one that recasts the sources and purposes of managerial authority. The choice to automate will strike many as the easier and more expedient of the two. There are, however, fresh complexities that muddle and confound the seductive elegance of that solution.

Three years into the Cedar Bluff start-up, and three years after the first wave of major technological conversions at Piney Wood, a growing number of managers in each mill had tasted enough of the dynamics of machine dependency to identify a potential future that was all the more frightening for the way in which it no longer seemed outlandish. A top manager at Piney Wood described it this way:

> The fear is that people will become an extension of a machine, and in this way of someone else's logic process. I would just as soon throw some of these new systems away and invest our money in training people how to think. The operator has to understand the logic patterns. We need to equip machines to help us, not to replace us. Individuals literally become an extension of the tool. I have asked our other top managers, where does the computer fit in the hierarchy? Will we end up with thinkers at the top, the computer at the next level down, and then the masses who if it says jump, they jump? It's downright scary.

In Piney Wood, where an adversarial culture created a natural setting for the logic of automatic control, many managers were finally forced to acknowledge the way in which the lack of intellective skill development ultimately limited operational competence and prevented the organization from exploiting the opportunities created by so much new data. One manager framed the problem this way:

Source: "The Limits of Hierarchy in an Informed Organization," from *In the Age of the Smart Machine: The Future of Work and Power*, by Shoshana Zuboff. Copyright © 1988 by Basic Books, Inc. Reprinted by permission of BasicBooks, a division of HarperCollins Publishers, Inc.

As the plant becomes unified under a computer system, if the master computer screws up, no one else will know about it until there is actual physical evidence. Using computers to handle unmanageable amounts of information is necessary, but who will manage the computer? What will be the skills necessary to do that? What kind of training will people need?

Other managers voiced similar concerns. They spoke of the importance of troubleshooting and problem-solving skills at the data interface, in addition to a solid understanding of the process. There was a growing perception that instead of a gut feel, operators would be required to have a level of technical competence that would even exceed the current expectations for intellective skill within management. In short, intellective skill would become the new grounds for "knowing better" than the systems one operated. Intellective skill would be necessary if those closest to the point of production were to know when to say no. . . .

Most of Piney Wood's operators had arrived at a similar conclusion as they thought about what would constitute the basis of their expertise. Some insisted that only the hands-on knowledge honed by years of experience would provide an operator with enough judgment to be able to be critical of what the computer presented to him or her. Over the three-year period, however, I began to hear a new point of view, one that reflected a growing awareness of the profound and irreversible nature of the changes that were occurring. The operators seemed to feel that they faced a choice of either taking direction from the computer system in a kind of stupefied fog or developing a sophisticated understanding of the computer system that they could then use to express their in-depth knowledge of the production process.

A new sensibility was reflected in the belief that superior process skills would no longer have value if they could not be expressed in the terms of the computer system. Operators saw that if they did not make a serious attempt to develop intellective skill, any possibility of judgment and accountability would be lost to the systems that claimed to supplant human direction.

> I am used to using my own techniques and systems for how I run my job. Now they have put my hands into the computer, and I am just a puppet, a common laborer. Therefore, if I want to have value in this new environment, I have no choice but to learn the computer.

Management's growing recognition of the need for critical judgment at the information interface was accompanied by the realization that the emphasis on the smart machine prevented the organization from exploiting the vast quantity of new information for fundamental business improvement. One line manager complained:

> We have cut out so many people there is no one to do the neat things we could use the information for. It's like a vast crop and no one to harvest it.

Other managers agreed:

> We have concentrated exclusively on job elimination. But we are not dealing with the people we have left. We need to look at added value and we don't know how. Unfortunately, no one is considering the trade-offs.

The-ill-considered trade-offs involve the special characteristics of a technology that informates. As more and more managers throughout the three plants gained experience with advanced information technology, they began to see that dealing with the tidal wave of increased information in a timely and insightful way was likely to provide their most crucial source of comparative advantage in the emerging economic environment of global markets and cost-conscious consumers. Many managers had begun to sense that technology alone would not provide an enduring competitive edge, as it would become widely available and quickly equalize competition within the marketplace. If the full power of the data interface were to be exploited, then the organization would need people at each level who could analyze and respond to the data most relevant to their functional responsibilities. This implied a new vision of the organization and a strategy of technological deployment that gave preeminence to the informating capacities of the technology. . . .

Critical judgment means the capacity to ask questions, to say no when things are not right. It also creates the possibility of asking "why?" or "why not?" One of the Cedar Bluff managers most respected for his willingness to "pass the knowledge down," described what he called "the developmental learning process" that operators must go through if they are to become critically competent at the data interface. He recognized its implications for managerial authority.

At the first level, of course, people need to know how to keep the equipment running. But the next step is to ask, "Why am I doing what I am doing?" Only if people understand why, will they be able to make sense of the unknowns. The third step is process optimization and diagnostic problem solving. At that point, they can hone in on the real issues. Once this happens, the need for management goes down the drain and my job is over.

Some managers continued to struggle with their own sense of vulnerability; they recognized that subordinates' questions could all too easily unravel the painstakingly constructed facade of infallibility to which many still clung. . . .

Others had begun to discover new mechanisms of influence associated with this learning process, even as their conventional sources of influence were in decline. They had begun to see that the interpretive process itself could be a powerful vehicle for extending one's influence while encouraging learning.

In this environment, the key to influence is not telling people what to do but in helping to shape the way they interpret data. For example, in our unit, information is available to everyone, but I am the only one who can interpret it. I can either give them the result of my interpretations, or I can show them how to interpret it. If I choose the latter, I increase my influence. Now there are fifteen people who think like I do. And it is not just data. It is the priorities and philosophies that I bring to the analysis.

Questions, in a fundamental way, are inimical to authority. The question values change over tradition, doubt over reverence, fact over faith. The question responds to knowledge and creates new knowledge. The question initiates and reflects learning. The question is incompatible with the unity of imperative control. Yet the question is essential if information is to yield its full value. Obedience will not lead to and does not require a depth of understanding. But in a world where value is created through understanding, obedience no longer fulfills the demands of production. An operator at Cedar Bluff reflected:

We need to know the whys of this process. I can't just punch this button because I was told to. I have to do it because I know why and what happens. That's the only way I can run it better.

LIFE AT THE DATA INTERFACE

Work Is Invisible

An informating technology challenges the organization to recognize the skill demands associated with computer mediation and the redistribution of knowledge that intellective skill development implies. Yet the intricacies of life at the data interface can confound managerial assumptions in still other ways. Obedience has been the axial principle of task execution in the traditional environment of imperative control. The logic of that environment is reproduced when technology is used only to automate. When tasks require intellective effort, however, obedience can be dysfunctional and can impede the exploitation of information. Under such conditions, internal commitment and motivation replace obedience as the primary bond between the individual and the task.

As the work that people do becomes more abstract, the need for positive motivation and internal commitment becomes all the more crucial. It is far easier for a manager to determine that a worker has not properly repaired a boiler (it continues to malfunction) or has failed to adequately monitor the levels of a surge chest (it overflows). What will ensure that when an operator is face-to-face with a real-time array of relevant operating information, he or she will actually be responsive to it and will exert the intellective effort that is necessary to go beyond the surface of the data and learn from it? How does the manager evaluate the possibility of missed opportunities to learn more about the production process and to improve operations? In the world of industry, where workers' bodies have been the target for precise performance measures from time-and-motion studies to piecework rates, how does a manager measure the ability to solve problems, to analyze, or to think critically at the data interface?

The shortcomings of a traditional approach to supervision and evaluation were evident at both Piney Wood and Cedar Bluff, where computer mediation had altered the appearance of work. Even as managers exhorted operators to trust the computer system, they had difficulty accepting that when the worker finally did so, he or she was still "working." The complaints voiced by many managers revealed their conventional assumptions about the nature of effort. Work and skill were almost exclusively associated with those activities that require the active engagement of the worker's body.

As operators learned to rely on the computer systems, many managers saw them as having succumbed to a self-indulgent laziness. . . .

It is true that some operators experienced the computer as an excuse to escape tasks that were unpleasant and physically depleting. But many of them believed that they were simply beginning to accept the implications of the transformation of their work. The terrain of effort had shifted to what they could do with their minds, but it was difficult to fully comprehend that one could be working while sitting still. The trade-offs were perplexing, even for the operators themselves.

> I have thirty-six main screens to watch, and fifteen are really critical. I need to be mentally alert. On a bad day, I can look at the screen and ask myself, "Why am I looking at this?" If you want to get into it and do everything right, it takes a lot out of you. If I am in a bad mood, I would rather be out in the process. If I screw something up out there, no one will see it. But it is so much easier to be in here; it is hard to give that up. Why should I kill myself?

On the one hand, this operator recognized the pressure of the intellective demands he confronted in the control room. The consequences of "screwing up" can be far greater if one makes a mistake through the system than if one makes an error on a discrete piece of equipment. It is easier to be doing something physical when the stress begins to eat at you. Finally, it is hard to give up the gracefulness of work that does not use the body up. Like the ancient Siren, freedom from physical effort is almost impossible to resist.

Many operators felt confined by this paradox. They had been required to devalue their action-centered skills and the activities in which those skills were displayed. They had been pressured into trusting a medium that initially evoked suspicion, doubt, and frustration. Some came to embrace the new circumstances as an opportunity to escape from physical effort. Others took pride in discovering the new modalities through which they could have effects, and they found that the reduced physical requirements of the computer control room provided an extra measure of pleasure. Under these circumstances, are workers lazy, or are they simply living out the implications of the technological transformation that has rendered work abstract? Have they lost the motivation to make a contribution, or is that contribution now dependent upon one's quality of mind and intellective effort? Should we conclude that these operators had given up on work or that the very nature of life at the data interface had now come to define work? Operators at Piney Wood said:

> The managers see us sitting, and they think we are not doing anything. If I am not moving, they think I am lazy. If I am sitting, that means I have my mind on something out there in the process. Before, you had to walk around to see what was happening. Now we can see it from in here on the computer.
>
> My managers think I should wear my britches out all the time. But when I am watching the computer, I am working. They think I am goofing off, so I am afraid of being caught in the control room. Here in Piney Wood, people think that the only real work is physical work. But the key

man at the computer has the most responsibility.

. . . There were at least some managers in Cedar Bluff who realized that the abstraction of work necessitated a fundamental reappraisal of their methods of supervision and evaluation. They had begun to grapple with the notion of supervising what people were doing "in their heads," but the first step was to invent a way to make that activity more "visible." The plant manager regarded this as an issue of real importance, insisting that some of the most vital questions confronting him concerned how to effectively manage the operators' cognitive life.

> What are the operators really doing at the screens? What is actually going on in their heads? How are they reacting to the information they see? Where are their skills leveling out? What is the degree of concentration and full use of the individual that we are achieving? We need to know these things so that we can figure out how we structure their minds so that they are consistently aware of what is going on.

Cedar Bluff developed an elaborate "qualifications procedure" which required each hourly worker to appear before a panel of process experts drawn from the plant and from the wider company. The panel would pose a variety of open-ended questions designed to elicit the depth of the operator's process knowledge and problem-solving skills. People would be asked both what they would do under a particular set of operating conditions and why they would choose that course of action. The goal was "to understand how an operator sees the process, what is in their heads, their level of conceptual skills. The procedure asks them to say how they think."

Such a procedure puts a premium on an individual's capacity for verbal explication. It is unlikely that one would be seen as very proficient without a well-developed ability to articulate one's thoughts in what Bernstein called an "elaborated" linguistic code. Speech had become an important vehicle for making visible what was "in people's heads." . . . The qualifications sessions were charged with so much tension that on at least one occasion, a manager's office was burglarized. The notebooks containing questions for the qualifications examination in his area had been stolen in the night.

There were some managers and operators, however, who believed that the inability to "see" what was taking place inside someone's head encouraged managers to use more subjective, trivial, and even irrelevant criteria for judging an operator's competence.[1] Many workers complained:

> The people who get the highest rankings do the most talking, but it can be a real snow job. The managers can't see the work, but they can hear you talk, so that is what they pay attention to.
>
> Managers can't tell if you are operating the system right or wrong. They just see people with long hair or a beard, and they evaluate you on perceptions, not on actual fact.

. . . At the same time, more managers were beginning to discuss the need to manage the psychological relationship between the worker and the data interface. They had come to the conclusion that, in the final analysis, only the strength of an operator's commitment and motivation would ensure high-quality performance. This commitment would be developed as operators felt they had a real share in the business, an opportunity to learn, and the freedom to inquire without confronting arbitrary barriers of managerial authority. As one operator put it:

> The money for this job is very good, but that won't keep your enthusiasm high all the time. Around here, you get enthusias-

tic when you can talk about reoccurring problems with other people. When managers share information and help us track results that we would not normally have access to, that kind of information peaks enthusiasm.

A few managers had begun to see the implications of intellective work for their supervisory approach:

> There is just so much going on here that we call "work" but that you can't see. You can look busy and not be doing a damn thing. If someone is productive, they are asking questions, interested, and inquisitive.

As action becomes secondary to intellective effort, our images of work continue to draw upon a set of experiences that are as old as our species. It is the body that works, and until quite recently, no amount of mechanical assistance has overcome the central fact of bodily involvement. As long as the body defined the scene of work, face-to-face supervision had real meaning. When work is abstract, direct supervisory observation is not well equipped to discern the quality of performance. This quality is itself now an abstraction that must be deduced from more subtle behavioral cues, such as inquisitiveness, or from the objective record of operating results.

Work Is Responsibility

Another aspect of the transformation of work at the data interface concerns the heightened responsibility of jobs that demand continual responsiveness to a flow of data. In a traditional work system, job descriptions carefully define the range of a worker's responsibility and, together with considerations of seniority, are used as the index for decisions regarding promotions and compensation. The logic is such that increments in years of experience imply eligibility for increments in responsibility, which in turn imply increments of pay. Narrow definitions of occupational functions are feasible in a world of action, because events have observable boundaries. In a traditional manufacturing environment, machinery makes it possible to locate work, and to a large extent, responsibility could be defined concretely in terms of where one stood and the equipment with which one engaged. Actions make it possible to see work, so performance can be evaluated based on observation as well as output.

As work becomes computer mediated, it is difficult to distinguish responsibility from the work itself. Much of what now constitutes "work" involves the mindfulness and intellective effort necessary for continual responsiveness at the interface. What, finally, is the difference between being responsive and being responsible? *Webster's* defines *responsive* as "answering" and *responsible* as "liable to be called upon to answer." Looked at this way, responsibility implicates the worker as the one to respond: the capacity to comprehend and react to data becomes the essence of work. The limits of responsibility thus would be determined by the limits of what an individual could appropriately be expected to be responsive to. How should limits be drawn, when the obvious limitations of geography and action no longer apply? . . . The message underlying the emerging job structure is that being exposed to data implies that a person sees, comprehends, and is appropriately responsive. For example, in Piney Wood's bleach plant and powerhouse, operators found that instead of having data from local instrumentation regarding the discrete pieces of equipment for which they were responsible, they now routinely saw data that corresponded to many aspects of their unit's operations as well as data on operations in other parts of the plant. The assumption here, only occasionally made explicit, is that such newly visible data becomes the responsibility of those

who see it. It is further assumed that the individual who views the data actually sees the data and assumes responsibility for what is seen.

A manager at Piney Wood, who has worked closely with his operators in the conversion to the new microprocessor-based control system, explains:

> In computerizing the controls, we exposed people to data that had nothing to do with their jobs, but they couldn't ignore the data once they identified it. So they are taking the responsibility without being formally assigned the responsibility. Before, they were not allowed to touch the instrumentation and did not cross the borders between jobs.

. . . However, in a traditional workplace like Piney Wood, where even small increments of responsibility are treated in terms of their dollar value and seen as a reward for seniority, identifying the new work as "more responsible" meant that managers risked calling into question some fundamental tenets of the union contract. In Piney Wood's bleach plant, where the integration process was well under way and operators perceived the responsibility in their jobs as having dramatically increased, a grievance was filed and brought before the plant manager. The operators argued that more responsibility should translate into more pay. They also wanted the task of working at the interface to be confined to one or two control room positions, which would be assigned a pay rate at the upper end of the scale and opened to bidding by operators with the most seniority. The plant manager took as his primary objective maintaining the current pay levels and job definitions. He told the operators who brought the grievance:

> We have not increased your job responsibilities, and you are being paid for job responsibility. You do not have additional responsibilities; you simply have new equipment. You have new equipment, and

you are required to do your same job, simply with new equipment.

Maintaining this narrow objective meant that the plant manager was not free to concede publicly the demands associated with the new technology nor to explore ways to exploit its potential. In private discussions, however, he acknowledged that the new technology provided an opportunity to fulfill a general goal of American Paper Company's approach to manufacturing management—making the worker a part of the business. He viewed the technology as particularly well suited to "integrating the worker in the business," because exposure to data "increases the operator's responsibility" and ultimately his or her ability to make a contribution.

> Our desire is to make people part of the business. The technology helps that happen because it gives them the data, and this means responsibility. With this system, you push one button and it gives you all the data—trends, averages, comparisons. We choose to expose them to this integrative data because we think it will make them part of the business. . . . Let's get the responsibility more personalized so an operator can say, "On my shift, here is what I accomplished."

The problem wouldn't go away, largely because the operators in the control rooms believed that their jobs had changed fundamentally, not superficially. . . . They felt the weight of the demands of intellective effort and responsiveness, and wondered how the plant manager defined responsibility. . . .

Two years later, the issue was still a lively one in Piney Wood's bleach plant and had spread to the powerhouse as well. Workers across the plant were disgruntled. In part, their grievance focused on pay: they argued that their wages should be increased in proportion to the increase in responsibility. The unifying theme in their comments was one of a contract violated. Their "sense of contract" could not be reduced to the formal document signed by management and the union; rather, it reflected something deeper and more enduring—a coherent body of shared assumptions that seemed to be eroding rapidly without anyone ever having agreed to let them go.

This sense of contract played an important role in the operator's most intimate self-evaluation. Having a clear notion of what is expected of you on the job helps shape the personal criteria against which you inwardly assess your performance. It is as if a private competition against these standards provides the measure of one's competence. Some of the criteria that are applied in this judgment of the self come from the work group, from the collective sense of what constitutes being skillful. Other criteria, the promotions and wage increases that allow an operator to take on more comprehensive, responsible, and well-paying positions, are supplied by the formal organization.

The critical point is that the workers who draw sustenance from developing their competence seek measures that they believe will reflect their skills. These are the measures against which they want to be judged, and the reflections of competence provided by such judgments are critical to their own feelings of value. Throughout Piney Wood, operators complained, "They are not letting me do my job." For them, their jobs had been related specifically to pieces of equipment; since they no longer were able to use familiar skills, they had lost the certainty that "I can do a good job."

The sense of contract performs another psychological function: it sustains a belief in justice and fairness, allowing the worker to feel like an actor, not a victim. Under these conditions, one feels that "I know what I am getting into, I know what is expected of me, I know what I can expect in return. I have made a choice. It is fair."

The ambiguity that results from an erosion of this contractual equilibrium can evoke feelings of incompetence and victimization. When it does, reactions are hostile. In this situation, some workers focus on realigning structural elements in order to recreate a psychological equilibrium and a renewed feeling of control.

> We are a ship adrift at sea. We know where we want to be, but we don't know how to get there. Most of us are high school graduates, and we have been in the service. We are used to structures that let you know where you stand. The way we expect to get rewarded is by moving up one grade at a time in the mill. With all the changes that are taking place in my job, it's not fair, not just. It's like I hired you to rake my yard, and now I say I won't pay unless you also clean up the garage. They keep putting off addressing the tough issues: What is my pay? What is my responsibility? How will we be trained? They should not have implemented the new technology without taking care of these things, too. If it had been fair, there would not be trouble.

In the area of the mill where operators experienced the greatest sense of ambiguity and victimization, they fashioned their own methods of reestablishing order. These workers believed that their jobs had been unfairly expanded, that they were not being empowered with the skills they needed to cope with computerization, and that their managers had abdicated their leadership roles for a kind of technological fatalism. One solution was to redefine their own jobs in terms that they believed represented a fair work load. They simply stopped performing some of the tasks for which they had formal responsibility. . . .

A second adaptation was to challenge the notion that exposure to data demands responsiveness. Piney Wood's managers began to notice that in the most adversarial areas of the plant, operators had developed a new method of expressing their discontent. Why resort to the machine-breaking tactics of an earlier century when it was so much more elegant to simply ignore data?

> We are exposing them to all this data now, which means more responsibility because you can't ignore it. But in one module, the operators are digging their heels in. They want more pay and they are mad. So they are ignoring the data they see.

INFORMATING: AUTONOMOUS PROCESS OR CONSCIOUS STRATEGY?

Life at the data interface invites the worker into the abstract precincts of managerial work. It provides access to a broader view of the business as well as a deepened understanding of one's tasks and their role in the wider sphere of organizational functions. When work becomes synonymous with responsiveness to data, it engenders inquiry and dialogue, thus opening the way for workers to envision new possibilities and fresh alternatives to the reigning definitions of process, product, and organization.

The autonomous power of the informating process was clearly felt in each of the three pulp and paper plants by workers who frequently found themselves generating the kinds of data-based insights that their organizations had always expected from managers and engineers.

> It is a different kind of decision making now. The computer is already making the smaller process decisions that I used to make. So that means I have to make the larger decisions and I have to have the information to make those decisions.
>
> Having access to so much information makes you think ahead. There are always some problems that you have no control

over, but many problems can be avoided if you are just monitoring the information, concentrating on it, thinking about it, understanding what it means, seeing the patterns in it, and being alert to the things it is showing you. Once you gain confidence with the new technology, you have time to think about how to do the job better and how things could be done differently. That is the real potential of this equipment. That would never have occurred if we had just stayed with the old technology.

Thinking about "how things could be done differently" has not been part of the worker's function, at least not since the advances of Taylor's logic helped to build the management superstructures of the modern organization, nor has the worker had access to the kind of data that would facilitate such insight. In many industries, management itself has had to apply enormous diligence in order to compile the kind of data that could be subject to systematic analysis and to yield new insights into process or product improvements.

The significance of the new opportunity open to operators can be appraised only in light of the legacy of scientific management, which dramatically limited the worker's legitimate contribution to the production process. Consider again the logic of Taylorism: (1) the worker's implicit know-how is analyzed in order to generate data that contribute to (2) the development of a series of management functions that enable (3) management to take on responsibility for coordination and control of the production process.

The process of automation in these plants follows precisely the same course. Just as Taylor wanted to systematize the know-how that was "in the worker's head," so process engineers and managers discuss establishing the basic algorithms to duplicate "what an operator

does in his head." Automation also shares the same goal as Taylorism—to establish managerial control over a knowledge domain that serves as the basis for a division of labor that is minimally dependent upon the skills or disposition of a (shrinking) work force.

Like scientific management, computer-based automation provides a means for the managerial hierarchy to reproduce itself, because it can concentrate knowledge in the managerial domain and so be used to renew belief in the necessity of imperative control. It must be an unwritten law of social life that hierarchies will utilize any means available as a potential method for reproducing, extending, and heightening those experiences through which elite groups win legitimation. In this sense, computer-based technologies represent merely one more episode in a two-century-long effort to define, consolidate, and reproduce managerial authority.

When automation is the exclusive end of computerization, it not only repeats the structure and objectives of Taylorism but also replicates its inherent antagonisms. In one area of Piney Wood where automatic control and manning reductions were emphasized, the technology already had become the target of adversarial feelings. Operators there complained:

> . . . It robs my dignity; it robs my dignity of what I know how to do. They are removing my job, the job that lets me use my judgment. Now if you work on any one piece of the process, you have access to information about the entire bleach plant; you have access at your fingertips. That means that my knowledge—which used to be special knowledge—becomes open and available to a lot of people.

When the application of computer-based technology informates the task environment, the results can be dramatically different. Intelligent technology textualizes the production process. When that text is made accessible to operators, the essential logic of Taylorism is undermined. For the first time, technology returns to workers what it once took away—but with a crucial difference. The worker's knowledge had been implicit in action. The informating process makes that knowledge explicit: it holds a mirror up to the worker, reflecting what was known but now in a precise and detailed form. In order to reappropriate that reflection, the worker must be able to grapple with a kind of knowledge that now stands outside the self, externalized and public. Intellective skill becomes the means to interact competently with this now objectified text, to reappropriate it as one's own, and to engage in the kind of learning process that can transform data into meaningful information and, finally, into insight. . . .

The activities associated with both automating and informating represent intellectual effort; but their objectives, assumptions, and the nature of the organizational processes they entail are different. In the case of automation, intellectual effort is a fair accompli. Learning about the processes in question has already been completed by the time automation begins. Automation thus preserves what is already known and assumes that it knows best. It treats as negligible the potential value to be added from learning that occurs in the living situation. Automation reproduces the status quo and consolidates the managerial hierarchy's monopoly over knowledge.

The informating process takes learning as its pivotal experience. Its objective is to achieve the value that can be added from learning in the situation. Informating assumes that making the organization more transparent will evoke valuable communal insight. From this perspective, learning is never complete, as new data, new events, or new contexts create opportunities for additional insight, improvement, and innovation.

The value of an informating strategy varies in relation to the degree of necessity associated with learning and innovation—necessity that may derive from market conditions, the nature of the production process, or other organizational considerations. For example, rapidly changing markets that put a premium on flexibility and responsiveness, competitive conditions that offer opportunities for value-added products or services, substantial variation in customer needs, short production cycles or variability in raw materials, interdependence among production operations or between production and other business functions, the persistence of "unknowns" in the core production process, opportunities for increased quality or decreased costs of products or services, the need to avoid the high levels of cost and risk associated with error when computer systems are broadly integrated, and the perceived need to develop and maintain a motivated and committed work force—these are factors that contribute to the appropriateness of an informating strategy. Where these factors are *not* present to any significant degree, an automating strategy is likely to be most feasible.

In the case of the pulp and paper mills, most managers recognized the presence of several of these factors and believed that an alternative to conventional automation was required. One of the easiest factors to agree upon was the presence of many "unknowns" in the core production process. Pulp and paper making remains an imperfect science; there is as yet no complete explication of the entire production process. Managers and operators alike live with a certain awe for the terrifically complex process that refuses to yield much of its essence. "We can't measure most of the things that need to be measured on a piece of equipment" they say. Operational unknowns and variability in raw materials mean that it is impossible to put an entire operation on automatic control.

There were also many managers who believed that product and service innovations would become an increasingly crucial competitive variable. Pulp makers facing increased competition from a variety of synthetic products would need to discover new ways of combining materials or of utilizing less costly combinations of materials while maintaining similar levels of quality. They believed that pressures for more customized and flexible manufacturing were likely to develop, coupled with a greater emphasis on customer integration in production and distribution processes. Many managers at the corporate level in the American Paper Company, and a significant number within each plant, believed that these current and anticipated demands put a premium on information technology as a primary means by which to learn more and to do more with the manufacturing process. Further, they had compelling evidence to suggest that each level of the organization could make an important contribution to these objectives.

. . . The evidence indicates that informating typically unfolds as an objective, unplanned, autonomous process. Though a technology that informates invites learning, organizational members can find themselves confronting a system of imperative control that is inimical to learning. Under these conditions, intellectual skill development occurs only haltingly, as it battles wide-scale efforts to reproduce those everyday experiences that legitimate managerial

authority. . . . A manager at Cedar Bluff responsible for developing the strategic plan for the new technology offered an observation. The set of curves (see page 559) illustrates how he drew the distribution of what he called "intellectual, knowledge-based skills."

The first curve represented the distribution of operating skill in the daily plant environment. The third represented the distribution of skill that he believed the plant would require in the future. In between the two, he drew a curve representing how well the plant operated at night. He believed that the skill level was significantly greater at night, when the absence of managers freed operators to express and develop their intellective capabilities. There were many managers and operators who agreed with that assessment. . . .

If learning is a pivotal experience in the effort to utilize the value of new information, then the autonomous dynamics set into motion by a technology that informates will not be suiffcient to achieve its full realization. Learning requires a learning environment if it is to be nurtured as a core organizational process. Based upon what we have seen of life at the data interface, a learning environment would encourage questions and dialogue. It would assume shared knowledge and collegial relationships. It would support play and experimentation, as it recognized the intimate linkages between the abstraction of work and the requirements for social interchange, intellectual exploration, and heightened responsibility.

If the technology cannot shoulder the entire burden of strategic change, it nevertheless can set into motion a series of dynamics that present an important challenge to imperative control and the industrial division of labor. The more

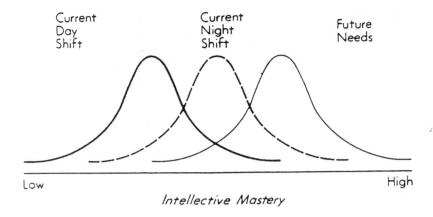

Current Day Shift

Current Night Shift

Future Needs

Low

High

Intellective Mastery

blurred the distinction between what workers know and what managers know, the more fragile and pointless any traditional relationships of domination and subordination between them will become.

The explication of meaning that is so central to the development of intellective skill requires that people become their own authorities. The communicative demands of abstract work compel once implicit and largely silent know-how to become psychologically active and individually differentiated. Without the consensual immediacy of a shared action context, individuals must construct interpretations of the information at hand and so reveal what they believe to be significant. In this way, authority is located in the process of creating and articulating meaning, rather than in a particular position or function. Under such conditions, it is unlikely that a traditional organization will achieve the efficiencies, standards of quality, or levels of innovation that have become mandatory in an environment marked by the competitive challenges of global markets and deregulation. . . .

The informating process may not be sufficient to transform authority, but it does appear to erode the pragmatic claims that have lent force and credibility to the traditional managerial role. If allegiance to the faith that sustains imperative control takes precedence over effectiveness, then that faith will inevitably find itself attempting to draw life from withered roots. . . .

A redistribution of authority is both the basis upon which intellective skill development can proceed and the necessary implication of its success. Unless informating is taken up as a conscious strategy, rather than simply allowed to unfold without any anticipation of its consequences, it is unlikely to yield up its full value. The centerpiece of such a strategy must be a redefinition of the system of authority that is expressed in and maintained by the traditional industrial division of labor. As long as organizational members are unwilling to critically examine their faith in this system, individuals at every level will remain like reeds in the wind, able to do only as much as their roles prescribe, seeking the psychological equivalent of the graveyard shift in order to test one's wings, only to be pulled back daily by the requirements of the faith.

Without a capacity to envision an alternative, it is likely that our work organizations will continue to reproduce relationships that impede a powerful understanding of the economic and social potential of new technology. . . .

The informating process sets knowledge and authority on a collision course. In the absence of a strategy to synthesize their force, neither can emerge a clear victor, but neither can emerge unscathed.

NOTES

1. The tendency to rely on social and subjective criteria in the face of uncertain standards or in the evaluation of abstract phenomena has been well documented in social psychology. For example, in an early article, Leon Festinger noted "the less 'physical reality' there is to validate the opinion or belief, the greater will be the importance of the social referent, the group, and the greater will be the forces to communicate" ("Informal Social Communication," *Psychology Review* 57 [1950]: 273). More recent empirical confirmation of this tendency can be found in Michael Kelley, "Subjective Performance Evaluation and Person-Role Conflict Under Conditions of Uncertainty," *Academy of Management Journal* 20, no. 2 (1977): 301–14; Jeffrey Pfeffer, Gerald Salancik, and Huseyin Leblebici, "The Effect of Uncertainty on the Use of Social Influence in Organization Decision Making," *Administrative Science Quarterly* 21 (1976): 227–45.

45

Technology as Equivoque: Sensemaking in New Technologies

Karl E. Weick

New technologies, such as complex production systems that use computers (Ettlie, 1988; Majchrzak, 1988; Susman and Chase, 1986; Zuboff, 1988), create unusual problems in sensemaking for managers and operators. For example, people now face the novel problem of how to recover from incomprehensible failures in production systems and computer systems. To solve this problem, people must assume the role of failure managers who are heavily dependent on their mental models of what might have happened, although they can never be sure because so much is concealed. Not only does failure take on new forms, but there is also continuous intervention, improvement, and redesign, which means that the implementation state of development never stops (Berniker and Wacker, 1988, p. 2).

Problems like these affect organizational structure in ways not previously discussed by organizational scholars. To understand new technologies and their impacts, we need to supplement existing concepts. Thus, the purpose of this chapter is to describe features of new technologies that necessitate a revision in the concepts we use to understand their place in organized life and then to suggest what some of those revised concepts might be.

The central idea is captured by the phrase *technology as equivoque*. An *equivoque* is something that admits of several possible or plausible interpretations and therefore can be esoteric, subject to misunderstandings, uncertain, complex, and recondite. New technologies mean many things because they are simultaneously the source of stochastic events, continuous events, and abstract events. Complex systems composed of these three classes of events make both limited sense and many different kinds of sense. They make limited sense because so little is visible and so much is transient, and they make many different kinds of sense because the dense interactions that occur within them can be modeled in so many different ways. Because new technologies are equivocal, they require ongoing structuring and sensemaking if they are to be managed.

The effects of these equivocal properties on organizations can be grasped more readily if analysts talk about structuration rather than structure, affect rather than analysis, dynamic interactive complexity rather than static interactive complexity, and premise control rather than behavioral control. . . .

DEFINITIONS OF TECHNOLOGY

Three definitions of technology provide a context that illustrates strengths and weaknesses of prevailing thought about technology:

1. "We define technology as the physical combined with the intellectual or knowledge processes by which materials in some form are transformed into outputs used by another organization or subsystem within the same organization" (Hulin and Roznowski, 1985, p. 47)
2. Technology is "a family of methods for associating and channeling other entities and forces, both human and nonhuman. It is a method, one method, for the conduct of heterogeneous engineering, for the construction of a relatively stable system of related bits and pieces with emergent properties in a hostile or indifferent environment" (Law, 1987, p. 115).
3. "Technology refers to a body of knowledge about the means by which we work on the world, our arts and our methods. Essentially, it is knowledge about the cause and effect relations of our actions. . . . Technology is knowledge that can be studied, codified, and taught to others" (Berniker, 1987, p. 10).

. . . As technologies become more automated, abstract, continuous, flexible, and complex, they may become less analyzable and encounter more exceptions. These changes in analyzability and exceptions should be patterned, but the question is whether our concepts and instruments are sufficiently sensitive to capture these patterns and to differentiate degrees of routineness (Perrow, 1986) and degrees of analyzability. The answer seems to be no.

PROPERTIES OF NEW TECHNOLOGIES

The purpose of this section is to single out three qualities of newer technologies—stochastic events, continuous events, and abstract events—that, while present in older technologies, seem now to be more prominent and to have distinctive organizational implications. . . .

Stochastic Events. Davis and Taylor (1976) suggest that previous industrial-era technologies were deterministic, with clear cause-effect relationships among what was to be done, how it was to be done, and when it was to be done. Newer automated technologies no longer are dominated by determinism. Instead, "people operate in an environment whose 'important events' are randomly occurring and unpredictable" (Davis and Taylor, 1976, p. 388). . . .

While technologies have always had stochastic events—for example, steam boilers did blow up (Burke, 1972)—the unique twist in new technologies is that the uncertainties are permanent rather than transient. All technologies surprise operators at first, but as learning develops, surprises recede. That normal development, however, occurs less often with new technologies, because of their poorly understood processes and raw material, continuous revision of the design of the process, and the fact that implementation often is the means by which the technology itself is designed. Furthermore, with increased dependence on computers, there is the dual problem that computers often do not give a complete and accurate picture of the state of the process and, when they do, "operator state identification and control activities gradually become decoupled from actual process state as a function of execution problems or the unexpected" (Woods, O'Brien, and Hanes, 1987, p. 1741). . . .

The skill requirements of a stochastic environment are unique. A large repertoire of skills must be maintained, even though they are used infrequently; people are usually on standby, giving special attention to startup and to anticipating faults that may lead to downtime; the distinction between operations and maintenance is blurred; skills in monitoring and diagnostics are crucial; people must be committed to do what is necessary on their own initiative and have the autonomy to do so; and people have now assumed the role of "variance absorber, dealing with and counteracting the unexpected" (Davis and Taylor, 1976, pp. 388–389).

As we noted earlier, stochastic environments represent a moving target for learning because they can change faster than people can accumulate knowledge about them. When recurrence is scarce, so is learning, which is why stochastic events have become a permanent fixture of new technologies. . . .

Continuous Events. An expanded version of Woodward's (1965) continuous process technology provides a prototype that captures additional properties of new technologies. Traditionally, process production has been illustrated by batch production of chemicals, by continuous-flow production of gases, liquids, and solids, and by description of the outputs as dimensional products measured by width, capacity, or volume, rather than as integral products that can be counted (Scott, 1981). Continuous process production tends to be more heavily automated than the mechanized process of mass production (Mintzberg, 1983), which means that some of the issues discussed as stochastic events still apply when we emphasize continuity rather than unpredictability. While continuity and stochastic events covary, we intend to pry them apart as much as possible because they represent distinct issues in new technologies.

Continuous processes impose their own imperative—the reliability imperative—and this sets them apart from stochastic events. This shift from efficiency to reliability may constitute the single most important change associated with new technologies. Reliability is salient in continuous processing because the overriding requirement is to keep the process doing what it is supposed to do. This means there is a premium on maintaining the continuity and integrity of the process. "Responsibility for assuring operations continuity is more important than responsibility for effort" (Adler, 1986, p. 20).

Reliability has recently been highlighted as an issue of safety in the context of dangerous technologies (for example, nuclear power plants), but the issue of reliability is larger than the question of safety. Most of the technologies associated with safety issues are part of a larger group of technologies, all of which involve continuous processes. The problems posed by continuous processing are more visible and consequential in such technologies as nuclear reactors, but the problems are indigenous to all members of this class. Thus, the current concern with issues of reliability is not just a reaction to an increase in the number of dangerous technologies; it is symptomatic of a larger set of unique issues associated with postindustrial technology in general. While efficiency was the hallmark of deterministic industrial-era technology, reliability is the hallmark of stochastic, continuous technology associated with the postindustrial era.

There are numerous examples of an upswing in continuous processing. Bank tellers now deal with a level of automation that is qualitatively higher than that of continuous-flow chemical refineries (Adler, 1986). When transaction entries are made, adjustments are made instantaneously to all relevant bank accounts. Since the data base is on line for entry and access, any error means that the bank uses inaccurate data for all subsequent operations and calculations. Air traffic control in heavily loaded sectors requires continuous processing (Finkelman and Kirschner, 1980). Activities that normally look like mass production, such as the production of soap operas (Intintoli, 1984), in fact turn out to resemble continuous production more closely.

Transaction processing in general has become more continuous, as is evident in automatic teller machines, computerized reservation systems, toll-free phone numbers that can be switched from one answering location to another according to the time of day, and point-of-sale debit machines that can support continuous transaction processing in direct sales. Unlike previous continuous process technologies, which were confined to one location (such as a factory or refinery), newer technologies use communication technology and construct organization without location. New technologies knit separate actors, transactions, and locations together into a continuous process.

One of the most interesting examples of continuous processing is flexible, automated manufacturing. The fascinating quality of this technology is that it allows continuous processing of customized products. Less standardized low-volume unique products, usually made in a job shop, can now be made by a quasi-continuous process (Adler, 1988). . . .

A technology that combines craft and continuous processing (a combination that is possible, given some of the similarities observed by Woodward) may provide a core image to understand newer technologies. Denison (personal communication) has suggested that reliability assurance becomes the craft. As the supervisor of continuous processing pays more attention to the process and the product than to people, he or she may often become the most skilled worker, or someone very much like a person involved in unit production (Davis and Taylor, 1976).

People confronted with problems of continuity and reliability need a different set of sensitivities and skills than do people confronted with problems of discreteness and efficiency. It is important, for example, for them to visualize and think in terms of processes rather than products. Burack (cited in Davis and Taylor, 1976) has suggested that such aptitudes as high attention to work processes, rapid response to emergencies, ability to stay calm in tense environments, and early detection of malfunctions are crucial. Adler (1986) argues that newer technologies, which put a premium on continuous processing, require that people assume higher task responsibility, deal comfortably with higher levels of abstraction, and develop a deeper appreciation for the qualitatively higher levels of interdependence involved in their work.

Perrow's (1984) diagnosis that the coincidence of tight coupling and technological complexity has created conditions of interactive complexity and a new family of failures (called "normal accidents") may be an early recognition that continuous processing in general presents unique problems that require unique structures. Classical examples of continuous processing technologies, such as chemical plants, are described by Perrow (1984, p. 97) as "interactively complex," although he describes other process technologies, such as drug and bread production, as "linear, tight." As we will argue shortly, a linear, tight system is vulnerable because if members lose some comprehension of cause and effect, the system becomes more interactively complex and more prone to failure. All agree that continuous processes, by definition, have no buffers, which compounds the problems created by more frequent stochastic events and higher mental workloads.

The coexistence of stochastic events and continuous events creates several problems of analysis. For example, it could be argued that stochastic events—which have been around as long as technology itself—are no more common in new technologies than they were before but simply seem that way because they stand out more vividly against the background of more continuous processing. The argument throughout this chapter is that the combination of increased cognitive demands, increased electronic complexity, and dense interdependence over larger areas increases the incidence of unexpected outcomes that ramify in unexpected ways. These unexpected ramifications need not be synonymous with failure because they may also be occasions for innovation and learning. The point is that we assume there are more stochastic events with new technologies, rather than more salience for relatively the same number of stochastic events as were associated with older technologies; but we could be wrong.

Abstract Events. More and more of the work associated with new technologies has disappeared into machines, which means that managers and operators experience increased cognitive demands for inference, imagination, integration, problem solving, and mental maps to monitor and understand what is going on out of sight. Buchanan and Bessant (1985, p. 303) argue that people who work with new technologies have to have a complex understanding of at least four components: "1. the process—its layout, sequence of events and interdependencies; 2. the product—its key characteristics, properties and variability of raw materials; 3. the equipment—its functions, capabilities and limitations; 4. the controls—their functions, capabilities and limitations, and the effects of control actions on performance." These four understandings are crucial be-

cause the technology is partially self-controlled, and people have to handle the unexpected and provide backup control when automatic control systems fail. People need sufficient understanding of abstract events so that they can intervene at any time and pick up the process or assemble a recovery.

The unique and sizable cognitive demands imposed by new technologies suggest that the concept of operator error is misleading and should be replaced. Part of the argument for replacement is that operators are often blamed for errors that lie with designers and systems (Perrow, 1984). In Berniker's (private communication) colorful language, "Operator error is the fig leaf of scoundrels promoting complex systems." Thus, at the minimum, we should talk about operating error rather than operator error.

Aside from that issue, I want to argue that new technologies foster operator *mistakes* rather than operator errors. The difference is not trivial. An error occurs when a person strays from a guide or a prescribed course of action through inadvertence and is blameworthy, whereas a mistake occurs when there is a misconception, a misidentification, or a misunderstanding. Some problems in new technologies do occur when operators stray from rote procedures and err in executing an intention, but a more frequent and more serious source of problems develops when people form their intentions in the first place. . . .

Mistakes in the formation of an intention tend to be surprisingly resistant to change, as was evident at Three Mile Island (Perrow, 1984); at Tenerife, when the pilot of KLM flight 4805 persisted in his hypothesis that the cloud-shrouded runway was clear for takeoff (Weick, 1988b); and in several studies of operator performance (Woods, O'Brien, and Hanes, 1987). These mistakes usually are not corrected until a "fresh viewpoint enters the situation" (Woods, O'Brien, and Hanes, 1987, p. 1745).

While we could cite numerous other examples of the ways in which new technologies have become more abstract, with a corresponding higher mental workload, we need instead to highlight the significance of this change. New technologies are basically dual rather than singular. They involve the self-contained, invisible material process that is actually unfolding, as well as the equally self-contained, equally invisible imagined process that is mentally unfolding in the mind of an individual or a team. There are relatively few points at which the mental representation can be checked against and corrected by the actual process. True, there are hundreds of discrete sensors that track fluctuations, but those readings do not convey a direct picture of relationships, be they cause-effect, goals-means, or physical relationships. Relational information is the most crucial information when the object being monitored is a continuous process.

Thus, unlike any other technologies that have been used previously as predictors by organizational theorists, the new technologies exist as much in the head of the operator as they do on the plant floor. This is not to argue that one technology is more important than another, but it is to argue that cognition and micro-level processes are keys to understanding the organizational impact of new technologies.

An operator's representation of a process technology, and the resulting formation of intentions and choice of control activities, can gradually become decoupled from the actual process state, so that the operator's control intervention literally creates a new technical system that is understood neither by the operator nor by the devices for self-control originally designed into the material

technology. The human construction is itself an intact and plausible view. The decoupling is gradual. The immediate consequences of decoupling are invisible except for dial fluctuations that could be errors, separate independent deviations of separate sensors, or a single problem with multiple symptoms. Therefore, it is not surprising that so-called mistakes persist.

New technologies are parallel technologies involving a technology in the head and a technology on the floor. Each is self-contained. Each is coordinated with the other intermittently rather than continuously. Each corrects the other discontinuously. Each can have a sizable effect on the other, and the parallel technologies have a constant amount of mystery that is due to the invisibility of the processes each contains.

CONCEPTUALIZING NEW TECHNOLOGIES

Such concepts as structure, analysis, complexity, and behavior control have been prominent in previous discussions of deterministic, mechanized, physical technologies that impose their imperatives on organizational functioning. As technologies become more stochastic, continuous, and abstract, those same concepts no longer explain as much as they used to. In their place, we now need to talk more about structuration, affect, dynamic interactive complexity, and premise control. The following discussion shows why.

From Structure to Structuration. Deterministic, stable technology is compatible with deterministic organizational structure, but the shift toward stochastic, automated technology requires that we pay more attention to structuration and structuring. Structuration is defined as "the production and reproduction of a social system through members' use of rules and resources in interaction" (Poole, n.d., p. 6). The important ideas in that statement are that systems are built from interactions and rules; that such resources as action are the tools people use to enact their organizations; and, most important, that structures are both the medium and the outcome of interaction. People create structural constraints, which then constrain them (Turner, 1987). Structuration pays equal attention to both sides of that structuring process (constraining and being constrained), whereas earlier notions emphasized one side and neglected the other.

The idea that structure constrains action (Khandwalla, 1974) dominated earlier discussions of mechanized technology, but this emphasis was flawed because it treated structure as a given and underestimated the degree to which human action can alter it. The opposite emphasis, represented by the idea that structure is an emergent property of ongoing action (Weick, 1969), made the opposite error. It suggested that ongoing action unfolds free of any preconceptions, and it underestimated the degree to which institutional patterns impose prior constraints on the action from which structures emerge.

The concept of structuration is exemplified by Goffman's marvelous observation that "in everyday life actors are simultaneously the marks as well as the shills of social order" (cited in Barley, 1986, p. 79): the same person is both the shill who constructs the game and the mark who is drawn in by the game that has been constructed; victimizer becomes victim through frameworks laid down during prior interaction.

An illustration of how technology affects structuration has been supplied by Barley's (1986) analysis of two radiology departments that adopted CAT scanners. In one department, initial expertise was lodged in the technicians (Suburban Hospital); in the other, expertise was lodged in radiologists (Urban Hospital). The new technology introduced in both settings was identical—a Technicare 2060 whole-body computed topography scanner. This technology is stochastic (for example, bone artifacts sometimes appear unpredictably in pictures of the basal brain area, which makes interpretation difficult) and continuous (for example, the timing of injections of dye to highlight portions of the body affects the conclusions that may be drawn), and the mental workload is substantial because the system uses novel diagnostic signs. The technology is hypothesized to affect structuration in the following manner. At first the technology is exogenous. When translated into a technical system, it either confirms ingrained interaction patterns or disturbs and reformulates them. These patterns are carried by scripts—"standard plots of types of encounters whose repetition constitutes the setting's interaction order" (Barley, 1986, p. 83)—which create reciprocal links between structure and action. Thus, the technology ratifies or alters scripts that have grown up as a result of previous structuring. When the new body-imaging technologies were introduced to both departments, radiologists and technicians alike drew on traditional, institutionalized patterns of signification, legitimation, and domination (see Riley, 1983) to construct roles to deal with this technology and to interpret the strange products that it produced. However, the traditional pattern of technicians' deference to professional radiologists proved inadequate, especially at Suburban, because radiologists had only modest understanding of the technology. The puzzling technology introduced slippage between the idealized patterns of dominance and legitimation built up from past practice and the immediate problem of trying to discover what the novel diagnostic signs meant. Given this slippage, new patterns of action emerged and were incorporated into scripts that made a lasting change in institutional structure.

To understand how structures were both created and altered by interactions between radiologists and technicians, we need to look more closely at the scripts that emerged from actions involving the new technology. Some of these scripts, such as direction giving, countermands, usurping the controls, direction seeking, and expected criticisms, ratified traditional institutional forms. Other scripts, such as preference stating, clandestine teaching, role reversal, and mutual execution, modified these traditional forms. Each script was built from actions evoked by the technology, but the influence of the technology on structure occurred through the ratio of ratification scripts to modification scripts, not through some more static vehicle, such as workflow rigidity. For example, the ratio of preference stating (a modification script) to direction giving (a ratification script) was lower at Suburban

(1 : 1.7) than at Urban (1 : 4.7), which meant that the same technology produced more structural change at Suburban than at Urban and did so because it led to the construction of a different social order. Direction giving is a straightforward enactment of the prevailing institutionalized dominance of radiologists over technologists; direction giving is a pure expression of existing structure. But as the frequency of this pure enactment is moderated by scripts that place greater emphasis on collegiality, the traditional form is changed. Ongoing affirmations and modifications such as these are the means by which technology both shapes structure and is itself shaped by structure when different techniques are built and used to run it.

The relationships between structuration and technology can be diagrammed into the deviation-amplifying system shown in Figure 1. The linkage from C to D represents action as a constraint on structure. The linkage from E to B represents institutional constraints on action. Scripts are found at steps B and C, and either ratification or modification can occur at each of those two stages.

FIGURE 1 • STRUCTURATION AND TECHNOLOGY

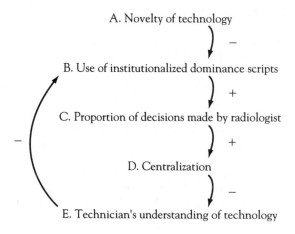

A. Novelty of technology

B. Use of institutionalized dominance scripts

C. Proportion of decisions made by radiologist

D. Centralization

E. Technician's understanding of technology

Notice that when we depict the structural effects of technology in this way, once technology provides the initial "kick" to the process, its effects are then dependent on how it becomes woven into the process of action. This embedding is a mixture of action, scripts, and institutional forms, but the technology itself becomes something different, according to how these three components interact. That is the central point of the structuration hypothesis, and it is an important point to maintain as technologies become more fluid and more difficult to comprehend, with less transparent effects on shifting organizational structures.

There are several ways to enlarge Barley's (1986) analysis and bring in additional dimensions of technology. The point at which technology is introduced is the point at which it is most susceptible to influence (Winner, 1986), and Barley's analysis shows why. When conceptualized in the context of structure, technologies are treated as self-evident artifacts to which people accommodate, rather than as open-ended artifacts that accommodate to interactions. Structuration sensitizes the observer to look for an ongoing redefinition among structure, action, and technology. Beginnings are of special importance for structuration because they constrain what is learned about the technology and how fast it is learned (for example, Urban Hospital technicians learned less and learned more slowly, even though it was assumed that they understood the technology). . . .

While there are other ways than structuration to understand Barley's data, none of them preserve quite so succinctly the point that technology is both a cause and a consequence of structure. This dual role of technology occurs because structuring is an ongoing process that shapes the meaning of artifacts through scripts, interaction, and tradition and is itself shaped by those meanings. The ability to treat structure in this manner is an important conceptual change that we need for understanding the effects of new technologies.

From Analysis to Affect. Throughout the preceding discussion, we have implied that new technologies trigger strong feelings. These feelings have a substantial effect on the operation of the technologies. Thus, we need to understand not only how operators solve problems within the bounds of their mental maps but also how they do so under pressure. Problem solving under pressure means coping both with interruptions and with excessive arousal. We review these two issues in that order.

When a continuous process begins to fail, in an environment where excessive deviation in one measurement-one indication is signaled by one alarm, operators are hit with an "avalanche" of alarms (Woods, O'Brien, and Hanes, 1987, p. 1735). In the first few minutes after a sudden change in a parameter, two hundred alarm points may be active. Since the alarms are hardwired and not conditioned by multivariable patterns, the operator gets no help in pattern recognition from the alarms themselves. Furthermore, the search for patterns is carried out amidst considerable distraction.

The theorizing about emotion done by Berscheid (1983) and Mandler (1984) suggests that interruptions, similar to those that alarms create, are a sufficient and possibly necessary condition for arousal and emotional experience. Since interruption is a chronic threat to continuous processing, and since stochastic events are a chronic source of interruptions, we may expect that strong emotions are coexistent with new technologies.

This conjunction of strong emotions and new technologies can be understood if we look more closely at the relationship between arousal and interruption. A necessary condition for emotion is arousal, or discharge in the autonomic nervous system. Arousal has physiological significance because it prepares people for fight-or-flight reactions. Of even more importance is the fact that arousal also has psychological significance. The perception of arousal provides a warning that there is some stimulus to which attention must be paid in order to initiate appropriate action. This signal suggests that one's well-being may be at stake. . . .

If we apply these propositions to new technologies, we start by asking, "What is the distribution of interruption in technology? Where are interruptions most likely to occur, and how organized are the actions and plans that are likely to be interrupted?" If we can describe this, then we can predict where emotional experiences are most likely to occur and how intense they will be. For example, systems with newer, less well organized response sequences, settings with fewer standard operating procedures, and settings that are more loosely coupled should be settings in which there is less emotion because interruptions are less disruptive. Settings in which there are few developed plans should be less interruptible and therefore should elicit less emotion. . . .

Other than redoubled effort, what other behavioral consequences of emotion might we expect in new technologies? To ask this question is to confront the venerable issue of whether emotion disrupts adaptive functioning or energizes it. Given the staying power of this controversy, we must assume that both views are partially correct. . . .

The key point for technology is that the breadth of attention varies in response to fluctuations in emotion (Weltman, Smith, and Egstrom, 1971; Berkun, 1964; Wachtel, 1967). This variation could affect both task conceptions and performance. Assuming that people try to make sense of whatever they notice, as the breadth of their attention varies, so should their descriptions of what they are doing. Thus, task conceptions themselves, not just task performance, should change as arousal changes. Unreliable performance may persist because the operator is performing a different task than observers realize. The point is that this discrepancy in conception may be due to differences in pressure rather than to differences in authority and position.

There is a clear example of this possibility in Barley's (1986) data. Technicians at Urban Hospital were the object of a steady stream of directives, imperative speech, puzzling countermands, sarcasm, and usurped control generated by radiologists. These could easily have raised the level of threat and arousal experienced by technicians, which in turn could have narrowed their attention, made complex learning more difficult, and actually altered their conception of what kind of task CAT-scanner technology posed for them. These effects could have slowed their learning, which should then have intensified the pressure that radiologists imposed, making further learning even more difficult.

This scenario of obstructed learning produced by heightened arousal places less emphasis on differences in position, authority, and structure and more emphasis on the disruptive effects of emotions, such as threat and fear, when they occur under conditions of high arousal and complex technology. Since ongoing learning is so much a part of new technologies, anything that obstructs learning, such as arousal, is of considerable importance.

Since new technologies make greater demands for abstract mental work, we must pay as much attention to the fact that there is an increase in demands as to the fact that those demands are mental. To cope with mental workload is an arousing, emotional experience, which means that mental processes will be modified by affect. New technologies have properties that seem likely to intensify affect. If that intensification occurs, then affect can shape the technology because it attenuates the attention directed at it. As attention varies, so do conceptions of the technology and the effectiveness and reliability of performance. To change how people cope with this technology requires an understanding of these fluctuations in attention. As we have suggested, these fluctuations are driven by uncertainties that seem to affect people in a manner analogous to those postulated for the concept of global arousal.

From Static to Dynamic Interactive Complexity. . . . Interactive complexity is not a fixed commodity tied to specific technologies, such as nuclear reactors. Since arousal tends to increase when control and prediction become problematic, and since newer technologies alter many of the processes of control and prediction that people are accustomed to, arousal is likely to accompany many of the newer technologies much of the time. What makes this so serious is that virtually all of the effects of arousal on the already complex newer technology are in the direction of making it even more complex. Stochastic events become even more so when the few patterns that are still visible in them vanish in the face of perceptual narrowing.

When we argue that interactive complexity is dynamic rather than static, this does not give researchers license to study perception and ignore material artifacts and structure. Material artifacts set sensemaking processes in motion; sensemaking is constrained by actions, which themselves are constrained by artifacts; and sensemaking attempts to diagnose symptoms emitted by the technology. What we are trying to emphasize in recasting the concept of interactive complexity is that the increased mental workload created by new technologies forces people to impose more of their own interpretations to understand what is occurring. These interpretations are necessarily incomplete, which means that a greater number of material events interact longer, with potentially more severe consequences—out of sight but, more seriously, out of mind. When people use fallible models to cope with stochastic, continuous, abstract events under conditions of excessive arousal, interactive complexity is one consequence.

The gradual decoupling of a mental model of a process from the actual steps that occur in that process allows events to unfold that ramify in their consequences and grow increasingly incomprehensible. These outcomes potentially occur whenever excessive arousal contracts attention and allows events to interact unnoticed and unmonitored, so that a new technical system and a new set of interactions are created, without any person intending it. It is in this sense that humans can transform a simple linear system into one that is interactively complex, and it is in this sense that interactive complexity and new technologies are closely associated.

The point of all this is not to lay one more shortcoming at the door of the human operator; quite the opposite. What we are suggesting is that the design of technical systems often fails to moderate arousal levels, make complex judgment tasks simpler, distribute responsibilities among team members, reduce distractions, provide incentives for early reporting of error and problem solving, reduce production pressure, heighten perceptions of control, and add slack capacity to attention.

Considering what they face, it is remarkable that operators do as well as they do. If, after three years, teams of professional analysts still were not completely certain of what had happened at Three Mile Island, then we can hardly fault a handful of operators who had thirteen seconds to decide what had happened. As Frijda (1986, pp. 476-477) observes, "A human being cannot have been made to stand and withstand all contingencies life presents. What can you expect from a system that only takes nine months to produce and merely weighs about 70 kilograms? . . . One may assume that humans have been fitted out with provisions to deal effectively with a number of important contingencies. There is necessarily a cost to this. Several emotion provisions, for instance, are emergency provisions. They produce response fast, and upon a minimum of information processing. If the system can do that, one should not complain that its information processing on these occasions is truncated, or that response is being made when finer meaning analysis might have shown it to be unnecessary."

From Behavior and Output Control to Premise Control. As new technologies increasingly take on the form of abstract working knowledge, they move deeper inside the operator's head, which means that effective control over these technologies will be exerted by cognitive variables and unobtrusive controls. Obtrusive controls, such as orders, rules, regulations, specialization, or hierarchy (Perrow, 1977), require more observables than are ordinarily present with new technologies. For example, behavior control (Ouchi and McGuire, 1975)

is more difficult in new technologies because visible behaviors comprise a smaller portion of the actual inputs. Thus, behavior is a less meaningful object of control: there is less behavior to monitor, the effects of observed behaviors are mystified by interactive complexity, and the same behaviors may be mediated by private diagnoses that vary widely in their accuracy. All of these complications mean that observed behaviors are less diagnostic of how well the process is progressing.

Output control is also difficult, for many of the same reasons. Visible outputs are less meaningful because so many unobservable determinants other than operators' actions can affect them. While an operator can be held accountable for the output, that accountability is empty if neither the operator nor the monitor understand what is occurring or why.

Obtrusive managerial controls, such as direct surveillance and standardization, are relatively ineffective ways to influence the operation of new technologies because less obtrudes to be monitored or standardized. This does not mean that obtrusive controls have disappeared in organizations with new technologies, but it does mean that unobtrusive controls in the form of decision premises (for example, managerial psychosocial assumptions incorporated into work arrangements) should have more impact. Decision premises have become more crucial now that more of the organization is carried in the head and less of it is carried by visible, sensible, transparent artifacts. Cognition is an increasingly important determinant of organizational outcomes because, with fewer visible artifacts, more of the organization has to be imagined, visualized, and filled in from cryptic cues. All of this fleshing out is cognitive and is affected by decision premises. . . .

Premise controls are often created when managerial psychosocial assumptions are incorporated into technological and organizational designs. As Dornbusch and Scott (1975, p. 89) note, work arrangements, which consist of such components as allocation of responsibility, procedures for the evaluation of performance, and rules governing task performance, usually "are messages concerning the nature of the tasks from those who control to those who perform." At the center of these messages is either a delegation premise (that performers can make nontrivial decisions regarding a course of action) or a directive premise (that they cannot). These premises may be unconsidered choices by managers, but that does not make them any less potent.

Much of the potency of managerial assumptions derives from the fact that they act like self-fulfilling prophecies. Davis and Taylor (1976, p. 412) provide the example of "when assumptions are held that a system is comprised [sic] of reliable technical elements and unreliable social elements, then in order to provide total system reliability, the technical design must call for parts of people as replaceable machine elements to be regulated by the technical system or by a superstructure of personal control. On the other hand, if the system designers' assumptions are that the social elements are reliable, learning, self-organizing, and committed elements, then the technical system will require whole, unique people performing the regulatory activities. Experience has shown that in the latter case such a technical system design produces effects markedly different than [in] the former."

It becomes more plausible to link technology with determination by self-fulfilling prophecies when a sizable portion of the technology exists in the form of decision premises. Self-fulfilling prophecies are themselves decision premises, which become realized when they are treated as if they were true.

An interesting current puzzle in technology may be the result of a self-fulfilling prophecy incorporated into managerial assumptions. American implementation of flexible manufacturing systems differs dramatically from Japanese implementation of the same systems. Thurow (1987) observes that the average American system makes ten parts while the average Japanese system makes ninety-three different parts. Adler (1988) cites data showing that American systems produce eight parts, on average, whereas those in Japan produce an average of thirty parts and those in Germany as many as eighty-five parts. In other words, flexible manufacturing systems in the United States show a remarkable lack of flexibility. Although flexible manufacturing is more like batch or continuous processing, managers may still assume it is a long-linked assembly line and embed the system in a mechanistic structure, which fulfills the prophecy that it is simply an electronic assembly line. Again, the imposed premises define, flesh out, and actualize a portion of the technology.

It does not matter that the operators are more sensitive to nonroutine qualities of the technology that the manager overlooks. Managerial assumptions typically dominate, and this is especially serious when managers underestimate the skills required for operation of new systems (Adler, 1986). This underestimation is not trivial, since it is backed up with directives rather than with delegation. These directives either squeeze out the flexibility that was designed into the technology or, more seriously, restrict perception and make it harder for people to operate the technology in a reliable manner.

Our point is that managers and designers are able to exert substantial influence over the form of new technologies because key parts of these technologies exist in the form of decision premises, which makes these forms more vulnerable to the premises imposed by managers.

If those premises are imposed by managers who feel threatened by the potential loss of their authority (Davis and Taylor, 1976) or by designers who want to centralize decisions, promulgate rules, and differentiate tasks (Scott, 1981), then technologies will be run with less judgment than is necessary to manage and comprehend their complexity. As a result, these technologies will become more interactively complex because directives will make it harder for operators to monitor, learn about, and respond to the full range of states that a machine can assume. The artificial restriction of perception and action by directives does not stop elements of the technology from interacting, but it does curtail comprehension of these interactions, which means the technology becomes more complex and more puzzling.

Thus, interactive complexity can be a social construction, as well as an indigenous feature of new technologies. This is why, throughout this chapter, it is assumed that interactive complexity is more common, more easily created, and more pervasive as an accompaniment of newer technologies than has previously been recognized. Furthermore, decision premises are an important source of interactive complexity. Designers whose assumptions issue in directives create more interactive complexity than do designers whose assumptions issue in delegations.

CONCLUSIONS

The preceding analysis suggests that an important pathway by which new technology affects organizations is variation in the ability of people to reason about the deep structure of new systems. Reasoning of some sort is mandatory because the systems are equivocal. The adequacy of reasoning depends on the extent to which the mental models used by people who work with new technologies are equivalent to the processes they model. These models represent an imagined technology that people assume parallels the actual technology, which they can see only through its punctate sensors.

Reasoning about new technologies can have a consequential effect on the way those technologies function. Our recurrent theme has been that technical systems and organizational constraints can reduce meaning, control, and predictability, which raises arousal, which affects the material interactions that are set in motion, which affects the outcome, which then feeds back and has a further effect on meaning, control, and predictability. The cycle can be broken, reversed, or dampened at any one of these points. Part of what we have tried to articulate is ways in which people can gain some control over the increasingly private, increasingly equivocal new technologies, which often test the limits of human comprehension.

This rephrasing of the main argument is an attempt to articulate the implications for individuals, as well as for organizations, of a set of technological qualities that we have not seen together before in quite this combination. Just as the novel combination of complex structures and tight coupling has produced interactive complexity and normal accidents at the organizational level, so has the novel combination of stochastic events and continuous processes produced cognitiveemotional complexity and operator mistakes at the individual level. More important, normal accidents and operator mistakes derive from analogous assumptions and mechanisms, the one set emphasizing macro material determinants and the other emphasizing micro perceptual determinants.

New technologies are fascinating because, in their complex equivocality, they force us to grapple with a key issue in technology—namely, how to apply perceptual perspectives to a material world. . . .

New technologies are paradoxical, as well as equivocal. These descriptions are not intended merely as clever phrases. Instead, they speak to the core issues we need to resolve if we want to understand technologies in which mental representation plays a central role in operation. . . .

REFERENCES

Adler, P. "New Technologies, New Skills." *California Management Review*, 1986, *29*, 9–28.

Adler, P. S. "Managing Flexible Automation." *California Management Review*, 1988, *30*, 34–56.

Barley, S.R. "Technology as an Occasion for Structuring: Evidence from Observations of CT Scanners and the Social Order of Radiology Departments." *Administrative Science Quarterly*, 1986, *31*, 78–108.

Berkun, N. M. "Performance Decrement Under Psychological Stress." *Human Factors*, 1964, *6*, 21–30.

Berniker, E. "Understanding Technical Systems." Paper presented at Symposium on Management Training Programs: Implications of New Technologies, Geneva, Switzerland, Nov. 1987.

Berniker, E., and Wacker, G. "Advanced Manufacturing Systems." Unpublished manuscript, 1988.

Berscheid, E. "Emotion." In H. H. Kelley and others (eds.), *Close Relationships*. New York: W. H. Freeman, 1983.

Berscheid, E., Gangestad, S. W., and Kulakowski, D. "Emotion in Close Relationship: Implications for Relationship Counseling." In *Handbook of Counseling Psychology*. New York: Wiley, forthcoming.

Broadhurst, P. L. "Emotionality and the Yerkes-Dodson Law." *Journal of Experimental Psychology*, 1957, *54*, 345–352.

Buchanan, D. A., and Bessant, J. "Failure, Uncertainty, and Control: The Role of Operators in a Computer-Integrated Production System." *Journal of Management Studies*, 1985, *22*, 292–308.

Burke, J. G. "Bursting Boilers and the Federal Power." In M. Kranzberg and W. H. Davenport (eds.), *Technology and Culture: An Anthology*. New York: Schocken, 1972.

Campbell, D. J. "Task Complexity: A Review and Analysis." *Academy of Management Review*, 1988, *13*, 40–52.

Davis, L. E., and Taylor, J. C. "Technology, Organization, and Job Structure." In R. Dubin (ed.), *Handbook of Work, Organization, and Society*. Skokie, Ill.: Rand-McNally, 1976.

Dornbusch, S. M., and Scott, W. R. *Evaluation and the Exercise of Authority*. San Francisco: Jossey-Bass, 1975.

Easterbrook, J. A. "The Effect of Emotion on Cue Utilization and the Organization of Behavior." *Psychological Review*, 1959, *66*, 183–201.

Ettlie, J. E. *Taking Charge of Manufacturing: How Companies Are Combining Technological and Organizational Innovations to Compete Successfully*. San Francisco: Jossey-Bass, 1988.

Eysenck, M. W. *Attention and Arousal*. New York: Springer-Verlag, 1982.

Finkelman, J. M., and Kirschner, C. "An Information-Processing Interpretation of Air Traffic Control Stress." *Human Factors*, 1980, *22*, 561–567.

Frijda, N. F. *The Emotions*. New York: Cambridge University Press, 1986.

Hancock, W. M., Macy, B. A., and Peterson, S. "Assessment of Technologies and Their Utilization." In S. E. Seashore, E. E. Lawler III, P. H. Mirvis, and C. Cammann (eds.), *Assessing Organizational Change*. New York: Wiley, 1983.

Hermann, C. E "Some Consequences of Crisis Which Limit the Viability of Organizations." *Administrative Science Quarterly*, 1963, *8*, 61–82.

Hickson, D. J., and others. "A Strategic-Contingencies Theory of Intraorganizational Power." *Administrative Science Quarterly*, 1971, *16*, 216–229.

Hulin, C. L., and Roznowski, M. "Organizational Technologies: Effects on Organizations' Characteristics and Individuals' Responses." In L. L. Cummins and B. M. Staw (eds.), *Research in Organizational Behavior*. Vol. 7. Greenwich, Conn.: JAI Press, 1985.

Intintoli, M. J. *Taking Soaps Seriously: The World of "Guiding Light."* New York: Praeger, 1984.

Khandwalla, P. N. "Mass-Output Orientation of Operations Technology and Organizational Structure." *Administrative Science Quarterly*, 1974, *19*, 74–97.

Law, J. "Technology and Heterogeneous Engineering: The Case of Portuguese Expansion." In W. E. Bijker, T. P. Hughes, and T. J. Pinch (eds.), *The Social Construction of Technological Systems*. Cambridge, Mass.: MIT Press, 1987.

Lawrence, P. R., and Dyer, D. *Renewing American Industry*. New York: Free Press, 1983.

Lynch, B. P. "An Empirical Assessment of Perrow's Technology Construct." *Administrative Science Quarterly*, 1974, *19*, 338–356.

McGrath, J. E. "Stress and Behavior in Organizations." In M. D. Dunnette (ed.), *Handbook of Industrial and Organizational Psychology*. Skokie, Ill.: Rand-McNally, 1976.

Majchrzak, A. *The Human Side of Factory Automation: Managerial and Human Resource Strategies for Making Automation Succeed*. San Francisco: Jossey-Bass, 1988.

Mandler, G. *Mind and Body: Psychology of Emotion and Stress*. New York: Norton, 1984.

March, J. G., and Olsen, J. P. "Garbage Can Models of Decision Making in Organizations." In J. G. March and R. Weissinger-Baylon (eds.), *Ambiguity and Command*. Marshfield, Mass.: Pitman, 1986.

Metcalf, J., III. "Decision Making and the Grenada Rescue Operation." In J. G. March and R. Weissinger-Baylon (eds.), *Ambiguity and Command*. Marshfield, Mass.: Pitman, 1986.

Miles, R. H. *Macro Organizational Behavior*. Santa Monica, Calif.: Goodyear, 1980.

Mintzberg, H. *Structure in Fives*. Englewood Cliffs, N.J.: Prentice-Hall, 1983.

Neiss, R. "Reconceptualizing Arousal: Psychobiological States in Motor Performance." *Psychological Bulletin*, 1988, *103*, 345–366.

Ouchi, W. G., and McGuire, M. A. "Organizational Control: Two Functions." *Administrative Science Quarterly*, 1975, *20*, 559–569.

Perrow, C. "A Framework for the Comparative Analysis of Organizations." *American Sociological Review*, 1967, *32*, 194–208.

Perrow, C. "The Bureaucratic Paradox: The Efficient Organization Centralizes in Order to Decentralize." *Organizational Dynamics*, Spring 1977, pp. 3–14.

Perrow, C. *Normal Accidents: Living with High-Risk Technologies*. New York: Basic Books, 1984.

Perrow, C. *Complex Organizations.*(3rd ed.) New York: Random House, 1986.

Poole, M. S. "Communication and the Structuring of Organizations." Unpublished manuscript, n.d.

Riley, P. "A Structurationist Account of Political Culture." *Administrative Science Quarterly*, 1983, *28*, 414–437.

Roberts, K. H. "Bishop Rock Dead Ahead: The Grounding of U.S.S. *Enterprise.*" *Naval Institute Proceedings*, forthcoming.

Scott, W. R. *Organizations: Rational, Natural, and Open Systems*. Englewood Cliffs, N.J.: Prentice-Hall, 1981.

Scott, W. R. *Organizations: Rational, Natural, and Open Systems*. (2nd ed.) Englewood Cliffs, N.J.: Prentice-Hall, 1987.

Susman, G. I., and Chase, R. B. "A Sociotechnical Analysis of the Integrated Factory." *Journal of Applied Behavioral Science*, 1986, *22*, 257–270.

Thompson, J. D., and Tuden, A. "Strategies, Structures, and Processes of Organization Decision." In J. D. Thompson (ed.), *Comparative Studies in Administration*. Pittsburgh, Pa.: University of Pittsburgh Press, 1959.

Thurow, L. C. "A Weakness in Process Technology." *Science*, 1987, *238*, 1659–1663.

Turner, J. H. "Analytical Theorizing." In A. Giddens and J. H. Turner (eds.), *Social Theory Today*. Stanford, Calif.: Stanford University Press, 1987.

Van de Ven, A. H., Delbecq, A. L., and Koenig, R. "Determinants of Coordination Modes Within Organizations." *American Sociological Review*, 1976, *41*, 322–338.

Wachtel, P. L. "Conceptions of Broad and Narrow Attention." *Psychological Bulletin*, 1967, *68*, 417–429.

Weick, K. E. *The Social Psychology of Organizing*. Reading, Mass.: Addison-Wesley, 1969.

Weick, K. E. "Enacting Sensemaking in Crisis Situations." *Journal of Management Studies*, 1988a, *25*, 305–317.

Weick, K. E. "We Are at Takeoff: Lessons from Tenerife." Paper presented at Stanford University, Nov. 1988b.

Weltman, G., Smith, J. E., and Egstrom, G. H. "Perceptual Narrowing During Simulated Pressure-Chamber Exposure." *Human Factors*, 1971, *13*, 99–107.

Winner, L. *The Whale and the Reactor*. Chicago: University of Chicago Press, 1986.

Withey, M., Daft, R. L., and Cooper, W. H. "Measures of Perrow's Work-Unit Technology: An Empirical Assessment and a New Scale." *Academy of Management Journal*, 1983, *26*, 45–63.

Woods, D. P., O'Brien, J. E, and Hanes, L. F. "Human Factors Challenges in Process Control: The Case of Nuclear Power Plants." In G. Salvendy (ed.), *Handbook of Human Factors*. New York: Wiley, 1987.

Woodward, J. *Industrial Organization: Theory and Practice*. London: Oxford University Press, 1965.

Zuboff, S. *In the Age of the Smart Machine: The Future of Work and Power*. New York: Basic Books, 1988.

46

Postmodern Thought in a Nutshell: Where Art and Science Come Together

William Bergquist

The postmodern world is in the midst of being born. It does not yet have clear definition, other than its origins in and difference from the modern era. Hence the term *postmodern*: the concept is still defined with reference to its mother (modernism) rather than reflecting a free and independent movement or set of ideas and images with its own distinctive name. In many ways, postmodernism is a fad—and is at the same time about fads. Even though postmodernism is characterized by superficial, facile, and often internally contradictory analyses, it must not be dismissed, for these analyses offer insightful and valuable (even essential) perspectives on and critiques of an emerging era: "The postmodern moment had arrived and perplexed intellectuals, artists, and cultural entrepreneurs wondered whether they should get on the bandwagon and join the carnival, or sit on the sidelines until the new fad disappeared into the whirl of cultural fashion. Yet postmodernism refused to go away. . . . At first, there was no clear sense as to what constituted postmodernism, when it arrived, what it meant, and what effects it was having and would be likely to have in the future. Eventually, more systematic and sustained discussion took place" (Kellner, 1989, p. 2).

In the postmodern camp, there is neither interest in the systematic building of theory (through what Thomas Kuhn, 1962, calls "normal science") nor in a warfare between competing paradigms (what Kuhn calls "scientific revolutions"). Rather, everything is preparadigmatic. Tom Peters acknowledges that in the early 1980s he knew something about how organizations achieved excellence (Peters and Waterman, 1982). By the late 1980s, he discovered that he had been mistaken. Many of the "excellent" organizations of the early 1980s had become troubled institutions by the late 1980s. Other theorists and social observers have been similarly humbled by the extraordinary events of the 1980s and early 1990s. They simply haven't been as forthcoming (or opportunistic) as Tom Peters. "Postmodernism at its deepest level," notes Andreas Huyssen (1987, p. 217), "represents not just another crisis within the perpetual cycle of boom and bust, exhaustion and renewal, which has characterized the trajectory of modernist culture." Rather, the postmodern condition "represents a new type of crisis of that modernist culture itself."

If postmodernism is to provide a solid base for useful social analysis and if it is to contribute to the formulation of a new theory of organizations, then it must move beyond the status of fad and find roots in the soil of history and precedent. The origins of postmodernism can be traced to many different sources, ranging from the Marxist-based analyses of Frederick Jameson (1991) to the more conservative observations and predictions of

Source: Adapted from Bergquist, William. *The Postmodern Organization: Mastering the Art of Irreversible Change*, pp. 15–36. Copyright 1993 Jossey-Bass Inc., Publishers. Reprinted by permission.

Peter Drucker (1989), from Cristo's art-as-event performances to Peter Vaill's (1989) spiritual leadership. To trace the origins of postmodernism is to review the cultural history of twentieth-century America and possibly of our entire contemporary world. Since this task is impossible. . . . I will focus briefly in this chapter on four different sources of postmodernism. . . .

A first source of postmodernism is the intellectual debates and dialogues in Europe (primarily in France) regarding structuralism, poststructuralism, deconstruction, postcapitalism, critical theory, and feminism. Much of this work is very difficult to understand, let alone summarize or typify. Some say it is difficult because the ideas are subtle, elusive, and complex. Others say it is difficult because the authors purposefully make their points in obscure or convoluted manners.

The second source of postmodern thought is the much more accessible (some would say popularized) critique of contemporary art forms (particularly architecture, literature, and painting) and contemporary life-styles (for example, advertising, fashion, and the colloquial use of language). This line of thought relates to many of the critiques offered by the first source, in particular those involving deconstructionist and feminist reinterpretations of cultural history. Some of the clearest, and most controversial, writers in this feminist tradition are those who study and write about alternative versions of world (especially Western) history (for example, Eisler, 1987) and alternative ways of knowing (for example, Gilligan, 1982; Belenky and others, 1986).

A third source is social analysis of the workplace and economy, as represented by the work of Daniel Bell (1976), who first coined the phrase "post-industrial era," and Peter Drucker, notably in his recent book, *The New Realities* (1989).

Popular books written by Naisbitt (1984) and Toffler (1971, 1980) also have contributed, as has Tom Peters (particularly in *Thriving on Chaos*, 1987), who accurately portrays the inadequacies of the current response to postmodern conditions. Finally, postmodernism is beholden, in a somewhat more indirect manner, to work in the physical sciences that is usually labeled *chaos theory*. This work has been made accessible to the lay public through the journalistic writing of James Gleick (1987) and the more technical, but nevertheless fascinating, writing of Ilya Prigogine (Prigogine and Stengers, 1984).

In the remainder of this chapter, I briefly summarize the contributions made by each of these four sources, thereby setting the stage for our subsequent discussion of the postmodern characteristics of contemporary organizations. I specifically focus on four themes often associated with postmodernism and briefly indicate how one or more of the four postmodern sources have contributed to the elucidation of each theme.

OBJECTIVISM VERSUS CONSTRUCTIVISM

Two different perspectives compete in the postmodern era. They may be as important in the postmodern world as the liberal versus conservative distinction has been in the modern world. These two views, in fact, are often inaccurately equated with liberalism and conservatism. Advocates for *objectivism*, on the one hand, assume that there is a reality out there that we can know and articulate. There are universal truths—or at least universal principles—that can be applied to the improvement of the human condition, resolution of human conflicts, restoration of human rights, or even to the construction of a global order and community.

Advocates for *constructivism*, on the other hand, believe that we construct our own social realities, based in large part on the traditions and needs of the culture and socioeconomic context in which we find ourselves. There are no universal truths or principles, nor are there any global models of justice or order that can be applied in all settings, at all times, with all people. There are rather specific communities that espouse their own unique ways of knowing. Furthermore, these ways of knowing may themselves change over time and in differing situations.

These two perspectives do not simply involve different belief systems. They encompass different notions about the very nature of a belief system and in this sense are profoundly different from one another. While the objectivist perspective was prevalent during the modern era, the constructivist perspective is a recent, postmodern phenomenon. The emergence of the constructivist perspective represents a revolutionary change in the true sense of the term. . . . "But the problem with this modern tendency to disenchant the world was that it turned the old religious drive upside down. The traditional man of faith seeks transcendence. He wants contact with God, the One, the Truth. The modern thinker, inspired by Marx and Freud, found truth in repressed or hidden impulses, but he *found truth* nonetheless. Similarly, modern artists and critics found organic cohesion, autonomy—a form of truth, perhaps—in the grand works, works like Joyce's *Ulysses* or Eliot's *The Waste Land*" (Edmundson, 1989, p. 63).

Thus, according to Edmundson, the central challenge for a postmodernist is to retain a healthy skepticism about all purported truths—including the "truths" offered by the postmodernists themselves:

The postmodern man sees religious residues in *any* way of thinking that affirms the Truth. He reads the modern period as the time when transcendentalism gave way, yes, but to a kind of thinking that sought to penetrate the depths, there to find bedrock reality. The spirit of the . . . postmodern movement in the arts, literary criticism, and philosophy might, assuming one were determined to shrink it to bumper-sticker size, be expressed like this: "If you want to be genuinely secular, then give up on transcendence in every form." Or, if your bumper's too small for that: "Accept no substitutes—for God." In other words, don't replace the deity with some other idol, like scientific truth, the self, the destiny of America, or what have you. And (front bumper) "Don't turn your postmodernism into a faith. Don't get pious about your impiety" [1989, p. 63].

As a result of this postmodern commitment to the shattering of epistemological icons, the traditional distinction between liberal and conservative breaks down. While the capitalist and Communist offer quite different versions about what the world is like and what it should be like, they both begin with the assumption that there is a reality they can describe and assess with greater or lesser fidelity and that there are stable standards and values against which one can test alternative futures. Many of the postmodernists place a curse on both of these houses.

According to the constructivists, we must construct models of social reality and social value that are fluid, or at least flexible, and open to new data and to social conditions that change in rapid and unpredictable fashion. The postmodernist (and Marxist) Frederick Jameson (1991, p. 198) disagrees with Daniel Bell's assessment that ideology (in particular, liberal ideology) is dead because of improved social conditions in society; he does agree (for alternative reasons) that postmodernism has brought about "the end of ideology."

As with so much else, it is an old 1950s acquaintance, "the end of ideology," which has in the postmodern returned with a new and unexpected kind of plausibility. But ideology is now over, not because class struggle has ended and no one has anything class-ideological to fight about, but rather because the fate of "ideology" in this particular sense can be understood to mean that conscious ideologies and political opinions, particular thought systems along with the official philosophical ones which laid claim to a greater universality—the whole realm of consciousness, argument, and the very appearance of persuasion itself (or of reasoned dissent)— has ceased to be functional in perpetuating and reproducing the system.

Social psychologist Milton Rokeach (1960) provided insight regarding this new way of thinking about social and political models of society. Rokeach pointed out that in certain important ways, the far left and the far right tend to think alike. They search for absolutes and often portray their adversaries in what William Perry (1970) later described as a "dualistic" framework: either you agree with me or you disagree with me. Either you are right or I am right. Which is it? Both liberals and conservatives often believe that their own models of social justice and governance can be applied throughout the world (with a few adjustments for culture). They are both missionary in their zeal for dissemination of the truths they hold. The dualistic frameworks of both conservatives and liberals no longer hold up. The world is changing to a more constructivist perspective, particularly with regard to its most prized fictions—such as freedom. "Man's freedom is a fabricated freedom and he pays a price for it. He must at all times defend the utter fragility of his delicately constituted fiction, deny its artificiality. . . . Man's fictions are not superfluous creations that could be 'put aside' so that the 'more serious' busi-

ness of life could continue" (Becker, 1971, p. 139).

Elaboration of the new, constructivist perspective has been accelerated by several contemporary social scientists who have written about the "social construction of reality"—notably Berger and Luckmann (1967)—and by feminists who have written about unique ways many women and some men become knowledgeable about their world (Gilligan, 1982; Belenky and others, 1986). The new constructivism has also been aided by the emergence of a critical perspective on absolute knowledge in the physical sciences, culminating in the establishment of chaos theory. Something as simple as the measurement of length and circumference is subject to debate and the particular interest and purpose of the person doing the measurement (Gleick, 1987), in addition to the effect the measurer has on the phenomenon being measured (the so-called Heisenberg Principle).

One of the earliest and most articulate scientific spokespersons for this constructivist perspective was Michael Polanyi (1969), who wrote of the problem associated with the act of "attending to" and "attending from" any phenomenon. We can never attend to that from which we are attending. The base of our perception must always remain hidden from our perception; otherwise, we will be perceiving this base from yet another base. Thus, there is the danger of infinite regression among the social constructivists: the relativistic "social construction of reality" may itself be a social construction; Thomas Kuhn's observation about paradigms may itself be a social scientific paradigm of history that will soon be overturned by yet another paradigm; Michel Foucault's (1965) critique regarding the social/political origins of knowledge must itself be placed in a social/political context.

The Polanyi dilemma becomes particularly poignant when considering, as the French psychoanalyst Lacon did, the act of self-reflection. When one is attending to oneself in a mirror, one is attending back (in Polanyi's terms) to that from which one attends. Similarly, in psychoanalysis (or in any organization's attempt to study and understand itself), the subject is observing himself or herself in the mirror. Yet, the base from which one is attending can never be the subject of analysis, unless the base itself is changed. If the base is changed, then the new base will still remain elusive and incapable of simultaneous review.

Thus, an organization that brings in an outside consultant to study its culture will be subject to the particular perspectives (including distortions) of the consultant's own culture. To turn around and study the consultant's culture in order to gain a better perspective on the consultant's report would require the hiring of yet another consultant to study the first consultant—or would require that the client organization study the consultant's culture. The first approach would lead to infinite external regression (a consultant for the consultant for the consultant, ad infinitum); the second would lead to a never-ending internal regression (like looking at mirror images of mirror images of mirror images, ad infinitum). Hence, according to the constructivists, one can never obtain an objective assessment of an institution, even with the help of a skilled and honest external consultant.

LANGUAGE IS ITSELF REALITY

According to Huyssen (1987, p. 179), the postmodern world is a bit "softer" than the modern world. It is less a world of facts and figures and more a world of story and performance. We are moving from a modern world that was primarily mediated by visual communication (descriptive writing, television, and movies) to a postmodern world that is once again (as in the premodern world) mediated primarily by auditor communication (speech and narrative writing). We are moving from a world that uses metaphors of sight ("having a vision of a future world," "imagining an alternative") to one using metaphors of speech ("finding one's voice," "telling one's own story"). According to the postmodernist voices of the literary critics who do deconstruction, language gains primacy in the understanding of any text (be it literature, history, or philosophy). Rather than (to use Polanyi's term) attending *from* the language used in any text, the deconstructionists attend *to* the language, thereby making language much more visible than is typically the case in other forms of literary criticism. Deconstructionists (led by Derrida) believe that the language used in a text is itself the reality, rather than being the means by which some other reality (for example, the reality of history or the reality of a literary figure) is described.

A shift from objectivity and vision to subjectivity and voice is prevalent in our postmodern world. In its embracing of a constructivistic notion of reality, postmodernism takes a significant step in positing that language—or more generally, the use of symbols and signs—is not simply a vehicle for commenting on the reality that underlies and is the reference point for this language. This stance is opposed to an objectivist view, which is based on the assumption that there is a constant reality to which one can refer (through the use of language and other symbol/sign systems). If reality is a social construction, then the language being used to describe this elusive and changing reality is itself a major source of this social construction.

The postmodernists often take this analysis one step further by proposing that language is itself the primary reality in our daily life experiences. Language begins to assume its own reality, much as money, credit cards, electronic transfers, options, and so forth are perceived as reality. Language, like money, ceases to be an abstract sign that substitutes for the real things of value. Money used to be a substitute for gold or property; now, it is itself important. Similarly, language used to substitute for that which it denoted. Now it is important in and of itself.

In our large and complex postmodern world we are often distant from many of the most important events that affect our lives: war, the death of significant others, the use of our money by the government (taxation). Living in a global community, we no longer have direct experience of, or influence over, many of the things that were accessible when we lived in much smaller and more directly experienced communities. As a result, we often talk about things rather than actually experiencing them. We listen to a lecture on Asian art rather than actually seeing the art. Language itself becomes the shared experience. Conversation itself becomes the reality. This may have always been the case, to some extent. Language and conversation may have always played a central role in our society. Who we are—our sense of self—may have always been conveyed by the stories that we tell about ourselves. We may only be returning to a sense of reality inherent in the premodern world.

Perhaps our stories about self themselves constitute our sense of self. This means that my stories about childhood, about major adult accomplishments, and about difficult life-long disappointments may be the basic building blocks of my self-image—whether or not they are accurate. Not only are we influenced by

a broad *social* construction of reality—conveyed through the stories of the society in which we find ourselves—but also by a more narrowly based *personal* construction of reality, which is conveyed through our stories about ourself (and perhaps through stories that we inherit about our own family and immediate community).

One of the major implications of this notion of language as reality is that language—and therefore reality—is ephemeral. Once we have spoken, the reality that was created when we spoke is no longer present. Even if we say the same words, they are spoken in a different context and therefore have a somewhat different meaning. Thus, even when our speaking comes in the form of written words or in the form of other images (visual, tactile, and so on), these words or images will have different meaning depending on who hears them, the setting in which the communication takes place, and the words or images that have preceded and will follow these efforts at communication. From this perspective, therefore, reality is a shifting phenomenon subject to change and uncertainty.

GLOBALIZATION AND SEGMENTALISM

According to the postmodernists, our world is becoming progressively more global, while at the same time becoming progressively more segmented and differentiated. Though many of the postmodernist theorists spoke of this contradictory trend in our world at least ten to fifteen years ago, it is remarkable how contemporary this perspective seems to be, given the developments in Europe (and elsewhere in the world) over the past five years. While European countries are moving, in a globalizing manner, toward a unified common market and community, we also see movement (particularly in Eastern Europe) toward increased nationalism and factionalism among specific national, ethnic, and racial groups. From one perspective, globalism thrives. We are increasingly successful in saying a few things that are universal for all people. Walter Truett Anderson (1990, pp. 21–22) suggests that the following "ordinary ideas" are held by most people in the world (or at least in the Western world):

- That there is a human species, all of its members biologically capable of interbreeding with all the others, but not with members of different species.
- That the world is divided up into nation-states.
- That there are such things as atomic weapons, and that a global atomic war is possible.
- That there are many different religions, and that some people do not take any of them very seriously.
- That societies change and keep changing.

Communality arises in part from shared experiences, which in turn are the product of the electronically mediated "global community" of which Marshall McLuhan (1964) spoke prophetically over twenty-five years ago. We can create world-encompassing computer-based models that predict the flow of resources, the growth of population, and the destruction of our ecology with frightening accuracy (Meadows and others, 1972). Similarly, we can now trace worldwide trends in fashion, movies, and so on. This point is vividly confirmed in the specter of a young man in China or a young woman in Iraq wearing a T-shirt with a picture of an American sports hero or cartoon character. These young people are trying to defy U.S. society while expressing its culture and values. We now have global life-styles and many more "inter-sect" cultures that readily borrow from many different societies and

social values. The bohemian, international society of Paris during the 1920s is replicated in the 1990s, in settings ranging from Hong Kong and Singapore to London and now even Moscow.

At a much deeper level, there is even the possibility (or is it only a hope?) that the Eastern and Western worlds are beginning to come together. There is a growing awareness in at least some Western countries that "cultures, non-European, non-Western cultures must be met by means other than conquest and domination" (Huyssen, 1987, p. 220). In the non-Western world, there is growing recognition that issues of ecology and the environment are not just capitalistic or imperialistic artifacts, nor primarily a matter of politics. There is a deepening sense that the ecological perspective itself offers a penetrating critique of the modern world, a world the Eastern world both wants and does not want to embrace.

From a quite different perspective, the world seems to be highly segmented. We are becoming increasingly less successful in saying much that is generally valid about even our local communities or nation, let alone the world. We are confronted with discrepancies, diversity, and unpredictability. Huyssen (1987, p. 187) describes an "appropriation of local venaculars and regional traditions" in postmodern societies. Robert Bellah and his colleagues (Bellah and others, 1985) write about new forms of community in the United States. In the modern world, men, women, and children lived in small, geographically contained communities (villages, towns, small cities). According to Bellah and his colleagues, they now find postmodern community in "life-style enclaves." These enclaves are composed of people who usually don't live near each other (except in the case of enclaves that are age related, such as singles-oriented condos or retirement communities). Rather, members of the enclave, according to Bellah, have something in common that brings them together on occasion. These life-style enclaves may be found in Porsche-owner clubs or among those who regularly attend specific sporting events. They are also found among churchgoers and those who attend fashionable night clubs. Regardless of the type, enclaves contribute to the diversity and ultimately the unpredictability of the larger social system.

Physical scientists describe diverse and unpredictable systems as chaotic, in the sense that behavior inside each system and between systems is neither predictable nor readily described. While computer models have been highly successful in predicting and describing the general trends in our postmodern world (Meadows and others, 1972), they have not been very successful at predicting the precise impact of global events (such as the availability of food or temperature changes) on specific geographic regions or societies in the world. Global computer-based models have now generally been replaced by models that acknowledge broad worldwide dynamics, while also recognizing that each of these dynamics plays out somewhat differently and at a different rate in each of several geographic regions of the world (Mesarovic and Pestel, 1974). While Meadows and her colleagues attempted to build a unified, world-based model of various ecological dynamics, Mesarovic and Pestel described and modeled a world in which subsystems offer their own distinctive, "self-organizing" dynamics (Loye and Eisler, 1987, p. 59).

Similarly, we have been unsuccessful in using global models to predict weather. We are not much better at making predictions than we were ten years ago (Gleick, 1987). Specific, localized aberrations or "rogue events" (what chaos theorists call the "butterfly effect") that can neither be predicted nor adequately described apparently have a major influence on the weather in parts of the world remote from the events. In North America, we have seen the influence of El Niño (a change in the circulation of Pacific ocean currents, occurring every four to seven years), much as we have seen the impact the invasion of a very small country (Kuwait) had on the entire world community. Are there many El Niños that directly affect our daily lives? Are there other influential events that are far removed and unknown (and perhaps unknowable) to us? Perhaps we live with the contradiction between globalism and localism in many aspects of our daily lives.

FRAGMENTED AND INCONSISTENT IMAGES

In a newspaper article entitled "Hip Deep in Post-Modernism," Todd Gitlin (1988) describes the blurring and juxtaposition of forms, moods, stances, and cultural levels in the postmodern world. According to Gitlin, we have moved into a form of global capitalism (perhaps better labeled postcapitalism) that requires high levels of consumption, which in turn requires "ceaseless transformation in style, a connoisseurship of surface, an emphasis on packaging and reproducibility" (p. 35). A widely seen bumper sticker—"The one who dies with the most toys wins"—illustrates this point.

Frederick Jameson (1991, p. 25) similarly speaks of the "heaps of fragments" in the production of postmodern culture, although he later declares that "The description of postmodernism [is] something for which the word fragmentation remains much too weak and primitive a term . . . particularly since it is now no longer a matter of the breakup of some preexisting older organic totality, but rather the emergence of the multiple in new and unexpected ways, unrelated strings of events, types of discourse, modes of classification, and compartments of reality."

In the postmodern world, we find hand-me-down scraps of culture and images from the modern and even premodern eras, according to Jameson. These remnants are inextricably interwoven with new and surprising cultural elements to produce fragmented and inconsistent images of our time. Such a world tends to deny the continuity of tradition and underminds the certainty of specific social constructions of reality. History, according to both Jameson and Gitlin, has been ruptured. We live in an era that need pay little attention to the past, for as Jameson (1991, p. 36) has observed, over half the people who have ever lived on earth are still alive; "the present is thus like some new thriving and developing nation-state, whose numbers and prosperity make it an unexpected rival for the old traditional ones." Yet, in spite of the absence of any postmodern attention to the lessons that might be learned from the past—from history—the postmodern era is defined primarily by what it isn't and by what it used to be. According to Gitlin, we are now experiencing our world as an aftermath. In the United States, we label our era as post-60s, post-Viet Nam, post-New Left, post-hippie, post-Watergate, post-Marxist. Jameson (1991) believes that we live in a new world of "historicism." Rather than there being a careful analysis of past historical events and careful planning for future events based on this analysis, there is a replication of the past in the nostalgic touches on buildings and furniture, in the proliferation of museums, and in the recreation of past settings (Disneyland and other theme parks).

Rather than learning from the past, we replicate it and pretend that nothing has changed or that there is no hope for the future anyway—hence, a regressive, sedating appeal to the past. Fifty thousand men and women gather each August in Pebble Beach, California, to show off, admire, race, buy, sell, and talk about old cars (Flint, 1991, p. 196). While malls lose business, consumers flock to informal markets and bazaars from the past that feature everything from potatoes to fur coats. The 1960s in particular, according to Jameson, exploded our American belief in progress, in the linear order of things, and in moral clarity. We look for truth in our search for the "real" past, yet find the past revealed in distorted and confusing manner through the postmodern mixture of premodern, modern, and postmodern cultures. Huyssen (1987, p. 196) similarly notes, specifically with regard to the arts, that "all modernist and avant-garde techniques, forms and images are now stored for instant recall in the computerized memory banks of our culture. But the same memory also stores all of premodernist art as well as the genres, codes and image worlds of popular cultures and modern mass culture."

Huyssen speaks of a cultural anesthesia that protects us from the abyss and uncertainty that undergird (or fail to undergird) our society. We collectively dull our senses with variety because the underneath hurts too much. We become "couch potatoes," mainlining our television while simultaneously mocking it. Everything appears to have already been done in some form or other in our postmodern world. Culture becomes a process of recycling. We have gradually begun to embrace a much more Eastern sense about time as a cyclical notion. Instead of believing in progress, we believe in a world that replicates itself again and again—hence the use and distortion of the past and history. Everything in the fragmented postmodern world is seen as a faint resemblance of reality, a private vision that knows no public substance. We are living in an era of edginess with an accompanying sense of unreality and an "unbearable lightness of being" (Kundera, 1984). This edginess may in turn lead to disengagement and dissociation.

Postmodernists are enthralled with the superficial and trendy. Television, the primary conveyer of postmodern culture, knows only the present tense; there are no beginnings or ends, only sound bits and isolated images. Newly constructed buildings offer additional examples of the postmodern emphasis on surfaces. While they provide interesting surfaces of varying texture, they also tend to be constructed without any apparent underlying theme or order (Jameson, 1991). The computerized goggles and gloves used in "virtual reality" machines can make a Boeing engineer or executive think and feel as if he or she were actually flying a plane or hooking two molecules together (Bylinsky, 1991a, p. 138). These machines convey the sense of depth, yet like holographic devices, they actually replicate only the surface, never the depth of the experience. We are tricked into believing that we have experienced depth or virtual reality when in fact we have seen only the surface. While the three-dimensional glasses of the later stages of the modern era never really captured our imagination, the virtual reality of computerized gloves, holographic images, a replicated mainstreet in Disneyland, or, for that matter, a new corporate emphasis on "the core values of our organization" lure us into belief and eventually produce a state of confusion about what is real and what is phony.

In the postmodern world, fragmented visions are coupled with fragmented attention. Fred Wydler, an astute, high-tech manager who works in a large high-tech company, speaks of the fragmentation and superficiality of his own company as it tries to change "from the environment of farmers market through industrialization and standardization back into postmodernism while preserving industrial-age pricing. We are doing this in [an] industry which is not nearly as flexible in terms of manufacturing as we would like to be. We are doing this by means of superficial measures which are barely deep enough as to not appear as a subterfuge but which are successful with our customers."

While Gitlin (1988) believes that postmodern fragmentation is global in scope and character, he also believes it is particularly prevalent in the United States. He writes of "American eclecticism" and notes the lack of a distinctive American culture. A federation of cultures (the American "variety show") has emerged in the United States, bolstered by a sense that "anything goes." Postmodern terms and concepts are defined by lists of examples rather than by any formal definition. According to Gitlin, the postmodern world in the United States consists of shopping malls, suburban strips, Disneyland, the Isuzu "He's Lying" commercial, MTV, David Letterman, Hyatt Regency hotels, Doctorow, Foucault, Lacan, Derrida, Baudrillard, and remote control-equipped viewers "grazing" around the television dial. American postmodernism is Tom Peters' description of a manufacturing firm that is able to change its product line every four hours with the assistance of computers and robotics. Nothing remains the same for very long, and what does remain must reside alongside things that are very old, very new, or short-lived. The rest of the world is following in the footsteps of the United States and will soon be just as fragmented and inconsistent.

THE STATE OF POSTMODERN THEORY AND ANALYSIS

The inconsistency and fragmentation of the postmodern world make it very difficult to build a coherent theory or to recommend specific strategies or courses of action in response to these new societal conditions. Each of the pressing themes of postmodernism (constructivism, language as reality, globalism, and segmentalism) contribute to an even more basic theme that often makes the very analysis of the postmodern condition particularly difficult. In essence, it is virtually impossible to make a definitive statement about our contemporary world because this world is filled with contradictions and discrepancies. We are living in a world that is simultaneously premodern, modern, and postmodern. For every new phenomenon that can be identified as postmodern, we can find another phenomenon that is clearly modern or even premodern.

Ironically, all of these diverse phenomena provide evidence of the universal presence of a postmodern world. The inconsistencies of the hypothesized postmodern era allow the postmodern analyst to never be proven wrong. Any data (other than absolute uniformity, which will never be the case) fit into the postmodern model, for the more discrepant the data, the more confirming these data are of the postmodern hypothesis. Show me evidence of modernism and I will declare it amenable to my postmodern analysis. Show me premodern styles and forms, and I will be equally convinced that my postmodern hypothesis is correct. As in the case of a Freudian analysis of dreams, all evidence can be used in a way that confirms the initial hypothesis.

Thus, in some ways, the world picture conveyed by postmodernists can't be disproven, for contradictory evidence is itself part of the postmodern premise.

The postulation of a fragmented and inconsistent postmodern world, however, seems to be more than just a semantic or intellectual ploy to avoid any disproof of the postmodern perspective. There is ample evidence to suggest that this is a central (if not *the* central) characteristic of our contemporary world. The postmodern world is filled with fragmented and incoherent images of the future, as well as fragmented images of art, politics, and the sciences. This is most concretely and perhaps clearly exemplified in the calvacade of events that many of us experience as we transact our daily work. Several days ago, for instance, I was walking down a street in an American city and passed a man with a flower in his lapel, who was tap-dancing and encouraging each of us passing by to "smile and be happy." A second man, twenty feet beyond the tap dancer, wore a sandwich board on his back that solemnly declared that human kind and the American government were irredeemably corrupt and that our world was about to come to an end.

These two messages were received in a very confusing context. Wealthy businesspeople were walking rapidly past other men, women, and children in torn clothes who were begging for money. Newspaper headlines spoke of candidates no one wants to elect and of gross mismanagement of public and corporate funds. Yet, it was a beautiful day. The air was fresh because pollution control standards were beginning to work; a nearby park had been successfully restored by concerned citizens. Should I be happy? Should I be sad? Should I be angry? Is the world (at least, as we know it) coming to an end? How did we ever come to a state where there is such a discrepancy in the living conditions of American citizens? These fragmented and contradictory images must either be ignored, on a daily basis, or somehow comprehended in a manner that makes sense to me and my fellow city dwellers.

The fragmented and inconsistent image is also exemplified in the emergence of postmodern architecture. Whereas modern architecture tended to stress uniformity and order, postmodern architects have emphasized diversity and complexity. Postmodern buildings in many cities blend classic Greco-Roman columns and cornices with clean modern lines and neobaroque bric-a-brac. Rough cement slabs are placed next to smooth marble walls and wood-inlaid ceilings. Water spills out over highly abstract brass forms, while tourists and workers on lunch break sit on nineteenth-century New England-style wrought iron benches, watching brightly colored balls roll through plastic tubes in order to set off quarter-hour chimes or bang against Japanese-style resonant wood blocks. Corporations throughout the United States, such as Nike and Trivona, have built postmodern facilities in suburban areas that include lakes, beautiful grounds laced with walking and jogging trails, fitness centers, and gourmet lunchrooms, usually intermixed with rather sterile-looking concrete buildings filled with confining cubicles and mauve or gray-colored modularized furnishings. Optimistically, we are told (Alpert, 1991, pp. 141–142) that a new era of more user-friendly office buildings has come: "Unlike most office parks built in the past three decades—anonymous-looking blocks of steel and glass, many of them Darth Vader black—the new suburban complexes will be designed on a smaller, more human, even homey, scale. Often they will resemble farms or college campuses."

The people who fill these urban and suburban buildings are diverse with regard to gender, age, nationality, and physical challenges, as are their customers. Members of the organization even participate in a variety of premodern celebrations: companywide Christmas and Hanukkah gift giving, Fourth of July picnics, and departmental birthday parties. Yet, in true postmodern fashion, one wonders to what extent the premodern celebrations are a bit phony and, even more important, to what extent there really are postmodern equity and equal access for these people to the career opportunities of this organization. A postmodern canopy of diversity often seems to be draped over a very modern and Waspish culture of privilege and discrimination.

At an even deeper level, one wonders if this fragmentation and inconsistency—and the accompanying edginess—are temporary. Does postmodernism suggest that we are in a major transition between a modern society and some new society that has not yet become clear or at least been properly named? Alternatively, is the postmodern world in which we now live a long-lasting phenomenon? We may be moving into a fragmented world that will not readily change. We may never (at least in our lifetime) be able to return to a world of greater simplicity. Regional or national coherence and consistency may be nostalgic remnants of the past.

The implications of a long-lasting fragmented and inconsistent society are great. Remarkable futurist Fred Polak (1972) proposed several decades ago that the continuation of any society depends in large part on the presence in the society of a sustaining and motivating image of its own collective future. For instance, European communities thrived for many centuries under a clearly articulated, Christian-based image of personal and collective salvation. Similarly, many Asian countries have been guided for centuries by a coherent set of propositions about the nature of the world and society that were offered by Confucius (or Buddha). According to Polak, when a society has lost an image of its future, then this society will soon crumble, and a new society will rise in its place that does have a clear and guiding sense of some collective future. Polak assembled an impressive collection of historical facts and figures to buttress his argument.

If Polak is correct, one wonders about the survival of our fragmented and inconsistent postmodern societies. Where do we find the clear and coherent images to guide us in preparing for our own collective future? Will we lose our way and our vitality at this critical point in our history? Perhaps Polak is only partially correct. We may find that many small, microcommunities will form, each with its own image of the future and its own sustaining vision of the proper order for society. If this is the case, then the question shifts slightly: can our world continue to exist in such a fragmented state? What will prevent these microcommunities from constant conflict regarding the validity and universality of their different visions? To what extent is the recent Persian Gulf War a preliminary vision of a neofeudal world to come?

Any easy answers to the questions posed by Polak diminish the importance and profundity of his analysis. I will not, therefore, attempt to provide these kinds of answers. What I offer . . . are several preliminary suggestions concerning how our postmodern world will play out in organizational settings and what actions we might take to address these problems of fragmentation and potential dissolution. These matters are not easy to assimilate, as one of my students has candidly noted:

For me, as well as most present generation managers, postmodern theory has a rather disconcerting feel to it. We have been schooled in modern theories that are strongly grounded in systems approaches, scientific methods, and the benefits of increasing efficiency. Postmodern theory, though not invalidating these concepts, holds that they are only part of the solution to the social and economic work that organizations are formed to do. The modern manager sees systems as the ultimate tool for making sense out of chaos. The postmodern manager sees chaos as what is to be managed and systems, though very useful, as merely one aspect of the chaotic environment. To the postmodern manager chaos is not bad. It is what is.

If this book makes a valuable contribution to our new dialogues about postmodernism, it will help find the order that underlies much of the chaos in contemporary organizations. If this book is intellectually honest, it will also help expose and analyze the chaos that inevitably underlies much of the apparent order in contemporary organizations. . . .

REFERENCES

Alpert, M. "Office Buildings for the 1990s." *Fortune*, Nov. 18, 1991, pp. 140–150.

Anderson, W. *Reality Isn't What It Used To Be.* San Francisco: Harper San Francisco, 1990.

Becker, E. *The Birth and Death of Meaning.* New York: Free Press, 1971.

Belenky, M., and others. *Women's Ways of Knowing.* New York: Basic Books, 1986.

Bell, D. *Coming of Post-Industrial Society: A Venture in Social Forecasting.* New York: Basic Books, 1976.

Bellah, R., and others. *Habits of the Heart.* Berkeley: University of California Press, 1985.

Berger, P., and Luckmann, T. *Social Construction of Reality.* New York: Doubleday, 1967.

Bylinsky, G. "The Marvels of 'Virtual Reality.'" *Fortune*, Jun. 3, 1991a, pp. 138–150.

Drucker, P. *The New Realities.* New York: HarperCollins, 1989.

Edmundson, M. "Prophet of a New Postmodernism: The Greater Challenge of Salman Rushdie." *Harper's Magazine*, December 1989, pp. 62–71.

Eisler, R. *The Chalice and the Blade*. San Francisco: Harper San Francisco, 1987.

Flint, J. "They Don't Build 'em Like They Used To." *Forbes*, Oct. 28, 1991, pp. 196–197.

Foucault, M. *Madness and Civilization*. New York: Random House, 1965.

Gilligan, C. *In a Different Voice*. Cambridge, Mass.: Harvard University Press, 1982.

Gitlin, T. "Hip-Deep in Post-Modernism." *New York Times Book Review*, Nov. 6, 1988, pp. 1, 35, 36.

Gleick, J. *Chaos: Making A New Science*. New York: Viking Penguin, 1987.

Huyssen, A. *After the Great Divide*. Bloomington: Indiana University Press, 1987.

Jameson, F. *Postmodernism or the Cultural Logic of Late Capitalism*. Durham, N.C.: Duke University Press, 1991.

Kellner, D. "Introduction: Jameson, Marxism and Postmodernism." In D. Kellner (ed.), *Postmodernism/Jameson/Critique*. Washington, D.C.: Maisonneuve Press, 1989.

Kuhn, T. *The Structure of Scientific Revolutions*. Chicago: University of Chicago Press, 1962.

Kundera, M. *The Unbearable Lightness of Being*. New York: HarperCollins, 1984.

Loye, D., and Eisler, R. "Chaos and Transformation: Implications of Nonequilibrium Theory for Social Science and Society." *Behavioral Science*, 1987, *32*, 53–65.

McLuhan, M. *Understanding Media: The Extensions of Man*. New York: McGraw-Hill, 1964.

Meadows, D., and others. *The Limits to Growth*. New York: Signet, 1972.

Mesarovic, M., and Pestel, E. *Mankind at the Turning Point: The Second Report to the Club of Rome*. New York: Dutton, 1974.

Naisbitt, J. *Megatrends*. New York: Warner, 1984.

Perry, W. *Form of Intellectual and Ethical Development in the College Years: A Scheme*. Troy, Mo.: Holt, Rinehart & Winston, 1970.

Peters, T. *Thriving on Chaos*. New York: HarperCollins, 1987.

Peters, T., and Waterman, R. H. *In Search of Excellence: Lessons from America's Best-Run Companies*. New York: HarperCollins, 1982.

Polak, F. *The Image of the Future*. San Francisco: Jossey-Bass, 1972.

Polanyi, M. *Knowing and Being*. Chicago: University of Chicago Press, 1969.

Prigogine, I., and Stengers, I. *Order Out of Chaos*. New York: Bantam Books, 1984.

Rokeach, M. *The Open and Closed Mind*. New York: Basic Books, 1960.

Toffler, A. *Future Shock*. New York: Bantam Books, 1971.

Toffler, A. *The Third Wave*. New York: Morrow, 1980.

Turner, V. *The Ritual Process*. Hawthorne, N.Y.: Aldine, 1969.

Vaill, P. *Managing as a Performing Art: New Ideas for a World of Chaotic Change*. San Francisco: Jossey-Bass, 1989.

47

Nonlinear Dynamical Analysis: Assessing Systems Concepts in a Government Agency

L. Douglas Kiel

Human phenomena generally reveal varying levels of activity over time. For example, automobile traffic in metropolitan areas evidences rather rhythmic activity over time. Increased levels of traffic occur during consistent times of the day and week, whereas considerably less activity occurs during other times. Other phenomena, however, may display less rhythmic behavior. For example, levels of activity in stock markets, such as shares traded, may fluctuate and oscillate erratically over time.

The varying work activities of individuals and groups in government organizations also fluctuate and oscillate over time. Organizations such as the Internal Revenue Service clearly must evidence peaks and valleys in the levels of various work activities during a fiscal year. The work activity of police officers also fluctuates in levels of activity and intensity contingent on the time of day and the day of the week.

For service organizations, these fluctuations in activity are often dependent on the level and nature of the service requests imposed on the organization. From this perspective, variations in the level and type of external service requests may generate oscillatory behavior in the work activities of organizations. In short, the varying tides of service requests may generate varying levels of in-ternal activity in response to those requests. If such oscillations become extreme or erratic, the responding internal work system may, over time, appear chaotic and disorderly. One task of management is, however, to maintain a degree of order within the apparent chaos of fluctuations in service requests. This is particularly true in government organizations where maintaining orderly and stable service provision carries high value.

. . . In the vernacular of systems theory, management must maintain a dynamic equilibrium, or dynamic stability, that incorporates a dynamism adequate for adjustment to change, while maintaining an equilibrium necessary for stable operational performance (Kast and Rosenzweig, 1970, p. 574). Management may thus strive to smooth operations by damping or minimizing troughs and peaks in the demands on organizational resources for the purposes of order and stability (Thompson, 1967). Administrative and work processes thus may serve to preserve the structure of the existing system via adjustment to environmental and internal change. . . .

Nonlinear dynamics may aid in simplifying the complexities inherent in examining these concepts in organization and management studies. Nonlinear dynamics, furthermore, represents the re-

Source: Reprinted with permission from *Public Administration Review* 53 (2) pp. 143–53 (Mar–Apr. 1993).

cent culmination of efforts, within the systems paradigm, to develop an integrative framework with relevance to a variety of disciplines that examine evolving and complex phenomena. The study of nonlinear dynamics is now spilling into fields ranging from economics (Baumol and Berthabib, 1989) to management science (Rasmussen and Mosekilde, 1988) to planning (Cartwright, 1991). . . .

Human organizations are dearly nonlinear systems where the relationships between variables are dynamic and where complex behavior occurs over time. Such nonlinear behavior also generates a potential for structural and behavioral change. The fact that, as Jay Forrester notes, "we live in a highly nonlinear world" (1987, p. 4) emphasizes the challenge of administration. Management must, in short, bring order out of the apparent chaos of the changing dynamics of external and internal milieus.

This study has two purposes. First, this article presents nonlinear dynamics as a method of analysis for organization and administrative studies in public administration. Second, the tools of nonlinear dynamics are presented as the means for examining systems concepts in organizations. Terms such as *equilibrium, chaos,* and *order* are often used in a metaphorical vein in reference to organizations and management (Peters, 1987). This new analytical paradigm may provide insight into the empirical verification of these systems concepts in organizations. I attempt to "bring to earth" some of the metaphorical abstractions of the systems paradigm. This effort may afford a means for assessing both the temporal behavior of organizational work activities and the character of management systems.

This article presents a quantitative and graphical perspective of managed equilibrium (Dunsire, 1978) in a government organization as the foundation for this analysis. Rather than focusing primarily on the process of generating a managed equilibrium, I examine the qualitative structure that describes the outcome of this process. Such analysis may afford information as to the level of control or self-regulation (Dunsire, 1978) exhibited by a management system.

UNDERSTANDING NONLINEAR DYNAMICS

Nonlinear dynamics, often labeled chaos theory and emanating from the natural sciences, is the study of the temporal behavior of nonlinear systems (Thompson and Stewart, 1986; Stein, 1989). Nonlinear systems are typified by dynamic relationships between variables that may generate very complex behavior over time. In nonlinear systems, both external and internal "disturbances" may alter significantly the behavior and structure of such systems. Nonlinear systems may also appear disorderly and chaotic yet maintain an underlying order.

Nonlinear dynamics is also well suited to the analysis of managed equilibrium because nonlinear dynamics is founded on the examination of the behavior of systems over time. The examination of the existence of an equilibrium requires longitudinal assessment in order to determine a system's response to varying conditions that occur over time. The longitudinal analysis of organizational work, using this approach, allows the observer to view organizational work as if it were under an oscilloscope.

Perhaps the best way to understand the dynamics of nonlinear systems is to compare the behavior of such systems with that of linear systems. In linear systems, the relationships between relevant variables remains stable over time. This means that the dynamics of linear systems will typically show smooth, regular, and well-behaved motion. Linear systems respond to changes in their parameters, or to external shocks, in a proportionate and consistent manner.

Nonlinear systems are typified by a potential for dynamic relationships between variables during the life of the system. As these relationships change, the temporal behavior of the system may change from smooth to unstable and even to seeming randomness, referred to as chaos. The changing relationships between variables may consequently generate new system behaviors and structures.

At certain times, either external or internal disturbances to a nonlinear system may generate a disproportionate relationship between cause and effect. Such nonlinear interactions may lead to small causes generating large effects and significant system change. Alternatively, nonlinear systems may minimize or damp the impact of a seemingly large disturbance, thus maintaining the behavior and structure of the existing system.

Nonlinear systems exhibit four distinct types of temporal behavior. These behaviors can be labeled as (1) convergence to a stable equilibrium, (2) stable oscillation, (3) unstable and explosive, and (4) chaotic. Each regime can appear within the long-term behavior of a nonlinear system. Importantly, each behavior type does not reflect permanent commitment only to that behavioral type but rather reflects one possible type that may occur over the life of a system. . . .

Convergence to an equilibrium (Figure 1A) represents behavior from which an initial point reaches and maintains a mathematically stable point This behavior suggests minimal or no change in the system over time. If change is desired in such a stable phase, appropriate action would appear to require either a significant jolt to the system or the identification and manipulation of relevant variables capable of altering system structure

and behavior. In a nonlinear world, one must also wonder how many actual working systems will show such stable behavior over time.

Nonlinear behavior typified by stable oscillation refers to system behavior that shifts between stable parameters in a periodic, or patterned, fashion (Figure 1B). Systems revealing this behavior may be representative of many social systems in which oscillations typify the systems' long-term behavior. One example may be daily traffic flows in metropolitan areas as traffic waxes and wanes from peaks to nadirs in a generally consistent and rhythmic manner.

Unstable and explosive behavior represents behavioral regimes that may oscillate stably and then explode into instability (Figure 1C). The time evolution of the system initially reveals considerable uncertainty. Just beyond the midpoint of the time frame shown, the system appears to seek a stable phase for approximately four cycles. However, the system destabilizes and explodes into a new unstable phase. Such explosive behavior may occur via internal dynamics or external disturbances. An example of such behavior may be the activity level of a police patrol officer. At some times, activity levels may be relatively stable while punctuated periods of extreme activity levels may interrupt such stable periods.

Chaos (Figure 1D) has received the most attention of the behavioral regimes evidenced in the time evolution of nonlinear systems (Gleick, 1987; Mosekilde *et al.*, 1988; Baumol and Bernhabib, 1989). Chaotic behavior occurs within definable parameters but is typified by temporal behavior devoid of pattern. A nonliner system in a chaotic phase does not retrace previous identifiable sequences of behavior. In short, chaotic behavior appears quite random and without pattern. Chaotic behavior thus

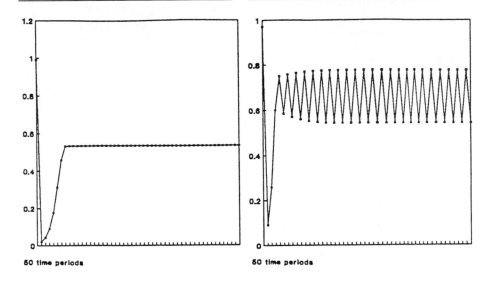

FIGURE 1A • CONVERGENCE TO
AN EQUILIBRIUM
w = 2.14, y = .99

FIGURE 1B • STABLE
OSCILLATION
w = 3.13, y = .97

50 time periods

50 time periods

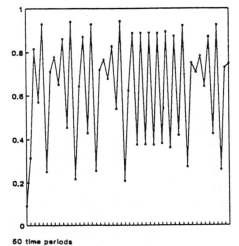

FIGURE 1C • UNSTABLE AND
EXPLOSIVE
w = 3.79, y = .091

50 time periods

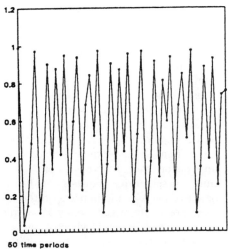

FIGURE 1D • CHAOS
w = 3.895, y = .99

50 time periods

appears extremely disorderly because patterns over time, one symbol of orderliness, are nonexistent. Studies of chaos, however, reveal an underlying order or structure in such behavior.[1]

One might imagine the chaotic activities of a government executive. The executive engages in a variety of activities for differing periods of time. Even if the activities are repetitive, the time series of activities does not repeat itself exactly. The flow of activities each day is genuinely unique.

THE ORGANIZATION AND UNITS OF ANALYSIS

The organization studied for this analysis is the communications division of a state government.[2] The mission of this agency is to provide telecommunications service, maintenance, and equipment to all state agencies. The agency also handles requests for new telecommunications services and equipment installation. Service updates and equipment repair are also handled. The requests made for service are continuous throughout the year. The number of service requests, however, varies from week to week. The unique state of the telecommunications technology of each agency also means that the content and work effort required to complete service requests varies considerably. . . .

From the perspective of nonlinear dynamics, each service request represents a disturbance with the potential for altering the behavior and structure of the work system. Such disturbances are not to be viewed in a negative light but rather from the objective perspective as impacts on the observed system. Over time, these service requests, or disturbances, have varying impacts on the response of the impacted agency. From this perspective, a dynamic view of one aspect of the environment's impact on the

organization's internal operations is presented.

THE WORK EFFORT ATTRACTOR: A GRAPHICAL PORTRAYAL OF WORK SYSTEM EQUILIBRIUM

. . . The qualitative analysis of a nonlinear system is, however, initiated via an examination of its attractors (Mosekilde et al., 1988, p. 21). Baumol and Benhabib (1989, p. 91) define an attractor as, "a set of points toward which complicated time paths starting in its neighborhood are attracted." Pool (1989, p. 1292) defines an attractor as, "the set of points in a phase space corresponding to all the different states of the system."

More simply, the term attractor is used because the system's temporal evolution appears to be consistently "pulled" to identifiable mathematical points. The attractor functions as an abstract representation of the flow or motion of a system. In short, the attractor stores information about a system's temporal behavior. The attractor is used as a means for examining the structure of the underlying order within a nonlinear system.

The examination of an attractor is conducted by a mapping of the data onto a phase space (Thompson and Stewart, 1986). A phase space represents a graphic backdrop for presenting the motion of time-based data. The examination of an attractor is conducted in a t/t-1 phase space (Baumol and Benhabib, 1989, p. 91). In this case, t (time) represents the percentage of labor costs devoted to work orders during a week, while t-1 (time-1) represents the previous week's percentage of labor costs devoted to work orders. The t is plotted on the vertical axis and t-1 is plotted on the horizontal axis. This method of plotting the data reveals the relationship between last weeks efforts devoted to service requests and the associated current week's work efforts devoted to service requests. The temporal relationship between these data elements is mapped in Figure 2.

Figure 2 shows the data are attracted to a clear range on the phase space.[3] The attractor is identified by the circular flow between the parameters of 5 percent and 20 percent of total labor costs. If the data were randomly distributed a wider dispersion of the data in the phase space would be apparent. The phase map in Figure 2 shows a stable periodic orbit, sometimes labeled a limit cycle (Shaw, 1981, p. 82). Figure 2 also evidences periods in which the motion of the system appears erratic and exits the attractor. However, close observation shows that the system behavior adjusts down to the attractor, where it oscillates within stable, yet oscillating, parameters.

The circular oscillation of the attractor in Figure 2 represents the equilibrium of the work system examined. This equilibrium is identified by an oscillation around stable parameters. A close inspection of Figure 2 shows two smaller attractors within the larger attractor. This result is not surprising as multiple attractors are common in nonlinear systems (Thompson and Stewart, 1986, p. 10). These smaller attractors are identifiable at the parameters of 4 percent to 10 percent and 12 percent to 20 percent.

The oscillation of the larger attractor represents the steady state of the system. Yet, as Katz and Kahn noted, "A steady state is not a motionless or true equilibrium" (1966, p. 26). Thus, in a dynamic system, an equilibrium is represented by oscillation within parameters. In the case presented here, the movement of the equilibrium is represented by the motion of the larger attractor and the motion of the smaller subsystem attractors. The parameters of equilibria can, of course, vary markedly between divergent work activities. What is of importance

FIGURE 2 • ATTRACTOR-WORK EFFORT RESPONSE (AS A PERCENT OF TOTAL LABOR COSTS) TO SERVICE REQUESTS OVER A 51-WEEK PERIOD

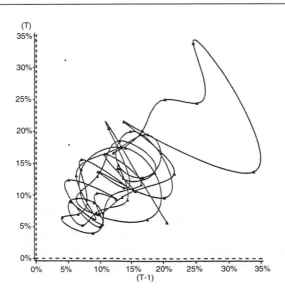

to the verification of such equilibria is an oscillation around definable parameters.

The minimal periods of erratic behavior in Figure 2 may be viewed as disturbances to the system that push the system out of its normal functioning parameters. This erratic behavior also evidences that disturbances to a nonlinear system may change the system's structure. The geometry of the phase map is clearly altered during this disturbance. The work system under investigation, however, settles down to the oscillating limit cycle after the erratic behavior generated by disturbances. The work system adapts to extreme cases while self-adjusting to a consistent pattern of behavior.

The work system examined thus reveals homeostatic properties as it adjusts around the identifiable steady state. The result of these homeostatic properties is a dynamic equilibrium in which the system preserves its internal structure in spite of a changing environment. This changing environment is represented by the disturbances to the "normal" functioning parameters of the system.

The attractor also reveals the relative order, or structure, in the work system examined. The concept of order is a global concept that refers to a system as a whole (Davies, 1988, p. 74). The system examined here shows an order with some disturbance. The order in the system is represented by the circular oscillation of the work system during most of its temporal evolution. The use of the attractor as a means for assessing system order also minimizes the subjective assessment of the notion of order. The attractor provides a quantitative and geometric view of the relative order, or structure, of the equilibrium in the system examined.

As noted, nonlinear systems may evidence chaotic and seemingly random behavior, yet an underlying order appears

to exist. The apparent disorder in the work system investigated shows an underlying order as represented by its attractor (Figure 2). The attractor of work systems in general may show the degree of order and stability in organizational work activities.

THE INPUT-PROCESSING RELATIONSHIP: IS IT LINEAR OR NONLINEAR?

The view of equilibrium, represented by the working parameters of the system under investigation, raises a question concerning the nature of the impact of service requests (input) on the work system (processing). In short, is this impact linear or nonlinear? One initial response is to assume that for each service request or input, a direct and proportionate cause-and-effect chain of processing is generated. From this perspective, the attractor (Figure 2) simply represents the smooth and proportionate relationship between requests and the concomitant service response. Yet, the mapping of such a linear system would result in a series of very symmetric straight lines not exhibited in the work system examined.

The control engineering perspective of management is a result of commitment to linearized operations. In other words, management's efforts to damp oscillations are aimed at predictability in operations. The totally automated manufacturing organization epitomizes this perspective. Service organizations also demonstrate this perspective as control mechanisms are used in an effort to stabilize time and costs devoted to service responses (Thompson, 1967). However, even in service organizations, work activities will evidence oscillations in response to variances in requests for service. In the specific case noted here, each service request would appear unique as each requesting agency possesses divergent telecommunications needs.

An analysis of the number of work order requests completed on a corresponding weekly basis was conducted. This analysis was conducted to determine the existence of proportionality and linearity between the number of work orders or service requests completed and the total work order costs as a proportion of total costs. . . .

Figure 3 shows a varying relationship between the number of service requests completed each week and the work activity and costs generated. Each singular request has a variable impact on the work of the service-providing organization. The unique nature of service requests would appear to generate a dynamic relationship between the variables of service requests and the eventuating work effort.

A further test for proportionality was also conducted using linear regression analysis. Linear regression analysis examines the movement, or relative changes in the values of the related variables analyzed. This test was used to determine if the relationships between service requests completed and associated labor costs is linear and proportional. In short, does an increase in the number of service requests completed generate an increase in the work efforts to these service requests in the organization? Regression analysis was conducted using the number of service requests completed as the independent variable and

FIGURE 3 • NUMBER OF SERVICE REQUESTS COMPLETED AND CORRESPONDING WORK EFFORT (AS A PERCENT OF TOTAL LABOR COSTS) OVER A 51-WEEK PERIOD

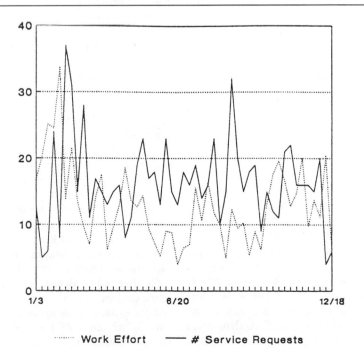

the total of work order costs as a proportion of total labor costs as the dependent variable. This test resulted in a coefficient of determination or $r^2 = .009$. This linear analysis of the number of service requests completed per week appears to explain only a vary negligible proportion of the variance in the work efforts, or labor costs, devoted to service requests.

However, polynomial regression analysis[4] indicates a quadratic and curvilinear relationship.[5] These data fit a shallow U-shaped curve at a statistically significant level ($F = 3.22$, $p < .05$). There is a peak at the beginning of the calendar year that drops to a low point during midyear and then rise toward the end of the calendar year. The U-shaped nature of the service order and work effort relationship suggests the oscillatory behavior of the work system examined as activities wax and wane between peaks and troughs. Assuming the data used are typical of other years in this agency, one can imagine an oscillating time-series of activities characterizing the dynamics of work activities.

However, the large proportion of unexplained variance even in the quadratic relationship ($r^2 = .118$) is likely due to the unique nature of service requests and to the unique response necessary to each request. Service requests and the corresponding work efforts, in this case, actually appear as nonlinear phenomena. Some service orders may entail considerable work and labor costs to the organization, while others require only minimal effort and cost. No consistently proportionate, or linear, relationship exists between the cause, or the service request, and the effect, or work activity generated. Most significantly, the work effort in response to service requests shows considerable dynamism. This dynamism may also result from management-defined priorities that define the relative

immediacy of response to particular service requests.

MANAGED EQUILIBRIUM: AN ASSESSMENT

The apparent order, as represented by the work effort attractor, in a seemingly disorderly regime of work activity is not a mystical occurrence. The fact that a direct linear relationship between service requests and service response does not exist appears to verify the existence of some managed effort to maintain a degree of equilibrium in the work system. Clearly, a control mechanism of some sort exists that maintains the parameters of the system in a consistent, yet oscillating, regime. Control systems can exist, of course, in a variety of forms throughout the organizational hierarchy.

The maintenance of a dynamic equilibrium may be carried out by a variety of means. For example, Thompson (1967) noted the use of smoothing as a means for minimizing dramatic troughs and peaks in the demands on organizational resources. From the systems perspective, this phenomena may be labeled damping as organizations strive to maintain a level of service stability by minimizing the extent and impact of system oscillations. Managers in public organizations thus may damp external or internal disturbances that threaten to overwhelm the system's capacity to maintain a level of service stability. Or, public organizations must generate order from the apparent chaos that often appears to typify related external and internal activities.

How can such damping be verified? Nonlinear dynamics provides relevant tools that aid in determining the existence of damping in a system. Damping can be examined by an analysis of the various attractors of the system examined (Thompson and Stewart, 1986, p. 20). For the organization examined here, this test requires visual examination of the attractors of both the work activities of the system (Figure 2) and the motion or flow of service requests completed during the same time period.

Figure 4 shows the phase map of the number of service requests completed on a weekly basis during the 47-week period. Visual analysis of the two phase maps shows that the work effort attractor (Figure 2) reveals a very consistent oscillation around the parameters of 4 percent to 20 percent of total labor costs. The attractor for the service requests completed (Figure 4) shows a more erratic pattern relative to the work effort attractor. There is in Figure 4, however, a definable attractor oscillation around the parameters of 8 and 24 completed service requests.

Both the service requests completed and the work effort phase maps show identifiable attractors. Previous analysis

also showed that the relationship between these two variables is not linear. These facts point to the existence of some damping mechanism directed at minimizing excessive oscillations thus maintaining an equilibrium in service response activities. What this visual evidence suggests is the use of some sort of filtering technique ensuring consistency of both service requests completed and service response activity. The definable parameters of the service request completed attractor (Figure 4) also reflect an attempt to smooth the number of service requests completed during the weekly time periods examined.

Equilibrium is attained via a maintenance of service response activity within definable parameters. Regardless of the number of service requests completed, the work effort activities retain a stable, but oscillating equilibrium. The dynamism of the work system is, however,

FIGURE 4 · ATTRACTOR-SERVICE REQUESTS OVER A 51-WEEK PERIOD

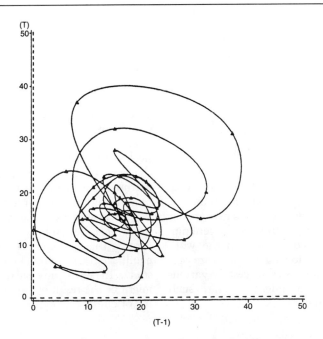

(T)

(T-1)

reflected in its ability to cope with change while adjusting back to a definable equilibrium. The management action appears consequently as a damping of system nonlinearities in order to generate a consistency in work effort. Equilibrium, in nonlinear systems such as organizations, may sometimes require that management damp nonlinearities to maintain order and avoid instability.

The degree of equilibrium evidenced in a work system also reveals the level of control in the system. For example, Dunsire's (1978) assessment of control in a bureaucracy is based on definable behavior that remains within designated parameters. Dunsire (1978) noted the importance of "threshold avoidance" as a means of ensuring that a system's limits are not exceeded. This approach allows normal oscillations within defined parameters while maintaining control. The case presented in this work suggests an example of such control, characterized by a temporary period where its normal operating parameters, or its attractor, are altered by the increased activity of a new legislative session.[6] The fundamental control in this work system, however, is seen by its return to its normal operating parameters, or attractor state, once it responded to the disturbance of the legislative session.

ALTERNATIVE SCENARIOS: UNDERSTANDING THE UNDERLYING ORDER IN WORK ACTIVITIES

Several varying views of the underlying order, in the seemingly chaotic behavior, of the work activities studied here appear plausible. Many factors could generate the apparent equilibrium in the work system. The following scenarios are presented as a means of suggesting various possibilities that might generate such an equilibrium.

The Learning Curve as the Underlying Order in Work Activities

Initially, the attractor that represents the equilibrium of work order activities may represent a rational attempt not to overload the carrying capacity of the agency. Such knowledge is gained through experience. The relatively well-defined parameters of the work effort attractor (Figure 2) may represent the flattening of the learning curve. Agency employees may understand both the nature of incoming work and the carrying capacity of the agency to such an extent that even when the number of service orders increases, work order activities, in terms of hours of labor, are smoothed. . . .

Soldiering as the Underlying Order in Work Activities

One cynical response to the data examined in this article is the possible assertion that a Tayloristic "systematic soldiering" (Taylor, 1911) is in process. Soldiering is indicative of employee norm setting rounded on a common commitment to minimal levels of work activity and intensity. The concept of systematic soldiering suggests, then, that soldiering is supported by a definable system for work. In the present study, the agency filter, the employee who assigns work orders to workers, simply allocates work orders in such a manner as to ensure a consistent yet relatively slow pace of work. From this perspective, a bottleneck is intentionally created that eases the work pressure on employees to the detriment of those agencies seeking prompt responses to service requests.

The systematic soldiering scenario, however, raises an important issue concerning the nature of an organizational equilibrium such as that identified in this study. In short, any such equilibrium might be the result of systematic soldiering or efforts to create a stable system of service delivery may lead to some level of soldiering of employees. Without exacting knowledge of the full carrying capacity or full potential work effort of the work system, such soldiering is difficult to determine.

The work system examined in this study obviously responded to the peak disturbance of a new legislative session and followed by a movement back to an oscillating equilibrium. This recognition suggests also that the response to the new legislative session may be viewed as the use of available slack resources during periods of peak activity. After such peak activity, work order activities are smoothed and technicians engage some of their efforts in other duties. This understanding raises issues concerning the importance of slack resources in government organizations. . . .

ADMINISTRATIVE APPLICATIONS: ATTRACTORS AND SYSTEM PERFORMANCE

The approach to data gathering and analysis presented in this study may also serve as an analytic tool for quality management systems such as the Total Quality Management (TQM) system. The total quality management approach relies both on the gathering and presentation of operational and activity data over time. One goal of contemporary quality management is to define optimal parameters of a work process based on average performance and then provide means for maintaining service or activity levels, for example, within those parameters (Carr and Littman, 1990). The total quality methodology acknowledges that statistical variation occurs in all systems and accepts normal variation within defined parameters.

The parameters defined in quality management systems may be viewed as

the attractor of the work process. It should be noted that an attractor does not represent average behavior as does the baseline used in statistical process control charts in quality management systems. Instead the attractor represents a set of points which, via oscillation, define a system's parameters. However, by using phase diagrams such as those in Figures 2 and 4, managers and staff may differentiate between normal variation, or routine fluctuations in a system's attractor or usual regime of performance, versus abnormal variation that exceeds system parameters. Such abnormal variation may represent special causes or events that jolt the process outside its normal parameters. In this study, the onset of the new legislative session represents such an abnormal variation. From the perspective of quality management, such abnormal variation serves as a clear signal warranting examination in order to remove or perhaps diminish the sources or events causing such variation.

Improvement in performance is measured by decreasing the sources of normal variation in the process and thus decreasing the acceptable parameters of variation (Carr and Littman, 1990, p. 74). The examination of the attractors of a work process may serve as a means to determine the relative effectiveness of intended improvements. Examining attractors in nonlinear systems affords a view of qualitative change in such systems. The goal of continuous improvement in TQM would be to consistently "tighten" the geometric pattern, or the extent of normal fluctuations, of the attractor of a work process. Of course, a single point attractor (zero errors or zero defects) cannot be achieved in a statistical system because variation is inevitable.

The identification of an attractor represents behavior within defined parameters indicating control within the system. On the other hand, a phase diagram showing no apparent attractor phase and wildly distributed data points suggests a system either out of control or, perhaps, beyond control. If managed equilibrium is a desired goal, the methodology presented here is offered as means for testing the evidence of its existence.

Furthermore, the change from an existing attractor to a new attractor signals a definitive transformation in a nonlinear system. Thus, if management desires to alter an existing equilibrium, as represented by a system's attractor, management can evaluate the results of the intended change via an examination of the system's attractors over time.

Examination of the attractors of work systems can also serve to identify instances of instability in a work system. Movement away from an existing attractor, or equilibrium, suggests a work system is leaving its previous parameters and seeking new levels of activity or performance. Identification of such instability allows management to respond either to damp the instability or perhaps allow an intended change to express itself. The relative success of an intended change can also be examined by the shape of the new geometric structure created.

CONCLUSION

This article views organizations as dynamic systems. People in motion engaged in various activities for various periods of time represent these dynamics. This perspective allows the analyst to examine organizational work as if it were some biological or chemical system examined on an oscilloscope. This approach interjects time into organizational analyses allowing the observer to view the oscillation and rhythms of organizational work. Furthermore, the approach used in this work allows for the measurement of systems concepts that

require the incorporation of longitudinal analysis for proper examination. . . .

This study also shows that, although work activities may appear disorderly, order may exist at the foundation of these work activities. This means that such managed equilibrium, as assessed by the system attractor, evidences what might be labeled the "deep structure" of the work. The methodology used in this work should aid in the examination of the extent of such structure in government organizations. Such research has considerable potential for examining the degree of equilibrium or even disorder and chaos in organizational systems.

The analytical approach used in this work might also initiate the development of a typology of organizational subunit work by the structure or degree of oscillation in the work activities in the subunit. Such analysis also may lead to a typology of work systems based on factors such as the range of system parameters or the nature of systems attractors. For example, work systems might be categorized on a continuum from loose to tightly coupled attractors. Such information possesses practical value as a means for managers to determine the degree of control resulting from management systems and as a means for determining when the working parameters of a management system change.

It also is important to recognize that work dynamics may not lead to an equilibrium but rather may generate consistently erratic behavior without clear evidence of an attracting phase. Organizations may not find an equilibrium where work activities appear stable over time. Such erratic behavior, however, may expedite learning. For it is through continuous exploration of the parameters of their capacity for service provision that managers and organizations learn the scope and depth of their capabilities.

The research approach here emphasizes the importance of direct observation of the subject. In short, such research requires direct information on the actual activities of government employees. Such information is not always readily available to the researcher. Examination of the dynamics of organizations will certainly require extensive efforts to investigate in detail what actually occurs in organizations. A combination of micro-level organizational information and the tool of nonlinear dynamics should provide an enhanced view of the dynamics of organizational work. Further research may also aid in developing models that capture the variety of nonlinear behavior in organizations. . . .

NOTES

The author is grateful to Alexander Holmes, former Director of State Finance, State of Oklahoma, for his support of the data gathering necessary for his paper. Jerry Stillwell and Nancy Ivins, Oklahoma Office of State Finance, also provided valuable support. A special thanks to Ray Penrod, Nolan Kelly and all of the employees of the Communications Division, for their cooperation with this project.

1. Chaotic behavior is not inherently negative behavior. Chaos is simply a mathematical description of the temporal behavior of a system. Chaos may simply be a system's adaptive response to its environment (Mosekilde, et al. 1988, p. 52). The existence of apparent mathematical disorder, or chaos, in a system does not necessarily mean that the system is malfunctioning or headed toward disintegration. Instead, chaos may represent exploration of a variety of possibilities in an effort to adapt to changing circumstances.

2. The communications division is an agency of the Office of State Finance, State of Oklahoma.

3. The smooth curves from point to point on the phase map are referred to as splining.

Splining is based on approximation theory and is generated via calculations on the rate of change in pairs of adjacent points. This approach expedites the identification of oscillation in a system and avoids drawing straight lines between points that may not represent the dynamism in a human system.

4. Polynomial (or power) regression analysis is a form of multiple regression used to fit a line to data that is not linear. In polynomial regression, successive powers (exponents) of the independent variable X are used in an effort to determine the best fit of a relationship that appears curvilinear. Thus, X combined with X^2 produces a (multiple) curvilinear regression referred to as quadratic, while the curvilinear regression combining X, X^2, and X^3 is called cubic. See, Meier and Brudney (1987), for a brief review of this approach. The selection of the "best" fitting curve in polynomial regression is based on a statistical test measuring the contribution of each polynomial to the fit of the curve. See, Cohen and Cohen (1983), for a discussion of the means for making this selection.

5. The nonlinearity of a curvilinear relationship is not the same as that represented by genuinely chaotic systems. The difference concerns the underlying mathematics that generates each form of nonlinearity. Curvilinear relationships can be generated by simultaneous equations, whereas chaotic systems are generated by nonlinear differential equations. Chaotic systems may, however, reveal periods that can be "fit" by curvilinear regression. Both forms of nonlinearity, however, evidence the dynamism in the relationships between variables that generates oscillatory behavior. The research challenge is to identify the mathematical approaches that will aid in the modeling of the dynamics of organizations.

6. This insight was provided by an experienced state administrator.

REFERENCES

Baumol, William J. and Jess Benhabib, 1989. "Chaos: Significance, Mechanism, and Economic Applications." *Journal of Economic Perspectives*, vol. 3, no. 1, pp. 77-105.

Carr, David K. and Ian D. Littman, 1990. *Excellence in Government.* Arlington, VA: Coopers & Lybrand.

Cartwright, T. J., 1991. "Planning and Chaos Theory." *Journal of the American Planning Association*, vol. 57 (Winter), pp. 45-56.

Cohen, Jacob and Patricia Cohen. 1983. *Applied Multiple Regression/Correlation Analysis for the Behavioral Sciences*, 2d ed. Hillsdale, NJ: Lawrence Erlbaum.

Daneke, Gregory A., 1988. "On Paradigmatic Progress in Public Policy and Administration." *Policy Studies Journal*, vol. 17 (Winter 1988-89), pp. 277-296.

————, 1990. "A Science of Public Administration." *Public Administration Review*, vol. 50 (May/June), pp. 383-392.

Daives, Paul, 1988. *The Cosmic Blueprint: New Discoveries in Nature's Creative Ability to Order the Universe*. New York: Simon and Schuster.

Dunsire, Andrew, 1978. *Control in a Bureaucracy*. New York: St. Martin's Press.

Forrester, Jay W., 1987. "Nonlinearity in High-Order Models of Social Systems." *European Journal of Operational Research*, vol. 30, pp. 104-109.

Gleick, James, 1987. *Chaos: Making a New Science*. New York: Viking.

Harrison, E. Frank, 1978. *Management and Organizations*. Boston; Houghton Mifflin.

Kast, Fremont E, and James E. Rosenzweig, 1970. *Organization and Management: A Systems Approach*. New York: McGraw-Hill.

Katz, Daniel, and Robert L. Kahn, 1966. *The Social Psychology of Organizations*. New York: John Wiley & Sons.

Kiel, L. Douglas, 1989. "Nonequilibrium Theory and Its Implications for Public Administration." *Public Administration Review*, vol. 49 (November/December), pp. 544-551.

Meier, Kenneth J. and Jeffrey L. Brudney, 1987. *Applied Statistics for Public Administration*, rev. ed. Monterey, CA: Brooks/Cole Publishing.

Mericle, Mary F., 1980. "The External Environment: Effects of Change in Environment Dynamics and Complexity." In Daniel Katz, Robert L. Kahn, and J. Stacey Adams, eds., *The Study of Organizations*. San Francisco: Jossey-Bass, pp. 59-65.

Mosekilde, Erik, Javier Aracil, and Peter M. Allen, 1988. "Instabilities and Chaos in Nonlinear Dynamic Systems." *System Dynamics Review*, vol. 4, pp. 14-55.

Peters, Thomas J., 1987. *Thriving on Chaos: Handbook for a Management Revolution*. New York: Knopf.

Pool, Robert, 1989. "Where Strange Attractors Lurk." *Science*, vol. 243, p. 1292.

Rasmussen, Dan R. and Erik Moskilde, 1988. "Bifurcations and Chaos in a Generic Management Model." *European Journal of Operational Research*, vol. 35, pp. 80-88.

Schumacher, B. G., 1986. *On the Origin and Nature of Management*. Norman, OK: Eugnosis Press.

Scott, William G., 1981. *Organizations: Rational, Natural and Open Systems*. Englewood Cliffs, NJ: Prentice-Hall.

Scott, William G., Terence R. Mitchell, and Philip H. Birnbaum, 1981. *Organization Theory: a Structural and Behavioral Analysis*. Homewood, IL: Richard D. Irwin.

Shaw, Robert, 1981. "Strange Attractors, Chaotic Behavior, and Information Flow." *Zeitschrift für Naturforschung*, vol. 36a, pp. 80-112.

Stein, Daniel L., ed., 1989. *Lectures in the Sciences of Complexity*. Reading, MA: Addison-Wesley.

Taylor, Frederick W., 1911. *The Principles of Scientific Management*. New York: Harper & Brothers.

Thompson, James D., 1967. *Organizations in Action*. New York: McGraw-Hill.

Thompson, J. M. T. and H. B. Stewart, 1986. *Nonlinear Dynamics and Chaos*. New York: John Wiley and Sons.

48

Reengineering the Corporation: The Enabling Role of Information Technology

Michael Hammer & James Champy

A company that cannot change the way it thinks about information technology cannot reengineer. A company that equates technology with automation cannot reengineer. A company that looks for problems first and then seeks technology solutions for them cannot reengineer.

Information technology plays a crucial role in business reengineering, but one that is easily miscast. Modern, state of the art information technology is part of any reengineering effort, an *essential enabler* . . . since it *permits* companies to reengineer business processes. But, to paraphrase what is often said about money and government, merely throwing computers at an existing business problem does not cause it to be reengineered. In fact, the *misuse* of technology can block reengineering altogether by reinforcing old ways of thinking and old behavior patterns. . . .

LEARNING TO THINK INDUCTIVELY

To recognize the power inherent in modern information technology and to visualize its application requires that companies use a form of thinking that businesspeople usually don't learn and with which they may feel uncomfortable.

Most executives and managers know how to think *deductively*. That is, they are good at defining a problem or problems, then seeking and evaluating different solutions to it. But applying information technology to business reengineering demands *inductive* thinking —the ability to first recognize a powerful solution and then seek the problems it might solve, problems the company probably doesn't even know that it has. . . .

The fundamental error that most companies commit when they look at technology is to view it through the lens of their existing processes. They ask, "How can we use these new technological capabilities to enhance or streamline or improve what we are already doing?" Instead, they should be asking, "How can we use technology to allow us to do things that we are *not* already doing?" Reengineering, unlike automation, is about innovation. It is about exploiting the latest capabilities of technology to achieve entirely new goals. One of the hardest parts of reengineering lies in recognizing the new, unfamiliar capabilities of technology instead of its familiar ones.

Even Thomas J. Watson, Sr., the founder of IBM, fell victim to this common shortsightedness when he proclaimed that the worldwide demand for data-processing computers would come to fewer than fifty machines. Twenty years later, mainframe computer makers and corporate computer managers both dismissed the minicomputer as a toy. Ten years after that, the personal computer received the same reception: "We're already meeting our needs with large machines," the conventional thinking went, "so why would we need small ones?" The answer, as we can see now, was that the great power of minicomputers, and then of PCs, did not lie in doing what larger machines already did but in giving birth to entirely new classes of applications.

Thinking deductively about technology not only causes people to ignore what is really important about it, it also gets them excited about technologies and applications that are, in fact, trivial and unimportant. Not long ago, for instance, someone thought it would be a terrific idea to integrate the personal computer and the telephone. The integrated unit would save space on desktops and be less expensive than buying separate units. That may be true, but combining the two machines into one doesn't offer any breakthroughs in capability. It doesn't let people do important things that they couldn't do before. It was at best a marginal improvement.

A lack of inductive thinking about technology is not a new problem, nor one confined to laypeople. Early on, many people thought that the greatest potential for the telephone lay in reducing the loneliness of the farmer's wife. Thomas Edison once said he thought the value of the phonograph, which he invented, was its capability to allow "dying gentlemen" to record their last wishes. Marconi, the developer of the radio, viewed it as a wireless telegraph that would operate point-to-point; he didn't recognize its potential as a broadcast medium. The real power of xerography was completely missed by no less a company than IBM.

In the late 1950s, when Xerox was performing the basic research on the 914, its first commercial copying machine, the company was hard pressed for money and wanted to cash out of the project. It offered its patents to IBM, which hired Arthur D. Little (ADL), the Cambridge, Massachusetts–based consulting firm, to do a market research study. ADL concluded that even if the revolutionary machine captured 100 percent of the market for carbon paper, dittograph, and hectograph—the techniques used for copying documents at the time—it still would not repay the investment required to get into the copier business. IBM, on the best evidence available, decided to turn down the Xerox patents and stay out of copiers. Despite the downbeat forecast, Xerox decided to persevere, on the assumption that *someone* would find a use for the machines.

We know now—indeed, it seems obvious—that the power of the Xerox copier did not lie in its capability to replace carbon paper and other existing copying technologies, but in its ability to perform services beyond the reach of these technologies. The 914 created a market for convenience copies that had previously not existed. Thirty copies of an existing document to share with a group of coworkers was not a need people knew they had before the invention of xerography. Since people couldn't make thirty easily and inexpensively, no one articulated doing so as a "need."

What we see operating in these cases of technology creating its own previously undreamed of uses is a variant of Say's Law. Jean Baptiste Say, an early nineteenth-century French economist, observed that in many situations, supply creates its own demand. People do not know they want something until they see that they can have it; then they feel they can't live without it. Alan Kay, often referred to as the father of the personal computer and now Apple Fellow at Apple Computer, puts it this way: "An important technology first creates a problem, and then solves it." No one "needed" the 914 copier—no one knew that they had a problem it solved—until the 914 appeared. Then the latent, unarticulated need suddenly became tangible and overwhelming.

It is, therefore, no use simply asking people how they would use a technology in their business. They will inevitably reply in terms of how that technology might improve a task they do already. One can usefully inquire of people whether they prefer their milk in glass bottles or cardboard cartons. Consumers are familiar with milk and with the two types of containers, and they can provide good information about their preferences and the reasons for them. If, though, a market researcher were to ask people in the pre-xerography days about copy machines, as they did, the respondents would say that it was hardly worth the price just to replace carbon paper.

Similarly, if a market research firm asks a person who travels frequently on business what would make his life easier, he might reply that he would like a faster way to reach the airport, or might express a yearning for a private plane. What he *will not* say he needs is a Star Trek-style teleportation device. He won't, because such a device is outside his frame of reference. When the market researcher mentions business travel to him, the business traveler's mind thinks of the familiar process: Get stuck in traffic on the way to the airport, stand in line, scrunch into seat, eat terrible food. Those are the problems of which he is *aware* and the ones to which he will seek solutions. The true power of technology is to offer answers to problems he does

not *know* he has—how, for example, to eliminate air travel completely.

Sony Corporation has achieved a good measure of its success by paying attention to this fundamental precept— that market research done for a product that does not yet exist is useless. When Sony developers first envisioned the Walkman, management did not order up a market research survey to see if the product would be embraced by consumers. Realizing that people are unable to conceptualize what they do not know, Sony gave the Walkman the green light based on developers' insights into people's needs and the capabilities of the technology. The Walkman transformed, rather than responded to, people's ideas about where and how they could listen to music.

The larger point we want to make is that needs, as well as aspirations, are shaped by people's understanding of what is possible. Breakthrough technology makes feasible activities and actions of which people have not yet dreamed. The challenge that most corporations fail to meet is recognizing the business possibilities that lie latent in technology. This shortcoming is understandable if not excusable.

Take, for instance, teleconferencing. This technology allows people located in specially equipped rooms in remote locations to hear and see each other and to work together almost as though they were in the same room. Initially, most organizations saw the value of teleconferencing as a means of reducing travel costs; people would be able to meet without having to fly. In this respect, teleconferencing has, by and large, proved a monumental failure. People travel to be with other people for many reasons. A trip, whether it's across town or across the country, in its very undertaking says something about the importance attached to the message ultimately delivered, of the subject eventually discussed. The nonverbal communication that takes place in a face-to-face meeting is probably more important than most of the words actually spoken. No surprise, then, that teleconferencing has had little effect on corporate travel costs.

That doesn't mean, however, that teleconferencing is without value. It means that its worth lies in transforming how work is done, not in lowering its costs. For instance, one company we know has used teleconferencing to cut its product development cycle by six months. How?

This company's engineering and marketing staffs are based in two different states, so once a month one group would fly to the other's location and, face to face, they would iron out their problems. Now the company has installed teleconferencing facilities, but the engineers and marketers still fly to see one another once a month, because they have found it difficult to resolve all their differences over television. The medium is too cool, and teleconferencing is no substitute for hand-to-hand combat. However, the engineers and marketers do use teleconferencing for weekly discussion sessions, which, previously, they could nor hold because of the inconvenience, lost time, and costs associated with travel.

During their weekly teleconferences, the two groups can follow up on the points they discussed at the last face-to-face meeting. Moreover, they can include more people in their discussions. Before teleconferencing, the senior managers were too busy to devote three days—one day to get there, one day to meet, and one day to get home—to a monthly meeting, and it proved too expensive to buy airline tickets for the junior staff involved in the projects. That meant that only the mid-level people met face to face. With teleconferencing,

everyone can "meet" once a week, stay informed, and have his or her routine questions answered. As a result, product developers and marketers keep in better touch, problems get resolved earlier and faster, fewer trips get taken down blind alleys, projects are completed faster, and the products they produce are better suited to their markets.

In short, the value of teleconferencing to this company lay in allowing it to do something it had *not* done before: keep marketers and designers in weekly contact. This use had not occurred to the people promoting teleconferencing, because they had not broken out of their old, deductive thinking mode.

To reiterate, the real power of technology is not that it can make the old processes work better, but that it enables organizations to break old rules and create new ways of working—that is, to re-engineer.

In building a brand new facility in which to manufacture its Saturn cars, General Motors enjoyed the opportunity to reengineer old work processes without the constraints imposed on it by existing plants. Consequently, GM, which had great ambitions for the Saturn facility, could break rules in a wholesale fashion by capitalizing on the enabling capabilities of information technology.

GM designed the Saturn plant, located in Spring Hill, Tennessee, to include an on-line manufacturing database that is accessible by the company's component suppliers. The suppliers do not wait for GM to send them a purchase order; they simply consult the car maker's production schedule, which is included in the database. Then they take it upon themselves to deliver the appropriate parts to the assembly plant as needed. By knowing how many cars GM plans to make in the following month, for instance, the company supplying Saturn's brakes knows how to configure its own production and shipping schedule. It is the brake manufacturer's responsibility to show up at 8:30 in the morning at the right door at the right plant with the right brakes for the right cars, palletized in linesequence order. Nobody at Saturn has to instruct the vendor explicitly to do so.

In this process, there is no paper—no purchase order and no invoice. After the parts are shipped, the vendor sends an electronic message to Saturn saying, in effect, "These are the parts we have sent to you." When the box of goods arrives, the receiving clerk scans the bar code printed on it with an electronic wand. The computer can then tell the receiving clerk to what part of the plant the goods should go. The scanning also initiates payment to the vendor.

In essence, information technology—in this case, the production schedule database and electronic data interchange (EDI)—has enabled Saturn and its supplier to operate as one company, to eliminate overhead in both organizations, and to break one of the oldest rules in any corporation's unwritten rule book: Treat vendors as adversaries.

In fact, breaking rules is how we recommend that people learn to think inductively about technology during the reengineering process: Find the long-standing rule or rules that technology allows the company to break, then see what business opportunities are created by breaking those rules. Teleconferencing, for example, breaks the rule that remotely located people can meet only infrequently and at great cost. Now it's possible for those people to meet often and inexpensively in an environment where limitations of geographical separation no longer count.

That insight gives a company a powerful tool for transforming its operations. It is one that can be applied in many areas and to many processes, not just

to product development. Several mass merchandisers, such as Wal-Mart and K Mart, are using teleconferencing to allow headquarters-based merchandisers to provide store managers in the field with guidance and advice. Teleconferencing enables them to combine local initiative with centralized expertise.

IBM Credit, Ford, and Kodak used technology to break rules as well. The rules, explicit or not, were neither frivolous nor absurd when they were first articulated. They were expressions of the wisdom people had derived from experience. A smart plant manager runs short of parts only a few times because of unexpected demand before he learns to order a little extra. In the absence of forecasting technology, this practice makes perfect sense. But the advent of that technology breaks the reigning rule about the need for safety stocks to buffer demand.

It is this *disruptive* power of technology, its ability to break the rules that limit how we conduct our work, that makes it critical to companies looking for competitive advantage.

Following are some illustrations of additional rules about the organization of work that can be broken by various information technologies, some of them familiar and some state of the art.

Old rule: Information can appear in only one place at one time
Disruptive technology: Shared databases
New rule: Information can appear simultaneously in as many places as it is needed

It is sobering to reflect on the extent to which the structure of our business processes has been dictated by the limitations of the file folder. When information is captured on paper and stored in a folder, only one person can use it at a time. Making copies and distributing them is not always feasible and, in any event, leads to the creation of multiple and eventually inconsistent versions of the file. Consequently, work involving this information tends to be structured sequentially, with one individual completing his or her tasks, then passing the folder to the next in line.

Database technology changes this rule. It allows many people to use the information simultaneously.

In an insurance business, for instance, Clerk A can be calculating an applicant's premium rate while Clerk B checks his or her credit—both of them using the same application form—since neither job depends upon the other. By allowing one document to exist in several places at once, database technology can free a process from the artificial limitations of sequencing.

> *Old rule:* Only experts can perform complex work
> *Disruptive technology:* Expert systems
> *New rule:* A generalist can do the work of an expert

When expert systems technology appeared on companies' radar screens in the early 1980s, most envisioned its utility in straightforward and simplistic terms: They would exploit it to automate the work of highly sophisticated experts by capturing their expertise in computer software. This was an extraordinarily foolish idea for several reasons: The technology is not really up to it; we need to retain the experts anyway, so they can continue to learn and advance in their field; and it is not clear why such clever people would participate in sharing all their knowledge with a computer designed to replace them.

In time, though, more sophisticated organizations have learned that there is more money in not being dumb than in being smart. That is, the real value of expert systems technology lies in its allowing relatively unskilled people to operate at nearly the level of highly trained experts.

A major chemical company, for example, has given each of its customer service representatives an expert system that advises them on product features and relationships. This system has allowed each of them to treat every customer inquiry as a cross-selling opportunity, something that previously only the very best had done.

Generalists supported by integrated systems can do the work of many specialists, and this fact has profound implications for the ways in which we can structure work. As illustrated by the changes at IBM Credit, systems technology allows the introduction of a *case worker*, who can handle all steps in a process from beginning to end. By eliminating the handoffs, delays, and errors inherent in a traditional sequential process, a *case worker*–based process can achieve order-of-magnitude improvements in cycle time, accuracy, and cost.

> *Old rule:* Businesses must choose between centralization and decentralization
> *Disruptive technology:* Telecommunications networks
> *New rule:* Businesses can simultaneously reap the benefits of centralization and decentralization

Businesspeople "know" that manufacturing plants, service facilities, and sales offices located far from headquarters must be treated as separate, decentralized, autonomous organizations if they are to function effectively and efficiently. Why? Because if every question that cropped up in the field had to be referred back to headquarters for an answer, little would get accomplished—and even that little would be late. Experience teaches that people in the field generally work best if they can make their own decisions.

If companies are relying on old technologies—the U.S. mail, the telephone, or even overnight express—to move their information back and forth, they must sacrifice central management control in order to achieve flexible and responsive field operations.

New technologies, however, free companies from this trade-off. High-bandwidth communications networks allow headquarters to have the same information that field offices have and to see the data that field offices see—and vice versa—in real time. With this shared capability, every field office can effectively be part of headquarters, and headquarters can be part of every field office. That means companies can utilize whatever arrangement—centralization, decentralization, or some combination—best serves their markets.

Information technology enabled Hewlett-Packard, the Palo Alto, California–based designer and manufacturer of instruments and computer systems, to break the time-honored rule that centralization and decentralization are mutually exclusive.

In materials procurement, as in most of its activities, Hewlett-Packard was highly decentralized. It granted its operating divisions virtually complete autonomy in purchasing, because they knew their own needs best. But the virtues of decentralization (flexibility, customization, responsiveness) are purchased at a cost (lack of economies of scale and reduced control). At Hewlett-Packard, decentralized purchasing meant that the company could not take advantage of high-volume discounts available from its vendors. For that reason, Hewlett-Packard estimated that it was spending $50 million to $100 million more each year than necessary on raw materials. Centralizing purchasing would not have "solved" the problem of high cost; it would merely have exchanged it for the twin problems of unresponsiveness and bureaucracy. Instead, Hewlett-Packard found a third way, through the use of a common purchasing software system.

Under Hewlett-Packard's new approach, each manufacturing division continues to order parts for its division. Now, however, each purchasing unit uses a standard purchasing system. These systems all provide data to a new database, which a corporate procurement unit oversees. Corporate procurement negotiates block contracts and volume discounts with suppliers of selected products on behalf of Hewlett-Packard as a whole. Corporate procurement can do so, because the database gives the unit complete information about the divisions' planned and actual purchases. Once contracts are established, purchasing agents check the database to locate approved suppliers and place orders.

The new process gives Hewlett-Packard the best of centralization—volume discounts—and the best of decentralized buying—meeting local needs locally.

Information technology, used imaginatively, has eliminated the need for separate, fully formed field units with their own overheads, and the banking industry, for one, has already begun to recognize this reality. For years, banks treated branches as P&L centers, but now many banks see a branch only as a point of sale and not as a self-contained organization. The availability of automated teller machines and other high-capacity, real-time data net-work devices means that branch transactions show up in the central bank's books immediately. Since a branch now becomes just a point sale, banks can keep people close to the customer without having to relinquish central control of operations.

Old rule: Managers make all decisions
Disruptive technology: Decision support tools (database access, modeling software)
New rule: Decision-making is part of everyone's job

Part of the Industrial Revolution model is the notion of hierarchical decision-making. The worker performing a task is expected only to do the job, not to think or make decisions about it. These prerogatives are reserved for management. These rules were not simply manifestations of industrial feudalism. Managers did in fact have broader perspectives, based on more information, than did lower-level workers. This better information presumably allowed them to make superior decisions.

The costs of hierarchical decision-making, however, are now too high to bear. Referring everything up the ladder means decisions get made too slowly for a fast-paced market. Today, companies say they realize that frontline workers must be empowered to make their own decisions, but empowerment cannot be achieved simply by giving people the authority to make decisions. They need the tools as well.

Modern database technology allows information previously available only to management to be made widely accessible. When accessible data is combined with easy-to-use analysis and modeling tools, frontline workers—when properly trained—suddenly have sophisticated decision-making capabilities. Decisions can be made more quickly and problems resolved as soon as they crop up.

> *Old rule:* Field personnel need offices where they can receive, store, retrieve, and transmit information
> *Disruptive technology:* Wireless data communication and portable computers
> *New rule:* Field personnel can send and receive information wherever they are

With wide-band, wireless data communications and portable computers, field people of whatever occupation can request, view, manipulate, use, and transmit data almost anywhere without ever having to run back to the office.

Wireless data communication relies on technology similar to that used in cellular telephones, with the important difference that it allows users to send data instead of, or in addition, to voice. With increasingly miniaturized terminals and computers, people can connect to information sources wherever they are. Otis Elevator's service people, for instance, carry with them small portable terminals. After they repair an elevator, they update the customer's service record on the spot, then send the information via modem to headquarters in Connecticut. Avis has applied the same principle to its rental operations. When a customer returns a car to an Avis lot, an attendant, equipped with a tiny computer, meets the car, pulls up the record of the rental transaction, and enters the charge. The customer never has to visit the office.

Earlier, we noted that high-bandwidth communication lets companies break the old rule that says field offices must be autonomous organizations. Wireless data communication goes further and begins to eliminate the need for field offices entirely. Processes such as job progress reporting, insurance claims adjusting, and onsite equipment repair consultation will not depend upon a fieldworker's having to find a phone or a computer terminal. Headquarters can know what the people onsite know when they know it—and vice versa.

> *Old rule:* The best contact with a potential buyer is personal contact
> *Disruptive technology:* Interactive videodisk
> *New rule:* The best contact with a potential buyer is effective contact

Some companies have started using interactive videodisks, which allow viewers to watch a video segment on a computer screen and then ask questions or answer them on screen. The initial application of this technology was in training, but the potential power of interactive video far transcends this domain.

Several retailers, for example, are experimenting with interactive video to augment their retail sales force. Customers at these stores can select a product from a menu, watch a video presentation about it, ask questions, then order it with a credit card—all without human intervention. The process may seem cold and impersonal, but customers find it preferable to the usual retail experience: waiting forever for a salesperson only to discover that he or she is uninformed.

Banks have begun using interactive video to explain their increasingly complex services to customers, who can ask the machine to clarify points that they don't understand. Some information is *best* communicated visually—real estate, for instance. Interactive video gives prospective buyers a tour of entire houses—and lets them return to see the master bedroom again if they ask—without their having to leave the broker's office.

Old rule: You have to find out where things are
Disruptive technology: Automatic identification and tracking technology
New rule: Things tell you where they are

Combined with wireless data communication, automatic identification technology lets things—trucks, for instance—tell you constantly where they are. You do not have to look for them, and when you want them to go someplace else, they get the word instantaneously. No more waiting for drivers to hit the next truck stop so they can telephone the dispatcher.

A company that knows in real time where its trucks are, or rail cars or service technicians for that matter, does not need as many of them. It does not require as much redundancy in personnel, equipment, and materials to cover the delays inherent in locating and rerouting things and people in transit.

Some railroads, for instance, are implementing satellite systems to tell them where a given train is at any given moment. The old method of tracking trains involved painting bar-code like symbols on the sides of the rail car. As the train pulled through the station, a machine—in theory, at least—would read the bar code and transmit the train's location to headquarters. We say "in theory" because the system never worked. Not surprisingly, the bar codes became so covered with dust and grime that they were unreadable. With the satellite system in place, the railroad companies will be able to deliver freight cars with the same precision with which overnight carriers deliver packages.

Old rule: Plans get revised periodically
Disruptive technology: High performance computing.
New rule: Plans get revised instantaneously

The sheer capacity of increasingly *affordable* computing power creates new application possibilities for companies. Take manufacturing, for instance. Today a manufacturer gathers data on product sales, raw materials price and availability, labor supply, and so on and once a month (or once a week) produces a master production schedule. A computer supplied with real-time data from point-of-sale terminals, commodity markets, and perhaps even weather forecasts, among other information sources, could constantly adjust the schedule to match real-time, not historic, needs.

It should be clear from these examples that further advances in technology will break more rules about how we conduct business. Rules that still appear inviolate today may become obsolete in a year or less.

Consequently, exploiting the potential of technologies to change a company's business processes and move it dramatically ahead of its competitors is not a one-time event. Nor is it something a company can do occasionally, say, once a decade. On the contrary, staying on top of new technology and learning how to recognize and incorporate it into an organization must be an ongoing effort—no different from research and development or marketing. It takes a practiced eye and imaginative mind to spot the potential in a technology that does not at first appear to have any obvious application to a company's work or to see past the obvious to the novel applications of a technology that superficially seems useful only for marginally improving the *status quo*.

Companies need to make technology exploitation one of their core competencies if they are to succeed in a period of ongoing technological change. Those better able to recognize and realize the potentials of new technology will enjoy a continuing and growing advantage over their competitors.

Our view is that if you can buy a technology, it is not new. We subscribe to what might be called the Wayne Gretzky School of Technology. Gretzky, who became the National Hockey League's all-time leading scorer at age twenty-eight, was once asked what made him a great hockey player. He was exceptional, he answered, "because I go where the puck is *going* to be, not where it *is*." The same rule applies to technology. Building a strategy around what one can buy in the market today means that a company will always be playing catch up with

competitors who have already anticipated it. These competitors know what they are *going* to do with technology *before* it becomes available, so they will be ready to deploy it when it does become available.

Companies that have had great success with applying technology—American Express, for instance, whose image processing system allows it to send digitized copies of original receipts to both corporate cardholders and their accounting departments and Chrysler with its satellite communications system for helping dealers manage their parts inventories—were asking for the technology they needed well before it appeared on the market. Year after year, Chrysler sent out requests for proposals (RFPs) that outlined what it wanted; when a vendor eventually responded with the needed capabilities, Chrysler was ready to implement. Management knew what rules they wanted to break with the technology before the technology was even at hand.

Companies cannot see or read about a new technology today and deploy it tomorrow. It takes time to study it, to understand its significance, to conceptualize its potential uses, to sell those uses inside the company, and to plan the deployment. An organization that can execute these preliminaries before the technology actually becomes available will inevitably gain a significant lead on its competition—in many cases, three years or more.

It is entirely possible to stay three years ahead of the market on technology. It takes time to move from laboratory to market; there does not exist a technology that will become important in 1996 that is not yet demonstrable today. Smart companies can be figuring out how they will use a technology, even while its developers are still polishing their prototypes.

As an essential enabler in reengineering, modern information technology has an importance to the reengineering process that is difficult to overstate. But companies need to beware of thinking that technology is the only essential element in reengineering.

To reengineer a company is to take a journey from the familiar into the unknown. This journey has to begin somewhere and with someone. Where and with whom? . . .